Mar Caribe
OCÉANO ATLÁNTICO
Barranquilla
Cartagena
Maracaibo
Caracas
Barquisimeto
Río Orinoco
VENEZUELA
CORDILLERA DE LOS ANDES
Medellín
Manizales
Bogotá
Cali
COLOMBIA
Salto Ángel
Georgetown
GUYANA
Paramaribo
SURINAM
Cayenne
GUAYANA FRANCESA (Francia)
Quito
ECUADOR
Ecuador
Guayaquil
Cuenca
Islas Galápagos (Ec.)
Iquitos
Río Amazonas
Manaus
Belém
Fortaleza
Río Madeira
Cajamarca
Trujillo
PERÚ
Río Branco
BRASIL
Recife
Lima
Machu Picchu
Cuzco
Ayacucho
Lago Titicaca
BOLIVIA
Salvador
Arequipa
La Paz
Brasília
Santa Cruz
Cochabamba
Arica
Sucre
Potosí
Belo Horizonte
Iquique
Desierto de Atacama
PARAGUAY
Río de Janeiro
São Paulo
Santos
Antofagasta
Salta
Asunción
Salto Iguazú
Trópico de Capricornio
CHILE
San Miguel de Tucumán
ARGENTINA
Río Paraná
Río Uruguay
Coquimbo
Pôrto Alegre
Córdoba
Rivera
Rosario
URUGUAY
Valparaíso
Santiago
Mendoza
Buenos Aires
La Plata
Montevideo
Río de la Plata
OCÉANO ATLÁNTICO
Concepción
Bahía Blanca
Puerto Montt
OCÉANO PACÍFICO
Estrecho de Magallanes
Islas Malvinas (Br.)
Punta Arenas
TIERRA DEL FUEGO
Cabo de Hornos
OCÉANO PACÍFICO
I. Pinta
I. Fernandina
I. Marchena
I. San Salvador
I. Isabela
Santa Cruz
I. Santa Cruz
Puerto Ayora
Puerto Villamil
I. San Cristóbal
Puerto Baquerizo Moreno
ISLAS GALÁPAGOS (ECUADOR)
OCÉANO PACÍFICO
Cabo Norte
Volcán Katiki
Hanga Roa
Cabo Cumming
Mataveri
ISLA de PASCUA (CHILE)
América del Sur

GUIDE TO *¡ANDA! CURSO ELEMENTAL* ICONS

Vocabulary Zoom Tool	Indicates that students can find the vocabulary digital zoom tool in ***¡Anda!* online** to zoom in on images and listen to the pronunciation of vocabulary words.
Vocabulary Tutorial	Indicates that vocabulary tutorials are available in ***¡Anda!* online**.
También se dice…	Clicking on this icon from the eText will send students to the *También se dice…* lists in Appendix 3, where they can find alternative vocabulary words from those presented in the vocabulary chunk.
Pronunciación	Indicates that prounciation practice can be found in ***¡Anda!* online**.
Readiness Check in *¡Anda!* online	This icon, located in the first grammar section of each chapter, reminds students to take the Readiness Check in ***¡Anda!* online** to test their understanding of the English grammar related to the Spanish grammar concepts in the chapter.
Grammar Tutorial	Indicates that grammar tutorials are available in ***¡Anda!* online**.
¡Explícalo tú!	Indicates that answers to the *¡Explícalo tú!* questions are available for students to review in Appendix 1.
Preparación y práctica	Indicates that *Preparación y práctica* activities for each vocabulary and grammar chunk can be found in ***¡Anda!* online**.
eText Activity	This icon indicates that an electronic version of this activity is available in ***¡Anda!* online**.
Text Audio Program	This icon indicates that recorded material to accompany ***¡Anda! Curso elemental*** is available in ***¡Anda!* online** or on the Companion Website (www.pearsonhighered.com/anda).
Pair Activity	This icon indicates that the activity is designed to be done by students working in pairs.
Group Activity	This icon indicates that the activity is designed to be done by students working in small groups or as a whole class.
Recycling	Indicates that the concept is being recycled from another section of the program.
Video	This icon indicates that a video episode is available for the *Club cultura* video series in ***¡Anda!* online**.
MediaShare	Indicates that the activity can be completed using MediaShare either in ***¡Anda!* online** or with the MediaShare app.

DEDICATION

To John, Jack, and Kate
—Glynis

To David, the love of my life
—Audrey

¡Anda! Curso elemental

THIRD EDITION

Glynis S. Cowell • Audrey L. Heining-Boynton

The University of North Carolina at Chapel Hill

With

Jean LeLoup

PEARSON

Boston Columbus Indianapolis New York San Francisco
Amsterdam Cape Town Dubai London Madrid Milan Munich Paris Montréal Toronto
Delhi Mexico City São Paulo Sydney Hong Kong Seoul Singapore Taipei Tokyo

Editor in Chief: Bob Hemmer
Senior Acquisitions Editor: Denise Miller
Editorial Assistant: Janelle McGill
Senior Digital Product Manager: Samantha Alducin
Digital Editorial Assistant: Sandra Fisac Rodríguez
Director of Editorial Development: Scott Gravina
Lead Senior Development Editor: Gisela Aragón-Velthaus
Development Editors: Gabriela Ferland, Sarah Link, Andrew Bowen, Patricia Acosta, Kristen Chapron, Nina Tunac Basey
Director of Program Management: Lisa Iarkowski
Team Lead Program Management: Amber Mackey
Program Manager: Annemarie Franklin
Team Lead Project Management: Melissa Feimer
Project Manager: Millie Chapman
Full-Service Project Manager: Melissa Sacco, Lumina Datamatics, Inc.
Front Cover Design: Lumina Datamatics, Inc.
Design Lead: Kathryn Foot
Operations Manager: Mary Fischer
Operations Specialist: Roy Pickering
Marketing Director: Steve Debow
Marketing Assistant: Jon Feuchter
Director of Market Development: Kristine Suárez
World Languages Consultants: Mellissa Yokell, Yesha Brill, Raúl J. Vázquez López
Cover Printer: Phoenix Color/Hagerstown
Interior Printer/Bindery: RR Donnelley / Willard

This book was set in Times LT Pro 9.5/11.

Acknowledgements of third-party content appear on pages A47–A49, which constitute an extension of this copyright page.

Library of Congress Cataloging-in-Publication Data

Cowell, Glynis S., author. | Heining-Boynton, Audrey L., author. | Leloup, Jean, 1949- author.
Anda! : curso elemental / Audrey L. Heining-Boynton ; Glynis S. Cowell ; with Jean Leloup.
Third Edition / Glynis S. Cowell ; Audrey L. Heining-Boynton ; with Jean Leloup. | Boston : Pearson, [2016] |
Previous edition: ¡Anda! : curso elemental / Audrey L. Heining-Boynton ; Glynis S. Cowell ; with Jean Leloup, 2nd ed., 2013. |
Includes bibliographical references and index.
LCCN 2016001408 (print) | LCCN 2016002624 (ebook) | ISBN 9780134146775 (Student Edition) | ISBN 0134146778 (Student Edition) | ISBN 9780134146799 (Annotated Instructor's Edition) | ISBN 0134146794 (Annotated Instructor's Edition) | ISBN 0134244877 ()
LCSH: Spanish language—Textbooks for foreign speakers—English. | Spanish language—Grammar.
LCC PC4129.E5 H428 2016 (print) | LCC PC4129.E5 (ebook) | DDC 468.2/421—dc23
LC record available at http://lccn.loc.gov/2016001408

10 9 8 7 6 5 4 3 2 1

Student Edition, ISBN-10: 0-13-414677-8
Student Edition, ISBN-13: 978-0-13-414677-5
Annotated Instructor's Edition, ISBN-10: 0-13-414679-4
Annotated Instructor's Edition, ISBN-13: 978-0-13-414679-9
a la Carte Edition, ISBN-10: 0-13-414683-2
a la Carte Edition, ISBN-13: 978-0-13-414683-6

BRIEF CONTENTS

SCOPE & SEQUENCE FIRST

(The numbers that precede the grammar and vocabulary sections indicate their numerical sequence within the chapter.)	A **Para empezar**	1 **¿Quiénes somos?**	2 **La vida universitaria**
VOCABULARIO	1 Saludos, presentaciones y despedidas, p. 4 2 Expresiones útiles para la clase, p. 8 4 Los cognados, p. 10 7 Los adjetivos de nacionalidad, p. 14 8 Los números 0–30, p. 16 9 La hora, p. 18 10 Los días, los meses y las estaciones, p. 21 11 El tiempo, p. 23	1 La familia, p. 32 6 Gente, p. 41 9 Los números 31–100, p. 50	1 Las materias y las especialidades, p. 66 2 La sala de clase, p. 69 5 Los números 100–1.000, p. 78 6 En la universidad, p. 80 8 Las emociones y los estados, p. 86 10 Los deportes y los pasatiempos, p. 89
GRAMÁTICA	3 El alfabeto, p. 9 5 Los pronombres personales, p. 11 6 El verbo **ser**, p. 13 12 **Gustar**, p. 25	2 El verbo **tener**, p. 35 3 Sustantivos singulares y plurales, p. 36 4 El masculino y el femenino, p. 37 5 Los artículos definidos e indefinidos, p. 38 7 Los adjetivos posesivos, p. 42 8 Los adjetivos descriptivos, p. 44	3 Presente indicativo de verbos regulares, p. 71 4 La formación de preguntas y las palabras interrogativas, p. 75 7 El verbo **estar**, p. 83 9 El verbo **gustar**, p. 87
PRONUNCIACIÓN		Vowels, p. 33	Word stress and accent marks, p. 67
NOTA CULTURAL	Cómo se saluda la gente, p. 7 ¿**Tú** o **usted**?, p. 12 Los hispanos, p. 16 El mundo hispano, p. 17	Los apellidos en el mundo hispano, p. 34 El español, lengua diversa, p. 49	Las universidades hispanas, p. 68 Los deportes en el mundo hispano, p. 91
ESCUCHA		Presentaciones, p. 52 **Estrategia:** Determining the topic and listening for words you know	Una conversación, p. 93 **Estrategia:** Listening for the gist
¡CONVERSEMOS!		Communicating about people you know, p. 53	Communicating about university life, p. 94
ESCRIBE		Un poema, p. 54 **Estrategia:** Organizing ideas / Preparing to write	Una descripción, p. 94 **Estrategia:** Creating sentences
VISTAZO CULTURAL		**LOS ESTADOS UNIDOS**, p. 56 **Club cultura:** *La vida de los hispanos*	**MÉXICO**, p. 96 **Club cultura:** *La vida universitaria*
LECTURA		*El perfil de Adriana*, p. 58 **Estrategia:** Recognizing cognates	*Una carta de la universidad*, p. 98 **Estrategia:** Skimming

SEMESTER

SCOPE & SEQUENCE

SECOND

(The numbers that precede the grammar and vocabulary sections indicate their numerical sequence within the chapter.)	B **Para repasar**	7 **¡A comer!**	8 **¿Qué te pones?**
VOCABULARIO	**Capítulo A,** p. 242 **Capítulo 1,** p. 242 **Capítulo 2,** p. 244 **Capítulo 3,** p. 250 **Capítulo 4,** p. 256 **Capítulo 5,** p. 261	**1** La comida, p. 268 **4** La preparación de las comidas, p. 281 **6** En el restaurante, p. 290	**1** La ropa, p. 308 **5** Las telas y los materiales, p. 324
GRAMÁTICA	**Capítulo A,** p. 242 **Capítulo 1,** p. 242 **Capítulo 2,** p. 244 **Capítulo 3,** p. 250 **Capítulo 4,** p. 256 **Capítulo 5,** p. 261	**2** Repaso del complemento directo, p. 275 **3** Algunos verbos irregulares en el pretérito (Parte I), p. 277 **5** Algunos verbos irregulares en el pretérito (Parte II), p. 284	**2** Los pronombres de complemento indirecto, p. 313 **3** **Gustar** y verbos como **gustar**, p. 317 **4** Los pronombres de complemento directo e indirecto usados juntos, p. 321 **6** El imperfecto, p. 328
PRONUNCIACIÓN		The different pronunciations of **r** and **rr**, p. 269	The letters **ll** and **ñ**, p. 309
NOTA CULTURAL		Las comidas en el mundo hispano, p. 274 La comida hispana, p. 283	Zara: la moda internacional, p. 312 Los centros comerciales en Latinoamérica, p. 327
ESCUCHA		Las compras en el mercado, p. 295 **Estrategia:** Combining strategies	En el centro comercial, p. 333 **Estrategia:** Guessing meaning from context
¡CONVERSEMOS!		Communicating about food shopping and party planning, p. 296	Communicating about clothing and fashion, p. 334
ESCRIBE		Una descripción, p. 297 **Estrategia:** Topic sentence and conclusion	Un e-mail, p. 335 **Estrategia:** Circumlocution
VISTAZO CULTURAL		**CHILE Y PARAGUAY**, p. 298 **Club cultura:** *Una tierra muy fértil, El tereré: la tradición más paraguaya*	**ARGENTINA Y URUGUAY**, p. 336 **Club cultura:** *La vida cultural de Buenos Aires, Uruguay y Argentina: una historia fascinante*
LECTURA		*Solicitud para un concurso de cocina*, p. 300 **Estrategia:** Predicting	*Consejos de moda*, p. 338 **Estrategia:** Guessing meaning from context

SEMESTER

NEW TO *¡ANDA! CURSO ELEMENTAL*, THIRD EDITION

Students and instructors will benefit from a wealth of new content and features in this edition. Detailed, contextualized descriptions are provided in the features walk-through that follows.

- **Revised *Scope and Sequence*** creates a better balance between the first and second half of the text and across the full *¡Anda!* program.
- **Chapter openers have been redesigned** to highlight the warm-up activities and facilitate class discussion through three captioned photos, a cultural introduction to the chapter, and a *¿Sabías qué?* fun fact.
- **Learning Outcomes** in the chapter openers focus students on what they will be able to do successfully by the end of each chapter. These are also tied to the *¿Cómo andas?* self-checks at the end of each *Comunicación* section.
- A ***vocabulary digital zoom tool*** in ***¡Anda!* online** allows students to zoom in on images and listen to the pronunciation of vocabulary words as they learn outside of class, helping them to quickly assimilate meanings and improve their pronunciation.
- ***Preparación y práctica*** activities for each vocabulary and grammar chunk in ***¡Anda!* online** will give your students a quick comprehension check before they come to class for communicative practice. An icon and directions in the text alert students when they should complete these activities.
- **A new cultural video program, *Club cultura*,** integrated with the revised *Vistazo cultural* section (formerly *Cultura*), brings the Spanish-speaking world to life through vibrant video episodes shot on location in 22 Spanish-speaking countries, including the United States. New activities written especially for ***¡Anda!* online** are language-controlled and offer a process approach to help students understand and gain insight into the countries they are studying. Pop-up eText activities offer in-class discussion questions about the integrated *Club cultura* videos for each country.

104

Vista de Madrid, capital de España

Apartamentos en Barcelona

3 Estamos en casa

From modern skyscrapers in large cities to the narrow streets of medieval towns and small farms in rural areas, homes in Spain reflect the varied climate, history, and lifestyles of the Spanish people. Homes in southern cities like Córdoba or Sevilla often have a Mediterranean feel, while in big cities like Madrid or Barcelona residents may opt to be in the middle of the action in a downtown apartment or choose a quieter, less expensive home on the outskirts of the city.

Preguntas

1. Is there Spanish-inspired architecture in the region where you live?
2. How do you think that geography and environment affect the design and construction of homes?
3. Observe the housing styles shown in the photos. How are these similar or different from those in your area?

¿Sabías que...?
Fifty percent of Spaniards between the ages of 20 and 25 live with their parents.

Carmona, un pueblo del su

Learning Outcom

By the end of this chapter

- express actions.
- create an ad.
- read a blog and view contemporary video from Spain.

132

Vistazo cultural

España

Explore more about Spain with *Club cultura* online.

Les presento mi país

Mi nombre es Mariela Castañeda Ropero y soy de Madrid, la capital de España. Estudio literatura en la Universidad Complutense de Madrid y vivo con mis padres en un piso en el centro. **¿Dónde vives tú? ¿En una casa, en un apartamento o en una residencia estudiantil?** La vida en la capital es muy interesante porque hay mucha actividad. Me gusta salir con mis amigos por la tarde para comer tapas y tomar algo. La Plaza Mayor es nuestro lugar favorito. **¿Cuál es tu lugar favorito para conversar y pasar tiempo con tus amigos?** Frecuentemente, hablamos de las clases en la universidad o de nuestros pasatiempos favoritos. En mi tiempo libre, practico deportes, escucho música y salgo a bailar con amigos los fines de semana. Hay muchos lugares para bailar: ¡la vida nocturna es excelente en Madrid! **¿Qué haces en tu tiempo libre?**

Mariela Castañeda Ropero

El flamenco es un estilo de baile y música con orígenes en Andalucía, una comunidad autónoma en el sur del país.

La Plaza Mayor de Madrid es un lugar agradable para comer tapas, tomar una bebida y conversar con amigos.

Don Quijote y Sancho Panza son personajes del autor Miguel de Cervantes Saavedra.

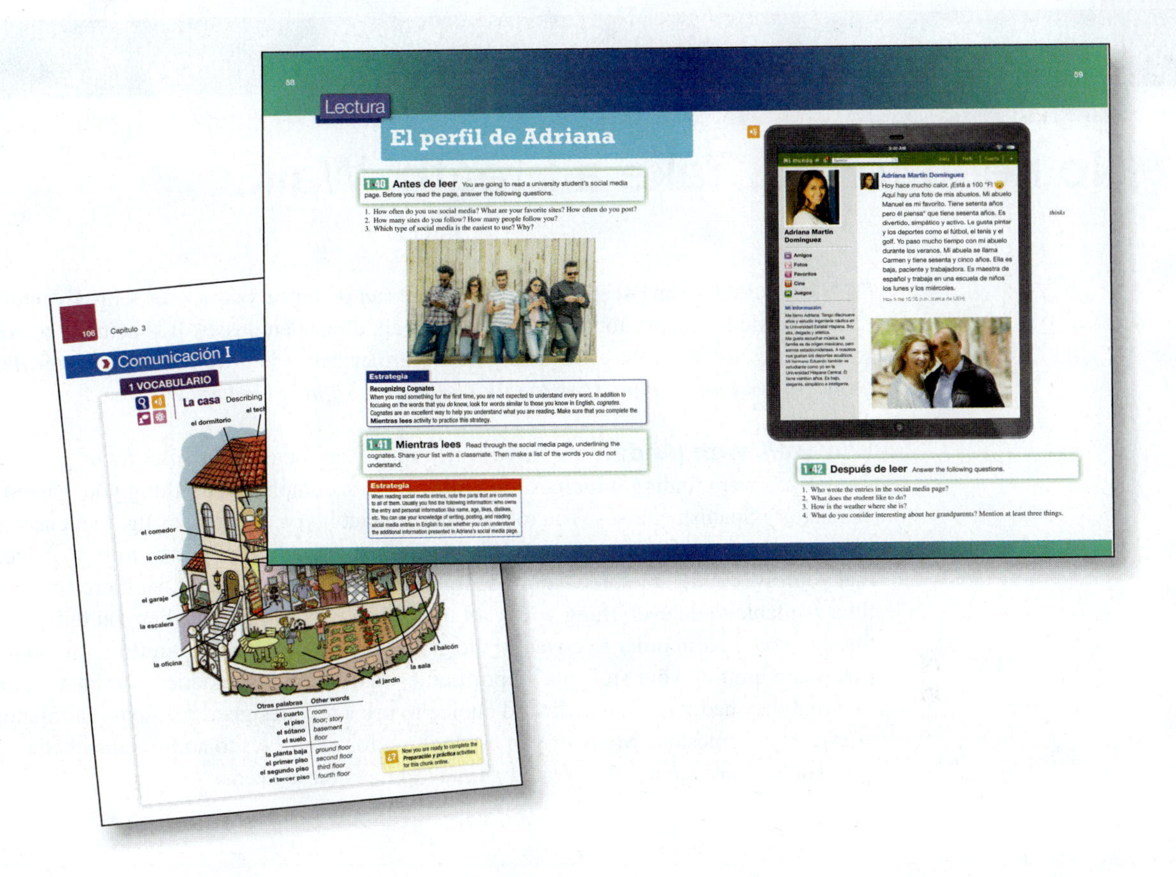
Lectura

El perfil de Adriana

1.40 Antes de leer

Estrategia

1.41 Mientras lees

1.42 Después de leer

106 Capítulo 3

Comunicación I

1 VOCABULARIO

La casa

- **A brand-new section, *Lectura*,** introduces students to reading through various styles that are familiar to them, like social media and blogs. Students work with authentic text selections in *Capítulos 10* and *11*. At the end of each *Lectura* section, new *MediaShare* presentation activities give students the opportunity to practice the presentational mode of communication in the digital environment. The integrated video-capture functionality allows learners and instructors to record and upload video directly from a webcam, smartphone, or tablet using the *MediaShare* app.
- **Two additional audio-based** activities in each chapter offer further listening comprehension practice for students.
- **Digital tools in *¡Anda!* online** to increase out-of-class communication opportunities include *LiveChat*, a pair/group video recording tool, *MediaShare*, a video sharing site, and *WeSpeke*, a website that allows students to connect virtually with native speakers.
- Grammar tutorials and vocabulary flashcards are now **mobile** and ready for study on the go with new apps for smartphones.
- An icon in the vocabulary presentations links to the *También se dice…* Appendix from the eText for additional personalization of vocabulary.
- Many new teacher annotations (*Lectura*, *Club cultura*, Expansion, Suggestion, Note, and Planning Ahead) have been added to provide additional guidance and options for instructors and to aid in lesson planning and implementation for the new sections of the program.
- The *Student Activities Manual,* fully revised for **¡Anda! online,** is now optimized for the best digital experience. New activity types—including *LiveChat*, drag-and-drop, and more—help students engage in homework to improve preparedness for class.
- The *Testing Program* had been revised to better reflect the goals of the ***¡Anda!*** program. Clearer direction lines and new activities allow instructors to personalize assessments for their courses.

PREFACE

No need to run. Take a breath. Walk.

The natural human pace is walking. We can run or sprint, but not for long. Eventually, we are exhausted and have to stop. But we can walk almost endlessly. It is actually amazing how far we can go when we walk—ultimately much farther than when we run. *So take a walk… a walk with* **¡Anda!**… *and have* ***ample time to talk*** *and* ***see the sights*** *along the way.*

***Why walk with* ¡Anda!?** In survey after survey, in focus group after focus group, you told us that you were finding it increasingly difficult to accomplish everything you wanted in your elementary Spanish courses. You told us that contact hours are decreasing, that class sizes are increasing, and that more and more courses are being taught partially or totally online. You told us that your lives and your students' lives are busier than ever. You said that there simply isn't enough time available to do everything you want to do. Some of you told us that you felt compelled to rush through your text in order to cover all the grammar and vocabulary, omitting important cultural topics and limiting your students' opportunities to develop and practice communication skills. Others said that they had made the awkward choice to use a text designed for first-year Spanish over three or even four semesters. Many of you are looking for new ways to address the challenges you and your students are facing. We created *¡Anda!* to meet these needs.

The *¡Anda!* Story

The entire *¡Anda!* program was designed to increase the opportunity for student and instructor success by giving them **more of what they need… and less of what they don't! *¡Anda!*** is designed to be **ready to go!** Its innovations center around four key areas:

1. **Realistic goals with a realistic approach**
2. **Increasing student talk time inside and outside the classroom**
3. **Focus on student motivation**
4. **Tools to promote success**

REALISTIC GOALS WITH A REALISTIC APPROACH

Realistic goals are the *first step* in achieving success!

A realistic assessment of the basic language sequence

¡Anda! is the first college-level Spanish program created as a seamless sequence of materials to be completed in two academic years. The *¡Anda!* program is divided into two halves, ***¡Anda! Curso elemental*** and ***¡Anda! Curso intermedio,*** each of which can be completed in one academic year.

Each volume's scope and sequence has been carefully designed, based on advice and feedback from hundreds of instructors and users at a wide variety of institutions. Each volume introduces a realistic number of new vocabulary words, and the traditional basic language grammar sequence has been spread over two volumes so that students have adequate time throughout each course to focus on communication, culture, and skills development, and to master the vocabulary and grammar concepts to which they are introduced.

Each volume of ***¡Anda!***, for both ***Curso elemental*** and ***Curso intermedio***, has been structured to optimize learning through thoughtful presentation, preparation, recycling, and review within the context of a multi-term sequence of courses. The ten regular chapters are complemented by *two preliminary* chapters and *two recycling* chapters.

- *Capítulo A Para empezar* is designed with **ample vocabulary** to get students up and running and to give them a **sense of accomplishment** quickly. Many students will already be familiar with some of this vocabulary. It also has students reflect on the question "Why study Spanish?"
- *Capítulo B Para repasar* is a **review** of *Capítulo A* through *Capítulo 5* and allows those who join the class midyear, or those who need a refresher, to get up to speed at the beginning of the second half of the book.
- *Capítulos 1–5* and *7–11* are **regular** chapters.
- *Capítulos 6* and *12* are **recycling** chapters. No new material is presented. Designed for in-class use, these chapters recycle and recombine previously presented vocabulary, grammar, and culture, giving students more time to practice communication without the burden of learning new grammar or vocabulary. Rubrics are provided in these chapters to assess student performance. They provide clear expectations for students as they review.

240

B Para repasar

Learning Outcomes

By the end of this chapter, you will be able to:

- describe people, homes, and household chores.
- impart information about student life, sports and pastimes, and service opportunities.
- identify places in and around town.
- relate likes and dislikes, things that happen, and things that have to be done.
- convey some past actions as well as expected actions in the near future.
- share information and preferences about music, movies, and television programs.

This chapter is a review of vocabulary and grammatical concepts that you are already familiar with in Spanish. Some of you are continuing with *¡Anda! Curso elemental*, while others may be coming from a different program. As you begin the second half of *¡Anda!*, it is important for all students to feel confident about what they already know about the Spanish language as they continue to acquire knowledge and proficiency. This chapter will help you determine what you already know, and also help you focus on what you personally need to improve upon.

If you are new to *¡Anda!*, you will not only want to review the grammar concepts already introduced, but also familiarize yourself with the active vocabulary used in the textbook.

¡Anda! recycles vocabulary and grammar concepts frequently to help you learn better, and this chapter will help you with what we consider to be the basics of the preceding chapters.

Before you begin this chapter, you may wish to review the study and learning strategies on page 220 in Capítulo 6. These strategies are applicable to your other subjects as well. So on your mark, get set, let's review!

¿Sabías que...?

El 50% de los estudiantes de lenguas en Estados Unidos estudia español.

A realistic approach for the achievement of realistic goals

- **Vocabulary and grammar presented in manageable chunks:** Vocabulary and grammar are presented in manageable amounts, or small **chunks**. Practice activities follow each presentation so that students get immediate practice on a manageable amount of material. Additionally, vocabulary and grammar explanations are interspersed, each introduced at the point of need.
- **Realistic vocabulary load:** ***Not more or less than is needed!*** Vocabulary has been selected for its relevance and support with the overall vocabulary load of approximately 100 words per chapter.
- **A nuanced approach to grammar:** Grammar explanations are **written in clear and concise English**, and include many supporting examples in Spanish followed by practice activities. Explanations vary between an inductive and a deductive approach. The inductive presentations provide students with examples of a grammar concept. Students then must formulate the rule(s) through the use of guiding questions. The inductive presentations are accompanied by an *¡Explícalo tú!* heading and an icon that directs them to Appendix 1 where answers to the questions in the presentations may be found. Research has shown that the inductive method enables students to **better remember and internalize the rules**. For those grammar concepts that are more difficult for students to learn, the more direct deductive approach is used.

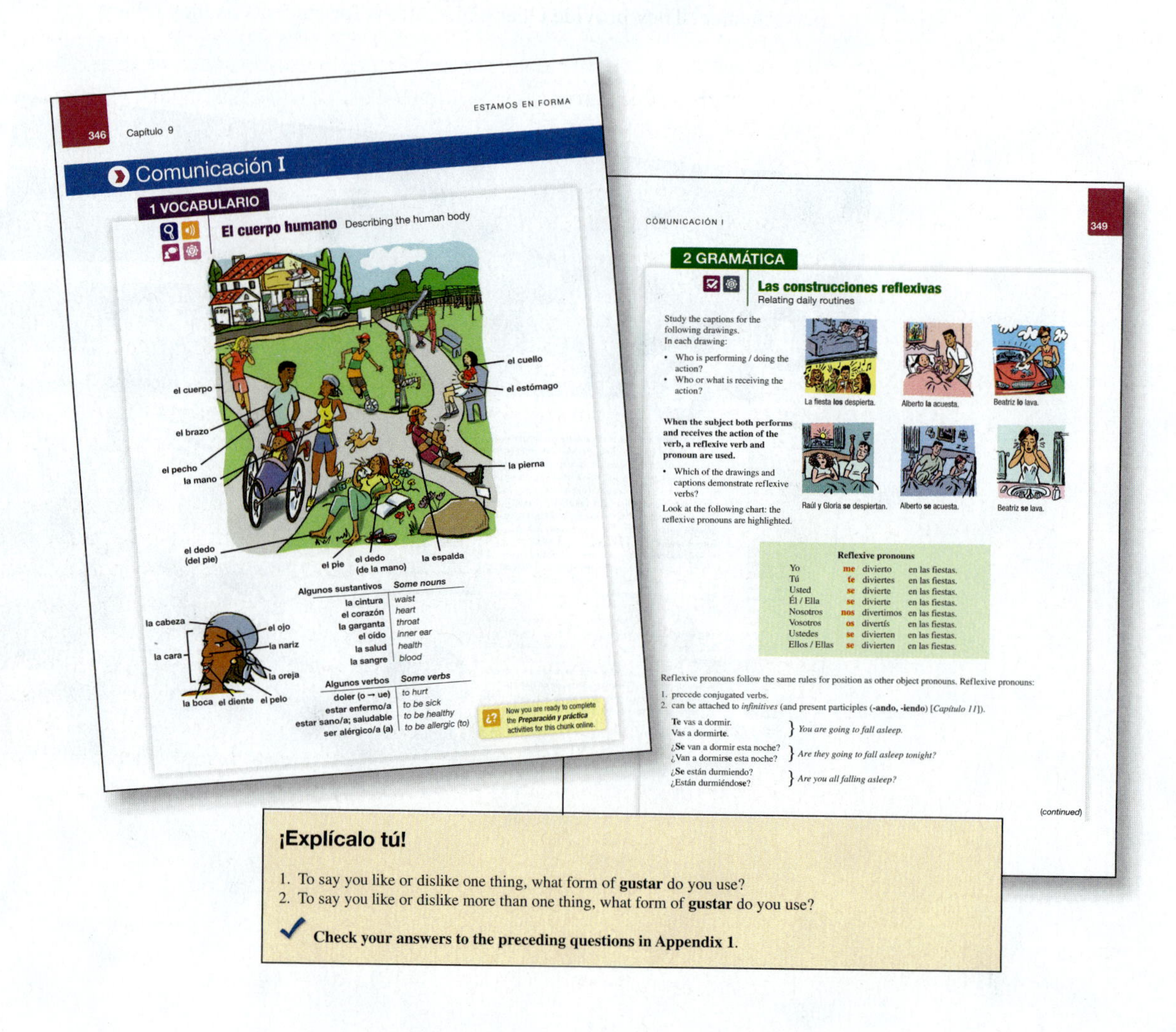

346 Capítulo 9 ESTAMOS EN FORMA

Comunicación I

1 VOCABULARIO

El cuerpo humano Describing the human body

Algunos sustantivos	Some nouns
la cintura	waist
el corazón	heart
la garganta	throat
el oído	inner ear
la salud	health
la sangre	blood

Algunos verbos	Some verbs
doler (o → ue)	to hurt
estar enfermo/a	to be sick
estar sano/a; saludable	to be healthy
ser alérgico/a (a)	to be allergic (to)

Now you are ready to complete the ***Preparación y práctica*** activities for this chunk online.

COMUNICACIÓN I 349

2 GRAMÁTICA

Las construcciones reflexivas
Relating daily routines

Study the captions for the following drawings. In each drawing:

- Who is performing / doing the action?
- Who or what is receiving the action?

La fiesta **los** despierta. Alberto **la** acuesta. Beatriz **lo** lava.

When the subject both performs and receives the action of the verb, a reflexive verb and pronoun are used.

- Which of the drawings and captions demonstrate reflexive verbs?

Raúl y Gloria **se** despiertan. Alberto **se** acuesta. Beatriz **se** lava.

Look at the following chart: the reflexive pronouns are highlighted.

Reflexive pronouns

Yo	me	divierto	en las fiestas.
Tú	te	diviertes	en las fiestas.
Usted	se	divierte	en las fiestas.
Él / Ella	se	divierte	en las fiestas.
Nosotros	nos	divertimos	en las fiestas.
Vosotros	os	divertís	en las fiestas.
Ustedes	se	divierten	en las fiestas.
Ellos / Ellas	se	divierten	en las fiestas.

Reflexive pronouns follow the same rules for position as other object pronouns. Reflexive pronouns:

1. precede conjugated verbs.
2. can be attached to *infinitives* (and present participles (**-ando, -iendo**) [*Capítulo 11*]).

Te vas a dormir. / Vas a dormir**te**. } *You are going to fall asleep.*

¿**Se** van a dormir esta noche? / ¿Van a dormir**se** esta noche? } *Are they going to fall asleep tonight?*

¿**Se** están durmiendo? / ¿Están durmiéndo**se**? } *Are you all falling asleep?*

(*continued*)

¡Explícalo tú!

1. To say you like or dislike one thing, what form of **gustar** do you use?
2. To say you like or dislike more than one thing, what form of **gustar** do you use?

✓ **Check your answers to the preceding questions in Appendix 1.**

INCREASING STUDENT TALK TIME

Promoting student communication inside and outside of class!

With so many real-life barriers to promoting oral proficiency—more students in each class, fewer contact hours, new course models like hybrid and fully online, students busier than ever—how can you make more time for speaking in the classroom? The *¡Anda!* program offers practical solutions that work. It gives students *more time to talk inside and outside the classroom* so that the opportunities for achieving oral proficiency increase dramatically.

¿? Now you are ready to complete the ***Preparación y práctica*** activities for this chunk online.

- **NEW** to this edition, online ***Preparación y práctica*** activities give students the practice they need before coming to class to actively participate in pair and group work. Virtually all of the in-class practice is comprised of pair and group activities, thereby ensuring students spend their class time speaking. However, note that there is a realistic approach to the activity sequence; not all activities are open-ended (more demanding), but rather practice begins with the **online *Preparación y práctica*** comprehension activities, followed in class by more **mechanical** exercises. Practice then progresses through more **meaningful, structured** activities in which the student is guided but has some flexibility in determining the appropriate response, and ends with **communicative** activities in which students are manipulating language to create personalized responses. With ***¡Anda!,*** the goal is for students to speak 20–30 minutes per class period.
- **NEW!** A wealth of online tools that provide students with options for **out-of-class communicative practice** include ***LiveChat***, a pair/group video recording tool, ***MediaShare***, a video sharing site, and ***WeSpeke***, the website that allows students to connect virtually with native speakers.
  - **NEW *LiveChat*** activities in ***¡Anda!* online** give students the opportunity to speak with other students online using chapter vocabulary, grammar, and cultural knowledge. The *LiveChat* tool offers synchronous audio and video recording capability, so instructors can **easily facilitate oral practice outside the classroom**. The *LiveChat* tool transmits the video and audio recording to the grade book where instructors can then review, comment or leave feedback, and assign a grade.
  - **NEW *MediaShare*** activities at the end of each *Lectura* section give students valuable practice in the presentational mode of communication. *MediaShare* **increases out-of-class talk time** by allowing language learners to create and post videos of assignments, role-plays, group projects, and more in a variety of formats including video, Word, PowerPoint, and Excel. Structured much like a social networking site, *MediaShare* helps promote a sense of community among learners. Instructors can create and post assignments—or copy and use preloaded assignments—and then evaluate and comment on learners' submissions online. Instructors also have the option of allowing peer review of submissions. Integrated video-capture functionality allows learners and instructors to record video directly from a webcam, smartphone, or tablet using the *MediaShare* app and easily upload their assignment.

- In collaboration with *WeSpeke*, **NEW** chapter-specific activities enable students to **practice new language "live" with native speakers** of their choosing from around the world. Learners select native speaking partners and complete activities that put newly acquired language to use in the "real" world, which increases curiosity, cross-cultural communication, engagement, and motivation.

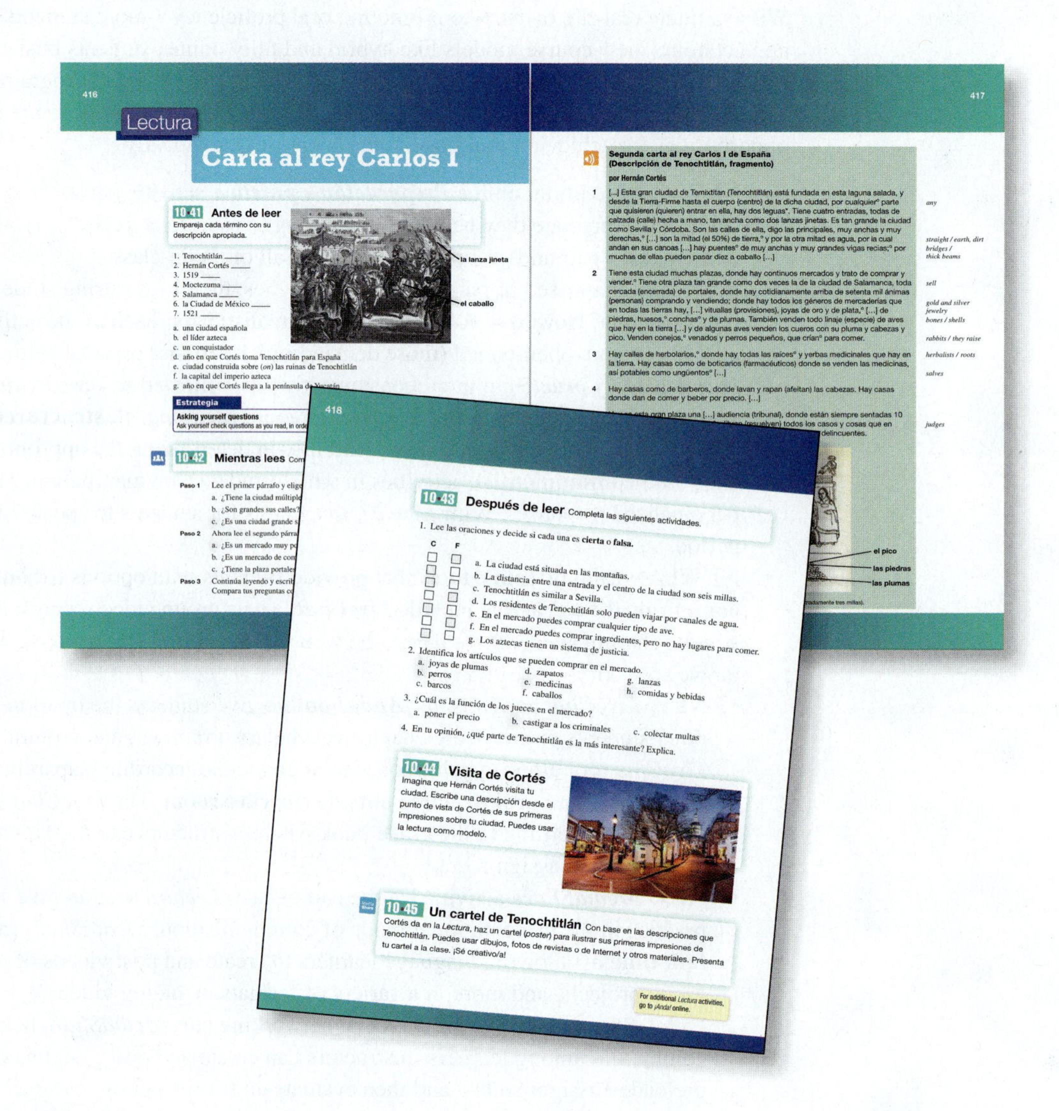

416

Lectura

Carta al rey Carlos I

10-41 Antes de leer Empareja cada término con su descripción apropiada.

1. Tenochtitlán _____
2. Hernán Cortés _____
3. 1519 _____
4. Moctezuma _____
5. Salamanca _____
6. la Ciudad de México _____
7. 1521 _____

a. una ciudad española
b. el líder azteca
c. un conquistador
d. año en que Cortés toma Tenochtitlán para España
e. ciudad construida sobre (*on*) las ruinas de Tenochtitlán
f. la capital del imperio azteca
g. año en que Cortés llega a la península de Yucatán

Estrategia

Asking yourself questions
Ask yourself check questions as you read, in orde

10-42 Mientras lees Com

Paso 1 Lee el primer párrafo y elige
a. ¿Tiene la ciudad múltiple
b. ¿Son grandes sus calles?
c. ¿Es una ciudad grande s

Paso 2 Ahora lee el segundo párra
a. ¿Es un mercado muy po
b. ¿Es un mercado de com
c. ¿Tiene la plaza portales

Paso 3 Continúa leyendo y escrib
Compara tus preguntas co

417

Segunda carta al rey Carlos I de España (Descripción de Tenochtitlán, fragmento)

por Hernán Cortés

1 [...] Esta gran ciudad de Temixtitan (Tenochtitlán) está fundada en esta laguna salada, y desde la Tierra-Firme hasta el cuerpo (centro) de la dicha ciudad, por cualquier° parte que quisieren (quieren) entrar en ella, hay dos leguas*. Tiene cuatro entradas, todas de calzada (calle) hecha a mano, tan ancha como dos lanzas jinetas. Es tan grande la ciudad como Sevilla y Córdoba. Son las calles de ella, digo las principales, muy anchas y muy derechas,° [...] son la mitad (el 50%) de tierra,° y por la otra mitad es agua, por la cual andan en sus canoas [...] hay puentes° de muy anchas y muy grandes vigas recias;° por muchas de ellas pueden pasar diez a caballo [...]

2 Tiene esta ciudad muchas plazas, donde hay continuos mercados y trato de comprar y vender.° Tiene otra plaza tan grande como dos veces la de la ciudad de Salamanca, toda cercada (encerrada) de portales, donde hay cotidianamente arriba de setenta mil ánimas (personas) comprando y vendiendo; donde hay todos los géneros de mercaderías que en todas las tierras hay, [...] vituallas (provisiones), joyas de oro y de plata,° [...] de piedras, huesos,° conchas° y de plumas. También venden todo linaje (especie) de aves que hay en la tierra [...] y de algunas aves venden los cueros con su pluma y cabezas y pico. Venden conejos,° venados y perros pequeños, que crían° para comer.

3 Hay calles de herbolarios,° donde hay todas las raíces° y yerbas medicinales que hay en la tierra. Hay casas como de boticarios (farmacéuticos) donde se venden las medicinas, así potables como ungüentos° [...]

4 Hay casas como de barberos, donde lavan y rapan (afeitan) las cabezas. Hay casas donde dan de comer y beber por precio. [...]

esta gran plaza una [...] audiencia (tribunal), donde están siempre sentadas 10 (resuelven) todos los casos y cosas que en delincuentes.

any
straight / earth, dirt
bridges / thick beams
sell
gold and silver jewelry
bones / shells
rabbits / they raise
herbalists / roots
salves
judges

418

10-43 Después de leer Completa las siguientes actividades.

1. Lee las oraciones y decide si cada una es **cierta** o **falsa.**

C	F	
☐	☐	a. La ciudad está situada en las montañas.
☐	☐	b. La distancia entre una entrada y el centro de la ciudad son seis millas.
☐	☐	c. Tenochtitlán es similar a Sevilla.
☐	☐	d. Los residentes de Tenochtitlán solo pueden viajar por canales de agua.
☐	☐	e. En el mercado puedes comprar cualquier tipo de ave.
☐	☐	f. En el mercado puedes comprar ingredientes, pero no hay lugares para comer.
☐	☐	g. Los aztecas tienen un sistema de justicia.

2. Identifica los artículos que se pueden comprar en el mercado.
   a. joyas de plumas
   b. perros
   c. barcos
   d. zapatos
   e. medicinas
   f. caballos
   g. lanzas
   h. comidas y bebidas
3. ¿Cuál es la función de los jueces en el mercado?
   a. poner el precio
   b. castigar a los criminales
   c. colectar multas
4. En tu opinión, ¿qué parte de Tenochtitlán es la más interesante? Explica.

10-44 Visita de Cortés Imagina que Hernán Cortés visita tu ciudad. Escribe una descripción desde el punto de vista de Cortés de sus primeras impresiones sobre tu ciudad. Puedes usar la lectura como modelo.

10-45 Un cartel de Tenochtitlán Con base en las descripciones que Cortés da en la *Lectura*, haz un cartel (*poster*) para ilustrar sus primeras impresiones de Tenochtitlán. Puedes usar dibujos, fotos de revistas o de Internet y otros materiales. Presenta tu cartel a la clase. ¡Sé creativo/a!

For additional *Lectura* activities, go to *¡Anda!* online.

FOCUS ON STUDENT MOTIVATION

Students will *stride with enthusiasm* if they are engaged with the content and are not intimidated!

The many innovative features of ***¡Anda!*** that have made it such a successful program continue in the third edition to help instructors generate and sustain interest on the part of their students, whether they be of traditional college age or adult learners:

- **Jump-start chapters: *¡Anda!*** has two preliminary chapters, one at the beginning of each term. A preliminary chapter at the beginning is designed to get students speaking quickly and experience the magic of communication in a new language right away. The purpose of the second preliminary chapter, for the beginning of the second term, is to help students remember what they learned in the first term or to help those students who placed into second term by giving them a catch-up or review.
- **A refined approach to vocabulary:** A reasonable, basic vocabulary load was selected and tested for relevance and support throughout the development of ***¡Anda!*** Furthermore, **additional words and phrases** are offered so that **students can personalize their responses** and acquire the vocabulary that is most meaningful to them. An icon in the vocabulary presentations allows students to link to the *También se dice…* lists in Appendix 3 from the eText for additional personalization of vocabulary.
- **No assumptions** are made concerning previous experience with Spanish or with language learning in general. Readiness Checks in ***¡Anda!* online** check for student understanding of English grammar concepts to ensure that they understand the basic concepts of language learning. Based on their performance on the Readiness Check diagnostic quiz, English Grammar Tutorials help to fill in the gaps in their grammar knowledge. In the chapters themselves, Student Notes provide additional explanations and guidance in the learning process. Throughout the program, explicit and transparent recycling reminds students where they can review vocabulary and previous grammar topics. The focus is on motivating students by ensuring that they have the tools that they need to succeed.

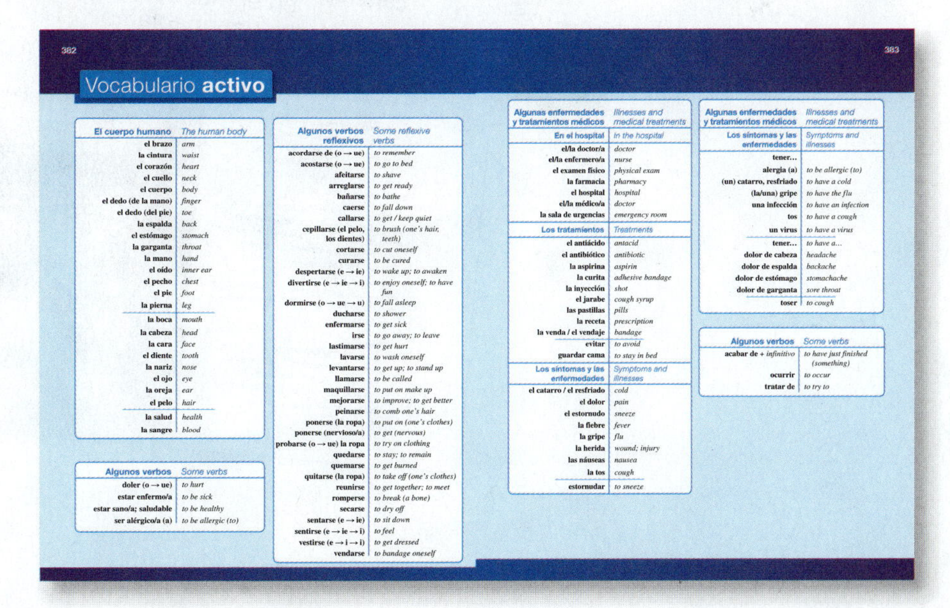

382

Vocabulario **activo**

El cuerpo humano	The human body
el brazo	arm
la cintura	waist
el corazón	heart
el cuello	neck
el cuerpo	body
el dedo (de la mano)	finger
el dedo (del pie)	toe
la espalda	back
el estómago	stomach
la garganta	throat
la mano	hand
el oído	inner ear
el pecho	chest
el pie	foot
la pierna	leg
la boca	mouth
la cabeza	head
la cara	face
el diente	tooth
la nariz	nose
el ojo	eye
la oreja	ear
el pelo	hair
la salud	health
la sangre	blood

Algunos verbos	Some verbs
doler (o → ue)	to hurt
estar enfermo/a	to be sick
estar sano/a; saludable	to be healthy
ser alérgico/a (a)	to be allergic (to)

Algunos verbos reflexivos	Some reflexive verbs
acordarse de (o → ue)	to remember
acostarse (o → ue)	to go to bed
afeitarse	to shave
arreglarse	to get ready
bañarse	to bathe
caerse	to fall down
callarse	to get / keep quiet
cepillarse (el pelo, los dientes)	to brush (one's hair, teeth)
cortarse	to cut oneself
curarse	to be cured
despertarse (e → ie)	to wake up; to awaken
divertirse (e → ie → i)	to enjoy oneself; to have fun
dormirse (o → ue → u)	to fall asleep
ducharse	to shower
enfermarse	to get sick
irse	to go away; to leave
lastimarse	to get hurt
lavarse	to wash oneself
levantarse	to get up; to stand up
llamarse	to be called
maquillarse	to put on make up
mejorarse	to improve; to get better
peinarse	to comb one's hair
ponerse (la ropa)	to put on (one's clothes)
ponerse (nervioso/a)	to get (nervous)
probarse (o → ue) la ropa	to try on clothing
quedarse	to stay; to remain
quemarse	to get burned
quitarse (la ropa)	to take off (one's clothes)
reunirse	to get together; to meet
romperse	to break (a bone)
secarse	to dry off
sentarse (e → ie)	to sit down
sentirse (e → ie → i)	to feel
vestirse (e → i → i)	to get dressed
vendarse	to bandage oneself

383

Algunas enfermedades y tratamientos médicos	Illnesses and medical treatments
En el hospital	*In the hospital*
el/la doctor/a	doctor
el/la enfermero/a	nurse
el examen físico	physical exam
la farmacia	pharmacy
el hospital	hospital
el/la médico/a	doctor
la sala de urgencias	emergency room
Los tratamientos	*Treatments*
el antiácido	antacid
el antibiótico	antibiotic
la aspirina	aspirin
la curita	adhesive bandage
la inyección	shot
el jarabe	cough syrup
las pastillas	pills
la receta	prescription
la venda / el vendaje	bandage
evitar	to avoid
guardar cama	to stay in bed
Los síntomas y las enfermedades	*Symptoms and illnesses*
el catarro / el resfriado	cold
el dolor	pain
el estornudo	sneeze
la fiebre	fever
la gripe	flu
la herida	wound; injury
las náuseas	nausea
la tos	cough
estornudar	to sneeze

Algunas enfermedades y tratamientos médicos	Illnesses and medical treatments
Los síntomas y las enfermedades	*Symptoms and illnesses*
tener…	
alergia (a)	to be allergic (to)
(un) catarro, resfriado	to have a cold
(la/una) gripe	to have the flu
una infección	to have an infection
tos	to have a cough
un virus	to have a virus
tener…	to have a…
dolor de cabeza	headache
dolor de espalda	backache
dolor de estómago	stomachache
dolor de garganta	sore throat
toser	to cough

Algunos verbos	Some verbs
acabar de + *infinitivo*	to have just finished (something)
ocurrir	to occur
tratar de	to try to

- **NEW! Relatable readings and activities** help students put activities that they do in their own lives, like updating social media pages, writing e-mails, reading blogs, and more, into practice in Spanish. Authentic texts in *Capítulos 10* and *11* introduce students to the richness of the Spanish language and serve as a portal to authentic culture while preparing students further literature study in ***¡Anda! Curso intermedio***.
- **NEW!** In the ***Club cultura*** video program in the *Vistazo cultural* section, six native speaker hosts **introduce students to contemporary cultural customs and daily life**—traditions, geography, history, and festivals—among other engaging aspects of Hispanic culture. Students are immersed in the nuances of culture and the Spanish language while being exposed to topics that are dynamic and exciting. New activities written especially for ***¡Anda!* online** are language-controlled and offer a process approach to help students understand and gain insight into the countries they are studying.
- Both **"high" and "popular" culture** are woven throughout the chapters to enable students to learn to recognize and appreciate cultural diversity as they explore behaviors and values of the Spanish-speaking world.

376

Vistazo cultural

Explore more about Bolivia with *Club cultura* online.

Bolivia

Les presento mi país

Fíjate: The abbreviation *m.s.n.m* means *metros sobre el nivel del mar*, or meters above sea level.

Mi nombre es Jorge Gustavo Salazar y soy de Sucre, una de las dos capitales de mi país y la sede (*headquarters*) constitucional de Bolivia. La Paz, la capital administrativa, es la capital más alta del mundo, a unos 3.650 m.s.n.m. en los Andes. **¿A qué altura está tu ciudad?** En Bolivia más del cincuenta por ciento de la población es indígena, como los aymara que viven en la zona del altiplano cerca del lago Titicaca. Desde tiempos remotos, los pueblos indígenas usaron las plantas y los rituales para tratar enfermedades, y el uso de la medicina tradicional es común en Bolivia hoy día. Por ejemplo, algunos bolivianos mastican (*chew*) las hojas de coca (*coca leaves*) para aliviar el hambre, el cansancio y el mal de altura (*altitude sickness*) **¿Es popular la medicina tradicional donde vives tú?**

Jorge Gustavo Salazar

El lago Titicaca está en la frontera entre Bolivia y Perú y es el lago navegable más alto del mundo.

Una mujer aymara con ropa tradicional

Unas hojas de coca a la venta en un mercado de La Paz

375

Vistazo cultural

Explore more about Peru with *Club cultura* online.

Perú

Les presento mi país

Mi nombre es Diana Ávila Peralta y soy de Ayacucho, Perú. Hay muchas ruinas de la civilización incaica en mi país, como las de Machu Picchu y Cuzco, la antigua capital del imperio inca. Cuando era más joven, visité Cuzco con mi familia y la arquitectura e historia de esta ciudad me inspiraron mucho. Ahora estudio historia en la Universidad Nacional Mayor de San Marcos en Lima y quiero ser profesora para compartir mi pasión con otras personas. **¿Qué profesión quieres tener en el futuro?** Perú es un país de extremos geográficos: tenemos la costa, las montañas impresionantes de los Andes, cañones profundos, la selva y el nacimiento (*source*) del río Amazonas con flora y fauna magníficas. ¡Puedes hacer mucho ejercicio caminando por estas zonas! **¿Qué haces tú para mantenerte en forma?**

Diana Ávila Peralta

En Cuzco se puede apreciar la arquitectura inca y colonial.

Loros en la selva amazónica

Miraflores, en las afueras de Lima, Perú

Preguntas

1. ¿Qué estudia Diana?
2. ¿Por qué se dice que Perú es un país de geografía muy variada?
3. ¿Qué otros países comparten algunas de las características geográficas de Perú?

Nota cultural

Las farmacias en el mundo hispanohablante

En Latinoamérica, las farmacias son, por la mayor parte, dispensarios de medicina únicamente. El farmacéutico (*pharmacist*) muchas veces ofrece consejos sobre los medicamentos (medicinas). Es fácil conseguir muchos tipos de medicina sin receta en las farmacias. Por ejemplo, puedes ir a la farmacia, describir los síntomas que tienes (como tos y fiebre) y pedir que te den unos antibióticos. Todo ello sin consultar al médico. Muchos países tienen *farmacias de turno* o *de guardia* que atienden al público las veinticuatro horas del día.

En algunos países (como Argentina, Chile y Perú) hay un nuevo tipo de farmacia al estilo estadounidense, que vende de todo. Estas farmacias pertenecen a grandes cadenas (Farmacity en Argentina, Farmacias Ahumada [FASA] en Chile, Inka Farma en Perú) que atraen a los consumidores con una gran variedad de productos, aparte de los medicamentos.

Preguntas

1. ¿Qué es una "farmacia de turno" o "farmacia de guardia"? ¿Existe este sistema en los Estados Unidos?
2. ¿Qué diferencias hay entre las farmacias hispanas tradicionales y las de los Estados Unidos?

TOOLS TO PROMOTE SUCCESS

Students and instructors will walk *with confidence* when they have the support tools when and where they need them!

The *¡Anda!* program includes many unique features and components designed to help students succeed at language learning and their instructors at language teaching.

Student learning support

- An online **"walking tour"** of the *¡Anda!* text and ***¡Anda!* online** tools helps students navigate their language program materials and understand better the "whys" and "hows" of learning Spanish.
- **A digital zoom tool for vocabulary** in ***¡Anda!* online** allows students to zoom in and see the vocabulary images more clearly and hear the words pronounced.
- One of the hallmarks of the *¡Anda!* program is the **transparent and comprehensive recycling system** that helps students link current learning to previously studied materials in earlier chapters or sections. Deliberate and explicit recycling makes students aware of the fact that language learning continually builds upon what they know and reuses what they know in different contexts:
  - Within chapters: vocabulary and grammar are carried from one chunk to another whenever possible and appropriate.
  - From chapter to chapter: There are many recycling activities in each chapter. Icons indicate this and give a reference to the student of exactly where the recycled concept is referenced earlier in the text.
  - There are two chapters entirely devoted to recycling. *Capítulo 6* recycles materials from *Capítulo A* through *Capítulo 5* and *Capítulo 12* recycles material from *Capítulo 7* through *Capítulo 11.* No new material is presented in these chapters. Rubrics have been provided for these chapters to assess student performance.
- **Periodic review and self-assessment** boxes (*¿Cómo andas I?* and *¿Cómo andas II?*) help students gauge their understanding and retention of the material presented. A final assessment in each chapter *(Y por fin, ¿cómo andas?)* offers a comprehensive review and ties to the Learning Outcomes at the beginning of each chapter. Practice activities available in ***¡Anda!* online** allow students to self-assess their understanding of chapter concepts, including full-length practice tests with remediation.

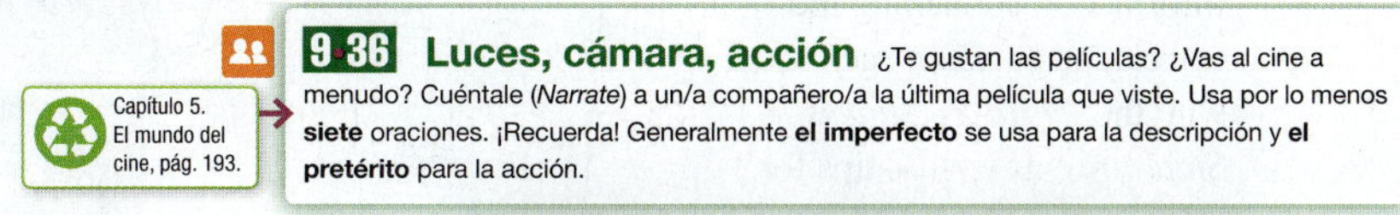

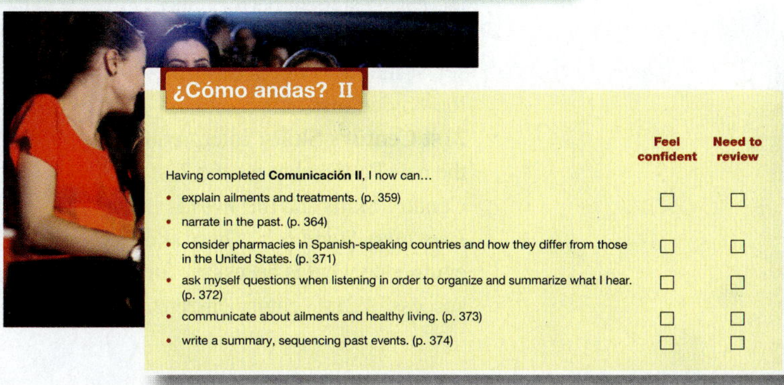

- **Student notes** provide additional explanations and guidance in the learning process. These notes offer learning strategies (*Estrategia*) and additional information (*Fíjate*).
- ***¡Anda!* online** offers students a wealth of online resources and a supportive environment for completing homework assignments and self-study. Extra resources appear at the point-of-need to support students as they complete online homework activities; providing links to English and Spanish grammar tutorials, eText sections, and additional practice activities—all directly relevant to the task at hand. Hints, verb charts, a glossary, and many other resources are available as well.

Instructor teaching support

One of the most important keys to student success is instructor success. The ***¡Anda!*** program has all of the support that you have come to expect and, based on our research, it offers many other enhancements!

- The **Annotated Instructor's Edition** of ***¡Anda!*** offers an abundance of materials designed to help instructors teach effectively and efficiently. Strategically placed annotations explain the text's methodology and function as **a built-in course in language teaching methods.**
- **Estimated time indicators** for presentational materials and practice activities help instructors create class plans.
- Other annotations provide **additional activities** and **suggested answers**.
- **The annotations are color-coded** and labeled for ready reference and ease of use.
- A treasure trove of supplemental activities, available for download in ***¡Anda!* online**, allows instructors to choose additional materials for in-class use.
- **NEW: Learning Catalytics™** offers instructors an easy way to engage students, incorporate quick checks, implement peer-to-peer learning in class, and track student performance through real-time analytics. Included in ***¡Anda!* online**, this interactive classroom tool uses students' smartphones, tablets, and laptops to engage them in sophisticated tasks and thinking in the classroom. Instructors can create their own activities or use activities especially prepared for ***¡Anda!***

Teacher annotations

The teacher annotations in the ***¡Anda!*** program fall into several categories:

- **Section Goals:** Set of student objectives for each section.
- ***World-Readiness Standards:*** Information containing the correlation between each section with the *World-Readiness Standards,* as well as tips for increasing student performance.
- **Methodology:** A deep and broad set of methods notes designed for the novice instructor.
- **21st Century Skills:** Interpreting the new Partnership for the 21st Century Skills and the *World-Readiness Standards*. These skills enumerate what is necessary for successful 21st century citizens.

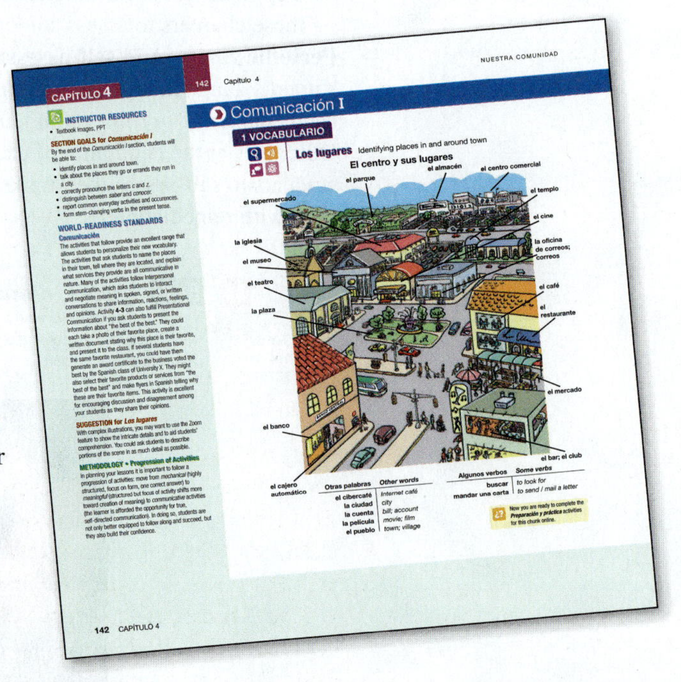

CAPÍTULO 4

142 Capítulo 4 NUESTRA COMUNIDAD

INSTRUCTOR RESOURCES
- Textbook Images, PPT

SECTION GOALS for *Comunicación I*
By the end of the *Comunicación I* section, students will be able to:
- identify places in and around town.
- talk about the places they go or errands they run in a city.
- correctly pronounce the letters *c* and *z*.
- distinguish between *saber* and *conocer*.
- report common everyday activities and occurences.
- form stem-changing verbs in the present tense.

WORLD-READINESS STANDARDS
Comunicación
The activities that follow provide an excellent range that allows students to personalize their new vocabulary. The activities that ask students to name the places in their town, tell where they are located, and explain what services they provide are all communicative in nature. Many of the activities follow Interpersonal Communication, which asks students to interact and negotiate meaning in spoken, signed, or written conversations to share information, reactions, feelings, and opinions. Activity **4-3** can also fulfill Presentational Communication if you ask students to present the information about "the best of the best." They could each take a photo of their favorite place, create a written document stating why this place is their favorite, and present it to the class. If several students have the same favorite restaurant, you could have them generate an award certificate to the business voted the best by the Spanish class of University X. They might also select their favorite products or services from "the best of the best" and make flyers in Spanish telling why these are their favorite items. This activity is excellent for encouraging discussion and disagreement among your students as they share their opinions.

SUGGESTION for *Los lugares*
With complex illustrations, you may want to use the Zoom feature to show the intricate details and to aid students' comprehension. You could ask students to describe portions of the scene in as much detail as possible.

METHODOLOGY • Progression of Activities
In planning your lessons it is important to follow a progression of activities: move from *mechanical* (highly structured, focus on form, one correct answer) to *meaningful* (structured but focus of activity shifts more toward creation of meaning) to *communicative* activities (the learner is afforded the opportunity for true, self-directed communication). In doing so, students are not only better equipped to follow along and succeed, but they also build their confidence.

Comunicación I

1 VOCABULARIO

Los lugares Identifying places in and around town

El centro y sus lugares

Otras palabras	Other words
el cibercafé	*Internet café*
la ciudad	*city*
la cuenta	*bill; account*
la película	*movie; film*
el pueblo	*town; village*

Algunos verbos	Some verbs
buscar	*to look for*
mandar una carta	*to send / mail a letter*

Now you are ready to complete the ***Preparación y práctica*** activities for this chunk online.

142 CAPÍTULO 4

- **Planning Ahead:** Suggestions for instructors included in the chapter openers to help prepare materials in advance for certain activities in the chapter. Also provided is information regarding which activities to assign to students prior to them coming to class.
- **Warm-Up:** Suggestions for setting up an activity or how to activate students' prior knowledge relating to the task at hand.
- **Suggestion:** Teaching tips that provide ideas that will help with the implementation of activities and sections.
- **Expansion:** Ideas for variations of a topic that may serve as wrap-up activities.
- **Follow-Up:** Suggestions to aid instructors in assessing student comprehension.
- **Notes:** Information on people, places, and things that aid in the completion of activities and sections by providing background knowledge.
- **Additional Activity:** Independent activities related to the ones in the text that provide further practice.
- **Alternate Activity:** Variations of activities provided to suit individual classrooms and preferences.
- **Heritage Language Learners:** Suggestions for the heritage language learners in the classroom that provide alternatives and expansions for sections and activities based on prior knowledge and skills.
- **Audioscript:** Written script of all audio recordings.

The authors' approach

Learning a language is an exciting, enriching, and sometimes life-changing experience. The development of the *¡Anda!* program, now in its third edition, is the result of many years of teaching and research that guided the authors independently to make important discoveries about language learning, the most important of which center on the student. Research-based and pedagogically sound, *¡Anda!* is also the product of extensive information gathered firsthand from numerous focus group sessions with students, graduate instructors, adjunct faculty, full-time professors, and administrators in an effort to determine the learning and instructional needs of each of these groups.

The importance of the *World-Readiness Standards* in *¡Anda!*

The *¡Anda!* program continues to be based on the *World-Readiness Standards.* The five organizing principles (the 5 Cs) of the Standards for language teaching and learning are at the core of *¡Anda!*: **Communication, Cultures, Connections, Comparisons,** and **Communities**. Each chapter opener identifies for the instructor where and in what capacity each of the 5 Cs are addressed. The **Weave of Curricular Elements** of the *World-Readiness Standards* provide additional organizational structure for *¡Anda!* The components of the **Curricular Weave** are: **Language System, Cultural Knowledge, Communication Strategies, Critical Thinking Skills, Learning Strategies, Other Subject Areas,** and **Technology**. Each of the Curricular Weave elements is omnipresent and, like the 5 Cs, permeates all aspects of each chapter of *¡Anda!*

- The **Language System**, which is comprised of components such as grammar, vocabulary, and phonetics, is at the heart of each chapter.
- The **Comunicación** sections of each chapter present vocabulary, grammar, and pronunciation at the point of need and maximum usage. Streamlined presentations are utilized that allow the learner to be immediately successful in employing the new concepts.
- **Cultural Knowledge** is approached thematically, making use of the chapter's vocabulary and grammar. Many of the grammar and vocabulary activities are presented in a cultural context. Cultural presentations begin with the two-page chapter openers and always start with what the students already know about the cultural theme/concept from their home, local, regional,

or national cultural perspective. The *Nota cultural* and *Vistazo cultural* sections provide rich cultural information about each Hispanic country.

- **Communication and Learning Strategies** are abundant with tips for both students and instructors on how to maximize studying and in-class learning of Spanish, as well as how to utilize the language outside of the classroom.
- **Critical Thinking Skills** take center stage in ***¡Anda!*** Questions throughout the chapters, in particular tied to the cultural presentations, provide students with the opportunities to respond to more than discrete-point questions. The answers students are able to provide do indeed require higher-order thinking, but at a linguistic level completely appropriate for a beginning language learner.
- With regard to **Other Subject Areas, *¡Anda!*** is diligent with regard to incorporating **Connections** to other disciplines via vocabulary, discussion topics, and suggested activities.
- Finally, **Technology** is taken to an entirely new level with ***¡Anda!* online**. The authors and Pearson believe that technology is a means to the end, not the end in itself, and so the focus is not on the technology per se, but on how that technology can facilitate learning and deliver great content in better, more efficient, more interactive, and more meaningful ways.

By embracing the *World-Readiness Standards* and as a result of decades of experience teaching Spanish, the authors believe that:

- A **student-centered classroom** is the best learning environment.
- Instruction must **begin where the learner is**, and all students come to the learning experience with prior knowledge that needs to be tapped.
- All students can learn in a **supportive environment** where they are encouraged to take risks when learning another language.
- **Critical thinking** is an important skill that must constantly be encouraged, practiced, and nurtured.
- **Learners** need to **make connections** with other disciplines in the Spanish classroom.

With these beliefs in mind, the authors have developed hundreds of creative and meaningful language-learning activities for the text and supporting components that employ students' imagination and engage the senses. For both students and instructors, they have created an instructional program that is **manageable, motivating,** and **clear**.

¡Que lo disfruten! Enjoy!

THE AUTHORS

Glynis Cowell

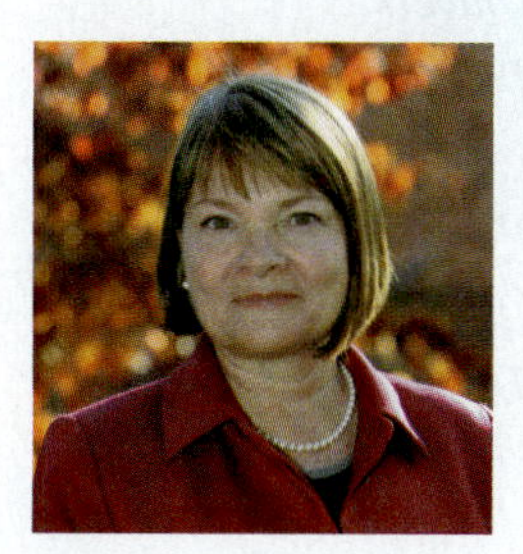

Glynis Cowell is the Director of Spanish Language Instruction and the Director of Undergraduate Studies in the Department of Romance Studies at the University of North Carolina at Chapel Hill. She has taught first-year seminars, honors courses, and numerous face-to-face and hybrid Spanish language courses. She also team-teaches a graduate course on the theories and techniques of teaching foreign languages. Dr. Cowell received her M.A. in Spanish Literature and her Ph.D. in Curriculum and Instruction, with a concentration in Foreign Language Education, from the University of North Carolina at Chapel Hill. Prior to joining the faculty at UNC-CH in August 1994, she coordinated the Spanish Language Program in the Department of Romance Studies at Duke University. She has also taught Spanish at both the high school and community college level. At UNC-CH she has received the Students' Award for Excellence in Undergraduate Teaching as well as the Graduate Student Mentor Award for the Department of Romance Studies.

Dr. Cowell has directed teacher workshops on Spanish language and cultures and has presented papers and written articles on the teaching of language and literature, the transition to blended and online courses in language teaching, and teaching across the curriculum. She is the co-author of two other college textbooks.

Audrey Heining-Boynton

Audrey Heining-Boynton received her Ph.D. from Michigan State University and her M.A. from The Ohio State University. Her career spans K–12 through graduate school teaching, most recently as Professor of Education and Spanish at the University of North Carolina at Chapel Hill. She has won many teaching awards, including the prestigious ACTFL Anthony Papalia Award for Excellence in Teacher Education, the Foreign Language Association of North Carolina (FLANC) Teacher of the Year Award, and the UNC ACCESS Award for Excellence in Working with LD and ADHD students. Dr. Heining-Boynton is a frequent presenter at national and international conferences, has published more than one hundred articles, curricula, textbooks, and manuals, and has won nearly $4 million in grants to help create language programs in North and South Carolina. Dr. Heining-Boynton has also held many important positions: President of the American Council on the Teaching of Foreign Languages (ACTFL), President of the National Network for Early Language Learning, Vice President of Michigan Foreign Language Association, board member of the Foreign Language Association of North Carolina, committee chair for Foreign Language in the Elementary School for the American Association of Teachers of Spanish and Portuguese, and elected Executive Council member of ACTFL. She is also an appointed two-term *Foreign Language Annals* Editorial Board member and guest editor of the publication.

Faculty Reviewers

Elizabeth Adams, *State University of New York, Geneseo*
Melba Amador, *Western Kentucky University*
Teresa Arrington, *Blue Mountain College*
Julie Augustinaitis, *Schoolcraft College*
Shaun Bauer, *University of Central Florida*
Hilda Benton, *University of Arkansas*
Isabel Brown, *University of South Alabama*
Aurora Castillo-Scott, *Georgia College State University*
Esther Castro, *San Diego State University*
Zoila Castro, *University of Rhode Island*
Miguel Dominguez, *California State University, Dominguez Hills*
Cory Duclos, *Spring Hill College*
Marla Estes, *University of North Texas*
Miguel Estrada, *Houston Baptist University*
Dina A. Fabery, *University of Central Florida*
Jenny Faile, *University of South Alabama*
Benito Gomez, *California State University, Dominguez Hills*
Viviannette Gonzalez, *Indiana University, Bloomington*
Joe Guerra, *Navarro College*
Heather Hinds, *University of Arkansas*
Cari Jiménez, *University of Florida*
Catherine Kraft, *Navarro College*
Veronica Marquez, *University of North Florida*
Kyle Matthews, *State University of New York, Geneseo*
Monica Montalvo, *University of Central Florida*
Iris Myers, *Roanoke College*
Carla Naranjo, *Montgomery College*
Rosalinda Nericcio, *San Diego State University*
Lisa Noetzel, *College of Coastal Georgia*
Andrea Nofz, *Schoolcraft College*
Diego Pascual, *Texas Tech University*
Robin Reeves, *Indiana University*
Manuela Rodriguez-Morales, *University of North Florida*
Paul Roggendorff, *Abilene Christian University*
Steven Sheppard, *University of North Texas*
Christine Stanley, *Roanoke College*
Silvina Trica-Flores, *Nassau Community College*
Phoebe Vitharana, *Le Moyne College*
Consuelo Wallace, *Navarro College*
Richard Wallace, *Crowder College*

Walk with Us Advisory Board

Susana Ackerman, *Santa Rosa Junior College*
Tyler Anderson, *Colorado Mesa University*
Alejandra Balestra, *University of Houston*
Melissa Birkhofer, *University of North Dakota*
Brian Boisvert, *State University of New York, Fredonia*
Kristy Britt, *University of South Alabama*
Rebecca Cottrell, *Metropolitan State University of Denver*
Allen Davis, *Indiana University*
Juan De Urda Anguita, *State University of New York, Fredonia*
Dorian Dorado, *Louisiana State University*
Laura Fox, *Grand Valley State University*
Lisa Fraguada-Pileggi, *Delaware County Community College*
Alejandra Galindo, *University of Tennessee, Knoxville*
Inma Gomez-Soler, *University of Memphis*
Shannon Hahn, *Durham Technical Community College*
Milvia Hernandez, *University of Maryland, Baltimore County*
Courtney Lanute, *Florida Southwestern State*
Jeff Longwell, *New Mexico State University*
Maria Manni, *University of Maryland, Baltimore County*
Elizabeth Morais, *Community College of Rhode Island*
Jennifer Rathbun, *Ashland University*
Terri Rice, *University of South Alabama*
Carmen Rivera, *State University of New York, Fredonia*
Ruth Sanchez, *Sewanee: University of the South*
Carmen Sparrow, *University of Tennessee, Knoxville*
Gwen Stickney, *North Dakota State University*
Erika Sutherland, *Muhlenberg College*
Linda Tracy, *Santa Rosa Junior College*
Gheorghita Tres, *Oakland Community College*
Victoria Uricoechea, *Winthrop University*
Paul Worley, *Western Carolina University*

ACKNOWLEDGMENTS

The third edition of ***¡Anda! Curso elemental*** is the result of careful planning between ourselves and our publisher and ongoing collaboration with students and you, our colleagues. We look forward to continuing this dialogue and sincerely appreciate your input. We owe special thanks to the many members of the Spanish-teaching community whose comments and suggestions helped shape the pages of every chapter—you will see yourselves everywhere. We gratefully acknowledge the reviewers for this third edition, and we thank them for their invaluable support, input, and feedback.

We are especially thankful for the unwavering support of Jean LeLoup. We are also grateful to those who have collaborated with us in the writing of ***¡Anda!*** Thank you to Josefa Lindquist for her outstanding work on the new *Lectura* section. We also thank Robin Reeves for the excellent integration of the new *Club cultura* video with the *Vistazo cultural*. We also thank her for the wonderful activities written to accompany the new video program. Thanks to Donna Binkowski for her work on the chapter openers and the *Notas culturales*. For ***¡Anda!*** **online**, we thank Marta Tecedor for her hard work on the digital Student Activities Manual, Jon Aske for the thoughtful revision of the Testing Program, Jeff Longwell for creating the *LiveChat* Activities, Mónica Montalvo for the creation of the *MediaShare* activities, and Rob Martinsen for his work on the *WeSpeke* activities for ***¡Anda!***

Equally important are the contributions of the highly talented individuals at Pearson Education. We wish to express our gratitude and deep appreciation to the many people at Pearson who contributed their ideas, tireless efforts, and publishing experience to this third edition of ***¡Anda! Curso elemental.*** First, we thank Bob Hemmer, Editor in Chief, and Denise Miller, Senior Acquisitions Editor, whose support and guidance have been essential. We are indebted to Gisela Aragón-Velthaus, Senior Development Editor, for all of her hard work, suggestions, attention to detail, and dedication to the programs. We have also been fortunate to have Scott Gravina, Director of Editorial Development, who brings his special talents to the project, helping to create the outstanding final product. We send our thanks to the development team of Sarah Link, Gabriela Ferland, Andrew Bowen, Patricia Acosta, Nina Tunac Basey, and Kristen Chapron for their focus and attention on the myriad details of the program. We would also like to thank Samantha Alducin for all of the hard work on the integration of technology for the ***¡Anda!*** program. Thanks to Elle McGill, Editorial Assistant, for attending to many administrative details.

Our thanks also go to Steve Debow, Marketing Director, and the World Language Consultants, Yesha Brill, Raúl Vásquez López, and Mellissa Yokell, for their strong support of ***¡Anda!,*** and for creating and coordinating all marketing and promotion for this third edition. Thank you to Millie Chapman and Marlene Gassler, Project Managers, and Annemarie Franklin, Program Manager, who guided ***¡Anda!*** through the many stages of production. We continue to be indebted to Andrew Lange for the amazing illustrations that translate our vision.

We also thank our colleagues and students from across the country who inspire us and from whom we learn.

And finally, our love and deepest appreciation to our families for all of their support during this journey: John, Jack, Kate; and David.

Glynis S. Cowell
Audrey L. Heining-Boynton

Para empezar

You are about to begin the exciting journey of studying the Spanish language and learning about Hispanic culture. Learning a language is a skill much like learning to ski or playing an instrument. Developing these skills takes practice and in the beginning, perfection is not expected. Research has shown that successful language learners are willing to take risks and experiment with the language.

What is essential in learning Spanish is to keep trying and be willing to risk making mistakes, knowing that the practice will garner results. *¡Anda! Curso elemental* will be your guide and provide you with key essentials for becoming a successful language learner.

Why should you study Spanish, or for that matter, any language other than English? For some of you, the answer may be quite frankly, "because it is a graduation requirement!" Bear in mind, however, that Spanish is one of the most widely spoken languages in the world. You may find that knowledge of the Spanish language is a useful professional and personal tool.

If you have never studied Spanish before, this chapter will provide you with some basic words and expressions you will need to begin to use the language in meaningful ways. If you have already learned or studied some Spanish, this chapter can serve as a quick review.

Preguntas

1. Why is it important to study Spanish?
2. How might Spanish play a role in your future?

¿Sabías que...?

Spanish is the official language of 21 countries and over 400 million people speak Spanish as a native language.

Learning Outcomes

By the end of this chapter, you will be able to:

- ✔ greet, introduce, and say good-bye to someone.
- ✔ understand and respond appropriately to basic classroom expressions and requests.
- ✔ count from 0–30, state the time, elicit the date and season, and report the weather.
- ✔ share personal likes and dislikes.
- ✔ summarize the diversity of the Spanish-speaking world.

Comunicación

1 VOCABULARIO

Saludos, presentaciones y despedidas

Greeting, introducing, and saying good-bye to someone

Los saludos	*Greetings*
¡Hola!	*Hi! Hello!*
Buenos días.	*Good morning.*
Buenas tardes.	*Good afternoon.*
Buenas noches.	*Good evening; Good night.*
¿Cómo estás?	*How are you?* (familiar)
¿Cómo está usted?	*How are you?* (formal)
¿Qué tal?	*How's it going?*
Más o menos.	*So-so.*
Regular.	*Okay.*
Bien, gracias.	*Fine, thanks.*
Bastante bien.	*Just fine.*
Muy bien.	*Really well.*
¿Y tú?	*And you?* (familiar)
¿Y usted?	*And you?* (formal)

Las despedidas	*Farewells*
Adiós.	*Good-bye.*
Chao.	*Bye.*
Hasta luego.	*See you later.*
Hasta mañana.	*See you tomorrow.*
Hasta pronto.	*See you soon.*

—¿Qué tal?
—Bien.

—¿Cómo estás?
—Bien, gracias.

—Hasta mañana.
—Adiós.

Las presentaciones	*Introductions*
¿Cómo te llamas?	*What is your name?* (familiar)
¿Cómo se llama usted?	*What is your name?* (formal)
Me llamo...	*My name is...*
Soy...	*I am...*
Mucho gusto.	*Nice to meet you.*
Encantado/Encantada.	*Pleased to meet you.*
Igualmente.	*Likewise.*
Quiero presentarte a...	*I would like to introduce you to...* (familiar)
Quiero presentarle a...	*I would like to introduce you to...* (formal)

- The expressions **¿Cómo te llamas?** and **¿Cómo se llama usted?** both mean *What is your name?* but the former is used among students and other peers (referred to as *familiar*). You will learn about the differences between these *familiar* and *formal* forms later in this chapter. Note that **Encantado** is said by a male, and **Encantada** is said by a female.
- Spanish uses special punctuation to signal a question or an exclamation. An upside-down question mark begins a question and an upside-down exclamation mark begins an exclamation, as in **¿Cómo te llamas?** and **¡Hola!**

A-1 Saludos y despedidas Match each greeting or farewell with its logical response. Compare your answers with those of a classmate.

1. ______ ¿Qué tal?
2. ______ Hasta luego.
3. ______ ¿Cómo te llamas?
4. ______ Encantada.

a. Me llamo Julia.
b. Bastante bien.
c. Igualmente.
d. Hasta pronto.

A-2 **¡Hola! ¿Qué tal?** Greet five classmates, and ask how each is doing. After you are comfortable with one greeting, try a different one.

MODELO E1: *¡Hola! ¿Cómo estás?*
E2: *Bien, gracias. ¿Y tú?*
E1: *Muy bien.*

A-3 **¿Cómo te llamas?** Introduce yourself to three classmates.

MODELO E1: *¡Hola! Soy… ¿Cómo te llamas?*
E2: *Me llamo… Mucho gusto.*
E1: *Encantado/a.*
E2: *Igualmente.*

A-4 **Quiero presentarte a…** Now, introduce one person you have just met to another classmate.

MODELO E1: *John, quiero presentarte a Mike.*
MIKE: *Mucho gusto.*
JOHN: *Igualmente.*

A-5 **Una fiesta** Imagine that you are at a party. In groups of five, introduce yourselves to each other. Use the model as a guide.

MODELO AMY: *Hola, ¿qué tal? Soy Amy.*
ORLANDO: *Hola, Amy. Soy Orlando. ¿Cómo estás?*
AMY: *Muy bien, Orlando. ¿Y tú?*
ORLANDO: *Bien, gracias. Amy, quiero presentarte a Tom.*
TOM: *Encantado.*
E4: …

Cómo se saluda la gente

How do you generally greet acquaintances? Do you use different greetings for different people?

When native speakers of Spanish meet, they greet each other, ask each other how they are doing, and respond using phrases like the ones you just learned. In most of the Spanish-speaking world, men usually shake hands when greeting each other, although close male friends may greet each other with an **abrazo** (*hug*). Between female friends, the usual greeting is a **besito** (*little kiss*) on one or both cheeks (depending on the country) and a gentle hug. The **besito** is a gentle air kiss. When men and women greet each other, depending on their ages, how well they know each other, and what country they are in, they either simply shake hands and/or greet with a **besito.** While conversing, Spanish speakers may stand quite close to each other.

Preguntas

1. How do people in the Spanish-speaking world greet each other?
2. How do your male friends generally greet each other? And your female friends?
3. In general, how much distance is there between you and the person(s) with whom you are speaking?

2 VOCABULARIO

Expresiones útiles para la clase

Understanding and responding appropriately to basic classroom expressions and requests

The following list provides useful expressions that you and your instructor will use frequently.

Preguntas y respuestas	Questions and answers
¿Cómo?	*What? How?*
¿Cómo se dice... en español?	*How do you say... in Spanish?*
¿Cómo se escribe... en español?	*How do you write... in Spanish?*
¿Qué significa?	*What does it mean?*
¿Quién?	*Who?*
¿Qué es esto?	*What is this?*
Comprendo.	*I understand.*
No comprendo.	*I don't understand.*
Lo sé.	*I know.*
No lo sé.	*I don't know.*
Sí.	*Yes.*
No.	*No.*

Expresiones de cortesía	Polite expressions
De nada.	*You're welcome.*
Gracias.	*Thank you.*
Por favor.	*Please.*

Mandatos para la clase	Classroom instructions (commands)
Abra(n) el libro en la página...	*Open your book to page...*
Cierre(n) el/los libro/s.	*Close your book/s.*
Conteste(n).	*Answer.*
Escriba(n).	*Write.*
Escuche(n).	*Listen.*
Lea(n).	*Read.*
Repita(n).	*Repeat.*
Vaya(n) a la pizarra.	*Go to the board.*

In Spanish, commands can have two forms. The singular form (**abra, cierre, conteste,** etc.) is directed to one person, while the plural form (those ending in **-n: abran, cierren, contesten,** etc.) is used with more than one person.

A-6 Práctica Take turns saying which expressions or commands would be used in the following situations.

Estrategia

When working with a partner, always listen carefully. If your partner gives an incorrect response, help your partner arrive at the correct response.

1. You don't know the Spanish word for something.
2. Your teacher wants everyone to listen.
3. You need your teacher to repeat what he/she has said.
4. You don't know what something means.
5. Your teacher wants students to turn to a certain page.
6. You don't understand something.

A-7 Más práctica Play the roles of instructor **(I)** and student **(estudiante / E)**. The instructor either tells the student to do something or asks a question; the student responds appropriately. Practice with at least **five** sentences or questions, using the expressions that you have just learned; then change roles.

MODELO I: *Abra el libro.*
E: (Student opens the book.)
I: *¿Cómo se dice* hello?
E: *Se dice "hola".*

Estrategia

To learn Spanish more quickly, you should attempt to speak only Spanish in the classroom.

3 GRAMÁTICA

El alfabeto Spelling in Spanish

The Spanish alphabet is quite similar to the English alphabet except in the ways the letters are pronounced. Learning the proper pronunciation of the individual letters in Spanish will help you pronounce new words and phrases.

LETTER	LETTER NAME	EXAMPLES	LETTER	LETTER NAME	EXAMPLES
a	a	**a**diós	**ñ**	eñe	ma**ñ**ana
b	be	**b**uenos	**o**	o	c**ó**mo
c	ce	**c**lase	**p**	pe	**p**or favor
d	de	**d**ía	**q**	cu	**q**ué
e	e	**e**spañol	**r**	ere	seño**r**a
f	efe	por **f**avor	**s**	ese	**s**aludos
g	ge	lue**g**o	**t**	te	**t**arde
h	hache	**h**ola	**u**	u	**u**sted
i	i	señor**i**ta	**v**	uve	nue**v**e
j	jota	**j**ulio	**w**	doble ve o uve doble	**W**ashington
k	ka	**k**ilómetro	**x**	equis	e**x**amen
l	ele	**l**uego	**y**	ye o i griega	**y**o
m	eme	**m**adre	**z**	zeta	pi**z**arra
n	ene	**n**oche			

A-8 En español

Take turns saying the following abbreviations in Spanish, helping each other with pronunciation if necessary.

1. CD-RW
2. IBM
3. CNN
4. MTV
5. MCI
6. UPS
7. WWW
8. QVC
9. CBS
10. ABC

A-9 ¿Qué es esto?

Complete the following steps.

Paso 1 Take turns spelling the following words for a partner, who will write what you spell. Then pronounce each word.

1. hola
2. mañana
3. usted
4. igualmente
5. que
6. noches

Paso 2 Now spell your name for your partner as he/she writes it down. Your partner will pronounce your name, based on your spelling. Use **otra palabra** (*another word*) to indicate the beginning of a new word.

MODELO E1: *de, a, uve, i, de, otra palabra, ese, eme, i, te, hache*

E2: (escribe y repite) *D-a-v-i-d S-m-i-t-h*

4 VOCABULARIO

Los cognados Identifying cognates

Cognados, or *cognates,* are words that are similar in form and meaning to their English equivalents. As you learn Spanish you will discover many cognates. Can you guess the meanings of the following words?

inteligente **septiembre** **familia** **universidad**

A-10 Práctica

Take turns giving the English equivalents for the following words.

1. importante
2. animal
3. programa
4. mapa
5. atractivo
6. favorito
7. especial
8. fantástico
9. famoso
10. diferente

A-11 ¿Hablas español?

Read the classified ad and make a list of all of the cognates; then answer the following questions.

1. What job is advertised?
2. What are the requirements?
3. How much does it pay?
4. How can you get more information?

Administrador/a
Departamento de Servicio Público.
Hospital General de Mesa Grande, AR.
Experiencia necesaria.
Fluidez en inglés y español.
$45,000–$60,000.
Teléfono: 480-555-2347

5 GRAMÁTICA

Los pronombres personales Expressing subject pronouns

Can you list the subject pronouns in English? When are they used? The following chart lists the subject pronouns in Spanish and their equivalents in English. As you will note, Spanish has several equivalents for *you*.

yo	*I*	**nosotros/as**	*we*
tú	*you* (familiar)	**vosotros/as**	*you* (plural, Spain)
usted	*you* (formal)	**ustedes**	*you* (plural)
él	*he*	**ellos**	*they* (masculine)
ella	*she*	**ellas**	*they* (feminine)

Tú

Generally speaking, **tú** (you, singular) is used for people with whom you are on a first-name basis, such as family members and friends.

Usted

Usted, abbreviated **Ud.,** is used with people you do not know well, or with people with whom you are not on a first-name basis. **Usted** is also used with older people, or with those to whom you want to show respect.

Spanish shows gender more clearly than English. **Nosotros** and **ellos** are used to refer to either all males or to a mixed group of males and females. **Nosotras** and **ellas** refer to an all-female group.

¿Tú o usted?

Languages are constantly evolving. Words are added and deleted, they change in meaning, and the use of language in certain situations may change as well. For example, the use of **tú** and **usted (Ud.)** is changing dramatically in Spanish. **Tú** may now be used more freely in situations where **usted** was previously used. In some Spanish-speaking countries, it has become acceptable for a shopper to address a young store clerk with **tú.** Just a few years ago, only **usted** would have been appropriate in that context. Nevertheless, the traditional use of **tú** and **usted** still exists. Regarding your choice between **tú** and **usted,** a good rule of thumb is: *When in doubt, be more formal.*

There are a few regional differences in the use of pronouns. Spanish speakers in Spain use **vosotros** ("you all") when addressing more than one person with whom they are on a first-name basis. Elsewhere in the Spanish-speaking world, **ustedes,** abbreviated **Uds.,** is used when addressing more than one person on a formal or informal basis. In Costa Rica, Argentina, and other parts of Latin America, **vos** replaces **tú,** but **tú** would be perfectly understood in these countries.

Preguntas

1. When in doubt, do you use **tú** or **usted**?
2. What new words have been added to the English language in the past twenty years?
3. What are some words and expressions that we do not use in English anymore?

A-12 ¿Cómo se dice?

Take turns expressing the following in Spanish.

1. we (all men)
2. I
3. you (speaking to a friend)
4. they (just women)
5. we (all women)
6. you (speaking to a professor)
7. they (just men)
8. they (fifty women and one man)
9. we (men and women)
10. they (men or women)

A-13 ¿Tú o usted?

Determine whether you would most likely address the following people with **tú** or **usted**. State your reasons, using the categories below.

A respect
B family member
C someone with whom you are on a first-name basis
D someone you do not know well

1. your sister
2. your mom
3. your Spanish professor
4. your grandfather
5. your best friend's father
6. a clerk in a department store
7. your doctor
8. someone you've just met who is older
9. someone you've just met who is your age
10. a child you've just met

6 GRAMÁTICA

El verbo *ser* Using *to be*

You have already learned the subject pronouns in Spanish. It is time to put them together with a verb. First, consider the verb *to be* in English. The *to* form of a verb, as in *to be* or *to see*, is called an *infinitive*. Note that *to be* has different forms for different subjects.

to be			
I	**am**	we	**are**
you	**are**	you (all)	**are**
he, she, it	**is**	they	**are**

Verbs in Spanish also have different forms for different subjects.

ser (*to be*)					
Singular			**Plural**		
yo	**soy**	*I am*	nosotros/as	**somos**	*we are*
tú	**eres**	*you are*	vosotros/as	**sois**	*you (all) are*
Ud.	**es**	*you are*	Uds.	**son**	*you (all) are*
él, ella	**es**	*he/she is*	ellos/as	**son**	*they are*

- In Spanish, subject pronouns are not required, but rather used for clarification or emphasis. Pronouns are indicated by the verb ending. For example:

  Soy means *I am.*

  Es means either *he is, she is*, or *you* (formal) *are.*

- If you are using a subject pronoun, it will appear first, followed by the form of the verb that corresponds to the subject pronoun, and then the rest of the sentence, as in the examples:

  Yo **soy** Mark. **Soy** Mark.

  Él **es** inteligente. **Es** inteligente.

As you continue to progress in ***¡Anda! Curso elemental,*** you will learn to form and respond to questions, both orally and in writing, and you will have the opportunity to create longer sentences.

A-14 Vamos a practicar Take turns saying the forms of the verb **ser** that you would use with the following pronouns. Correct your partner's answers as necessary.

1. nosotras
2. usted
3. yo
4. él
5. ellas
6. tú
7. ustedes
8. ella

A-15 "Ser o no ser… " Take turns changing these forms of **ser** to the plural if they are singular, and vice versa. Listen to your partner for accuracy and help him/her if necessary.

MODELO E1: yo soy
E2: *nosotros somos*

1. usted es 2. nosotros somos 3. ella es 4. ellos son 5. tú eres

7 VOCABULARIO

Los adjetivos de nacionalidad Stating nationalities

Nacionalidad	Estudiantes
alemán	Hans
alemana	Ingrid
canadiense	Jacques/Alice
chino	Tsong
china	Xue Lan
cubano	Javier
cubana	Pilar
español	Rodrigo
española	Guadalupe
estadounidense (norteamericano/a)	John/Kate
francés	Jean-Paul
francesa	Brigitte
inglés	James
inglesa	Diana
japonés	Yasu
japonesa	Tabo
mexicano	Manuel
mexicana	Milagros
nigeriano	Yena
nigeriana	Ngidaha
puertorriqueño	Ernesto
puertorriqueña	Sonia

In Spanish:

- adjectives of nationality are not capitalized unless one is the first word in a sentence.
- most adjectives of nationality have a form for males, and a slightly different one for females. (You will learn more about this in **Capítulo 1.** For now, simply note the differences.)
- when referring to more than one individual, you make the adjectives plural by adding either an **-s** or an **-es.** (Again, in **Capítulo 1** you will formally learn more about forming plural words.)
- some adjectives of nationality have a written accent mark in the masculine form, but not in the feminine, like **inglés/inglesa** and **francés/francesa.** For example: **Mi papá es *inglés* y mi mamá es *francesa*.**

A-16 ¿Cuál es tu nacionalidad?

Describe the nationalities of the students listed on page 14. Form complete sentences using either **es** or **son,** following the model. Then practice spelling the nationalities in Spanish with your partner.

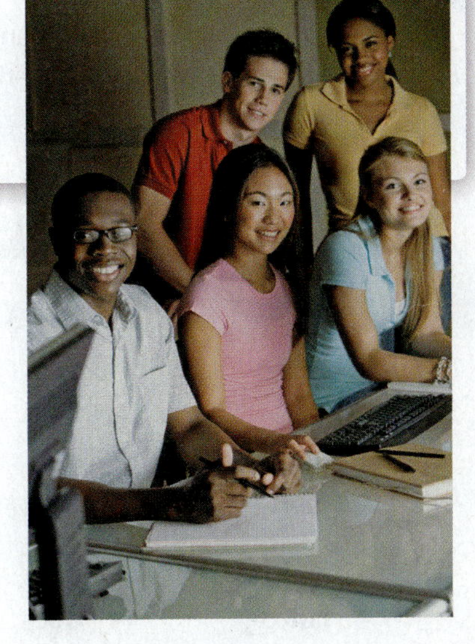

MODELO E1: china
E2: *Xue Lan es china.*
E1: chinos
E2: *Xue Lan y Tsong son chinos.*

1. francesa
2. japonés
3. estadounidenses
4. canadiense
5. mexicanos
6. alemán

A-17 ¿Qué son?

Take turns naming the nationalities of the people listed. Make sure you use the correct form of **ser** in each sentence. Follow the model.

MODELO E1: Yena
E2: *Yena es nigeriano.*
E1: Yena y Ngidaha
E2: *Yena y Ngidaha son nigerianos.*

1. Jacques
2. Xue Lan y Tsong
3. Ingrid
4. Brigitte
5. Kate
6. Hans
7. Javier y Pilar
8. Jean-Paul
9. yo
10. mi familia y yo

Los hispanos

Many terms are associated with people from the Spanish-speaking world, most commonly *Hispanic* and *Latino*. While there is some controversy regarding the use of these terms, typically *Hispanic* refers to all people who come from a Spanish-speaking background. *Latino,* on the other hand, implies a specific connection to Latin America. Whichever term is used, the people denoted are far from homogeneous. Some are racially diverse, most are culturally diverse, and some do not even speak Spanish.

Preguntas

1. Briefly explain the terms *Latino* and *Hispanic.*
2. Name two people who are of Spanish-speaking heritage, and state how they are similar, and how they are different.

8 VOCABULARIO

Los números 0–30 Counting from 0–30

0 **cero**	7 **siete**	13 **trece**	19 **diecinueve**	25 **veinticinco**
1 **uno**	8 **ocho**	14 **catorce**	20 **veinte**	26 **veintiséis**
2 **dos**	9 **nueve**	15 **quince**	21 **veintiuno**	27 **veintisiete**
3 **tres**	10 **diez**	16 **dieciséis**	22 **veintidós**	28 **veintiocho**
4 **cuatro**	11 **once**	17 **diecisiete**	23 **veintitrés**	29 **veintinueve**
5 **cinco**	12 **doce**	18 **dieciocho**	24 **veinticuatro**	30 **treinta**
6 **seis**				

A-18 ¿Qué número? Take turns saying what number comes before and after each of the numbers below. Your partner will check your accuracy.

MODELO 1 *cero, dos*

1. 2
2. 5
3. 8
4. 11
5. 15
6. 17
7. 20
8. 23
9. 24
10. 28

A-19 ¿Cuál es la secuencia? Take turns reading the number patterns aloud while filling in the missing numbers.

1. 1, 3, 5, ______, 9, ______, 13, ______, ______
2. 2, 4, ______, 8, ______, 12, ______, 16, ______, 20, ______
3. 3, ______, 9, ______, 15, ______, 21, ______, 27, ______
4. 1, 3, 6, ______, 15, ______, 28

El mundo hispano

PAÍS	POBLACIÓN
ARGENTINA	41.343.201
BOLIVIA	9.947.418
CHILE	16.746.491
COLOMBIA	44.205.293
COSTA RICA	4.516.220
CUBA	11.477.459
ECUADOR	14.790.608
EL SALVADOR	6.052.064
ESPAÑA	46.505.963
GUATEMALA	13.550.440
GUINEA ECUATORIAL	650.702
HONDURAS	7.989.415
MÉXICO	112.468.855
NICARAGUA	5.995.928
PANAMÁ	3.410.676
PARAGUAY	6.375.830
PERÚ	29.907.003
PUERTO RICO	3.978.702
LA REPÚBLICA DOMINICANA	9.823.821
URUGUAY	3.510.386
VENEZUELA	27.223.228

*CIA World Factbook, 2010

Fíjate

Spanish uses a period to indicate thousands and millions, rather than the comma used in English.

Fíjate

Spanish is the official language of the countries listed in the chart. In the United States, over 50 million people speak Spanish; it is home to the world's second largest Spanish-speaking community.

(continued)

Preguntas

Use the map and chart of the Spanish-speaking world to answer the following questions in Spanish. Then, compare your answers with your partner's.

1. Fill in the chart with the names of the Spanish-speaking countries in the appropriate columns. How many such countries are there in each of these areas? How many are there in the world?

AMÉRICA DEL NORTE	CENTROAMÉRICA	EL CARIBE	AMÉRICA DEL SUR	EUROPA	ÁFRICA

2. How many continents contain Spanish-speaking countries? What are they?
3. How many countries have a Spanish-speaking population of 25,000,000 or more? Name them and their continents.

9 VOCABULARIO

La hora Stating the time

Es (la) medianoche.

Es (el) mediodía.

Es la una.

Son las diez y cinco.

Son las tres y cuarto.

Son las seis y media.

Son las nueve menos cuarto.

Son las diez menos veinticinco.

La hora	*Telling time*
¿Qué hora es?	*What time is it?*
Es la una. / Son las…	*It's one o'clock. / It's… o'clock.*
¿A qué hora… ?	*At what time…?*
A la… / A las…	*At… o'clock.*
…de la mañana	*… in the morning*
…de la tarde	*… in the afternoon, early evening*
…de la noche	*… in the evening, at night*

la medianoche	*midnight*
el mediodía	*noon*
menos cinco	*five minutes to the hour*
y cinco	*five minutes after the hour*

When telling time in Spanish:

- use **Es la…** to say times between 1:00 and 1:30.
- use **Son las…** to say times *except* between 1:00 and 1:30.
- use **A la…** (between 1:00 and 1:30) or **A las…** to say *at* what time.
- use the expressions **mediodía** and **medianoche** to say *noon* and *midnight*.
- **de la tarde** tends to mean from noon until 7:00 or 8:00 p.m.
- **cuarto** and **media** are equivalent to the English expressions *quarter* (fifteen minutes) and *half* (thirty minutes). **Cuarto** and **media** are interchangeable with the numbers **quince** and **treinta**.
- use **y** for times that are before and up to the half-hour mark.
- use **menos** for times that are beyond the half-hour mark.

A 20 ¿Qué hora es? Look at the clocks, and take turns asking and responding to **¿Qué hora es?**

MODELO E1: *¿Qué hora es?*
E2: *Son las nueve de la mañana.*

1. 

2. 

3. 

4. 

5. 

6. 

7. 

8. 

A-21 ¿A qué hora...?

Take turns asking and answering at what time the following occur.

MODELO la clase de matemáticas (8:00 a.m.)

E1: ¿A qué hora es la clase de matemáticas?

E2: Es a las ocho de la mañana.

1. la clase de español (10:15 a.m.)
2. el programa de televisión (5:45 p.m.)
3. la fiesta (8:30 p.m.)
4. la clase de arte (2:40 p.m.)
5. la clase de biología (8:05 a.m.)

A-22 Tu horario

Think about your daily schedule. Then, take turns asking and telling your partner at what times you do the following activities.

MODELO E1: *¿A qué hora?*

E2: *a la una y media*

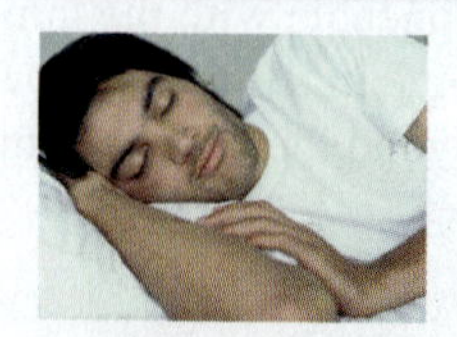

1. 

2. 

3. 

4. 

5. 

6. 

7. 

8. 

A-23 ¿Y el fin de semana?

What is your schedule for the weekend? Take turns telling your partner at what times you plan to do the activities from **A-22** this coming weekend.

10 VOCABULARIO

Los días, los meses y las estaciones

Eliciting the date and season

Los meses y las estaciones (*Months and seasons*)

la primavera

marzo, abril y mayo

el verano

junio, julio y agosto

el otoño

septiembre, octubre y noviembre

el invierno

diciembre, enero y febrero

Los días de la semana	*Days of the week*
lunes	*Monday*
martes	*Tuesday*
miércoles	*Wednesday*
jueves	*Thursday*
viernes	*Friday*
sábado	*Saturday*
domingo	*Sunday*

Expresiones útiles	*Useful expressions*
¿Qué día es hoy?	*What day is today?*
¿Cuál es la fecha de hoy?	*What is today's date?*
Hoy es lunes.	*Today is Monday.*
Hoy es el 1° (primero) de septiembre.	*Today is September first.*
Mañana es el 2 (dos) de septiembre.	*Tomorrow is September second.*

Unlike in English, the days of the week and the months of the year are not capitalized in Spanish. Also, in the Spanish-speaking world, in some countries, Monday is considered the first day of the week. On calendars the days are listed from Monday through Sunday.

A-24 Antes y después Which days come directly before and after the ones listed? Take turns saying the days in Spanish.

1. sábado
2. lunes
3. viernes
4. domingo
5. jueves
6. miércoles

A-25 Y los meses Which months come directly before and after the ones listed? Take turns saying the months in Spanish.

1. octubre
2. febrero
3. mayo
4. agosto
5. diciembre
6. junio
7. septiembre
8. enero
9. octubre
10. marzo

A-26 ¿Cuándo es? Look at the activities included in the **Guía del ocio.** Take turns determining what activity takes place and at what time on the following days.

Fíjate

In Spanish, ***h*** is the abbreviation for ***hora***.

GUÍA DEL OCIO MADRID

MÚSICA

Sábado 4

- **XVI Festival de Jazz:**

Joe Henderson
La Riviera. 21 h.

- **Alonso y Williams**
La Madriguera. 24 h.

Domingo 5

- **Pedro Iturralde**
Clamores. Pases: 22.45 y 0.45 h. Libre.

Lunes 6

- **Moreiras Jazztet**
Café Central. 22 h.

CINE

Ocho apellidos vascos
(2014, España)****
Género: Comedia
Director: Emilio Martínez-Lázaro
Interpretación: Clara Lago, Dani Rovira…
Un sevillano (Dani Rovira) decide salir de Andalucía para seguir a una joven vasca (Clara Lago).

Piratas del Caribe: En mareas misteriosas
(2011, EE. UU.) ****
Género: Acción, fantasía, comedia
Director: Rob Marshall
Interpretación: Johnny Depp, Penélope Cruz, Ian McShane…
La continuación de la historia del capitán Jack Sparrow quien guía una expedición a la fuente de la juventud.

Volver (2006, España)*****
Género: Comedia dramática
Director: Pedro Almodóvar
Interpretación: Penélope Cruz, Carmen Maura…
Se basa en la vida y los recuerdos del director sobre su madre y el lugar donde se crió.

EXPOSICIONES

- **Museo Nacional Centro de Arte Reina Sofía**
Santa Isabel, 52.
Metro Atocha
Tel. 91 467 50 62
Horario: de 10 a 21 h. Domingo de 10 a 14.30 h.
Martes cerrado.

Un recorrido del arte del siglo XX, desde Picasso. Salas dedicadas a los comienzos de la vanguardia. Además, exposiciones temporales.

- **Museo del Prado**
Paseo del Prado, s/n. Metro Banco de España.
Tel. 91 420 36 62 y 91 420 37 68
Horario: martes a sábado de 9 a 19 h. Domingo de 9 a 14 h.
Lunes cerrado.

Todas las escuelas españolas, desde los frescos románicos hasta el siglo XVIII. Grandes colecciones de Velázquez, Goya, Murillo, etc. Importante representación de las escuelas europeas (Rubens, Tiziano, Durero, etc.). Escultura clásica griega y romana y Tesoro del Delfín.

MODELO E1: el lunes por la noche
E2: *El Moreiras Jazztet es a las veintidós horas / a las diez.*

1. el sábado por la noche
2. el miércoles por la mañana
3. el domingo
4. el sábado por la noche
5. el martes por la tarde

11 VOCABULARIO

El tiempo Reporting the weather

¿Qué tiempo hace? (*What's the weather like?*)

el sol

Hace sol.

Hace buen tiempo.

la lluvia

Llueve.

Hace mal tiempo.

la nube

Está nublado.

el viento

Hace viento.

la nieve

Nieva.

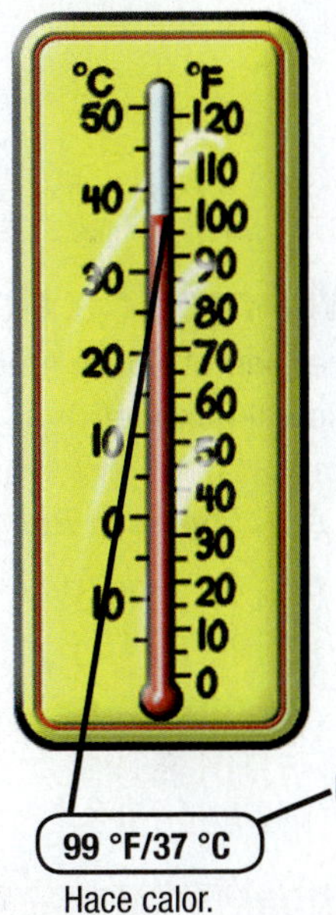

la temperatura

99 °F/37 °C

Hace calor.

14 °F/-10 °C

Hace frío.

A-27 ¿Qué tiempo hace?

Take turns asking and answering what the most typical weather is during the following seasons where you go to school.

MODELO E1: ¿Qué tiempo hace… en (el) verano?

E2: *En (el) verano hace sol.*

¿Qué tiempo hace…?

1. en (el) otoño
2. en (el) invierno
3. en (la) primavera
4. en (el) verano

A-28 España Take turns answering the question **¿Qué tiempo hace?** based on the map of Spain.

MODELO E1: ¿Qué tiempo hace en Sevilla?

E2: *Hace calor.*

1. ¿Qué tiempo hace en Mallorca?
2. ¿Qué tiempo hace en Pamplona?
3. ¿Qué tiempo hace en Barcelona?
4. ¿Qué tiempo hace en Madrid?
5. ¿Qué tiempo hace en Córdoba?

A-29 Y América del Sur Take turns making statements about the weather based on the map of South America. You can say what the weather is like, and also what it is not like. Follow the model.

MODELO E1: *Llueve en Bogotá.*

E2: *No hace frío en Venezuela.*

Fíjate

To make a negative statement, simply place the word **no** before the verb: *No llueve en Caracas. No nieva en Buenos Aires. No hace calor en Punta Arenas.*

12 GRAMÁTICA

Gustar Sharing personal likes and dislikes

To express likes and dislikes, you say the following:

Me gusta la primavera.

No me gusta el invierno.

Me gustan los viernes.

No me gustan los lunes.

¡Explícalo tú!

1. To say you like or dislike one thing, what form of **gustar** do you use?
2. To say you like or dislike more than one thing, what form of **gustar** do you use?

Check your answers to the preceding questions in Appendix 1.

A-30 **¿Qué te gusta?** Ask your partner whether he/she likes or dislikes the following things.

Estrategia
Say *¿Te gusta… ?* to ask "Do you like… ?"

MODELO la primavera

E1: *¿Te gusta la primavera?*

E2: *Sí, me gusta la primavera.*

1. el otoño
2. el invierno
3. el verano
4. los lunes
5. los sábados
6. los domingos
7. los viernes
8. la clase de español

A-31 **¿Qué más te gusta?** Take turns asking your partner about the following places and things.

MODELO E1: *¿Te gustan las hamburguesas?*

E2: *No, no me gustan las hamburguesas.*

1. Las Vegas, Nevada

2. las guitarras

3. 

las camionetas

4. 

la pizza

5. 

San Antonio, Texas

6. 

los teléfonos celulares

7. 

el béisbol

8. 

el fútbol

Y por fin, ¿cómo andas?

Estrategia

The *¿Cómo andas?* and *Y por fin, ¿cómo andas?* sections are designed to help you assess your understanding of specific concepts. In *Capítulo A Para empezar*, there is one opportunity for you to reflect on how well you understand the concepts. Beginning with *Capítulo 1* there will be three opportunities per chapter for you to stop and reflect on what you have learned. These checklists help you become accountable for your own learning, and help you determine what you need to review. Use the checklist as a way to communicate with your instructor about any concepts you still need to review. Additionally, you might also use your checklist as a way to study with a peer group or peer tutor. If you need to review a particular concept, more practice is available in *¡Anda!* online.

Each of the coming chapters of ***¡Anda! Curso elemental*** will have three self-check sections for you to assess your progress. A **¿Cómo andas? I** (*How are you doing?*) section will appear one third of the way through each chapter; another, **¿Cómo andas? II,** will appear at the two-thirds point, and a third and final one will appear at the end of the chapter, called **Y por fin, ¿cómo andas?** (*Finally, how are you doing?*) Use the checklists to measure what you have learned in the chapter. Place a check in the *Feel confident* column of the topics you feel you know, and a check in the *Need to review* column of those that you need to practice more. Be sure to go back and practice because it is the key to your success!

Having completed this chapter, I now can...	Feel confident	Need to review
Comunicación		
• greet, introduce, and say good-bye to someone. (p. 4)	☐	☐
• understand and respond appropriately to basic classroom expressions and requests. (p. 8)	☐	☐
• spell in Spanish. (p. 9)	☐	☐
• identify cognates. (p. 10)	☐	☐
• express subject pronouns. (p. 11)	☐	☐
• use *to be*. (p. 13)	☐	☐
• state nationalities. (p. 14)	☐	☐
• count from 0–30. (p. 16)	☐	☐
• state the time. (p. 18)	☐	☐
• elicit the date and season. (p. 21)	☐	☐
• report the weather. (p. 23)	☐	☐
• share personal likes and dislikes. (p. 25)	☐	☐
Cultura		
• compare and contrast greetings in the Spanish-speaking world and in the United States. (p. 7)	☐	☐
• explain when to use the familiar and formal *you*. (p. 12)	☐	☐
• summarize the diversity of the Spanish-speaking world. (p. 16)	☐	☐
• name the continents and countries where Spanish is spoken. (p. 17)	☐	☐
Comunidades		
• use Spanish in real-life contexts. (online)	☐	☐

Vocabulario **activo**

Los saludos	*Greetings*
Buenos días.	*Good morning.*
Buenas noches.	*Good evening; Good night.*
Buenas tardes.	*Good afternoon.*
¡Hola!	*Hi! Hello!*
¿Cómo está usted?	*How are you?* (formal)
¿Cómo estás?	*How are you?* (familiar)
¿Qué tal?	*How's it going?*
Bastante bien.	*Just fine.*
Bien, gracias.	*Fine, thanks.*
Más o menos.	*So-so.*
Muy bien.	*Really well.*
Regular.	*Okay.*
¿Y tú?	*And you?* (familiar)
¿Y usted?	*And you?* (formal)

Las despedidas	*Farewells*
Adiós.	*Good-bye.*
Chao.	*Bye.*
Hasta luego.	*See you later.*
Hasta mañana.	*See you tomorrow.*
Hasta pronto.	*See you soon.*

Las presentaciones	*Introductions*
¿Cómo te llamas?	*What is your name?* (familiar)
¿Cómo se llama usted?	*What is your name?* (formal)
Encantado/a.	*Pleased to meet you.*
Igualmente.	*Likewise.*
Mucho gusto.	*Nice to meet you.*
Me llamo…	*My name is…*
Soy…	*I am…*
Quiero presentarle a…	*I would like to introduce you to…* (formal)
Quiero presentarte a…	*I would like to introduce you to…* (familiar)

Expresiones útiles para la clase	*Useful classroom expressions*
Preguntas y respuestas	*Questions and answers*
¿Cómo?	*What? How?*
¿Cómo se dice… en español?	*How do you say… in Spanish?*
¿Cómo se escribe… en español?	*How do you write… in Spanish?*
¿Qué es esto?	*What is this?*
¿Qué significa?	*What does it mean?*
¿Quién?	*Who?*
Comprendo.	*I understand.*
Lo sé.	*I know.*
No.	*No.*
No comprendo.	*I don't understand.*
No lo sé.	*I don't know.*
Sí.	*Yes.*

Expresiones de cortesía	*Polite expressions*
De nada.	*You're welcome.*
Gracias.	*Thank you.*
Por favor.	*Please.*

Mandatos para la clase	*Classroom instructions (commands)*
Abra(n) el libro en la página…	*Open your book to page…*
Cierre(n) el/los libro/s.	*Close your book/s.*
Conteste(n).	*Answer.*
Escriba(n).	*Write.*
Escuche(n).	*Listen.*
Lea(n).	*Read.*
Repita(n).	*Repeat.*
Vaya(n) a la pizarra.	*Go to the board.*

Las nacionalidades	Nationalities
See pages 14–15.	

Los números 0–30	Numbers 0–30
See page 16.	

La hora	Telling time
A la... / A las...	*At... o'clock.*
Es la... / Son las...	*It's... o'clock.*
¿A qué hora... ?	*At what time... ?*
¿Qué hora es?	*What time is it?*
...de la mañana	*... in the morning*
...de la noche	*... in the evening, at night*
...de la tarde	*... in the afternoon, early evening*
la medianoche	*midnight*
el mediodía	*noon*
menos cinco	*five minutes to the hour*
y cinco	*five minutes after the hour*

Expresiones del tiempo	Weather expressions
Está nublado.	*It's cloudy.*
Hace buen tiempo.	*The weather is nice.*
Hace calor.	*It's hot.*
Hace frío.	*It's cold.*
Hace mal tiempo.	*The weather is bad.*
Hace sol.	*It's sunny.*
Hace viento.	*It's windy.*
Llueve.	*It's raining.*
la lluvia	*rain*
Nieva.	*It's snowing.*
la nieve	*snow*
la nube	*cloud*
¿Qué tiempo hace?	*What's the weather like?*
el sol	*sun*
la temperatura	*temperature*
el viento	*wind*

Los días, los meses y las estaciones	Days, months, and seasons
Los días de la semana	**Days of the week**
See page 21.	
Las estaciones	**Seasons**
el invierno	*winter*
la primavera	*spring*
el otoño	*autumn; fall*
el verano	*summer*
Expresiones útiles	**Useful expressions**
¿Cuál es la fecha de hoy?	*What is today's date?*
¿Qué día es hoy?	*What day is today?*
Hoy es el 1° (primero) de septiembre.	*Today is September first.*
Hoy es lunes.	*Today is Monday.*
Mañana es el dos de septiembre.	*Tomorrow is September second.*

Los meses del año	Months of the year
enero	*January*
febrero	*February*
marzo	*March*
abril	*April*
mayo	*May*
junio	*June*
julio	*July*
agosto	*August*
septiembre	*September*
octubre	*October*
noviembre	*November*
diciembre	*December*

Algunos verbos	Some verbs
gustar	*to like*
ser	*to be*

La familia Sánchez, San Antonio, Texas

1 ¿Quiénes somos?

Families can be big or small, and family members can be similar or very diverse. What makes us who we are? What makes each of us unique? What impact does your family or where you grow up have on the person you are?

We may come from different geographical locations and represent different cultures, races, and religions, yet in many respects we are much the same. We have the same basic needs, share common likes and dislikes, and possess similar hopes and dreams.

Preguntas

1. Whom do you resemble most in your family? In what ways are you alike?
2. What are some different nationalities and cultures you encounter on a regular basis in your community? What do you have in common with them?
3. What are some activities families do together in your community?

¿Sabías que...?

At least 13% of U.S. residents speak Spanish in their homes.

Luis con su papá

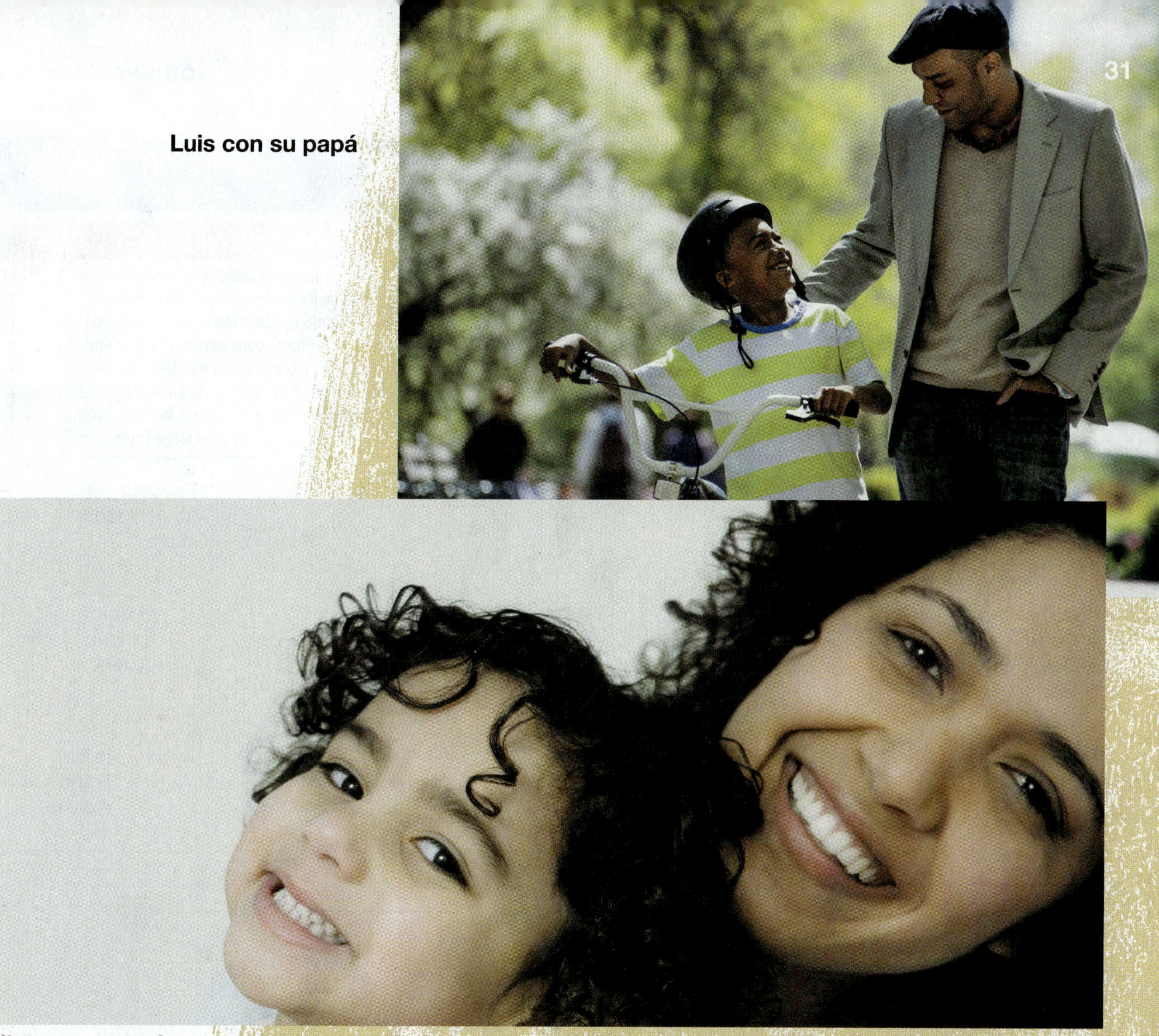

Nina y su mamá

Learning Outcomes

By the end of this chapter, you will be able to:

- ✔ describe families.
- ✔ express what someone has.
- ✔ give details about yourself and others.
- ✔ state possession and give details about people, places, and things.
- ✔ communicate about people you know.
- ✔ organize ideas to write a poem.
- ✔ exchange interesting facts about the size, location, and makeup of the Hispanic population in the United States.
- ✔ read a social media page.

Comunicación I

1 VOCABULARIO

Fíjate

Your instructor assigned this *Vocabulario* to be learned before you come to class. Therefore, when you come to class, you can immediately work with a partner to practice the vocabulary in context. Your instructor will assign all *Vocabulario* to be learned before class. This practice will help you become a highly successful Spanish-language learner.

La familia Describing families

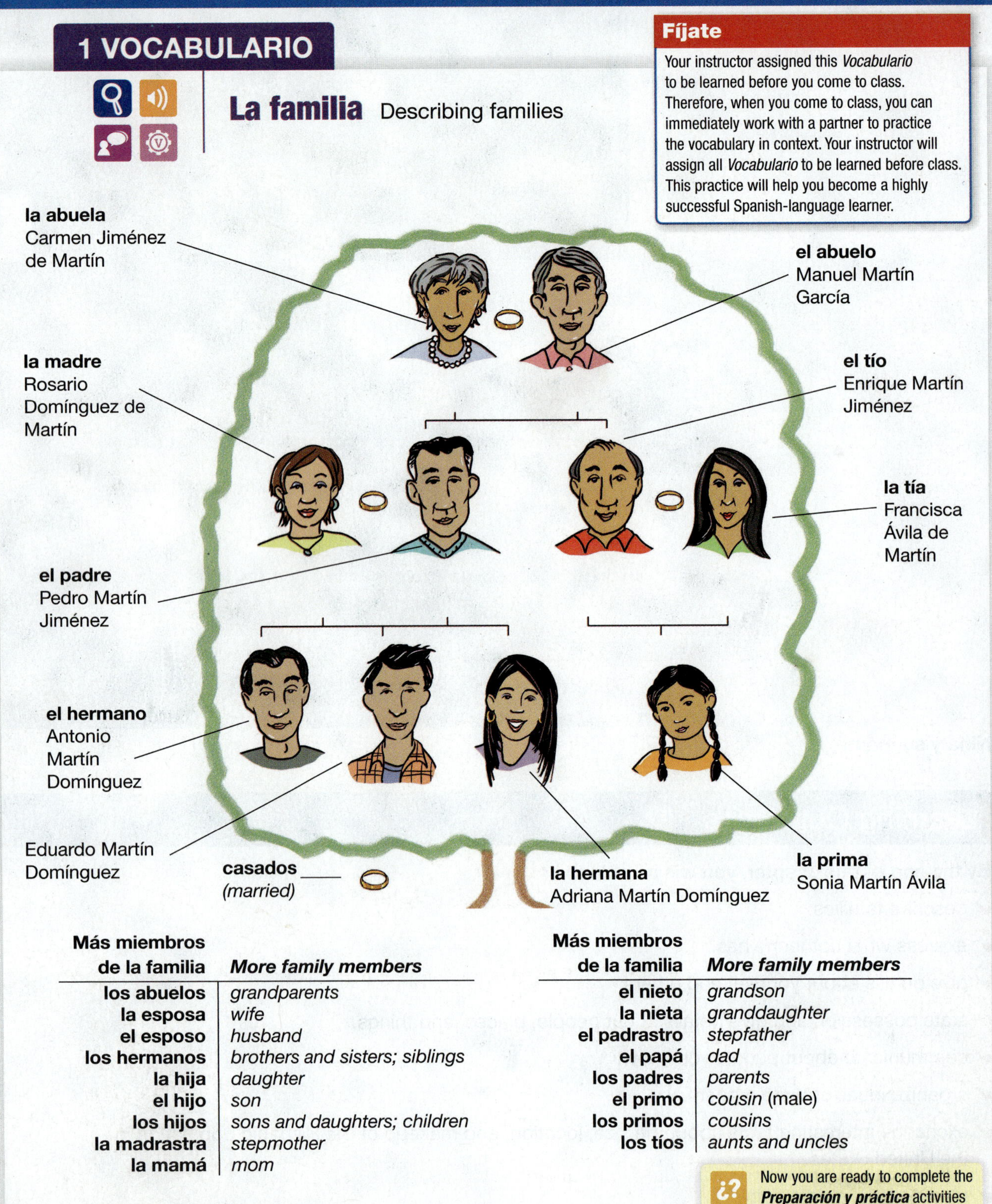

Más miembros de la familia	*More family members*
los abuelos	*grandparents*
la esposa	*wife*
el esposo	*husband*
los hermanos	*brothers and sisters; siblings*
la hija	*daughter*
el hijo	*son*
los hijos	*sons and daughters; children*
la madrastra	*stepmother*
la mamá	*mom*

Más miembros de la familia	*More family members*
el nieto	*grandson*
la nieta	*granddaughter*
el padrastro	*stepfather*
el papá	*dad*
los padres	*parents*
el primo	*cousin* (male)
los primos	*cousins*
los tíos	*aunts and uncles*

¿? Now you are ready to complete the ***Preparación y práctica*** activities for this chunk online.

PRONUNCIACIÓN

Vowels

Go to *¡Anda!* online to learn about the pronunciation of vowels.

Fíjate

You will find this *Pronunciación* section, and accompanying activities, in *¡Anda!* online.

Capítulo A Para empezar. El verbo *ser*, pág. 13.

Estrategia

¡Anda! Curso elemental has provided you with recycling references to help guide your continuous review of previously learned material. Make sure to consult the indicated pages if you need to refresh your memory about the topic.

1-1 La familia de Eduardo

Look at Eduardo's family tree. Take turns with a partner to ask and answer questions about the family members.

MODELO Antonio

E2: *¿Quién es Antonio?*

E2: *Es su* (his) *hermano.*

1. Francisca
2. Carmen
3. Enrique
4. Manuel
5. Pedro
6. Rosario
7. Sonia
8. Adriana

1-2 ¿Cierto o falso?

Roberto is a friend of Eduardo, but does he really know Eduardo's family? Listen to Roberto's statements. Using Eduardo's family tree on page 32, indicate **C** for **Cierto** (*true*) or **F** for **Falso** (*false*) for each statement you hear.

MODELO [*you hear*] Sonia es la prima de Eduardo.

[*you mark*] C

	C	F		C	F
1.	☐	☐	4.	☐	☐
2.	☐	☐	5.	☐	☐
3.	☐	☐			

1-3 Mi familia

Complete the following steps.

Paso 1 Draw and label in less than one minute **three** generations of your own family tree, or create a fictitious one. Then share your information with a partner, following the model. Please save your drawing! You will need it for **1-7.**

MODELO E1: *Mary es mi* (my) *hermana.*

E2: *George es mi papá.*

Paso 2 Finally, quickly write at least **five** of the sentences that you shared orally with your partner, or **five** different sentences about your family members. Follow the **modelo**.

Estrategia

For additional vocabulary choices, consult Appendix 3, *También se dice…*

MODELO ____________ ____________ mi ________________.

(Subject) ***(verb)*** ***(family member)***

Los apellidos en el mundo hispano

In Spanish-speaking countries, it is customary for people to use both paternal and maternal last names (surnames). For example, Eduardo's father is **Pedro Martín Jiménez** and his mother's maiden name is **Rosario Domínguez Montalvo**. Eduardo's first last name is his father's first last name (**Martín**); Eduardo's second last name is his mother's first last name (**Domínguez**). Therefore, Eduardo's full name is **Eduardo Martín Domínguez**. In most informal situations, though, Eduardo would use only his first last name, so he would call himself **Eduardo Martín**.

In most Spanish-speaking countries, a woman usually retains the surname of her father upon marriage, while giving up her mother's surname. She takes her husband's last name, preceded by the preposition **de** (*of*). For example, when Eduardo's mother married his father, her name became **Rosario Domínguez de Martín**. Therefore, if a woman named **Carmen Torres López** married **Ricardo Colón Montoya**, her name would become **Carmen Torres de Colón**.

Preguntas

1. It may seem unusual to use more than one last name at a time, but this custom is not unique to Spanish-speaking cultures. Are there any equivalents in the United States or in other countries?
2. Can you think of any advantages to using both the mother's and the father's last names?

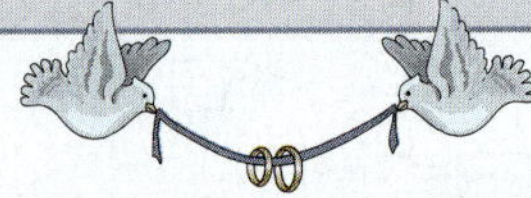

Sr. Pablo Valenzuela Domínguez *Sr. Roberto Rebolledo Sánchez*
Sra. Alicia Ochoa de Valenzuela *Sra. Rosario Menéndez de Rebolledo*

Tienen el gusto de invitarles al matrimonio de sus hijos

José Luis y María Luisa

que se celebrará el sábado, día 14 de junio de 2008,
a las 3:00 de la tarde,
en la Iglesia Santa Margarita

Iglesia Santa Margarita
Avenida Juárez, nº 32
Colonia Escobar
Cholula

Fíjate

Your instructor assigned this *Nota cultural* to be read before you come to class. In class you will then be prepared to answer the *Preguntas* with a partner. All *Nota cultural* should be read before coming to class.

Fíjate

Below are some common Spanish first names and nicknames.

Hombres (*men*)

Antonio	Toño, Toni
Francisco	Paco, Pancho, Cisco
Guillermo	Memo, Guillo, Guille
Jesús	Chu, Chuito, Chucho, Chus
José	Pepe
Manuel	Manolo, Mani
Ramón	Moncho, Monchi

Mujeres (*women*)

Antonia	Toñín, Toña, Toñi(ta)
Concepción	Concha, Conchita
Guadalupe	Lupe, Lupita
María Soledad	Marisol
María Teresa	Maite, Marité, Maritere
Pilar	Pili
Rosario	Charo

2 GRAMÁTICA

El verbo *tener* Expressing what someone has

Fíjate

Your instructor assigned this *Gramática* to be read, studied, and learned before you come to class. Therefore, when you come to class, you can immediately work with a partner to practice the grammar in context via the activities in your text. Your instructor will assign all *Gramática* to be learned before class. This practice will help you become a highly successful Spanish-language learner.

In **Capítulo A Para empezar** you learned the present tense of **ser.** Another very common verb in Spanish is **tener** (*to have*). The present tense forms of the verb **tener** follow.

¿? Now you are ready to complete the ***Preparación y práctica*** activities for this chunk online.

tener (*to have*)

Singular			Plural		
yo	**tengo**	*I have*	nosotros/as	**tenemos**	*we have*
tú	**tienes**	*you have*	vosotros/as	**tenéis**	*you all have*
Ud.	**tiene**	*you have*	Uds.	**tienen**	*you all have*
él, ella	**tiene**	*he/she has*	ellos/as	**tienen**	*they have*

1-4 ¿Quién tiene familia?

Take turns giving the correct form of the verb **tener** for each subject listed.

MODELO E1: *la prima*
E2: *tiene*

1. tú
2. los padres
3. nosotros
4. Pedro, Carmen y Rosario
5. yo
6. el tío

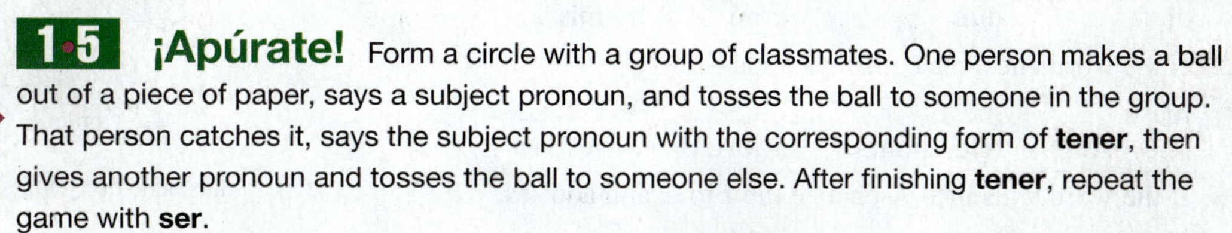

1-5 ¡Apúrate!

Form a circle with a group of classmates. One person makes a ball out of a piece of paper, says a subject pronoun, and tosses the ball to someone in the group. That person catches it, says the subject pronoun with the corresponding form of **tener**, then gives another pronoun and tosses the ball to someone else. After finishing **tener**, repeat the game with **ser**.

Capítulo A Para empezar. El verbo *ser*, pág. 13.

MODELO E1: *yo*
E2: *yo tengo; ellas*
E3: *ellas tienen; usted*
E4: *usted tiene;...*

1-6 La familia de José

Complete the paragraph with the correct forms of **tener.** Share your answers with a partner. Based on what you learned in the **Nota cultural** on page 34, what is José's father's last name? What is José's mother's maiden name?

Yo soy el primo de José Ruiz López. Él (1) ______ una familia grande. (2) ______ tres hermanos. Su hermano Pepe está casado (*is married*) y (3) ______ dos hijos. También (*Also*) José y sus hermanos (4) ______ muchos tíos, siete en total. La madre de José (5) ______ tres hermanos y dos están casados. El padre de José (6) ______ una hermana y ella está casada con mi padre: ¡es mi madre! Nosotros (7) ______ una familia grande. ¿Y tú? ¿(8) ______ una familia grande?

1-7 Mi árbol familiar

Create **three** sentences with **tener** based on your family tree from **1-3**, page 33. Tell them to your partner, who will then share what you said with another classmate.

MODELO E1 (ALICE): *Tengo un hermano, Scott. Tengo dos tíos, George y David. No tengo abuelos.*

E2 (JEFF): *Alice tiene un hermano, Scott. Tiene dos tíos, George y David. No tiene abuelos.*

Fíjate

The word *un* is the shortened form of the number *uno*. It is used before a masculine noun—a concept that will be explained later in this chapter.

3 GRAMÁTICA

Sustantivos singulares y plurales

Using singular and plural nouns

To pluralize nouns and adjectives in Spanish, follow these guidelines.

1. If the word ends in a vowel, add **-s.**

hermana → hermanas		abuelo → abuelos	
día → días		mi → mis	

2. If the word ends in a consonant, add **-es.**

mes → meses	ciudad → ciudades
televisión → televisiones	joven → jóvenes

3. If the word ends in a **-z**, change the **z** to **c**, and add **-es.**

lápiz → lápices	feliz → felices

Raúl tiene dos primas y Jorge tiene una prima.

Now you are ready to complete the ***Preparación y práctica*** activities for this chunk online.

Fíjate

Note that *televisión* loses its accent mark in the plural. Also, note the plural of *joven* is *jóvenes*. You will learn about accent marks in *Capítulo 2*.

1-8 Te toca a ti
Take turns making the following singular nouns plural.

MODELO E1: primo
E2: *primos*

1. padre
2. tía
3. taxi
4. francés
5. nieto
6. alemán
7. abuela
8. sol
9. emoción

1-9 De nuevo
Now take turns making the following plural nouns singular.

MODELO E1: primos
E2: *primo*

1. hijos
2. días
3. discusiones
4. madres
5. lápices
6. jóvenes
7. familias
8. libertades
9. nietos

4 GRAMÁTICA

El masculino y el femenino
Identifying masculine and feminine nouns

In Spanish, all nouns (people, places, and things) have gender; they are either masculine or feminine. Use the following rules to help you determine the gender of nouns. If a noun does not belong to any of the following categories, you must memorize the gender as you learn that noun.

1. Most words ending in **-a** are feminine.

   la hermana, la hija, la mamá, la tía

   *Some exceptions: **el día**, **el papá**, and words of Greek origin ending in **-ma,** such as
   el problema and **el programa.**
2. Most words ending in **-o** are masculine.

   el abuelo, el hermano, el hijo, el nieto

   *Some exceptions: **la foto** (*photo*), **la mano** (*hand*), **la moto** (*motorcycle*)

   *Note: **la foto** and **la moto** are shortened forms for **la fotografía** and **la motocicleta.**
3. Words ending in **-ción** and **-sión** are feminine.

   la discusión, la recepción, la televisión

   *Note: The suffix **-ción** is equivalent to the English *-tion.*
4. Words ending in **-dad** or **-tad** are feminine.

   la ciudad (*city*), **la libertad, la universidad**

   *Note: these suffixes are equivalent to the English *-ty.*

El abuelo y las tías

Estrategia

Making educated guesses about the meanings of unknown words will help to make you a successful Spanish learner!

Now you are ready to complete the ***Preparación y práctica*** activities for this chunk online.

As you learned in **Capítulo A Para empezar,** words that look alike and have the same meaning in both English and Spanish, such as **discusión** and **universidad,** are known as *cognates*. Use them to help you decipher meaning and to form words. For example, **prosperidad** looks like what English word? What is its gender?

1-10 ¿Recuerdas? Take turns determining which of the following nouns are masculine (**M**) and which are feminine (**F**).

1. ______ hijas
2. ______ discusión
3. ______ mapa
4. ______ nacionalidad
5. ______ hermano
6. ______ manos
7. ______ mamá
8. ______ abuelos

1-11 Para practicar Take turns deciding whether these cognates are masculine or feminine. Can you guess their English equivalents?

1. guitarra
2. teléfono
3. computadora
4. drama
5. cafetería
6. educación

5 GRAMÁTICA

Los artículos definidos e indefinidos

Conveying *the*, *a*, *one*, and *some*

Like English, Spanish has two kinds of articles, definite and indefinite. The definite article in English is *the*; the indefinite articles are *a*, *an*, and *some*.

In Spanish, articles and other adjectives mirror the gender (masculine or feminine) and number (singular or plural) of the nouns to which they refer. For example, an article referring to a singular masculine noun must also be singular and masculine. Note the forms of the articles in the following charts.

Eduardo tiene una hermana. La hermana de Eduardo se llama Adriana.

Los artículos definidos

el hermano	*the brother*	**los** hermanos	*the brothers/the brothers and sisters*
la hermana	*the sister*	**las** hermanas	*the sisters*

Los artículos indefinidos

un hermano	*a/one brother*	**unos** hermanos	*some brothers/some brothers and sisters*
una hermana	*a/one sister*	**unas** hermanas	*some sisters*

1. ***Definite articles*** are used to refer to **the** person, place, or thing.
2. ***Indefinite articles*** are used to refer to **a** or **some** person, place, or thing.

¿? Now you are ready to complete the ***Preparación y práctica*** activities for this chunk online.

Adriana es **la** hermana de Eduardo y **los** abuelos de él se llaman Carmen y Manuel.	*Adriana is Eduardo's sister, and his grandparents' names are Carmen and Manuel.*
Jorge tiene **una** tía y **unos** tíos.	*Jorge has an aunt and some uncles.*

Fíjate

Note that *el* means "the," and *él* means "he."

1-12 Vamos a practicar

Complete the following steps.

Paso 1 Take turns giving the correct form of the *definite* article for each of the following nouns.

MODELO E1: tías
E2: *las tías*

1. tío
2. padres
3. mamá
4. papá
5. hermanas
6. hijo
7. abuela
8. primo

Paso 2 This time provide the correct form of the *indefinite* article.

MODELO E1: tías
E2: *unas tías*

1-13 Una concordancia

Take turns matching the family members with the corresponding articles. Each family member will have **two** articles: one definite and one indefinite.

1. __el__ hijo	a. el
2. __las__ hermanas	b. la
3. ______ tía	c. los
4. ______ primas	d. las
5. ______ abuelos	e. un
6. ______ nieta	f. una
7. ______ padres	g. unos
8. ______ madre	h. unas

1-14 ¿Quiénes son?

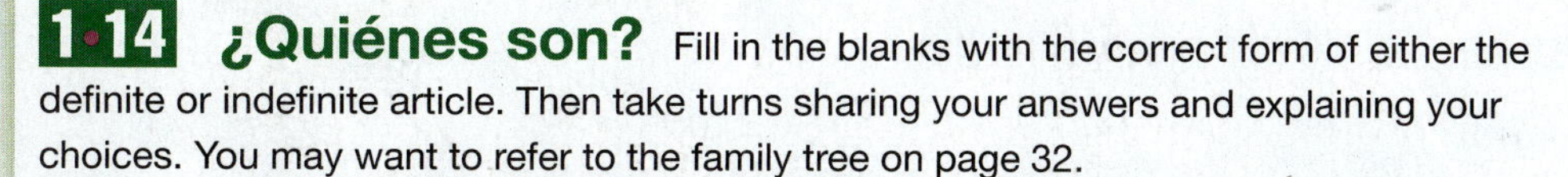
Fill in the blanks with the correct form of either the definite or indefinite article. Then take turns sharing your answers and explaining your choices. You may want to refer to the family tree on page 32.

Estrategia

To say "Eduardo's sister" or "Eduardo's grandparents," you add *de Eduardo* to each of your sentences: *Es la hermana de Eduardo. Son los abuelos de Eduardo.*

MODELO Adriana es *la* hermana de Eduardo.

(1) ______ abuelos se llaman Manuel y Carmen. Eduardo tiene (2) ______ tío. (3) ______ tío se llama Enrique. Eduardo tiene (4) ______ prima; se llama Sonia. (5) ______ hermano de Eduardo se llama Antonio.

¿Cómo andas? I

Each chapter has three places at which you will be asked to assess your progress. This first assessment comes as you have completed approximately one third of the chapter. How confident are you with your progress to date?

Having completed **Comunicación I**, I now can…	Feel confident	Need to review
• describe families. (p. 32)	☐	☐
• pronounce vowels. (p. 33 and online)	☐	☐
• illustrate formation of Hispanic last names. (p. 34)	☐	☐
• express what someone has. (p. 35)	☐	☐
• use singular and plural nouns. (p. 36)	☐	☐
• identify masculine and feminine nouns. (p. 37)	☐	☐
• convey *the*, *a*, *one*, and *some*. (p. 38)	☐	☐

Comunicación II

6 VOCABULARIO

Gente Giving details about yourself and others

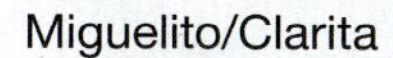

Miguelito/Clarita

el niño/la niña

Daniel/Mariela

el chico, el muchacho/ la chica, la muchacha

Javier/Ana

el joven/la joven

Manuel/Manuela

el hombre/la mujer

la Sra. Torres/la Srta. Sánchez/el Sr. Martín

la señora/la señorita/ el señor

Manolo/Pilar

el amigo/la amiga

Pepita/Roberto

la novia/el novio

El hombre and **la mujer** are terms for *man* and *woman*. **Señor, señora,** and **señorita** are often used as titles of address; in that case, they may also be abbreviated as **Sr., Sra.,** and **Srta.,** respectively.

—Buenos días, **Sr.** Martín.	*Good morning, Mr. Martín.*
—¿Cómo está Ud., **Sra.** Sánchez?	*How are you, Mrs. Sánchez?*

Fíjate

The abbreviations *Sr.*, *Sra.*, and *Srta.* are always capitalized, just like their equivalents in English.

¿? Now you are ready to complete the ***Preparación y práctica*** activities for this chunk online.

1·15 Los opuestos Take turns giving the gender opposites for the following words. Include the appropriate articles.

MODELO E1: el novio
E2: *la novia*

1. el chico
2. un hombre
3. la joven
4. un señor
5. una amiga
6. la niña

1-16 ¿Cómo se llama? Take turns answering the following questions, based on the drawings on page 41.

Capítulo A Para empezar. *Saludos, presentaciones y despedidas*, pág. 4.

MODELO E1: ¿Cómo se llama el hombre?

E2: *El hombre se llama Manuel.*

1. ¿Cómo se llama la joven?
2. ¿Cómo se llama el niño?
3. ¿Cómo se llaman los novios?
4. ¿Cómo se llama la señora?

7 GRAMÁTICA

Los adjetivos posesivos Stating possession

You have already used the possessive adjective **mi** (*my*). Other forms of possessive adjectives are also useful in conversation.

Look at the following chart to see how to personalize talk about your family (*our* dad, *his* sister, *our* cousins, etc.) using possessive adjectives.

Fíjate

Vuestro/a/os/as is only used in Spain.

Los adjetivos posesivos

mi, mis	*my*	**nuestro/a/os/as**	*our*
tu, tus	*your*	**vuestro/a/os/as**	*your*
su, sus	*your*	**su, sus**	*your*
su, sus	*his, her, its*	**su, sus**	*their*

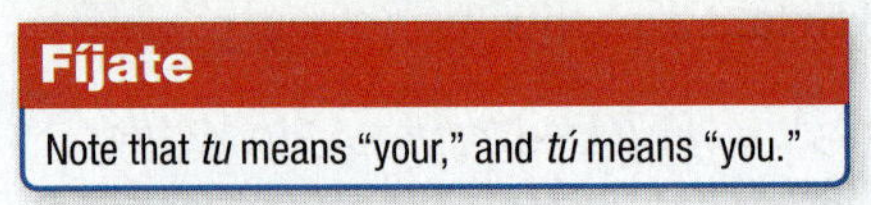
Fíjate

Note that *tu* means "your," and *tú* means "you."

Note:

1. Possessive adjectives agree in form with the person, place, or thing possessed, *not with the possessor.*
2. Possessive adjectives agree in number (singular or plural), and in addition, **nuestro** and **vuestro** indicate gender (masculine or feminine).
3. The possessive adjectives **tu/tus** (*your*) refer to someone with whom you are familiar and/or on a first name basis. **Su/sus** (*your*) is used when you are referring to people to whom you refer with *usted* and *ustedes*: that is, more formally and perhaps not on a first-name basis. **Su/sus** (*your* plural or *their*) is used when referring to individuals whom you are addressing with *ustedes* or when expressing possession with *ellos* and *ellas*.

mi hermano	*my brother*	**mis** hermanos	*my brothers/siblings*
tu primo	*your cousin*	**tus** primos	*your cousins*
su tía	*her/his/your/their aunt*	**sus** tías	*her/his/your/their aunts*
nuestra familia	*our family*	**nuestras familias**	*our families*
vuestra mamá	*your mom*	**vuestras** mamás	*your moms*
su hija	*her/his/your/their daughter*	**sus** hijas	*his/her/your/their daughters*

Eduardo tiene una novia. — *Eduardo has a girlfriend.*
Su novia se llama Julia. — *His girlfriend's name is Julia.*

Nuestros padres tienen dos amigos. — *Our parents have two friends.*
Sus amigos son Jorge y Marta. — *Their friends are Jorge and Marta.*

¿? Now you are ready to complete the ***Preparación y práctica*** activities for this chunk online.

1-17 ¿De quién es? Take turns supplying the correct possessive adjectives for the family members listed.

MODELO E1: (*our*) papás
E2: *nuestros papás*

1. (*your*/familiar) novia
2. (*my*) hermanos
3. (*our*) mamá
4. (*your*/formal) tío
5. (*her*) amiga
6. (*his*) hermanas

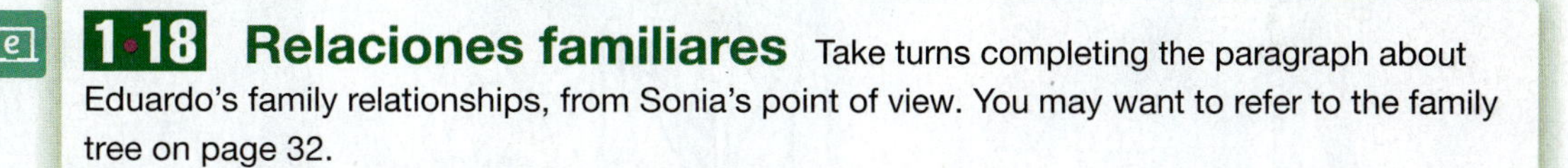

1-18 Relaciones familiares Take turns completing the paragraph about Eduardo's family relationships, from Sonia's point of view. You may want to refer to the family tree on page 32.

Yo soy Sonia. Eduardo es (1) ______ primo. Antonio y Adriana son (2) ______ primos también (*also*). (3) ______ padres, Pedro y Rosario, son (4) ______ tíos. (5) ______ padres se llaman Enrique y Francisca. Además (*Furthermore*), (6) ______ amiga Pilar es como (*like*) parte de (7) (*our*) ______ familia.

1-19 Tu familia Using at least **three** different possessive adjectives, talk to your partner about your family. You may want to refer to the family tree you drew for **1-3**.

MODELO En mi familia somos cinco personas. Mi padre se llama John y mi madre es Marie. Sus amigos son Mary y Dennis. Tengo dos hermanos, Clark y Blake. Nuestros tíos son Alice y Ralph y nuestras primas se llaman Gina y Glynis.

Estrategia

Using your own friends and family will help you remember the vocabulary. Write the names of your immediate family or your best friends. Then write a description of how those people are connected to each other. E.g., *Karen es la madre de Brian* or *Brian es el hijo de Karen*.

8 GRAMÁTICA

Los adjetivos descriptivos Supplying details about people, places, and things

Descriptive adjectives are words that describe people, places, and things.

1. In English, adjectives usually come before the words they describe (e.g., **the *red* car**), but in Spanish, they usually follow the words (e.g., **el coche *rojo***).
2. Adjectives in Spanish agree with the nouns they modify in number (singular or plural) and in gender (masculine or feminine).

Carlos es un **chico** simpátic**o.**	*Carlos is a nice boy.*
Adela es una **chica** simpátic**a.**	*Adela is a nice girl.*
Carlos y Adela son (unos) **chicos** simpátic**os.**	*Carlos and Adela are (some) nice children.*

3. A descriptive adjective can also follow the verb **ser** directly. When it does, it still agrees with the noun to which it refers, which is the subject in this case.

Carlos es simpátic**o.**	*Carlos is nice.*
Adela es simpátic**a.**	*Adela is nice.*
Carlos y Adela son simpátic**os.**	*Carlos and Adela are nice.*

Las características físicas, la personalidad y otros rasgos

La personalidad	*Personality*
aburrido/a	*boring*
antipático/a	*unpleasant*
bueno/a	*good*
cómico/a	*funny; comical*
interesante	*interesting*
malo/a	*bad*
paciente	*patient*
perezoso/a	*lazy*
responsable	*responsible*
simpático/a	*nice*
tonto/a	*silly; dumb*
trabajador/a	*hard-working*

Las características físicas	*Physical characteristics*
bonito/a	*pretty*
feo/a	*ugly*
grande	*big; large*
pequeño/a	*small*

Otras palabras	*Other words*
muy	*very*
(un) poco	*(a) little*

¿? Now you are ready to complete the ***Preparación y práctica*** activities for this chunk online.

1-20 ¿Cómo son? Take turns describing the following people to a classmate.

Capítulo A Para empezar. El verbo *ser*, pág. 13.

MODELO E1: Jorge

E2: *Jorge es débil.*

Jorge

Estrategia

Review *Los adjetivos de nacionalidad* on p. 14 in *Capítulo A Para empezar* in order to describe people in more detail.

1. Juan

2. María

3. Lupe y Marco

4. Roberto

5. Beatriz

6. yo

1-21 ¿Cierto o falso? Juana is describing her friends and family. Listen to what she says and look at the images to determine if she is correct in her descriptions. Indicate **C** for **Cierto** (*true*) or **F** for **Falso** (*false*).

	C	F
1.	☐	☐
2.	☐	☐
3.	☐	☐
4.	☐	☐
5.	☐	☐

1-22 Al contrario Student 1 creates a sentence using the cues provided, and Student 2 expresses the opposite. Pay special attention to adjective agreement.

MODELO los hermanos González / guapo

E1: *Los hermanos González son guapos.*

E2: *¡Ay no, son muy feos!*

1. los abuelos / pobre
2. la señora López / antipático
3. Jaime / delgado
4. la tía Claudia / mayor
5. Tomás y Antonia / alto
6. nosotros / perezoso

1-23 ¿Cómo los describes? Circulate among your classmates, asking for descriptions of the following people. Write what each person says, along with his/her name.

MODELO E1: *¿Cómo es Jon Stewart?*

E2: *Jon Stewart es cómico, inteligente y muy trabajador.*

E1: *¿Cómo te llamas?*

E2: *Mi nombre* (name) *es Rubén.*

PERSONA(S)	DESCRIPCIÓN	NOMBRE DEL ESTUDIANTE
Jon Stewart	Es cómico, inteligente y muy trabajador.	Rubén
1. Bruno Mars		
2. tus padres		
3. tu mejor (*best*) amigo/a y tú		
4. Shakira		
5. los estudiantes en la clase de español		

1-24 ¿Cómo eres? Imagine you are signing up for a dating service. Complete the following steps.

Capítulo A Para empezar. El verbo *ser*, pág. 13.

Paso 1 Describe yourself to your partner using at least **three** adjectives, and then describe your ideal date.

MODELO *Me llamo Julie. Soy joven, muy inteligente y alta. La persona ideal para mí (*for me*) es inteligente, paciente y cómica.*

Paso 2 How similar are you and your partner and how similar are your ideal dates?

MODELO *Rebeca y yo somos jóvenes, altas y muy inteligentes. Nuestras personas ideales son cómicas y pacientes.*

1-25 ¿Es verdad?

Describe **five** famous (or infamous!) people or characters. Your partner can react by saying **Es verdad** (*It's true*) or **No es verdad** (*It's not true*). If your partner disagrees with you, he/she must correct your statement.

MODELO E1: *Santa Claus es gordo y un poco feo.*
E2: *No es verdad. Sí, es gordo pero no es feo. Es guapo.*

> **Estrategia**
>
> Being an "active listener" is an important skill in any language. *Active listening* means that you hear and understand what someone is saying. Being able to repeat what someone says helps you practice and perfect the skill of active listening.

1-26 ¿Cuáles son sus cualidades?

Think of the qualities of your best friend and those of someone you do not particularly like (**una persona que no me gusta**). Using adjectives that you know in Spanish, write at least **three** sentences that describe each of these people. Share your list with a partner.

MODELO

MI MEJOR (*BEST*) AMIGO/A	UNA PERSONA QUE NO ME GUSTA
1. Es trabajador/a.	1. Es antipático/a.
2. Es inteligente.	2. No es paciente.
3. …	3. …

1-27 Describe a una familia

Bring family photos (personal ones or some taken from the Internet or a magazine) to class and describe the family members to a classmate, using at least **five** sentences.

Capítulo A Para empezar. *Los pronombres personales*, pág. 11.

MODELO *Tengo dos hermanas, Kate y Ana. Ellas son simpáticas y bonitas. Mi papá no es aburrido y es muy trabajador. Tengo seis primos…*

El español, lengua diversa

The title of this chapter, **¿Quiénes somos?**, suggests that we are all a varied combination of many factors, one of which is language. As you know, the English language is rich in state, regional, and national variations. For example, what word do you use when referring to soft drinks? Some people in the United States say *soda,* others say *pop,* and still others use *Coke* as a generic term for all brands and flavors of soft drinks.

The Spanish language also has many variations. For example, to describe someone as *funny* you could say **cómico/a** in many Latin American countries, but **divertido/a** or **gracioso/a** in Spain. Similarly, there are multiple ways to say the word *bus*: in Mexico, **camión**; in Puerto Rico and Cuba, **guagua**; in Spain, **autobús**. In ***¡Anda! Curso elemental,*** such variants will appear in the **También se dice**… section in Appendix 3.

The pronunciation of English also varies in different parts of the United States and throughout the rest of the English-speaking world, and so it is with Spanish across the Spanish-speaking world. Nevertheless, wherever you go you will find that Spanish is still Spanish, despite regional and national differences. You should have little trouble understanding native speakers from different countries or making yourself understood. You may have to attune your ears to local vocabulary or pronunciation, but that's part of the intrigue of communicating in another language.

Preguntas

1. What are some characteristics of the English spoken in other countries, such as Canada, Great Britain, Australia, and India?
2. What are some English words that are used where you live that are not necessarily used in other parts of the country?

9 VOCABULARIO

Los números 31–100 Counting from 31 to 100

The numbers 31–100 function in much the same way as the numbers 0–30. Note how the numbers 30–39 are formed. This pattern will repeat itself up to 100.

31	**treinta y uno**	37	**treinta y siete**	51	**cincuenta y uno…**
32	**treinta y dos**	38	**treinta y ocho**	60	**sesenta**
33	**treinta y tres**	39	**treinta y nueve**	70	**setenta**
34	**treinta y cuatro**	40	**cuarenta**	80	**ochenta**
35	**treinta y cinco**	41	**cuarenta y uno…**	90	**noventa**
36	**treinta y seis**	50	**cincuenta**	100	**cien**

Estrategia

Practice the numbers in Spanish by reading and pronouncing any numbers you see in your daily routine (e.g., highway signs, prices on your shopping receipts, room numbers on campus, phone numbers, etc.).

¿? Now you are ready to complete the ***Preparación y práctica*** activities for this chunk online.

1-28 Examen de matemáticas Are you ready to test your math skills?

Take turns reading and solving the problems aloud. Then create your own math problems to test your partner.

más	*plus*
menos	*minus*
son	*equals*
por	*times; by*
dividido por	*divided by*

MODELO E1: 97 – 53 =

E2: *Noventa y siete menos cincuenta y tres son cuarenta y cuatro.*

1. 81 + 13 =
2. 65 – 26 =
3. 24 + 76 =
4. 99 – 52 =
5. 12 × 8 =
6. 8 × 7 =
7. 65 ÷ 5 =
8. 100 ÷ 2 =

1-29 **¿Qué número es?** Look at the pages from the telephone book. Say **five** phone numbers and have your partner tell you whose numbers they are. Then switch roles.

MODELO E1: *Ochenta y ocho, sesenta y ocho, setenta y cinco*

E2: *Adelaida Santoyo*

SANTOS JAIME-SIERRA 12I 12 SM 3 CP 77500....**84-0661**
SANTOS JAVIER L1 Y 12 M10 SM43 PEDREGAL CP 77500....**80-5138**
SANTOS SEGOVIA FREDDY CALLE 45 NTE MANZ 34 LTE 3 COL 77528....**80-2242**
SANTOS SEGURA ALBA ROSA COL LEONA VICARIO M 8 L SM 74 77500....**80-0861**
SANTOS SOLIS FELIPE CALLE 20 OTE NO 181 SM 68 M 12 L 28 CP 77500....**80-1330**
SANTOS VELÁZQUEZ MARÍA JESÚS CALLE 3 NO 181 77537....**86-6949**
SANTOS VILLANUEVA ARMINDA CALLE 46 PTE MANZ 20 77510....**88-3999**
SANTOS JOSÉ E CALLE 33 OTE 171 L 14 M 25 CP 77500....**80-1175**
SANTOSCOY LAGUNES ELIZABETH CERRADA FLAMBOYANES 2 SM23....**87-6204**
SANTOYO ADELAIDA CALLE 75 NTE DEPTO 7 EDIF 2 SM 92 CP 77500....**88-6875**
SANTOYO BETANCOURT PEDRO ARIEL HDA NUM 12 NABZ 61 77517....**88-7941**
SANTOYO CORTEZ LIGIA EDIFICIO QUETZAL DEPTO C-1 SM 32 77500....**87-4676**
SANTOYO MARTÍN AIDA MARÍA NANCE DEP 4 MZA 12 NUM 13....**87-3799**

1-30 **¿Su número de teléfono?** Imagine that you work in a busy office. You take messages with the following phone numbers. Say the numbers to a partner, who will write them. Then switch roles, mixing the order of the numbers.

MODELO E1: 223-7256

E2: *dos, veintitrés, setenta y dos, cincuenta y seis*

1. 962-2136
2. 615-9563
3. 871-4954
4. 414-4415
5. 761-7920
6. 270-2325

Capítulo A
Para empezar.
Los números
0–30, pág. 16.

1-31 Los hispanos en los EE. UU.

Use the information from the pie chart to answer the following questions in Spanish.

por ciento	*percent*

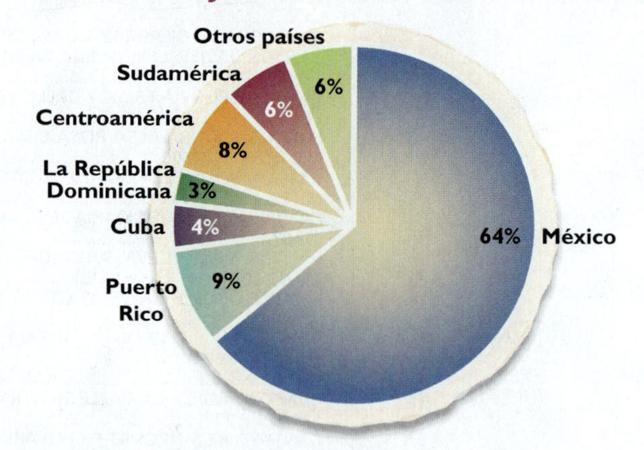

Source: US Census Bureau State & County QuickFacts

1. What percentage of U.S. Hispanics is from Cuba?
2. What percentage of U.S. Hispanics is from Puerto Rico?
3. What percentage of U.S. Hispanics is from Mexico?
4. What percentage of U.S. Hispanics is from South America?
5. What percentage of U.S. Hispanics comes from countries other than Mexico?

Escucha

Presentaciones

Estrategia

Determining the topic and listening for words you know

The first steps to becoming a successful listener are to determine the topic and then listen for words that you know. If you are in a social situation, you can determine the topic by looking for visual cues (body language, pictures, etc.) or by asking the speaker(s) for clarification. When listening to passages in ***¡Anda! Curso elemental,*** look at the activities or questions connected with the passage to help you determine the topic. Remember that words that you know include *cognates* which are words that look and sound like words in English.

Aural comprehension is critical in learning to communicate in Spanish. You are working on developing your listening skills every time your instructor speaks or when you work in pairs or groups in class. You will also practice this skill when you watch the *Club cultura* video series, which is part of the *Vistazo cultural* section in ***¡Anda! Curso elemental***.

In ***¡Anda! Curso elemental*** you will have the opportunity to learn and practice strategies to assist you in developing listening skills in Spanish. Let's begin with listening for words you know, including cognates.

1·32 Antes de escuchar In the following segment, Alejandra introduces her family. Write two things that you expect to hear.

____

____

1·33 A escuchar Listen as Alejandra introduces her family. Use the following steps to help you.

a. First, look at the incomplete sentences in item c below. They will give you an idea about the topic of the passage.
b. Listen to the passage, concentrating on the words you know. Make a list of those words.
c. Listen one more time and complete the following sentences.
   1. La familia de Alejandra es ______________.
   2. Los nombres de sus padres son ______________.
   3. Alejandra tiene ______________ hermanos y ______________ hermanas.

1·34 Después de escuchar Take turns saying **three** sentences about you and your family to a partner. Your partner will tell you the words he/she knows.

¡Conversemos!

1·35 Jefe nuevo With a partner, imagine that your new boss came to your office today to introduce himself/herself. Call your best friend, and describe your new boss in at least **four** sentences.

1·36 Mucho gusto You have just met a new neighbor. Imagine that your partner is your new neighbor, and describe yourself and your family to him/her. Use at least **six** sentences. In addition to **ser** and **tener,** create sentences using *Me gusta / No me gusta,* etc.

Escribe

Un poema

Estrategia

Organizing ideas / Preparing to write

Whether you are writing informally or formally, organizing your ideas before you write is important. The advance preparation will help you express yourself clearly and concisely. Jotting notes or ideas helps in the organizational process.

1-37 Antes de escribir Write all the Spanish nouns and adjectives you can think of that describe you. Start by reviewing the vocabulary lists for **Capítulo 1** and **También se dice…,** Appendix 3.

1-38 A escribir Complete the following steps in order to write your first poem in Spanish.

Paso 1 Using either your first, middle, or last name, match a noun or descriptive adjective with each letter of that name. For example:

*"Sarah": **S** = simpática, **a** = alta, **r** = responsable, **a** = amiga, **h** = hermana*

With these words, create what is known as an *acrostic* poem.

Paso 2 Now build phrases or sentences around your letters, using **tener, ser,** possessive adjectives, and numbers.

MODELO

***S**impática*	***SARAH***
***A**lta*	*es **S**impática*
***R**esponsable*	*no es baja; es **A**lta*
***A**miga*	*es **R**esponsable*
***H**ermana*	*tiene cien **A**migas*
	*es mi **H**ermana.*

1-39 Después de escribir Read your poem to a classmate.

¿Cómo andas? II

This is your second self-assessment. You have now completed two thirds of the chapter. How confident are you with the following topics and concepts?

Having completed **Comunicación II**, I now can…	**Feel confident**	**Need to review**
• give details about myself and others. (p. 41)	☐	☐
• state possession. (p. 42)	☐	☐
• supply details about people, places, and things. (p. 44)	☐	☐
• compare and contrast several regional and national differences in the English and Spanish languages. (p. 49)	☐	☐
• count from 31 to 100. (p. 50)	☐	☐
• determine the topic and listen for known words. (p. 52)	☐	☐
• communicate about people I know. (p. 53)	☐	☐
• organize ideas to write a poem. (p. 54)	☐	☐

Vistazo cultural

Explore more about Hispanics in the United States with *Club cultura* online.

Los Estados Unidos

Les presento mi país

Rafael Sánchez Martínez

Mi nombre es Rafael Sánchez Martínez y soy de El Barrio, una comunidad en la ciudad de Nueva York. Soy bilingüe: hablo inglés y español. Soy estadounidense y tengo herencia hispana. Mis abuelos son puertorriqueños. Hay (*There are*) muchos hispanohablantes (*Spanish speakers*) en mi barrio, y en los Estados Unidos también. **¿Puedes (*Can you*) identificar otras cuatro o cinco ciudades en el mapa con grandes poblaciones hispanohablantes?** Hay hispanohablantes famosos de muchas carreras diferentes, como Soledad O'Brien y Aarón Sánchez. El padre de Soledad es cubano y la madre de Aarón es mexicana. **¿Por qué son famosas estas personas?** También se nota la influencia hispana en los restaurantes y en los supermercados donde se ofrecen productos hispanos de compañías como Goya, Ortega, Corona, Marinela y Tecate. Mi restaurante favorito se llama Fonda Boricua. **¿Cuál es tu restaurante favorito?**

Los Estados Unidos

Una señora prepara tortillas en un restaurante en San Diego, California.

San Francisco, California, como otras ciudades en los Estados Unidos, tiene un centro para mujeres hispanas.

El mes de la herencia hispana se celebra entre el 15 de septiembre y el 15 de octubre en muchas ciudades de los Estados Unidos.

St. Augustine es la primera ciudad europea en los Estados Unidos, fundada en el año 1565 por los españoles.

ESTADO

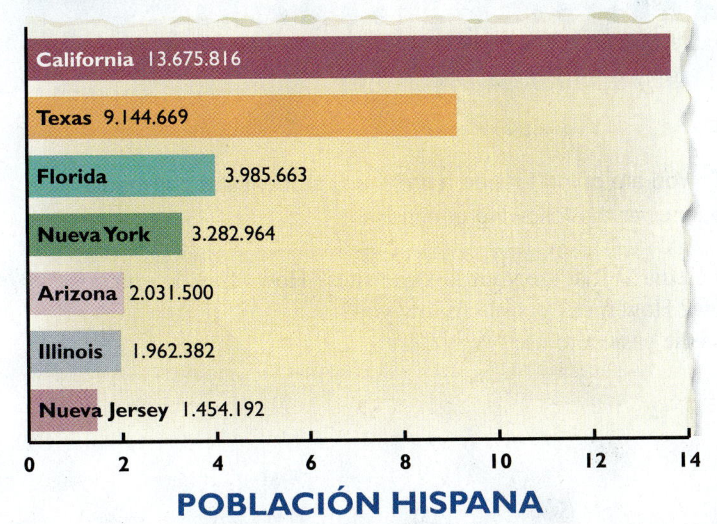

POBLACIÓN HISPANA

Source: US Census Bureau State & County QuickFacts

Fíjate

In most of the Spanish-speaking world, commas are used where the English-speaking world uses decimal points, and vice versa. For example, in English one says "six point four percent," in Spanish, *seis coma cuatro por ciento.*

CIUDAD

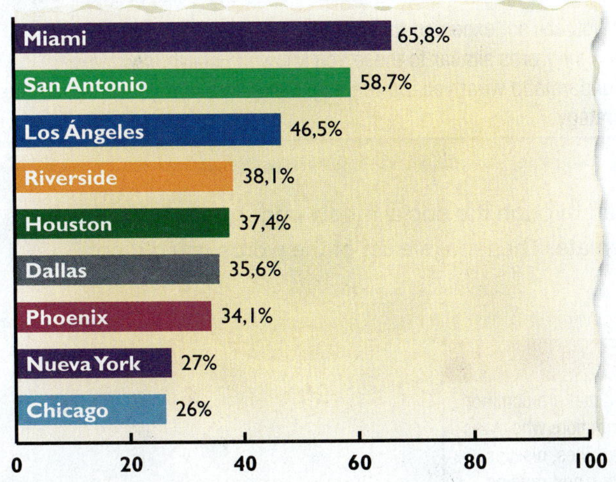

PORCENTAJE DE POBLACIÓN HISPANA

Source: Brookings Institution

ALMANAQUE

Nombre oficial:	Estados Unidos de América
Gobierno:	República constitucional y federal
Población:	307.006.550 (2010)
Población de origen hispano:	15,8% (2010)
Moneda:	el dólar ($)

¿Sabías que...?

- Para el año 2050, una de cada cuatro personas en los Estados Unidos va a ser de origen hispano.
- Los hispanos tienen una gran presencia en el béisbol profesional en los Estados Unidos. Según (*According to*) un censo del deporte del 2014, los hispanos representan más del 28% de los jugadores de las grandes ligas de béisbol. De los beisbolistas hispanos, el 44% son de origen dominicano y el 32% son de origen venezolano. En las pequeñas ligas de béisbol hay aún más (*even more*) participación hispana, con más del 40% de los jugadores de origen hispano en años recientes.

Preguntas

1. What is the importance of St. Augustine, Florida?
2. What states have the largest Hispanic population?
3. Who are some famous Hispanics in the United States? Which do you admire most? What do you know about his or her heritage?
4. Which sport in the United States has a large Hispanic presence? What do you know about the origins of those players?

Lectura

El perfil de Adriana

1-40 Antes de leer You are going to read a university student's social media page. Before you read the page, answer the following questions.

1. How often do you use social media? What are your favorite sites? How often do you post?
2. How many sites do you follow? How many people follow you?
3. Which type of social media is the easiest to use? Why?

Estrategia

Recognizing Cognates

When you read something for the first time, you are not expected to understand every word. In addition to focusing on the words that you *do* know, look for words similar to those you know in English, *cognates*. Cognates are an excellent way to help you understand what you are reading. Make sure that you complete the **Mientras lees** activity to practice this strategy.

1-41 Mientras lees Read through the social media page, underlining the cognates. Share your list with a classmate. Then make a list of the words you did not understand.

Estrategia

When reading social media entries, note the parts that are common to all of them. Usually you find the following information: who owns the entry and personal information like name, age, likes, dislikes, etc. You can use your knowledge of writing, posting, and reading social media entries in English to see whether you can understand the additional information presented in Adriana's social media page.

9:40 AM

Mi mundo | buscar | Inicio | Perfil | Cuenta

Adriana Martín Domínguez

- Amigos
- Fotos
- Favoritos
- Cine
- Juegos

Mi información

Me llamo Adriana. Tengo diecinueve años y estudio ingeniería náutica en la Universidad Estatal Hispana. Soy alta, delgada y atlética.
Me gusta escuchar música. Mi familia es de origen mexicano, pero somos estadounidenses. A nosotros nos gustan los deportes acuáticos. Mi hermano Eduardo también es estudiante como yo en la Universidad Hispana Central. Él tiene veintiún años. Es bajo, elegante, simpático e inteligente.

Adriana Martín Domínguez

Hoy hace mucho calor. ¡Está a 100 °F! Aquí hay una foto de mis abuelos. Mi abuelo Manuel es mi favorito. Tiene setenta años pero él piensa° que tiene sesenta años. Es divertido, simpático y activo. Le gusta pintar y los deportes como el fútbol, el tenis y el golf. Yo paso mucho tiempo con mi abuelo durante los veranos. Mi abuela se llama Carmen y tiene sesenta y cinco años. Ella es baja, paciente y trabajadora. Es maestra de español y trabaja en una escuela de niños los lunes y los miércoles.

Hoy a las 15:35 p.m. (cerca de UEH)

thinks

1·42 Después de leer

Answer the following questions.

1. Who wrote the entries in the social media page?
2. What does the student like to do?
3. How is the weather where she is?
4. What do you consider interesting about her grandparents? Mention at least three things.

1·43 Experiencia personal

Your favorite family member is coming to visit you at school. You want to explain to your friends what he/she is like. Write a brief social media announcement for your friends to present your favorite family member.

Paso 1 Make a list of the things you would like to write about your family member:

- Who is he/she?
- What is his/her nationality?
- Is he/she your age?
- Is he/she attending school like you?
- What does he/she like to do?

Paso 2 With the information from *Paso 1*, write a message to post on social media to share with your friends.

1·44 Tus compañeros de clase

Your family wants to know about your new Spanish class. Create a presentation in which you describe your class to your family. Make sure to include the following information:

- where and when your Spanish class is
- number of classmates
- a description of two of your classmates (names, likes, dislikes, and origin)

For additional *Lectura* activities, go to *¡Anda!* online.

Y por fin, ¿cómo andas?

Each chapter will end with a checklist like the one that follows. This is the third time in the chapter that you are given the opportunity to check your progress. Use the checklist to measure what you have learned in the chapter. Place a check in the *Feel confident* column for the topics you feel you know, and a check in the *Need to review* column for the topics that you need to practice more.

Having completed this chapter, I now can...	Feel confident	Need to review
Comunicación I		
• describe families. (p. 32)	☐	☐
• pronounce vowels. (p. 33 and online)	☐	☐
• express what someone has. (p. 35)	☐	☐
• use singular and plural nouns. (p. 36)	☐	☐
• identify masculine and feminine nouns. (p. 37)	☐	☐
• convey *the*, *a*, *one*, and *some*. (p. 38)	☐	☐
Comunicación II		
• give details about myself and others. (p. 41)	☐	☐
• state possession. (p. 42)	☐	☐
• supply details about people, places, and things. (p. 44)	☐	☐
• count from 31 to 100. (p. 50)	☐	☐
• determine the topic and listen for known words. (p. 52)	☐	☐
• communicate about people I know. (p. 53)	☐	☐
• organize ideas to write a poem. (p. 54)	☐	☐
Cultura		
• illustrate formation of Hispanic last names. (p. 34)	☐	☐
• compare and contrast several regional and national differences in the English and Spanish languages. (p. 49)	☐	☐
• discuss the size, location, and makeup of the Hispanic population in the United States. (p. 56)	☐	☐
Lectura		
• read a social media page in Spanish. (p. 58)	☐	☐
Comunidades		
• use Spanish in real-life contexts. (online)	☐	☐

Vocabulario activo

La familia	Family
el/la abuelo/a	*grandfather/grandmother*
los abuelos	*grandparents*
el/la esposo/a	*husband/wife*
el/la hermano/a	*brother/sister*
los hermanos	*brothers and sisters; siblings*
el/la hijo/a	*son/daughter*
los hijos	*sons and daughters; children*
la madrastra	*stepmother*
la madre/la mamá	*mother/mom*
el/la nieto/a	*grandson/granddaughter*
el padrastro	*stepfather*
el padre/el papá	*father/dad*
los padres	*parents*
el/la primo/a	*cousin*
los primos	*cousins*
el/la tío/a	*uncle/aunt*
los tíos	*aunts and uncles*

La gente	People
el/la amigo/a	*friend*
el/la chico/a	*boy/girl*
el hombre	*man*
el/la joven	*young man/young woman*
el/la muchacho/a	*boy/girl*
la mujer	*woman*
el/la niño/a	*little boy/little girl*
el/la novio/a	*boyfriend/girlfriend*
el señor (Sr.)	*man; gentleman; Mr.*
la señora (Sra.)	*woman; lady; Mrs.*
la señorita (Srta.)	*young woman; Miss*

Los adjetivos descriptivos	Descriptive adjectives
La personalidad y otros rasgos	**Personality and other characteristics**
aburrido/a	*boring*
antipático/a	*unpleasant*
bueno/a	*good*
cómico/a	*funny; comical*
inteligente	*intelligent*
interesante	*interesting*
malo/a	*bad*
paciente	*patient*
perezoso/a	*lazy*
pobre	*poor*
responsable	*responsible*
rico/a	*rich*
simpático/a	*nice*
tonto/a	*silly; dumb*
trabajador/a	*hard-working*
Otras palabras	**Other words**
muy	*very*
(un) poco	*(a) little*
Las características físicas	**Physical characteristics**
alto/a	*tall*
bajo/a	*short*
bonito/a	*pretty*
débil	*weak*
delgado/a	*thin*
feo/a	*ugly*
fuerte	*strong*
gordo/a	*fat*
grande	*big; large*
guapo/a	*handsome/pretty*
joven	*young*
mayor	*old*
pequeño/a	*small*

Los números 31–100	*Numbers 31–100*
treinta y uno	*thirty-one*
treinta y dos	*thirty-two*
treinta y tres	*thirty-three*
treinta y cuatro	*thirty-four*
treinta y cinco	*thirty-five*
treinta y seis	*thirty-six*
treinta y siete	*thirty-seven*
treinta y ocho	*thirty-eight*
treinta y nueve	*thirty-nine*
cuarenta	*forty*
cuarenta y uno	*forty-one*
cincuenta	*fifty*
cincuenta y uno	*fifty-one*
sesenta	*sixty*
setenta	*seventy*
ochenta	*eighty*
noventa	*ninety*
cien	*one hundred*

Un verbo	*Verb*
tener	*to have*

If you are interested in discovering additional vocabulary for the topics studied in each chapter, consult Appendix 3, **También se dice…,** for additional words. It contains expanded vocabulary that you may need for your own personal expression, including regionally used words and slang. Enjoy!

Unos estudiantes en San Miguel de Allende, México

2 La vida universitaria

The majority of universities throughout the Spanish-speaking world tend to be public, with vast student enrollments, minimal tuition, if any, and rigorous admission exams. In many countries, exam results can determine career choices and generally students begin to take courses in their major area in their first year. As a rule, students live off-campus and universities are often in large urban areas.

Preguntas

1. Do you live on campus or commute to classes? Is your college or university in a city or small town? How might these factors impact your experience?
2. How large is your college or university? What are the advantages and/or disadvantages of studying at an institution of this size?
3. Why do many U.S. colleges and universities require general education courses prior to entering courses for majors? Why do many schools have language requirements?

¿Sabías que...?

In Mexico, a bachelor's degree is called *licenciatura.*

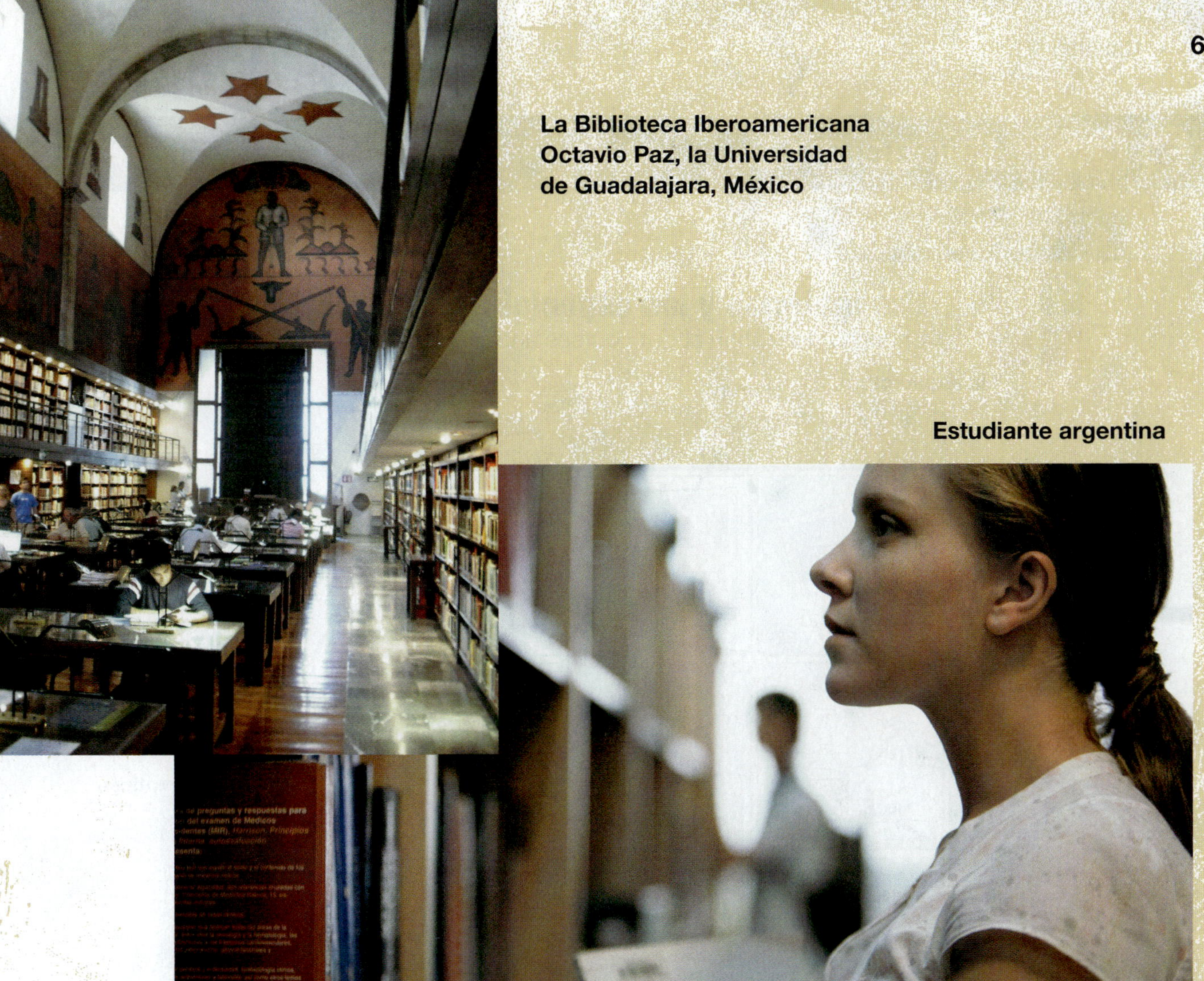

La Biblioteca Iberoamericana Octavio Paz, la Universidad de Guadalajara, México

Estudiante argentina

Learning Outcomes

By the end of this chapter, you will be able to:

- ✔ state places, majors, and items associated with university life.
- ✔ relate daily activities.
- ✔ articulate emotions and states of being, and convey likes and dislikes.
- ✔ offer opinions on sports and pastimes.
- ✔ communicate about university life.
- ✔ craft a personal description.
- ✔ exchange interesting facts about Mexico and university life there.
- ✔ read a letter from an academic advisor.

Comunicación I

1 VOCABULARIO

Las materias y las especialidades

Sharing information about courses and majors

Otras palabras	*Other words*
la administración de empresas	*business administration*
el curso	*course*
la pedagogía	*education*
el periodismo	*journalism*
el semestre	*semester*

REMINDER: There is additional enrichment vocabulary that you may find useful for your own personal expression in Appendix 3.

Now you are ready to complete the ***Preparación y práctica*** activities for this chunk online.

PRONUNCIACIÓN

Word stress and accent marks

Go to *¡Anda!* online to learn about word stress and accent marks.

2-1 ¿Cuál es su especialidad? Complete the following steps.

Paso 1 Take turns matching the following famous people with the majors they may have studied in college.

1. <u>B</u> Pablo Picasso
2. <u>e</u> Maya Angelou
3. <u>f</u> Marie Curie
4. <u>c</u> Sigmund Freud
5. <u>h</u> el presidente de Coca-Cola
6. <u>G</u> Supreme Court Justice Sonia Sotomayor
7. <u>A</u> Taylor Swift
8. <u>D</u> Bill Gates

a. la música
b. el arte
c. la psicología
d. la informática
e. la literatura
f. las ciencias
g. el derecho
h. la administración de empresas

Paso 2 Now, can you name the majors the following famous Hispanics may have studied in college?

1. Ellen Ochoa (astronauta)
2. Jorge Ramos (periodista *[journalist]*)
3. Isabel Allende (autora)
4. Carlos Santana (músico)

2-2 ¿Qué clases tienes? Complete the following chart, and then share your schedule with a partner.

HORARIO DE CLASES

CLASES	DÍAS DE LA SEMANA	HORA
matemáticas	martes y jueves	1:30

MODELO *Este semestre tengo cinco cursos. Tengo la clase de matemáticas los martes y jueves a la una y media... ¿Y tú?*

Estrategia

If the meaning of any of the vocabulary words is not clear, verify the definition in the *Vocabulario activo* at the end of this chapter.

2-3 Estereotipos

In your opinion, the following characteristics are stereotypically associated with students majoring in which fields? Share your responses with your group of three or four students, and then report the group findings to the class.

Capítulo 1. El verbo *tener*, pág. 35; Los adjetivos descriptivos, pág. 44.

Estrategia

Go to Appendix 3, *También se dice…*, for an expanded list of college majors. *También se dice…* includes additional vocabulary and regional expressions for all chapters. Although not exhaustive, the list will give you an idea of the variety and richness of the Spanish language.

MODELO Los estudiantes ______________ son ricos.

E1: *Tengo "Los estudiantes de administración de empresas son ricos". ¿Qué tienes tú?*

E2: *También tengo "Los estudiantes de administración de empresas son ricos".*

E3: *Tengo "Los estudiantes de informática son ricos".*

GRUPO: *Tenemos "Los estudiantes de administración de empresas y los estudiantes de informática son ricos".*

Los estudiantes de…

1. ______________ son ricos.
2. ______________ son simpáticos.
3. ______________ son trabajadores.
4. ______________ son cómicos.
5. ______________ son responsables.
6. ______________ son pacientes.
7. ______________ son interesantes.
8. ______________ son muy inteligentes.

Las universidades hispanas

There are many similarities and differences between the system of higher education in the United States and that of the Spanish-speaking world. For example, students in universities across the Spanish-speaking world usually begin their career courses immediately, as opposed to having several years of liberal arts courses. Also, although many universities have student housing, it is common for students to live at home or rent apartments with other students.

La Universidad Nacional Autónoma de México (UNAM)

With regard to collegiate sports and pastimes, there are usually varieties of extracurricular activities available in the form of clubs. For example, clubs can be sports-related, or they can be centered around other organized activities such as socially conscious volunteerism groups.

Technology permeates Hispanic universities. As in the United States, it is not uncommon for students to take online courses or have opportunities for some type of distance learning.

Preguntas

1. What are similarities between your life as a college student and that of a student in the Spanish-speaking world?
2. Where in the Spanish-speaking world would you like to study? Find the university's web site and share with the class the programs and opportunities that the school has to offer.

2 VOCABULARIO

La sala de clase

Describing your classroom and classmates

Otras palabras	*Other words*
los apuntes *(pl.)*	*notes*
la composición	*composition*
el examen	*exam*
el papel	*paper*
la tarea	*homework*
la compañera de clase	*female classmate*
el compañero de clase	*male classmate*
la profesora	*female professor*

¿? Now you are ready to complete the ***Preparación y práctica*** activities for this chunk online.

2-4 ¿Cómo es tu sala de clase?

Using the numbers 0–30, take turns indicating how many there are in your classroom of each of the items presented in **La sala de clase.** You and your partner should each create at least **five** sentences following the model.

Capítulo A Para empezar. Los números 0–30, pág. 16.

Fíjate

Hay is a little word that carries a lot of meaning. It means both "there is" and "there are."

MODELO E1: *Hay veinticinco mochilas y tres ventanas.*

E2: *Sí, y también hay diecinueve cuadernos.*

hay	*there is; there are*
pero	*but*
también	*too; also*
y	*and*

2-5 ¿Qué tiene Miguel?

Miguel is running late for class again. He has remembered some things and forgotten others. Make a list of **five** things he possibly has and does not have for class, using the verb **tener**. Share your list with a classmate.

Capítulo 1. El verbo *tener*, pág. 35.

Fíjate

To make a negative statement, simply place the word *no* before the verb: *Miguel tiene los apuntes. Miguel* no *tiene los apuntes.*

MODELO *Miguel tiene los apuntes, pero no tiene el libro de matemáticas. También tiene...*

2-6 ¿Cierto o falso?

After class, Miguel meets Claudia in the library. Claudia wants to know if he has the necessary materials for their study session. Listen to the conversation and, based on the drawing in **2-5**, determine if Miguel's answers are **Cierto** (*true*) or **Falso** (*false*).

Capítulo 1. El verbo *tener*, pág. 35.

	C	F		C	F
1.	☐	☐	4.	☐	☐
2.	☐	☐	5.	☐	☐
3.	☐	☐			

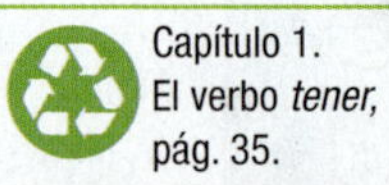

2-7 **¿Qué tienen tus compañeros?** Randomly choose three students and complete the chart below. Then take turns having your partner identify the classmates as you state **five** things each one has or does not have for class.

Fíjate

As in English, when listing a series of things, the word *y* (*and*) is placed just before the last item. In Spanish, however, note that you do not place a comma before *y*.

MODELO E1: *La estudiante 1 tiene dos cuadernos, un libro, un bolígrafo y dos lápices. ¡No tiene la tarea!*

E2: *¿Es Sarah?*

E1: *Sí, es Sarah. / No, no es Sarah.*

ESTUDIANTE 1	ESTUDIANTE 2	ESTUDIANTE 3
(NO) TIENE...	(NO) TIENE...	(NO) TIENE...
1.	1.	1.
2.	2.	2.
3.	3.	3.
4.	4.	4.
5.	5.	5.

3 GRAMÁTICA

Presente indicativo de verbos regulares

Relating daily activities

Mario es un estudiante de derecho. ¿Qué hace (*does he do*) todos los días (*every day*)?

Llega a la clase a las nueve de la mañana.

Lee en la biblioteca.

Habla con sus compañeros.

Trabaja dos horas como tutor.

Come en la cafetería con amigos.

A las 6:30 **espera** el autobús y **regresa** a su apartamento.

Spanish has three groups of verbs, which are categorized by the ending of the infinitive. Remember that an infinitive is expressed in English by the word *to: to have, to be*, and *to speak* are all infinitive forms of English verbs. Spanish infinitives end in **-ar, -er,** or **-ir.** Look at the lists of infinitives on the next page.

(continued)

Verbos que terminan en *-ar*

comprar	*to buy*	**preguntar**	*to ask (a question)*
contestar	*to answer*	**preparar**	*to prepare; to get ready*
enseñar	*to teach; to show*	**regresar**	*to return*
esperar	*to wait for; to hope*	**terminar**	*to finish; to end*
estudiar	*to study*	**tomar**	*to take; to drink*
hablar	*to speak*	**trabajar**	*to work*
llegar	*to arrive*	**usar**	*to use*
mirar	*to look (at); to watch*		
necesitar	*to need*		

Verbos que terminan en *-er*

aprender	*to learn*	**correr**	*to run*
comer	*to eat*	**creer**	*to believe*
comprender	*to understand*	**leer**	*to read*

Verbos que terminan en *-ir*

abrir	*to open*	**recibir**	*to receive*
escribir	*to write*	**vivir**	*to live*

To talk about daily or ongoing activities or actions, you need to use the present tense. You can also use the present tense to express future events.

Mario **lee** en la biblioteca. { *Mario reads in the library.* / *Mario is reading in the library.*

Mario **lee** en la biblioteca mañana. *Mario will read in the library tomorrow.*

To form the present indicative, drop the **-ar, -er,** or **-ir** ending from the infinitive, and add the appropriate ending. The endings are in blue in the following chart. Follow this simple pattern with all regular verbs.

Estrategia

If you would like to review the difference between the formal "you" and the informal "you," return to the cultural reading *¿Tú o usted?* on page 12 of *Capítulo A Para empezar.*

	hablar (*to speak*)	**comer** (*to eat*)	**vivir** (*to live*)
yo	hablo	como	vivo
tú	hablas	comes	vives
Ud.	habla	come	vive
él, ella	habla	come	vive
nosotros/as	hablamos	comemos	vivimos
vosotros/as	habláis	coméis	vivís
Uds.	hablan	comen	viven
ellos/as	hablan	comen	viven

¿? Now you are ready to complete the ***Preparación y práctica*** activities for this chunk online.

2-8 Vamos a practicar Take ten small pieces of paper and write a different noun or pronoun (**yo, tú, él,** etc.) on each one. On another five small pieces of paper write five infinitives, one on each piece of paper. Take turns drawing a paper from each pile. Give the correct form of the verb you selected to match the noun or pronoun you picked from the pile. Each person should say at least **five** verbs in a row correctly.

MODELO INFINITIVE: *preguntar*

PRONOUN OR NOUN: *mi madre*

E1: *mi madre pregunta*

2-9 El e-mail de Carlos Complete Carlos's e-mail message to his mother using the correct form of the verbs in parentheses.

Enviar | Enviar más tarde | Guardar | Borrar | Adjuntar | Contactos

Para: Mamá

De: Carlos

Asunto: La universidad

Hola mamá:

¡Qué difícil es la universidad! Me gusta mucho pero (1) ________ (trabajar) mucho. Por ejemplo, mañana (2) ________ (tomar) un examen de biología. Ahora mismo (*Right now*) mi amigo Tim y yo (3) ________ (estudiar) en la biblioteca. Generalmente, cuando estudiamos juntos (*together*) (4) ________ (leer: nosotros) de nuevo (*again*) los capítulos y (5) ________ (hablar) de la información que la profesora (6) ________ (enseñar) en clase. Gracias a Tim, yo (7) ________ (comprender) casi todo (*almost everything*). Todos los estudiantes (8) ________ (trabajar) mucho. Es curioso, sus padres (9) ________ (vivir) muy cerca de la tía Julia.

Bueno, es todo por ahora. (10) ________ (necesitar) terminar. ¿A qué hora (11) ________ (llegar) tú mañana para visitarme?

Hasta pronto,

Carlos

2-10 Dime quién, dónde y cuándo Look at the three columns below. Create **five** sentences by combining an element from each column. Share your sentences with a classmate.

MODELO nosotros/as / usar un microscopio / ciencias
Usamos un microscopio en la clase de ciencias.

Fíjate

Remember that subject pronouns (*yo, tú, él, ella,* etc.) are used for emphasis or clarification, and therefore do not always need to be expressed.

PRONOMBRE	ACTIVIDAD	CLASE
yo	preparar una presentación	matemáticas
nosotros/as	leer mucho	literatura
ellos/as	necesitar una calculadora	español
ella	estudiar leyes (*laws*)	periodismo
tú	escribir muchas composiciones	historia
Uds.	contestar muchas preguntas	derecho
él	aprender mucho	arquitectura

2-11 ¿A quién conoces que...? Who do you know whom displays the following characteristics? Complete the following questions. Then, take turns asking and answering in complete sentences to practice the new verbs.

MODELO ¿Quién _________ (hablar) mucho?
E1: *¿Quién habla mucho?*
E2: *Mi hermano Tom habla mucho. También mis hermanas hablan mucho.*

1. ¿Quién _________ (correr) mucho?
2. ¿Quién _________ (estudiar) muy poco?
3. ¿Quién _________ (escribir) muchos e-mails?
4. ¿Quién _________ (llegar) tarde (*late*) a la clase?
5. ¿Quién _________ (abrir) su mochila?
6. ¿Quién _________ (usar) los apuntes de sus amigos?
7. ¿Quién _________ (comprender) todo cuando el/la profesor/a habla español?
8. ¿Quién _________ (creer) en Santa Claus?

4 GRAMÁTICA

La formación de preguntas y las palabras interrogativas Creating and answering questions

Asking *yes/no* questions

Yes/no questions in Spanish are formed in two different ways:

1. Adding question marks to the statement.

   Antonio habla español. → ¿Antonio habla español?
   Antonio speaks Spanish. *Does Antonio speak Spanish?* or *Antonio speaks Spanish?*

   As in English, your voice goes up at the end of the sentence. Remember that written Spanish has an upside-down question mark at the beginning of a question.

2. Inverting the order of the subject and the verb.

   Antonio habla español. → ¿Habla Antonio español?
   SUBJECT + VERB VERB + SUBJECT
   Antonio speaks Spanish. *Does Antonio speak Spanish?*

Antonio: ¿Cuántos idiomas hablas?
Silvia: Hablo dos, español y francés. ¿Y tú?
Antonio: Solo hablo español, pero mi loro habla cinco idiomas.

Answering *yes/no* questions

Answering questions is also like it is in English.

¿Habla Antonio español?	*Does Antonio speak Spanish?*
Sí, habla español.	*Yes, he speaks Spanish.*
No, no habla español.	*No, he does not speak Spanish.*

Notice that in the negative response to the question above, both English and Spanish have two negative words.

Information questions

Information questions begin with interrogative words. Study the list of question words below and remember, accents are used on all interrogative words and also on exclamatory words: **¡Qué bueno!** (*That's great!*)

Las palabras interrogativas

¿Qué?	*What?*	**¿Qué** idioma habla Antonio?	*What language does Antonio speak?*
¿Por qué?	*Why?*	**¿Por qué** no trabaja Antonio?	*Why doesn't Antonio work?*
¿Cómo?	*How?*	**¿Cómo** está Antonio?	*How is Antonio?*
¿Cuándo?	*When?*	**¿Cuándo** es la clase?	*When is the class?*
¿Adónde?	*To where?*	**¿Adónde** va Antonio?	*(To) Where is Antonio going?*
¿Dónde?	*Where?*	**¿Dónde** vive Antonio?	*Where does Antonio live?*

(continued)

Las palabras interrogativas

¿De dónde?	*From where?*	**¿De dónde** regresa Antonio?	*Where is Antonio coming back from?*
¿Cuánto/a?	*How much?*	**¿Cuánto** estudia Antonio para la clase?	*How much does Antonio study for the class?*
		¿Cuánta tiza hay?	*How much chalk is there?*
¿Cuántos/as?	*How many?*	**¿Cuántos** idiomas habla Antonio?	*How many languages does Antonio speak?*
		¿Cuántas compañeras llegan tarde?	*How many classmates arrive late?*
¿Cuál?	*Which (one)?*	**¿Cuál** es su clase favorita?	*Which is his favorite class?*
¿Cuáles?	*Which (ones)?*	**¿Cuáles** son sus clases favoritas?	*Which are his favorite classes?*
¿Quién?	*Who?*	**¿Quién** habla cinco idiomas?	*Who speaks five languages?*
¿Quiénes?	*Who?* (pl.)	**¿Quiénes** hablan cinco idiomas?	*Who speaks five languages?*

Note that, although the subject is not always necessary, when it is included in the sentence it follows the verb.

¿? Now you are ready to complete the ***Preparación y práctica*** activities for this chunk online.

2-12 ¿Sí o no? Take turns asking and answering the following yes/no questions in complete sentences.

MODELO E1: ¿Estudias francés?

E2: *Sí, estudio francés. / No, no estudio francés.*

1. ¿Hablas español?
2. ¿Estudias mucho?
3. ¿Aprendes mucho?
4. ¿Escribes mucho en clase?
5. ¿De dónde es tu profesor/a?
6. ¿Trabajas?
7. ¿Vives con tus padres?
8. ¿Lees muchas novelas?

2-13 Preguntas, más preguntas

With a partner, determine which interrogative word would elicit each of the following responses and create a question that would elicit each statement.

MODELO E1: Estudio **matemáticas.**
E2: *¿Qué estudias?*

Fíjate

Porque written as one word and without an accent mark means "because."

1. Martín estudia **en la sala de clase.**
2. Estudiamos español **porque es interesante.**
3. **Susana y Julia** estudian.
4. Estudian **por la noche.**
5. Leen **rápidamente.**
6. Leo **tres libros.**

2-14 ¿Y tú?

Interview your classmates using the following questions about Spanish class.

MODELO E1: ¿Cuántas sillas hay en la clase?
E2: *Hay veinte sillas.*

difícil	*difficult*
fácil	*easy*

1. ¿Quién enseña la clase?
2. ¿Dónde enseña la clase?
3. ¿Quiénes hablan en la clase generalmente?
4. ¿Cuántos estudiantes hay en la clase?
5. ¿Qué libro(s) usas en la clase?
6. ¿Tomas muchos apuntes en la clase?
7. ¿Es la clase fácil o difícil?
8. ¿Trabajas mucho en la clase de español?

2-15 ¿Y tu familia o amigos?

Write **five** questions you could ask classmates about their families or friends. Then move around the room asking those questions of as many people as possible.

Capítulo 1. La familia, pág. 32; El verbo *tener*, pág. 35; Los adjetivos descriptivos, pág. 44.

MODELO E1: *¿Cómo se llaman tus padres? ¿Dónde viven tus abuelos?*
E2: *¿Cuántos hermanos tienes?...*

5 VOCABULARIO

Los números 100–1.000

Counting from 100–1,000

100	**cien**	200	**doscientos**	600	**seiscientos**
101	**ciento uno**	201	**doscientos uno**	700	**setecientos**
102	**ciento dos**	300	**trescientos**	800	**ochocientos**
116	**ciento dieciséis**	400	**cuatrocientos**	900	**novecientos**
120	**ciento veinte**	500	**quinientos**	1.000	**mil**

1. The conjuction **y** is used to connect only 31–39, 41–49, 51–59, 61–69, 71–79, 81–89, and 91–99.

   32 = treinta **y** dos, 101 = ciento uno, 151 = ciento cincuenta **y** uno

2. **Ciento** is shortened to **cien** before any noun.

   cien hombres **cien** mujeres

3. Multiples of **cientos** agree in number and gender with the nouns they modify.

   doscientos estudiantes **trescientas** jóvenes

4. Note the use of a decimal instead of a comma in **1.000.**

¿? Now you are ready to complete the ***Preparación y práctica*** activities for this chunk online.

2-16 ¡Dinero! Take turns saying the following amounts of money aloud, in the currencies listed below.

U.S. dollar (dólares) = USD Euro (euros) = EUR

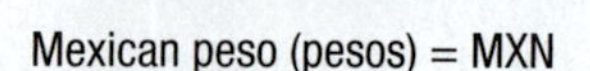

Mexican peso (pesos) = MXN

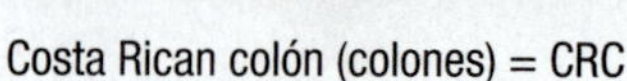

Costa Rican colón (colones) = CRC

MODELO E1: 325 USD

E2: *trescientos veinticinco dólares*

1. 110 USD	3. 376 CRC	5. 638 MXN	7. 763 CRC
2. 415 MXN	4. 822 EUR	6. 544 USD	8. 999 EUR

2-17 Vamos a adivinar On a popular TV show, *The Price is Right*, contestants must guess the prices of different items. Bring in **five** ads of items priced between $100 and $1,000 and cover the prices. In groups of three or four, take turns guessing the prices in U.S. dollars. The person who comes closest without going over the price wins each item!

Fíjate

If the item you are pricing is plural, the verb form will be *cuestan*.

MODELO E1: *¿Cuesta* (Does it cost) *ciento cincuenta y cinco dólares?*
E2: *No.*
E1: *Cuesta ciento ochenta dólares.*
E2: *Sí.*

¿Cómo andas? I

Having completed **Comunicación I**, I now can...	Feel confident	Need to review
• share information about courses and majors. (p. 66)	☐	☐
• indicate the stressed syllables in words. (p. 67 and online)	☐	☐
• examine Hispanic university life. (p. 68)	☐	☐
• describe my classroom and classmates. (p. 69)	☐	☐
• relate daily activities. (p. 71)	☐	☐
• create and answer questions. (p. 75)	☐	☐
• count from 100–1,000. (p. 78)	☐	☐

Comunicación II

6 VOCABULARIO

En la universidad

Elaborating on university places and objects

Los lugares

Otras palabras	*Other words*
el apartamento	*apartment*
el edificio	*building*
el laboratorio	*laboratory*
la tienda	*store*

La residencia

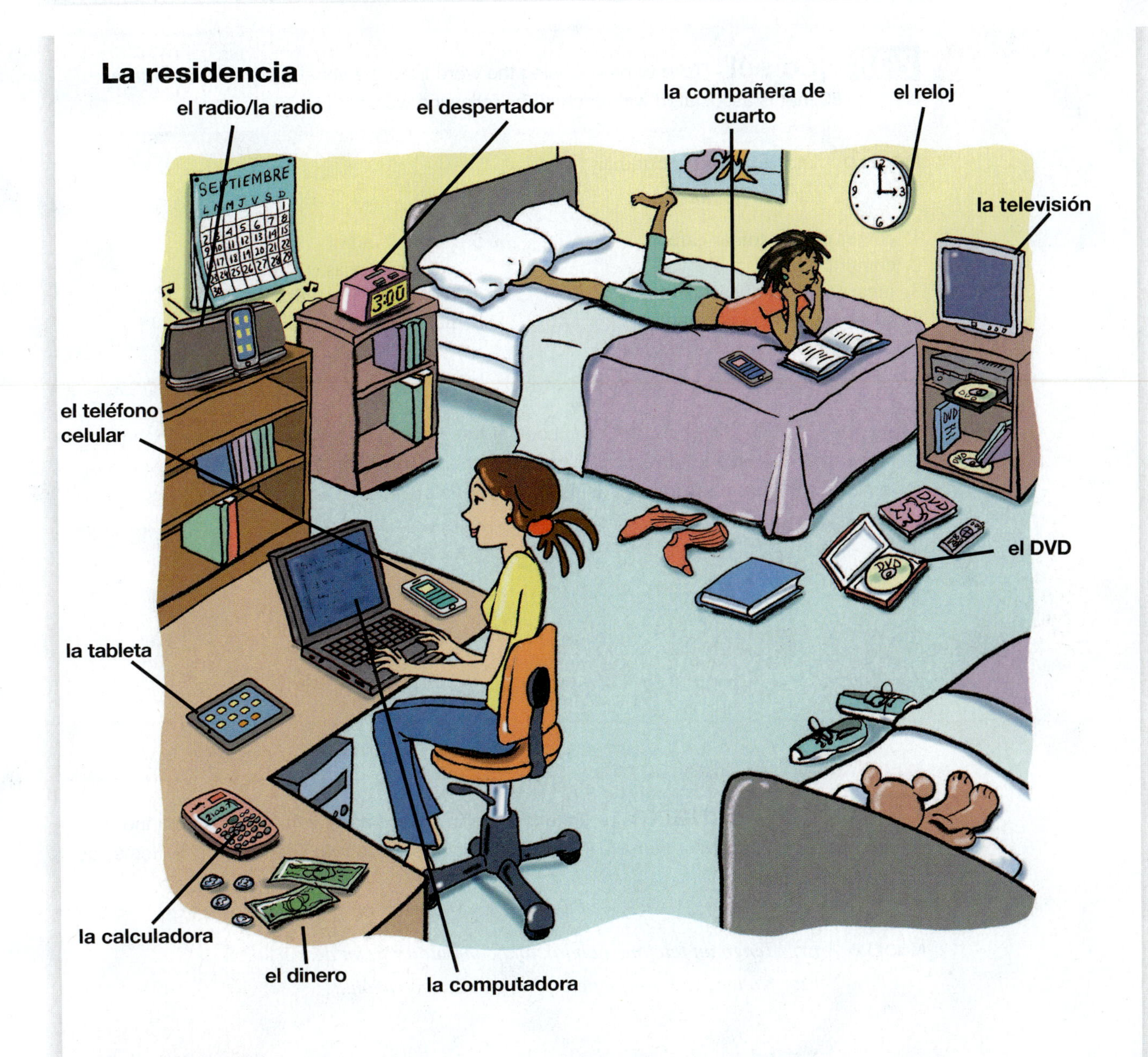

Otras palabras	*Other words*
el compañero de cuarto	*male roommate*
el horario (de clases)	*schedule (of classes)*

Fíjate

El radio is the radio; *la radio* is the broadcast.

Now you are ready to complete the ***Preparación y práctica*** activities for this chunk online.

2-18 ¡Lo sé! Take turns choosing the word from the vocabulary list **Los lugares** on page 80 that is associated with each of the following words.

MODELO E1: leer libros, estudiar
E2: *la biblioteca*

1. comer pasta y tomar café
2. comprar libros
3. jugar (*to play*) al básquetbol
4. hacer experimentos científicos
5. jugar al fútbol
6. comprar cosas (*things*) en general
7. leer libros y estudiar
8. hablar con amigos

2-19 ¿Cierto o falso? Look at the drawing on page 81. Gabriela (in the red T-shirt) and Consuelo (in the yellow T-shirt) are in their dorm room. Listen to the following statements and indicate **C** for **Cierto** (*true*) or **F** for **Falso** (*false*) based on the drawing.

	C	F
1.	☐	☐
2.	☐	☐
3.	☐	☐
4.	☐	☐
5.	☐	☐

2-20 En mi cuarto... Take turns telling your partner which items from the list **La residencia** on page 81 you have in your room or where you live. Then say which items you do not have.

MODELO E1: *Tengo un teléfono celular, una computadora, un despertador...*
E2: *No tengo un radio, pero sí tengo una televisión...*

2-21 Datos personales You are a foreign exchange student in Mexico, living with a family. Your Mexican little "brother" wants to know all about you! Answer his questions, which follow, then ask a classmate the same questions.

1. ¿De dónde eres?
2. ¿Qué estudias?
3. ¿Dónde estudias?
4. ¿Dónde comes?
5. ¿Dónde compras tus libros?
6. ¿Dónde vives?
7. ¿Qué necesitas para tu clase de español?
8. ¿Qué necesitas para una clase de matemáticas?
9. ¿Qué tienes en tu mochila?

7 GRAMÁTICA

El verbo *estar* Expressing *to be*

Another verb that expresses *to be* in Spanish is **estar.** Like **tener** and **ser, estar** is not a regular verb; that is, you cannot simply drop the infinitive ending and add the usual **-ar** endings.

estar (***to be***)

Singular		Plural	
yo	**estoy**	nosotros/as	**estamos**
tú	**estás**	vosotros/as	**estáis**
Ud.	**está**	Uds.	**están**
él, ella	**está**	ellos/as	**están**

Ser and **estar** are not interchangeable because they are used differently. Two uses of **estar** are:

1. To describe the location of someone or something.

   Manuel **está** en la sala de clase. — *Manuel is in the classroom.*
   Nuestros padres **están** en México. — *Our parents are in Mexico.*

2. To describe how someone is feeling or to express a change from the norm.

   Estoy bien. ¿Y tú? — *I'm fine. And you?*
   Estamos tristes hoy. — *We are sad today. (Normally we are upbeat and happy.)*

Now you are ready to complete the ***Preparación y práctica*** activities for this chunk online.

2-22 ¿Cuál es la palabra? Take turns giving the correct form of **estar** for each subject.

1. nosotras
2. el estudiante
3. tú
4. la pizarra y la tiza
5. yo
6. los profesores

2-23 Busco... You are on campus and you want to know where you can find the following items, people, and places. Take turns creating questions to determine the location of each person or thing. Your partner provides a response using the correct form of **estar + en** (*in*, *on*, or *at*).

Estrategia

You have noted that the majority of the classroom activities are with a partner. So that each person has equal opportunities, one of you should do the even-numbered items in an activity, the other do the odd-numbered items.

MODELO el mapa / el libro

E1: *¿Dónde está el mapa?*

E2: *El mapa está en el libro.*

1. las calculadoras / la mochila
2. los apuntes / el cuaderno
3. tú / el laboratorio
4. el despertador / la mesa
5. yo / la residencia
6. mi amigo y yo / el centro estudiantil

2-24 ¡Ahora mismo! With a partner, determine what the following people may be doing, using the following verbs.

aprender	comer	comprar	escribir	estudiar
hablar	leer	preparar	tomar	trabajar

MODELO E1: Marta está en la sala de clase.

E2: *Toma apuntes.*

1. Juan y Pepa están en la biblioteca.
2. Mi hermana está en la librería.
3. El profesor está en su casa.
4. Los estudiantes están en la cafetería.
5. María está en su apartamento.
6. Patricia está en el centro estudiantil.
7. Tú estás en el laboratorio.
8. Mi amiga y yo estamos en la clase de español.

2-25 La clase de geografía

Take turns asking a partner in which countries the following capitals are located.

MODELO E1: *¿Dónde está Washington, D.C.?*
E2: *Washington, D.C., está en los Estados Unidos.*

Fíjate

Knowledge of geography is increasingly important in our global community. Activity **2-25** presents an opportunity to review the countries and capitals of the Spanish-speaking world.

1. Madrid
2. México, D.F.
3. Lima
4. San Juan
5. La Paz
6. Buenos Aires
7. Santiago
8. Tegucigalpa
9. Santo Domingo
10. La Habana

8 VOCABULARIO

Las emociones y los estados

Articulating emotions and states of being

Chema/Gloria

aburrido/a

Roberto/Mayra

cansado/a

Samuel/Tina

contento/a

Ruy/Carmen

enfermo/a

Memo/Eva

enojado/a

Carlos/Patricia

nervioso/a

Ramón/Raquel

preocupado/a

Fernando/Silvia

triste

Carlos/Rebeca

feliz

Now you are ready to complete the ***Preparación y práctica*** activities for this chunk online.

2-26 ¿Cómo están?

Look at the drawings from **Las emociones y los estados** and take turns answering the following questions.

MODELO E1: ¿Cómo está Silvia?
E2: *Silvia está triste.*

1. ¿Cómo están Ruy y Carmen?
2. ¿Cómo está Roberto?
3. ¿Quién está preocupada?
4. ¿Quiénes están nerviosos?
5. ¿Cómo están Chema y Gloria?
6. ¿Cómo estás tú?

2-27 ¿Qué pasa?

Which adjectives from the drawings above best describe how you might feel in each of the following situations? Share your responses with a partner.

MODELO E1: recibes $1.000
E2: *Estoy contento/a.*

1. Estás en el hospital.
2. Tienes un examen muy difícil hoy.
3. Corres quince millas (*miles*).
4. Tu profesor de historia lee un libro por (*for*) una hora y quince minutos.
5. Esperas y esperas pero tu amigo no llega. (¡Y no te llama por teléfono!)
6. Sacas una "A" en tu examen de español.

2-28 ¿Dónde y cómo? Together, look at the following drawings and determine where the people are, what they are doing, and how they might be feeling.

Tomás

Tina

Ana y Mirta

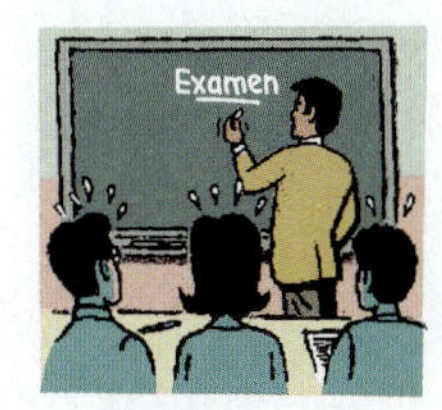

El profesor Martín y sus estudiantes

MODELO E1: el profesor Martín

E2: *El profesor Martín está en la clase. Enseña matemáticas. Está contento.*

1. Tomás
2. Tina
3. Ana y Mirta
4. Los estudiantes del profesor Martín

9 GRAMÁTICA

El verbo *gustar*

Conveying likes and dislikes

Estrategia

You may have noticed that there are two types of grammar presentations in *¡Anda! Curso elemental:*

1. You are given the grammar rule.
2. You are given guiding questions to help *you* construct the grammar rule, and to state the rule in your own words.

No matter which type of presentation, educational researchers have found it is *always* important for you to state the rules orally. Accurately stating the rules demonstrates that you are on the road to using the grammar concept(s) correctly in your speaking and writing.

Fíjate

You can go back to page 25 in *Capítulo A Para empezar* for more information on *gustar*.

To express likes and dislikes you say the following:

Me gusta la profesora.	*I like the professor.*
Me gustan las clases de idiomas.	*I like language classes.*
¿**Te gustan** las novelas de Sandra Cisneros?	*Do you like Sandra Cisneros's novels?*
Te gusta el arte abstracto.	*You like abstract art.*
No **le gusta** estudiar.	*He does not like to study.*

(continued)

¡Explícalo tú!

1. To say you like or dislike one thing, what form of **gustar** do you use?
2. To say you like or dislike more than one thing, what form of **gustar** do you use?
3. Which words in the examples mean *I? You? He/she?*
4. If a verb is needed after **gusta,** what form of the verb do you use?

✓ To check your answers to the preceding questions, see Appendix 1.

¿? Now you are ready to complete the ***Preparación y práctica*** activities for this chunk online.

2-29 ¿Qué te gusta?

Decide whether or not you like the following items, and share your opinions with a classmate.

MODELO E1: las clases difíciles

E2: *(No) Me gustan las clases difíciles.*

1. el centro estudiantil
2. los sábados
3. vivir en un apartamento
4. la informática
5. aprender idiomas
6. la cafetería
7. correr
8. los libros de Harry Potter

2-30 Te toca a ti

Now change the cues from **2-29** into questions, and ask a different classmate to answer.

Estrategia

Remember, if you answer negatively, you will need to say *no* twice. If you need to review, check *La formación de preguntas* on page 75 of this chapter.

MODELO E1: *¿Te gustan las clases difíciles?*

E2: *No, no me gustan las clases difíciles.*

10 VOCABULARIO

Los deportes y los pasatiempos

Offering opinions on sports and pastimes

bailar

caminar

escuchar música

ir de compras

jugar al básquetbol

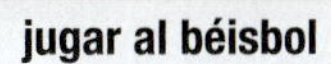

jugar al béisbol

jugar al fútbol

jugar al fútbol americano

jugar al golf

jugar al tenis

nadar

montar en bicicleta

(continued)

patinar

tocar un instrumento

ver la televisión

tomar el sol

Otras palabras	*Other words*
el equipo	*team*
hacer ejercicio	*to exercise*
la pelota	*ball*

Now you are ready to complete the ***Preparación y práctica*** activities for this chunk online.

Capítulo A Para empezar. Los días, los meses y las estaciones, pág. 21.

2-31 ¿En qué mes te gusta...? For a fan or a participant, sports and pastimes can be seasonal. Complete the following steps.

Paso 1 Make a list of the top **three** sports or pastimes you enjoy in the months listed below.

enero	mayo	julio	octubre

MODELO enero

1. patinar, 2. bailar, 3. tocar un instrumento

Paso 2 Circulate around the classroom and compare your preferences with those of your classmates. Do you see any trends?

MODELO E1: *¿Qué deportes y pasatiempos te gusta practicar más en enero?*

E2: *Me gusta patinar, bailar y tocar un instrumento.*

2-32 **¿Cuánto te gusta?** What activities do you enjoy in your spare time? Write **ten** activities in the chart and rank the sports and pastimes by placing a mark in the column that best describes your feeling toward the sport or pastime. What do you suppose **¡Lo odio!** means? Share your answers with your partner, following the model.

Fíjate

Remember that *gustar* is formed differently from regular verbs.

MODELO E1: *Me gusta mucho el fútbol.*

E2: *No me gusta patinar.*

	ME GUSTA MUCHO	ME GUSTA	NO ME GUSTA	¡LO ODIO!
1. el fútbol	X			
2. patinar			X	
3. …				

Los deportes en el mundo hispano

Estrategia

Remember to use your reading strategy *Recognizing cognates* from *Capítulo 1* to assist you with this and all future reading passages.

Los Juegos Panamericanos ocurren cada cuatro años.

El fútbol es el deporte más popular en el mundo hispanohablante. Sin embargo (*Nevertheless*), los hispanos participan en una gran variedad de actividades físicas y deportivas como el béisbol, el boxeo, el básquetbol (o baloncesto), el tenis, el vóleibol y el atletismo (*track and field*). España y los países latinoamericanos participan en los Juegos Olímpicos. Además (*Furthermore*), los países latinoamericanos, junto con Canadá y los Estados Unidos, participan en los Juegos Panamericanos que ocurren cada cuatro años, siempre (*always*) un año antes de los Juegos Olímpicos.

Los deportes forman una parte importante de la vida universitaria, especialmente en la Universidad Nacional Autónoma de México (la UNAM). Además de tener el equipo de fútbol Club Universidad Nacional, ofrecen (*they offer*) más de 40 disciplinas deportivas que incluyen los deportes mencionados y también el fútbol americano, el judo, el karate, el ciclismo, la natación, la lucha libre (*wrestling*) y más. Hay varios gimnasios, dos estadios, piscinas (*pools*) y muchas otras áreas para practicar estos deportes.

Preguntas

1. What is the most important sport in the Spanish-speaking world?
2. Does your college/university offer the same sports as the UNAM? What are some differences?

2-33 ¿Eres activo/a? Just how active are you? Complete the chart with activities that should, or do, occupy your time. Share your results with a partner. So… are you leading a well-balanced life?

a menudo	*often*
a veces	*sometimes; from time to time*
nunca	*never*

A MENUDO	A VECES	NUNCA	NECESITO HACERLO (*TO DO IT*) MÁS
1. jugar al golf	1. patinar	1. jugar al fútbol americano	1. jugar al tenis
2.	2.	2.	2.
3.	3.	3.	3.
4.	4.	4.	4.
5.	5.	5.	5.

MODELO *A menudo me gusta jugar al golf.*
A veces me gusta patinar.
Nunca me gusta jugar al fútbol americano.
Necesito jugar más al tenis.

2-34 Tus preferencias Select your **three** favorite sports and/or pastimes (**que más me gustan**) and then select your **three** least favorite (**que menos me gustan**) from **2-33.** Then complete the following steps.

Paso 1 Write your choices in the chart. Then, create **two** sentences summarizing your choices.

LOS DEPORTES/PASATIEMPOS QUE MÁS ME GUSTAN	LOS DEPORTES/PASATIEMPOS QUE MENOS ME GUSTAN
1. *patinar*	1.
2. *bailar*	2.
3. *leer*	3.

MODELO *Los deportes o pasatiempos que más me gustan son patinar, bailar y leer. Los deportes o pasatiempos que menos me gustan son…*

Paso 2 Circulate around the classroom to find classmates with the same likes and dislikes as you. Follow the model. When you find someone with the same likes or dislikes, write his/her name in the chart that follows.

MODELO E1: *¿Qué deporte o pasatiempo te gusta más?*
E2: *El deporte que me gusta más es el tenis.*
E1: *¿Qué deporte o pasatiempo te gusta menos?*
E2: *El pasatiempo que me gusta menos es ir de compras.*

NOMBRE DE TU COMPAÑERO/A	EL DEPORTE/PASATIEMPO QUE MÁS LE GUSTA
1.	
2.	
3.	
NOMBRE DE TU COMPAÑERO/A	**EL DEPORTE/PASATIEMPO QUE MENOS LE GUSTA**
1.	
2.	
3.	

Escucha

Una conversación

Estrategia

Listening for the gist

When *listening for the gist,* you listen for the main idea(s). You do not focus on each word, but rather on the overall meaning. Practice summarizing the gist in several words or a sentence.

2-35 Antes de escuchar In the following segment Eduardo, a university student, is talking on the phone with his mother. Write a question you might possibly hear in their conversation.

La mamá de Eduardo escucha a su hijo.

2-36 A escuchar Listen as Eduardo and his mother converse.

1. The first time you listen, concentrate on the questions she asks, noting key words and ideas.
2. In the second listening, focus on Eduardo's answers, again noting key words and ideas.
3. During the third listening, indicate whether these sentences are **C** for **Cierto** (*true*) or **F** for **Falso** (*false*).
   a. Eduardo's mother calls Eduardo to see how he is doing. ___
   b. Eduardo does not have classes on Tuesday. ___
   c. Eduardo's mother ends the conversation abruptly. ___

2-37 Después de escuchar In one sentence, what is the gist of their conversation? Share your sentence with a partner.

¡Conversemos!

2-38 La vida universitaria

Imagine that you are at a gathering on campus for exchange students from Mexico. Introduce yourself by completing the following steps.

Paso 1 Create at least **five sentences** about yourself. Then create at least **five questions** to ask the person you are meeting. Include the following information:

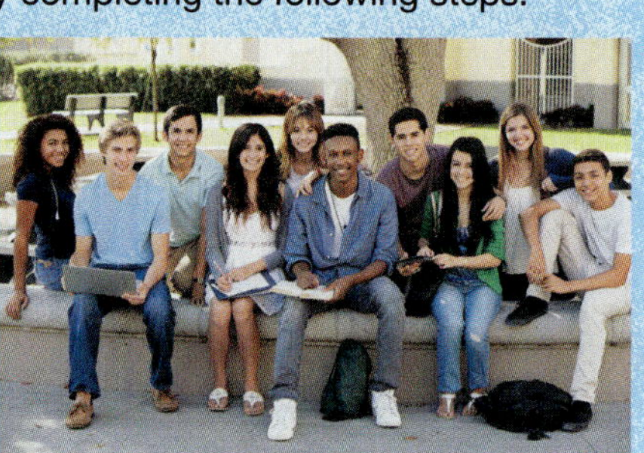

- Introductions from *Capítulo A Para empezar* (p. 5)
- Vocabulary including majors, courses, professions, campus places, emotions and states of being, and sports and pastimes
- New **-ar, -er,** and **-ir** verbs from this chapter.

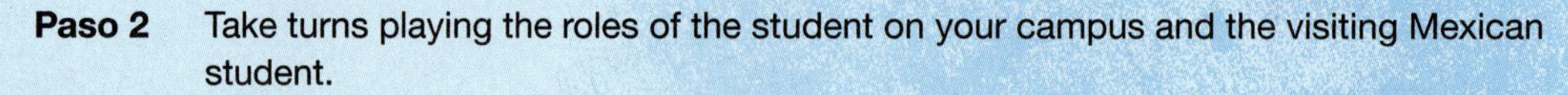

Paso 2 Take turns playing the roles of the student on your campus and the visiting Mexican student.

Escribe

Una descripción

Estrategia

Creating sentences

You have been practicing speaking in sentences. Remember:

1. Basic sentences need: (subj.) + verb + (rest of the sent.)
2. A sentence can express a complete idea with just a verb form, e.g., *Corren*. Subjects clarify, e.g., *Ellos corren* or *Juan y Marta corren.*
3. To make a sentence negative, place ***no*** before the verb, e.g., *No nadamos.*
4. Make sure that your intended subject and verb ending agree, e.g., **yo** = **–o**, etc. *Yo corr**o**.*
5. Make sure that adjectives agree with their corresponding nouns, e.g., *amig**os** inteligent**es**.*

2-39 Antes de escribir

Imagine that you are applying for a job on campus—either to work in the library, the student center, or the athletic department. Make a list in Spanish of what makes you a viable applicant.

MODELO (athletic department)

Lista: ✓ Me gustan los deportes; nado y corro muy bien.

✓ Soy buena estudiante, inteligente, creativa, organizada y trabajadora.

✓ Me gustan las cosas nuevas (new) / las personas nuevas.

2-40 A escribir

Using your list, create a personal description using the model.

MODELO Tengo veinte años y soy buena estudiante. Soy organizada y trabajadora. Me gustan mucho...

2-41 Después de escribir

Your instructor will collect the descriptions, and read some of them to the class. He/She may ask you to guess who wrote each one.

¿Cómo andas? II

Having completed **Comunicación II**, I now can…	**Feel confident**	**Need to review**
• elaborate on university places and objects. (p. 80)	☐	☐
• express *to be*. (p. 83)	☐	☐
• articulate emotions and states of being. (p. 86)	☐	☐
• convey likes and dislikes. (p. 87)	☐	☐
• offer opinions on sports and pastimes. (p. 89)	☐	☐
• compare and contrast sports. (p. 91)	☐	☐
• glean the main idea. (p. 93)	☐	☐
• communicate about university life. (p. 94)	☐	☐
• craft a personal description. (p. 94)	☐	☐
• engage in additional communication practice. (online)	☐	☐

Vistazo cultural

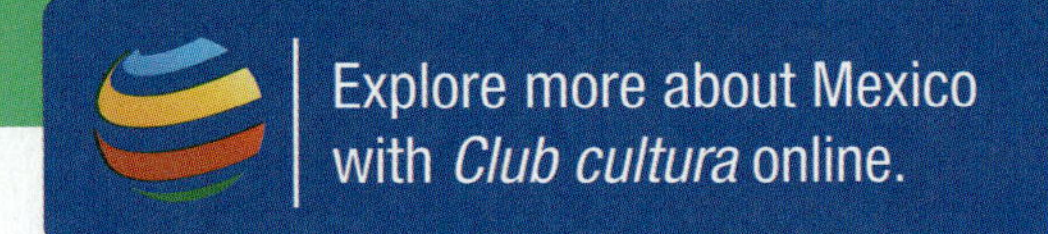

México

Les presento mi país

Mi nombre es Gabriela García Cordera y soy de Coyotepec, México. Yo estudio periodismo en la Universidad Nacional Autónoma de México (la UNAM) que está en la Ciudad de México. Vivo cerca de (*near*) la universidad con la familia de mi tía porque normalmente hay pocas residencias estudiantiles en las universidades y muchos estudiantes viven con sus parientes (*relatives*). La UNAM es la universidad más grande de México y de América Latina, con aproximadamente 340.000 estudiantes. **¿Cuántos estudiantes hay en tu universidad?** En la UNAM, tenemos un equipo de fútbol, los Pumas. El fútbol es muy popular en mi país: es el pasatiempo nacional. **¿Qué deporte es muy popular en tu país?** Mi ciudad natal, Coyotepec, está en el estado de Oaxaca, un centro famoso de artesanía. En particular, hay hojalatería (*tin work*), cerámicas de barro negro (*black clay*), cestería (*basket weaving*), fabricación de textiles y de alebrijes (*painted wooden animals*) y mucho más. **¿Qué tipo de artesanía hay en tu región?**

Gabriela García Cordera

La biblioteca de la Universidad Nacional Autónoma de México. La fachada tiene un mosaico de la historia de México.

En Oaxaca, un centro famoso de artesanía, venden alebrijes. Estas figuras de madera son una forma de arte popular.

El fútbol es el pasatiempo nacional del país.

El Palacio Nacional de Bellas Artes es un centro cultural muy importante de México.

El tianguis de Tepotzlán en Morelos se instala los sábados y domingos con una variedad de artículos como comida y ropa.

ALMANAQUE

Nombre oficial:	Estados Unidos Mexicanos
Gobierno:	República federal
Población:	111.211.789 (2010)
Idiomas:	español (oficial); maya, náhuatl
Moneda:	peso mexicano ($)

¿Sabías que...?

- El origen del chicle (*gum*) es el látex del chicozapote (*sapodilla tree* en inglés), un árbol tropical de la península de Yucatán. Los mayas, tribu antigua y muy importante de Yucatán, usaban (*used*) el látex como chicle.
- La planta "cabeza de negro", del estado mexicano de Veracruz, forma la base del proceso para crear la cortisona y "la píldora", el contraceptivo oral.

Preguntas

1. What is the most popular sport in Mexico?
2. What is a **tianguis**? What do we have in the United States that is similar?
3. What are the origins of cortisone and the birth control pill?
4. What are some of the handcrafted items from Mexico? What are similar handcrafted items made in your region?
5. What are some differences between the UNAM and your school?

Lectura

Una carta de la universidad

2-42 Antes de leer You will read a letter that Adriana received from her university. Before you read, complete the following activities.

1. Note that there are a limited number of key words in the reading passage you may not know. They are written below with the English equivalents and are listed in order of appearance. They are also boldfaced in the body of the reading.

me gustaría	*I would like*
solicitud	*application*
primer	*first*
siguientes	*following*
equipo	*team*

2. Based on the list of words, can you begin to guess what the context of the reading will be?
3. What other words from the reading can you associate with these words?

Estrategia

Skimming

When you skim, or read quickly, you generally do so to capture the gist of the passage. Practice with skimming helps you learn to focus on the main ideas in your reading.

2-43 Mientras lees To boost your comprehension, it is helpful to skim the passage for the first reading and then ask yourself what key information you have learned.

1. Skim the first paragraph, and then answer the following questions.
   a. Why is Dr. Bermúdez writing the letter?
   b. How long do classes last?
   c. What does Adriana need to do?
2. Now skim the entire letter and write down the key points for each paragraph.
3. Then, reread the letter, this time carefully, to add details to those main ideas. Do not forget to take advantage of cognates like **ingeniería** and **educación** to boost your comprehension.

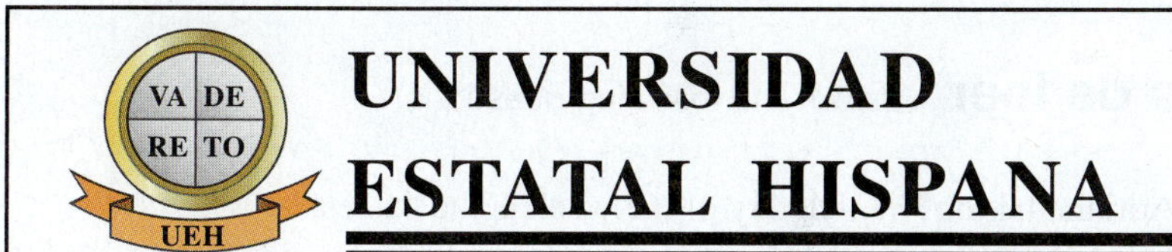

Centro de Matrículas
616 Avenida Principal
Springfield, CA 95370

3 de mayo

Estimada señorita Martín Domínguez:

En esta carta° **me gustaría** darle la bienvenida° una vez más a la Universidad Estatal Hispana. Según° la información en su **solicitud**, usted quiere estudiar ingeniería náutica. Las clases de los lunes, miércoles y viernes son de cincuenta minutos. Las clases de los martes y jueves son de hora y media. Aquí tiene usted su horario inicial. Necesita leer cuidadosamente° su horario.

letter / to welcome you
According to
carefully

En el **primer** semestre tiene las **siguientes** clases: Inglés 105 – Literatura norteamericana, los lunes, miércoles y viernes. La clase de inglés es en el edificio Dante, sala 450 a las 8:00 de la mañana. En el mismo° edificio y en la misma sala tiene Psicología 200 a las 11:00 de la mañana, los lunes, miércoles y viernes. Todos los estudiantes necesitan tomar idiomas. Su clase de Francés 150 – Francés elemental es a la 1:00 de la tarde los lunes, miércoles y viernes en el edificio Cervantes, sala 216. Los martes y jueves tiene clase de Matemáticas 265 – Cálculo I en el edificio de química, sala 203 a las 9:30 de la mañana. La clase de Introducción a la ingeniería 124 es los martes y jueves al mediodía en el centro Newton, sala 1137.

same

Un requisito de la universidad es que necesita una clase de Educación Física. En su solicitud, usted menciona que le gusta nadar y que tiene experiencia con un **equipo** estatal de natación. Natación olímpica 366 es de la 6:30 de la tarde hasta las 8:00 de la tarde los lunes y los jueves en el estadio Nautilos.
Si tiene preguntas, llámeme° al 1-877-554-0877.

call me

Le saludo atentamente°,

Best regards

Augusto Bermúdez

Dr. Augusto Bermúdez
Consejero Académico
Universidad Estatal Hispana

2•44 Después de leer

Answer the following questions.

1. How many classes is Adriana taking? Which day of the week is the busiest?
2. Why is she taking Natación olímpica 366?
3. Re-read the academic advisor's letter and complete the following chart with Adriana's classes for the week.

hora	lunes	martes	miércoles	jueves	viernes
8:00–8:50 a.m.					
9:30–10:45 a.m.					
11:00–11:50 a.m.					
12:00–12:50 p.m.					
1:00–1:50 p.m.					
6:30–8:00 p.m.					

2•45 El horario de tu compañero/a de clase

Interview a classmate and find out what his/her schedule is and what he/she likes to do on the weekend.

2•46 Tu declaración de solicitud (*application statement*)

You are applying to Universidad Estatal Hispana, and need to create a personal statement. Make sure to include the following information:

- full name
- your field of studies
- schedule preferences
- dorm preferences

For additional *Lectura* activities, go to *¡Anda!* online.

Y por fin, ¿cómo andas?

Having completed this chapter, I now can...

	Feel confident	Need to review
Comunicación I		
• share information about courses and majors. (p. 66)	☐	☐
• indicate the stressed syllables in words. (p. 67 and online)	☐	☐
• describe my classroom and classmates. (p. 69)	☐	☐
• relate daily activities. (p. 71)	☐	☐
• create and answer questions. (p. 75)	☐	☐
• count from 100–1,000. (p. 78)	☐	☐
Comunicación II		
• elaborate on university places and objects. (p. 80)	☐	☐
• express *to be*. (p. 83)	☐	☐
• articulate emotions and states of being. (p. 86)	☐	☐
• convey likes and dislikes. (p. 87)	☐	☐
• offer opinions on sports and pastimes. (p. 89)	☐	☐
• glean the main idea. (p. 93)	☐	☐
• communicate about university life. (p. 94)	☐	☐
• craft a personal description. (p. 94)	☐	☐
Cultura		
• examine Hispanic university life. (p. 68)	☐	☐
• compare and contrast sports. (p. 91)	☐	☐
• share information about Mexico. (p. 96)	☐	☐
Lectura		
• read a letter from an academic advisor. (p. 98)	☐	☐
Comunidades		
• use Spanish in real-life contexts. (online)	☐	☐

Vocabulario activo

Las materias y las especialidades — *Subjects and majors*

la administración de empresas	*business administration*
la arquitectura	*architecture*
el arte	*art*
la biología	*biology*
las ciencias (*pl.*)	*science*
el derecho	*law*
los idiomas (*pl.*)	*languages*
la informática	*computer science*
la literatura	*literature*
las matemáticas (*pl.*)	*mathematics*
la medicina	*medicine*
la música	*music*
la pedagogía	*education*
el periodismo	*journalism*
la psicología	*psychology*
el curso	*course*
el semestre	*semester*

En la sala de clase — *In the classroom*

los apuntes (*pl.*)	*notes*
el bolígrafo	*ballpoint pen*
el borrador	*eraser*
el/la compañero/a de clase	*classmate*
la composición	*composition*
el cuaderno	*notebook*
el escritorio	*desk*
el/la estudiante	*student*
el examen	*exam*
el lápiz	*pencil*
el libro	*book*
el mapa	*map*
la mesa	*table*
la mochila	*book bag; backpack*
el papel	*paper*
la pared	*wall*
la pizarra (interactiva)	*chalkboard; (interactive) whiteboard*
el/la profesor/a	*professor*
la puerta	*door*
la sala de clase	*classroom*
la silla	*chair*
la tarea	*homework*
la tiza	*chalk*
la ventana	*window*

Los verbos — *Verbs*

abrir	*to open*
aprender	*to learn*
comer	*to eat*
comprar	*to buy*
comprender	*to understand*
contestar	*to answer*
correr	*to run*
creer	*to believe*
enseñar	*to teach; to show*
escribir	*to write*
esperar	*to wait for; to hope*
estar	*to be*
estudiar	*to study*
hablar	*to speak*
leer	*to read*
llegar	*to arrive*
mirar	*to look (at); to watch*
necesitar	*to need*
preguntar	*to ask (a question)*
preparar	*to prepare; to get ready*
recibir	*to receive*
regresar	*to return*
terminar	*to finish; to end*
tomar	*to take; to drink*
trabajar	*to work*
usar	*to use*
vivir	*to live*

Las palabras interrogativas — *Interrogative words*

See page 75.

Los números 100–1.000 — *Numbers 100–1,000*

See page 78.

Los lugares	Places
el apartamento	*apartment*
la biblioteca	*library*
la cafetería	*cafeteria*
el centro estudiantil	*student center; student union*
el cuarto	*room*
el edificio	*building*
el estadio	*stadium*
el gimnasio	*gymnasium*
el laboratorio	*laboratory*
la librería	*bookstore*
la residencia estudiantil	*dormitory*
la tienda	*store*

La residencia	The dorm
la calculadora	*calculator*
el/la compañero/a de cuarto	*roommate*
la computadora	*computer*
el despertador	*alarm clock*
el dinero	*money*
el DVD	*DVD*
el horario (de clases)	*schedule (of classes)*
el radio/la radio	*radio*
el reloj	*clock; watch*
la tableta	*tablet*
el teléfono celular	*cell phone*
la televisión	*television*

Los deportes y los pasatiempos	Sports and pastimes
bailar	*to dance*
caminar	*to walk*
el equipo	*team*
escuchar música	*to listen to music*
hacer ejercicio	*to exercise*
ir de compras	*to go shopping*
jugar al básquetbol	*to play basketball*
jugar al béisbol	*to play baseball*
jugar al fútbol	*to play soccer*
jugar al fútbol americano	*to play football*
jugar al golf	*to play golf*
jugar al tenis	*to play tennis*
montar en bicicleta	*to ride a bike*
nadar	*to swim*
patinar	*to skate*
la pelota	*ball*
tocar un instrumento	*to play an instrument*
tomar el sol	*to sunbathe*
ver la televisión	*to watch television*

Emociones y estados	Emotions and states of being
aburrido/a	*bored (with* **estar***)*
cansado/a	*tired*
contento/a	*content; happy*
enfermo/a	*ill; sick*
enojado/a	*angry*
feliz	*happy*
nervioso/a	*upset; nervous*
preocupado/a	*worried*
triste	*sad*

Vista de Madrid, capital de España

3 Estamos en casa

From modern skyscrapers in large cities to the narrow streets of medieval towns and small farms in rural areas, homes in Spain reflect the varied climate, history, and lifestyles of the Spanish people. Homes in southern cities like Córdoba or Sevilla often have a Mediterranean feel, while in big cities like Madrid or Barcelona residents may opt to be in the middle of the action in a downtown apartment or choose a quieter, less expensive home on the outskirts of the city.

Preguntas

1. Is there Spanish-inspired architecture in the region where you live?
2. How do you think that geography and environment affect the design and construction of homes?
3. Observe the housing styles shown in the photos. How are these similar or different from those in your area?

¿Sabías que...?

Fifty percent of Spaniards between the ages of 20 and 25 live with their parents.

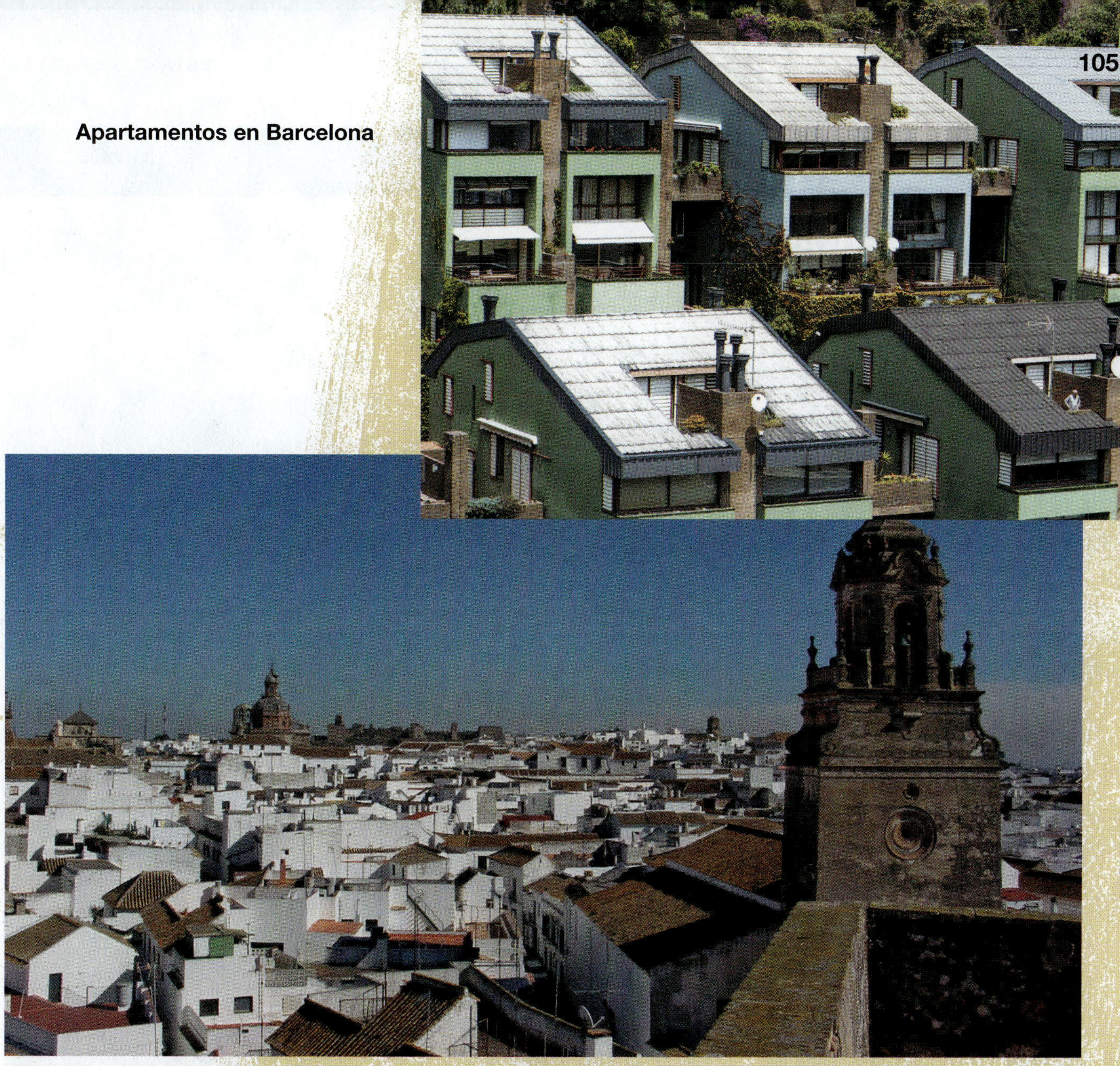

Apartamentos en Barcelona

Carmona, un pueblo del sur

Learning Outcomes

By the end of this chapter, you will be able to:

- ✔ describe homes and elaborate on their rooms.
- ✔ express actions.
- ✔ share information about household chores.
- ✔ depict states of being and state *there is* / *there are* and *it's necessary to…*
- ✔ create an ad.
- ✔ explore housing in Spain as well as other interesting facts about the country.
- ✔ read a blog and view contemporary video from Spain.

Comunicación I

1 VOCABULARIO

La casa Describing homes

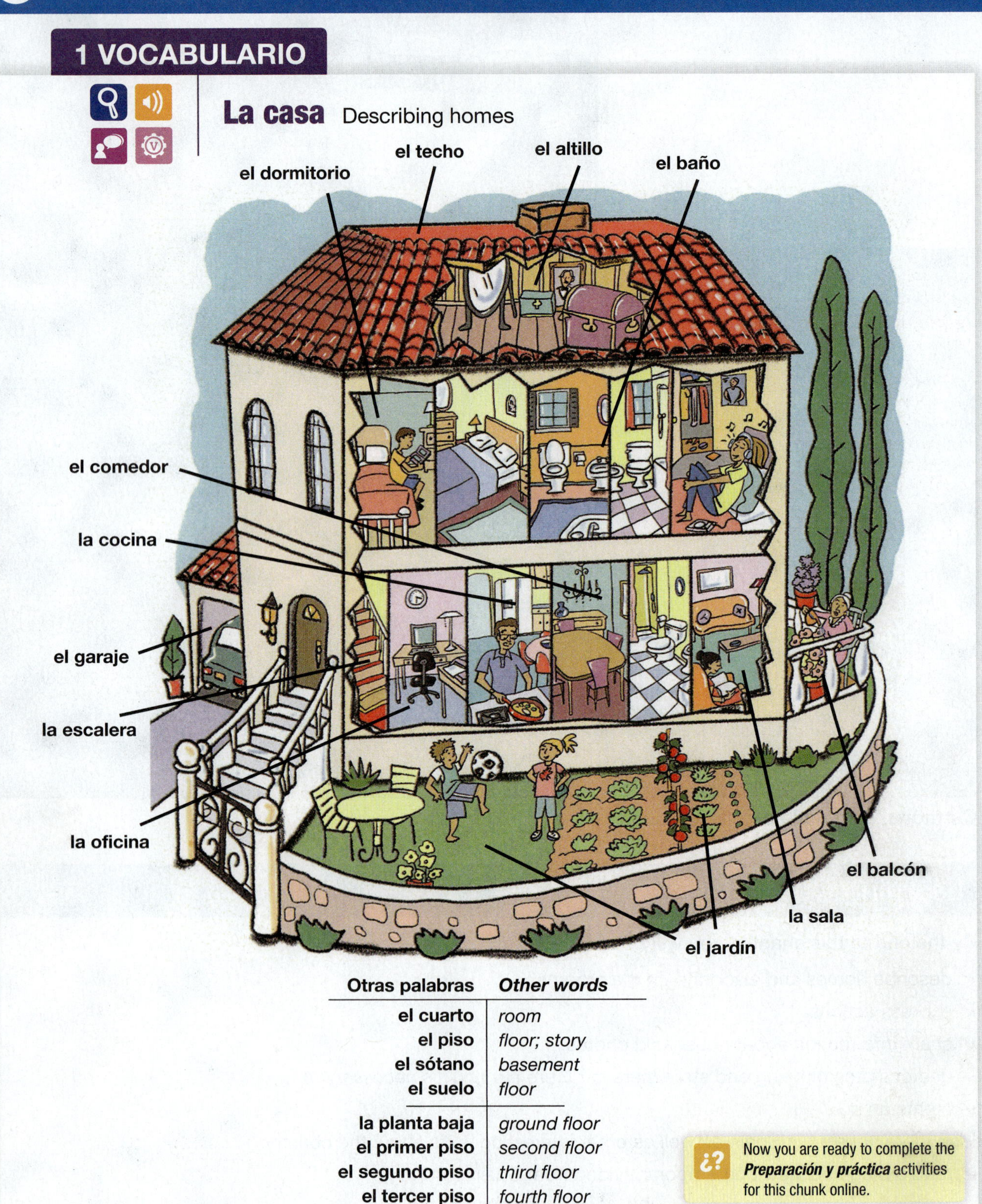

Otras palabras	*Other words*
el cuarto	*room*
el piso	*floor; story*
el sótano	*basement*
el suelo	*floor*
la planta baja	*ground floor*
el primer piso	*second floor*
el segundo piso	*third floor*
el tercer piso	*fourth floor*

¿? Now you are ready to complete the ***Preparación y práctica*** activities for this chunk online.

PRONUNCIACIÓN

The letters *h, j,* and *g*

Go to *¡Anda!* online to learn to pronounce the letters **h, j,** and **g.**

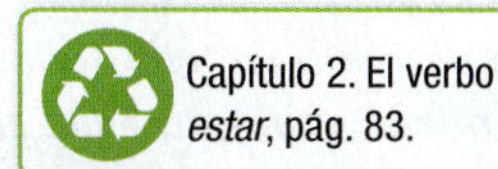

Capítulo 2. El verbo *estar*, pág. 83.

3-1 ¿Dónde están los cuartos? Miren (*Look at*) el dibujo (*drawing*) de la casa en la página 106 y túrnense (*take turns*) para decir dónde están los siguientes (*following*) cuartos.

Estrategia

In *Capítulo 3* many of the directions for the activities are written in Spanish. New words that appear in the directions will be translated for you the first time they are used. Keep a list of those words to refer to; it helps you increase your vocabulary.

MODELO E1: *el garaje*
E2: *El garaje está en la planta baja.*

Fíjate

The first floor, or ground floor, is generally called *la planta baja; el primer piso* actually refers to the second floor. What is the third floor called?

	EN LA PLANTA BAJA	EN EL PRIMER PISO	EN EL SEGUNDO PISO
la sala			
el baño			
el dormitorio			
la cocina			
la oficina			
el altillo			

3-2 ¿Cierto o falso? Look at the drawing on page 106. Then listen to Marta talking on the phone as she tells her friend where she thinks all of her family members are. Indicate **C** for **Cierto** (true) or **F** for **Falso** (false) for each statement you hear.

C	F	Miembro de la familia
☐	☐	1. hermanos Marco y Ana
☐	☐	2. mamá
☐	☐	3. hermano Gregorio
☐	☐	4. papá
☐	☐	5. abuela

3-3 Las partes de la casa Dile (*Tell*) a tu compañero/a en qué parte de la casa haces (*you do*) las siguientes actividades.

Capítulo 2. Los deportes y los pasatiempos, pág. 89.

MODELO estudiar
E1: *Yo estudio en la oficina. ¿Y tú?*
E2: *Yo estudio en mi dormitorio.*

1. hablar por teléfono
2. leer un libro
3. ver la televisión
4. organizar papeles
5. preparar enchiladas
6. tocar un instrumento
7. escuchar música
8. tomar el sol

Fíjate

In the directions, words like *miren, túrnense, comparen,* and *usen* are plural—they refer to both you and your classmate.

3-4 ¿Y tu casa...?

Túrnense para describir sus casas (o la de un miembro de su familia o de un amigo) y compararlas con la casa de la página 106. Usen el modelo para crear por lo menos (*at least*) **cinco** oraciones (*sentences*).

MODELO *En la casa del dibujo, la sala está en la planta baja y mi sala está en la planta baja también. En la casa del dibujo, el dormitorio está en el segundo piso, pero mi dormitorio está en la planta baja. No tenemos altillo...*

Capítulo 2. Presente indicativo de verbos regulares, pág. 71; Capítulo 1. El verbo *tener*, pág. 35

3-5 Es una casa interesante...

Look at the following photos and, with a partner, create a short description of one of the houses. Imagine the interior, and the person(s) who may live there. Share your description with the class.

MODELO *La casa está en México y es grande y muy moderna. Tiene seis dormitorios, cuatro baños, una cocina grande y moderna, una sala grande y un balcón. Gastón y Patricia viven allí. Tienen tres hijos. Ellos trabajan en la ciudad...*

antiguo/a	*old*	**humilde**	*humble*
la calle	*street*	**moderno/a**	*modern*
el campo	*country*	**nuevo/a**	*new*
la ciudad	*city*	**tradicional**	*traditional*
contemporáneo/a	*contemporary*	**viejo/a**	*old*

1. 

Oviedo, España

2. 

México

3. 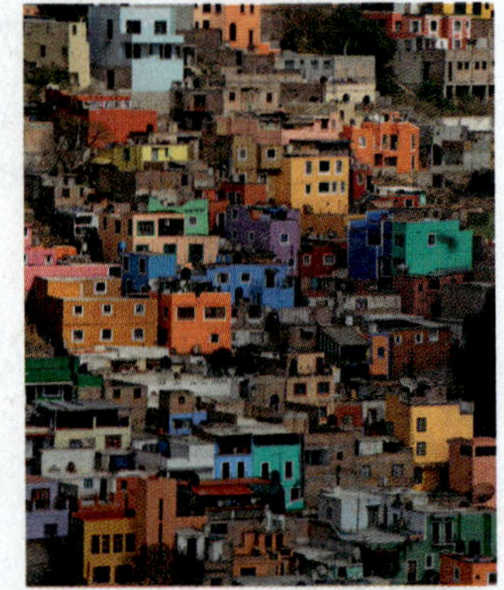

Guanajuato, México

4.

Cartagena, Colombia

5. 

las islas flotantes de los Uros, Perú

6. 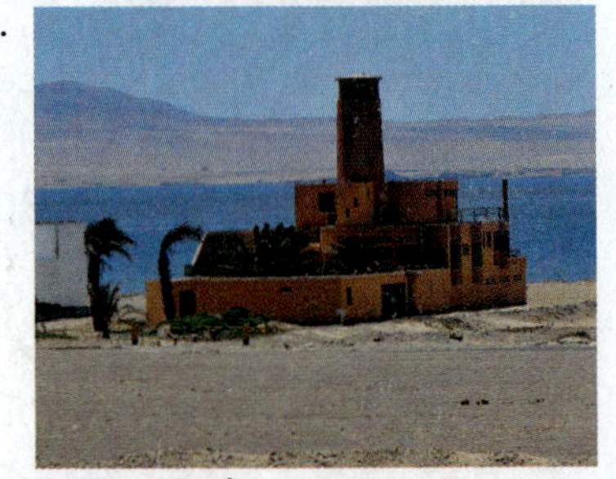

Paracas, Perú

2 GRAMÁTICA

Algunos verbos irregulares Expressing actions

Estrategia

Memorizing information is easier to do when the information is arranged in chunks. You will notice that some of the *yo* forms end in *-go*, such as *salgo, traigo,* and *pongo*. Learning the information as a chunk of "*go*" verbs may make it easier to remember.

Look at the present tense forms of the following verbs. In the first group, note that they all follow the same patterns that you learned in **Capítulo 2** to form the present tense of regular verbs, *except* in the **yo** form.

Group 1

	conocer (*to be acquainted with*)	**dar** (*to give*)	**hacer** (*to do; to make*)	**poner** (*to put; to place*)
yo	cono**zco**	d**oy**	ha**go**	pon**go**
tú	conoces	das	haces	pones
Ud.	conoce	da	hace	pone
él, ella	conoce	da	hace	pone
nosotros/as	conocemos	damos	hacemos	ponemos
vosotros/as	conocéis	dais	hacéis	ponéis
Uds.	conocen	dan	hacen	ponen
ellos/as	conocen	dan	hacen	ponen

Estrategia

Organize the new verbs you are learning in your notebook. Note whether each verb is regular or irregular, what it means in English, if any of the forms have accents, and if any other verbs follow this pattern. You might want to highlight or color code the verbs that follow patterns.

	salir (*to leave; to go out*)	**traer** (*to bring*)	**ver** (*to see*)
yo	sal**go**	tra**igo**	v**eo**
tú	sales	traes	ves
Ud.	sale	trae	ve
él, ella	sale	trae	ve
nosotros/as	salimos	traemos	vemos
vosotros/as	salís	traéis	veis
Uds.	salen	traen	ven
ellos/as	salen	traen	ven

In the second group, note that **venir** is formed similarly to **tener,** which you learned about in **Capítulo 1,** on p. 35.

Group 2

	venir (*to come*)
yo	vengo
tú	vienes
Ud.	viene
él, ella	viene
nosotros/as	venimos
vosotros/as	venís
Uds.	vienen
ellos/as	vienen

In the third group of verbs, note that all of the verb forms have a spelling change except in the **nosotros** and **vosotros** forms.

Group 3

	decir (*to say; to tell*)	**oír** (*to hear*)	**poder** (*to be able to*)	**querer** (*to want; to love*)
yo	digo	oigo	puedo	quiero
tú	dices	oyes	puedes	quieres
Ud.	dice	oye	puede	quiere
él, ella	dice	oye	puede	quiere
nosotros/as	decimos	oímos	podemos	queremos
vosotros/as	decís	oís	podéis	queréis
Uds.	dicen	oyen	pueden	quieren
ellos/as	dicen	oyen	pueden	quieren

¿? Now you are ready to complete the ***Preparación y práctica*** activities for this chunk online.

3·6 La ruleta

How competitive are you? Listen as your instructor explains how to play this fast-paced game designed to practice the new verb forms. When you finish with this list, repeat the activity with different verbs and include **estar, ser,** and **tener.**

Capítulo A Para empezar. El verbo *ser*, pág. 13; Capítulo 1. El verbo *tener*, pág. 35; Capítulo 2. El verbo *estar*, pág. 83.

1. traer
2. hacer
3. oír
4. querer
5. conocer
6. dar
7. decir
8. venir
9. poder
10. poner
11. ver
12. salir

3·7 ¿Qué hacen?

Empareja los elementos de las dos columnas para formar oraciones lógicas. Compara tus oraciones con las de tu compañero/a (*with those of your partner*).

1. ______ Hoy mis hermanos…
2. ______ Mis amigos y yo…
3. ______ Mi abuelo…
4. ______ Yo…
5. ______ Mi perro (*dog*)…
6. ______ Mi profesor/a…
7. ______ Tú…

a. pone los recuerdos (*mementos*) de nuestra familia en el altillo.
b. conoce bien la arquitectura de España.
c. hacemos fiestas en el jardín.
d. ves la televisión en tu dormitorio.
e. no pueden salir de casa.
f. quiero una casa con dos pisos, tres baños y un garaje.
g. siempre viene a la cocina para comer.

3·8 Combinaciones

Completa los siguientes pasos.

Paso 1 Escribe una oración lógica con cada (*each*) verbo, combinando elementos de las tres columnas.

MODELO (A) nosotros, (B) hacer, (C) la tarea en el dormitorio
Nosotros hacemos la tarea en el dormitorio.

COLUMNA A	COLUMNA B	COLUMNA C
Uds.	(no) hacer	estudiar en el balcón
mamá y papá	(no) ver	programas interesantes en la televisión los domingos
yo	(no) conocer	de la casa
tú	(no) oír	la tarea en el dormitorio
el profesor	(no) querer	los libros al segundo piso
nosotros/as	(no) salir	ruidos (*noises*) en el altillo por la noche
ellos/ellas	(no) traer	bien el arte de España

Paso 2 En grupos de tres, lean las oraciones y corrijan (*correct*) los errores.

Paso 3 Escriban juntos (*together*) **dos** oraciones nuevas y compártanlas (*share them*) con la clase.

3-9 Confesiones

Time for true confessions! Take turns asking each other how often you do the following things.

Capítulo 2. La formación de preguntas y las palabras interrogativas, pág. 75.

siempre	*always*
a menudo	*often*
a veces	*sometimes*
nunca	*never*

MODELO venir tarde (*late*) a la clase de español

E1: *¿Vienes tarde a la clase de español?*

E2: *Nunca vengo tarde a la clase de español. ¿Y tú?*

E1: *Yo vengo tarde a veces.*

1. querer estudiar
2. oír lo que (*what*) dice tu profesor/a
3. poder contestar las preguntas de tu profesor/a de español
4. escuchar música en la clase de español
5. hacer preguntas tontas en clase
6. traer tus libros a la clase
7. salir temprano (*early*) de tus clases
8. querer comer en la sala para ver la televisión

3-10 Firma aquí

Complete the following steps.

Paso 1 Circulate around the room, asking your classmates appropriate questions using the cues provided. Ask those who answer **sí** to sign on the corresponding line in the chart.

MODELO venir a clase todos los días

E1: *Roberto, ¿vienes a clase todos los días?*

E2: *No, no vengo a clase todos los días.*

E1: *Amanda, ¿vienes a clase todos los días?*

E3: *Sí, vengo a clase todos los días.*

E1: *Muy bien. Firma aquí, por favor.* Amanda

¿QUIÉN… ?	
1. ver la televisión todas las noches	______
2. hacer la tarea siempre	______
3. salir con los amigos los jueves por la noche	______
4. estar enfermo/a hoy	______
5. conocer Madrid	______
6. poder estudiar con música fuerte (*loud*)	______
7. querer ser arquitecto	______
8. tener una nota muy buena en la clase de español	______

Fíjate

Part of the enjoyment of learning another language is getting to know other people. Your instructor structures your class so that you have many opportunities to work with different classmates.

Paso 2 Report some of your findings to the class.

MODELO *Joe ve la televisión todas las noches. Toni siempre hace la tarea. Chad está enfermo hoy…*

3-11 Entrevista

Complete the following steps.

Paso 1 Ask a classmate you do not know the following questions. Then change roles.

1. ¿Haces ejercicio? ¿Con quién? ¿Dónde?
2. ¿Cuándo ves la televisión? ¿Cuál es tu programa favorito?
3. ¿Con quién(es) sales los fines de semana (*weekends*)? ¿Qué hacen ustedes?
4. ¿Qué días vienes a la clase de español? ¿A qué hora?
5. ¿Dónde pones tus libros?
6. ¿Siempre dices la verdad (*the truth*)?

Paso 2 Share a few of the things you have learned about your classmate with the class.

MODELO *Mi compañero sale los fines de semana con sus amigos y no hace ejercicio.*

¿Dónde viven los españoles?

En Madrid, la capital de España, al igual que en Barcelona, una ciudad cosmopolita en el noreste del país, la vida es tan rápida y vibrante como en la ciudad de Nueva York y otras grandes ciudades. Muchas personas viven en pisos (apartamentos) en edificios grandes, mientras que muchas otras viven ahora en las afueras (*outskirts*) en complejos (grupos) de casas llamados "urbanizaciones", y van a la ciudad para trabajar. Para muchas personas, el costo de vivir en los centros urbanos resulta demasiado caro. Para otras, es preferible vivir donde la vida es un poco más tranquila y tener algo de naturaleza (*nature*) cerca de su vivienda.

Sin embargo (*Nevertheless*), en los pueblos pequeños y en el campo la vida es diferente. Generalmente, las casas son bajas y algunas (*some*) tienen corrales con animales. Muchas personas se dedican a la agricultura y la vida es más lenta (*slow*).

Preguntas

1. ¿Dónde viven generalmente las personas que residen en Barcelona y en Madrid? ¿Qué es una "urbanización"?
2. ¿Cómo es diferente la vida en el campo?
3. ¿Dónde prefieres vivir tú, en el campo o en la ciudad?

3 VOCABULARIO

Los muebles y otros objetos de la casa

Elaborating on rooms

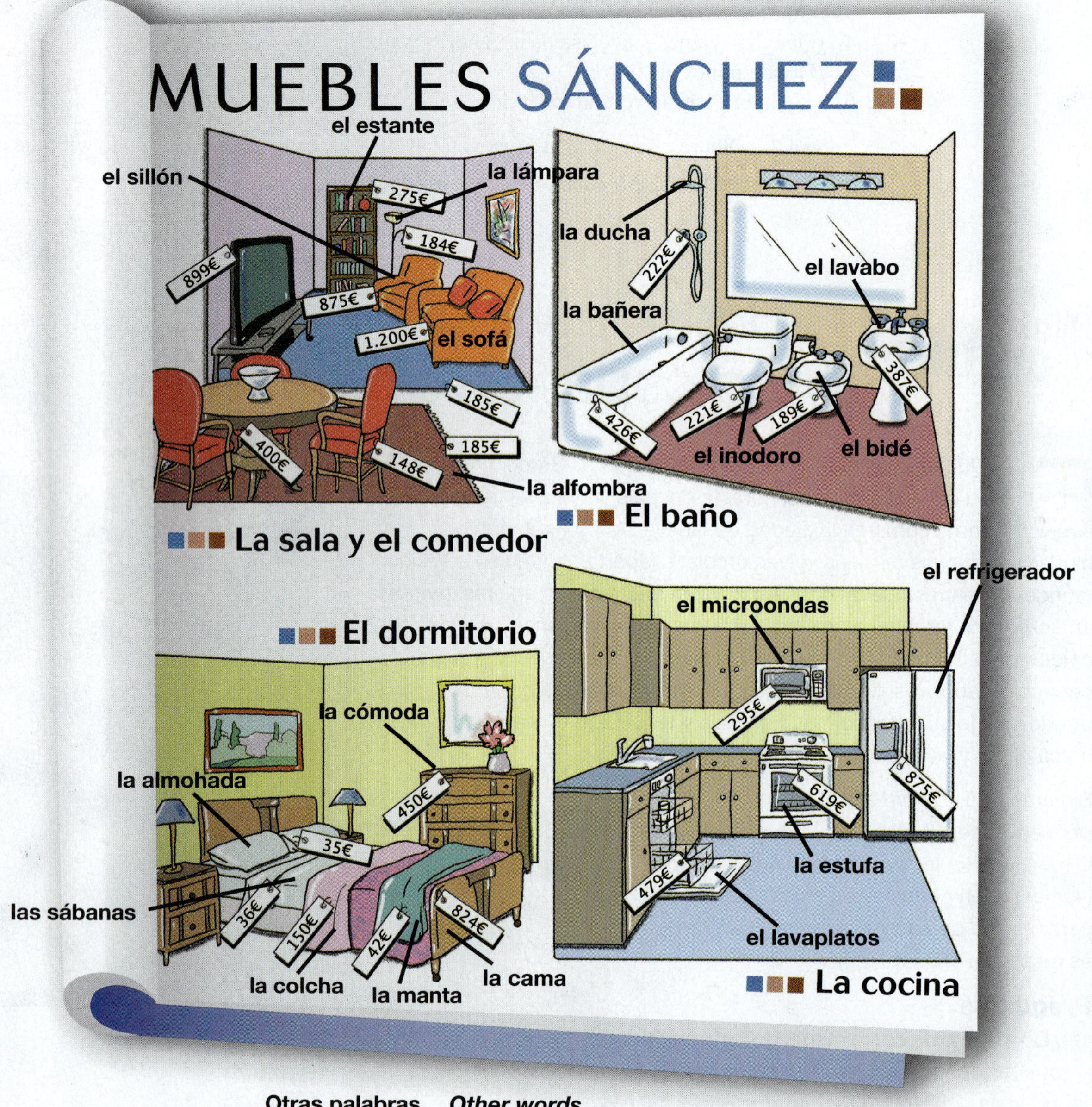

Otras palabras	*Other words*
el armario	*armoire; closet; cabinet*
la cosa	*thing*
el cuadro	*picture; painting*
el mueble	*piece of furniture*
los muebles	*furniture*
el objeto	*object*
amueblado/a	*furnished*

¿? Now you are ready to complete the ***Preparación y práctica*** activities for this chunk online.

3-12 En mi casa

Túrnense para describir qué muebles y objetos tienen en sus casas.

Capítulo 1. El verbo *tener*, pág. 35.

MODELO E1: *Yo tengo una cama y dos sillas en mi dormitorio. ¿Qué tienes tú?*

E2: *Yo tengo una cama, un cuadro, una lámpara y una televisión. ¿Qué tienes en tu cocina?*

3-13 El dormitorio de Cecilia

Mira (*Look at*) la foto y con un/a compañero/a determina dónde está o no está cada objeto.

Fíjate

The preposition *de* combines with the masculine definite article *el* to form the contraction *del*. The feminine article *la* does not contract. Note the following examples.

La cómoda está a la derecha **de la** puerta.	*The dresser is to the right of the door.*
La cómoda está a la derecha **del** armario.	*The dresser is to the right right of the closet.*

a la derecha (de)	*to the right (of)*
a la izquierda (de)	*to the left (of)*
al lado (de)	*beside*
encima (de)	*on top (of)*
sobre	*on; on top (of); over*

MODELO E1: ¿Dónde está la manta?

E2: *La manta está sobre la cama.*

¿Dónde está(n)...?

1. la cama
2. el armario
3. la lámpara
4. la cómoda
5. las sábanas
6. los cuadros
7. las almohadas
8. la ventana

3-14 ¿Quieres un apartamento estupendo? You have received a grant to study abroad in Sevilla, Spain! Now you need to find a place to live. Look at the three apartment ads below, and select one of them. Give your partner at least **three** reasons for your choice. Use expressions like **Quiero…, Me gusta(n)…** or **Tiene un/a…** Be creative!

Capítulo 2. El verbo *gustar*, pág. 87.

MODELO *Me gusta el edificio nuevo y tiene un apartamento con muebles. No me gustan…*

Piso. Plaza de Cuba, Los Remedios. Edificio nuevo: dos dormitorios, baño, cocina, sala grande y balcón. Amueblado. 750€ al mes. Tel. 95 446 04 55.

Piso. Colonia San Luis. Sala, cocina, dormitorio y baño. Sin muebles. 400€ al mes. Tel. 95 448 85 32.

Alquilo piso de lujo en casa patio rehabilitada del siglo XVIII. Dos plantas, sala, cocina con zona de comedor, baño y dormitorio. Totalmente amueblado (junto a la Plaza Nueva, a dos minutos de la Catedral, Alcázar). Para más información por favor ponte en contacto con Teresa Rivas. Tel. 95 422 47 03.

¿Cómo andas? I

Having completed **Comunicación I,** I now can…	Feel confident	Need to review
• describe homes. (p. 106)	☐	☐
• pronounce the letters **h, j,** and **g**. (p. 107 and online)	☐	☐
• express actions. (p. 109)	☐	☐
• describe general differences in housing in Spain. (p. 113)	☐	☐
• elaborate on rooms. (p. 114)	☐	☐

Comunicación II

4 VOCABULARIO

Los quehaceres de la casa

Sharing information about household chores

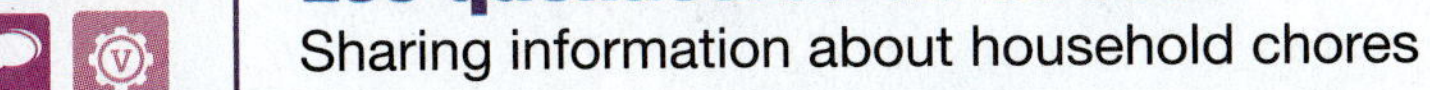

Otras palabras	*Other words*
arreglar	*to straighten up; to fix*
ayudar	*to help*
cocinar; preparar la comida	*to cook; to prepare a meal*
guardar	*to put away; to keep*
hacer la cama	*to make the bed*
lavar los platos	*to wash dishes*
limpiar	*to clean*
pasar la aspiradora	*to vacuum*
poner la mesa	*to set the table*
sacar la basura	*to take out the garbage*
sacudir los muebles	*to dust*
la ropa	*clothes; clothing*
desordenado/a	*messy*
limpio/a	*clean*
sucio/a	*dirty*

¿? Now you are ready to complete the ***Preparación y práctica*** activities for this chunk online.

3-15 ¡Mucho trabajo! Mira el dibujo en la página 117 y con un/a compañero/a determina qué hacen las siguientes personas.

MODELO E1: *Carmen*

E2: *Carmen hace la cama.*

1. El Sr. Sánchez
2. Hosun
3. Javier
4. Reyes
5. Donato y Leticia
6. Lourdes
7. Lina y Carlos
8. Teresa
9. Felipe y Alfonso
10. Juan y Carmen

3-16 Responsabilidades ¿Cuáles son tus responsabilidades? ¿Cuánto tiempo dedicas a (*do you devote to*) estas tareas? ¿Cuándo? Completa el cuadro y comparte (*share*) oralmente tus respuestas con un/a compañero/a.

Fíjate

The expression *tener que* + (infinitive) means "to have to do" something. *¿Qué tienes que hacer?* means "What do you have to do?" Later in this chapter you will learn more expressions with *tener.*

tener que + (***infinitive***) *to have to* + (*verb*)

MODELO *Tengo que limpiar mi dormitorio y sacar la basura los lunes. Dedico dos horas porque está muy sucio y tengo mucha basura.*

LUGAR	¿QUÉ TIENES QUE HACER?	¿CUÁNDO?	¿CUÁNTO TIEMPO DEDICAS?
1. mi dormitorio	limpiar mi dormitorio y sacar la basura	el lunes	dos horas
2. el baño			
3. la cocina			
4. la sala			
5. el garaje			
6. el comedor			

5 VOCABULARIO

Los colores Illustrating objects using colors

una casa sevillana

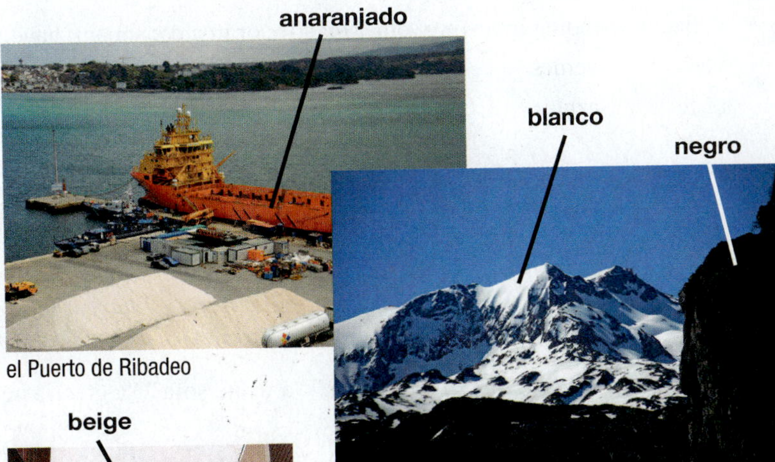

el Puerto de Ribadeo

los Picos de Europa

beige

una casa urbana española

el mar al lado de Baiona

la catedral en Bilbao

un viñedo en La Rioja

una casa privada

las botellas para la sidra

un autobús

Colors are descriptive adjectives, and as such, they must agree with the nouns they describe in number and gender.

Fíjate

You learned in *Capítulo 1* (p. 44) that adjectives normally follow nouns in Spanish, e.g. el coche *rojo.*

- Adjectives ending in **-o** have four forms.

  roj**o** roj**a** roj**os** roj**as**
- Adjectives ending in a vowel other than **-o,** or in a consonant, have two forms.

  verd**e** verd**es**

  azu**l** azu**les**

¿De qué color es...?	***What color is ... ?***
La cas**a** es blanc**a** y tiene un tech**o** roj**o**.	*The house is white and has a red roof.*
Las cas**as** son blanc**as** y tienen tech**os** roj**os**.	*The houses are white and have red roofs.*
Tengo un armari**o** marr**ón**.	*I have a brown armoire.*
Tengo una alfombr**a** marr**ón**.	*I have a brown rug.*
Tengo dos sillon**es** marron**es**.	*I have two brown armchairs.*

How would you say "a black refrigerator," "a white sofa," "a green kitchen," and "some yellow chairs?"

Now you are ready to complete the ***Preparación y práctica*** activities for this chunk online.

3-17 La casa ideal

Termina (*Finish*) las siguientes oraciones para describir tu casa ideal, incluyendo los colores. Comparte tus respuestas con un/a compañero/a.

MODELO E1: *Quiero una casa con... una cocina...*

E2: *Quiero una casa con una cocina amarilla.*

Quiero una casa con...

1. una alfombra...
2. una bañera...
3. un inodoro y un lavabo...
4. un refrigerador...
5. un comedor...
6. unos sillones...
7. un techo...
8. ¿?

3-18 ¿Cómo son?

Túrnense para comparar la sala de Luis con la tuya (*yours*) o la sala de un/a amigo/a. Usen los verbos **ser** y **tener**.

Capítulo A Para empezar. El verbo *ser*, pág. 13; Capítulo 1. El verbo *tener*, pág. 35; Capítulo 2. El verbo *estar*, pág. 83.

MODELO E1: *Luis tiene una sala grande, pero yo tengo una sala pequeña.*

E2: *La sala de Luis es grande y mi sala es grande también.*

la sala de Luis

3-19 Buena memoria Bring in colorful pictures of a house or rooms in a house. Select one picture and take a minute to study it carefully. Turn it over and relate to a partner as much detail as you can remember about the picture, especially pertaining to colors. Then listen to your partner talk about his or her picture. Who remembers more?

3-20 En la casa de Dalí Go to the Internet to take a virtual tour of the home of a famous Spaniard, such as the house of the artist Salvador Dalí, the Castillo Gala Dalí in Púbol, Spain. While you are exploring his house, or the house of another Spaniard, answer the following questions. Then compare your answers with those of a classmate.

1. ¿Qué ves en el jardín?
2. ¿Qué muebles ves o imaginas en cada cuarto?
3. ¿Cuáles son los colores principales de cada cuarto?
4. ¿Qué te gusta más de esta casa? ¿Qué te gusta menos?

el Castillo Gala Dalí

6 GRAMÁTICA

Algunas expresiones con *tener*

Depicting states of being using *tener*

The verb **tener,** besides meaning *to have*, is used in a variety of expressions.

Susana tiene 19 años.

tener… años	*to be… years old*
tener calor	*to feel hot*
tener cuidado	*to be careful*
tener éxito	*to be successful*
tener frío	*to be cold*
tener ganas de + (*infinitive*)	*to feel like + (verb)*
tener hambre	*to be hungry*
tener miedo	*to be afraid*
tener prisa	*to be in a hurry*
tener que + (*infinitive*)	*to have to + (verb)*
tener razón	*to be right*
tener sed	*to be thirsty*
tener sueño	*to be sleepy*
tener suerte	*to be lucky*
tener vergüenza	*to be embarrassed*

Fíjate

When you use expressions like *tener frío* or *tener éxito,* please note that words like *frío* and *éxito* are nouns and do not change. For example: *Nosotras tenemos frío. Ellas tienen éxito.*

—Mamá, **tengo hambre.** ¿Cuándo comemos?
—**Tienes suerte,** hijo. Salimos para el restaurante Tío Tapas en diez minutos.

Mom, I'm hungry. When are we eating?
You are lucky, son. We are leaving for Tío Tapas Restaurant in ten minutes.

Now you are ready to complete the ***Preparación y práctica*** activities for this chunk online.

3-21 ¿Qué pasa?

Mira los dibujos y, con un/a compañero/a, crea una oración para cada persona. Usa expresiones con **tener.**

MODELO

Susana tiene 19 años.

Rosario Alicia

Beatriz Julián

Pilar

Jorge Ramón Roberto

Carmen David

3-22 ¿Qué haces cuando...?

¿Qué haces en casa en las siguientes situaciones? Contesta la pregunta emparejando los elementos de las dos columnas de la forma más lógica. Compara tus respuestas con las de un/a compañero/a.

MODELO E1: tener ganas de descansar ver la televisión

E2: *Cuando tengo ganas de descansar, veo la televisión.*

Cuando...

1. _____ tener hambre
2. _____ tener suerte
3. _____ tener cuidado
4. _____ tener prisa
5. _____ tener frío
6. _____ tener éxito
7. _____ tener sed
8. _____ tener ganas de descansar

a. estar muy feliz
b. preparar comida en la cocina
c. hacer una limonada
d. no tener que limpiar la casa
e. ver la televisión
f. salir rápidamente en mi carro
g. no hacer errores
h. tomar el sol en el jardín

Capítulo A Para empezar. Los días, los meses y las estaciones, pág. 21; Capítulo 2. Presente indicativo de verbos regulares, pág. 71.

3-23 ¿Qué tengo yo?

Expresa cómo te sientes (*you feel*) en las siguientes ocasiones usando (*using*) expresiones con **tener.** Compara tus respuestas con las de un/a compañero/a.

MODELO E1: antes de comer
E2: *Antes de comer tengo hambre.*

1. temprano en la mañana
2. los viernes por la tarde
3. después de correr mucho
4. en el verano
5. en el invierno
6. cuando tienes tres minutos para llegar a clase
7. cuando sacas una "A" en un examen
8. cuando lees un libro de Stephen King o ves una película (*movie*) de terror

3-24 Pobre Pablo

Poor Pablo, our friend from Madrid, is having one of those days! With a partner, retell his story using **tener** expressions.

MODELO

Pablo tiene prisa.

El despertador de Pablo no funciona (*does not work*). Tiene una clase a las 8:00 y es tarde. Sale de casa a las 8:10.

1. Es invierno y Pablo no tiene abrigo (*coat*).

2. Pablo tiene un insuficiente (60% en los Estados Unidos) en un examen.

3. Pablo recibe una oferta (*offer*) de trabajo increíble.

4. Pablo ve que no tiene dinero para comer.

5. Pablo está en casa y quiere una botella de agua. En el refrigerador no hay ninguna (*none*).

3-25 Datos personales

Túrnense para hacerse esta entrevista (*interview*).

1. ¿Cuántos años tienes?
2. ¿Qué tienes que hacer hoy?
3. ¿Tienes ganas de hacer algo diferente? ¿Qué?
4. ¿En qué clase tienes sueño?
5. ¿En qué clase tienes mucha suerte?
6. ¿Siempre tienes razón?
7. ¿Cuándo tienes hambre?
8. ¿Cuándo tienes sueño?
9. Cuando tienes sed, ¿qué tomas?
10. ¿En qué tienes éxito?

7 VOCABULARIO

Los números 1.000–100.000.000 y los números ordinales

Counting from 1,000 to 100,000,000 and ranking people and things

1.000	mil	**100.000**	cien mil
1.001	mil uno	**400.000**	cuatrocientos mil
1.010	mil diez	**1.000.000**	un millón
2.000	dos mil	**2.000.000**	dos millones
30.000	treinta mil	**100.000.000**	cien millones

1. **Mil** is never used in the plural form when counting.

   mil dos mil tres mil

Fíjate

To express "a/one thousand," use *mil.* Do not use the word *un* with *mil.*

2. To state numbers in the thousands (such as the following dates), use mil, followed by hundreds in the masculine form (if needed).

   1492 mil cuatrocientos noventa y dos
   1950 mil novecientos cincuenta
   2012 dos mil doce

3. The plural of **millón** is **millones** and when followed by a noun, both take the preposition **de.**

   un millón de autos cinco millones de personas

Fíjate

Note that *millón* has an accent mark in the singular form but loses the accent mark in the plural form, *millones.*

4. **Cien** is used before **mil** and **millones (de).**

   cien mil euros cien millones de euros

5. Decimal points are used instead of commas in some Hispanic countries to group three digits together, and commas are used to replace decimal points.

   1.000.000 (un millón) $2.000,00 (dos mil dólares)

6. **Ordinal numbers** indicate position in a series or order. The first ten ordinal numbers are listed below. Ordinal numbers beyond *décimo* are rarely used.

primer, primero/a	*first*	**sexto/a**	*sixth*
segundo/a	*second*	**séptimo/a**	*seventh*
tercer, tercero/a	*third*	**octavo/a**	*eighth*
cuarto/a	*fourth*	**noveno/a**	*ninth*
quinto/a	*fifth*	**décimo/a**	*tenth*

7. Ordinal numbers are adjectives and agree in number and gender with the nouns they modify. They usually *precede* nouns.

   el **cuarto** piso — *the fourth floor*
   la **quinta** casa — *the fifth house*

8. Before masculine, singular nouns, **primero** and **tercero** are shortened to **primer** and **tercer.**

   el **primer** coche — *the first car*
   el **tercer** curso — *the third course*

9. After *décimo,* a cardinal number is used and *follows* the noun.

   el piso **catorce** — *the fourteenth floor*
   el siglo **veintiuno** — *the 21st century*

¿? Now you are ready to complete the ***Preparación y práctica*** activities for this chunk online.

3-26 ¿Cuánto cuesta? Look at the ads for houses in Spain. Complete the following steps.

Paso 1: Take turns asking for the price and other details for each of the houses.

MODELO E1: *¿Cuánto cuesta la casa en Carmona?*
E2: *Cuesta* (It costs) *ochocientos noventa y cinco mil euros.*
E1: *¿Cuántos dormitorios tiene?*
E2: *Tiene dos dormitorios.*

Paso 2: Rank the houses from your first to fourth favorite.

MODELO E1: *Para mí, la primera es la casa en Costa Brava.*
E2: *Para mí, la primera es la casa en Los Gigantes.*
E1: *Para mí, la segunda es....*
E2: *Para mí...*

Casa en venta

2 dormitorios,
2 baños,
calefacción,
aire acondicionado.

Cerca de la calle Santa Ana.

Carmona, España.

Precio: 895.000€ Tel: (+34) 954 190 576

Casa independiente en venta

6 dormitorios, 3 baños, cocina amueblada, terrazas, piscina.

Los Gigantes, Tenerife, España.

Precio: 2.620.000€ Tel: (+34) 922 787 718

Casa independiente en venta

3 dormitorios, 2 baños, cocina amueblada, calefacción, terrazas, chimenea. Jardín grande. Posibilidad de ampliación de dormitorios.

Costa Brava, España.

Precio: 960.607€ Tel: (+34) 972 212 315

Casa unifamiliar en venta

Casa señorial de cuatro plantas.

La construcción data del año 1800.

En buen estado de conservación.

5 dormitorios, 2 baños, chimenea, terrazas, jardín grande.

Oviedo, España.

Precio: 620.000€ Tel: (+34) 984 223 591

3-27 ¿Cuánto? Listen as Miguel, a real estate agent, tells you the prices of luxury homes available for purchase. Write the prices you hear.

1. ______________

3. ______________

2. ______________

4. ______________

3-28 ¿Cuál es su población? Lee las poblaciones de las siguientes ciudades de España mientras (*while*) tu compañero/a te escucha y corrige. Después, cambien de papel (*change roles*).

1. Madrid	2.824.000
2. Barcelona	1.454.000
3. Valencia	736.000
4. Sevilla	695.000
5. Granada	242.000

3-29 **¿Qué compras?** Your rich uncle left you an inheritance with the stipulation that you use the money to furnish your house. Refer to the pictures on page 114 to spend 5.500€ on your house. Make a list of what you want to buy, assigning prices to any items without tags. Then share your list with your partner, who will keep track of your spending. Did you overspend?

Fíjate

The sentence in the model includes two verbs; the second verb is an infinitive (*-ar*, *-er*, *-ir*).

Quiero compra**r** un televisvor. *I want to buy a television.*

MODELO *Quiero comprar una televisión por* (for) *ochocientos noventa y nueve euros.*

3-30 **Preguntas de trivia** Túrnense para hacerse las siguientes preguntas y contestarlas.

1. ¿En qué piso está tu clase de español?
2. ¿A qué hora es tu primera clase los lunes? ¿Y la segunda?
3. ¿Cuál es el tercer mes del año? ¿Y el sexto?
4. ¿Cuál es el séptimo día de la semana?
5. ¿Cuál es el nombre del primer presidente de los Estados Unidos?
6. ¿Cómo se llama la cuarta persona de la tercera fila (*row*) en la clase de español?

Nota cultural

Las casas "verdes"

El norte de España (Galicia, Asturias, Cantabria y el País Vasco) se llama "la España verde" a causa del color verde del paisaje (*countryside*). Hay suficiente lluvia y los árboles y la otra vegetación responden bien a la madre naturaleza.

Pero verde significa otra cosa también. España y otros países hispanohablantes tratan de (*try to*) vivir una vida verde. "Vivir una vida verde" significa valorar, cuidar (*care for*) y preservar los recursos naturales. Por ejemplo, usan el viento para producir energía. España produce entre 30 y 50 por ciento de su electricidad del viento. También hay casas con paneles solares.

En el sur de España, muchas casas son de color blanco. Es una tradición muy vieja. El color blanco refleja los rayos del sol y conserva la casa más fresca. Es aún otra manera para vivir una vida verde.

Preguntas

1. Explica los dos sentidos (*meanings*) de la palabra "verde".
2. ¿Dónde hay edificios o casas verdes en los Estados Unidos?

8 GRAMÁTICA

Hay y hay que + (infinitivo) Stating *There is / There are*. Stating what needs to be accomplished.

1. In **Capítulo 2,** you became familiar with **hay** when you described your classroom. To say *there is* or *there are* in Spanish you use **hay.** The irregular form **hay** comes from the verb **haber.**

Hay un baño en mi casa.	*There is one bathroom in my house.*
Hay cuatro dormitorios también.	*There are also four bedrooms.*
—¿**Hay** tres baños en tu casa?	*Are there three bathrooms in your house?*
—No, no **hay** tres baños.	*No, there aren't three bathrooms.*

2. Earlier in this chapter you learned that a form of *tener* + *que* + (infinitive) means *to have to do something.* Another way of expressing the idea of needing to do something is *hay que* + (infinitive).

Hay que limpiar el baño.	*It's necessary to clean the bathroom.*
Hay que poner la mesa.	*It's necessary to set the table.*
¿**Hay que sacar** la basura?	*Is it necessary to take out the garbage?*

Now you are ready to complete the ***Preparación y práctica*** activities for this chunk online.

¿Qué hay en ese cuarto?

3-31 ¡Escucha bien!

Descríbele un cuarto de tu casa (real o imaginaria) a un/a compañero/a en **tres** oraciones. Él/Ella tiene que repetir las oraciones. Después, cambien de papel.

MODELO E1: *En mi dormitorio hay una cama, una lámpara y una cómoda. También hay dos ventanas. No hay una alfombra.*
E2: *En tu dormitorio hay una cama, una lámpara y una cómoda…*

3-32 ¿Qué hay en tu casa?

Descríbele tu casa a un/a compañero/a. Usen todas las palabras que puedan (*you can*) del vocabulario de **La casa**, p. 106, y **Los muebles y otros objetos de la casa**, p. 114.

MODELO E1: *En mi casa hay un garaje. ¿Hay un garaje en tu casa?*
E2: *No, en mi casa no hay un garaje.*
E2: *En mi baño hay una bañera y una ducha. ¿Qué hay en tu baño?*
E1: *Hay una ducha, un inodoro y un lavabo grande.*

3-33 ¿Qué hay que hacer?

Contesta las siguientes preguntas usando *hay que.*

MODELO ¿Tienes que limpiar el baño? *Sí, hay que limpiar el baño.*

1. ¿Tenemos que arreglar la sala?
2. ¿Tengo que pasar la aspiradora?
3. ¿Tiene Miguelito que guardar sus cosas?
4. ¿Tengo que sacar la basura?
5. ¿Tienen Uds. que poner la mesa?

3-34 ¿Cuántos hay?

Túrnense para preguntar y contestar cuántos objetos y personas hay en su clase aproximadamente.

Capítulo A Para empezar. Los números 0–30, pág. 16; Capítulo 2. La formación de preguntas y las palabras interrogativas, pág. 75.

MODELO libros de español

E1: *¿Cuántos libros de español hay?*

E2: *Hay treinta libros de español.*

1. puertas
2. escritorios
3. mochilas azules
4. cuadernos negros
5. estudiantes contentos
6. estudiantes cansados
7. computadoras
8. estudiantes a quienes les gusta jugar al fútbol
9. estudiantes a quienes les gusta ir a fiestas (*parties*)
10. estudiantes a quienes les gusta estudiar

Escucha

Una descripción

Estrategia	
Listening for specific information	To practice listening for specific information, first determine the context of the passage and then decide what information you need about that topic. For example, if you are listening to an ad about an apartment to rent, you may want to focus on size, location, and price. In ***¡Anda! Curso elemental,*** the **Antes de escuchar** section will provide you with tools for successfully listening to and comprehending each passage.

3-35 Antes de escuchar

A real estate agent is describing one of the homes listed as a possibility to sell to the Garrido family. Mr. Garrido asks for a few details. Write a question Mr. Garrido might ask the agent.

3-36 A escuchar

Listen to the passage and complete the following list based on the information the agent provides. Listen a second time to verify your answers.

1. Number of floors: _____
2. Number of bedrooms: _____
3. Number of bathrooms: _____
4. Size of kitchen: _____
5. Size of living room: _____
6. Price: __________

Los señores Garrido quieren comprar una casa.

3-37 Después de escuchar

With a partner, play the roles of Mr. Garrido and a friend. The friend asks questions about the house, and Mr. Garrido describes the house using the information from **3-36**.

¡Conversemos!

3-38 Su casa Look at the drawing below, and create a story about the family who lives there. Your partner will ask you the following questions as well as additional ones he/she may have.

- When does your story take place?
- What is the weather?
- What is the name of the family?
- Describe furniture and household objects using colors.

Also make sure that your story includes the following components.

- Include at least *eight* different verbs.
- Use at least *three* new **tener** expressions (p. 121).

3-39 Mi casa ideal Describe tu casa ideal. Di por lo menos (*at least*) **diez** oraciones, usando palabras descriptivas (adjetivos) en cada oración. Tu compañero/a de clase va a hacer por lo menos **tres** preguntas sobre tu descripción.

Escribe

Un anuncio (*ad*)

Estrategia	
Noun → adjective agreement	Remember that most adjectives follow nouns, and that adjectives agree with their corresponding nouns in gender (*masculine/feminine*) and number (*singular/plural*). Keep this in mind when creating your ad.

3-40 Antes de escribir You have accepted a new job in a different town and you are uncertain regarding the permanence of the position. Therefore, you decide to sublet your apartment, listing it on the Internet. Before creating the posting, make a detailed list of the features you want to include.

3-41 A escribir Organize your list and create your ad, making it as informative and attractive as possible. The ad should include the following information:

- Location (city, country, street, etc.)
- Type of house or building
- Number and types of rooms
- Appliances in the kitchen
- Pieces of furniture included
- Colors
- Price and contact information
- Special features

3-42 Después de escribir Circulate among your classmates sharing your ads, and determine which you would most like to sublet.

¿Cómo andas? II

Having completed **Comunicación II**, I now can...	Feel confident	Need to review
• share information about household chores. (p. 117)	☐	☐
• illustrate objects using colors. (p. 119)	☐	☐
• depict states of being using **tener**. (p. 121)	☐	☐
• count from 1,000–100,000,000 and use ordinal numbers. (p. 124)	☐	☐
• discover green initiatives. (p. 127)	☐	☐
• state *There is / There are* and *It's necessary to...* (p. 128)	☐	☐
• listen for specific information. (p. 129)	☐	☐
• communicate about homes and life at home. (p. 130)	☐	☐
• create an ad. (p. 131)	☐	☐

Vistazo cultural

España

Les presento mi país

Mariela Castañeda Ropero

Mi nombre es Mariela Castañeda Ropero y soy de Madrid, la capital de España. Estudio literatura en la Universidad Complutense de Madrid y vivo con mis padres en un piso en el centro. **¿Dónde vives tú? ¿En una casa, en un apartamento o en una residencia estudiantil?** La vida en la capital es muy interesante porque hay mucha actividad. Me gusta salir con mis amigos por la tarde para comer tapas y tomar algo. La Plaza Mayor es nuestro lugar favorito. **¿Cuál es tu lugar favorito para conversar y pasar tiempo con tus amigos?** Frecuentemente, hablamos de las clases en la universidad o de nuestros pasatiempos favoritos. En mi tiempo libre, practico deportes, escucho música y salgo a bailar con amigos los fines de semana. Hay muchos lugares para bailar: ¡la vida nocturna es excelente en Madrid! **¿Qué haces en tu tiempo libre?**

El flamenco es un estilo de baile y música con orígenes en Andalucía, una comunidad autónoma en el sur del país.

La Plaza Mayor de Madrid es un lugar agradable para comer tapas, tomar una bebida y conversar con amigos.

Don Quijote y Sancho Panza son personajes del autor Miguel de Cervantes Saavedra.

El patio de los leones de La Alhambra muestra la influencia árabe en Granada.

La tortilla española es una tapa (un aperitivo) muy típica y popular.

Los *castells* —o castillos (*castles*) en español— son impresionantes construcciones humanas.

La Pedrera (la Casa Milà) en Barcelona es un ejemplo de la arquitectura creativa de Antonio Gaudí.

ALMANAQUE

Nombre oficial:	Reino de España
Gobierno:	Monarquía parlamentaria
Población:	46.505.963 (2010)
Idiomas oficiales:	español, catalán, gallego, euskera (vasco)
Moneda:	euro (€)

¿Sabías que…?

- España tiene una diversidad de culturas, regiones y arquitectura. Para un país que tiene el doble del tamaño (*size*) del estado de Oregon, tiene una gran variedad.
- Los *castells* forman parte de una tradición empezada en Cataluña en el siglo (*century*) XVIII que consiste en competir por hacer la torre (*tower*) humana más alta. ¡Actualmente el récord es un castillo de nueve pisos!

Preguntas

1. ¿Qué es una tapa?
2. ¿Qué región de España se asocia con el flamenco?
3. ¿Qué evidencia hay de la presencia histórica de los árabes en España?
4. ¿Por qué son impresionantes los *castells*? Nombra una competencia famosa de tu país.
5. Describe la arquitectura de Antonio Gaudí. ¿Te gusta? ¿Por qué?
6. ¿Qué tienen en común España y México? ¿Cómo son diferentes?

Lectura

Un blog de decoración

3-43 Antes de leer You will read a blog about decorating. Before you begin to read, consider the following questions.

1. ¿Te ayudan tu familia y tus amigos en la decoración de tu dormitorio en la residencia estudiantil, tu apartamento o tu casa?
2. ¿Miras programas de televisión sobre decoración? ¿Lees o escribes blogs de decoración?

Estrategia

Scanning

To enhance comprehension, you can scan or search a reading passage for specific information. When skimming you read quickly to get the gist of the passage, the main ideas. With scanning, you already know what you need to find out, so you concentrate on searching for that information.

3-44 Mientras lees Complete the following steps.

1. Scan the first paragraph, looking for specific information:
   a. the location of the apartment
   b. why the location of the apartment is important
   c. why Ana María is unable to decorate the room
2. Read the entire blog post to determine Ana María's style preferences and the decorator's response.

DECORADORES, ¡NECESITO AYUDA!

Me llamo Ana María Jiménez. Ahora hago mi residencia médica en el hospital general universitario. Puedo llegar al trabajo en quince minutos en autobús. No tengo tiempo para decorar porque trabajo turnos° de doce horas en el hospital. Tengo suerte porque vivo en un apartamento antiguo en el centro de la ciudad°. Mi compañera es una modelo de ropa° que tiene el apartamento decorado de estilo moderno. Ella me dice que puedo redecorar mi dormitorio. La habitación no tiene espacio. Los muebles en la habitación son muy anticuados, feos y muy grandes. Hay una cama horrible. ¡Es marrón! No me gustan los colores fuertes, especialmente el marrón y el negro. Quiero ver los colores transparentes del mar Mediterráneo en mi cuarto. Tengo un presupuesto° de 3.500 euros. A mí me gusta la música, el cine y el arte moderno. Necesito ayuda porque no sé dónde hay tiendas de muebles en el centro de la ciudad.
¿Qué me recomiendan?

shifts

city
fashion model

budget

Comentarios

¡Ay, qué horror! ¡No puedo creer lo que veo!
Ana María, aquí tienes mi recomendación. Primero, necesitas dar los muebles a un centro de caridad°. Segundo, puedes pintar las paredes con una combinación de blanco y azul. Tercero, tienes suerte porque conozco varias tiendas de muebles baratos° como *Compra aquí, Muebles baratos y Todo moderno,* y están en el centro.
Si quieres mi ayuda, llámame al 1-800-DECORAS.
Marisa López

charity

inexpensive

3-45 Después de leer Contesta las siguientes preguntas.

1. ¿Dónde trabaja Ana María?
2. ¿Cómo es la habitación de Ana María?
3. ¿Por qué no puede decorar su habitación?
4. ¿Cuánto dinero tiene para decorar su habitación?
5. ¿Qué colores le gustan a Ana María?
6. Según Marisa López, ¿qué tiene que hacer Ana María?

3-46 ¡A decorar! Imagina que tú trabajas para una compañía de decoradores. Describe en detalle tus recomendaciones para Ana María.

3-47 Muebles gratis (*free*) Ganas (*You win*) la lotería y compras un apartamento. Quieres comprar todo nuevo y quieres dar tus cosas. Necesitas crear una presentación en la que describes las cosas que quieres dar gratis.

For additional *Lectura* activities, go to *¡Anda!* online.

Y por fin, ¿cómo andas?

Having completed this chapter, I now can…	Feel confident	Need to review
Comunicación I		
• describe homes. (p. 106)	☐	☐
• pronounce the letters **h, j,** and **g**. (p. 107 and online)	☐	☐
• express actions. (p. 109)	☐	☐
• elaborate on rooms. (p. 114)	☐	☐
Comunicación II		
• share information about household chores. (p. 117)	☐	☐
• illustrate objects using colors. (p. 119)	☐	☐
• depict states of being using **tener.** (p. 121)	☐	☐
• count from 1,000–100,000,000 and use ordinal numbers. (p. 124)	☐	☐
• state *There is / There are* and *It is necessary to…* (p. 128)	☐	☐
• listen for specific information. (p. 129)	☐	☐
• communicate about homes and life at home. (p. 130)	☐	☐
• create an ad. (p. 131)	☐	☐
Cultura		
• describe general differences in housing in Spain. (p. 113)	☐	☐
• discover green initiatives. (p. 127)	☐	☐
• share information about Spain. (p. 132)	☐	☐
Lectura		
• scan a blog about decoration. (p. 134)	☐	☐
Comunidades		
• use Spanish in real-life contexts. (online)	☐	☐

Vocabulario **activo** 

La casa	*The house*
el altillo	*attic*
el balcón	*balcony*
el baño	*bathroom*
la cocina	*kitchen*
el comedor	*dining room*
el cuarto	*room*
el dormitorio	*bedroom*
la escalera	*staircase*
el garaje	*garage*
el jardín	*garden*
la oficina	*office*
el piso	*floor; story*
la sala	*living room*
el sótano	*basement*
el suelo	*floor*
el techo	*roof*
la planta baja	*ground floor*
el primer piso	*second floor*
el segundo piso	*third floor*
el tercer piso	*fourth floor*

Los verbos	*Verbs*
conocer	*to be acquainted with*
dar	*to give*
decir	*to say; to tell*
hacer	*to do; to make*
oír	*to hear*
poder	*to be able to*
poner	*to put; to place*
querer	*to want; to love*
salir	*to leave; to go out*
traer	*to bring*
venir	*to come*
ver	*to see*

Los muebles y otros objetos de la casa	*Furniture and other objects in the house*
La sala y el comedor	*The living room and dining room*
la alfombra	*rug; carpet*
el estante	*bookcase*
la lámpara	*lamp*
el sillón	*armchair*
el sofá	*sofa*
La cocina	*The kitchen*
la estufa	*stove*
el lavaplatos	*dishwasher*
el microondas	*microwave*
el refrigerador	*refrigerator*
El baño	*The bathroom*
la bañera	*bathtub*
el bidé	*bidet*
la ducha	*shower*
el inodoro	*toilet*
el lavabo	*sink*
El dormitorio	*The bedroom*
la almohada	*pillow*
la cama	*bed*
la colcha	*bedspread; comforter*
la cómoda	*dresser*
la manta	*blanket*
las sábanas	*sheets*
Otras palabras	*Other words*
el armario	*armoire; closet; cabinet*
la cosa	*thing*
el cuadro	*picture; painting*
el mueble	*piece of furniture*
los muebles	*furniture*
el objeto	*object*
la ropa	*clothes*
amueblado/a	*furnished*

Los quehaceres de la casa	Household chores
arreglar	*to straighten up; to fix*
ayudar	*to help*
cocinar, preparar la comida	*to cook; to prepare a meal*
guardar	*to put away; to keep*
hacer la cama	*to make the bed*
lavar los platos	*to wash dishes*
limpiar	*to clean*
pasar la aspiradora	*to vacuum*
poner la mesa	*to set the table*
sacar la basura	*to take out the garbage*
sacudir los muebles	*to dust*
desordenado/a	*messy*
limpio/a	*clean*
sucio/a	*dirty*

Los colores	Colors
amarillo	*yellow*
anaranjado	*orange*
azul	*blue*
beige	*beige*
blanco	*white*
gris	*gray*
marrón	*brown*
morado	*purple*
negro	*black*
rojo	*red*
rosado	*pink*
verde	*green*

Un verbo	A verb
hay	*There is / There are.*
hay que + (*infinitive*)	*It's necessary to…*

Expresiones con tener	Expressions with tener
tener… años	*to be . . . years old*
tener calor	*to be hot*
tener cuidado	*to be careful*
tener éxito	*to be successful*
tener frío	*to be cold*
tener ganas de + (*infinitive*)	*to feel like + (verb)*
tener hambre	*to be hungry*
tener miedo	*to be afraid*
tener prisa	*to be in a hurry*
tener que + (*infinitive*)	*to have to + (verb)*
tener razón	*to be right*
tener sed	*to be thirsty*
tener sueño	*to be sleepy*
tener suerte	*to be lucky*
tener vergüenza	*to be embarrassed*

Los números 1.000–100.000.000 y los números ordinales	Numbers 1,000–100,000,000 and ordinal numbers
1.000	*mil*
1.001	*mil uno*
1.010	*mil diez*
2.000	*dos mil*
30.000	*treinta mil*
100.000	*cien mil*
400.000	*cuatrocientos mil*
1.000.000	*un millón*
2.000.000	*dos millones*
100.000.000	*cien millones*
primer, primero/a	*first*
segundo/a	*second*
tercer, tercero/a	*third*
cuarto/a	*fourth*
quinto/a	*fifth*
sexto/a	*sixth*
séptimo/a	*seventh*
octavo/a	*eighth*
noveno/a	*ninth*
décimo/a	*tenth*

Sacatepéquez, Guatemala

4 Nuestra comunidad

No importa si vivimos en el campo (*countryside*), en un pueblo (*town*), en una ciudad o en otro país: tenemos mucho en común. Todos comemos, trabajamos, hacemos compras, pasamos tiempo con la familia y los amigos y ayudamos a los demás (*others*). Nuestra vida en comunidad es similar.

Preguntas

1. Adónde van las personas de tu comunidad para divertirse (*to have fun*)? ¿Dónde hacen las compras? ¿Hay muchas o pocas opciones donde vives?
2. Piensa en tu país. ¿Dónde prefiere vivir la gente: en el campo, los pueblos o las ciudades grandes? ¿Cómo se compara con la tendencia en Centroamérica?
3. ¿Conoces a personas de otros países o culturas? ¿Cuáles son sus actividades típicas? ¿Qué tienes en común con las personas de otros países?

¿Sabías que...?

Más del 25% de los residentes urbanos de Honduras, Guatemala y El Salvador vive en la capital de su país.

Cartagena, Colombia

Plaza de Mayo y la Casa Rosada, Buenos Aires, Argentina

Learning Outcomes

By the end of this chapter, you will be able to:

- ✔ identify places in and around town.
- ✔ relate actions, where you and others are going, and what will happen in the future.
- ✔ impart information about service opportunities.
- ✔ articulate concepts and ideas both affirmatively and negatively.
- ✔ communicate about different aspects of your town.
- ✔ write a postcard and proofread it for accuracy.
- ✔ exchange interesting facts about Honduras, Guatemala, and El Salvador.
- ✔ read a volunteer brochure.

Comunicación I

1 VOCABULARIO

Los lugares Identifying places in and around town

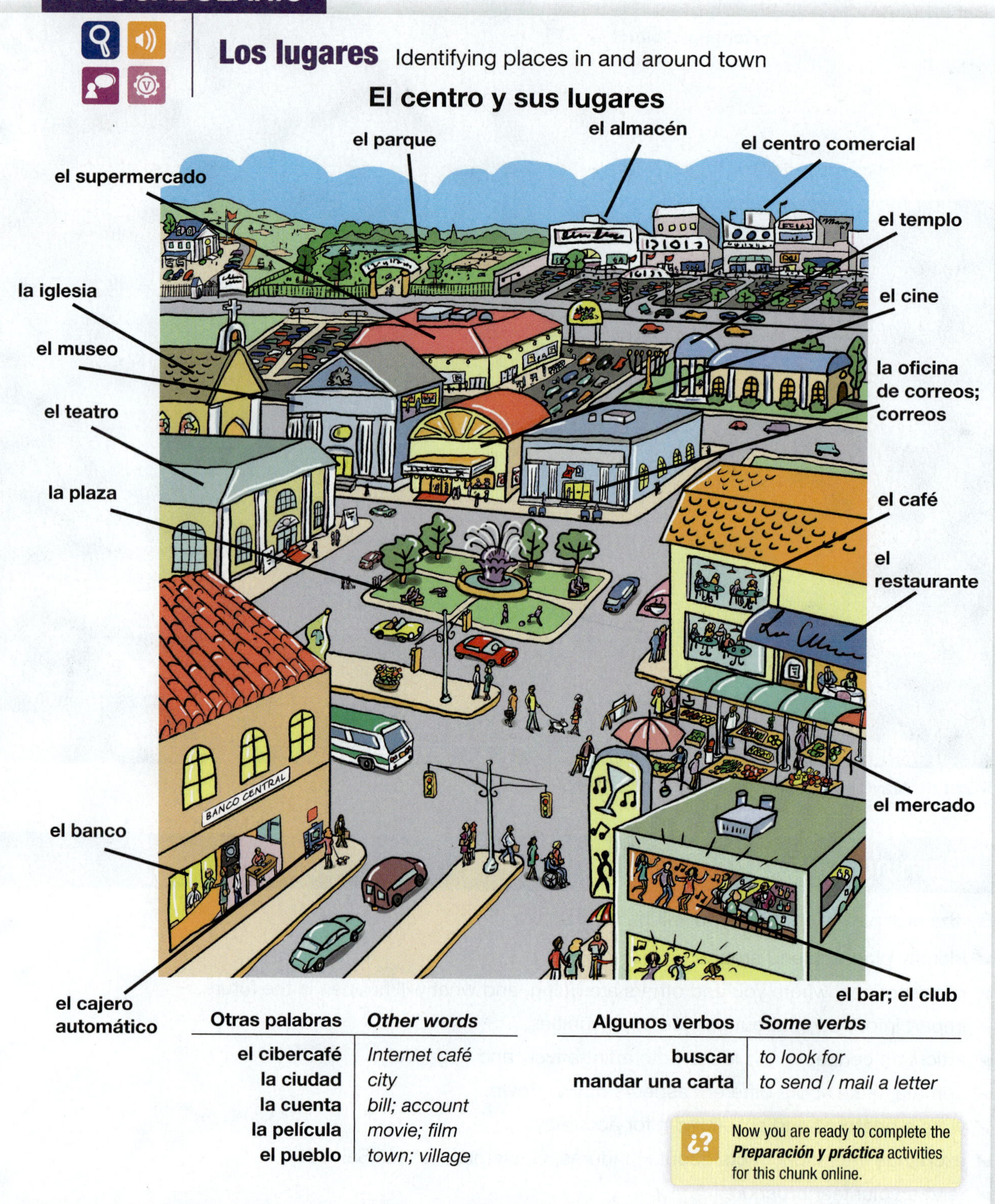

Otras palabras	*Other words*
el cibercafé	*Internet café*
la ciudad	*city*
la cuenta	*bill; account*
la película	*movie; film*
el pueblo	*town; village*

Algunos verbos	*Some verbs*
buscar	*to look for*
mandar una carta	*to send / mail a letter*

¿? Now you are ready to complete the ***Preparación y práctica*** activities for this chunk online.

PRONUNCIACIÓN

The letters *c* and *z*

Go to *¡Anda!* online to learn how to pronounce the letters *c* and *z*.

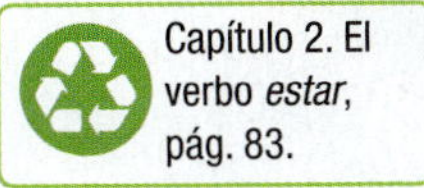

Capítulo 2. El verbo *estar*, pág. 83.

4-1 ¿Dónde está?

Tu amigo está muy ocupado. Túrnate con un/a compañero/a para decir dónde está en este momento.

MODELO E1: Quiere mandar una carta.
E2: *Está en la oficina de correos.*

1. Quiere ver una película.
2. Necesita dinero para la cuenta.
3. Quiere comer algo (*something*).
4. Quiere ver una exposición de arte.
5. Quiere caminar y hacer ejercicio.
6. Tiene sed y quiere tomar algo.
7. Quiere mandar un e-mail.
8. Tiene que ir a una boda (*wedding*).

Fíjate

Note that you use a form of *querer* + *infinitive* to express "to want to ______."
For example:

Quiero mandar… = I want to send…

Queremos ver… = We want to see…

4-2 Ciudad Fantasía

Marco visita la Ciudad Fantasía que vemos en la página 142. Escucha e indica el lugar que él visita.

1. a. el club
   b. el banco
   c. el centro comercial
2. a. el almacén
   b. el cine
   c. el supermercado
3. a. el correos
   b. el mercado
   c. el banco
4. a. la plaza
   b. la iglesia
   c. el cajero automático
5. a. el restaurante
   b. el museo
   c. el centro comercial

4-3 El mejor de los mejores

¿Cuáles son, en tu opinión, los mejores lugares en tu comunidad? Completa los siguientes pasos.

Capítulo A Para empezar. El verbo *ser*, pág. 13; Capítulo 2. El verbo *estar*, pág. 83.

Paso 1 Haz (*Make*) una lista de los mejores lugares de tu pueblo o ciudad según las siguientes categorías.

MODELO E1: restaurante

E2: *El mejor restaurante es The Lantern.*

a la derecha (de)	*to the right (of)*	**enfrente (de)**	*in front (of)*
a la izquierda (de)	*to the left (of)*	**estar de acuerdo**	*to agree*
al lado (de)	*next (to)*	**mejor**	*best*
detrás (de)	*behind*	**peor**	*worst*

1. almacén
2. banco
3. centro comercial
4. cine
5. café
6. teatro
7. tienda
8. restaurante
9. supermercado

El mejor de los mejores
Las mejores TIENDAS
Los mejores CINES
Los mejores RESTAURANTES

Paso 2 Compara tu lista con las listas de los otros estudiantes de la clase. ¿Están de acuerdo?

MODELO E1: *En mi opinión, el mejor restaurante es The Lantern. ¿Estás de acuerdo?*

E2: *No, no estoy de acuerdo. El mejor restaurante es The Cricket.*

Fíjate

A reminder from *Capítulo 3*: The preposition *de* combines with the masculine singular definite article *el* to form the contraction *del*. The feminine article *la* does not contract.

Paso 3 Túrnense para explicar dónde están los mejores lugares.

MODELO E1: *Busco el mejor restaurante.*

E2: *El mejor restaurante es The Lantern.*

E1: *¿Dónde está?*

E2: *Está al lado del Banco Nacional.*

4-4 Chiquimula y mi ciudad...

Chiquimula es una ciudad de aproximadamente 41.000 personas que está en el este de Guatemala. Completa los siguientes pasos.

Paso 1 Túrnense para describir el centro del pueblo. Mencionen dónde están los edificios principales.

MODELO *El Hotel Victoria está al lado del Restaurante el Dorado…*

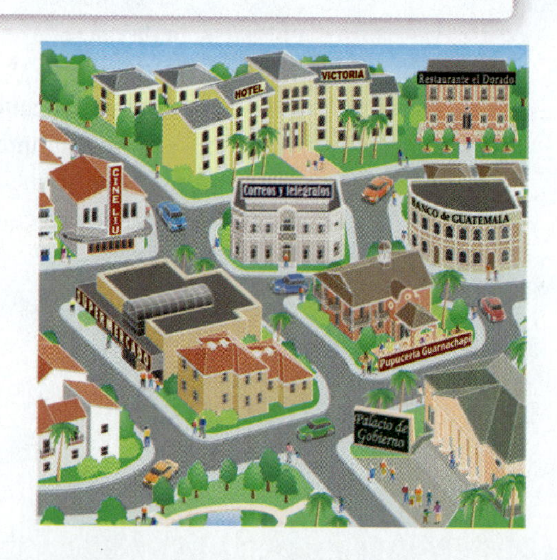

Paso 2 Ahora dibuja (*draw*) un mapa del centro de tu pueblo o ciudad. El dibujo debe incluir los edificios principales. Después, túrnense para describirlo oralmente.

Paso 3 Túrnense para describir sus dibujos mientras tu compañero/a dibuja lo que dices.

Actividades cotidianas: Las compras y el paseo

En los Estados Unidos, la gente hace gran parte de las compras en los centros comerciales. En los países hispanohablantes, también se hacen las compras en los centros comerciales, especialmente en las ciudades grandes. En Guatemala, Honduras y El Salvador algunos de los más conocidos son Miraflores, Altara y Centro Comercial Basilea.

En los pueblos pequeños la gente va al centro de la ciudad. En el centro están los supermercados y el mercado al aire libre, y hay muchas tiendas además de la oficina de correos, el banco y los restaurantes. Se puede encontrar gente de todas las clases sociales y muchos vendedores ambulantes (*roving*).

Otro lugar importante en el centro de los pueblos es la plaza. Allí se encuentra la gente (*people meet*) para conversar, pasear, ir de compras o ir a la iglesia. Además, los lugareños (*locals*) pasean a diario por las calles principales y los parques del pueblo. En los pueblos hispanos siempre hay mucho bullicio (*hubbub*) y actividad, especialmente los fines de semana.

Preguntas

1. En los países hispanohablantes, ¿qué hay en las ciudades grandes? ¿Cómo son los pueblos pequeños? ¿Qué hace la gente todos los días?
2. ¿Dónde prefieres comprar, en las tiendas pequeñas o en los centros comerciales? ¿Por qué?

Fíjate

Note that the word *gente*, unlike the word *people* in English, is singular: *La gente* ***va*** *al centro de la ciudad. Gente,* although made up of more than one person, is considered a collective noun like the singular nouns *la clase, el equipo,* and *la familia.*

2 GRAMÁTICA

Saber* y *conocer Stating whom and what is known

In **Capítulo 3,** you learned that **conocer** means *to know*. Another verb, **saber,** also expresses *to know*.

Fíjate

Note that *conocer* and *saber* both have irregular *yo* forms: *conozco* and *sé* respectively.

saber (*to know*)

Singular		Plural	
yo	**sé**	nosotros/as	**sabemos**
tú	**sabes**	vosotros/as	**sabéis**
Ud.	**sabe**	Uds.	**saben**
él, ella	**sabe**	ellos/as	**saben**

The verbs are not interchangeable. Note when to use each.

Conocer

- Use **conocer** to express ***being familiar or acquainted with people, places, and things.***

Ellos **conocen** los mejores restaurantes de la ciudad.	*They know the best restaurants in the city.*
Yo **conozco** a tu hermano, pero no muy bien.	*I know your brother, but not very well.*

Note:

1. When expressing that *a person* is known, you must use the personal **a**. For example: **Conozco *a* tu hermano**…
2. When **a** is followed by **el, a + el = al**. For example: **Conozco *al* señor (a + el señor)**…

Saber

- Use **saber** to express ***knowing facts, pieces of information,*** or ***how to do something.***

¿Qué **sabes** sobre la música de Guatemala?	*What do you know about Guatemalan music?*
Yo **sé** tocar la guitarra.	*I know how to play the guitar.*

Fíjate

A form of *saber* + *infinitive* expresses knowing how to do something. For example:
Sé nadar. = I know how to swim.
Sabemos tocar la guitarra. = We know how to play the guitar.

Now you are ready to complete the ***Preparación y práctica*** activities for this chunk online.

4-5 ¿Sabes o conoces? Completa las preguntas usando **sabes** o **conoces**. Después, túrnate con un/a compañero/a para hacer y contestar las preguntas.

MODELO E1: *¿Conoces San Salvador?*
E2: *Sí, conozco San Salvador. / No, no conozco San Salvador.*

1. ¿ ______ usar una computadora?
2. ¿ ______ al presidente del Banco Central?
3. ¿ ______ dónde hay un cajero automático?
4. ¿ ______ Tegucigalpa, Honduras?
5. ¿ ______ el mejor restaurante mexicano?
6. ¿ ______ llegar a la oficina de correos?
7. ¿ ______ las películas de James Cameron?
8. ¿ ______ cuál es el mejor café de esta ciudad?

4-6 ¿Qué sabemos de Honduras? Completen juntos el diálogo con las formas correctas de **saber** y **conocer**.

PROF. DOMÍNGUEZ: ¿Qué (1) __________ ustedes sobre Honduras?

DREW: Yo (2) __________ que la capital de Honduras es Tegucigalpa.

DREW Y TANYA: Nosotros (3) __________ mucho sobre el país.

PROF. DOMÍNGUEZ: ¿Y (4) __________ ustedes cómo se llaman las personas de Honduras?

TANYA: Sí, se llaman *hondureños*. (5) __________ la cultura hondureña bastante bien. Nuestra hermana, Gina, es una estudiante de intercambio allí este año y nos manda muchas fotos y cartas. Ella (6) __________ a mucha gente interesante, incluso al hijo del Presidente.

PROF. DOMÍNGUEZ: ¡No me digan! (*No way!*) ¿Estudia allí su hermana? ¿(7) __________ ustedes que hay dos universidades muy buenas en Tegucigalpa?

TANYA: Sí, el novio de Gina estudia allí, pero yo no (8) __________ en qué universidad. Él es salvadoreño y nuestros padres no lo (9) __________ todavía. Gina dice que no quiere volver a los Estados Unidos. Yo (10) __________ que mis padres van a estar (*they are going to be*) muy tristes si ella no vuelve.

PROF. DOMÍNGUEZ: Yo (11) __________ a tu hermana y (12) __________ que es una mujer inteligente. Va a pensarlo bien antes de tomar una decisión.

4-7 ¿Me puedes ayudar? Sofía acaba de llegar a San Salvador y se siente un poco perdida (*she is feeling a little lost*). Túrnense para hacer y contestar sus preguntas de manera creativa. Luego, creen (*create*) y contesten **dos** preguntas más usando **saber** y **conocer**.

MODELO SOFÍA: *¿Sabes dónde hay una iglesia?*
TÚ: *Sí, sé que hay una iglesia en la plaza.*

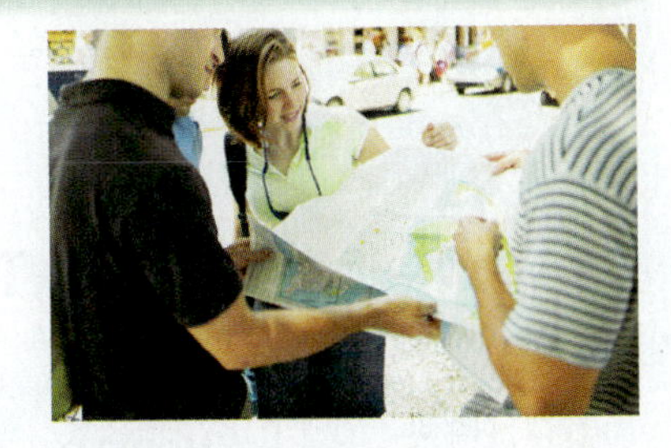

1. ¿Conoces un buen restaurante típico?
2. ¿Sabes dónde está el restaurante?
3. ¿Sabes qué tipo de comida (*food*) sirven en el restaurante?
4. ¿Conoces al cocinero (*chef*)?
5. ¿?
6. ¿?

3 VOCABULARIO

Actividades y acciones cotidianas Relating common everyday activities and occurrences

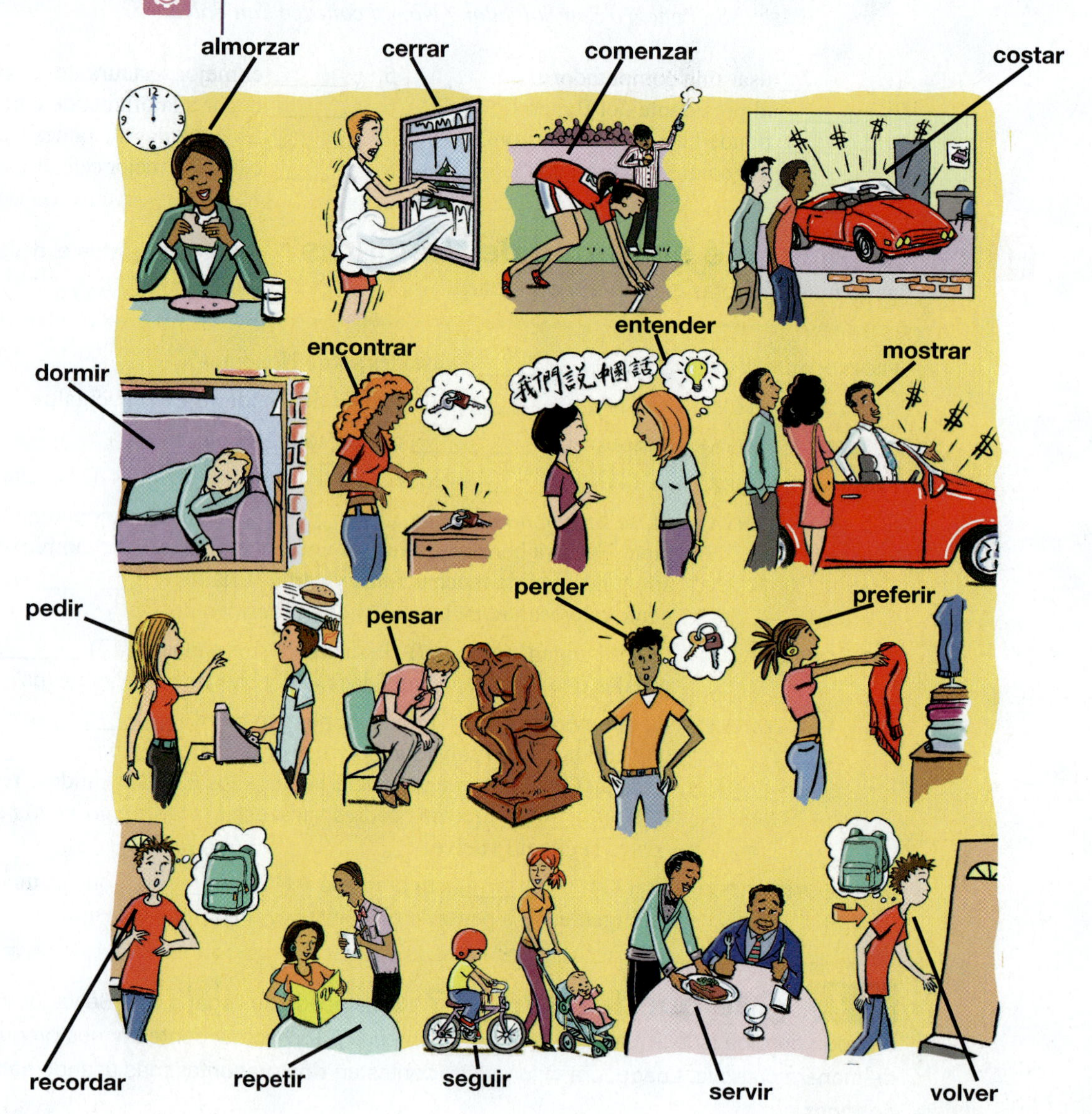

Now you are ready to complete the ***Preparación y práctica*** activities for this chunk online.

4-8 Tres en línea Escucha mientras tu instructor/a explica el juego del *tic-tac-toe*.

Capítulo 1. El verbo *tener*, pág. 35.

MODELO E1: *¿Tienes "volver"?*

E2: *Sí, tengo "volver". / No, no tengo "volver".*

4-9 ¿Y lo opuesto?

Decidan juntos qué verbo expresa lo opuesto (*opposite*) de cada una de las palabras o expresiones de la siguiente lista.

MODELO E1: no comer por la tarde
E2: *almorzar*

repetir	encontrar	volver	entender	pedir
perder	comenzar	querer	cerrar	almorzar

1. salir
2. terminar
3. abrir
4. perder
5. decir una vez (*once*)
6. dar
7. encontrar
8. no comprender

4-10 ¿Qué tienen que hacer?

Terminen las oraciones de manera lógica para expresar qué tienen que hacer.

Estrategia

Make an attempt to work with a different partner in every class. This enables you to help and learn from a variety of your peers, an important and highly effective learning technique.

Fíjate

Remember that in *Capítulo 3* you learned that *tener* + *que* + *infinitive* means "to have to do something."

MODELO Tengo que encontrar…
E1: *Tengo que encontrar mi libro de español.*
E2: *Tengo que encontrar los apuntes para la clase de español.*

1. Tengo que comenzar…
2. Tengo que repetir…
3. Tengo que pedir…
4. Tengo que recordar…
5. Tengo que almorzar…
6. Tengo que dormir…

4-11 Entrevistas

Entrevista a tres compañeros para averiguar si (*to find out whether*) hacen cosas similares. Después, comparte la información con la clase. ¿Qué tienen ustedes en común?

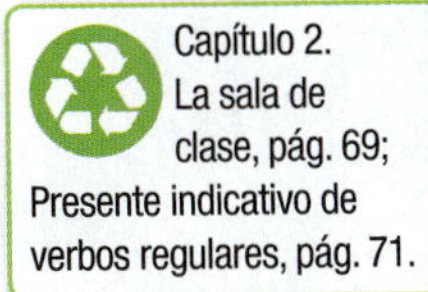
Capítulo 2. La sala de clase, pág. 69; Presente indicativo de verbos regulares, pág. 71.

1. ¿Qué tienes que hacer para prepararte bien para las clases?
2. ¿Qué tienes que hacer durante la clase de español para sacar buenas notas (*to get good grades*)?
3. Generalmente, ¿qué tienes que hacer cuando terminas con tus clases?

4 GRAMÁTICA

Los verbos con cambio de raíz

Expressing actions

In **Capítulo 3,** you learned a variety of common verbs that are irregular. Two of those verbs were **querer** and **poder,** which are irregular due to some changes in their stems. Look at the following verb groups and answer the questions regarding each group.

Change e → ie

cerrar (*to close*)

Singular		Plural	
yo	cierro	nosotros/as	cerramos
tú	cierras	vosotros/as	cerráis
Ud.	cierra	Uds.	cierran
él, ella	cierra	ellos/as	cierran

¡Explícalo tú!

1. Which verb forms look like the infinitive **cerrar**?
2. Which verb forms have a spelling change that differs from the infinitive **cerrar**?

✓ Check your answers to the preceding questions in Appendix 1.

Other verbs like **cerrar** (**e → ie**) are:

comenzar	*to begin*	**mentir**	*to lie*	**preferir**	*to prefer*
empezar	*to begin*	**pensar**	*to think*	**recomendar**	*to recommend*
entender	*to understand*	**perder**	*to lose; to waste*		

Change e → i

pedir (*to ask for*)

Singular		Plural	
yo	pido	nosotros/as	pedimos
tú	pides	vosotros/as	pedís
Ud.	pide	Uds.	piden
él, ella	pide	ellos/as	piden

¡Explícalo tú!

1. Which verb forms look like the infinitive **pedir**?
2. Which verb forms have a spelling change that differs from the infinitive **pedir**?

✓ Check your answers to the preceding questions in Appendix 1.

Other verbs like **pedir** (e → **i**) are:

repetir	*to repeat*	**seguir***	*to follow; to continue* (*doing something*)	**servir**	*to serve*

*Note: The **yo** form of **seguir** is **sigo**.

Change o → ue

encontrar (*to find*)

Singular		Plural	
yo	encuentro	nosotros/as	encontramos
tú	encuentras	vosotros/as	encontráis
Ud.	encuentra	Uds.	encuentran
él, ella	encuentra	ellos/as	encuentran

¡Explícalo tú!

1. Which verb forms look like the infinitive **encontrar**?
2. Which verb forms have a spelling change that differs from the infinitive **encontrar**?

✓ Check your answers to the preceding questions in Appendix 1.

Other verbs like **encontrar** (**o** → **ue**) are:

almorzar	*to have lunch*	**dormir**	*to sleep*	**mostrar**	*to show*	**volver**	*to return*
costar	*to cost*	**morir**	*to die*	**recordar**	*to remember*		

Change u → ue

jugar (*to play*)

Singular		Plural	
yo	juego	nosotros/as	jugamos
tú	juegas	vosotros/as	jugáis
Ud.	juega	Uds.	juegan
él, ella	juega	ellos/as	juegan

¡Explícalo tú!

1. Which verb forms look like the infinitive **jugar**?
2. Which verb forms have a spelling change that differs from the infinitive **jugar**?
3. Why does **jugar** not belong with the verbs like **encontrar**?

✓ Check your answers to the preceding questions in Appendix 1.

¡Explícalo tú!

To summarize…

1. What rule can you make regarding all four groups of stem-changing verbs and their forms?
2. With what group of stem-changing verbs would you put **querer**?
3. With what group of stem-changing verbs would you put each of the following verbs?

demostrar	*to demonstrate*	**encerrar**	*to enclose*
devolver	*to return* (*an object*)	**perseguir**	*to chase*

✓ Check your answers to the preceding questions in Appendix 1.

¿? Now you are ready to complete the ***Preparación y práctica*** activities for this chunk online.

4-12 Categorías

Complete the following steps.

Paso 1 With a partner, write the stem-changing verbs that were just presented on individual slips of paper. Next, make a chart with four categories: **e → ie, e → i, o → ue,** and **u → ue**.

Paso 2 Join another pair of students. When your instructor says **¡Empiecen!**, place each verb under the correct category (**e → ie, e → i, o → ue**, or **u → ue**). Do several rounds of this activity, playing against different doubles partners.

4-13 Nuestras preferencias

Averigua cuáles son las preferencias de tu compañero/a. Luego, comparte tus respuestas con la clase.

MODELO el cine o el teatro

E1: *¿Qué prefieres, el cine o el teatro?*

E2: *Prefiero el cine.*

¿Qué prefieres,...?

1. correr en el parque o en el gimnasio
2. comer en un restaurante o en un café
3. visitar un gran almacén o un centro comercial
4. comprar comida (*food*) en un supermercado o en un mercado al aire libre (*open-air*)
5. trabajar en un banco o en una oficina de correos
6. conversar con amigos en un bar o en una plaza

4-14 ¿Quién hace qué?

Túrnense para decir qué personas que ustedes conocen hacen las siguientes cosas.

MODELO E1: siempre perder la tarea

E2: *Mi hermano Tom siempre pierde la tarea.*

1. pensar ser profesor/a
2. almorzar en McDonald's a menudo
3. querer visitar Sudamérica
4. siempre entender al/a la profesor/a de español
5. preferir dormir hasta el mediodía
6. volver tarde a casa a menudo
7. perder dinero
8. pensar que Santa Claus existe
9. nunca mentir
10. comenzar a hacer la tarea de noche

4-15 **¿Quién eres?** Escribe las respuestas a las siguientes preguntas en forma de párrafos.

Capítulo A Para empezar. La hora, pág. 18; Capítulo 2. Las materias y las especialidades, pág. 66; La formación de preguntas y las palabras interrogativas, pág. 75; Los deportes y los pasatiempos, pág. 89.

Primer párrafo

1. ¿Qué clases tienes este semestre?
2. ¿A qué hora empieza tu clase preferida? ¿Cuándo termina?
3. ¿Qué prefieres hacer si (*if*) tienes tiempo entre (*between*) tus clases?
4. ¿A qué hora vuelves a tu dormitorio/apartamento/casa?

Segundo párrafo

1. ¿Qué carro tienes (o quieres tener)? ¿Cuánto cuesta un carro nuevo?
2. ¿Cómo vienes a la universidad? (Por ejemplo, ¿vienes en carro?)
3. ¿Dónde prefieres vivir, en una residencia estudiantil, en un apartamento o en una casa?
4. ¿Dónde quieres vivir después de graduarte?

Tercer párrafo

1. ¿Qué deporte o pasatiempo prefieres?
2. Si es un deporte, ¿juegas a ese deporte? ¿Ves ese deporte en la televisión?
3. Normalmente, ¿cuándo y con quién(es) juegas el deporte / disfrutas (*enjoy*) el pasatiempo?
4. ¿Qué otros deportes y pasatiempos te gustan?

¿Cómo andas? I

Having completed **Comunicación I**, I now can...	Feel confident	Need to review
• identify places in and around town. (p. 142)	☐	☐
• pronounce the letters *c* and *z*. (p. 143 and online)	☐	☐
• describe shopping and other daily activities in Spanish-speaking countries. (p. 145)	☐	☐
• state whom and what is known. (p. 146)	☐	☐
• relate common everyday activities and occurrences. (p. 148)	☐	☐
• express actions. (p. 150)	☐	☐

Comunicación II

5 GRAMÁTICA

El verbo *ir*

Sharing where you and others are going

Another important verb in Spanish is **ir**. Note its irregular present tense forms.

ir (*to go*)

Singular		Plural	
yo	**voy**	nosotros/as	**vamos**
tú	**vas**	vosotros/as	**vais**
Ud.	**va**	Uds.	**van**
él, ella	**va**	ellos/as	**van**

Voy al parque. ¿**Van** ustedes también? *I'm going to the park. Are you all going too?*

No, no **vamos** ahora. Preferimos **ir** más tarde. *No, we're not going now. We prefer to go later.*

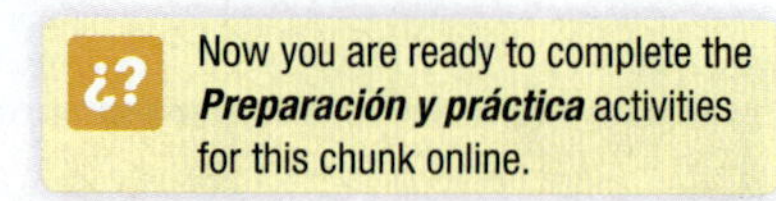
Now you are ready to complete the ***Preparación y práctica*** activities for this chunk online.

4-16 ¿Adónde vas? Túrnense para completar la conversación que tienen Memo y Esteban al salir de la clase de música. Usen las formas correctas del verbo **ir**.

Fíjate

In *Capítulo 2* you learned two words for the question word "Where?" Use *¿Adónde?* with *ir*.

Fíjate

Remember that *a* + *el* = *al*.

MEMO: Hola, Esteban. ¿Adónde (1) __________ ahora?
ESTEBAN: ¿Qué hay? Pues, (2) __________ a la clase de física.
MEMO: Ah sí. Bueno, mi compañero de cuarto y yo (3) __________ al gimnasio. Tenemos un torneo *(tournament)* de tenis.
ESTEBAN: Buena suerte. Oye, ¿tú (4) __________ a la fiesta de Isabel esta noche?
MEMO: No sé. ¿Quiénes (5) __________? Creo que (yo) (6) __________ al cine para ver la película nueva de Steven Spielberg.
ESTEBAN: ¿Por qué no (7) __________ primero a la fiesta y después al cine?
MEMO: Buena idea. ¿(8) __________ (tú y yo) juntos?
ESTEBAN: Muy bien. Mi amigo Roberto (9) __________ también. Hablamos después del torneo.
MEMO: Bueno, hasta luego.

4·17 Los "¿porqués?" Esperanza tiene una sobrina que está en la etapa de los "¿porqués?" Tiene muchas preguntas. Túrnense para darle las respuestas de Esperanza a Rosita.

MODELO ROSITA: ¿Por qué va mi papá al gimnasio?

ESPERANZA: *Tu papá va al gimnasio porque quiere hacer ejercicio.*

1. ¿Por qué va mi mamá al mercado?
2. ¿Por qué va mi hermana a la oficina de correos?
3. ¿Por qué van mis hermanos al parque?
4. ¿Por qué vas a la universidad?
5. ¿Por qué no vamos al cine ahora?

4·18 ¿Adónde van? Miren los horarios de las siguientes personas. Túrnense para decir adónde van, a qué hora y qué hacen en cada (*each*) lugar.

Capítulo A Para empezar. La hora, pág. 18.

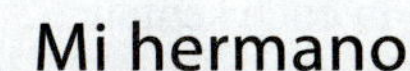

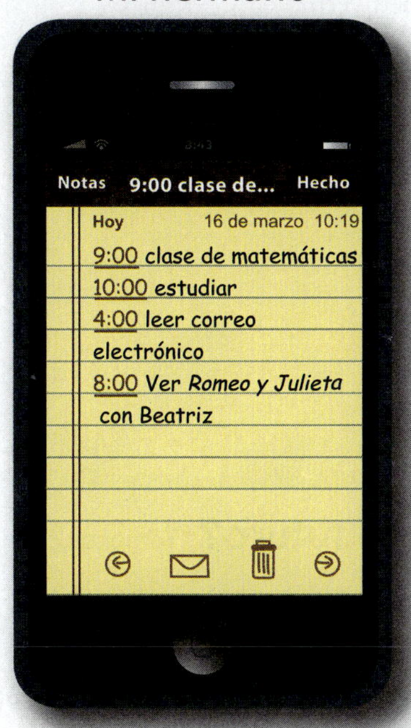

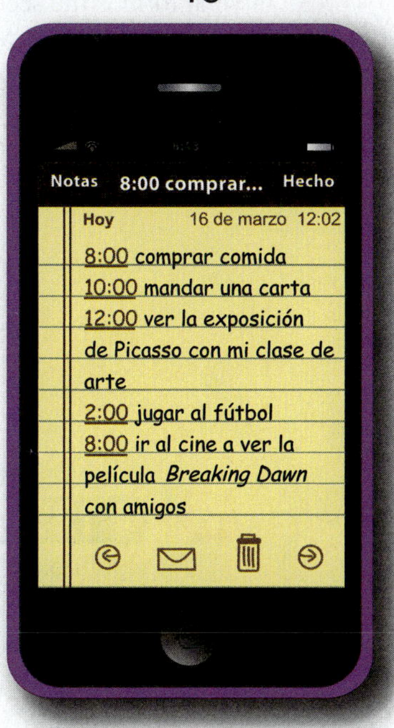

MODELO *A las diez mis padres van a la librería para comprar unos libros. Luego…*

GRAMÁTICA 6

Ir + a + infinitivo Conveying what will happen in the future

Study the following sentences and then answer the questions that follow.

—**Voy a mandar** esta carta. ¿Quieres ir?	*I'm going to mail this letter. Do you want to go?*
—Sí. Luego, **¿vas a almorzar?**	*Yes. Then, are you going to have lunch?*
—Sí, **vamos a comer** comida guatemalteca.	*Yes, we are going to eat Guatemalan food.*
—¡Perfecto! **Voy a pedir** unos tamales.	*Perfect! I am going to order some tamales.*
—Pero primero, **¡vamos a ir** al banco!	*But first we are going to the bank!*

¡Explícalo tú!

1. When do the actions in the previous sentences take place: in the *past*, *present*, or *future*?
2. What is the first bold type verb you see in each sentence?
3. In what form is the second bolded verb?
4. What word comes between the two verbs? Does this word have an equivalent in English?
5. What is your rule, then, for expressing future actions or statements?

Check your answers to the preceding questions in Appendix 1.

Now you are ready to complete the ***Preparación y práctica*** activities for this chunk online.

4-19 ¿Y en el futuro? Túrnense para contestar las siguientes preguntas sobre el futuro.

1. ¿Vas a dedicar más tiempo a tus estudios?
2. Después de terminar con tus estudios, ¿vas a vivir en una ciudad, un pueblo pequeño o en el campo?
3. ¿Vas a comprar una casa grande?
4. ¿Tus amigos y tú van a visitar Honduras u otro país en Centroamérica?
5. ¿Van los científicos a encontrar la cura para el cáncer?
6. ¿Vamos a poder acabar con (*end*) el terrorismo?

Capítulo A Para empezar. Los días de la semana, los meses y las estaciones, pág. 21.

4-20 Mi agenda

¿Qué planes tienes para la semana que viene? Termina las siguientes frases sin (*without*) repetir las actividades.

MODELO E1: El lunes…

E2: *El lunes voy a ir al cajero automático.*

1. El lunes…
2. El martes…
3. El miércoles…
4. El jueves…
5. El viernes…
6. El sábado…
7. El domingo…
8. El fin de semana…

4-21 El futuro…

¿Qué tiene el futuro para ti, tus amigos y tu familia? Escribe **cinco** predicciones de lo que va a ocurrir en el futuro.

MODELO *Mi primo va a ir a la Universidad Autónoma el año que viene. Mis padres van a limpiar el armario y el altillo este fin de semana. Yo voy a estudiar en Sudamérica…*

7 VOCABULARIO

Servicios a la comunidad

Imparting information about service opportunities

Al aire libre

trabajar como consejero/a

viajar en canoa

trabajar en el campamento de niños

hacer una hoguera

montar una tienda de campaña

Para el bienestar

trabajar como voluntario/a en la residencia de ancianos

ayudar a las personas mayores/los mayores

hacer artesanía

dar un paseo

repartir comidas

llevar a alguien al médico

ir de excursión

Para la política

participar en una campaña política

apoyar a un/a candidato/a

organizar

circular una petición

Algunos verbos	*Some verbs*
deber	*ought to; should*
ir de camping	*to go camping*
trabajar en política	*to work in politics*

Otras palabras	*Other words*
el deber	*obligation; duty*
el voluntariado	*volunteerism*

Now you are ready to complete the ***Preparación y práctica*** activities for this chunk online.

4-22 Definiciones Túrnense para leer las definiciones y decir cuál de las palabras o expresiones del vocabulario de **Servicios a la comunidad** corresponde a cada una.

MODELO E1: personas que tienen muchos años
E2: *las personas mayores*

1. salir en un bote (*boat*) para una o dos personas
2. dar un documento a personas para obtener firmas (*signatures*)
3. "construir" una estructura portátil (no permanente) que se usa para dormir fuera de casa
4. acompañar a una persona a una cita (*appointment*) con el médico
5. trabajar con niños en un campamento
6. servir a las personas sin recibir dinero a cambio (*in exchange*)
7. disfrutar de (*enjoy*) un tipo de arte que puedes crear con materiales diversos
8. un lugar donde van los niños, en el verano, para hacer muchas actividades diferentes
9. trabajar para un candidato político
10. un lugar donde viven las personas mayores

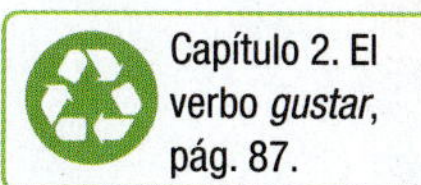
Capítulo 2. El verbo *gustar*, pág. 87.

4-23 En tu opinión... Termina las siguientes oraciones sobre el voluntariado. Después, comparte tus respuestas con un/a compañero/a.

MODELO *Yo soy una consejera perfecta porque me gustan los niños. También sé escuchar muy bien...*

1. Yo (no) soy un/a consejero/a perfecto/a porque...
2. Dos trabajos (*jobs*) voluntarios que me gustan son...
3. Hay muchas residencias de ancianos en los Estados Unidos porque...
4. Yo apoyo al candidato _______ porque...
5. Cuando repartes comidas, puedes...

4-24 Elaborando el tema En grupos de tres o cuatro, discutan las siguientes preguntas.

1. ¿Cuáles son las actividades más interesantes en los campamentos de niños?
2. ¿Cuáles son las oportunidades de voluntariado que existen en tu universidad/iglesia/templo?
3. ¿Cuáles son los trabajos voluntarios que se asocian más con apoyar a un candidato?
4. ¿Crees que servir a la comunidad es un deber y por qué?

La conciencia social

Tanto en los Estados Unidos como en los países hispanohablantes, la gente se interesa cada día más en servir a la comunidad. Su conciencia social se puede manifestar tanto en un trabajo remunerado (*paid*) como en trabajos voluntarios: por ejemplo, ser entrenadores de deportes, llevar a los ancianos a pasear por los centros comerciales, trabajar para los congresistas, etc. En los Estados Unidos muchos trabajos voluntarios tienen que ver con (*are related to*) las personas mayores o con los jóvenes.

Preguntas

1. ¿Cuáles son algunos trabajos voluntarios comunes en los Estados Unidos?
2. ¿Cómo sirves a tu comunidad?

Tanto… como means "as much… as."

8 GRAMÁTICA

Las expresiones afirmativas y negativas

Articulating concepts and ideas both affirmatively and negatively

In the previous chapters, you have seen and used a number of the affirmative and negative expressions listed on the following page. Study the list, and learn the ones that are new to you.

Expresiones afirmativas		Expresiones negativas	
a veces	*sometimes*	**jamás**	*never; not ever* (emphatic)
algo	*something; anything*	**nada**	*nothing*
alguien	*someone*	**nadie**	*no one; nobody*
algún	*some; any*	**ningún**	*none*
alguno/a/os/as	*some; any*	**ninguno/a/os/as**	*none*
o... o	*either... or*	**ni... ni**	*neither... nor*
siempre	*always*	**nunca**	*never*

Look at the following sentences, paying special attention to the position of the negative words, and answer the questions that follow.

—¿Quién llama?	*Who is calling?*
—**Nadie** llama. (**No** llama **nadie**.)	*No one is calling.*
—¿Vas al gimnasio todos los días?	*Do you go to the gym every day?*
—No, **nunca** voy. (No, **no** voy **nunca**.)	*No, I never go.*

Fíjate

Unlike English, Spanish can have two or more negatives in the same sentence. A double negative is actually quite common. For example, *No tengo nada que hacer* means *I don't have anything to do.*

¡Explícalo tú!

1. When you use a negative word (**nadie, nunca,** etc.) in a sentence, does it come before or after the verb?
2. When you use the word **no** and then a negative word in the same sentence, does **no** come before or after the verb? Where does the negative word come in these sentences?
3. Does the meaning change depending on where you put the negative word (e.g., **Nadie llama** *vs.* **No llama nadie**)?

 Check your answers to the preceding questions in Appendix 1.

Algún and *ningún*

1. Forms of **algún** and **ningún** need to agree in gender and number with the nouns they modify.
2. **Alguno** and **ninguno** are shortened to **algún** and **ningún** when they are followed by *masculine, singular nouns*.
3. When no noun follows, use **alguno** or **ninguno** when referring to masculine, singular nouns.
4. The plural form **ningunos** is rarely used.

Study the following sentences.

MARÍA: ¿Tienes **alguna** clase fácil este semestre?
JUAN: No, no tengo **ninguna**. ¡Y **ningún** profesor es simpático!
MARÍA: Vaya (*Wow*), ¿y puedes hacer **algún** cambio (*change*)?
JUAN: No, no puedo hacer **ninguno**. (No, no puedo tomar **ningún** otro curso.)

¿? Now you are ready to complete the ***Preparación y práctica*** activities for this chunk online.

4-25 ¿Con qué frecuencia? Entrevista a tus compañeros/as de clase para saber con qué frecuencia hacen las siguientes actividades. Escribe el nombre de cada compañero/a debajo de la columna apropiada y comparte los resultados con la clase.

MODELO ir de excursión con niños
A veces Josefina va de excursión con niños.

	SIEMPRE	A VECES	NUNCA
1. ir de excursión con niños		Josefina	
2. participar en una campaña política			
3. hacer una hoguera			
4. circular una petición			
5. firmar una petición			
6. repartir comidas a los mayores			
7. visitar una residencia de ancianos			
8. trabajar en un campamento para niños			
9. trabajar como voluntario/a en un hospital o una clínica			
10. dormir en una tienda de campaña			

4-26 El/La profesor/a ideal Túrnense para decir si las siguientes características son ciertas (*true*) o no en un/a profesor/a ideal.

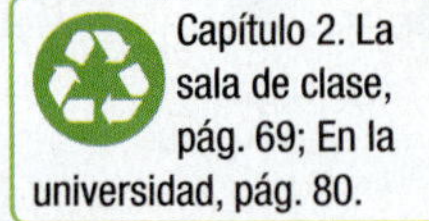

Capítulo 2. La sala de clase, pág. 69; En la universidad, pág. 80.

MODELO E1: a veces duerme en su trabajo
E2: *No. Un profesor ideal nunca duerme en su trabajo.*
E1: jamás va a clase sin sus apuntes
E2: *Sí, un profesor ideal jamás va a clase sin sus apuntes.*

Un/a profesor/a ideal…

1. siempre está contento/a en su trabajo.
2. a veces llega a clase cinco minutos tarde.
3. prepara algo interesante para cada clase.
4. piensa que sabe más que nadie.
5. falta (*misses*) a algunas clases.
6. nunca pone a los estudiantes en grupos.
7. jamás asigna tarea para la clase.
8. siempre prefiere leer sus apuntes.
9. no pierde nada (la tarea, los exámenes, etc.).
10. no habla con nadie después de la clase.

4-27 Siempre/A veces/Nunca Gloria nos habla de sus servicios a la comunidad. Escucha e indica si ella hace los siguientes servicios a la comunidad **siempre, a veces** o **nunca**.

SERVICIO A LA COMUNIDAD	SIEMPRE	A VECES	NUNCA
1. repartir comidas			
2. hacer artesanías			
3. participar en campañas políticas			
4. viajar en canoa y montar una tienda			
5. hacer una hoguera			

4-28 ¿Sí o no? Túrnense para contestar las siguientes preguntas.

MODELO E1: *¿Siempre almuerzas a las cuatro de la tarde?*
E2: *No, nunca almuerzo a las cuatro de la tarde. / No, no almuerzo nunca/jamás a las cuatro de la tarde.*

1. ¿Pierdes algo cuando vas de vacaciones?
2. ¿Siempre encuentras las cosas que pierdes?
3. ¿Siempre montas una tienda de campaña cuando vas de camping?
4. ¿A veces vas de excursión con tus amigos?
5. ¿Prefieres almorzar en un restaurante elegante o en casa?
6. ¿Conoces a alguien de El Salvador?
7. ¿Siempre piensas en el amor (*love*)?
8. ¿Hay algo más importante que el dinero?

4-29 No tienes razón Tu amigo/a es muy idealista. Túrnense para decirle (*tell him/her*) que debe ser más realista, usando expresiones negativas.

MODELO

1. Tengo que buscar una profesión sin estrés.
2. Quiero el carro perfecto.
3. Voy a tener hijos perfectos.
4. Pienso que no voy a estudiar la semana que viene.
5. Voy a encontrar unos muebles muy baratos (*cheap*) y elegantes.

9 GRAMÁTICA

Un repaso de *ser* y *estar*

Describing states of being, characteristics, and location

You have learned two Spanish verbs that mean ***to be*** in English. These verbs, **ser** and **estar,** are contrasted here.

Ser

Ser is used:

- **To describe physical or personality characteristics that remain relatively constant**

Gregorio **es** inteligente.	*Gregorio is intelligent.*
Yanina **es** guapa.	*Yanina is pretty.*
Su tienda de campaña **es** amarilla.	*Their tent is yellow.*
Las casas **son** grandes.	*The houses are large.*

- **To explain what or who someone or something is**

El Dr. Suárez **es** profesor de literatura.	*Dr. Suárez is a literature professor.*
Marisol **es** mi hermana.	*Marisol is my sister.*

- **To tell time, or to tell when or where an event takes place**

¿Qué hora **es**?	*What time is it?*
Son las ocho.	*It's eight o'clock.*
Mi clase de español **es** a las ocho y **es** en Peabody Hall.	*My Spanish class is at eight o'clock and is in Peabody Hall.*

- **To tell where someone is from and to express nationality**

Somos de Honduras.	*We are from Honduras.*
Somos hondureños.	*We are Honduran.*
Ellos **son** de Guatemala.	*They are from Guatemala.*
Son guatemaltecos.	*They are Guatemalan.*

Estar

Estar is used:

- **To describe physical or personality characteristics that can change, or to indicate a change in condition**

María **está** enferma hoy.	*María is sick today.*
Jorge y Julia **están** tristes.	*Jorge and Julia are sad.*
La cocina **está** sucia.	*The kitchen is dirty.*

- **To describe the locations of people, places, and things**

El museo **está** en la calle Quiroga.	*The museum is on Quiroga Street.*
Estamos en el centro comercial.	*We're at the mall.*
¿Dónde **estás** tú?	*Where are you?*

¡Explícalo tú!

Compare the following sentences and answer the questions that follow.

Su hermano **es** simpático.

Su hermano **está** enfermo.

1. Why do you use a form of **ser** in the first sentence?
2. Why do you use a form of **estar** in the second sentence?

 Check your answers to the preceding questions in Appendix 1.

Estrategia

Review the forms of *ser* (p. 13) and *estar* (p. 83).

You will learn several more uses for **ser** and **estar** by the end of ***¡Anda! Curso elemental.***

¿? Now you are ready to complete the ***Preparación y práctica*** activities for this chunk online.

4-30 ¿Y Margarita?

Ester y Margarita son estudiantes de la Universidad Francisco Marroquín en la ciudad de Guatemala. Ellas tienen clase ahora, pero Margarita no llega. Completen juntos el siguiente párrafo con las formas correctas de **ser** o **estar** para saber qué pasó.

Paso 1

(1) __________ las siete y media de la mañana. Nuestra clase de física (2) __________ a las ocho y siempre vamos juntas. Bueno, ¿dónde (3) __________ Margarita? Es raro porque ella (4) __________ muy puntual y no le gusta llegar tarde. Yo (5) __________ su mejor amiga y sé que (6) __________ preocupada por sus abuelos.

Ellos (7) __________ mayores y a veces (8) __________ enfermos. Margarita (9) __________ muy responsable y ayuda mucho a sus abuelos. Toda su familia (10) __________ de la ciudad de Antigua y siempre piensa en ellos. Aquí viene Margarita, ¡menos mal (*thank goodness*)!

Paso 2 Expliquen por qué usaron (*you used*) **ser** o **estar** en **Paso 1**.

MODELO 1. (*Son*) telling time

4-31 Nuestro conocimiento

¿Qué sabes de Guatemala, Honduras y El Salvador? Túrnense para hacer y contestar las siguientes preguntas.

1. ¿Dónde están estos países: en Norteamérica, Centroamérica o Sudamérica?
2. ¿Cuál está más cerca de México? ¿Cuál está más cerca de Panamá?
3. ¿Son países grandes o pequeños?
4. ¿Cuáles son sus capitales?

4-32 ¡A jugar!

Vamos a practicar **ser** y **estar**. Completa los siguientes pasos.

Paso 1 Draw two columns on a piece of paper labeling one **ser** and the other **estar**. Write as many sentences as you can in the three minutes you are given.

Paso 2 Form groups of four to check your sentences and uses of the verbs.

4-33 Somos iguales

Completa los siguientes pasos.

Paso 1 Draw **three** circles, as per the model below, and ask each other questions to find out what things you have in common and what sets you apart. In the center circle write sentences using **ser** and **estar** about things you have in common, and in the side circles write sentences about things that set you apart.

MODELO E1: *¿Cuál es tu color favorito?*
E2: *Mi color favorito es el negro.*
E1: *Mi color favorito es el negro también.*
E2: *Hoy estoy nerviosa. ¿Cómo estás tú?*
E1: *Yo estoy cansado.*

Paso 2 Share your diagrams with the class. What are some of the things that all of your classmates have in common?

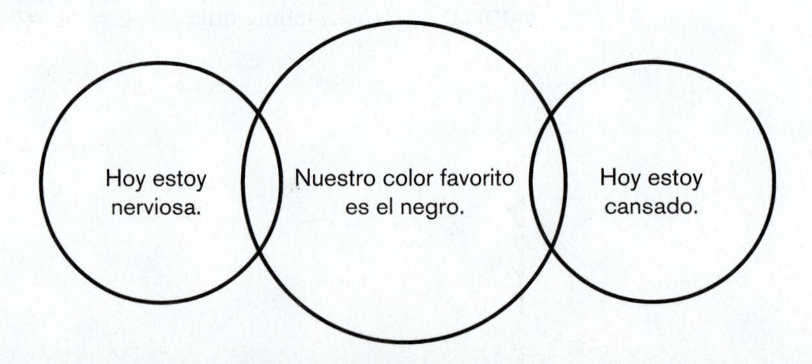

Escucha

El voluntariado

Estrategia

Paraphrasing what you hear

When you know the context and listen carefully, you can repeat or paraphrase what you hear. Start by saying one or two words about what you hear and work up to complete sentences.

4-34 Antes de escuchar Do you volunteer? What service opportunities exist in your city/town? You are going to hear a conversation between Marisol and Lupe, in which Marisol shares her experiences with volunteering. Think of three Spanish words dealing with volunteering that you might hear.

4-35 A escuchar After listening to the conversation for the first time, note three main points, words, or topics. After listening a second time, paraphrase their conversation with at least **three** complete sentences. You may use the following questions to guide your listening.

1. ¿Quién hace trabajo voluntario?
2. ¿Qué trabajo hace ella en la escuela? ¿Qué más quiere hacer?
3. ¿Adónde va a ir mañana? ¿Con quién?

4-36 Después de escuchar Form **three** sentences about your volunteering experiences, and tell them to your classmate. Your classmate will paraphrase what you have said.

¡Conversemos!

4-37 Mi comunidad You and a partner are on the planning commission of your town. Take turns sharing your ideas with the other commissioners, stating at least **five** positive aspects of your town and **five** areas that could be improved. You should also respond to your partner's ideas, agreeing or disagreeing. Use vocabulary words from *Los lugares,* on page 142, and verbs from page 148, *Actividades y acciones cotidianas.*

4-38 Servicio a nuestra comunidad Your college has a community service component, and you are a coordinator for these services. With a partner, take turns describing the opportunities available to fellow students in your town(s) or school community. Create at least **ten** sentences using the vocabulary from *Servicios a la comunidad* on page 158.

Escribe

Una tarjeta postal (*A postcard*)

Estrategia

Proofreading

It is important to always carefully read over what you have written to check for meaning and accuracy. You want to minimally:

- verify spelling.
- check all verb forms.
- confirm that subjects and verbs, as well as nouns and adjectives, agree in number and gender.
- review for appropriate meaning.

4-39 **Antes de escribir** Escribe una lista de los lugares importantes o interesantes de tu pueblo o ciudad. Luego escribe por qué son importantes o interesantes. Usa el vocabulario de este capítulo y de **También se dice**… en el Apéndice (*Appendix*) 3.

4-40 **A escribir** Organiza tus ideas usando las siguientes preguntas como guía. Escribe por lo menos **cinco** oraciones completas. Puedes consultar el modelo.

1. ¿Qué lugares hay en tu pueblo o ciudad?
2. ¿Por qué son importantes o interesantes?
3. Normalmente, ¿qué haces allí?
4. ¿Adónde vas los fines de semana?
5. ¿Qué te gusta de tu pueblo?

Querido/a ___________:

Tienes que conocer mi pueblo, Roxborough. Hay __________. Me gusta(n) ___________. Es interesante porque ________. Los fines de semana ________________.

Con cariño,
(Tu nombre)

4-41 **Después de escribir** Tu profesor/a va a recoger las tarjetas y "mandárselas" (*mail them*) a otros miembros de la clase para leerlas. Luego, la clase tiene que escoger (*to choose*) los lugares que desean visitar.

¿Cómo andas? II

Having completed **Comunicación II**, I now can…	Feel confident	Need to review
• share where I and others are going. (p. 154)	☐	☐
• convey what will happen in the future. (p. 156)	☐	☐
• impart information about service opportunities. (p. 158)	☐	☐
• discuss the concept of social consciousness. (p. 160)	☐	☐
• articulate concepts and ideas both affirmatively and negatively. (p. 160)	☐	☐
• describe states of being, characteristics, and location. (p. 164)	☐	☐
• paraphrase what I hear. (p. 167)	☐	☐
• communicate about ways to serve the community. (p. 168)	☐	☐
• write a postcard and proofread it for accuracy. (p. 169)	☐	☐

Vistazo cultural

Honduras

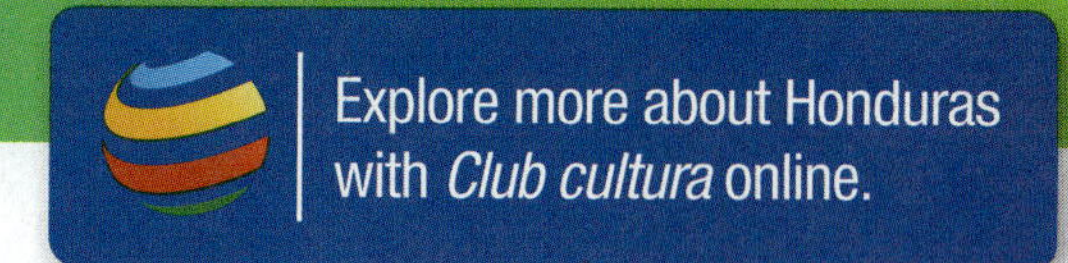

 Les presento mi país

César Alfonso Ávalos

Mi nombre es César Alfonso Ávalos y soy de La Ceiba, Honduras, una ciudad en el Mar Caribe. Mi lugar favorito para visitar es Utila, una isla bella (*beautiful*) y bien conocida en el mundo por el buceo (*scuba diving*). **¿Te gusta bucear?** Mi país tiene una diversidad cultural muy rica. Los garífunas son una comunidad de herencia africana e indígena que vive en la costa caribeña del país. También, los mayas y los lencas son grupos indígenas con mucha presencia. En Copán tenemos las ruinas mayas más importantes. **¿Hay ruinas importantes cerca de tu pueblo?**

La playa de Utila, Islas de la Bahía

Los garífunas preservan su cultura, música y lengua hoy en día.

Las ruinas de Copán

ALMANAQUE

Nombre oficial:	República de Honduras
Gobierno:	República democrática constitucional
Población:	7.989.415 (2010)
Idiomas:	español (oficial); miskito, garífuna, otros dialectos amerindios
Moneda:	Lempira (L)

¿Sabías que...?

- Al llegar a la costa norteña, Cristóbal Colón nombra la región *Honduras* a causa de la profundidad del agua en la bahía.
- Honduras tiene una diversidad de vida animal impresionante: en sus bosques viven más de 210 especies de mamíferos, más de 95 especies de anfibios y 715 especies de pájaros tropicales.

Preguntas

1. ¿Qué significa *Honduras*? ¿De dónde viene el nombre?
2. ¿Quiénes son los garífunas? ¿Dónde viven?
3. ¿Qué semejanzas (*similarities*) hay entre Honduras y México?

Vistazo cultural

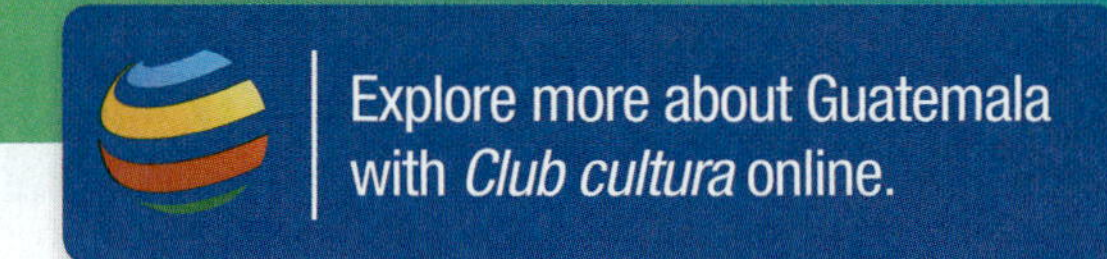

Guatemala

Les presento mi país

Luis Pedro Aguirre Maldonado

Mi nombre es Luis Pedro Aguirre Maldonado y soy de Antigua, Guatemala. Muchas personas vienen a mi ciudad para estudiar en nuestras excelentes escuelas de lengua española. **¿Visitan muchas personas tu ciudad o pueblo?** Mi país es montañoso (*mountainous*) con muchos volcanes, como el Pacaya y el gran Tajumulco. Además, es muy fácil conocer la cultura y arquitectura maya aquí. Tenemos varios sitios arqueológicos mayas como las ruinas de Tikal en el norte, y algunas de nuestras pirámides son las más altas de las Américas. **¿En qué otros lugares encuentras pirámides?**

Muchos descendientes de los mayas conservan sus lenguas y tradiciones.

El volcán de Pacaya está en constante erupción y es uno de los más visitados por turistas de todo el mundo.

Antigua, la primera capital de Guatemala

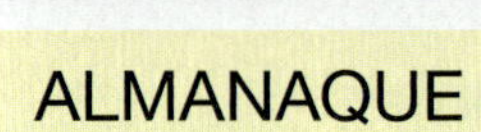

ALMANAQUE

Nombre oficial:	República de Guatemala
Gobierno:	República democrática constitucional
Población:	13.550.440 (2010)
Idioma:	español (oficial); idiomas amerindios (23 reconocidos oficialmente)
Moneda:	Quetzal (Q)

¿Sabías que...?

- Los mayas tienen un calendario civil, *El Haab*. Consiste en 18 "meses" de 20 días cada uno. Los últimos cinco días del año, conocidos como *el Wayeb*, se consideran de muy mala suerte.
- El volcán Tajumulco es el más alto de Centroamérica y la montaña más alta de Guatemala.

Preguntas

1. Nombra dos cosas que sabes de la geografía guatemalteca.
2. ¿Cuántos idiomas se hablan en Guatemala?
3. ¿Qué otros países tienen herencia maya?

Vistazo cultural

El Salvador

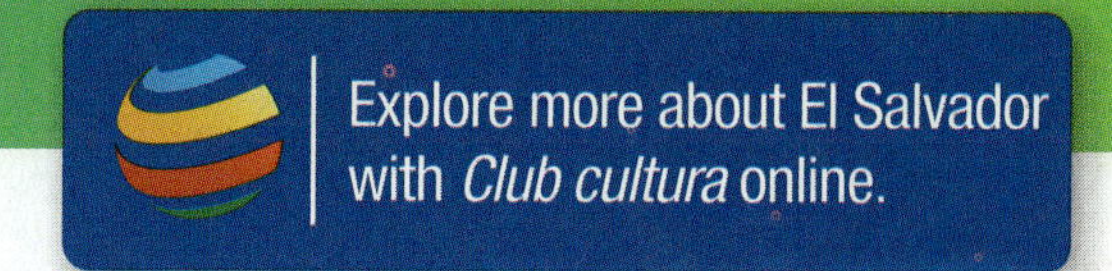

Les presento mi país

Claudia Figueroa Barrios

Mi nombre es Claudia Figueroa Barrios. Soy de La Libertad, al sur de nuestra capital San Salvador. Mi ciudad está en la costa del Pacífico donde hay muchas playas buenas para practicar los deportes acuáticos, como el buceo, el snorkeling y especialmente el surf. **¿Te gustan los deportes acuáticos?** El Salvador es el único país de Centroamérica que no tiene costa caribeña. En mi casa nos gusta mucho la comida típica salvadoreña, como los mariscos (*shellfish*) frescos o las pupusas. **¿Cuál es tu comida favorita?**

Las pupusas son la comida nacional de El Salvador.

En la antigüedad, los mayas usaron (*used*) granos de cacao como dinero.

Las playas salvadoreñas son unas de las mejores del mundo para hacer surf.

ALMANAQUE

Nombre oficial:	República de El Salvador
Gobierno:	República democrática constitucional
Población:	6.052.064 (2010)
Idiomas:	español (oficial)
Moneda:	Dólar estadounidense

¿Sabías que...?

- Algunos salvadoreños, sobre todo los que viven en las partes rurales del país, van a los curanderos (*folk healers*) para buscar ayuda médica.

Preguntas

1. ¿Qué importancia tiene el cacao en la historia maya?
2. ¿Qué deportes son populares en El Salvador? ¿Por qué?
3. ¿Qué cosas de El Salvador son únicas o diferentes a las de otros países hispanos?

Lectura

Trabajo voluntario en Honduras

4-42 Antes de leer Contesta las siguientes preguntas.

1. ¿Hay parques nacionales en donde vives?
2. ¿Qué servicios a la comunidad tiene tu ciudad?

Estrategia

Skimming and Scanning (II)

Continue to practice focusing on main ideas and important information. Remember, when you *skim* a passage you read quickly to get the gist of the passage. When you *scan* a passage you already know what you need to find out, so you concentrate on searching for that particular information.

4-43 Mientras lees Complete the following steps.

1. *Skim* the first paragraph, looking for the answers to the following questions.
   a. What is the paragraph about?
   b. Which of the following best describes the purpose of the program?
      Protection of wildlife
      Following international laws
      Eliminate sales of exotic animals
2. Now *scan* the reading, looking for the following information:
   a. What can people study through this program?
   b. Where can they live in the park?
   c. What is the closest city to the park?

El Parque Nacional Pico Bonito necesita voluntarios

El parque

Pico Bonito es un gran parque que empieza a nivel del mar° y va hasta los 7.500 pies de alto. Está en La Ceiba, la ciudad principal del ecoturismo en Honduras. Al parque llegan animales salvajes° que vienen de los traficantes ilegales de animales exóticos. El centro es una colaboración entre Estados Unidos y Honduras para proteger a estos animales. Estos dos países tienen un acuerdo° en el que es ilegal capturar y comercializar animales salvajes.

El parque es un centro de rehabilitación de aves°. Después de su recuperación, el centro los libera en su hábitat natural. El centro tiene un gran problema financiero, es decir, siempre necesita dinero para ayudar a los animales. Por eso prefieren ofrecer un programa de voluntariado nacional e internacional.

Programa de voluntarios

El programa está diseñado para estudiantes que quieren aprender español y a quienes les interesa la rehabilitación de animales.

El programa puede ser de una a cuatro semanas y cuesta aproximadamente 800 dólares por semana. Los estudiantes siguen un horario estricto. Por la mañana toman clases de español y ciencias durante 55 minutos. Después de las clases, los estudiantes salen al parque a explorar y a ayudar a limpiar el parque, estudiar la naturaleza, tomar notas y catalogar a los animales salvajes. Por la tarde organizan sus notas y las ponen en el banco de datos del centro.

Incluido en el precio

Los estudiantes de voluntariado viven en una cabaña central en el parque y reciben tres comidas al día. El precio también incluye el transporte de La Ceiba al parque, un examen de nivel de español, seguro médico, el certificado de realización de curso° y una o dos actividades organizadas.

sea level

wild life

agreement

birds

course completion

4-44 Después de leer

Contesta las siguientes preguntas.

1. ¿Qué tipo de parque es?
2. ¿Qué servicios ofrece el parque?
3. ¿Qué ofrece el parque para financiar su programa?
4. ¿Cuánto cuesta el programa? Además de (*Besides*) la residencia y la comida, ¿qué incluye el precio?
5. ¿Participas en servicios a la comunidad? ¿Cuáles? Si no lo haces, ¿por qué no?

Fíjate

In the *Escribe* section of this chapter, you learned how to open and close an informal message. In more formal writing, such as a letter or e-mail, use *Estimado/a____:* (Dear) to address the person at the beginning and *Atentamente* (Sincerely) to close your message.

4-45 Voluntarios en Pico Bonito

Quieres solicitar (*to apply*) entrar al programa de voluntarios del Parque Nacional Pico Bonito. Escríbele un e-mail al director del programa para expresar tu interés. Explica por qué quieres trabajar con ellos y cuáles son los aspectos del programa que consideras más interesantes. También debes hacer una o dos preguntas adicionales sobre el trabajo o los cursos.

4-46 En el campamento de niños

Vas a trabajar en un campamento de niños en el verano. Después de la entrevista de trabajo envías (*you send*) un mensaje a tu familia. En este mensaje describes en detalle qué vas a hacer en el campamento de niños.

For additional *Lectura* activities, go to *¡Anda!* online.

Y por fin, ¿cómo andas?

Having completed this chapter, I now can...	Feel confident	Need to review
Comunicación I		
• identify places in and around town. (p. 142)	☐	☐
• pronounce the letters *c* and *z*. (p. 143 and online)	☐	☐
• state whom and what is known. (p. 146)	☐	☐
• relate common everyday activities and occurrences. (p. 148)	☐	☐
• express actions. (p. 150)	☐	☐
Comunicación II		
• share where I and others are going. (p. 154)	☐	☐
• convey what will happen in the future. (p. 156)	☐	☐
• impart information about service opportunities. (p. 158)	☐	☐
• articulate concepts and ideas both affirmatively and negatively. (p. 160)	☐	☐
• describe states of being, characteristics, and location. (p. 164)	☐	☐
• paraphrase what I hear. (p. 167)	☐	☐
• communicate about ways to serve the community. (p. 168)	☐	☐
• write a postcard and proofread it for accuracy. (p. 169)	☐	☐
Cultura		
• describe shopping and other daily activities. (p. 145)	☐	☐
• discuss the concept of social consciousness. (p. 160)	☐	☐
• share information about Honduras, Guatemala, and El Salvador. (pp. 171–173)	☐	☐
Lectura		
• read a brochure for volunteer work in Honduras. (p. 174)	☐	☐
Comunidades		
• use Spanish in real-life contexts. (online)	☐	☐

Vocabulario **activo** 

Los lugares	*Places*
el almacén	*department store*
el banco	*bank*
el bar; el club	*bar; club*
el café	*café*
el cajero automático	*ATM machine*
el centro	*downtown*
el centro comercial	*mall; business/shopping district*
el cibercafé	*Internet café*
el cine	*movie theater*
la iglesia	*church*
el mercado	*market*
el museo	*museum*
la oficina de correos; correos	*post office*
el parque	*park*
la plaza	*town square*
el restaurante	*restaurant*
el supermercado	*supermarket*
el teatro	*theater*
el templo	*temple*

Algunos verbos	*Some verbs*
buscar	*to look for*
ir	*to go*
mandar una carta	*to send/mail a letter*
saber	*to know*

Otras palabras	*Other words*
la ciudad	*city*
la cuenta	*bill; account*
la película	*movie; film*
el pueblo	*town; village*

Actividades y acciones cotidianas	*Common everyday activities and occurrences*
(Verbos con cambio de raíz)	*(Stem-changing verbs)*
almorzar (ue)	*to have lunch*
cerrar (ie)	*to close*
comenzar (ie)	*to begin*
costar (ue)	*to cost*
demostrar (ue)	*to demonstrate*
devolver (ue)	*to return (an object)*
dormir (ue)	*to sleep*
empezar (ie)	*to begin*
encerrar (ie)	*to enclose*
encontrar (ue)	*to find*
entender (ie)	*to understand*
jugar (ue)	*to play*
mentir (ie)	*to lie*
morir (ue)	*to die*
mostrar (ue)	*to show*
pedir (i)	*to ask for*
pensar (ie)	*to think*
perder (ie)	*to lose; to waste*
perseguir (i)	*to chase*
preferir (ie)	*to prefer*
recomendar (ie)	*to recommend*
recordar (ue)	*to remember*
repetir (i)	*to repeat*
seguir (i)	*to follow; to continue (doing something)*
servir (i)	*to serve*
volver (ue)	*to return*

Servicios a la comunidad	*Community service*
apoyar a un/a candidato/a	*to support a candidate*
ayudar a las personas mayores/los mayores	*to help elderly people*
circular una petición	*to circulate a petition*
dar un paseo	*to go for a walk*
deber	*ought to; should*
el deber	*obligation; duty*
hacer artesanía	*to make arts and crafts*
hacer una hoguera	*to light a campfire*
ir de camping	*to go camping*
ir de excursión	*to take a short trip*
llevar a alguien al médico	*to take someone to the doctor*
montar una tienda de campaña	*to put up a tent*
organizar	*to organize*
participar en una campaña política	*to participate in a political campaign*
repartir comidas	*to hand out/deliver food*
trabajar como consejero/a	*to work as a counselor*
trabajar como voluntario/a en la residencia de ancianos	*to volunteer at a nursing home*
trabajar en el campamento de niños	*to work in a summer camp*
trabajar en política	*to work in politics*
viajar en canoa	*to canoe*
el voluntariado	*volunteerism*

Expresiones afirmativas y negativas	*Affirmative and negative expressions*
a veces	*sometimes*
algo	*something; anything*
alguien	*someone*
algún	*some; any*
alguno/a/os/as	*some; any*
o… o	*either… or*
siempre	*always*
jamás	*never; not ever* (emphatic)
nada	*nothing*
nadie	*no one; nobody*
ni… ni	*neither… nor*
ningún	*none*
ninguno/a/os/as	*none*
nunca	*never*

El conductor Gustavo Dudamel de Venezuela

5 ¡A divertirse!

En el mundo hispanohablante la gente trabaja pero también sabe divertirse (*enjoy themselves*). La música, el baile y el cine son formas de expresión y de distracción comunes. Estos pasatiempos, además de otros como los deportes o leer un buen libro, nos hacen la vida muy agradable. Sobre todo (*Above all*), es importante buscar maneras de relajarse y aliviar el estrés.

Preguntas

1. ¿Qué haces cuando no estudias? ¿Qué hacen tus amigos y tú para relajarse y aliviar el estrés?
2. ¿Vas a conciertos, obras de teatro (*plays*) o películas (*movies*) con frecuencia? ¿Participas en producciones en la universidad?
3. ¿Qué sabes de la música hispana?

¿Sabías que...?

Los Goyas son los premios (*awards*) cinematográficos más importantes del mundo hispano.

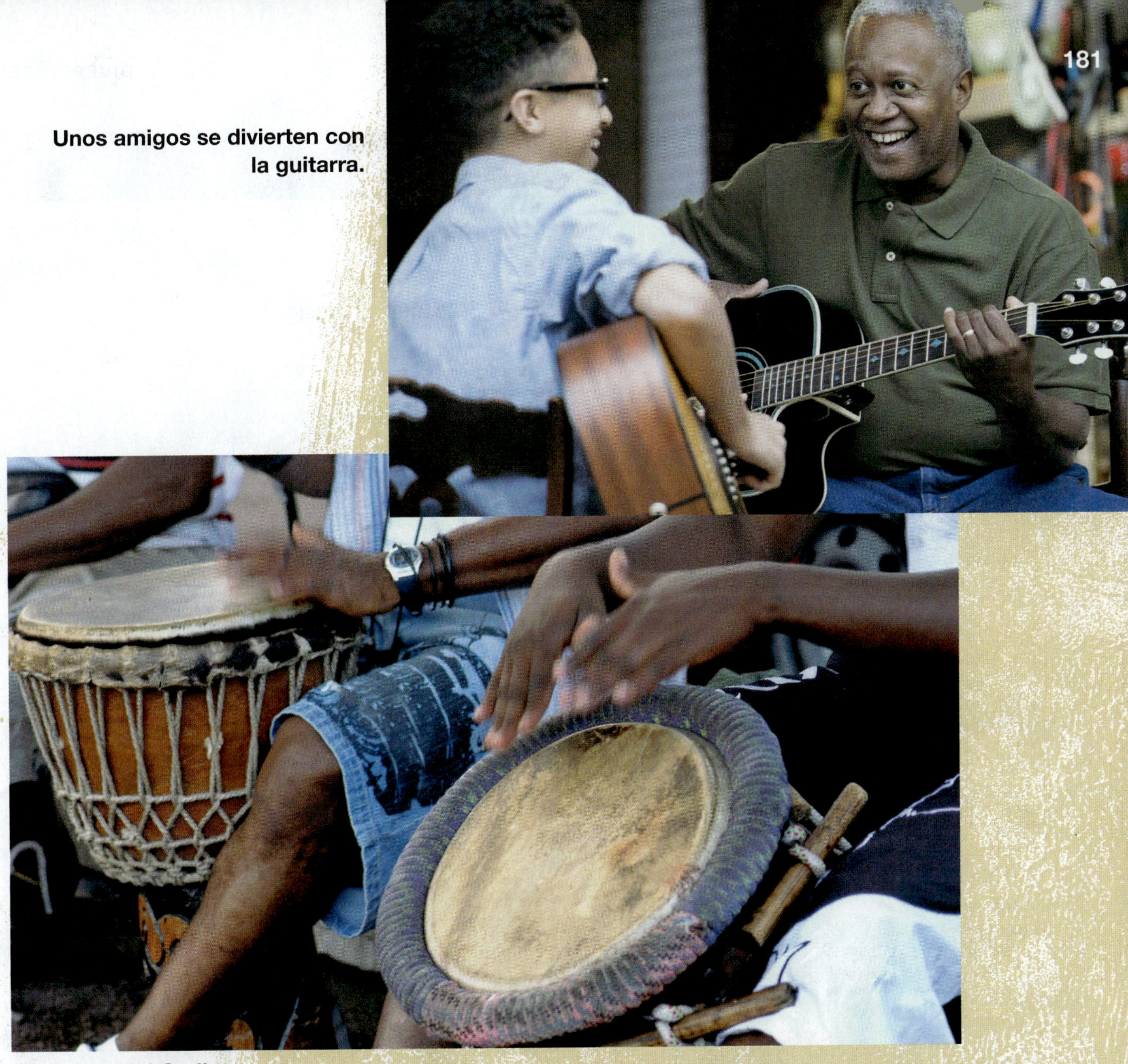

Unos amigos se divierten con la guitarra.

Tambores del Caribe

Learning Outcomes

By the end of this chapter, you will be able to:

- ✔ share information about music, movies, and television programs.
- ✔ identify people and things, and express *what* or *whom*.
- ✔ explain how something is done.
- ✔ describe things that happened in the past.
- ✔ write a movie review.
- ✔ exchange interesting facts about Nicaragua, Costa Rica, and Panama.
- ✔ read a cultural events guide.

Comunicación I

1 VOCABULARIO

El mundo de la música Discussing music

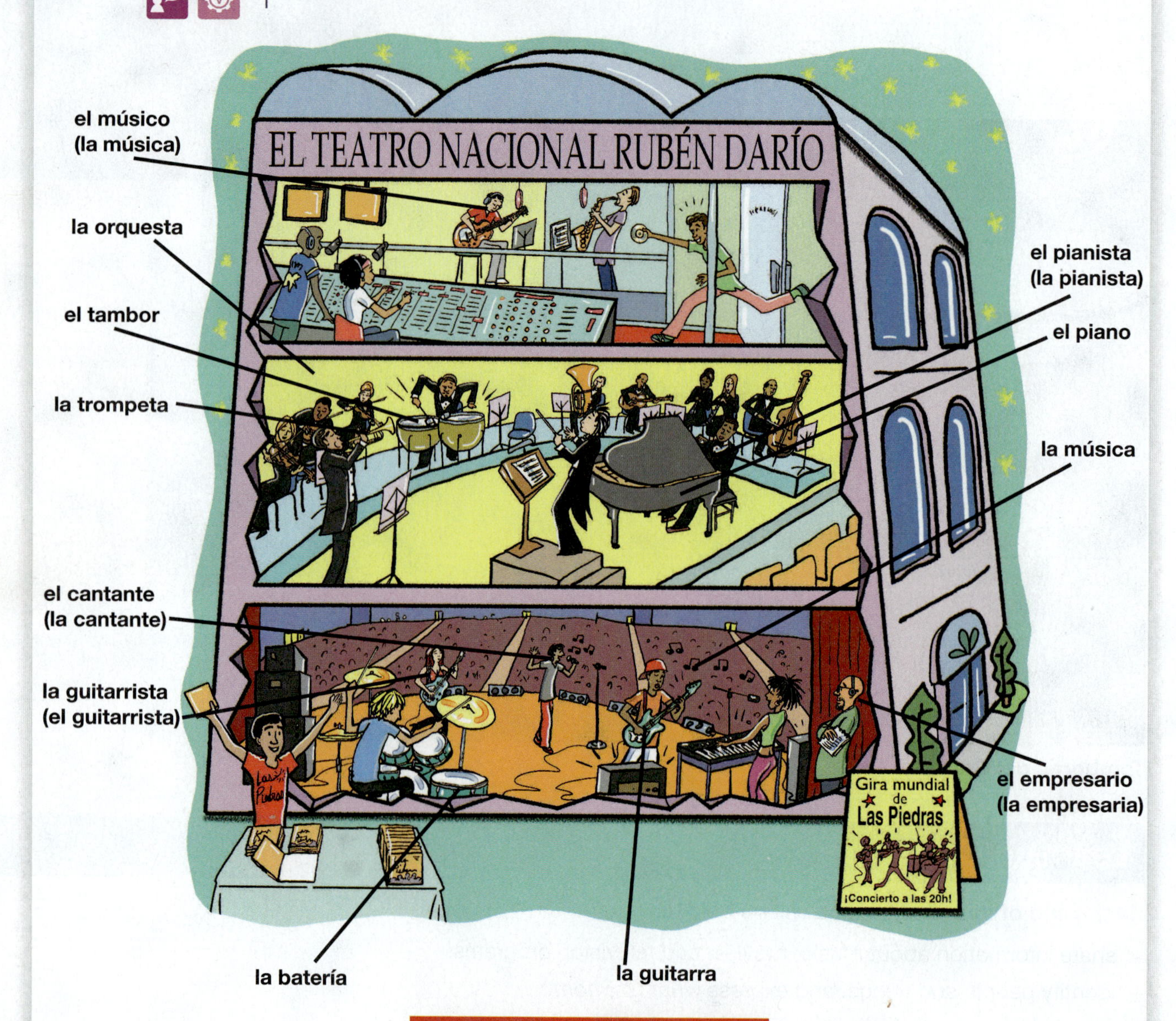

Estrategia

Have you noticed how the Spanish word for an instrument (*guitarra, piano*) is changed to become the word for the musician who plays that instrument (*guitarrista, pianista*)? With that in mind, how would you say *drummer*? *Trumpeter*?

Algunos géneros musicales	Some musical genres
el jazz	*jazz*
la música clásica	*classical music*
la música folklórica	*folk music*
la música popular	*pop music*
la música rap	*rap music*
la ópera	*opera*
el rock	*rock*
la salsa	*salsa*

Algunos verbos	Some verbs
cantar	*to sing*
dar un concierto	*to give / perform a concert*
ensayar	*to practice / rehearse*
grabar	*to record*
hacer una gira	*to tour*
sacar una canción	*to release a song*

Algunos adjetivos	Some adjectives
apasionado/a	*passionate*
fino/a	*fine; delicate*
lento/a	*slow*
suave	*smooth*

Otras palabras	Other words
el/la aficionado/a	*fan*
el/la artista	*artist*
el concierto	*concert*
el conjunto	*group; band*
la fama	*fame*
el género	*genre*
la gira	*tour*
la habilidad	*ability; skill*
la letra	*lyrics*
el ritmo	*rhythm*
la voz	*voice*

¿? Now you are ready to complete the ***Preparación y práctica*** activities for this chunk online.

PRONUNCIACIÓN

Diphthongs and linking

Go to *¡Anda!* online to learn about diphthongs and linking.

5-1 Dibujemos Escuchen mientras su profesor/a les da (*gives you*) las instrucciones de esta actividad.

5-2 Listas

Túrnense con un/a compañero/a para decir y escribir todas las palabras del vocabulario nuevo que recuerden (*you both remember*) de las categorías en el modelo. ¿Cuántas palabras pueden recordar?

MODELO

PERSONAS	TIPOS DE MÚSICA	INSTRUMENTOS	ADJETIVOS	VERBOS

5-3 Para conocerte mejor

Hazle las siguientes preguntas a un/a compañero/a. Toma apuntes y luego comparte las respuestas con otros dos compañeros.

1. ¿Con qué frecuencia vas a conciertos?
2. ¿Qué género de música prefieres?
3. ¿Cuál es tu grupo favorito?
4. ¿Cuál es tu cantante favorito/a? ¿Cómo es su voz?
5. ¿Qué instrumento te gusta?
6. ¿Cuál es tu canción favorita?
7. ¿Sabes tocar un instrumento? ¿Cuál?
8. ¿Sabes cantar bien? ¿Te gusta cantar? ¿Cuándo y dónde cantas?
9. ¿En qué tienes mucha habilidad o talento?
10. ¿Conoces algún conjunto o cantante hispano? ¿Cuál?

Fíjate

For a list of additional instruments, refer to *También se dice*.

Estrategia

When reporting your information, make complete sentences, and remember to use the *él* or *ella* form of the verb. Also, simply refer to your notes; do not read from them. This technique will help you to speak more fluidly and will help you speak in paragraphs, an important skill to perfect when learning a language.

5-4 Los famosos Completa los siguientes pasos.

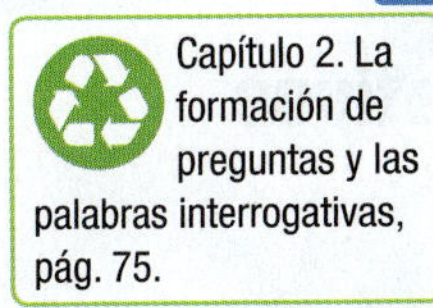
Capítulo 2. La formación de preguntas y las palabras interrogativas, pág. 75.

Paso 1 Como reportero/a de la revista *Rolling Stone* tienes la oportunidad de entrevistar a los hermanos Mejía, dos músicos populares de Nicaragua. Escribe por lo menos **cinco** preguntas que vas a hacerles.

Fíjate

Remember that if you are interviewing people whom you don't know, use the *usted/ustedes* form.

Paso 2 Haz una investigación en Internet para ver si puedes descubrir las respuestas a tus preguntas y para escuchar la música de Luis Enrique y Ramón Mejía. Después, comparte tus resultados y tu opinión con la clase; diles (*tell them*) qué canción te gusta más y por qué.

5-5 ¿Cierto o falso? Paco y Lucía son muy buenos amigos. Escucha mientras ellos hablan de un concierto de Juanes. Después, indica si las oraciones son ciertas (**C**) o falsas (**F**).

C	F	
☐	☐	1. El concierto de Juanes es el sábado a las tres de la tarde.
☐	☐	2. El concierto es en el teatro de la universidad.
☐	☐	3. Paco tiene una entrada (*ticket*) extra.
☐	☐	4. Lucía quiere ir aunque (*even though*) no le gustan mucho las canciones de Juanes.
☐	☐	5. Paco prefiere la música rap.
☐	☐	6. El primo de Lucía conoce a Pitbull personalmente.
☐	☐	7. Paco dice que Pitbull es un hombre muy simpático.
☐	☐	8. Lucía no puede ir al concierto porque tiene que trabajar.

2 GRAMÁTICA

Los adjetivos y los pronombres demostrativos

Identifying people and things

Los adjetivos demostrativos

When you want to point out a specific person, place, thing, or idea, you use a ***demonstrative adjective***. In Spanish, they are:

DEMONSTRATIVE ADJECTIVES	MEANING	FROM THE PERSPECTIVE OF THE SPEAKER, IT REFERS TO...
este, esta, estos, estas	*this, these*	something nearby
ese, esa, esos, esas	*that, those over there*	something farther away
aquel, aquella, aquellos, aquellas	*that, those (way) over there*	something even farther away in distance and/or time... perhaps not even visible

Since forms of **este, ese,** and **aquel** are adjectives, they must agree in gender and number with the nouns they modify. Note the following examples.

Este conjunto es fantástico. — *This group is fantastic.*
Esta orquesta es fenomenal. — *This orchestra is phenomenal.*
Estos conjuntos son fantásticos. — *These groups are fantastic.*
Estas orquestas son fenomenales. — *These orchestras are phenomenal.*

Ese conjunto es fantástico. — *That group is fantastic.*
Esa orquesta es fenomenal. — *That orchestra is phenomenal.*
Esos conjuntos son fantásticos. — *Those groups are fantastic.*
Esas orquestas son fenomenales. — *Those orchestras are phenomenal.*

Aquel conjunto es fantástico. — *That group (over there) is fantastic.*
Aquella orquesta es fenomenal. — *That orchestra (over there) is phenomenal.*
Aquellos conjuntos son fantásticos. — *Those groups (over there) are fantastic.*
Aquellas orquestas son fenomenales. — *Those orchestras (over there) are phenomenal.*

¡Explícalo tú!

In summary:

1. When do you use **este, ese,** and **aquel**?
2. When do you use **esta, esa,** and **aquella**?
3. When do you use **estos, esos,** and **aquellos**?
4. When do you use **estas, esas,** and **aquellas**?

 Check your answers to the preceding questions in Appendix 1.

Los pronombres demostrativos

Demonstrative pronouns take the place of nouns. They are identical in form and meaning to demonstrative adjectives.

Masculino	**Femenino**	***Meaning***
este	**esta**	*this one*
estos	**estas**	*these*
ese	**esa**	*that one*
esos	**esas**	*those*
aquel	**aquella**	*that one (way over there/not visible)*
aquellos	**aquellas**	*those (way over there/not visible)*

A demonstrative pronoun must agree in gender and number with the noun it replaces. Observe how demonstrative adjectives and demonstrative pronouns are used in the following sentences.

Yo quiero ir a **este concierto,** pero mi hermana quiere ir a **ese.**

I want to go to this concert, but my sister wants to go to that one.

—¿Te gusta **esa guitarra**?
—No, a mí me gusta **esta.**

Do you like that guitar?
No, I like this one.

Estos instrumentos son interesantes, pero prefiero tocar **esos.**

These instruments are interesting, but I prefer to play those.

En **esta** calle hay varios cines.
¿Quieres ir a **aquel**?

There are several movie theaters on this street. Do you want to go to that one over there?

Now you are ready to complete the ***Preparación y práctica*** activities for this chunk online.

5-6 En el centro estudiantil

Completen el diálogo de Lola y Tina con las formas correctas de **este, ese** y **aquel**.

LOLA: Tina, mira (1) __________ (*those*) estudiantes que acaban de (*have just*) entrar.

TINA: ¿Cuál de (2) __________ (*those*)? Creo que conozco a (3) __________ (*that*) hombre alto. Es guitarrista del trío de jazz Ritmos.

LOLA: Tienes razón. Y (4) __________ (*this*) mujer rubia es pianista en la orquesta de la universidad.

TINA: ¿Quiénes son (5) __________ (*those*) dos mujeres morenas (*dark-haired*)?

LOLA: Están en nuestra clase de química. ¿No las conoces? Y (6) __________ (*those, over there*) dos hombres de las camisas rojas ¡son muy guapos!

5-7 Amiga, tienes razón

Tu amigo/a te da su opinión y tú respondes con una opinión similar. Túrnense para dar la opinión (usando el adjetivo demostrativo) y para responder (usando el pronombre demostrativo). Sigue el modelo.

MODELO E1 (EL/LA AMIGO/A): Esta música es muy suave.
E2 (TÚ): *Sí, y esa es suave también.*

1. Este grupo es fenomenal.
2. Estos cantantes son muy jóvenes.
3. Esta gira empieza en enero.
4. Esta canción sale ahora.
5. Estas canciones son muy apasionadas.
6. Estos pianistas tocan muy bien.

5-8 ¿Qué opinas?

Miren el dibujo y expresen sus opiniones sobre las casas. Usen las formas apropiadas de **este, ese** y **aquel**.

Capítulo 2. El verbo *gustar*, pág. 87; Capítulo 3. La casa, pág. 106; Los colores, pág. 119; Capítulo 4. Los verbos con cambios de raíz, pág. 150.

MODELO *Me gusta esta casa blanca, pero prefiero esa porque es beige. Pienso que aquella es fea porque no me gustan las casas rojas. También creo que este jardín de la casa blanca es bonito.*

5-9 ¿Qué prefieres?

Tu compañero/a te propone (*proposes*) una cosa, pero tú siempre prefieres otra (*another one*). Responde a sus comentarios usando las formas correctas de los adjetivos y pronombres demostrativos.

MODELO E1: ¿Quieres comprar este tambor?
E2: *No, quiero comprar ese/aquel.*

1. ¿Quieres tocar esa guitarra?
2. ¿Te gustan esas trompetas?
3. ¿Prefieres este piano?
4. ¿Tus amigos van a tocar aquellas flautas (*flutes*)?
5. ¿Prefieres escuchar esos instrumentos?
6. ¿Estos instrumentos son tus favoritos?

5-10 ¡Vamos a un concierto!

¡Qué suerte! Tienes dos entradas gratis (*free tickets*) para ir a un concierto.

Paso 1 Escucha en Internet la música de Molotov, Marc Anthony, Enrique Iglesias y Calle 13.

Paso 2 Tu compañero/a y tú tienen que decidir a qué concierto quieren ir. Túrnense para describir a quién prefieren escuchar y por qué. Usen **este, ese** y **aquel** en sus descripciones.

MODELO *Prefiero ir al concierto de Enrique Iglesias. ¡Él canta muy bien! Pero es difícil decidir porque Marc Anthony es muy bueno también. Estos saben tocar y cantar muy bien. Y aquellos...*

La música latina en los Estados Unidos

La música latina abarca (*encompasses*) muchos géneros, estilos e intérpretes (músicos, cantantes). Entre los géneros más populares en los Estados Unidos se encuentran la salsa, el merengue, el Tex-Mex o norteño y otros. Algunos intérpretes de estos tipos de música son El Gran Combo, Marc Anthony, Juan Luis Guerra y Los Tigres del Norte.

Pitbull

El rock y el jazz son influencias que están presentes en la música latina en los Estados Unidos, aunque esta ha evolucionado (*has evolved*) y producido nuevos géneros como el rock latino, el pop latino, el rap en español, el jazz latino, la música urbana, el reggaetón y otros. De estos géneros algunos de los más conocidos son los grupos Molotov y Calle 13, Shakira, Enrique Iglesias, Juanes, Pitbull y Daddy Yankee, entre muchos otros.

Shakira

La influencia de los países hispanohablantes del Caribe —Cuba, Puerto Rico y la República Dominicana— y su herencia africana forman parte de los ritmos, las melodías y la instrumentación de la música y los bailes latinos. También les dan vida (*they give life*) a géneros como la plena, la cumbia y la bachata.

Juan Luis Guerra

Preguntas

1. ¿Cuáles son cuatro de los géneros de la música latina? ¿Cuáles conoces tú?
2. ¿Quiénes son los artistas latinos más conocidos en este momento?

3 GRAMÁTICA

Los adverbios

Explaining how something is done

Este baterista toca horriblemente.

An **adverb** usually describes a verb and **answers the question "how."** Many Spanish adverbs end in **-mente,** which is equivalent to the English *-ly*. These Spanish adverbs are formed as follows:

1. Add **-mente** to the ***feminine singular*** form of an ***adjective***.

Adjetivos			**Adverbios**
Masculino		**Femenino**	
rápido →		***rápida*** + -mente →	**rápidamente**
lento →		***lenta*** + -mente →	**lentamente**
tranquilo →		***tranquila*** + -mente →	**tranquilamente**

2. If an ***adjective*** ends in a ***consonant*** or in **-e,** simply add **-mente.**

Adjetivos		**Adverbios**
fácil →	*fácil* + -mente →	**fácilmente**
suave →	*suave* + -mente →	**suavemente**

NOTE: If an adjective has a written accent, it is retained when **-mente** is added.

Now you are ready to complete the ***Preparación y práctica*** activities for this chunk online.

5-11 Lógicamente

Túrnense para transformar en adverbios los siguientes adjetivos.

Capítulo 1. Los adjetivos descriptivos, pág. 44.

MODELO E1: normal

E2: *normalmente*

Estrategia

Remember to first determine the *feminine singular* form of the adjective and then add *-mente.*

1. interesante
2. perezoso
3. feliz
4. nervioso
5. fuerte
6. claro (*clear*)
7. seguro (*sure*)
8. apasionada
9. difícil
10. débil
11. rápida
12. paciente

5-12 Para conocerte

Túrnense para hacerse y contestar las siguientes preguntas. Pueden usar los adjetivos de la lista.

Capítulo 2. Presente indicativo de verbos regulares, pág. 71; Capítulo 2. La formación de preguntas y las palabras interrogativas, pág. 75.

alegre	constante	difícil	divino	fácil
horrible	paciente	perfecto	rápido	tranquilo

MODELO entender a tu profesor/a de español

E1: ¿Cómo entiendes a tu profesor/a de español?

E2: *Entiendo a mi profesor/a perfectamente.*

Estrategia

Answer in complete sentences when working with your partner. Even though it may seem mechanical at times, it leads to increased comfort speaking Spanish.

1. cantar
2. bailar
3. tocar el piano
4. aprender la letra de una canción
5. hablar español
6. dormir
7. jugar al béisbol
8. limpiar la casa
9. lavar los platos
10. manejar (*to drive*)

5-13 Di la verdad

Hazle (*Ask*) a tu compañero/a las siguientes preguntas. Después, cambien de papel.

MODELO E1: ¿Qué haces diariamente (todos los días)?

E2: *Limpio mi dormitorio, voy a clase, estudio, como, hago ejercicio y duermo.*

1. ¿Qué haces perfectamente?
2. ¿Qué haces horriblemente?
3. ¿Qué haces fácilmente?
4. ¿Qué debes hacer rápidamente?
5. ¿Qué debes hacer lentamente?

¿Cómo andas? I

Having completed **Comunicación I,** I now can...

	Feel confident	Need to review
• discuss music. (p. 182)	☐	☐
• practice pronouncing diphthongs and linking words. (p. 183 and online)	☐	☐
• identify people and things. (p. 186)	☐	☐
• discuss Hispanic music in the United States. (p. 190)	☐	☐
• explain how something is done. (p. 191)	☐	☐

Comunicación II

4 VOCABULARIO

El mundo del cine

Sharing information about movies and television programs

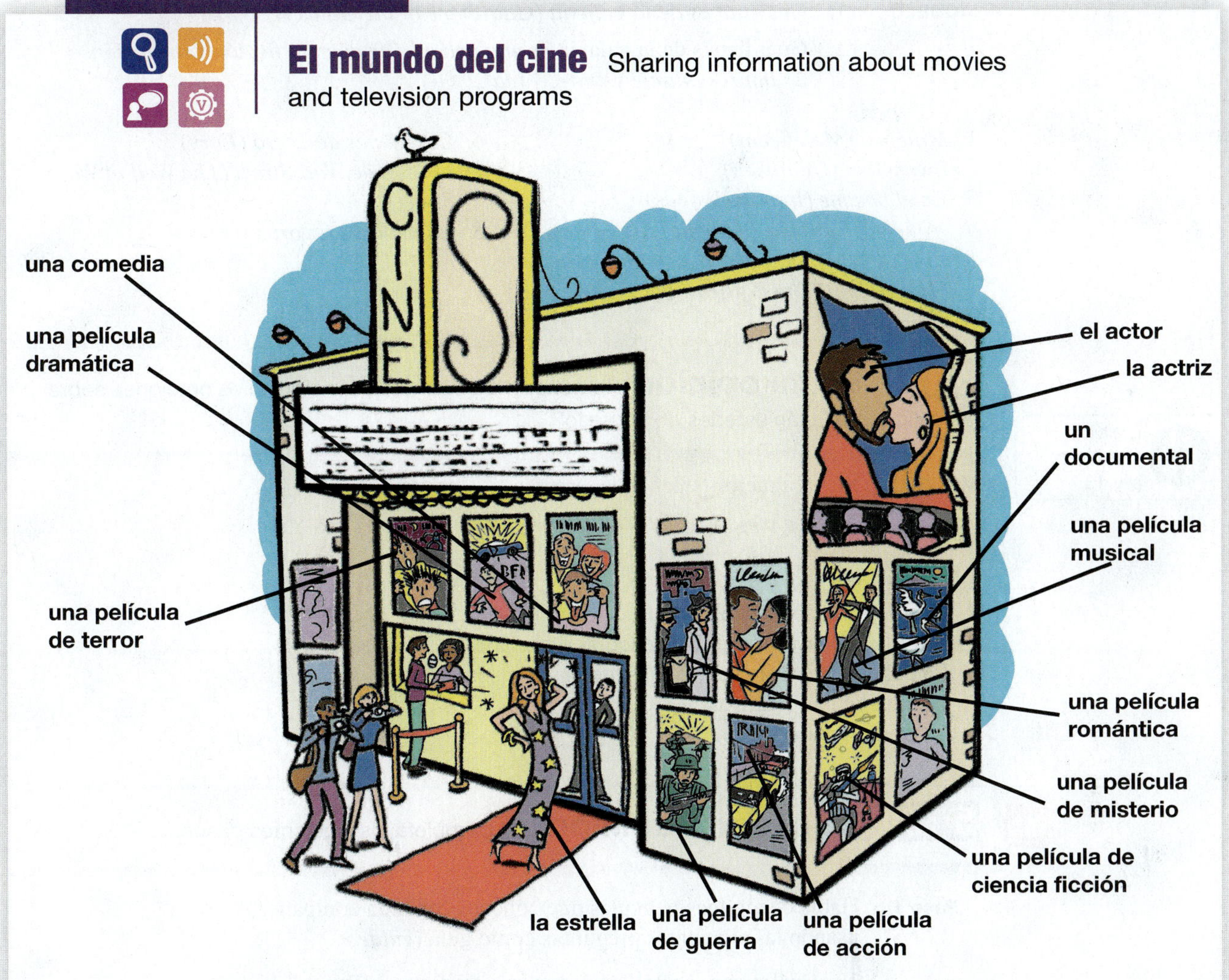

Otras palabras	*Other words*
la entrada	*ticket*
el estreno	*opening*
la pantalla	*screen*
una película...	*a ... movie*
aburrida	*boring*
animada	*animated*
conmovedora	*moving*
creativa	*creative*
deprimente	*depressing*
emocionante	*moving*
entretenida	*entertaining*
épica	*epic*
de espanto	*scary*
estupenda	*stupendous*
imaginativa	*imaginative*
impresionante	*impressive*
sorprendente	*surprising*
de suspenso	*suspenseful*
trágica	*tragic*

Algunos verbos	*Some verbs*
estrenar una película	*to release a film/movie*
presentar una película	*to show a film/movie*

¿? Now you are ready to complete the ***Preparación y práctica*** activities for this chunk online.

5-14 ¿Cuál es el género? Clasifiquen las siguientes películas según su género y usen el mayor (*the largest*) número de palabras posibles para describirlas.

MODELO E1: *Guardianes de la galaxia (Guardians of the Galaxy)*

E2: Guardianes de la galaxia *es una película de ciencia ficción y de acción. Es impresionante y entretenida…*

1. *Maléfica (Maleficent)*
2. *Invencible (Unbroken)*
3. *En el bosque (Into the Woods)*
4. *¿Qué pasó anoche? (About Last Night)*
5. *El Hobbit: La batalla de los cinco ejércitos (The Hobbit: The Battle of the Five Armies)*
6. *Corazones de acero (Fury)*
7. *El lobo de Wall Street (The Wolf of Wall Street)*
8. *(tu película favorita)*

5-15 En mi opinión Túrnense para completar las siguientes oraciones sobre las películas. ¿Están ustedes de acuerdo?

Capítulo A
El verbo *ser*, pág. 13.

MODELO E1: La mejor película de terror…

E2: *La mejor película de terror es* The Shining.

1. Las mejores comedias…
2. Una película épica deprimente…
3. Mis actores favoritos de las películas de acción…
4. La película de misterio que más me gusta…
5. Unas películas creativas…
6. El mejor documental…

5-16 En nuestra opinión… Completa los siguientes pasos.

Paso 1 Habla de algunas películas que conoces con un/a compañero/a, usando las siguientes preguntas como guía (*guide*).

1. ¿Cuáles son las películas que más te gustan? ¿Por qué?
2. ¿Quiénes son tus actores y actrices favoritos?
3. ¿Qué películas que van a estrenar pronto quieres ver?

Paso 2 Ahora hablen sobre programas de televisión.

5-17 Mis preferencias

Lee la información de las tres películas. Después, túrnate con un/a compañero/a para describir la película que prefieres ver y por qué.

MODELO *Prefiero ver __________. Es una película __________ y __________. Me gusta porque __________ …*

En el cine

Infiltrados en la universidad (2014, EE. UU.)
Género: Comedia, Acción
Director: Philip Lord y Christopher Miller
Interpretación: Channing Tatum, Jonah Hill
Los agentes de policía Jenko y Schmidt se infiltran encubiertos (*undercover*) en un campus universitario por una operación contra el narcotráfico.

El francotirador (2014, EE. UU.)
Género: Guerra, Drama
Director: Clint Eastwood
Interpretación: Bradley Cooper, Sienna Miller
Adaptación de la autobiografía del Navy SEAL Chris Kyle, el francotirador más letal del ejército americano.

El código Enigma (2014, EE. UU.)
Género: Drama
Director: Morten Tyldum
Interpretación: Benedict Cumberbatch, Keira Knightley
Basada en la biografía de Andrew Hodges sobre Alan Turing, un matemático, analista y héroe de guerra quien descifra, junto con su equipo, el código de la máquina Enigma de los alemanes durante la Segunda Guerra Mundial.

5-18 ¿Vemos una película?

Paul y Sara celebran su aniversario de dos años de novios. Quieren ir al cine pero… Escucha la conversación entre ellos y después indica si las oraciones son ciertas (**C**) o falsas (**F**).

C	F	
☐	☐	1. Para Paul, el cine es más importante que la película que presenta.
☐	☐	2. Es difícil para Sara decidir qué película ver porque no hay muchas películas buenas en los cines ahora.
☐	☐	3. Paul prefiere las películas de terror.
☐	☐	4. A Sara le gustan las películas románticas.
☐	☐	5. Paul decide ir a la película que Sara quiere ver.
☐	☐	6. Es cierto que Sara y Paul van a ir al cine esta noche.

Nota cultural La influencia hispana en el cine norteamericano

Javier Bardem

La influencia hispana en el cine estadounidense empieza a tener importancia en los años 50. Actores como Gilbert Roland, Anthony Quinn y Ricardo Montalbán se destacan (*stand out*) en películas de habla inglesa. Les siguen más tarde estrellas del cine y de la televisión como Raquel Welch y Rita Moreno y continúan hasta el presente con Antonio Banderas, Javier Bardem, Sofía Vergara, Jennifer López, John Leguizamo, Edward James Olmos, Benicio del Toro, Salma Hayek, Zoe Saldaña, Cameron Díaz, Diego Luna y Penélope Cruz, entre muchos otros. Su presencia en la industria representa el cambio demográfico de los Estados Unidos.

Preguntas

1. De los actores mencionados, ¿a cuáles conoces? ¿Qué sabes de ellos?
2. ¿Quiénes son los actores hispanos más populares en este momento?

Cameron Díaz

Benicio del Toro

Jennifer López

5 GRAMÁTICA

El pretérito: los verbos regulares *-ar*

Describing things that happened in the past

Up to this point, you have been expressing ideas or actions that take place in the present and future. To talk about something you did or something that occurred in the past, you can use the **pretérito** (*preterit*). Below are the endings for regular -ar verbs in the **pretérito**.

Los verbos regulares *-ar*

Note the endings for regular **-ar** verbs in the **pretérito** below and answer the questions that follow.

-ar: escuchar	
yo	escuch**é**
tú	escuch**aste**
Ud.	escuch**ó**
él, ella	escuch**ó**
nosotros/as	escuch**amos**
vosotros/as	escuch**asteis**
Uds.	escuch**aron**
ellos/as	escuch**aron**

—¿Dónde están las entradas que **compré** ayer? *Where are the tickets that I bought yesterday?*
—Mis primitos las **llevaron**. *My little cousins took them.*
—¿Ah, sí? ¿Las **llevaron** a su casa? *Really? Did they take them home?*
—No, las **llevaron** al colegio. ¡Las **regalaron** a su maestra! *No, they took them to school. They gave them to their teacher!*

Estrategia

Remember that there are two types of grammar presentations in *¡Anda!*:

1. You are given the grammar rule.
2. You are given guiding questions to help *you* construct the grammar rule, and state the rule in your own words.

¡Explícalo tú!

1. What do you notice about the endings?
2. Where are accent marks needed?

 Check your answers to the preceding questions in Appendix 1.

 Now you are ready to complete the ***Preparación y práctica*** activities for this chunk online.

5-19 De la teoría a la práctica Write these six infinitives on small pieces of paper: **cantar, escuchar, grabar, hablar,** and **presentar**. Next, write six different subject pronouns on different small pieces of paper. Take turns selecting a paper from each pile and give the correct **pretérito** form of the verb. Play several rounds.

5-20 ¡Una fiesta! Tu compañero/a y tú preparan una fiesta para después de un concierto. Para saber si todo está preparado, túrnense para contestar las siguientes preguntas usando el pretérito.

MODELO mandar las invitaciones

E1: *¿Mandaste las invitaciones?*

E2: *Sí, mandé las invitaciones.* o *No, no mandé las invitaciones.*

1. comprar las bebidas (*drinks*)
2. preparar la comida (*food*)
3. lavar los platos
4. limpiar la casa
5. encontrar música buena
6. guardar la ropa
7. hablar con los vecinos
8. abrir las ventanas

5-21 Creaciones

Completen los siguientes pasos.

Paso 1 Combinen elementos de las tres columnas para escribir **ocho** oraciones que describan lo que hicieron las siguientes personas (*what the following people did*).

MODELO mis padres comprar muchos instrumentos

Mis padres compraron muchos instrumentos.

Yolanda	escuchar	el concierto para sus padres
Ud.	comprar	la película nueva de Bradley Cooper
los estudiantes	preparar	siete niños a la tienda de música
yo	bailar	las entradas para la orquesta sinfónica
mi mejor amigo y yo	limpiar	música clásica antes de comer
tú	estrenar	siete películas nuevas el mes pasado
el Cine Cósmico	llevar	salsa en la fiesta
el empleado (*employee*)	presentar	el cine después del estreno

Paso 2 Túrnense para preguntarse cuándo ocurrió cada actividad mencionada en **Paso 1**.

E1: *¿Cuándo compraron muchos instrumentos tus padres?*

E2: *Compraron muchos instrumentos el año pasado.*

anoche	*last night*
anteayer	*the day before yesterday*
ayer	*yesterday*
el año pasado	*last year*
el fin de semana pasado	*last weekend*
el martes/viernes/domingo, etc. pasado	*last Tuesday/Friday/Sunday, etc.*
la semana pasada	*last week*

5-22 El hermano de Clara

Escribe la forma correcta del verbo apropiado para saber qué hicieron (*did*) Tina y Tomás anoche.

conversar hablar pasar preparar

El hermano de Clara se llama Antonio y tiene siete años. Anoche Tina y yo (1) _______________ cuatro horas con él porque Clara y sus padres fueron (*went*) al teatro para ver *Les Miserables*. Primero yo (2) _______________ unos sándwiches para todos. Después comimos y (3) _______________ con él sobre la escuela. Antonio (4) _______________ de su equipo de fútbol. Nos dijo (*he told us*) que le gusta el fútbol más que sus clases.

ayudar guardar lavar limpiar mirar terminar

A las siete yo (5) _______________ los platos, (6) _______________ la comida que sobró (*was left over*) y (7) _______________ la cocina en general. Tina (8) _______________ a Antonio con su tarea. Cuando nosotros (9) _______________, (10) _______________ la tele hasta las diez.

6 GRAMÁTICA

El pretérito: los verbos regulares *-er* e *-ir*

Describing things that happened in the past

You have just practiced verbs that end in **-ar** that are regular in the preterit. Now note the endings for regular **-er**/**-ir** verbs below and answer the questions that follow.

-er: aprender		**-ir: escribir**	
yo	aprend**í**	yo	escrib**í**
tú	aprend**iste**	tú	escrib**iste**
Ud.	aprend**ió**	Ud.	escrib**ió**
él, ella	aprend**ió**	él, ella	escrib**ió**
nosotros/as	aprend**imos**	nosotros/as	escrib**imos**
vosotros/as	aprend**isteis**	vosotros/as	escrib**isteis**
Uds.	aprend**ieron**	Uds.	escrib**ieron**
ellos/as	aprend**ieron**	ellos/as	escrib**ieron**

—¿Cuándo **aprendiste** a tocar la guitarra? *When did you learn to play the guitar?*
—**Aprendí** a tocar la guitarra el año pasado. *I learned to play the guitar last year.*
—¿Ah, sí? ¿Y tú **escribiste** la letra de aquella canción? *Really? And did you write the lyrics to that song?*
—No, mi novia **escribió** aquella. Ella **insistió** en escribir esa canción para nuestra boda. *No, my girlfriend wrote that one. She insisted on writing that song for our wedding.*

Now you are ready to complete the ***Preparación y práctica*** activities for this chunk online.

5-23 Tres en línea Make a grid, like one for tic-tac-toe. With a partner, select one regular **-ar**/**-er**/**-ir** verb. Write a different preterit form of the verb in each blank space on your grid. Each of you should write each preterit form with a different pronoun. Do not show your partner what you have written. Take turns randomly selecting pronouns and say the corresponding verb forms. When you say a form of the verb that your partner has, your partner marks an X over the word. The first person to get three X's either vertically, horizontally, or diagonally wins the round. After doing a round with **-er** and **-ir** verbs, repeat with **-ar** verbs.

MODELO E1: *tú comiste*
E2: (marks X over *tú comiste*)

~~tú comiste~~	ellos comieron	Ud. comió
yo comí	Uds. comieron	nosotros comimos
él comió	ellas comieron	ella comió

Capítulo 4. Los lugares, p. 142.

5·24 Emparejar Juntos emparejen los elementos de las dos columnas para decidir dónde estuvieron (*were*) estas personas cuando realizaron las actividades.

_____ 1. Fania mandó una carta.
_____ 2. Los estudiantes aprendieron mucho sobre las pinturas de Salvador Dalí.
_____ 3. Mis amigas y yo corrimos tres millas.
_____ 4. Yo tomé un café y escribí varios e-mails.
_____ 5. Los chicos compraron papel y lápices.
_____ 6. Ud. comió una pizza.
_____ 7. Tú cambiaste dinero.
_____ 8. Mis padres insistieron en ver *Twelfth Night* de Shakespeare.

a. la librería
b. el teatro
c. el parque
d. el restaurante
e. la oficina de correos
f. el banco
g. el museo
h. el cibercafé

5·25 ¿Sí o no? Entrevista a tres compañeros/as para saber si hicieron las siguientes cosas y cuándo.

MODELO comprar las entradas

E1: *¿Cuándo compraste las entradas?*

E2: *Compré las entradas el sábado pasado.*

o

E2: *No compré las entradas. / Nunca compré las entradas.*

¿Cuándo…?	E1	E2	E3
1. escuchar la música de Shakira			
2. comprender una película en español			
3. escribir una reseña (*review*) de una película			
4. comer palomitas (*popcorn*) en el cine			
5. insistir en ver una película de terror			
6. mirar todos los episodios de una serie en una noche			
7. bailar en un concierto			

5-26 ¡Qué curioso! Termina las oraciones con la forma correcta del pretérito del verbo apropiado de las listas para terminar la historia de Catalina. Después compara tus respuestas con un/a compañero/a.

aprender	comer	conocer	conversar	estudiar	volver

El mes pasado (1) ____________ a un hombre muy interesante en un restaurante en San José, Costa Rica. Según él, el verano pasado (2) ____________ el ecoturismo por seis semanas y este verano (3) ____________ a Costa Rica para filmar. Me dijo (*he told me*) que es director de cine y televisión. Juntos él y yo (4) ____________ en un café y (5) ____________ sobre muchas películas. Yo (6) ____________ mucho de él, sobre todo de la vida de un director.

estrenar	ganar	hablar	insistir	pasar	salir	terminar

El señor (7) ____________ en que, en este momento de su vida, está más interesado en documentales y series de televisión. (8) ____________ el documental *Cathedrals of Culture* recientemente y el año pasado él y su equipo (9) ____________ premios (*awards*) por las series *Death Row Stories* y *Chicagoland*. Cuando por fin (nosotros) (10) ____________ de comer, él (11) ____________ del café antes que yo. Cuando pagué (*paid*) la cuenta, una mujer me dijo: ¡Qué suerte! (12) ____________ mucho tiempo con ese actor tan famoso… ¡(tú) (13) ____________ por más de una hora con Robert Redford!

5-27 Conversaciones rápidas Túrnense para hacerse y contestar las siguientes preguntas. Después de tres preguntas, cambien de pareja y hagan tres preguntas más. Sigan hasta que hayan hablado (*continue until you have spoken*) con por lo menos tres personas diferentes. Contesten siempre en oraciones completas.

1. ¿Qué película te gustó más el año pasado?
2. ¿Qué concierto te gustó más en los últimos dos o tres años?
3. ¿Aprendiste a tocar un instrumento de niño/a? ¿Cuál?
4. ¿En qué clases estudiaste más el semestre pasado?
5. ¿En qué clase recibiste la mejor nota el semestre pasado?
6. ¿Cuándo conociste a tu mejor amigo/a?
7. ¿Cuándo hablaste en español por primera vez?
8. ¿Miraste la tele, estudiaste o saliste con amigos anoche?

Fíjate

Remember that if you did none of the things in 8 last night, your response would be *Ni miré la tele, ni estudié, ni salí con amigos anoche.*

7 GRAMÁTICA

Los pronombres de complemento directo y la *a* personal Expressing *what* or *whom*

Direct objects receive the action of the verb and answer the questions ***What?*** or ***Whom?*** Note the following examples.

A: I need to do *what?*
B: You need to buy *the concert tickets* by Monday.
A: Yes, I do need to buy *them*.

A: I have to call *whom*?
B: You have to call *your agent*.
A: Yes, I do have to call *him*.

Note the following examples of *direct objects* in Spanish.

María toca **dos instrumentos** muy bien.	*María plays two instruments very well.*
Sacamos **una canción nueva** el primero de septiembre.	*We are releasing a new song on September first.*
¿Tienes **las entradas**?	*Do you have the tickets?*
No conozco a **Benicio del Toro.**	*I do not know Benicio del Toro.*
Siempre veo a **Selena Gómez** en la televisión.	*I always see Selena Gómez on television.*

NOTE: In Capítulo 4, you learned that to express knowing a person, you put **a** after the verb (*conocer* + *a* + person). Now that you have learned about direct objects, a more global way of stating the rule is: When direct objects refer to *people*, you must use the personal **a.** Review the following examples.

People	Things
¡Veo **a** *Cameron Díaz*!	¡Veo *el coche* de Cameron Díaz!
Hay que ver **a** *mis padres*.	Hay que ver *la película*.
¿**A** qué *actores* conoces?	¿Qué *ciudades* conoces?

As in English, we can replace direct object nouns with ***direct object pronouns***. Note the following examples.

María **los** toca muy bien.	*María plays them very well.*
La sacamos el primero de septiembre.	*We are releasing it September first.*
¿**Las** tienes?	*Do you have them?*
No **lo** conozco.	*I do not know him.*
Siempre **la** veo en la televisión.	*I always see her on television.*

In Spanish, direct object pronouns ***agree in gender and number with the nouns they replace***. The following chart lists the direct object pronouns.

Singular		Plural	
me	*me*	**nos**	*us*
te	*you*	**os**	*you all*
lo, la	*you*	**los, las**	*you all*
lo, la	*him, her, it*	**los, las**	*them*

Placement of direct object pronouns

Direct object pronouns are:

1. Placed before the verb.
2. Attached to *infinitives*.

¿Tienes los tambores?	→	Sí, **los** tengo.
Tengo que traer los guiones.	→	**Los** tengo que traer. / Tengo que traer**los.**
Tiene que llevar su guitarra.	→	**La** tiene que llevar. / Tiene que llevar**la.**

¿? Now you are ready to complete the ***Preparación y práctica*** activities for this chunk online.

5-28 ¿Estás listo/a? ¿Te preparaste bien para el estreno de la nueva película de Bradley Cooper anoche? Túrnate con un/a compañero/a para confirmar que hiciste (*you did*) todas las actividades de la lista usando el pretérito y **lo, la, los** o **las**.

MODELO confirmar *la hora* del estreno

E1: ¿Confirmaste la hora del estreno?

E2: *Sí, la confirmé.*

1. comprar *las entradas*
2. invitar *a mis amigos*
3. mirar *el tráiler* de la película en Internet
4. compartir (*to share*) *el tráiler y una reseña (review) de la película* con mis amigos
5. tomar *muchas fotos de* Bradley Cooper
6. llevar mucho *dinero* extra para comprar comida en el cine

Bradley Cooper

5-29 ¿Hay deberes? El estreno de la película fue (*was*) increíble, pero hay que volver al mundo real. Siempre hay trabajo, sobre todo en la casa. Túrnate con un/a compañero/a para hacer y contestar las siguientes preguntas.

Capítulo 3. Los quehaceres de la casa, pág. 117.

MODELO E1: ¿Lavas los pisos?

E2: *Sí, los lavo. / No, no los lavo. / No, nunca los lavo.*

1. ¿Limpias la cocina?
2. ¿Arreglas tu cuarto?
3. ¿Lavas los platos?
4. ¿Guardas tus cosas?
5. ¿Sacudes los muebles?
6. ¿Haces las camas?
7. ¿Preparas la comida?
8. ¿Pones la mesa?
9. ¿Terminas el jardín?
10. ¿Sacas la basura?

5-30 Una hora antes

Carlos Santana, como muchos músicos, es una persona muy organizada. Antes de cada concierto repasa con su ayudante (*assistant*) personal todos los preparativos (*preparations*). Aquí tienes las preguntas del ayudante. Contesta como si fueras (*as if you were*) Santana, usando **lo, la, los** o **las.**

MODELO E1: ¿Tienes tu anillo (*ring*) de la buena suerte?
E2: *Sí, lo tengo.*

1. Juan está enfermo. ¿Conoces al trompetista que toca esta noche con el conjunto?
2. ¿Traes tu guitarra nueva?
3. ¿Los cantantes saben la letra de la canción nueva?
4. ¿Traemos todos los trajes (*suits, outfits*)?
5. ¿Quieres unas botellas de agua (*water*)?
6. ¿Oyes al público aplaudir?
7. ¿Me van a necesitar después del concierto?
8. ¿El empresario te va a anunciar?

Carlos Santana

5-31 ¿Te puedo hacer una pregunta?

Para cada actividad, primero indica si tú la terminaste o no (**sí** o **no**). Después entrevista a cuatro estudiantes diferentes y anota sus respuestas de **sí** o **no**. Finalmente, compara tus respuestas con las de los otros estudiantes de la clase. ¿Cuáles son las tendencias?

MODELO escuchar música clásica esta mañana
(Yo: Sí)
TÚ: *¿Escuchaste música clásica esta mañana?*
E1: *Sí, la escuché esta mañana.*
E2: *No, no, la escuché.*
E3: *Sí, escuché música clásica esta mañana.*
E4: *No, yo no la escuché, pero mi compañero la escuchó.*

	yo	E1	E2	E3	E4
1. escuchar música clásica esta mañana					
2. mirar la tele anoche					
3. bajar (*download*) música de Internet ayer					
4. terminar la tarea para todas las clases anoche					
5. llamar a tus padres anteayer					
6. viajar a la playa el verano pasado					
7. escribir un ensayo para la clase de inglés la semana pasada					
8. comer sushi el sábado pasado					

5-32 Mis preferencias

Túrnense para hacerse y contestar las siguientes preguntas usando **el pronombre de complemento directo** correcto. Debes hacer otra pregunta para pedir más información específica usando **por qué, cuándo, con quién(es),** etc.

Capítulo 2. La formación de preguntas y las palabras interrogativas, p. 75.

MODELO E1: ¿Lees los poemas de Rubén Darío?
E2: *No, no los leo.*
E1: *¿Por qué no los lees?*
E2: *No los leo porque no los conozco.*

1. ¿Escuchas música clásica?
2. ¿Tu amigo y tú tienen ganas de ver una película de acción de Zoe Saldaña?
3. ¿Tus amigos ven todas las películas de Javier Bardem?
4. ¿Escuchas las canciones de Shakira?
5. ¿Conoces a un/a director/a de cine o televisión, un actor, una actriz o un/a músico/a famoso/a?

Escucha

Planes para un concierto

Estrategia	
Anticipating content	Use all clues available to you to anticipate what you are about to hear. That includes photos, captions, and body language if you are looking at the individual(s) speaking. If there are written synopses, it is important to read them in advance. Finally, if you are doing listening activities such as these, look ahead at the comprehension questions to give you an idea of the topic and important points.

5-33 Antes de escuchar

Mira el título de esta sección y la foto. Contesta las siguientes preguntas.

1. ¿Quiénes están en la foto?
2. ¿De qué hablan Luis y Rodrigo?

Luis y Rodrigo

5-34 A escuchar

Escucha la conversación entre Luis y Rodrigo y averigua cuál es el tema (*topic*; *gist*). Después, escucha una vez más para contestar las siguientes preguntas.

1. ¿De qué concierto hablan Luis y Rodrigo?
2. A Luis le gusta el rock, pero ¿qué tipo de música prefiere Rodrigo?
3. Deciden no estudiar. ¿Adónde van a ir?

5-35 Después de escuchar

Describe una canción que te guste en **tres** oraciones y dibuja un cuadro (*picture*) que la represente. Preséntaselo a un/a compañero/a para ver si puede adivinar (*guess*) la canción.

¡Conversemos!

5-36 En mi opinión Hay un programa en el canal *E!* donde las personas expresan sus gustos y opiniones sobre la música y el cine ¡y tu compañero/a y tú van a participar esta semana! Entrevista a tu compañero/a sobre sus opiniones de los mejores grupos, las mejores películas, los mejores actores y actrices. Luego, cambien de papel.

5-37 Comparaciones En los **Capítulos 1–4** aprendieron información sobre los Estados Unidos (**Capítulo 1**), México (**Capítulo 2**), España (**Capítulo 3**) y Honduras, Guatemala y El Salvador (**Capítulo 4**). Con un/a compañero/a, compara estos países incluyendo la música y el cine, cuando sea posible. Usa información de los capítulos anteriores (*previous chapters*) e información de otras fuentes (*sources*).

MODELO *Los países son similares y diferentes. Por ejemplo, hablan español en todos los países. España tiene influencia árabe en ciudades como* (like) *Granada. México no tiene influencia árabe pero sí tiene influencia de los españoles. La música popular es similar, pero la música folklórica...*

Escribe

Una reseña (*A review*)

Estrategia

Peer review/editing

Reviewing the writing of a classmate teaches you valuable editing skills that can improve your classmate's paper as well as serve to build your confidence in your own writing by enhancing the content and syntax of your work, as well as boost your critical thinking skills.

5-38 Antes de escribir Piensa en una película que te gusta mucho. Anota algunas ideas sobre los aspectos que te gustan más de esa película.

- ¿Qué tipo de película es?
- ¿Para qué grupo(s) es apropiada?
- ¿Cuál es el tema?
- ¿Tiene una lección para el público?

5-39 A escribir Organiza tus ideas y escribe una reseña (*review*) de **cuatro** a **seis** oraciones. Puedes usar las siguientes preguntas para organizar tu reseña.

1. ¿Cómo se llama la película?
2. ¿De qué género es?
3. ¿Cómo la describes?
4. ¿A quiénes les va a gustar? ¿Por qué?
5. ¿La recomiendas? ¿Por qué?

5-40 Después de escribir En grupos de tres, compartan sus reseñas. Revisen las ideas tanto de la gramática como del vocabulario. Hagan los cambios necesarios. Después, tu profesor/a va a leer las reseñas. La clase tiene que adivinar cuáles son las películas.

¿Cómo andas? II

Having completed **Comunicación II,** I now can...	Feel confident	Need to review
• share information about movies and television programs. (p. 193)	☐	☐
• note Hispanic influences in North American film. (p. 196)	☐	☐
• describe things that happened in the past using **-ar** verbs. (p. 197)	☐	☐
• describe things that happened in the past using **-er** and **-ir** verbs. (p. 200)	☐	☐
• express *what* or *whom*. (p. 202)	☐	☐
• anticipate content when listening. (p. 206)	☐	☐
• communicate about music and film. (p. 207)	☐	☐
• write a movie review and practice peer editing. (p. 208)	☐	☐

Vistazo cultural

Nicaragua

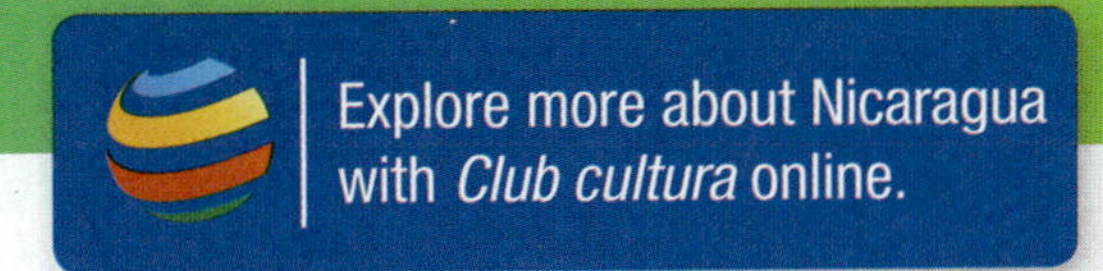

Les presento mi país

Mauricio Morales Prado

Mi nombre es Mauricio Morales Prado y soy de Managua, Nicaragua. Mi país es conocido como la tierra de lagos (*lakes*) y volcanes. Hay dos lagos principales y muchos volcanes. Siete están activos todavía y de ellos, San Cristóbal es el más alto y Masaya es el más activo. **¡Localiza estos volcanes en el mapa!** Mi familia y yo somos muy aficionados a la música. Vamos frecuentemente a los conciertos en La Concha Acústica en el lago Managua. **¿Asistes a conciertos con tu familia o amigos?**

ɘatro Nacional Rubén ario, Managua

Jnos visitantes en el Parque ɬacional Volcán Masaya

La Concha Acústica, Managua

ALMANAQUE

Nombre oficial:	República de Nicaragua
Gobierno:	República
Población:	5.995.928 (2010)
Idiomas:	español (oficial); misquito; otros idiomas indígenas
Moneda:	córdoba (C$)

¿Sabías que...?

- El lago de Nicaragua es el lago más grande de Centroamérica y es el único lago de agua dulce (*fresh water*) del mundo donde se encuentran tiburones (*sharks*) y atunes.
- El 23 de diciembre del año 1972, un terremoto (*earthquake*) desastroso de 6,5 en la escala Richter destruyó (*destroyed*) la ciudad de Managua.

Preguntas

1. ¿Por qué se llama Nicaragua la tierra de lagos y volcanes?
2. ¿Qué tiene el lago de Nicaragua de especial?
3. ¿Cuáles son dos lugares en Managua que ofrecen eventos culturales? ¿Puedes nombrar algunos eventos culturales posibles para estos lugares?

Vistazo cultural

Explore more about Costa Rica with *Club cultura* online.

Costa Rica

Les presento mi país

Laura Centeno Soto

Mi nombre es Laura Centeno Soto y soy *tica*. *Ticos* es el apodo (*nickname*) que tenemos todos los costarricenses. Soy de Sarchí, un pueblo muy conocido por su artesanía, especialmente por sus carretas que son un símbolo nacional de Costa Rica. **¿Cuáles son algunos símbolos de tu país?** La naturaleza es muy importante para los ticos y nuestro gobierno se dedica a la conservación y protección del medio ambiente (*environment*). Si quieres conocer la naturaleza pura costarricense, te recomiendo una visita a nuestros parques nacionales. Tienes muchas opciones: ¡hay 26 aquí! **¿Cuál es tu parque favorito?** ¡Costa Rica es pura vida!

El café es un producto principal de exportación.

Costa Rica tiene una naturaleza variada y exuberante.

Una carreta pintada de Sarchí

ALMANAQUE

Nombre oficial:	República de Costa Rica
Gobierno:	República democrática
Población:	4.516.220 (2010)
Idiomas:	español (oficial); inglés
Moneda:	colón (¢)

¿Sabías que...?

- El ejército (*army*) se abolió en Costa Rica en el año 1948. Los recursos monetarios desde aquel entonces apoyan (*support*) el sistema educativo. A causa de su dedicación a la paz (*peace*), la llaman "La Suiza de Centroamérica".

Preguntas

1. ¿Qué artesanía es un símbolo nacional costarricense?
2. ¿Cuál es un producto de exportación importante de Costa Rica? ¿Qué otros países exportan productos similares?
3. ¿Qué sabes sobre el gobierno de Costa Rica?

Vistazo cultural

Panamá

  Les presento mi país

Magdalena Quintero de Gracia

Mi nombre es Magdalena Quintero de Gracia y soy de Colón, una ciudad y puerto en la costa caribeña de Panamá. Mi país es famoso por el canal y mi ciudad está muy cerca de su entrada (*entrance*) atlántica. **¿Qué sabes tú de la historia del canal?** El canal es positivo para la economía de Panamá, que se basa principalmente en el sector de los servicios, la banca, el comercio y el turismo. Los turistas pueden ir al canal, a las playas o hasta pueden conocer grupos indígenas, como el pueblo emberá en el sureste o los gunas en la costa caribeña. **¿Dónde se localizan los pueblos indígenas en tu país?**

Unos barcos pasan por las esclusas (*locks*) del Canal de Panamá.

Una mujer guna vende molas, artesanía tradicional.

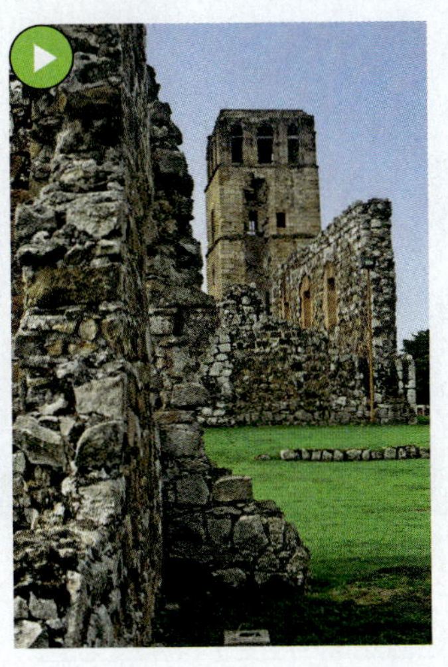
Las ruinas del Panamá Viejo

ALMANAQUE

Nombre oficial:	República de Panamá
Gobierno:	Democracia constitucional
Población:	3.410.676 (2010)
Idiomas:	español (oficial), inglés, otros idiomas indígenas
Moneda:	balboa (B/)

¿Sabías que…?

- Richard Halliburton nadó el canal en el año 1928 y la tarifa fue (*was*) 36 centavos. La tarifa más alta fue $375,000 para el crucero (*cruise ship*) Norwegian Pearl en el 2011.
- Hay un palíndromo famoso en inglés asociado con el canal: *A man, a plan, a canal: Panama!*

Preguntas

1. ¿Por qué es importante el canal?
2. Compara Panamá con Costa Rica y Nicaragua. ¿En qué son similares? ¿En qué son diferentes?
3. Compara Panamá, Costa Rica y Nicaragua con México. ¿En qué son similares? ¿En qué son diferentes?

Lectura

Una guía de eventos

5·41 Antes de leer Generalmente puedes encontrar información en Internet sobre los eventos culturales, sociales, musicales y deportivos en donde vives. Piensa en ellos y contesta las siguientes preguntas.

1. ¿Qué te gusta hacer cuando tienes tiempo libre? ¿Asistes a conciertos o eventos deportivos? ¿Vas al cine, al teatro o a otros eventos culturales?
2. ¿Dónde buscas información sobre eventos y actividades en tu ciudad o región?

Estrategia

Anticipating content
You can often anticipate the content of a reading passage by paying attention to the title and any available illustrations and by quickly reading through the comprehension questions that may follow a passage.

5·42 Mientras lees Complete the following activities.

1. Look at the title of the reading and answer the following questions.
   a. What do you anticipate the topic of this reading will be?
   b. How do you plan your free time on the weekend?
   c. Where do you find information about possible activities?
2. Now read the **Después de leer** questions on page 214. What do you glean from the questions? Employ this new reading strategy along with the others you have been learning (identifying cognates, skimming, and scanning).

SAN JOSÉ
GUÍA DE EVENTOS SEMANALES

Teatro Nacional en San José

El viernes a las 8:00 p.m. la Orquesta Sinfónica de la Universidad de Costa Rica y el Ballet Folclórico de Costa Rica con el director Norman Gamboa presentan un homenaje° a las compositoras costarricenses del siglo XX. Empiezan con Virginia Mata Alfaro y terminan con Mercedes O'Leary.

Entradas generales 2.000 ₡°
Entradas de estudiantes 1.000 ₡

¡Asedio en el Estadio Nacional! ¡Solamente una noche!

Este fin de semana Asedio va a estrenar su nuevo álbum en San José antes de presentarlo al próximo festival Headbangers Attack en la ciudad de Panamá. Según el baterista, Samuel Segura, "el nuevo álbum continúa con la tradición de Asedio de folk y rock metal". Este sábado puedes verlos a las 9:00 p.m. en el Estadio Nacional.

Entradas generales 3.000 ₡
Entradas de estudiantes 2.500 ₡

Música de jazz y baile de gala en el Museo de Oro

Gran concierto del Quinteto de Wynton Marsalis: el sábado a las 9:00 p.m. El músico estadounidense viene a dar un concierto exclusivo a San José. El jazzista viene al Museo de Oro para abrir la nueva exposición de arte afro-caribeño. Este concierto es parte de su gira internacional. Después del concierto hay un baile de gala donde puedes conocer a los artistas. La gala es para recaudar fondos° para el programa "Futuros niños artistas".

Entradas de adultos 15.000 ₡
Entradas de estudiantes 7.000 ₡

Cena y show en Luna Luna

El miércoles y el jueves el restaurante Luna Luna ofrece una cena-show con un menú típico de Costa Rica. El menú cuesta entre 5.400 y 6.900 colones. La banda de música se llama Byscaine y tiene tres saxofonistas, un tamborista y un baterista. Los clientes pueden aprender a bailar el "Diablo Chingo" o "La Cajeta", bailes tradicionales que cuentan leyendas tradicionales. Para hacer reservaciones, llame al (506) 2230-3022.

tribute

symbol for colón *(currency)*

raise money

5-43 Después de leer Contesta las siguientes preguntas.

1. ¿Qué programa ofrecen en el Teatro Nacional este fin de semana?
2. ¿Por qué va a tocar Wynton Marsalis en el Museo de Oro?
3. ¿Qué tipo de música toca Asedio?
4. ¿Dónde puedes aprender bailes tradicionales de Costa Rica?
5. Tienes la oportunidad de asistir a uno de los eventos de la guía. ¿Cuál es? ¿Por qué te interesa?

5-44 Un concierto Completa los siguientes pasos.

Paso 1 Piensa en un concierto al que asististe. ¿Quién cantó? ¿Qué tipo de música escuchaste? etc.

Paso 2 Escribe cinco preguntas para entrevistar (*to interview*) a tus compañeros de clase sobre los conciertos.

Paso 3 Entrevista a dos compañeros y después presenta la información a la clase.

5-45 Guía de eventos Completa los siguientes pasos.

Paso 1 Busca información sobre algunos eventos y actividades para hacer este fin de semana en tu ciudad. Escoge cuatro o cinco actividades interesantes.

Paso 2 Haz (*Make*) una guía de eventos. Incluye el día y la hora, el precio y una pequeña descripción de cada evento.

Paso 3 Presenta tu guía a un grupo de compañero/as. Deben hacer planes para ir a dos eventos este fin de semana.

For additional *Lectura* activities, go to *¡Anda!* online.

Y por fin, ¿cómo andas?

Having completed this chapter, I now can...	Feel confident	Need to review
Comunicación I		
• discuss music. (p. 182)	☐	☐
• practice pronouncing diphthongs and linking words. (p. 183 and online)	☐	☐
• identify people and things. (p. 186)	☐	☐
• explain how something is done. (p. 191)	☐	☐
Comunicación II		
• share information about movies and television programs. (p. 193)	☐	☐
• describe things that happened in the past using **-ar** verbs. (p. 197)	☐	☐
• describe things that happened in the past using **-er** and **-ir** verbs. (p. 200)	☐	☐
• express *what* or *whom*. (p. 202)	☐	☐
• anticipate content when listening. (p. 206)	☐	☐
• communicate about music and film. (p. 207)	☐	☐
• write a movie review and practice peer editing. (p. 208)	☐	☐
Cultura		
• discuss Hispanic music in the United States. (p. 190)	☐	☐
• note Hispanic influences in North American film. (p. 196)	☐	☐
• share information about Nicaragua, Costa Rica, and Panama. (pp. 209–211)	☐	☐
Lectura		
• read a cultural events guide. (p. 212)	☐	☐
Comunidades		
• use Spanish in real-life contexts. (online)	☐	☐

Vocabulario activo 

El mundo de la música	The world of music
el/la artista	*artist*
el/la cantante	*singer*
el conjunto	*group; band*
el/la empresario/a	*agent;, manager*
el/la guitarrista	*guitarist*
el/la músico/a	*musician*
el/la pianista	*pianist*
la batería	*drums*
el concierto	*concert*
la gira	*tour*
la guitarra	*guitar*
la música	*music*
la orquesta	*orchestra*
el piano	*piano*
el tambor	*drum*
la trompeta	*trumpet*

Algunos géneros musicales	Some musical genres
el jazz	*jazz*
la música clásica	*classical music*
la música folklórica	*folk music*
la música popular	*pop music*
la música rap	*rap music*
la ópera	*opera*
el rock	*rock*
la salsa	*salsa*

Algunos adjetivos	Some adjectives
apasionado/a	*passionate*
fino/a	*fine; delicate*
lento/a	*slow*
suave	*smooth*

Algunos verbos	Some verbs
cantar	*to sing*
dar un concierto	*to give/perform a concert*
ensayar	*to practice/rehearse*
grabar	*to record*
hacer una gira	*to tour*
sacar una canción	*to release a song*

Otras palabras	Other words
el/la aficionado/a	*fan*
la fama	*fame*
el género	*genre*
la habilidad	*ability; skill*
la letra	*lyrics*
el ritmo	*rhythm*
la voz	*voice*

El mundo del cine	The world of cinema
el actor	*actor*
la actriz	*actress*
la entrada	*ticket*
la estrella	*star*
la pantalla	*screen*
la comedia	*comedy*
el documental	*documentary*
una película...	*a ... film; movie*
de acción	*action*
de ciencia ficción	*science fiction*
dramática	*drama*
de guerra	*war*
de misterio	*mystery*
musical	*musical*
romántica	*romantic*
de terror	*horror*

Otras palabras	Other words
el estreno	*opening*
una película...	*a ... movie*
aburrida	*boring*
animada	*animated*
conmovedora	*moving*
creativa	*creative*
deprimente	*depressing*
emocionante	*moving*
entretenida	*entertaining*
épica	*epic*
de espanto	*scary*
estupenda	*stupendous*
imaginativa	*imaginative*
impresionante	*impressive*
sorprendente	*surprising*
de suspenso	*suspenseful*
trágica	*tragic*

Algunos verbos	Some verbs
estrenar una película	*to release a film/movie*
presentar una película	*to show a film/movie*

6 ¡Sí, lo sé!

This chapter is a recycling chapter, designed for you to see just how much Spanish you have learned thus far. The *major points* of **Capítulos 1–5** are included in this chapter, providing you with the opportunity to "put it all together." You will be pleased to realize how much you are able to communicate in Spanish.

Since this is a recycling chapter, no new vocabulary is presented. The intention is that you review the vocabulary of **Capítulos 1–5** thoroughly, focusing on the words that you personally have difficulty remembering.

Everyone learns at a different pace. You and your classmates will vary in terms of how much of the material presented thus far you have mastered and what you still need to practice.

Remember, language learning is a process. Like any skill, learning Spanish requires practice, review, and then more practice!

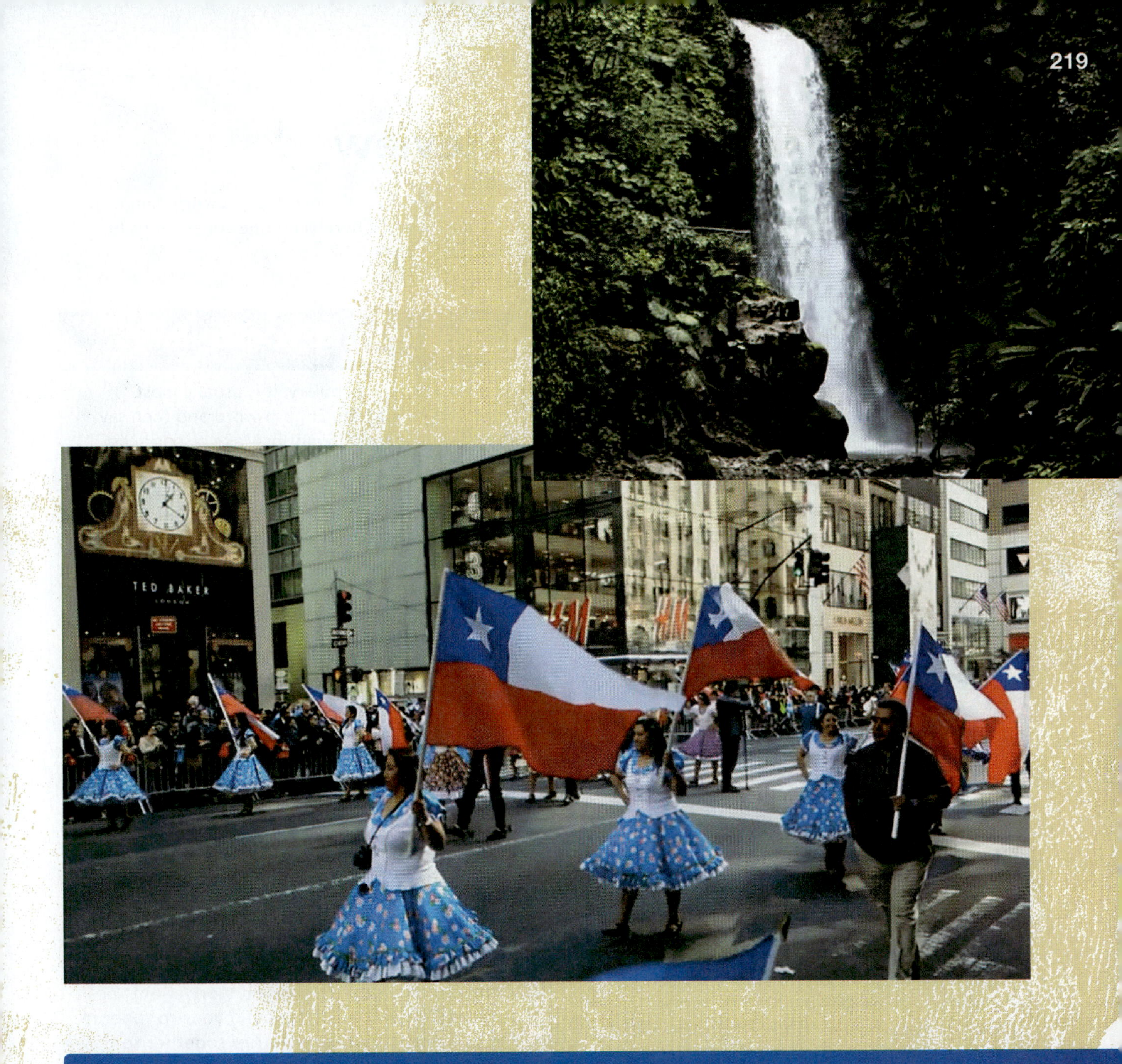

Learning Outcomes

After reviewing Chapters 1–5, you will be able to:

- ✔ describe your life at home, school, families, and things you need and like to do.
- ✔ report on service opportunities.
- ✔ discuss music, movies, and television.
- ✔ relate activities from the past.
- ✔ exchange interesting facts about Hispanic cultures in the United States, as well as Mexico, Spain, Honduras, Guatemala, El Salvador, Nicaragua, Costa Rica, and Panama.
- ✔ review and reflect on readings from these chapters.

Estrategia

Beyond reading these suggestions carefully, you will want to review the rubric for each section prior to beginning the activities. The first rubric can be found on page 223.

Organizing Your Review

There are processes used by successful language learners for reviewing a world language. The following tips can help you organize your review. There is no one correct way, but these are some suggestions that will best utilize your time and energy.

1 Reviewing Strategies

1. Make a list of the *major* topics you have studied and need to review, dividing them into three categories: *vocabulary, grammar,* and *culture*. These are the topics on which you need to focus the majority of your time and energy.
   Note: The two-page chapter openers can help you determine the *major* topics.
   After you create your list of major review topics, check Appendix 1, **Capítulo 6** to see if your list matches.
2. Allocate a minimum of an hour each day over a period of time to review. Budget the majority of your time for the major topics. After beginning with the most important grammar and vocabulary topics, review the secondary/supporting grammar topics and the culture. Cramming the night before a test is *not* an effective way to review and retain information.
3. Many educational researchers suggest that you start your review with the most recent chapter, or in this case, **Capítulo 5.** The most recent chapter is the freshest in your mind, so you tend to remember the concepts better, and you will experience quick success in your review.
4. Spend the most amount of time on concepts in which you determine *you* need to improve. Revisit the self-assessment tools **Y por fin, ¿cómo andas?** in each chapter to see how you rated yourself. Those tools are designed to help you become good at self-assessing what you need to work on the most.

2 Reviewing Grammar

1. When reviewing grammar, begin with the three tenses you learned: present, past, future. After feeling confident using the three main tenses (including the irregular verbs you learned in the present), proceed to the additional grammar points and review them.
2. Good ways to review include redoing activities in your textbook and (re)doing activities in *¡Anda!* online.

3 Reviewing Vocabulary

1. When studying vocabulary, it is usually most helpful to look at the English word and then say or write the word in Spanish. Make a special list of words that are difficult for you to remember, writing them in a small notebook or in an electronic file. Pull out your list every time you have a few minutes (in between classes, waiting in line at the grocery store, etc.) to review the words. The **Vocabulario activo** pages at the end of each chapter will help you organize the most important words of each chapter.
2. Saying vocabulary (which includes verbs) out loud helps you retain the words better.

4 Overall Review Technique

1. Get together with someone with whom you can practice speaking Spanish. If you need something to spark the conversation, take the drawings from each vocabulary presentation in ***¡Anda! Curso elemental*** and say as many things as you can about each picture. Have a friendly challenge to see who can make more complete sentences or create the longest story about the pictures. This will help you build your confidence and practice stringing sentences together to speak in paragraphs.
2. Yes, it is important for you to know "mechanical" pieces of information such as verb endings, or how to take a sentence and replace the direct object with a pronoun, *but* it is *much more important* that you are able to take those mechanical pieces of information and put them all together, creating meaningful and creative samples of your speaking and writing on the themes of the first five chapters.
3. You are well on the road to success if you can demonstrate that you can speak and write in paragraphs, using a wide variety of verbs and vocabulary words correctly. Keep up the good work!

Comunicación

Capítulo A Para empezar, Capítulo 1 y Capítulo 2

6-1 Nuestras familias

Completen los siguientes pasos en grupos de cuatro.

Fíjate

Most of the activities in this chapter are designed to be completed with a partner. Your instructor may modify the activity directions so that you do them on your own.

Estrategia

Before beginning each activity, make sure that you have reviewed the identified recycled concepts carefully so that you are able to move through the activities seamlessly as you put it all together! *¡Sí, lo sabes!*

Estrategia

Being a good listener is an important life skill. Repeating what your classmate said gives you practice in demonstrating how well you listen.

Paso 1 Con un/a compañero/a, túrnense para describir a varios miembros de sus familias usando por lo menos **diez** oraciones con un mínimo de **cinco** verbos diferentes. Incluyan (*Include*): aspectos de sus personalidades, descripciones físicas, qué hacen en su tiempo libre, cuántos años tienen, etc.

MODELO E1: *Mi familia no es muy grande. Mi madre es simpática, inteligente y trabajadora. Tiene cuarenta y cinco años…*

Paso 2 Ahora describe a la familia de tu compañero/a a otro miembro del grupo usando por lo menos **cinco** oraciones. Si no recuerdas bien los detalles o si necesitas clarificación, pregúntale (*ask him/her*).

MODELO E2: *La familia de Adriana es pequeña. Su madre es simpática y trabajadora… Adriana, perdón, pero ¿cuántos años tiene tu madre?…*

Estrategia

Although these activities are focusing on *Capítulos A Para empezar, 1*, and *2*, feel free to use additional vocabulary from later chapters to create your questions. For example, in **6-2,** you may want to use vocabulary from *Capítulo 5*.

6-2 ¿Cómo eres? Conoces un poco a los estudiantes que estudiamos en **Vistazo cultural** en los **Capítulos 1–5**. ¿Qué más quieres saber de ellos? Escribe por lo menos **diez** preguntas que quieres hacerles. Sé (*Be*) creativo/a.

MODELO
1. *¿Dónde estudias?*
2. *¿Te gusta leer libros de deportes?*
3. *¿Qué comes?*
4. *¿Qué idiomas hablan en tu país?*
5. …

Estrategia

Pay attention to the particular grammar point you are practicing. If you are supposed to write sentences using *tener*, underline each form of *tener* that you use, and then check to make sure it agrees with the subject. Using strategies such as underlining can help you focus on important points.

Rafael Sánchez Martínez

Gabriela García Cordera

Mariela Castañeda Ropero

César Alfonso Ávalos

Luis Pedro Aguirre Maldonado

Claudia Figueroa Barrios

Mauricio Morales Prado

Laura Centeno Soto

Magdalena Quintero de Gracia

6-3 Una gira Trabajas en tu universidad como guía para los estudiantes nuevos. Crea una gira para ellos. Incluye por lo menos **cinco** lugares y **dos** deportes.

MODELO *Esta universidad tiene diez mil estudiantes. Esta es la biblioteca. Los estudiantes estudian aquí y usan las computadoras. Allí está el gimnasio donde juegan al básquetbol. Tenemos las especialidades de matemáticas, español…*

aquí	*here*
allí	*there / over there*
allá	*over there (and potentially not visible)*

Rúbrica

Estrategia

You and your instructor can use this rubric to assess your progress for **6-1** through **6-3**.

All aspects of our lives benefit from self-reflection and self-assessment. Learning Spanish is an aspect of our academic and future professional lives that benefits greatly from just such a self-assessment. Also coming into play is the fact that, as college students, you personally are being held accountable for your learning and are expected to take ownership for your performance. Having said that, we instructors can assist you greatly by letting you know what we expect of you. It will help you determine how well you are doing with the recycling of **Capítulo A Para empezar, Capítulo 1,** and **Capítulo 2.** This rubric is meant first and foremost for you to use as a self-assessment tool, but you also can use it to peer-assess. Your instructor may use the rubric to assess your progress as well.

	3 EXCEEDS EXPECTATIONS	2 MEETS EXPECTATIONS	1 APPROACHES EXPECTATIONS	0 DOES NOT MEET EXPECTATIONS
Duración y precisión	• Has at least 8 sentences and includes all the required information. • May have errors, but they do not interfere with communication.	• Has 5–7 sentences and includes all the required information. • May have errors, but they rarely interfere with communication.	• Has 4 sentences and includes some of the required information. • Has errors that interfere with communication.	• Supplies fewer sentences than in *Approaches Expectations* and little of the required information. • If communicating at all, has frequent errors that make communication limited or impossible.
Gramática nueva de los *Capítulos A Para empezar, 1 y 2*	• Makes excellent use of the chapters' new grammar. • Uses a wide variety of verbs.	• Makes good use of the chapters' new grammar. • Uses a variety of verbs.	• Makes use of some of the chapters' new grammar. • Uses a limited variety of verbs.	• Uses little, if any, of the chapters' new grammar. • Uses few, if any, of the chapters' verbs.
Vocabulario nuevo de los *Capítulos A Para empezar, 1 y 2*	• Uses many of the vocabulary words new to these chapters.	• Uses a variety of the new vocabulary words.	• Uses some of the new vocabulary words.	• Uses few, if any, new vocabulary words.
Esfuerzo (*Effort*)	• Clearly the student made his/her best effort.	• The student made a good effort.	• The student made an effort.	• Little or no effort went into the activity.

Capítulo 3

6-4 Mi casa favorita Mira los dibujos y descríbele tu casa favorita a un/a compañero/a. Dile (*Tell him/her*) por qué te gusta la casa y explícale por qué no te gustan las otras (*the other*) casas.

Estrategia

As you study vocabulary or grammar, it might be helpful to organize the information into a word web. Start with the concept you want to practice, such as *la casa,* write the word in the center of the page, and draw a circle around it. Then, as you brainstorm how your other vocabulary fits into *la casa,* you can create circles that branch off from your main idea, for example, *la cocina, la sala, el dormitorio,* etc. and then list the furniture that belongs in each room.

6-5 Mi horario personal Escribe tu horario para una semana. Incluye por lo menos **siete** actividades que haces dentro de la casa, apartamento o residencia y usa por lo menos **siete** verbos diferentes. Después comparte tu horario con un/a compañero/a.

Estrategia

When you are reviewing vocabulary, one strategy is to fold your paper lengthwise and have one column dedicated to the words in English and another column in Spanish. That way, you can fold the page over and look at only one set of words, testing yourself to see whether you really know the vocabulary.

6-6 Quiero saber...

Completa los siguientes pasos para entrevistar a un/a compañero/a.

Paso 1 Escribe tus preguntas usando los siguientes verbos.

hacer	oír	querer	salir	venir
poder	poner	saber	traer	conocer

MODELO *¿Qué traes a tus clases todos los días?*

Paso 2 Entrevista a tu compañero/a.

MODELO E1: *¿Qué traes a tus clases todos los días?*

E2: *Traigo mi mochila a mis clases todos los días…*

Paso 3 Comparte la información con tus compañeros de clase.

MODELO *Mi compañero Jake trae su mochila a sus clases. También,…*

Estrategia

With situations like those in **6-6**, it is not essential that *all* details be remembered. Nor is it essential in this type of scenario to repeat *verbatim* what someone has said; it is totally acceptable to express the same idea in different words. When necessary, ask him/her to repeat or clarify information.

6-7 ¿Qué tienen?

Túrnense para describir a las personas de los dibujos usando expresiones con **tener**.

MODELO *Jorge recibe una buena nota en su examen. Tiene éxito en su clase de periodismo.*

Julia

Susana Mirta

Beatriz Jorge

Guadalupe

Guillermo Miguel Beto

Adriana David

Estrategia

You and your instructor can use this rubric to assess your progress for **6-4** through **6-7**.

Rúbrica

	3 EXCEEDS EXPECTATIONS	2 MEETS EXPECTATIONS	1 APPROACHES EXPECTATIONS	0 DOES NOT MEET EXPECTATIONS
Duración y precisión	• Has at least 8 sentences and includes all the required information. • May have errors, but they do not interfere with communication.	• Has 5–7 sentences and includes all the required information. • May have errors, but they rarely interfere with communication.	• Has 4 sentences and includes some of the required information. • Has errors that interfere with communication.	• Supplies fewer sentences than in *Approaches Expectations* and little of the required information. • If communicating at all, has frequent errors that make communication limited or impossible.
Gramática nueva del *Capítulo 3*	• Makes excellent use of the chapter's new grammar (e.g., **irregular present tense verbs, *tener* expressions,** and ***hay***). • Uses a wide variety of new verbs.	• Makes good use of the chapter's new grammar (e.g., **irregular present tense verbs, *tener* expressions,** and ***hay***). • Uses a variety of new verbs.	• Makes use of some of the chapter's new grammar (e.g., **irregular present tense verbs, *tener* expressions,** and ***hay***). • Uses a limited variety of new verbs.	• Uses little if any of the chapter's grammar (e.g., **irregular present tense verbs, *tener* expressions**, and ***hay***).
Vocabulario nuevo del *Capítulo 3*	• Uses many of the new vocabulary words (e.g., **house, furniture,** and **household chores**).	• Uses a variety of the new vocabulary words (e.g., **house, furniture,** and **household chores**).	• Uses some of the new vocabulary words (e.g., **house, furniture,** and **household chores**).	• Uses little, if any, new vocabulary (e.g., **house, furniture,** and **household chores**).
Gramática y vocabulario reciclado de los capítulos anteriores	• Does an excellent job using recycled grammar and vocabulary to support what is being said. • Uses a wide array of recycled verbs. • Uses some recycled vocabulary but focuses predominantly on new vocabulary.	• Does a good job using recycled grammar and vocabulary to support what is being said. • Uses an array of recycled verbs. • Uses some recycled vocabulary but focuses predominantly on new vocabulary.	• Does an average job using recycled grammar and vocabulary to support what is being said. • Uses a limited array of recycled verbs. • Uses mostly recycled vocabulary and some new vocabulary.	• If speaking at all, relies almost completely on a few isolated words. • Grammar usage is inconsistent.
Esfuerzo	• Clearly the student made his/her best effort.	• The student made a good effort.	• The student made an effort.	• Little or no effort went into the activity.

Capítulo 4

6-8 Lo conocemos y lo sabemos Juntos hagan un diagrama de Venn sobre lo que conocen y saben, y sobre lo que no conocen o no saben. Escriban por lo menos **diez** oraciones.

MODELO

Janet
1. Mi familia y yo sabemos hablar español.
2. Mi amiga Julia y sus hermanos saben tocar el piano.

Nosotras
1. Sabemos patinar.
2. No sabemos hablar chino.
3. Conocemos a la profesora.

Audrey
1. Mi amiga Sally y su familia conocen al presidente de la universidad.

6-9 Un cuento (*story*) divertido Escriban en grupos un cuento creativo usando los siguientes verbos en el presente. Empiecen con la oración en el modelo. ¡Incluyan muchos detalles!

almorzar (nosotros)	devolver (él)	mostrar (ella)	servir (ellos)
cerrar (ellas)	dormir (ellos)	pedir (tú)	volver (yo)
costar (los libros)	encontrar (nosotros)	seguir (yo)	comenzar (él)

MODELO

¡Qué día tan horrible! Primero pierdo la tarea para la clase de __________.

entonces	*then*
después	*afterward*
finalmente	*finally*
luego	*then*
sin embargo	*nevertheless*

6-10 Mi comunidad ideal

Eres un/a arquitecto/a urbano/a y planeas tu ciudad ideal.

Paso 1 Dibuja el plano de tu ciudad con los lugares más necesarios (mercados, bancos, parques, etc.).

Paso 2 Descríbele tu ciudad a un/a compañero/a. Usa por lo menos **diez** oraciones con una variedad de verbos y vocabulario.

MODELO *Mi ciudad ideal se llama Ciudad Feliz. Hay una plaza en el centro. Tiene…*

6-11 Querida familia: …

Trabajas como consejero/a en un campamento de niños. Un día ayudas a los niños a escribirles cartas a sus padres y piensas que es una buena idea escribirle a un amigo también. En tu carta o e-mail, incluye oraciones que incorporen todos los usos que puedas (*all of the uses that you can*) de **ser** y **estar**.

MODELO

Querido José:

Estoy muy, muy cansada hoy. Tengo ganas de dormir pero ¡solamente son las 9! Siempre estoy muy ocupada (*busy*). Cuando tengo tiempo libre, a veces nado, pero nunca hago artesanía.

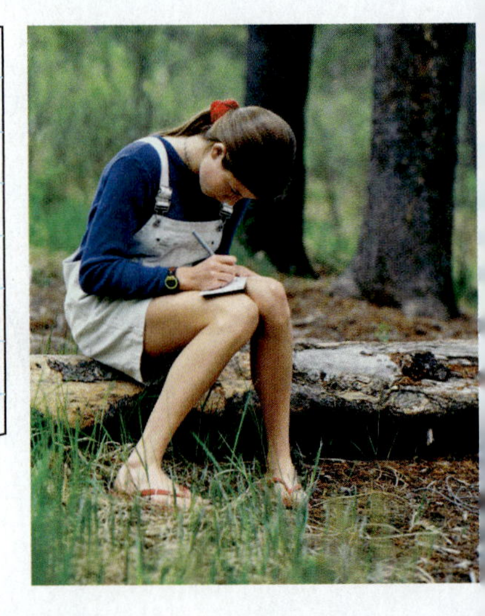

6-12 Mi tiempo libre ¡Tus compañeros y tú van a tener diez maravillosos días de vacaciones después de los exámenes! ¿Qué van a hacer? Túrnense **cinco** veces para decir oraciones usando **el futuro (*ir* + *a* + *infinitivo*)**. Después de decir tu oración, repite todo lo que dijeron (*you both said*) antes (*before*). Usen también diferentes pronombres (**yo, tú, ellos, nosotros**, etc.).

MODELO E1: *Voy a dormir diez horas cada día.*

E2: *Mis amigos van a ir a Cancún y tú vas a dormir diez horas cada día.*

E1: *Mi familia y yo vamos a nadar, tus amigos van a ir a Cancún, y voy a dormir diez horas cada día.*

E2: …

Estrategia

You and your instructor can use this rubric to assess your progress for **6-8** through **6-12**.

Rúbrica

	3 EXCEEDS EXPECTATIONS	2 MEETS EXPECTATIONS	1 APPROACHES EXPECTATIONS	0 DOES NOT MEET EXPECTATIONS
Duración y precisión	• Has at least 8 sentences and includes all the required information. • May have errors, but they do not interfere with communication.	• Has 5–7 sentences and includes all the required information. • May have errors, but they rarely interfere with communication.	• Has 4 sentences and includes some of the required information. • Has errors that interfere with communication.	• Supplies fewer sentences than in *Approaches Expectations* and little of the required information. • If communicating at all, has frequent errors that make communication limited or impossible.
Gramática nueva del *Capítulo 4*	• Makes excellent use of the chapter's new grammar (e.g., **stem-changing verbs, *ir, ir + a + infinitivo,*** and **affirmative and negative expressions**). • Uses a wide variety of new verbs.	• Makes good use of the chapter's new grammar (e.g., **stem-changing verbs, *ir, ir + a + infinitivo,*** and **affirmative and negative expressions**). • Uses a variety of new verbs.	• Makes use of some of the chapter's new grammar (e.g., **stem-changing verbs, *ir, ir + a + infinitivo, and* affirmative and negative expressions).** • Uses a limited variety of new verbs.	• Uses little if any of the chapter's grammar (e.g., **stem-changing verbs, *ir, ir + a + infinitivo,*** and **affirmative and negative expressions**). • Uses no new verbs.
Vocabulario nuevo del *Capítulo 4*	• Uses many of the new vocabulary words (e.g., **places** and **things to do**).	• Uses a variety of the new vocabulary words (e.g., **places** and **things to do**).	• Uses some of the new vocabulary words (e.g., **places** and **things to do**).	• Uses little, if any, new vocabulary (e.g., **places** and **things to do**).

(continued)

	3 EXCEEDS EXPECTATIONS	2 MEETS EXPECTATIONS	1 APPROACHES EXPECTATIONS	0 DOES NOT MEET EXPECTATIONS
Gramática y vocabulario reciclado de los capítulos anteriores	• Does an excellent job using recycled grammar and vocabulary to support what is being said. • Uses a wide array of recycled verbs. • Uses some recycled vocabulary but focuses predominantly on new vocabulary.	• Does a good job using recycled grammar and vocabulary to support what is being said. • Uses an array of recycled verbs. • Uses some recycled vocabulary but focuses predominantly on new vocabulary.	• Does an average job using recycled grammar and vocabulary to support what is being said. • Uses a limited array of recycled verbs. • Uses mostly recycled vocabulary and some new vocabulary.	• If speaking at all, relies almost completely on a few isolated words. • Grammar usage is inconsistent.
Esfuerzo	• Clearly the student made his/her best effort.	• The student made a good effort.	• The student made an effort.	• Little or no effort went into the activity.

Capítulo 5

6-13 ¡El concierto del siglo! Quieres ir al concierto de tu conjunto o cantante favorito, pero tu compañero/a no quiere ir. Creen un diálogo sobre su situación y preséntenlo a la clase. Su diálogo debe incluir por lo menos **doce** oraciones. Usen: formas de **este, ese, aquel**; unos adverbios (**-mente**); y pronombres de complemento directo (**me, te, lo, la, nos, los, las**).

MODELO E1: *David, quiero ir al concierto de Marc Anthony. Es este sábado a las ocho. Las entradas no cuestan mucho. Te invito.*

E2: *No gracias, Mariela. No quiero ir. Realmente, no puedo ir. Tengo mucha tarea.*

E1: *Pero David,…*

6-14 ¡Bienvenido/a, estrella! ¡Tienes el trabajo ideal! Puedes entrevistar a tu actor o actriz favorito/a del cine. Escribe **diez** preguntas que vas a hacerle. Después, con un/a compañero/a de clase, hagan los papeles de estrella y entrevistador/a para la clase.

6-15 El fin de semana Escribe un e-mail a un/a amigo/a. Dile (*tell him/her*) cómo pasaste (*how you spent*) el fin de semana pasado. Usa por lo menos 12 verbos de la lista.

apoyar	correr	grabar	montar	recibir
aprender	ensayar	guardar	participar	repartir
ayudar	escribir	lavar	preparar	trabajar
comer	estudiar	llevar	presentar	viajar

MODELO *Querido/a... :*
¡Qué fin de semana! El viernes...
Saludos,

____

Estrategia

You and your instructor can use this rubric to assess your progress for **6-13** through **6-15**.

Rúbrica

	3 EXCEEDS EXPECTATIONS	2 MEETS EXPECTATIONS	1 APPROACHES EXPECTATIONS	0 DOES NOT MEET EXPECTATIONS
Duración y precisión	• Has at least 8 sentences and includes all the required information. • May have errors, but they do not interfere with communication.	• Has 5–7 sentences and includes all the required information. • May have errors, but they rarely interfere with communication.	• Has 4 sentences and includes some of the required information. • Has errors that interfere with communication.	• Supplies fewer than 4 sentences and little of the required information. • Has frequent errors that make communication limited or impossible.
Gramática nueva del *Capítulo 5*	• Makes excellent use of the chapter's new grammar (e.g., **demonstrative adjectives and pronouns, adverbs, *Hay que...*, direct object pronouns,** and **regular verbs in the preterit**). • Uses a wide variety of new verbs.	• Makes good use of the chapter's new grammar (e.g., **demonstrative adjectives and pronouns, adverbs, *Hay que...*, direct object pronouns,** and **regular verbs in the preterit**). • Uses a variety of new verbs.	• Makes use of some of the chapter's new grammar (e.g., **demonstrative adjectives and pronouns, adverbs, *Hay que...*, direct object pronouns,** and **regular verbs in the preterit**). • Uses a limited variety of new verbs.	• Uses little, if any, of the chapter's new grammar (e.g., **demonstrative adjectives and pronouns, adverbs, *Hay que...*, direct object pronouns,** and **regular verbs in the preterit**). • Uses no new verbs.
Vocabulario nuevo del *Capítulo 5*	• Uses many of the new vocabulary words.	• Uses a variety of the new vocabulary words.	• Uses some of the new vocabulary words.	• Uses little, if any, new vocabulary.
Gramática y vocabulario reciclado de los capítulos anteriores	• Does an excellent job using recycled grammar and vocabulary to support what is being said. • Uses a wide array of recycled verbs. • Uses some recycled vocabulary but focuses predominantly on new vocabulary.	• Does a good job using recycled grammar and vocabulary to support what is being said. • Uses an array of recycled verbs. • Uses some recycled vocabulary but focuses predominantly on new vocabulary.	• Does an average job using recycled grammar and vocabulary to support what is being said. • Uses a limited array of recycled verbs. • Uses mostly recycled vocabulary and some new vocabulary.	• If speaking at all, relies almost completely on a few isolated words. • Grammar usage is inconsistent.
Esfuerzo	• The student made his/her best effort.	• The student made a good effort.	• The student made an effort.	• Little or no effort went into the activity.

Un poco de todo

6-16 ¡Ganaste la lotería!

Ganaste (*You won*) un millón de dólares en la lotería y te invitan a un programa de televisión para explicar qué vas a hacer con el dinero. Dile al/a la entrevistador/a (tu compañero/a) qué vas a hacer con el dinero en **diez** oraciones por lo menos. Después cambien de papel (*switch roles*).

6-17 Busco ayuda...

Con el dinero que ganaste en la lotería, decides buscar un ayudante personal (*personal assistant*) para ayudarte con los quehaceres de la casa y con algunos asuntos (*matters*) de tu trabajo. Entrevista a un/a compañero/a que hace el papel de ayudante. Después cambien de papel.

MODELO E1: *Debe mandar mis cartas y escribir unos e-mails.*

E2: *Bueno, pero no limpio las ventanas.*

E1: *¿Cómo? ¿No las limpia? ¿Pasa la aspiradora?*

E2: ...

6-18 Mi horario para la semana

Crea un horario para una semana ideal durante el verano. Usa por lo menos **diez** verbos diferentes para explicar lo que tienes que hacer. Comparte tu horario con un/a compañero/a.

julio

L	M	M	J	V	S	D
			1	2	3	4
5	6	7	8	9	10	11
12	13	14	15	16	17	18
19	20	21	22	23	24	25
26	27	28	29	30	31	

6-19 El verano pasado Escribe una entrada (*entry*) de blog de **ocho** a **diez** oraciones sobre algunas cosas que hiciste (*you did*) el verano pasado. Usa verbos de la lista de la Actividad **6-15**. Ojo: Incluye **cuándo, dónde** y **con quién** hiciste las cosas.

6-20 Para la comunidad Escribe un poema en verso libre o una canción sobre el voluntariado y sus beneficios para los que dan y para los que reciben ayuda.

MODELO *Ayudar a las personas es muy importante*
dar y recibir, dar y recibir
hay muchas maneras de hacer el voluntariado
en las residencias de ancianos…

6-21 Mi comunidad Túrnense para describir detalladamente su comunidad. Incluyan en su descripción oral detalles de su pueblo o ciudad (edificios, lugares de diversión, etc.), su casa y también las oportunidades que existen para hacer trabajo voluntario. Finalmente, hagan sus presentaciones para un grupo cívico como los Rotarios (*Rotary Club*).

México, D.F.

6-22 El juego de la narración

Túrnense para describir qué recuerdan de las **Lecturas** de los **Capítulos 1** a **5**. ¡Incluyan muchos detalles!

MODELO
E1: *En el **Capítulo 1** leemos información de Adriana en su perfil.*
E2: *Sí, ella tiene diecinueve años y es estudiante.*
E1: *Su familia es de origen mexicano. Adriana escribe de su familia en su perfil…*

Estrategia

The ability to retell information is an important language-learning strategy. Practice summarizing or retelling in your own words in Spanish the information presented in the *Lectura* section, chapter by chapter. Set a goal for yourself of saying or writing at least two things about each *Lectura*.

6-23 Su versión

En la actividad **6-22**, hablaron de las **Lecturas** de los **Capítulos 1** a **5**. Ahora es su turno como escritores. En grupos, van a escribir un cuento sobre Adriana, su familia y sus amigos. Pueden incluir información de su casa, sus actividades, sus preferencias, etc. Su instructor/a les va a explicar cómo hacerlo. Empiecen con la oración del modelo. ¡Sean muy creativos/as y diviértanse (*have fun*)!

MODELO *Adriana es una estudiante buena pero este semestre tiene algunas dificultades.*

6-24 Tu propia película documental

Eres director/a de cine y puedes crear tu propio video sobre tu universidad o tu pueblo/ciudad para un episodio de ***Club cultura*** de la sección de **Vistazo cultural**. Escribe una lista de los lugares y las personas que quieres incluir. Después escribe la introducción y los comentarios sobre cada lugar y persona.

6-25 Los hispanos en los Estados Unidos

Escribe **cinco** influencias hispanas en los Estados Unidos.

MODELO 1. *St. Augustine es la primera ciudad europea en los Estados Unidos.*

6-26 Aspectos interesantes

Escribe por lo menos **tres** cosas interesantes sobre cada uno de los siguientes países.

Estrategia

You have read numerous cultural notes throughout the first five chapters and have viewed corresponding episodes of *Club cultura*. To help you organize the material, make a chart of the most important information, or dedicate a separate page in your notebook for each country, recording the unique cultural items of that particular country.

MÉXICO	ESPAÑA	HONDURAS	GUATEMALA

EL SALVADOR	NICARAGUA	COSTA RICA	PANAMÁ

6-27 Un agente de viajes Durante el verano tienes la oportunidad de trabajar en una agencia de viajes (*travel agency*). Tienes unos clientes que quieren visitar un país hispanohablante. Escoge uno de los países que estudiamos y recomienda el país en **seis** oraciones por lo menos.

MODELO *Deben visitar Honduras, un país en el mar Caribe. Hay muchas cosas que pueden hacer. Por ejemplo, recomiendo las ruinas de Copán…*

6-28 Mi país favorito Describe tu país favorito entre los que hemos estudiado (*we have studied*). En **ocho** oraciones por lo menos explica por qué te gusta y lo que encuentras interesante e impresionante de ese país.

6-29 ¿Cómo son? Escoge dos países que estudiamos y escribe las diferencias y semejanzas (*similarities*) entre los dos.

MODELO *México es un país grande en Norteamérica. Nicaragua es un país pequeño y está en Centroamérica.*

6-30 ¡A jugar! Van a jugar ***¿Lo sabes?***, un juego como *Jeopardy!* Completen los siguientes pasos.

Paso 1 En grupos de tres o cuatro, preparen las respuestas para las siguientes categorías y después las preguntas correspondientes. (Pueden usar valores de dólares, pesos, euros, etc.)

Paso 2 Entre los grupos, intercambien (*exchange*) las respuestas y las preguntas. ¿Qué grupo va a ganar?

CATEGORÍAS

VOCABULARIO	**VERBOS**	**CULTURA**
la vida estudiantil	verbos regulares	Estados Unidos
las materias y las especialidades	verbos irregulares	México
los deportes y los pasatiempos	**saber** y **conocer**	España
la casa y los muebles	**ser** y **estar**	Honduras
los quehaceres de la casa	**ir**	Guatemala
el cine	**ir + a + infinitivo**	El Salvador
la música	verbos regulares en el pretérito	Nicaragua
el voluntariado		Costa Rica
		Panamá

MODELOS

CATEGORÍA: LA VIDA ESTUDIANTIL

Respuesta: en la residencia estudiantil
Pregunta: *¿Dónde viven los estudiantes?*

CATEGORÍA: LOS DEPORTES Y LOS PASATIEMPOS

Respuesta: Es Manny Machado.
Pregunta: *¿Quién juega al béisbol muy bien?*

¿LO SABES?
MÉXICO
ESPAÑA
HONDURAS
GUATEMALA

¿LO SABES? DOBLE
EL SALVADOR
NICARAGUA
COSTA RICA
PANAMÁ

Y por fin, ¿cómo andas?

Having completed this chapter, I now can...	Feel confident	Need to review
Comunicación		
• describe my family and other families.	☐	☐
• relate information about my school and campus.	☐	☐
• impart information about homes that my friends and I like and dislike.	☐	☐
• offer opinions on what will take place in the future.	☐	☐
• reveal what I and others like to do and what we need to do.	☐	☐
• report on service opportunities in my community.	☐	☐
• discuss music, movies, and television.	☐	☐
• share activities from the past.	☐	☐
• engage in additional communication practice (online).	☐	☐
Cultura		
• share information about the Spanish-speaking world in the United States, Mexico, Spain, Honduras, Guatemala, El Salvador, Nicaragua, Costa Rica, and Panama.	☐	☐
• compare and contrast the countries I learned about in **Capítulos 1–5**.	☐	☐
• explore further cultural themes (online).	☐	☐
Lecturas		
• share information about the readings from **Capítulos 1–5**.	☐	☐
Comunidades		
• use Spanish in real-life contexts (online).	☐	☐

B Para repasar

This chapter is a review of vocabulary and grammatical concepts that you are already familiar with in Spanish. Some of you are continuing with *¡Anda! Curso elemental*, while others may be coming from a different program. As you begin the second half of *¡Anda!*, it is important for all students to feel confident about what they already know about the Spanish language as they continue to acquire knowledge and proficiency. This chapter will help you determine what you already know, and also help you focus on what you personally need to improve upon.

If you are new to *¡Anda!*, you will not only want to review the grammar concepts already introduced, but also familiarize yourself with the active vocabulary used in the textbook.

¡Anda! recycles vocabulary and grammar concepts frequently to help you learn better, and this chapter will help you with what we consider to be the basics of the preceding chapters.

Before you begin this chapter, you may wish to review the study and learning strategies on page 220 in **Capítulo 6**. These strategies are applicable to your other subjects as well. So on your mark, get set, let's review!

¿Sabías que...?

El 50% de los estudiantes de lenguas en Estados Unidos estudia español.

Learning Outcomes

By the end of this chapter, you will be able to:

- ✔ describe people, homes, and household chores.
- ✔ impart information about student life, sports and pastimes, and service opportunities.
- ✔ identify places in and around town.
- ✔ relate likes and dislikes, things that happen, and things that have to be done.
- ✔ convey some past actions as well as expected actions in the near future.
- ✔ share information and preferences about music, movies, and television programs.

Comunicación

• Capítulo A Para empezar •

Greeting, introducing, and saying good-bye to others

1. Para empezar. This chapter provided an introduction to Spanish via the following topics: greetings and farewells; classroom expressions; the alphabet; cognates; subject pronouns and the verb **ser**; adjectives of nationality; numbers 1–30; telling time; days and months; the weather; and the verb **gustar**. If you need to review any of these topics before proceeding, consult pages 2–29.

• Capítulo 1 •

Describing yourself and others

2. La familia. Review the **La familia** vocabulary on page 32 and then do the following activities.

B-1 Mi familia

Túrnense para describir a sus familias o a una de las familias de las fotos. Digan por lo menos **cinco** oraciones.

Estrategia

In **B-1**, you are directed to write at least five sentences. See how many more than five you can write in the time allotted.

MODELO *George es mi tío. Mis primos son Stacy y Scott…*

3. El verbo *tener*. Review the verb **tener** on page 35. What are all the present tense forms of **tener**?

B-2 Y mis amigos... Túrnense para hablar de las familias de unos amigos o de una familia famosa usando el verbo **tener**. Digan por lo menos **ocho** oraciones.

MODELO *Mi amigo Joe tiene dos hermanos. Mis amigas Jennifer y Marty no tienen abuelos…*

4. El singular y el plural. Review how to make singular nouns plural on page 36 and explain the rules to your partner. Then complete the following activity.

B-3 Te toca a ti Si la palabra es singular, digan el plural y si es plural, digan el singular.

Fíjate

The rules for accents are listed in the *Pronunciación* section for *Capítulo 2* on *¡Anda!* online. As a reminder, some words keep their accent marks in the plural while other words lose or gain accent marks in the plural.

MODELO E1: primo
E2: *primos*

1. madres
2. francés
3. taxis
4. días
5. abuela
6. joven
7. educaciones
8. lápices
9. nieto
10. meses

5. El masculino y el femenino. Review the differences between masculine and feminine nouns on page 37. State the rules to a partner, and then do the following activity.

B-4 ¿Recuerdas? Digan si las siguientes palabras son masculinas o femeninas. **¡OJO!** Hay unas excepciones.

Fíjate

Some words that end in consonants, like *profesor*, also have feminine forms: *profesora*. Pay attention to the form when making the noun plural, as in the case of *profesores* or *profesoras*.

MODELO E1: tía
E2: *femenina*

1. padrastros
2. televisión
3. clase
4. universidad
5. hermano
6. mapa
7. sobrinas
8. hijo
9. foto
10. noche

6. Los artículos definidos e indefinidos. How do you say *the, a(n),* and *some* in Spanish? For a reminder, see page 38. Then do the following activity.

B-5 Vamos a practicar

Túrnense para añadir el equivalente de los artículos *the, a* o *some* a estas palabras.

MODELO E1: tías
E2: *las tías/unas tías*

1. abuelo
2. hermanas
3. madre
4. tío
5. hijos
6. primas
7. nieto
8. padres

7. Los adjetivos posesivos y descriptivos. How do you say *my, your, his, her, our*, and *their*? If you need help, see page 42. Also consult pages 44–45 to review words you may use to describe yourself and others. Then do the following activity.

B-6 Nuestras familias

Túrnense para describir a su familia y compararla con las familias de sus amigos. Digan por lo menos **ocho** oraciones.

MODELO *Mis padres son trabajadores. La mamá de mi amigo John es trabajadora también. Nuestros primos son simpáticos…*

Fíjate

When you see  by the activity number, you work with a partner. Words in the direction lines like *miren, túrnense, comparen*, and *usen* are plural—they refer to both of you.

• Capítulo 2 •

Sharing information about school and life as a student
Offering opinions about sports and pastimes that you and others like and dislike

8. Las materias y las especialidades. Review the **Las materias y las especialidades** vocabulary on page 66. Then practice the vocabulary words with the following activity.

B-7 ¿Cuál es más fácil?

Expresa tus opiniones sobre las materias y las especialidades. Comparte tus respuestas con un/a compañero/a. Puedes consultar **También se dice…** en el Apéndice 3.

MODELO *Las especialidades más difíciles son las matemáticas y los negocios. Las especialidades más fáciles son…*

LAS ESPECIALIDADES…

MÁS DIFÍCILES	MÁS FÁCILES	MÁS CREATIVAS	MÁS INTERESANTES	MÁS ABURRIDAS
1.	1.	1.	1.	1.
2.	2.	2.	2.	2.

Estrategia

For **B-7** about *Las materias y las especialidades*, change partners and find someone whose major is different from yours. See whether you have the same opinions.

9. La sala de clase. Review the **La sala de clase** vocabulary on page 69 and then do the following activity.

B-8 ¿Qué tienen tus compañeros/as?

Escoge (*Choose*) a unos/as de tus compañeros/as y completa el siguiente cuadro.

Estrategia

For **B-8**, you and your partner may wish to ask other classmates questions such as: *¿Qué tienes en tu mochila? ¿Qué tienes en tu escritorio?*

MODELO E1: *Hablamos de Melissa. ¿Qué tiene Melissa?*

E2: *Melissa tiene dos cuadernos, un libro, un bolígrafo y dos lápices.*

E3: *Pero Melissa no tiene la tarea.*

E2: *Ahora hablamos de _________ y _________. ¿Qué tienen _________ y _________?*

E1: *Tienen…*

ESTUDIANTE Melissa	ESTUDIANTES ____ Y ____	TÚ Y YO ____
(no) tiene	(no) tienen	(no) tenemos
1. tiene dos cuadernos	1.	1.
2. tiene un libro	2.	2.
3. tiene un bolígrafo	3.	3.
4. tiene dos lápices	4.	4.
5. no tiene la tarea	5.	5.

10. Presente indicativo de verbos regulares. How do you form the present tense of regular **-ar, -er,** and **-ir** verbs? If you need help, consult pages 71–72. Finally, before you complete the following activities, review the common verbs that are presented on those pages.

B-9 ¿A quién o quiénes conoces que…?

Túrnense para preguntarse y contestar para qué personas que ustedes conocen son ciertas las siguientes afirmaciones.

Estrategia

You will note that nearly all activities in *¡Anda! Curso elemental* are pair activities. You will be encouraged or required to change partners frequently, perhaps even daily. The purpose is for you to be able to practice Spanish with a wide array of speakers. Working with different classmates will help you improve your spoken Spanish more quickly.

MODELO hablar poco

E1: *¿Quién habla poco?*

E2: *Mi hermano Evan habla poco.*

E2: *¿Quiénes hablan poco?*

E1: *Mis padres hablan poco. / Mis hermanos y yo hablamos poco.*

1. hablar mucho
2. enseñar español
3. vivir en el campo
4. escribir muchos mensajes de texto
5. usar los apuntes de sus amigos
6. estudiar mucho
7. necesitar estudiar más
8. tomar un examen hoy
9. correr mucho

B-10 Dime quién, dónde y cuándo

Miren el dibujo y creen (*create*) juntos una historia sobre lo que ocurre en el edificio.

Estrategia

¡Anda! Curso elemental encourages you to be creative when practicing and using Spanish. One way is to create mini-stories about photos or drawings that you see. Being creative includes giving individuals in drawings names and characteristics.

MODELO E1: *Josefina escribe una carta.*
E2: *Ella escribe cartas todos los días.*
E1: *En otro apartamento Raúl y Mariela…*

11. La formación de preguntas y las palabras interrogativas. How do you form questions in Spanish? What are the question words in Spanish? To review this topic, consult pages 75–76 and then do the following activity.

B-11 Preguntas y más preguntas

Túrnense para formar una pregunta con cada oración.

Fíjate

Remember that all question words have accents. Also remember that when writing a question, there are two question marks, an inverted one at the beginning and one at the end of the question.

MODELO E1: Estudio **matemáticas**.
E2: *¿Qué estudias?*

1. Pilar estudia **en la biblioteca**.
2. **Guillermo y yo** estudiamos.
3. Comen **entre las 7:00 y las 8:00 de la noche**.
4. Aprendemos español **fácilmente**.
5. Leo **tres libros**.
6. Estudiamos español **porque nos gusta el profesor**.

12. Los números 1–1.000. Review the numbers 1–1,000, consulting pages 16, 50, and 78 if you need help. Then do the following activity.

B·12 ¡Dilo! Túrnense para decir los precios de los artículos en el catálogo.

MODELO E1: (325 €) *El precio del armario es trescientos veinticinco euros.*

E2: (999 €) *El precio del sofá es…*

13. El verbo *estar*. What are the present-tense forms of **estar**? When do you use **estar**? Check page 83 if you need help before doing the following activity.

B-13 ¿Dónde?

Túrnense para hacerse preguntas y contestar usando **estar**.

MODELO el mapa / libro

E1: *¿Dónde está el mapa?*

E2: *El mapa está en el libro.*

Fíjate

Remember that four forms of *estar* have accents in the present tense: *estás, está, estáis,* and *están.*

1. mis amigos y yo / la clase de ciencias
2. tú / el apartamento
3. los escritorios / la sala de clase
4. el papel / la silla
5. los apuntes / el cuaderno
6. Jorge y tú / la puerta
7. los libros / la mochila
8. José / bien
9. Lupe y Mariela / contento

14. Emociones y estados. Review the **Emociones y estados** vocabulary on page 86 and then do the following activity.

B-14 ¿Qué pasa?

Digan qué adjetivo describe cada una de las siguientes situaciones.

MODELO E1: Jorge y María reciben mil dólares.

E2: *Están contentos.*

Fíjate

In **B-14** you see *sus exámenes de español e informática.* The word *y* changes to *e* when the *i* sound appears immediately after the *y*, as in the case of the word *informática.*

1. Esperas y esperas pero tu amigo no llega. (¡Y no te llama por teléfono!)
2. Corres quince millas (*miles*).
3. Tus padres están en el hospital.
4. Tu novio/a está en Panamá y ¡no regresa!
5. El profesor de literatura lee sin parar durante (*during*) una hora y quince minutos.
6. Ustedes sacan "A" en sus exámenes de español e informática.
7. Ustedes tienen un examen muy difícil hoy.

15. En la universidad. Review the **En la universidad** vocabulary on pages 80–81 and do the following activity.

B-15 ¡Lo sé!

Digan qué lugares asocian con las siguientes palabras y acciones. Después formen una oración completa.

MODELO estudiar

E1: *Voy a la biblioteca para estudiar.*

E2: *Estudio en mi apartamento.*

1. jugar al fútbol
2. comprar libros
3. comer hamburguesas, pizza y sándwiches
4. jugar al básquetbol
5. hacer experimentos científicos
6. leer libros, estudiar, escribir composiciones, etc.

16. El verbo *gustar*. How do you say *to like* in Spanish? Review page 87 and then do the following activity.

B-16 Opiniones

¿Cuáles son tus opiniones sobre los siguientes temas (*topics*)? Completa los siguientes pasos.

Paso 1 Escribe tus opiniones de cada tema.

Paso 2 Pregunta a dos compañeros/as cuáles son sus opiniones.

MODELO E1: ¿Qué materias te gustan más?

E2: *Las materias que más me gustan son las ciencias y las matemáticas.*

	LAS MATERIAS…	LOS/LAS ESCRITORES/AS…	LAS PELÍCULAS…
	que más me gustan son:	que más me gustan son:	que más me gustan son:
YO	1.	1.	1.
ESTUDIANTE 1	2.	2	2
ESTUDIANTE 2	3.	3.	3.
	que menos me gustan son:	que menos me gustan son:	que menos me gustan son:
YO	1.	1.	1.
ESTUDIANTE 1	2	2	2
ESTUDIANTE 2	3.	3.	3.

Paso 3 Comparte las opiniones de tus compañeros/as.

MODELO *Las materias que más le gustan a David son las ciencias y las matemáticas. La escritora que más le gusta es J.K. Rowling…*

17. Los deportes y los pasatiempos. Review the **Los deportes y los pasatiempos** vocabulary on pages 89–90 and then do the following activity.

B-17 Tus preferencias

Selecciona los **tres** deportes o pasatiempos **que más te gustan** y luego los **tres que menos te gustan.** Después de completar el cuadro, comparte la información con un/a compañero/a, según el modelo.

MODELO *Los deportes o pasatiempos que más me gustan son patinar, bailar y leer. Los deportes o pasatiempos que menos me gustan son el fútbol, el fútbol americano y nadar.*

LOS DEPORTES Y PASATIEMPOS QUE MÁS ME GUSTAN	LOS DEPORTES Y PASATIEMPOS QUE MENOS ME GUSTAN
1.	1.
2.	2.
3.	3.

• Capítulo 3 •

Describing homes and household chores

18. La casa. Review the vocabulary about **La casa** on page 106 and do the following activities.

B-18 Las actividades

Túrnense para decir en qué parte o partes de la casa hacen las siguientes actividades.

MODELO E1: estudiar

E2: *Estudio en la oficina, en el dormitorio y en la cocina.*

1. escuchar música y ver la televisión
2. organizar papeles
3. tomar una siesta
4. preparar tacos
5. tocar el piano
6. hablar por teléfono
7. tomar el sol
8. trabajar en la computadora

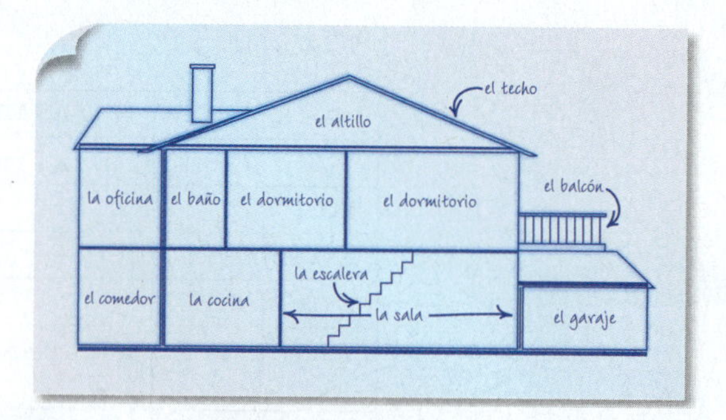

B-19 ¿Y tu casa...?

Descríbele tu casa o apartamento a un/a compañero/a. O si quieres, puedes describir tu casa ideal. Usa por lo menos **ocho** oraciones.

MODELO *Mi casa tiene dos pisos. Mi dormitorio está en la planta baja. No tenemos un altillo. Mi dormitorio está al lado del baño. La cocina es pequeña…*

19. Algunos verbos irregulares. Review the irregular verbs on pages 109–110 and then practice them with the following activities.

B-20 Otras combinaciones

Túrnense para formar oraciones completas combinando elementos de las tres columnas. Formen una oración distinta con cada verbo de la columna B.

MODELO *Nosotros hacemos la tarea todos los días.*

COLUMNA A	COLUMNA B	COLUMNA C
Uds.	(no) hacer	estudiar ciencias
el profesor	(no) oír	muchas películas
él, ella, Ud.	(no) querer	la tarea todos los días
nosotros/as	(no) salir	los libros a clase
ellos/ellas	(no) traer	temprano (*early*) a la universidad
yo	(no) venir	los viernes
tú	(no) ver	tocar la guitarra
mamá y papá	(no) poder	ruidos (*noises*) por la noche

B-21 Entrevista

Túrnense para hacerse la siguiente entrevista.

MODELO E1: ¿Qué haces cuando no tienes sueño?
E2: *Cuando no tengo sueño, leo o veo la televisión.*

1. ¿Qué haces cuando tienes sed?
2. ¿Cuándo haces ejercicio?
3. ¿Sales los fines de semana? ¿Con quién o quiénes sales?
4. ¿Qué quieres ser (o hacer) en el futuro?
5. ¿Conoces a una persona famosa?
6. ¿Cuándo ves la televisión?
7. ¿Qué traes a tus clases?
8. ¿Qué días vienes a la clase de español?
9. ¿A qué hora sales de tu casa, apartamento o residencia para la clase?
10. ¿Qué puedes hacer para tener más éxito en tus clases?

Estrategia

Getting to know your classmates helps you build confidence. It is much easier to interact with someone you know.

20. *Hay* y *hay que + infinitivo*. What do **hay** and **hay que + *infinitivo*** mean? When might you use each of these constructions? Review page 128 if you need help. Then do the following activities.

B-22 ¿Qué hay en tu casa?

Descríbele tu casa a un/a compañero/a y averigua (*find out*) cómo es la suya (*his/hers*) usando **hay**.

Fíjate

Remember that you can form questions by adding question marks to the statement or inverting the order of the subject and the verb.

MODELO E1: *En mi casa hay un garaje. ¿Hay un garaje en tu casa?*

E2: *Sí, en mi casa hay un garaje. / No, en mi casa no hay un garaje.*

E1: *Mi casa tiene dos pisos. ¿Cuántos pisos hay en tu casa?*

B-23 ¿Obligaciones?

Digan qué hay que hacer para tener una casa limpia y bien organizada.

MODELO el sótano

E1: *Hay que limpiar el piso.*

E2: *Hay que guardar todas las cosas.*

1. la cocina
2. el comedor
3. el dormitorio
4. la oficina
5. la sala
6. el baño

21. Los muebles y otros objetos de la casa. Review the **Los muebles y otros objetos de la casa** vocabulary on page 114. Then do the following activity.

B-24 En mi casa

¿Qué muebles y objetos tienen o no tienen en casa? Completen los siguientes pasos.

Paso 1 Túrnense para describir los muebles y los objetos de las fotos.

MODELO E1: *Hay un sofá blanco, una mesa con libros y un cuadro grande en la sala.*

E2: *En el comedor hay una mesa y ocho sillas…*

Paso 2 Ahora digan qué muebles y objetos tienen en sus casas, o en las casas de sus familias.

MODELO E1: *Yo tengo una cama y dos sillas en mi dormitorio. No tengo una televisión. ¿Qué tienes tú?*

E2: *Yo tengo un cuadro, una lámpara y una televisión.*

22. Los quehaceres de la casa y los colores. Review the vocabulary dealing with **Los quehaceres de la casa** and **Los colores** on pages 117 and 119. Then, do the following activities.

B-25 Responsabilidades

¿Cuáles son sus responsabilidades? Túrnense para contestar las siguientes preguntas y explicar cuándo hacen estos quehaceres y cuánto tiempo dedican a hacerlos.

MODELO E1: mi dormitorio

E2: *Tengo que limpiar mi dormitorio los lunes. Necesito dos horas porque está muy sucio.*

1. mi dormitorio
2. el baño
3. la cocina
4. la sala
5. el garaje
6. el comedor

Estrategia

Group the rooms of the house with the verbs associated with each room. For example, match *comer* and *el comedor, bañarse* and *el baño, dormir* and *el dormitorio, cocinar* and *la cocina.*

¿QUÉ TIENES QUE HACER?	¿CUÁNDO?	¿CUÁNTO TIEMPO?
limpiar mi dormitorio	los lunes	dos horas

B-26 La casa ideal ¿Cómo es tu casa ideal? ¿Y los colores? Descríbele tu casa ideal a un/a compañero/a en por lo menos **ocho** oraciones.

MODELO *Quiero una casa con una cocina amarilla...*

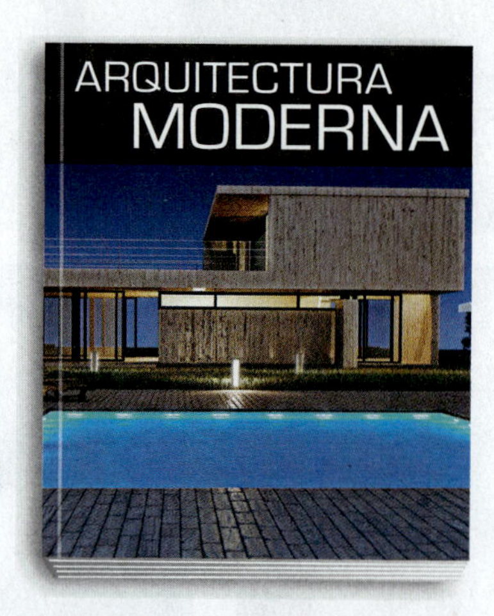

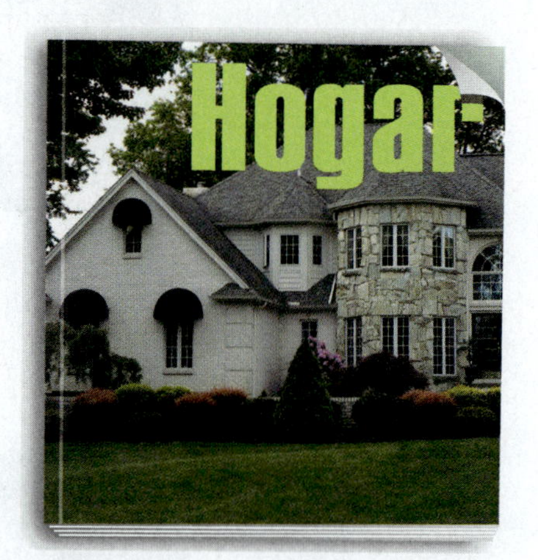

23. Algunas expresiones con *tener*. Review the **tener** expressions on page 121 and then do the following activities.

B-27 ¿Qué tengo yo? Túrnense para expresar cómo se sienten (*you feel*) en las siguientes situaciones. Usen las expresiones con **tener**.

MODELO E1: antes de comer

E2: *Antes de comer tengo hambre.*

1. los lunes
2. los sábados
3. tarde en la noche
4. temprano en la mañana
5. antes de tener un examen
6. cuando ves una película de terror
7. en el verano
8. en el invierno
9. durante (*during*) la semana de los exámenes finales
10. cuando sacas "A" en un examen

B-28 Datos personales Túrnense para hacerse esta entrevista.

1. ¿Cuántos años tienes?
2. ¿Cuándo tienes hambre?
3. ¿Qué tienes que hacer hoy?
4. ¿Qué tienes ganas de hacer?
5. ¿En qué clase tienes sueño?
6. ¿En qué clase tienes mucha suerte?
7. ¿Siempre tienes razón?
8. ¿Cuándo tienes sueño?
9. Cuando tienes sed, ¿qué tomas?

24. Los números 1.000–100.000.000. Review the numbers on page 124 and then do the following activity.

B-29 ¿Cuál es su población?

Túrnense para leer las poblaciones de las siguientes capitales del mundo hispano en voz alta.

1. Buenos Aires, Argentina	15.180.000
2. La Paz, Bolivia	1.816.000
3. Bogotá, Colombia	9.765.000
4. La Habana, Cuba	2.137.000
5. San José, Costa Rica	1.170.000
6. México, D.F., México	20.999.000

Source: CIA World Factbook

25. Los números ordinales. How do you say *first, second, third,* etc. in Spanish? Check your answers on page 124 and then do the following activity.

B-30 ¿En qué piso?

Túrnense para decir en qué piso están las siguientes personas y qué quehaceres hacen.

MODELO El Sr. Sánchez

El Sr. Sánchez está en la planta baja y sacude una lámpara.

1. Lourdes
2. Lina y Carlos
3. Hosun
4. Donato y Leticia
5. Juan y Carmen
6. Teresa
7. Reyes
8. Javier

• Capítulo 4 •

Identifying places in and around town
Relating things that happen and things that have to be done
Conveying what will take place in the immediate future
Imparting information about service opportunities

26. Los lugares. Review the **Los lugares** vocabulary on page 142 and then do the following activity.

B-31 ¿Dónde está?

Tus amigos y tú están muy ocupados. Túrnate con un/a compañero/a para decir dónde están.

MODELO E1: Mi amigo quiere mandar una carta.
E2: *Está en la oficina de correos.*

1. Marta quiere leer y necesita comprar un libro.
2. Dos de mis amigos necesitan dinero.
3. Julio tiene hambre y quiere comer algo.
4. Queremos ver una exposición de arte.
5. Ustedes quieren ver una película.
6. Jorge tiene sed y quiere tomar algo.
7. Tenemos que ir de compras.
8. Tienen que ir a una boda (*wedding*).

27. *Saber* y *conocer*. Make a list of when you use **saber** and when you use **conocer**. You can review the uses on page 146. Then do the following activity.

B-32 ¿Lo sabes o lo conoces?

Completa cada una de las siguientes preguntas usando **sabes** o **conoces**. Después, túrnate con un/a compañero/a para hacerse y contestar las preguntas.

MODELO E1: *¿Conoces Buenos Aires?*
E2: *Sí, conozco Buenos Aires. / No, no conozco Buenos Aires.*

1. ¿_______________ un buen lugar para comprar un teléfono celular?
2. ¿_______________ preparar tortillas?
3. ¿_______________ cuál es el mejor café de donde vives?
4. ¿_______________ San José, Costa Rica?
5. ¿_______________ jugar al golf?
6. ¿_______________ dónde están tus amigos ahora?
7. ¿_______________ al presidente de los Estados Unidos?
8. ¿_______________ el Wok, el mejor restaurante chino de esta comunidad?
9. ¿_______________ usar una computadora?
10. ¿_______________ las películas de Chris Hemsworth?

28. Actividades y acciones cotidianas. What are the things you usually do, and what do you have to do (**tener que** + **infinitivo**)? Review pages 121 and 148 if you have any questions before doing this activity.

B-33 Entrevistas

¿Hacen tus compañeros/as cosas similares? Completa los siguientes pasos.

Paso 1 Usando las siguientes preguntas, entrevista a tres compañeros/as.

1. ¿Cuáles son las cosas que haces para prepararte (*prepare yourself*) bien para tus clases?
2. Generalmente, ¿qué tienes que hacer después de terminar tus clases?

Paso 2 Comparte la información con otros/as compañeros/as de la clase. ¿Qué tienen ustedes en común?

MODELO *Para prepararse bien para las clases, Jack y ally tienen que estudiar cinco horas cada día. Sally repite las palabras nuevas. Jack pide ayuda a sus compañeros. Después de terminar nuestras clases, nosotros tenemos que limpiar nuestros apartamentos…*

29. Los verbos con cambio de raíz. Review the stem-changing verbs on pages 150–151 and then practice with the following activities.

B-34 ¿Quién es?

Túrnense para decir a qué personas conocen que hacen las siguientes actividades.

MODELO siempre perder la tarea

E1: *Mi novia Carmen siempre pierde la tarea.*

E2: *Mis primos siempre pierden la tarea.*

1. almorzar comida rápida (*fast food*) frecuentemente
2. siempre entender al/a la profesor/a de español
3. jugar al fútbol muy bien
4. preferir dormir hasta el mediodía
5. volver a casa tarde a menudo (*often*)
6. nunca tener dinero y siempre tener que pedirlo
7. nunca encontrar sus cosas
8. querer visitar Centroamérica
9. pensar que Santa Claus existe
10. nunca mentir

B-35 Un poco de mi vida

Escucha mientras tu compañero /a contesta las siguientes preguntas. Luego, repite la información a tu compañero/a. ¿Escuchaste bien? ¿Cuánta información puedes recordar?

Estrategia

Being an "active listener" is an important skill in any language. *Active listening* means that you have heard and understood what someone is saying. Being able to repeat what someone says helps you practice and perfect the skill of active listening.

1. ¿Qué clases tienes este semestre?
2. ¿A qué hora empieza tu clase preferida?
3. ¿Qué prefieres hacer si tienes tiempo entre (*between*) las clases?
4. ¿A qué hora vuelves a tu residencia/apartamento/casa?
5. ¿Qué carro tienes (o quieres tener)?
6. ¿Cuánto cuesta un carro nuevo?
7. ¿Cómo vienes a la universidad? Por ejemplo, ¿vienes en carro?
8. ¿Dónde prefieres vivir, en una residencia estudiantil, en un apartamento o en una casa?
9. ¿Dónde quieres vivir después de graduarte?
10. ¿Qué deporte prefieres?

30. El verbo *ir* e *ir* + *a* + *infinitivo*. What are the present tense forms of ***ir***? How do you express the future with **ir**? Consult pages 154 and 156 if you need to do so, and then do the following activities.

B-36 ¡Vámonos!

Completa las oraciones según el modelo. Después túrnate con un/a compañero/a para decir adónde van sus parientes (*relatives*) y sus amigos en las siguientes situaciones.

Estrategia

When you write sentences that require more than one verb, as in **B-36**, make sure that your verbs match your subject throughout the sentence.

MODELO E1: Cuando tengo que estudiar…
E2: *Cuando tengo que estudiar, voy a la biblioteca.*

1. Cuando quiere comer, mi compañero de cuarto…
2. Cuando queremos hacer ejercicio, nosotros…
3. Cuando tienes ganas de bailar, tú…
4. Para almorzar muy bien, mis amigos…
5. En la primavera me gusta…
6. Cuando mi hermana quiere comprar música, ella…
7. Para ver una película, tú…
8. Cuando llueve, yo…
9. Cuando hace frío, mis padres…
10. En el verano prefiero…

B-37 Nuestra agenda

¿Qué van a hacer la semana que viene? Termina las siguientes oraciones con planes diferentes usando **ir** + **a** + **infinitivo**. Compara tus respuestas con las de un/a compañero/a.

MODELO E1: El lunes, yo…
E2: *El lunes voy a devolver unos libros a la biblioteca.*

1. El lunes, yo…
2. El martes, la profesora…
3. El miércoles, mis amigos…
4. El jueves, tú y yo…
5. El viernes, mis primos…
6. El sábado, tú…
7. El domingo, mi madre…

B-38 ¿Qué van a hacer?

¿Qué va a ocurrir este año a ti, a tus amigos y a tu familia? Hagan **cinco** predicciones de lo que va a pasar y después compartan sus respuestas.

MODELO *Mi primo va a ir a la Universidad Autónoma en enero. Nosotros vamos a estudiar mucho para sacar buenas notas. Mis padres van a trabajar en Baltimore…*

31. Servicios a la comunidad. Review the vocabulary **Servicios a la comunidad** on page 158 and then do the following activity.

B-39 ¿A qué se refiere?

Túrnense para leer las siguientes definiciones y decir a qué palabra o expresión corresponde cada una.

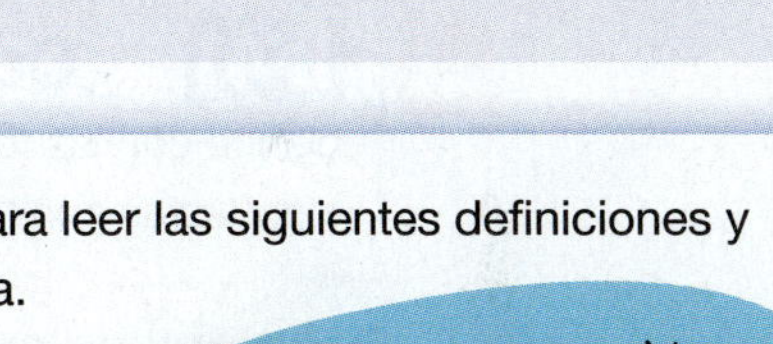

MODELO E1: personas que tienen muchos años
E2: *Las personas que tienen muchos años son los mayores.*

1. servir a las personas sin (*without*) recibir dinero a cambio (*in exchange*)
2. un lugar donde viven las personas mayores
3. acompañar a una persona a una cita (*appointment*) con el médico
4. dar un documento a las personas para obtener firmas
5. trabajar para un candidato político sin recibir dinero a cambio
6. una persona que trabaja con los niños en un campamento
7. salir en un barco (*boat*) para una o dos personas
8. disfrutar de (*enjoy*) un tipo de arte
9. "construir" una estructura portátil (no permanente) que se usa para dormir fuera de casa
10. un lugar adonde van los niños, generalmente en el verano, para hacer muchas actividades diferentes

32. Las expresiones afirmativas y negativas. Review the affirmative and negative expressions on pages 160–161 and then do the following activity.

B-40 El/La profesor/a ideal

Túrnense para decir si las siguientes características son ciertas o falsas en un profesor ideal. Usen las expresiones afirmativas y negativas en la página 161 para apoyar (*support*) sus opiniones.

MODELO Un/a profesor/a ideal… siempre da buenas notas.

E1: *A veces un profesor ideal da buenas notas.*

E2: *No, el profesor ideal no siempre da buenas notas. A veces tiene que dar malas notas.*

Un/a profesor/a ideal…

1. nunca falta (*misses*) a clase.
2. prepara algo interesante para cada clase.
3. siempre prefiere leer sus apuntes.
4. piensa que sabe más que nadie.
5. a veces organiza a sus estudiantes en grupos para discutir (*discuss*) ideas.
6. a veces llega a clase cinco minutos tarde.
7. jamás manda (da) tarea para la clase.
8. no pierde nada: por ejemplo, la tarea, los exámenes, las composiciones, etc.
9. no habla con nadie después de la clase.
10. siempre está contento/a con su trabajo.

33. Un repaso de *ser* y *estar*. When do you use **ser** and **estar**? Write the reasons on a sheet of paper, and then check your list against the one on pages 164–165. Next, do the following activities.

B-41 ¿Qué tal?

Adriana le escribe un e-mail a su familia. Llena los espacios en blanco con las formas correctas de **ser** y **estar** para conocerla mejor. Después comparte tus respuestas con un/a compañero/a.

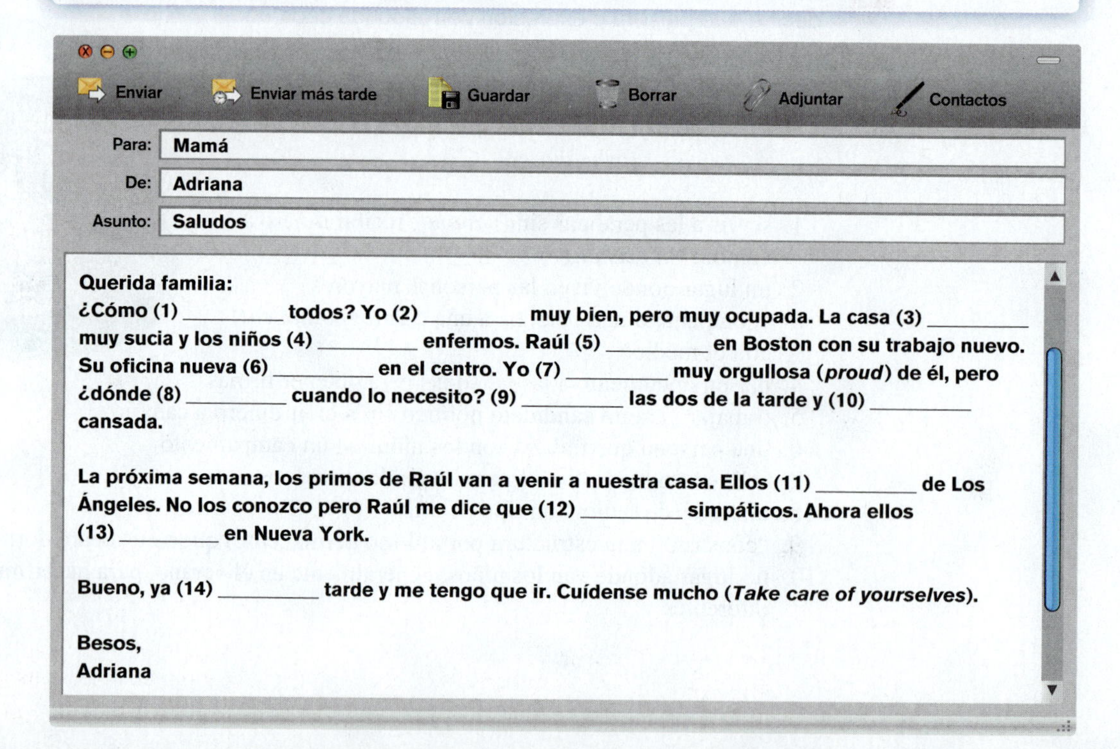

Enviar | Enviar más tarde | Guardar | Borrar | Adjuntar | Contactos

Para: Mamá
De: Adriana
Asunto: Saludos

Querida familia:

¿Cómo (1) ________ todos? Yo (2) ________ muy bien, pero muy ocupada. La casa (3) ________ muy sucia y los niños (4) ________ enfermos. Raúl (5) ________ en Boston con su trabajo nuevo. Su oficina nueva (6) ________ en el centro. Yo (7) ________ muy orgullosa (*proud*) de él, pero ¿dónde (8) ________ cuando lo necesito? (9) ________ las dos de la tarde y (10) ________ cansada.

La próxima semana, los primos de Raúl van a venir a nuestra casa. Ellos (11) ________ de Los Ángeles. No los conozco pero Raúl me dice que (12) ________ simpáticos. Ahora ellos (13) ________ en Nueva York.

Bueno, ya (14) ________ tarde y me tengo que ir. Cuídense mucho (*Take care of yourselves*).

Besos,
Adriana

B-42 Así es
Ahora expliquen por qué usaron **ser** o **estar** en cada parte de **B-41**.

MODELO 1. están *physical condition*

B-43 A conocernos mejor
Túrnense para hacerse y contestar las siguientes preguntas.

1. ¿De dónde eres?
2. ¿A qué hora son tus clases?
3. ¿Cómo es tu casa?
4. ¿Dónde está tu casa?
5. ¿Cómo es tu dormitorio?
6. ¿Dónde está tu dormitorio?
7. ¿De qué color es tu casa?
8. ¿Cuál es tu color favorito?
9. ¿Cómo es tu novio/a (esposo/a, mejor amigo/a)?
10. ¿Dónde está él/ella ahora (*now*)?
11. ¿Cómo eres?
12. ¿Cómo estás hoy?

• Capítulo 5 •

Sharing information about different types of music, movies, and television programs, including your personal preferences

Describing things that happened in the past

34. El mundo de la música. Review the **El mundo de la música** vocabulary on pages 182–183 and then do the following activities.

B-44 ¿Qué quiere decir?
Lee las siguientes descripciones. Después, túrnate con un/a compañero/a para decir a qué palabra o expresión se refieren.

MODELO E1: dar conciertos en varias ciudades

E2: *Dar conciertos en varias ciudades es "hacer una gira".*

1. ser muy popular y conocido entre muchas personas, como Shakira
2. las palabras que cantas en una canción
3. la música de Mozart y Beethoven, por ejemplo
4. una persona que canta
5. lo que usas para cantar y hablar
6. un instrumento de percusión
7. sinónimo de "grupo"
8. hacer sonido bonito con un instrumento
9. cuando haces algo muy bien, dicen que tienes mucha…
10. la música de Jay-Z y Nicky Minaj, por ejemplo

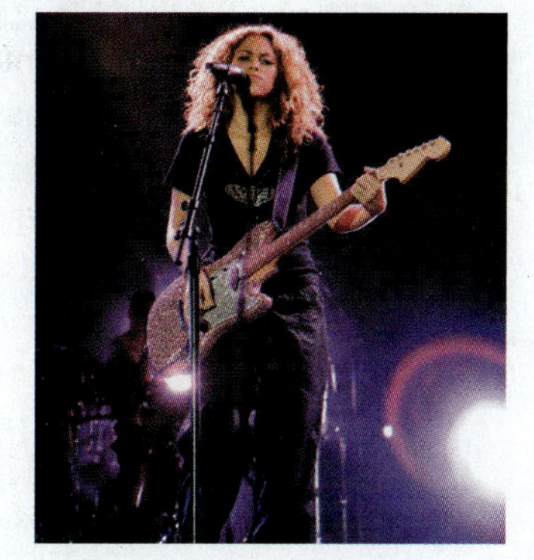

B-45 La música
Túrnense para hacerse esta entrevista.

1. ¿Cuál es tu grupo favorito?
2. ¿Cuál es tu cantante favorito/a?
3. ¿Cuál es tu instrumento favorito?
4. ¿Cuál es tu tipo de música favorito?
5. ¿Cuál es tu canción favorita?
6. ¿Sabes tocar un instrumento? ¿Cuál?
7. ¿Te gusta cantar? ¿Cuándo y dónde cantas?
8. ¿En qué tienes mucha habilidad o talento?

35. Los adjetivos y pronombres demostrativos. How do you say *this, that, these*, and *those* in Spanish? Review the demonstrative adjectives and pronouns on pages 186–187 and then do the following activities.

B-46 ¿Qué prefieres?

Tu mejor amigo/a te propone una cosa, pero tú siempre prefieres otra. Responde a sus comentarios usando la forma correcta de **este, ese** o **aquel**.

MODELO TU MEJOR AMIGO/A: ¿Quieres ir a este cine?
TÚ: *No, no quiero ir a este. Quiero ir a aquel.*

1. ¿Vamos a ir a ese teatro?
2. ¿Tus amigos van a tocar en aquel conjunto?
3. ¿Quieres escuchar a aquellas cantantes?
4. ¿Te gusta la letra de esta canción?
5. ¿Preparas una presentación sobre este género de música?
6. ¿Quieres ver a estos músicos en concierto?

B-47 En la universidad

Túrnense para hablar de lo que les gusta o no les gusta usando formas de **este, ese** y **aquel.** Hagan por lo menos **cinco** oraciones positivas y **cinco** oraciones negativas.

MODELO *Me gusta esta clase. Nuestro profesor de español es interesante, pero aquel profesor de sociología es un poco aburrido. Este libro es bueno, pero ese libro de matemáticas es difícil…*

36. Los adverbios. In Spanish, how do most adverbs end? How are they formed? Check page 191 to verify your answers. Then do the following activity.

B-48 ¿Qué ocurre en el concierto?

Vas a un concierto de varios conjuntos en el estadio de tu universidad. Para saber qué pasa, completa estas oraciones con los adverbios apropiados. Comparte tus respuestas con un/a compañero/a.

MODELO E1: Vamos al concierto (rápido, apasionado).
E2: *Vamos al concierto rápidamente.*

1. La gente espera a los conjuntos (paciente, rápido).
2. El primer conjunto toca (claro, feliz).
3. Un grupo llega tarde y entra al estadio (lento, nervioso).
4. Los otros músicos escuchan (atento, suave).
5. El conjunto toca una canción romántica y la gente empieza a bailar (lento, rápido).
6. Terminan el concierto (difícil, final).

37. El mundo del cine. Review the **El mundo del cine** vocabulary on page 193 and practice it with the following activity.

B-49 En mi opinión Termina las siguientes oraciones sobre las películas que tú has visto (*have seen*). Pueden ser películas viejas o nuevas, buenas o malas. Comparte tus respuestas con un/a compañero/a.

MODELO E1: La mejor película de terror…

E2: *La mejor película de terror es* Psycho.

1. La mejor comedia…
2. Una película dramática deprimente…
3. La película de misterio que menos me gusta…
4. Mi actor/actriz favorito/a de las películas de acción…
5. La película animada más creativa…
6. La película más conmovedora…

38. Los verbos regulares en el pretérito. When do you use the preterit tense? What are the endings for **-ar, -er,** and **-ir** verbs in the preterit? Check pages 197 and 200 to verify your answers. Then do the following activity.

B-50 Hoy es sábado Carolina les cuenta qué hicieron (*did*) ella y sus compañeros de apartamento esta mañana. Túrnense para formar las oraciones.

MODELO Juancho, lavar el carro, 10:30

Juancho lavó el carro a las 10:30 de la mañana.

1. yo, correr cinco millas, 6:45
2. nosotros, limpiar nuestros dormitorios, 11:00
3. Lola, llevar el carro al mecánico, 8:00
4. Antonio y Juancho, lavar los platos de anoche, 9:15
5. Antonio, escribir un ensayo para la clase de historia, 9:30
6. Lola y yo, tomar café en nuestro restaurante favorito, 7:30
7. yo, guardar la ropa limpia, 8:45
8. Lola y Juancho, repartir comida en la residencia de ancianos, 12:00

39. Los pronombres de complemento directo y la *a* personal. What is a *direct object*? What is a *direct object pronoun*? What are the direct object pronouns in Spanish? Where do you place direct object pronouns? Review pages 202–203 and then practice with the following activities.

B-51 ¿Estás listo/a?

¡Qué suerte! Vas al concierto del año en un anfiteatro. Revisa la lista de preparativos con un/a compañero/a usando **lo, la, los** o **las** y los verbos en el pretérito.

MODELO (nosotros) comprar las entradas del concierto

E1: ¿Compramos las entradas del concierto?

E2: *Sí, las compramos ayer.*

1. (nosotros) preparar la comida (*meal*) para llevar
2. (Juan) comprar las bebidas (*beverages*)
3. (tú) invitar a nuestros amigos
4. (los hermanos) entender las letras de las canciones en inglés
5. (Elena y Felipe) llevar la cámara
6. (yo) recibir el dinero para las entradas de todos

B-52 ¿Hay deberes?

Túrnense para hacer y contestar las siguientes preguntas. Sigan el modelo.

MODELO ¿Lavas los pisos todos los días?

E1: *Sí, tengo que lavarlos todos los días. / Sí, los tengo que lavar todos los días.*

E2: *No, nunca los lavo. / No, los lavo los fines de semana.*

1. ¿Sacudes los muebles cada (*each*) semana?
2. ¿Pones la mesa por la tarde?
3. ¿Limpias la cocina los sábados?
4. ¿Preparas la comida todos los días?
5. ¿Lavas los platos cada día?
6. ¿Haces las camas por la mañana?
7. ¿Guardas tus cosas por la noche?
8. ¿Arreglas tu cuarto cada semana?

Y por fin, ¿cómo andas?

Having completed this chapter, I now can…	Feel confident	Need to review
Comunicación		
• greet, introduce, and say good-bye to others.	☐	☐
• describe myself and others.	☐	☐
• share information about school and life as a student.	☐	☐
• offer opinions about sports and pastimes that I and others like and dislike.	☐	☐
• describe homes and household chores.	☐	☐
• identify places in and around town.	☐	☐
• relate things that happen and things that have to be done.	☐	☐
• convey what will take place in the immediate future.	☐	☐
• impart information about service opportunities.	☐	☐
• share information about different types of movies, music, and television programs, including my own personal preferences.	☐	☐
• describe things that happened in the past.	☐	☐
• express *what* or *whom.*	☐	☐
Comunidades		
• use Spanish in real-life contexts.	☐	☐

Estrategia

The *¿Cómo andas?* and *Y por fin, ¿cómo andas?* sections are designed to help you assess your understanding of specific concepts. In *Capítulo B Para repasar,* there is one opportunity for you to reflect on how well you understand the concepts. Beginning with *Capítulo 7* there will be three opportunities in each chapter for you to stop and reflect on what you have learned. These checks help you become accountable for your own learning, and help you determine what you need to review. Also use the checklist as a way to communicate with your instructor about any concepts you still need to review. Additionally, you might also use your checklist as a way to study with a peer group or peer tutor. If you need to review a particular concept, more practice is available on *¡Anda!* online.

El mercado de Chichicastenango, Guatema

7 ¡A comer!

Comer bien es un gran placer (*pleasure*). Dentro del mundo hispanohablante hay una gran variedad de comidas (*foods*) y la comida tiene una función social muy importante. También varía el lugar donde se compra la comida: hay tiendas pequeñas, supermercados y mercados al aire libre.

Preguntas

1. ¿Cuáles son tus platos (*dishes*) favoritos? ¿Te gusta comprar comida y prepararla en casa? ¿Dónde compras los ingredientes?
2. ¿Hay alguna comida típica de la región donde vives tú? ¿Cuáles son algunas comidas típicas de los Estados Unidos?
3. ¿Qué platos de otras culturas te gustan? ¿Qué platos hispanos te gustan?

¿Sabías que…?

El mercado de Chichicastenango abre los jueves y los domingos y es el mercado al aire libre más grande de Centroamérica.

Mercado de mariscos (*seafood*), Barcelona, España

Mercado de frutas en Chile

Learning Outcomes

By the end of this chapter, you will be able to:

- ✔ discuss food, its preparation, and restaurant activity.
- ✔ describe things that happened in the past.
- ✔ convey ideas and information with less repetition.
- ✔ communicate about food shopping and party planning.
- ✔ write about a memory.
- ✔ exchange interesting facts about Chile and Paraguay.
- ✔ read a completed application to appear on a cooking show.

Comunicación I

1 VOCABULARIO

La comida Discussing food

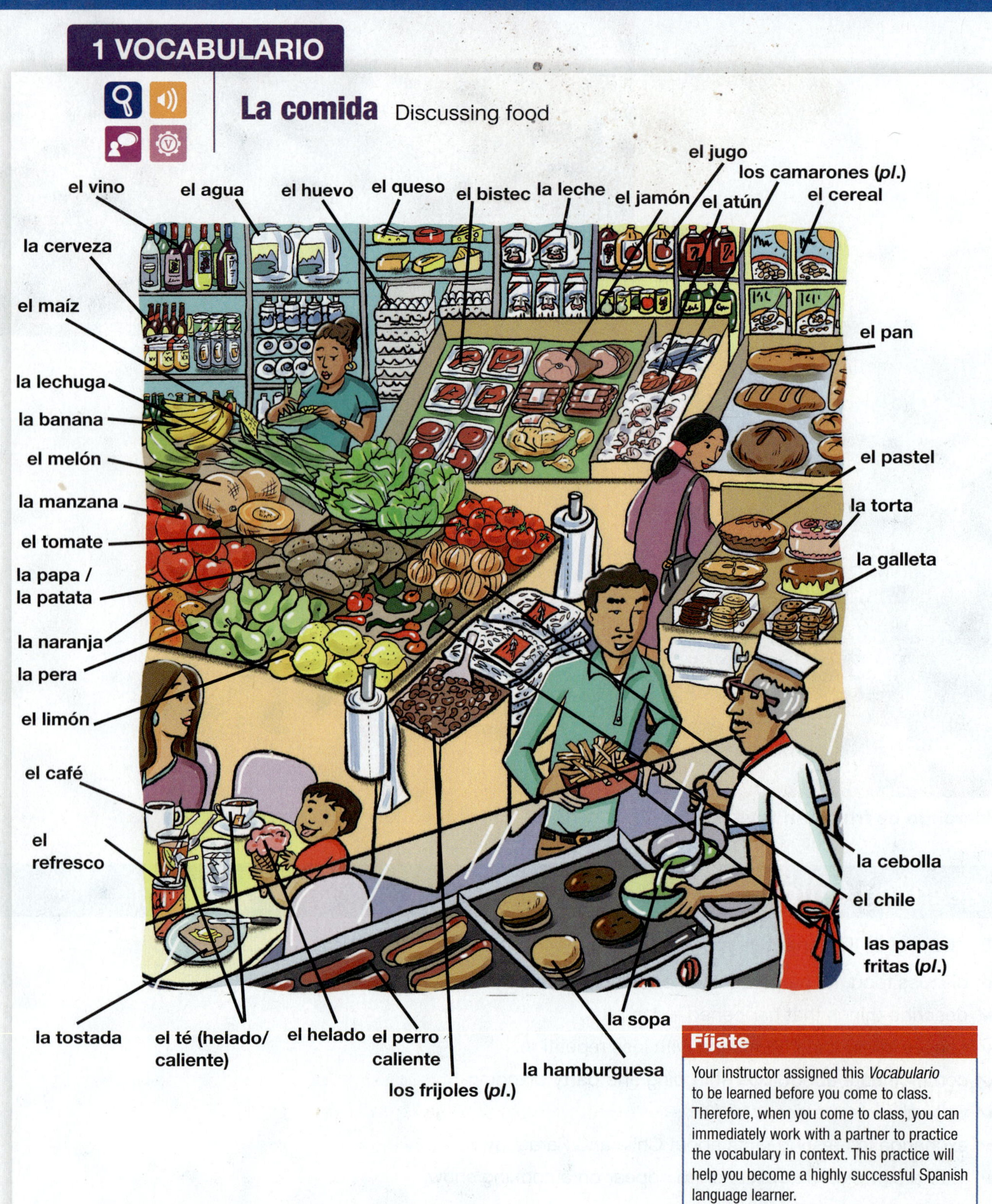

Fíjate

Your instructor assigned this *Vocabulario* to be learned before you come to class. Therefore, when you come to class, you can immediately work with a partner to practice the vocabulary in context. This practice will help you become a highly successful Spanish language learner.

Otras palabras	*Other words*
el desayuno	*breakfast*
el almuerzo	*lunch*
la merienda	*snack*
la cena	*dinner*
el ajo	*garlic*
el arroz	*rice*
los dulces	*sweets; candy*
el yogur	*yogurt*

Algunos verbos	*Some verbs*
beber	*to drink*
cenar	*to have dinner*
desayunar	*to have breakfast*
merendar (ie)	*to have a snack*

Fíjate

Remember that you learned the verb *almorzar* (*ue*), "to have lunch," in *Capítulo 4* when you learned stem-changing verbs.

Now you are ready to complete the ***Preparación y práctica*** activities for this chunk online.

PRONUNCIACIÓN

The different pronunciations of *r* and *rr*

Go to *¡Anda!* online to learn about the letters *r* and *rr*.

7-1 Concurso Escoge **cinco** letras diferentes. Bajo cada letra escribe todas las palabras del vocabulario de **La comida** que recuerdes. Después, compara tu lista con la de un/a compañero/a.

MODELO

a	d	p
arroz	desayuno	papas fritas
agua	dulce	

7-2 ¡Ay, las calorías! Túrnense para decir a qué comida corresponden las siguientes descripciones. Usen el cuadro de los valores nutritivos.

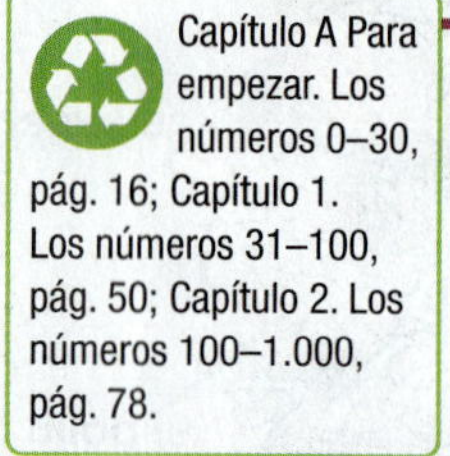
Capítulo A Para empezar. Los números 0–30, pág. 16; Capítulo 1. Los números 31–100, pág. 50; Capítulo 2. Los números 100–1.000, pág. 78.

Estrategia

¡Anda! Curso elemental has provided you with recycling references to help guide your continuous review of previously learned material. Make sure to consult the indicated pages if you need to refresh your memory about numbers.

CUADRO DE LOS VALORES NUTRITIVOS

Comida	Calorías	Proteínas (gramos)	Grasas (gramos)	Carbohidratos (gramos)	Vitaminas
bistec	455	27	36	0	A, B
hamburguesa con queso	950	50	60	54	B
jugo de naranja	100	1	0	16	A, B, C
naranja	50	1	0	16	A, B, C
pan	150	6	2	38	B
papa	100	3	0	23	B, C
perro caliente	200	5	14	1	B, C
salmón	200	24	10	0	A, B
torta	455	4	13	76	A, B, C
lechuga	10	1	0	2	A, B, C

MODELO E1: *Esta comida tiene mucha agua, es verde y tiene diez calorías.*

E2: *Es la lechuga.*

Esta comida tiene…

1. 60 gramos (*grams*) de grasas (*fat*), 50 gramos de proteínas y 950 calorías.
2. muchas proteínas, es un pescado y tiene 200 calorías.
3. vitamina C, es una verdura y tiene 100 calorías.
4. muchos carbohidratos y 150 calorías.
5. 27 gramos de proteínas, es una carne y tiene 455 calorías.
6. 50 calorías y es una fruta.
7. 16 gramos de carbohidratos y es una bebida.
8. las vitaminas B y C, sólo un gramo de carbohidratos y 14 gramos de grasa.

7-3 ¿Cuáles son tus preferencias? ¿Qué comidas te gustan?

Completa los siguientes pasos.

Capítulo 2. El verbo *gustar*, pág. 87.

Paso 1 Completa el cuadro según tus preferencias.

Estrategia

You may want to talk about foods that are not included here. Refer to the *También se dice*…section in Appendix 3 for additional vocabulary.

Fíjate

Although *agua* and *ave* are feminine nouns, the masculine singular article *el* is used with them (*el agua, el ave*), as a way to separate and differentiate the similar stressed vowel sounds in each word (*la* and *a*). *Las* is used with the plurals of these words (*las aguas, las aves*). All adjectives describing these words are feminine (*el agua fría / las aguas frías*).

1. Las carnes, las aves, el pescado y los mariscos que…	
a. más me gustan son…	b. menos me gustan son…
1.	1.
2.	2.
3.	3.
4.	4.
2. Las frutas y verduras que…	
a. más me gustan son…	b. menos me gustan son…
1.	1.
2.	2.
3.	3.
4.	4.

Paso 2 Ahora, compara tus preferencias con las de los compañeros de la clase: ¿Cuáles son sus comidas favoritas? ¿Qué comidas les gustan menos?

MODELO E1: *¿Cuál es tu carne favorita?*

E2: *No me gusta la carne, pero me gusta mucho el pollo. ¿Y a ti?*

7-4 ¿Qué necesito?

Julia llama a su madre para pedir consejos (*advice*) sobre la comida. Escucha la conversación y después escoge la opción correcta.

1. Hoy es el cumpleaños de…
   a. Carmen.
   b. Julia.
   c. la madre de Julia.
2. Para celebrar, las amigas van a…
   a. cenar en un restaurante elegante.
   b. ir al cine.
   c. preparar una cena para ella.
3. Según la madre, ¿qué más le gusta poner en la ensalada de frutas?
   a. hielo y yogur
   b. limón, yogur y azúcar
   c. yogur y azúcar
4. Según la madre, ¿qué NO le gusta poner en la ensalada de frutas?
   a. limón
   b. pera
   c. naranja
5. ¿Cuáles son las frutas que Julia necesita comprar para la ensalada?
   a. las peras
   b. ningunas (ella tiene todas las frutas mencionadas)
   c. todas (no tiene fruta en casa ahora)

7-5 La dieta de Nico

Nico es un estudiante universitario de Santiago de Chile. Mira lo que (*what*) come normalmente y cuándo lo come. Después completa los siguientes pasos.

Capítulo A Para empezar. La hora, pág. 18; Capítulo A Para empezar. Los días, los meses y las estaciones, pág. 21.

Fíjate

The word *galleta* means both "cookie" and "cracker." For "potato," *patata* is used in Spain, while *papa* is widely used in Latin America.

LA DIETA DE NICO

	DESAYUNO	ALMUERZO	MERIENDA	CENA
	8:30	1:00	5:30	8:00
DÍA 1:	té con galletas	ensalada, arroz con pollo y melón	manzana	atún con una ensalada de lechuga con tomate y fruta
DÍA 2:	té y pan con mantequilla	sopa, tortilla de papas y flan	galletas	pan con mermelada

Paso 1 Ahora completa el cuadro con tu información.

TU DIETA

	DESAYUNO	ALMUERZO	MERIENDA	CENA
DÍA 1:				
DÍA 2:				

Fíjate

To express "later than," you say *más tarde que* and to express "earlier than," you say *más temprano que*.

Paso 2 Con un/a compañero/a, comparen su información con la de Nico.

MODELO E1: *Yo nunca tomo té en el desayuno. Generalmente desayuno más temprano que* (earlier than) *Nico. ¿Y tú?*

E2: *Yo desayuno a las siete y media y generalmente como huevos y tostadas.*

Paso 3 Miren el plato de alimentación para determinar si todos los grupos están representados en sus dietas.

MODELO E1: *Comemos pan en el desayuno y a veces en la cena.*

E2: *Comemos papas y ensaladas de lechuga y tomate, pero no comemos muchas otras verduras.*

E1: *Tienes razón, pero comemos mucha fruta...*

7-6 ¿Qué comes tú? Túrnense para entrevistar a un/a compañero/a usando las siguientes preguntas.

1. ¿Comes bien o mal? Explica.
2. ¿Qué tipo de comida prefieres?
3. ¿Qué comidas no te gustan?
4. ¿Qué te gusta merendar?
5. ¿Qué comidas tienen vitamina C y calcio?
6. En tu opinión, ¿cuáles son las vitaminas más importantes para la salud? ¿De qué comidas sacamos estas vitaminas?
7. ¿Qué comidas tienen mucha grasa?
8. ¿Qué comidas tienen mucha proteína?
9. ¿Qué comidas sabes preparar?
10. Qué comidas conoces de los países hispanohablantes?

Las comidas en el mundo hispano

La palabra *comida* significa varias cosas en español: *food, meal* y *lunch* (*the main meal of the day*). Las comidas en los países hispanoamericanos son similares a las comidas norteamericanas pero también existen algunas diferencias. Por ejemplo, el desayuno en el mundo hispano normalmente consiste en café y pan o panes dulces. Generalmente es una comida ligera (*light*).

El almuerzo es normalmente la comida más grande y más fuerte del día. En lugares con una cultura más tradicional, el almuerzo puede empezar a eso de (*around*) las dos de la tarde. Los niños regresan de la escuela y los padres del trabajo (si trabajan fuera [*outside*] de casa) y comen juntos en casa. Entonces, hay tiempo para descansar (*to rest*) antes de volver al trabajo y a la escuela. En los países y las zonas con más industria y comercio puede haber un horario de almuerzo similar al horario de los Estados Unidos.

La cena generalmente es una comida más ligera. La gente en los países hispanohablantes cena más tarde que la mayoría de los norteamericanos. En España, por ejemplo, ¡muchas personas no cenan hasta las diez o las once de la noche!

Preguntas

1. ¿Cómo es un desayuno típico en el mundo hispano? ¿un almuerzo? ¿una cena?
2. Generalmente, ¿cuál es el horario de las comidas en los países hispanos?

Fíjate

Your instructor assigned this *Nota cultural* to be read before you come to class. In class you will then be prepared to answer the *Preguntas* with a partner.

2 GRAMÁTICA

Repaso del complemento directo

Communicating with less repetition

In **Capítulo 5** you learned to use **direct object pronouns** in Spanish. Return to pages 202–203 for a quick review, then answer the following questions:

¿Postre? Tenemos...

¡Los quiero todos!

¡Explícalo tú!

1. What are **direct objects**? What are **direct object pronouns**?
2. What are the pronouns (forms)? With what must they agree?
3. Where are direct object pronouns placed in a sentence?

 Check your answers to the preceding questions in Appendix 1.

Fíjate

Your instructor assigned this *Gramática* to be read, studied, and learned before you come to class. Therefore, when you come to class, you can immediately work with a partner to practice the grammar in context via the activities in your text. Your instructor will assign all *Gramática* to be learned before class. This practice will help you become a highly successful Spanish language learner.

¿? Now you are ready to complete the ***Preparación y práctica*** activities for this chunk online.

7-7 Las dietas

¿Piensas mucho en lo que comes? Completa los siguientes pasos.

Paso 1 Subraya (*Underline*) los complementos directos en las siguientes preguntas. Compara tus respuestas con las de un/a compañero/a.

MODELO ¿Conoces la dieta Weight Watchers?

1. ¿Sigues la dieta Nutrisystem?
2. ¿Prefieres los postres de chocolate?
3. ¿Sabes preparar bien el arroz?
4. ¿Comes muchas frutas diferentes?
5. ¿Preparas los huevos con queso?
6. ¿Lavas la lechuga bien antes de comerla?

Paso 2 Ahora túrnense para contestar las preguntas del **Paso 1,** usando los pronombres de complemento directo en sus respuestas.

MODELO E1: ¿Conoces la dieta Weight Watchers?

E2: *Sí, la conozco. / No, no la conozco.*

7-8 Cocinero/a

Tu compañero/a y tú van a preparar una cena especial para sus amigos. Para saber si todo está preparado, túrnense para contestar las siguientes preguntas usando el pretérito y un pronombre de complemento directo (**lo, la, los, las**).

Capítulo 5. El pretérito, págs. 197, 200.

MODELO E1: ¿Compraste la carne?
E2: *Sí, la compré.*

1. ¿Escribiste la lista de cosas que tenemos que hacer?
2. ¿Mandaste las invitaciones por e-mail?
3. ¿Limpiaste el comedor y el salón?
4. ¿Encontraste unas recetas (*recipes*) nuevas?
5. ¿Compraste la comida y las bebidas?
6. ¿Terminaste los postres?
7. ¿Preparaste una mesa bonita?
8. ¿Abriste el vino?

7-9 Las buenas decisiones

Túrnense para expresar cómo prefieren comer o tomar las siguientes comidas y bebidas y con qué frecuencia las toman.

nunca	algunas veces	generalmente	constantemente	siempre

MODELO E1: *la torta*
E2: *La como con helado. La como algunas veces. / No la como nunca.*

1. 
2. 
3. 
4. 
5. 
6. 
7. 
8. 
9. 

3 GRAMÁTICA

Algunos verbos irregulares en el pretérito (Parte I)

Talking about things that happened in the past

Los verbos que terminan en *-car*, *-zar* y *-gar* y el verbo *leer*

Several verbs have small spelling changes in the preterit. Look at the following charts.

Fíjate

The *-ar* and *-er* stem-changing verbs in the present tense do not have stem changes in the preterit. There may be spelling changes, however, as with *empezar* and *jugar*.

tocar (c → qu)	
yo	toqué
tú	tocaste
Ud.	tocó
él/ella	tocó
nosotros/as	tocamos
vosotros/as	tocasteis
Uds.	tocaron
ellos/ellas	tocaron

* (**sacar** and **buscar** have the same spelling change)

empezar (z → c)	
yo	empecé
tú	empezaste
Ud.	empezó
él/ella	empezó
nosotros/as	empezamos
vosotros/as	empezasteis
Uds.	empezaron
ellos/ellas	empezaron

* (**comenzar** and **organizar** have the same spelling change)

jugar (g → gu)	
yo	jugué
tú	jugaste
Ud.	jugó
él/ella	jugó
nosotros/as	jugamos
vosotros/as	jugasteis
Uds.	jugaron
ellos/as	jugaron

* (**llegar** has the same spelling change)

leer (i → y)	
yo	leí
tú	leíste
Ud.	leyó
él/ella	leyó
nosotros/as	leímos
vosotros/as	leísteis
Uds.	leyeron
ellos/as	leyeron

* (**creer** and **oír** have the same spelling change)

(continued)

—**Toqué** la guitarra con el conjunto de mariachi en un restaurante mexicano anoche.
—¿A qué hora **empezaste**?
—**Empecé** a las nueve.
—¿**Jugaron** tus hermanos al béisbol hoy?
—No, **leyeron** un libro de recetas porque van a preparar una cena especial para nuestros padres.

I played the guitar with a mariachi band at a Mexican restaurant last night.
At what time did you begin?
I began at nine.
Did your brothers play baseball today?
No, they read a recipe book because they are going to prepare a special dinner for our parents.

Some things to remember:

1. With verbs that end in **-car,** the **c** changes to **qu** in the **yo** form to preserve the sound of the hard **c** of the infinitive.
2. With verbs that end in **-zar,** the **z** changes to **c** before **e.**
3. With verbs that end in **-gar,** the **g** changes to **gu** to preserve the sound of the hard **g** (**g** before **e** or **i** sounds like the **j** sound in Spanish).
4. For **leer, creer,** and **oír,** change the **i** to **y** in the third-person singular and plural.
5. Useful words to discuss things that happened in the past:

anoche	*last night*
anteayer	*the day before yesterday*
ayer	*yesterday*
el año pasado	*last year*
el fin de semana pasado	*last weekend*
el martes / viernes / domingo, etc., pasado	*last Tuesday / Friday / Sunday, etc.*
la semana pasada	*last week*

Fíjate

Note that for the words "last weekend" (*el fin de semana pasado*), the adjective *pasado* agrees with the masculine noun *el fin* and not *semana.* In contrast, for "last week" (*la semana pasada*), the word *pasada* agrees with the feminine noun *semana.*

¿? Now you are ready to complete the ***Preparación y práctica*** activities for this chunk online.

7-10 ¡Apúrate! One person makes a ball out of a piece of paper, says a subject pronoun and one of the ***-car, -zar, -gar*** verbs or **leer** in its infinitive form, and tosses the ball to someone in the group. That person catches it, gives the corresponding form of the verb in the preterit, then says another pronoun and tosses the ball to someone else.

MODELO E1: *yo, jugar*
E2: *jugué; ellas, leer*
E3: *leyeron; usted, empezar*
E4: *empezó;...*

7·11 Creaciones Completen los siguientes pasos.

Paso 1 Juntos combinen elementos de las tres columnas para escribir **ocho** oraciones que describan lo que hicieron las siguientes personas.

MODELO Yolanda llegar al restaurante temprano
Yolanda llegó al restaurante temprano.

Yolanda	llegar	la televisión durante la cena
usted	tocar	la guitarra mientras el chef preparó la cena
los estudiantes	sacar	al restaurante temprano
yo	buscar	a comer antes del mediodía
mi mejor amigo y yo	leer	la comida en el refrigerador
tú	ver	la carne del congelador (*freezer*)
mis primos	organizar	el restaurante La Frontera en la Calle Diez
el/la profesor/a	empezar	el libro del gran cocinero Emeril Lagasse

Paso 2 Túrnense para preguntarse cuándo ocurrió cada actividad mencionada en **Paso 1.**

MODELO E1: *¿Cuándo llegó Yolanda al restaurante?*
E2: *Llegó a las ocho.*

7·12 Los quehaceres de Inés Completa los siguientes pasos.

Capítulo 3. La casa, pág. 106; Capítulo 3. Los quehaceres de la casa, pág. 117; Capítulo 4. Los lugares, pág. 142.

Paso 1 Escribe una oración sobre cada quehacer que terminó Inés.

MODELO *Inés lavó los platos.*

1. la ropa
2. la aspiradora
3. el baño
4. los muebles
5. la basura
6. el armario

Paso 2 Comparte tus oraciones con un/a compañero/a.

MODELO E1: *los platos*
E2: *Inés lavó los platos.*
E1: *Inés...*

Paso 3 Túrnense para decir qué hizo Inés en el centro después de terminar sus quehaceres. Sigan el modelo.

MODELO E1: el correo
E2: *Compró sellos.*

1. la librería
2. el cine
3. el banco
4. el cibercafé
5. la biblioteca
6. el café
7. el supermercado
8. la tienda

Capítulo 2. La formación de preguntas, pág. 75; Capítulo 5. Los pronombres de complemento directo, pág. 202.

7-13 ¿Te puedo hacer una pregunta? Entrevista a cinco estudiantes diferentes y anota sus respuestas (**sí** o **no**). Después, compara tus respuestas con las de los otros estudiantes de la clase. ¿Cuáles son las tendencias?

MODELO organizar el cuarto ayer

TÚ: *¿Organizaste tu cuarto ayer?*
E1: *Sí, lo organicé.*
E2: *No, no lo organicé.*
E3: *Sí, organicé mi cuarto.*
E4: *No, no organicé mi cuarto.*
E5: *No, yo no lo organicé, pero mi compañero lo organizó.*

	E1	E2	E3	E4	E5
1. buscar un libro en la biblioteca ayer					
2. empezar una dieta más sana el mes pasado					
3. leer una novela anoche					
4. jugar al tenis la semana pasada					
5. tocar un instrumento en una banda el año pasado					
6. llegar tarde a la clase hoy					
7. sacar dinero del cajero automático el fin de semana pasado					
8. comenzar la tarea antes de cenar anoche					

¿Cómo andas? I

Each chapter has three places at which you will be asked to assess your progress. This first assessment comes as you have completed approximately one third of the chapter. How confident are you with your progress to date?

Having completed **Comunicación I**, I now can...	**Feel confident**	**Need to review**
• discuss food. (p. 268)	☐	☐
• pronounce the different sounds of *r* and *rr*. (p. 269 and online)	☐	☐
• discuss eating habits in Spanish-speaking countries. (p. 274)	☐	☐
• communicate with less repetition using direct object pronouns. (p. 275)	☐	☐
• talk about things that happened in the past using irregular forms (Part I). (p. 277)	☐	☐

Comunicación II

4 VOCABULARIO

La preparación de las comidas Explaining food preparation

Algunos términos de cocina	*Some cooking terms*
cocinar	*to cook*
el aliño; el aderezo	*salad dressing*
al horno	*baked*
a la parrilla	*grilled*
asado/a	*roasted; grilled*
bien cocido/a	*well-done*
bien hecho/a	*well-cooked*
cocido/a	*boiled; baked*
crudo/a	*rare; raw*
duro/a	*hard-boiled*
fresco/a	*fresh*
frito/a	*fried*
hervido/a	*boiled*
picante	*spicy*
poco hecho/a	*rare*
término medio	*medium*

¿? Now you are ready to complete the ***Preparación y práctica*** activities for this chunk online.

7-14 La asociación Digan una palabra o expresión que asocian con cada condimento, especia o término de la siguiente lista.

MODELO E1: picante
E2: *salsa*

1. frito/a
2. la salsa de tomate
3. crudo/a
4. la mayonesa
5. el azúcar
6. a la parrilla
7. fresco/a
8. al horno
9. la mostaza
10. la mantequilla

7-15 ¡Cómo me gustan! Digan cómo les gusta preparar las siguientes comidas.

MODELO *Me gustan los perros calientes a la parrilla con mostaza y salsa de tomate.*

1.

2.

3.

4.

5.

6.

7.

8.

7-16 ¿Cómo lo prefieres? Entrevista a un/a compañero/a para conocer sus preferencias. Después cambien de papel.

Capítulo 4. Los verbos con cambio de raíz, pág. 150, Capítulo 5. Los pronombres de complemento directo, pág. 202.

MODELO E1: ¿Cómo prefieres tu hamburguesa?
E2: *La prefiero término medio.*

1. ¿Cómo prefieres tu bistec?
2. ¿Qué condimentos usaste la última vez que comiste bistec?
3. ¿Cómo pides tu refresco, con o sin hielo?
4. ¿Cómo preparaste los huevos la última vez que los comiste?
5. ¿Cómo prefieres la pizza?
6. ¿Cómo tomaste el té la última vez que lo bebiste, helado o caliente? ¿Lo tomaste con o sin azúcar?
7. ¿Cómo prefieres la sopa, con mucha o poca sal?
8. ¿Cómo tomaste el café esta mañana?

La comida hispana

La comida hispana es muy variada. En España se come mucho pescado y mariscos, pero cada región tiene sus platos típicos. Por ejemplo, en Asturias tienen la fabada (*bean stew*); en Valencia, la paella y en Andalucía, el gazpacho. La parte central de España es conocida por su carne asada.

La parrillada

La comida mexicana se define por sus técnicas y por los ingredientes propios del país. En México, el maíz y los chiles son ingredientes importantes en la cocina mexicana; también se destacan (*they distinguish themselves*) en la manera de cocinar verduras, carnes, mariscos, huevos, salsas, sopas y aves. Desde Baja California hasta la península de Yucatán, se encuentran platos típicos mexicanos de cada región.

Las islas del Caribe tienen en común la herencia de las culturas española, indígena y africana. Las comidas de estos países llevan una gran variedad de condimentos (*seasonings*) como la bija (*annatto*) o el achiote, el orégano, la cebolla, el ajo, el cilantro y muchos más. El arroz es indispensable en la dieta caribeña: también los plátanos, los mariscos y los frijoles (o habichuelas). El arroz es muy importante también en la dieta centroamericana, igual que el maíz, los frijoles, las tortillas, las enchiladas, las verduras, el pollo, los tamales y las frutas.

En los países de Sudamérica comen mucho arroz, frijoles, pollo, carne, frutas y mariscos. En Chile, Argentina, Paraguay y Uruguay las parrilladas o los asados (*mixed grills*) son muy populares. Las empanadas o empanadillas (un *turnover* de carne, legumbres, queso, mariscos o pollo) son famosas en toda América Latina, desde Cuba hasta Argentina.

Preguntas

1. ¿Cuáles de los platos típicos (o ingredientes) mencionados te gustan?
2. ¿Cómo se compara la comida del Caribe con la comida de otras partes del mundo hispanohablante?

5 GRAMÁTICA

Algunos verbos irregulares en el pretérito (Parte II)

Talking about things that happened in the past

In **Comunicación I** you learned that some verbs have spelling changes in the **pretérito**. The following verbs are also ***irregular*** in the **pretérito;** they follow patterns of their own. Study the verb charts to determine the similarities and differences among the forms.

Ayer anduvimos diez millas.

	andar (*to walk*)	**estar**	**tener**
yo	anduve	estuve	tuve
tú	anduviste	estuviste	tuviste
Ud.	anduvo	estuvo	tuvo
él/ella	anduvo	estuvo	tuvo
nosotros/as	anduvimos	estuvimos	tuvimos
vosotros/as	anduvisteis	estuvisteis	tuvisteis
Uds.	anduvieron	estuvieron	tuvieron
ellos/ellas	anduvieron	estuvieron	tuvieron

—El lunes pasado llegamos a Santiago y **anduvimos** mucho por la ciudad. — *Last Monday we arrived in Santiago and walked a lot throughout the city.*

—¿**Estuvieron** en un restaurante o bar interesante? — *Were you all in an interesting restaurant or bar?*

—Sí, **tuvimos** mucha suerte y comimos en el mejor restaurante de la ciudad. — *Yes, we were very lucky and we ate at the best restaurant in the city.*

	conducir (*to drive*)	**traer**	**decir**
yo	conduje	traje	dije
tú	condujiste	trajiste	dijiste
Ud.	condujo	trajo	dijo
él/ella	condujo	trajo	dijo
nosotros/as	condujimos	trajimos	dijimos
vosotros/as	condujisteis	trajisteis	dijisteis
Uds.	condujeron	trajeron	dijeron
ellos/as	condujeron	trajeron	dijeron

Fíjate

Note that the third-person plural ending of *conducir, decir,* and *traer* is *-eron.*

—¿**Condujiste** de Santiago a Valparaíso? — *Did you drive from Santiago to Valparaíso?*

—No pude conducir porque no **traje** mi licencia. — *I couldn't drive because I didn't bring my driver's license.*

—¿Qué te **dijeron** en la agencia Avis? — *What did they tell you at the Avis (car rental) agency?*

	ir	ser
yo	fui	fui
tú	fuiste	fuiste
Ud.	fue	fue
él/ella	fue	fue
nosotros/as	fuimos	fuimos
vosotros/as	fuisteis	fuisteis
Uds.	fueron	fueron
ellos/as	fueron	fueron

Fíjate

Note that *ser* and *ir* have the same forms in the preterit. You must rely on the context of the sentence or conversation to determine the meaning.

—¿Cómo **fue** el viaje a Chile? *How was the trip to Chile?*
—¡**Fue** increíble! Después de Valparaíso **fuimos** a la Patagonia. *It was incredible! After Valparaíso, we went to Patagonia.*

	dar	ver	venir
yo	di	vi	vine
tú	diste	viste	viniste
Ud.	dio	vio	vino
él/ella	dio	vio	vino
nosotros/as	dimos	vimos	vinimos
vosotros/as	disteis	visteis	vinisteis
Uds.	dieron	vieron	vinieron
ellos/as	dieron	vieron	vinieron

	hacer	querer
yo	hice	quise
tú	hiciste	quisiste
Ud.	hizo	quiso
él/ella	hizo	quiso
nosotros/as	hicimos	quisimos
vosotros/as	hicisteis	quisisteis
Uds.	hicieron	quisieron
ellos/as	hicieron	quisieron

Fíjate

The third-person singular form of *hacer* has a spelling change (*c* to *z*): *hizo*.

	poder	poner	saber
yo	pude	puse	supe
tú	pudiste	pusiste	supiste
Ud.	pudo	puso	supo
él/ella	pudo	puso	supo
nosotros/as	pudimos	pusimos	supimos
vosotros/as	pudisteis	pusisteis	supisteis
Uds.	pudieron	pusieron	supieron
ellos/as	pudieron	pusieron	supieron

—En Santiago **vimos** a mucha gente de la familia de Carlos. *In Santiago we saw a lot of people in Carlos's family.*
—Sí, ¿y les **diste** los regalos que tu familia mandó? *Yes, and did you give them the gifts your family sent?*
—Mi madre **vino** con nosotros y ella misma **pudo** darles los regalos. *My mother came with us and she was able to give them the gifts herself.*
—¿Qué **hiciste** después de visitar a la familia de Carlos? *What did you do after visiting Carlos's family?*

(continued)

Verbos con cambio de raíz

The next group of verbs also follows its own pattern. In these stem-changing verbs, the first letters next to the infinitives, listed in parentheses, represent the present-tense spelling changes; the last letter indicates the spelling change in the **Ud./él/ella** and **Uds./ellos/ellas** forms of the **pretérito.**

	dormir (o → ue → u)	**pedir** (e → i → i)	**preferir** (e → ie → i)
yo	dormí	pedí	preferí
tú	dormiste	pediste	preferiste
Ud.	durmió	pidió	prefirió
él/ella	durmió	pidió	prefirió
nosotros/as	dormimos	pedimos	preferimos
vosotros/as	dormisteis	pedisteis	preferisteis
Uds.	durmieron	pidieron	prefirieron
ellos/as	durmieron	pidieron	prefirieron

Fíjate

The *-ir* stem-changing verbs are irregular in the third-person singular and plural forms only.

—Cuando fuiste al restaurante en Valparaíso, ¿qué **pediste?**
What did you order when you went to the restaurant in Valparaíso?

—**Pedí** carne de res, pero mi madre **prefirió** pescado. Y después de comer mi madre **durmió** la siesta.
I ordered beef, but my mother preferred fish. and after eating, my mother took a nap.

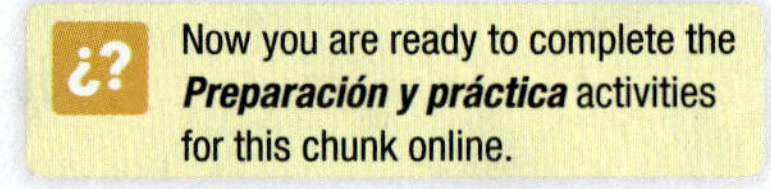
Now you are ready to complete the ***Preparación y práctica*** activities for this chunk online.

7-17 Más práctica Repite el juego de verbos de la actividad **7-10**, esta vez usando los nuevos verbos irregulares.

7-18 **¿Qué dijo?** Form groups of at least six students and sit in a circle. **Estudiante 1** starts by saying his/her name and something that he/she did yesterday, last week, or last year. **Estudiante 2** gives his/her name, says something he/she did, and then tells what the preceding person (**Estudiante 1**) did. **Estudiante 3** tells his/her name, says what he/she did, and then tells what **Estudiante 2** and **Estudiante 1** did (in that order). Follow the model.

MODELO E1: *Soy Fran y ayer fui a un restaurante mexicano.*

E2: *Soy Tom y ayer jugué al tenis. Fran fue a un restaurante mexicano.*

E3: *Soy Chris y ayer tuve que preparar la cena. Tom jugó al tenis y Fran fue a un restaurante mexicano.*

7-19 **El mercado** El año pasado, Amanda fue estudiante de intercambio y vivió con una familia en Asunción. Completa los siguientes párrafos sobre su primera visita al mercado y después compártelo con un/a compañero/a.

andar	traer	decidir	ir
pedir	poder	poner	tener

Ayer mis nuevas "hermanas", Patricia y Gloria, y yo (1) _____________ al mercado por primera vez. Como perdimos el autobús, (2) _____________ que ir caminando. ¡Nosotras (3) _____________ por más de media hora! Por fin llegamos y (4) _____________ tomar un café antes de entrar en el mercado. Yo pedí un café doble con leche y ellas (5) _____________ café con leche y tostada. Cuando el señor nos (6) _____________ los cafés, Patricia (7) _____________ seis cucharadas (*spoonfuls*) de azúcar en el suyo (*hers*). (Yo) No lo (8) _____________ creer: ¡demasiado dulce para mí!

comprar	decir	estar	poner
ser	tomar	ver	volver

Fíjate

Amanda refers to *medio kilo de papas*. Remember that in most parts of the world the metric system is the preferred system of measurement.

Al entrar en el mercado, yo (9) _____________ un montón (*a pile*) de verduras y frutas de muchos colores brillantes. (10) _____________ impresionante. Después yo les (11) _____________ varias fotos a las chicas. Primero compramos una lechuga, dos cebollas, ajo, medio kilo de papas y un pimiento verde. Hablamos unos cinco minutos con la vendedora (*seller*) sobre su sobrina. Ella (12) _____________ seis meses en los Estados Unidos como estudiante de intercambio. Después miramos las frutas y por fin escogimos dos melones y medio kilo de peras. Las chicas (13) _____________ las verduras en el bolso (*bag*) grande y la fruta en el bolso más pequeño. Entonces pasamos a la parte del pescado donde nosotras (14) _____________ atún. La señora lo envolvió (*wrapped*) en papel antes de ponerlo en una bolsa de plástico. Hicimos las compras en menos de media hora. A las nueve y cuarto les (15) _____________ adiós a todos y (16) _____________ a casa… esta vez en autobús.

7-20 ¿Hay rutina en tu semana?

¿Cuántas veces hiciste cada una de estas cosas la semana pasada? Completa los siguientes pasos.

Estrategia

Remember that *una vez* means *once* and *veces* means "times": *Yo fui al restaurante una vez, pero tú fuiste tres veces.* = "I went to the restaurant once, but you went three times."

Paso 1 Escribe cuántas veces tú hiciste las siguientes actividades la semana pasada. Sigue el modelo.

MODELO ver una película en la televisión

Vi una película en la televisión una vez (dos veces, tres veces, etc.).

La semana pasada, ¿cuántas veces… ?

1. hacer la tarea
2. dar la respuesta correcta en clase
3. venir a la clase de español
4. conducir a la universidad
5. dormir ocho horas
6. andar por el centro
7. ir al cine
8. jugar un deporte
9. ver un partido de fútbol americano en la televisión
10. comer comida rápida

Paso 2 Ahora pídele a tu compañero/a que adivine (*guess*) cuántas veces hiciste las actividades del **Paso 1.** Sigue el modelo.

MODELO
E1: *La semana pasada, ¿cuántas veces piensas que (yo) hice la tarea?*
E2: *Pienso que la hiciste tres veces.*
E1: *Sí, tienes razón. ¡La hice tres veces!*
E1: *¿Cuántas veces piensas que fui al cine?*
E2: *Pienso que no fuiste.*
E1: *No, no tienes razón. Fui una vez.*

7-21 ¿Adónde fui?

Hazle a tu compañero/a las siguientes preguntas para averiguar adónde fue de vacaciones. Después, cambien de papel. (**¡OJO!** *Before asking the last question, try to guess where he or she went.*)

Capítulo 2. Los deportes y los pasatiempos, pág. 89.

MODELO
E1: *¿Fuiste en verano?*
E2: *No, fui en otoño. / Sí, fui en verano.*

1. ¿Fuiste en carro?
2. ¿Visitaste un museo?
3. ¿Viste un partido de béisbol?
4. ¿Montaste en bicicleta?
5. ¿Qué compraste?
6. ¿Comiste mariscos?
7. ¿Tomaste el sol?
8. ¿Jugaste al golf?
9. ¿Nadaste?
10. ¿Dormiste en un hotel?
11. ¿Jugaste al tenis?
12. ¿Fuiste a un parque?
13. ¿Qué más hiciste?
14. ¿Tuviste que viajar muy lejos (*far*)?
15. ¿Adónde fuiste?

7-22 Chismes (*Gossip*) Imagina que eres el/la editor/a de la columna de chismes del periódico de tu universidad. Escribe tus respuestas a las siguientes preguntas. Después, entrevista a tres compañeros/as y anota sus respuestas. ¿Están de acuerdo?

1. ¿Qué película tuvo mucho éxito el año pasado?
2. ¿Qué actor salió en una película que **no** tuvo éxito?
3. ¿Qué miembro del gobierno (*member of the government*) dijo algo tonto?
4. ¿Quién sacó una canción nueva recientemente?
5. ¿Cuál de tus amigos estuvo en la playa recientemente?
6. ¿Quién vino tarde a la clase una vez?
7. ¿Quién no trajo sus libros a clase?
8. ¿Quién les dio un examen muy difícil la semana pasada?

YO	ESTUDIANTE 1	ESTUDIANTE 2	ESTUDIANTE 3
1.			
2.			
3.			
4.			
5.			
6.			
7.			
8.			

6 VOCABULARIO

En el restaurante Explaining restaurant activity

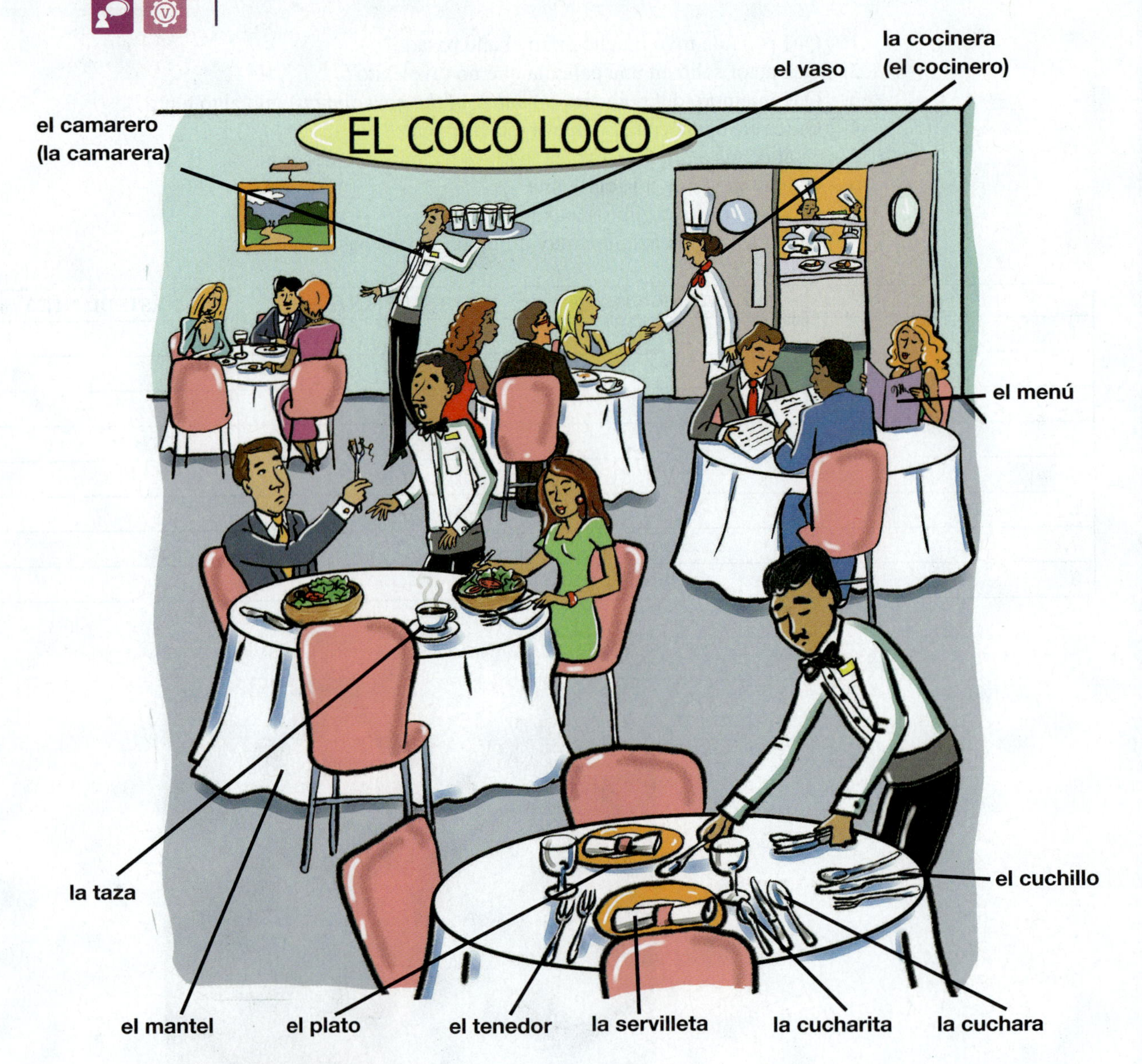

Fíjate

The word *plato* means both "plate" and "dish," as in *¿Cuál es tu plato favorito?* ("What is your favorite dish"?)

Otras palabras	*Other words*
barato/a	*cheap*
caro/a	*expensive*
delicioso/a	*delicious*
sabroso/a	*tasty*
el/la cliente/a	*customer; client*
la especialidad de la casa	*specialty of the house*
la propina	*tip*
la tarjeta de crédito	*credit card*
la tarjeta de débito	*debit card*
¡Buen provecho!	*Enjoy your meal!*
La cuenta, por favor.	*The check, please.*

Algunos verbos	*Some verbs*
pagar	*to pay*
pedir	*to order*
reservar una mesa	*to reserve a table*
saber bien/mal	*to taste good/bad*

Now you are ready to complete the ***Preparación y práctica*** activities for this chunk online.

7-23 La organización es clave Juntos escriban las siguientes categorías: **cosas en la mesa**, **pedir y pagar** y **personas en el restaurante**. Después, organicen el vocabulario de **En el restaurante** bajo esas categorías.

MODELO	COSAS EN LA MESA	PEDIR Y PAGAR	PERSONAS EN EL RESTAURANTE
	el cuchillo	la propina	el camarero

7-24 ¿Cómo se dice? Túrnense para decir qué palabra o frase corresponde a las siguientes descripciones.

Estrategia

As you acquire more Spanish in each chapter, try to write definitions in Spanish of your new vocabulary words as in the model. Learning new vocabulary will become easier the more you practice. Also, it will help you use your new vocabulary in sentences.

MODELO E1: el "Gran Especial"
E2: *la especialidad de la casa*

1. persona que sirve la comida
2. dinero que das por buen servicio
3. lista de comidas y bebidas
4. es necesario para limpiar las manos
5. persona que prepara la comida en un restaurante
6. es necesario para comer cereal
7. es necesario para beber café
8. persona que come en el restaurante

7-25 Una mesa bien puesta

Dibuja la mesa de tu familia o de la familia de un/a buen/a amigo/a para una cena especial con todo bien puesto (*well set*). Ahora, sin mostrar tu dibujo, descríbeselo a un/a compañero/a mientras él/ella lo dibuja. ¿Lo dibujó bien? Luego cambien de papel.

las flores	*flowers*
las velas	*candles*
al lado (de)	*beside; next to*
a la izquierda (de)	*to the left (of)*
a la derecha (de)	*to the right (of)*
cerca (de)	*near*
debajo (de)	*under; underneath*
encima (de)	*on top of; above*

7-26 ¿Qué pasó?

Miren el dibujo en la página 290 y digan por lo menos **cinco** oraciones acerca de lo que pasó anoche en el restaurante El Coco Loco.

7-27 En El Coco Loco

Mira otra vez el dibujo en la página 290. Gastón y Patricia cenaron anoche en el restaurante El Coco Loco. Escucha mientras Gastón habla con su amigo Pablo sobre la experiencia. Después completa las oraciones según lo que dice Gastón con la palabra o expresión apropiada.

1. Gastón dice que la comida fue ____________________.
2. Gastón y Patricia no estuvieron contentos con ____________________.
3. El camarero no trajo inmediatamente ____________________.
4. De primer plato, Patricia pidió ____________________.
5. El tenedor de Gastón estaba (*was*) ____________________.

7-28 Una comida Juntos escriban un párrafo sobre una comida que prepararon para un amigo. Describan los preparativos para la comida y la casa usando por lo menos **seis** verbos en el pretérito. Compartan su párrafo con otra pareja y comparen sus experiencias.

7-29 ¿Me puede servir…? Vas con dos amigos/as al restaurante más popular de Asunción para cenar. Completa los siguientes pasos.

Fíjate

Guaraní is the currency in Paraguay.

Paso 1 Miren el menú y determinen qué van a pedir sabiendo que juntos tienen 200.000 guaraníes.

EL RESTAURANTE BUEN PROVECHO

SOPAS Y CREMAS	
Sopa de cebolla gratinada	15.500 PYG
Sopa de pescado	32.000
Sopa de pollo y verduras	27.000
Consomé de pollo	17.000
ENSALADAS	
Mixta de verduras	19.500
Ensalada de jamón, pollo o atún	45.000
Ensalada de frutas	35.000
SÁNDWICHES CALIENTES	
Sándwich de queso	36.000
Sándwich de pollo, jamón y queso	48.000
Sándwich de jamón	38.000
SÁNDWICHES FRÍOS	
Sándwich de pollo, tomate y lechuga	43.000
Sándwich de ensalada de pollo	45.000
Sándwich de jamón y queso	46.000
HELADOS Y POSTRES	
Tres Marías	14.500
Helado de chocolate	12.000
Helado especial	12.000
Flan de la casa	14.500
BEBIDAS Y REFRESCOS	
Café	5.500
Vaso de leche	6.600
Chocolate en taza	7.200
Té caliente	5.500
Té frío	5.500
Refrescos fríos	7.000
Cervezas	12.500
Copa de vino	14.000

Paso 2 Ahora, utilizando esa información, realicen (*act out*) una escena en un restaurante para la clase. Una persona debe ser el/la camarero/a y las otras personas deben ser los clientes.

Capítulo 2. Presente indicativo de verbos regulares, pág. 71.

7-30 De compras en el mercado Algunos estudiantes van a hacer el papel de vendedores y otros de clientes. Tu profesor/a te va a dar una lista de los productos que tienes para vender (*sell*) o de los que necesitas comprar. Los vendedores deben ganar cincuenta mil guaraníes y los clientes solo pueden gastar cincuenta mil guaraníes. Va a haber competencia (*competition*) entre los vendedores y sí, ¡puedes regatear (*bargain; negotiate the price*)!

Escucha

Las compras en el mercado

Estrategia	
Combining strategies	To begin the new term it is useful to review and combine all the listening strategies you have practiced thus far. Remember to use all clues available to you to anticipate what you are about to hear, including photos, captions, and pre-listening synopses or questions. If you are performing a listening activity like the one to follow, also look ahead at the comprehension questions. Once you have an idea of the context, consider what you already know about it. Taking time to think about and practice these specific strategies will enhance your ability to listen effectively.

7-31 Antes de escuchar Contesta las siguientes preguntas.

1. Mira la foto. ¿Dónde está la mujer? ¿Qué hace?
2. ¿Haces las compras (*Do you shop*) en un mercado como este, donde hay muchos vendedores en un solo lugar, o en un supermercado?
3. ¿Qué tipo de vocabulario necesitas saber para poder hacer las compras en un mercado?

7-32 A escuchar Escucha la conversación entre la madre de Alejandra y un vendedor para averiguar el propósito (*purpose*) de la conversación. Después, escucha una vez más para contestar las siguientes preguntas.

1. ¿Qué compra? Marca (✓) delante de los ingredientes o condimentos que ella compra.

_______ mantequilla	_______ vinagre
_______ azúcar	_______ huevos
_______ queso	_______ pan
_______ mayonesa	_______ leche

2. Determina si las siguientes oraciones son ciertas (**C**) o falsas (**F**).

C	F	
☐	☐	a. La madre necesita ingredientes para preparar un plato nuevo.
☐	☐	b. El Sr. Gómez tiene huevos blancos y marrones.
☐	☐	c. La madre compra seis huevos.
☐	☐	d. El Sr. Gómez también vende verduras.
☐	☐	e. El Sr. Gómez tiene todo lo que la madre necesita comprar.

7-33 Después de escuchar Realiza (*Act out*) con un/a compañero/a la escena entre la madre y el Sr. Gómez.

¡Conversemos!

7-34 De compras Descríbele a un/a compañero/a lo que compraste la última vez que fuiste al supermercado. Di por lo menos **diez** oraciones e incluye detalles como los siguientes:

- lo que (no) tuviste que comprar (*tener que* + *infinitivo*)
- los precios de la comida y de las bebidas
- quién preparó la comida y cómo la preparó

Tu compañero/a va a comparar lo que él/ella compró con lo que tú compraste.

7-35 ¡Qué fiesta! Colin Cowie, un famoso organizador de fiestas para las grandes estrellas de Hollywood, te contrató para ayudarle a planear una fiesta para tu músico o actor favorito. Descríbele a un/a compañero/a (Colin Cowie) en por lo menos **diez** oraciones todo lo que tuviste que hacer. Incluye la comida que compraste, lo que preparaste para comer, cómo pusiste la mesa, quiénes vinieron a la fiesta, etc. Tu compañero/a (Colin Cowie) va a decirte si le gustó lo que hiciste. Después, cambien de papel.

Escribe

Una descripción

Estrategia	
Topic sentence and conclusion	In writing for any audience, it is important to both capture the interest of the reader with a strong topic sentence, preparing him/her for what he/she is about to read, and end with a strong conclusion, restating or summarizing the main points for the reader.

7-36 Antes de escribir Piensa en el mejor día festivo que pasaste. Haz una lista de los siguientes detalles:

- las personas con quienes celebraste o las que fueron a la fiesta
- lo que comieron y bebieron
- las cosas que hicieron
- los regalos que dieron y recibieron

7-37 A escribir Ahora, usando los detalles de la lista, escribe un párrafo bien desarrollado (*well-developed*) sobre ese día, con introducción y conclusión.

7-38 Después de escribir En grupos de cuatro o cinco estudiantes, lean los párrafos de la actividad **7-37**. Ofrezcan (*Offer*) ideas a sus compañeros para mejorar su trabajo. Después, escriban la versión final para entregársela (*turn it in*) a su profesor/a.

¿Cómo andas? II

This is your second self-assessment. You have now completed two thirds of the chapter. How confident are you with the following topics and concepts?

Having completed **Comunicación II**, I now can…	**Feel confident**	**Need to review**
• explain food preparation. (p. 281)	☐	☐
• survey foods from different parts of the Hispanic world. (p. 283)	☐	☐
• talk about things that happened in the past using irregular forms (Part II). (p. 284)	☐	☐
• explain restaurant activity. (p. 290)	☐	☐
• combine listening strategies. (p. 295)	☐	☐
• communicate about food shopping and party planning. (p. 296)	☐	☐
• relate a memory. (p. 297)	☐	☐

Vistazo cultural

Chile

 Les presento mi país

Gino Breschi Arteaga

Mi nombre es Gino Breschi Arteaga y soy de Viña del Mar, Chile, una ciudad turística en la costa con una playa hermosa. El país es muy largo y estrecho, con un promedio (*average*) de 180 kilómetros de ancho (*wide*) y aproximadamente 4.300 kilómetros de largo. Al oeste, tenemos el océano Pacífico y al este, la majestuosa cordillera de los Andes. **¿Prefieres vivir cerca del océano o de las montañas?** Al norte está el desierto de Atacama, el más árido del mundo, donde tenemos unas minas impresionantes de carbón, cobre, oro y otros minerales importantes. Al sur, hay una serie de glaciares en parques nacionales, como el glaciar San Rafael. Estudié viticultura y ahora trabajo para la Bodega Santa Rita en la provincia de Santiago. El vino es un producto de exportación importante en mi país, y también exportamos muchas frutas y verduras. **¿Qué productos agrícolas son importantes en tu región?**

Isla de Pascua

Una bodega en la provincia de Santiago

El pastel de choclo combina verduras y carne en una cazuela (*casserole*) de maíz.

El glaciar San Rafael, Patagonia

ALMANAQUE

Nombre oficial:	República de Chile
Gobierno:	República
Población:	16.746.491 (2010)
Idioma:	español
Moneda:	Peso chileno ($)

¿Sabías que...?

- Además del (*In addition to*) desayuno, el almuerzo y la cena, los chilenos toman una merienda llamada "las onces", que comen entre las 4:00 y las 7:00 de la tarde.
- El baile nacional de Chile es la cueca. Este baile se inspira en el rito de cortejo (*courting*) del gallo (*rooster*) y la gallina (*hen*).

Preguntas

1. ¿Qué extremos geográficos y climatológicos se mencionan? ¿Hay algo similar en los Estados Unidos?
2. ¿Cuáles son algunos productos de exportación importantes en Chile? ¿Y en tu región?
3. Un plato popular en Chile es el pastel de choclo. ¿Cuáles son algunos platos populares donde tú vives?

Vistazo cultural

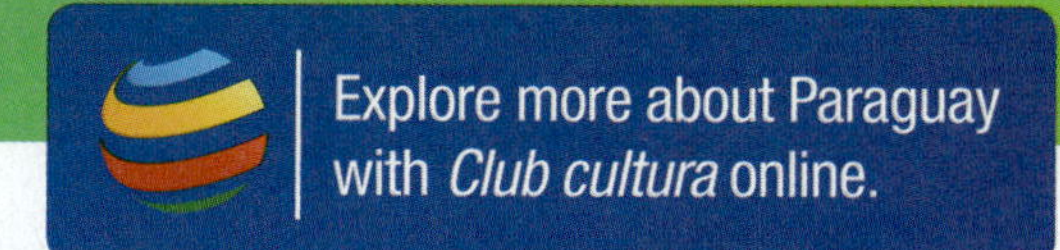

Paraguay

Les presento mi país

Sandra Manrique Esquivel

Mi nombre es Sandra Manrique Esquivel y vivo en Villarrica, Paraguay. Como un gran porcentaje de los paraguayos, soy bilingüe: hablo español y guaraní. **¿En qué otros países hay una población bilingüe?** El guaraní es el idioma hablado por los indígenas originales del país: los guaraníes. Hoy día, el noventa por ciento de los paraguayos somos **mestizos**, una mezcla (*mixture*) de los indígenas y los conquistadores españoles. Los indígenas cultivaron la mandioca (*yucca*), la batata (*yam*), el maíz y la yerba mate entre otras cosechas (*crops*), y estos productos todavía se cultivan hoy. Villarrica es importante por la producción de yerba mate, una hierba usada para preparar la infusión fría llamada tereré. El tereré es la bebida oficial de Paraguay y la que más les gusta tomar a los paraguayos. **¿Qué refresco te gusta tomar?**

La Represa Hidroeléctrica de Itaipú, en la frontera entre Paraguay y Brasil

El tereré es la bebida preferida de Paraguay.

El ñandú es una especie de ave nativa y amenazada (*endangered*) de El Chaco.

ALMANAQUE

Nombre oficial:	República del Paraguay
Gobierno:	República constitucional
Población:	6.375.830 (2010)
Idiomas:	español (oficial); guaraní (oficial)
Moneda:	Guaraní (₲)

¿Sabías que...?

- Muchos paraguayos son aficionados a los remedios caseros (*home-made remedies*), por ejemplo los usos de la planta guaraná, un arbusto (*bush; shrub*) indígena, para calmar los nervios y ayudar con la digestión.
- El Chaco cubre el 60% de la superficie de Paraguay pero contiene solamente el 5% de la población del país.

Preguntas

1. ¿Qué comidas y bebidas se asocian con Paraguay?
2. ¿Por qué son bilingües muchos paraguayos?
3. ¿En qué aspectos son Chile y Paraguay diferentes y similares? ¿Cómo se comparan con los países de Centroamérica?

Lectura

Solicitud para un concurso de cocina

7-39 **Antes de leer** Hoy día la cocina es muy popular en la televisión, el cine, los periódicos y las revistas. En televisión hay canales dedicados exclusivamente a la cocina y algunos cocineros famosos tienen programas en que muestran cómo hacer platos especiales.

1. ¿Qué programas de cocina son populares? ¿Miras alguno?
2. ¿Qué chefs famosos conoces? ¿Qué tipo de comida preparan?

Estrategia

Predicting
To predict what a reading passage is about, first anticipate the content by considering the title, visual cues (illustrations, photos), and comprehension questions. Once you have a general idea of what the passage is about, connect any personal knowledge or experience you have with it. Then, quickly skim the reading for the main idea(s). At that point you can predict what will happen in the reading.

7-40 **Mientras lees** Complete the following steps.

1. You will encounter the following boldfaced words in the reading.

caracolas	*conch*
olía	*smelled*
la cáscara	*peel*
crema batida	*whipped cream*
almendras	*almonds*
pelas	*you peel*
cazuela	*pot*

   Given these new words, what do you predict you will find in this reading?
2. Look at the title and logo. Scan the reading to find out what type of document this is, who filled it out, and what it is for.
3. Skim the reading to find out the applicant's work experience, a dish he makes well, and why he wants to participate.
4. Read the application again and predict whether the applicant will be accepted to the show.

SOLICITUD°
Concurso° de cocina
Viña del Mar, Chile

Application

Competition

Nombre del solicitante: Juan Carlos Machín

Restaurante en que trabaja ahora: El vasco

Correo electrónico: JCM@micocina.com

Número de teléfono: (2) 012 3456

¿Cuál es tu experiencia culinaria?

Empecé a trabajar en la cocina de Juan Mari Arzak como ayudante en 2005. En 2007 fui a trabajar en El Bulli en Barcelona para aprender a hacer salsas con Ferran Adrià. En 2011 regresé a Chile y empecé a trabajar con el chef Rodolfo Guzmán en el restaurante Boragó, donde aprendí la cocina del "naturalismo nacional". Esta filosofía culinaria se basa en cocinar exclusivamente con ingredientes nativos del país.

Describe tu estilo de cocina.

Desde que empecé a cocinar, supe que la comida tradicional de Chile podía competir con las internacionales. Me interesó siempre lo que yo llamo "la cocina de la abuela", es decir, la comida que se prepara en casa todos los días. El trabajar con estos famosos chefs me dio la oportunidad de conocer la industria culinaria y así poder ofrecer platos caseros de alta calidad.

¿Cuál es tu primer recuerdo en la cocina?

Mi primer recuerdo fue cuando tenía ocho años y mi abuelo Marcos quiso preparar un plato especial para mi abuela Ramona. Ellos viven en Isla Negra y a ella le gusta la paila marina, que es una sopa de mariscos. Recuerdo que tuve que limpiar pescado, gambas, mejillones y caracolas. La hicimos en media hora y toda la casa olía a pescado. Ese día me enamoré de° la cocina.

I fell in love with

¿Cuál es tu mejor plato? Describe brevemente cómo lo preparas.

Peras con salsa de naranja. Necesitas seis peras, 235 gramos de azúcar, tres tazas de jugo de naranja, una taza de agua fría, la cáscara de una naranja y media taza de licor de naranja. Para decorar, crema batida y almendras tostadas.

Instrucciones: Primero pelas las peras. Cortas finamente la cáscara de naranja. Mezclas el azúcar, el jugo de naranja y el agua en un bol. Después, en una cazuela, pones todos los ingredientes y los cocinas por 20 minutos. Por último sirves las peras acompañadas de crema batida y almendras.

Explica por qué quieres competir en Cocina Tour. Si ganas° el concurso, ¿qué quieres hacer después?

Sé que soy un buen cocinero y que necesito participar en el programa para obtener experiencia y hacerme conocer. Si gano el concurso, puedo abrir mi propio restaurante en Isla Negra cerca de la casa de mis abuelos.

you win

7·41 Después de leer

Contesta las siguientes preguntas.

1. ¿En qué tipo de concurso quiere participar Juan Carlos Machín? ¿Cómo lo sabes? Da evidencia del texto.
2. ¿Con qué cocineros famosos trabajó?
3. ¿Qué es el naturalismo nacional?
4. ¿Quién inspiró a Juan Carlos a ser cocinero?
5. ¿Cuál es el segundo paso para cocinar peras con salsa de naranja?
6. Juan Carlos fue aceptado al programa. ¿Por qué crees que lo aceptaron? Explica con ejemplos de la lectura.

7·42 Respuesta del director de Cocina Tour

Leíste la solicitud de Juan Carlos Machín para ser parte del concurso Cocina Tour. Imagina que eres uno de los jueces (*judges*) y debes escribir la carta de aceptación de Juan Carlos al programa. En la carta debes describir por qué lo aceptaron y dar más información para los participantes.

5 de noviembre del 2016

Juan Carlos Machín
Avenida Vitacura, 3913
Santiago, Chile

Estimado Señor Machín:
Le escribimos a usted para informarle…

Atentamente,
(nombre)

7·43 Tu solicitud a Cocina Tour

Después de leer la lectura decides participar en el concurso.

Paso 1 Completa la solicitud con tu información, siguiendo el modelo de la lectura.

Paso 2 Prepara una presentación con la información del **Paso 1** para convencer a los jueces que eres el/la candidato/a perfecto/a para Cocina Tour.

For additional *Lectura* activities, go to *¡Anda!* online.

Y por fin, ¿cómo andas?

Each chapter will end with a checklist like the one that follows. This is the third time in the chapter that you are given the opportunity to check your progress. Use the checklist to measure what you have learned in the chapter. Place a check in the "Feel confident" column for the topics you feel you know, and a check in the "Need to review" column for the topics that you need to practice more.

Having completed this chapter, I now can...	Feel confident	Need to review
Comunicación I		
• discuss food. (p. 268)	☐	☐
• pronounce *r* and *rr* correctly. (p. 269 and online)	☐	☐
• communicate with less repetition using direct object pronouns. (p. 275)	☐	☐
• talk about things that happened in the past using irregular forms (Part I). (p. 277)	☐	☐
Comunicación II		
• explain food preparation. (p. 281)	☐	☐
• talk about things that happened in the past using irregular forms (Part II). (p. 284)	☐	☐
• explain restaurant activity. (p. 290)	☐	☐
• combine listening strategies. (p. 295)	☐	☐
• communicate about food shopping and party planning. (p. 296)	☐	☐
• relate a memory. (p. 297)	☐	☐
Cultura		
• discuss eating habits in Spanish-speaking countries. (p. 274)	☐	☐
• survey foods from different parts of the Hispanic world. (p. 283)	☐	☐
• share information about Chile and Paraguay. (pp. 298–299)	☐	☐
Lectura		
• read a completed application to appear on a cooking show. (p. 300)	☐	☐
Comunidades		
• use Spanish in real-life contexts. (online)	☐	☐

Vocabulario **activo**

La comida	*Food*
Las carnes y las aves	*Meat and poultry*
las aves	*poultry*
el bistec	*steak*
la carne	*meat*
la hamburguesa	*hamburger*
el jamón	*ham*
el perro caliente	*hot dog*
el pollo	*chicken*
El pescado y los mariscos	*Fish and shellfish*
el atún	*tuna*
los camarones (*pl.*)	*shrimp*
los mariscos	*shellfish*
el pescado	*fish*
Las frutas	*Fruit*
la banana	*banana*
el limón	*lemon*
la manzana	*apple*
el melón	*melon*
la naranja	*orange*
la pera	*pear*
el tomate	*tomato*
Las verduras	*Vegetables*
el ajo	*garlic*
la cebolla	*onion*
el chile	*chili pepper*
la ensalada	*salad*
los frijoles (*pl.*)	*beans*
la lechuga	*lettuce*
el maíz	*corn*
la papa/la patata	*potato*
las papas fritas (*pl.*)	*french fries; potato chips*
la verdura	*vegetable*

La comida	*Food*
Los postres	*Desserts*
los dulces	*candy; sweets*
la galleta	*cookie; cracker*
el helado	*ice cream*
el pastel	*pastry; pie*
el postre	*dessert*
la torta	*cake*
Las bebidas	*Beverages*
el agua (con hielo)	*water (with ice)*
el café	*coffee*
la cerveza	*beer*
el jugo	*juice*
la leche	*milk*
el refresco	*soft drink*
el té (helado/caliente)	*tea (iced/hot)*
el vino	*wine*
Más comidas	*More foods*
el arroz	*rice*
el cereal	*cereal*
el huevo	*egg*
el pan	*bread*
el queso	*cheese*
la sopa	*soup*
la tostada	*toast*
el yogur	*yogurt*
Las comidas	*Meals*
el almuerzo	*lunch*
la cena	*dinner*
la comida	*food; meal*
el desayuno	*breakfast*
la merienda	*snack*

Verbos	*Verbs*
beber	*to drink*
cocinar	*to cook*
cenar	*to have dinner*
desayunar	*to have breakfast*
merendar	*to have a snack*

La preparación de comidas	*Food preparation*
Los condimentos y las especias	*Condiments and spices*
el aceite	*oil*
el aliño; el aderezo	*salad dressing*
el azúcar	*sugar*
la mantequilla	*butter*
la mayonesa	*mayonnaise*
la mermelada	*jam; marmalade*
la mostaza	*mustard*
la pimienta	*pepper*
la sal	*salt*
la salsa de tomate	*ketchup*
el vinagre	*vinegar*
Algunos términos de cocina	*Some cooking terms*
a la parrilla	*grilled*
al horno	*baked*
asado/a	*roasted; grilled*
bien cocido/a	*well done*
bien hecho/a	*well cooked*
caliente	*hot (temperature)*
cocido/a	*boiled; baked*
crudo/a	*rare; raw*
duro/a	*hard-boiled*
fresco/a	*fresh*
frito/a	*fried*
hervido/a	*boiled*
picante	*spicy*
poco hecho/a	*rare*
término medio	*medium*

En el restaurante	*In the restaurant*
el/la camarero/a	*waiter/waitress*
el/la cliente/a	*customer; client*
el/la cocinero/a	*cook*
la cuchara	*soup spoon; tablespoon*
la cucharita	*teaspoon*
el cuchillo	*knife*
la especialidad de la casa	*specialty of the house*
el mantel	*tablecloth*
el menú	*menu*
el plato	*plate; dish*
la propina	*tip*
la servilleta	*napkin*
la tarjeta de crédito	*credit card*
la tarjeta de débito	*debit card*
la taza	*cup*
el tenedor	*fork*
el vaso	*glass*
barato/a	*cheap*
caro/a	*expensive*
delicioso/a	*delicious*
sabroso/a	*tasty*
pagar	*to pay*
pedir	*to order*
reservar una mesa	*to reserve a table*
saber bien/mal	*to taste good/bad*
¡Buen provecho!	*Enjoy your meal!*
La cuenta, por favor.	*The check, please.*

De compras en Buenos Aires, Argentina

8 ¿Qué te pones?

En los países hispanohablantes la gente lleva ropa (*wear clothing*) muy similar a la que llevan por todo el mundo pero también se usa ropa más tradicional. Por ejemplo, en México se encuentran sarapes, ponchos y huaraches y en Colombia usan ruanas (ponchos) y alpargatas (*espadrilles*).

Preguntas

1. ¿Qué tipo de ropa te gusta? ¿Prefieres la ropa formal o la ropa informal? ¿Qué ropa llevas normalmente?
2. ¿Te interesa la moda (*fashion*)? ¿Te gusta experimentar con diferentes estilos de ropa? Explica.
3. ¿Cómo influye el lugar donde vive una persona en la ropa que lleva?

¿Sabías que...?

Así como la moda *cowboy* en Estados Unidos, los diseñadores argentinos usan elementos de la ropa típica de los gauchos: ponchos, pantalones anchos (*wide*) y bandanas.

En un almacén

Una modelo de ropa

Learning Outcomes

By the end of this chapter, you will be able to:

- ✔ describe clothing, fabrics, and materials.
- ✔ express likes, dislikes, and needs.
- ✔ convey information about people and things without repetition.
- ✔ share about situations in the past and how things used to be.
- ✔ write an e-mail and practice circumlocution.
- ✔ exchange interesting facts about Argentina and Uruguay.
- ✔ read an article from a fashion magazine.

Comunicación I

1 VOCABULARIO

La ropa Describing clothing

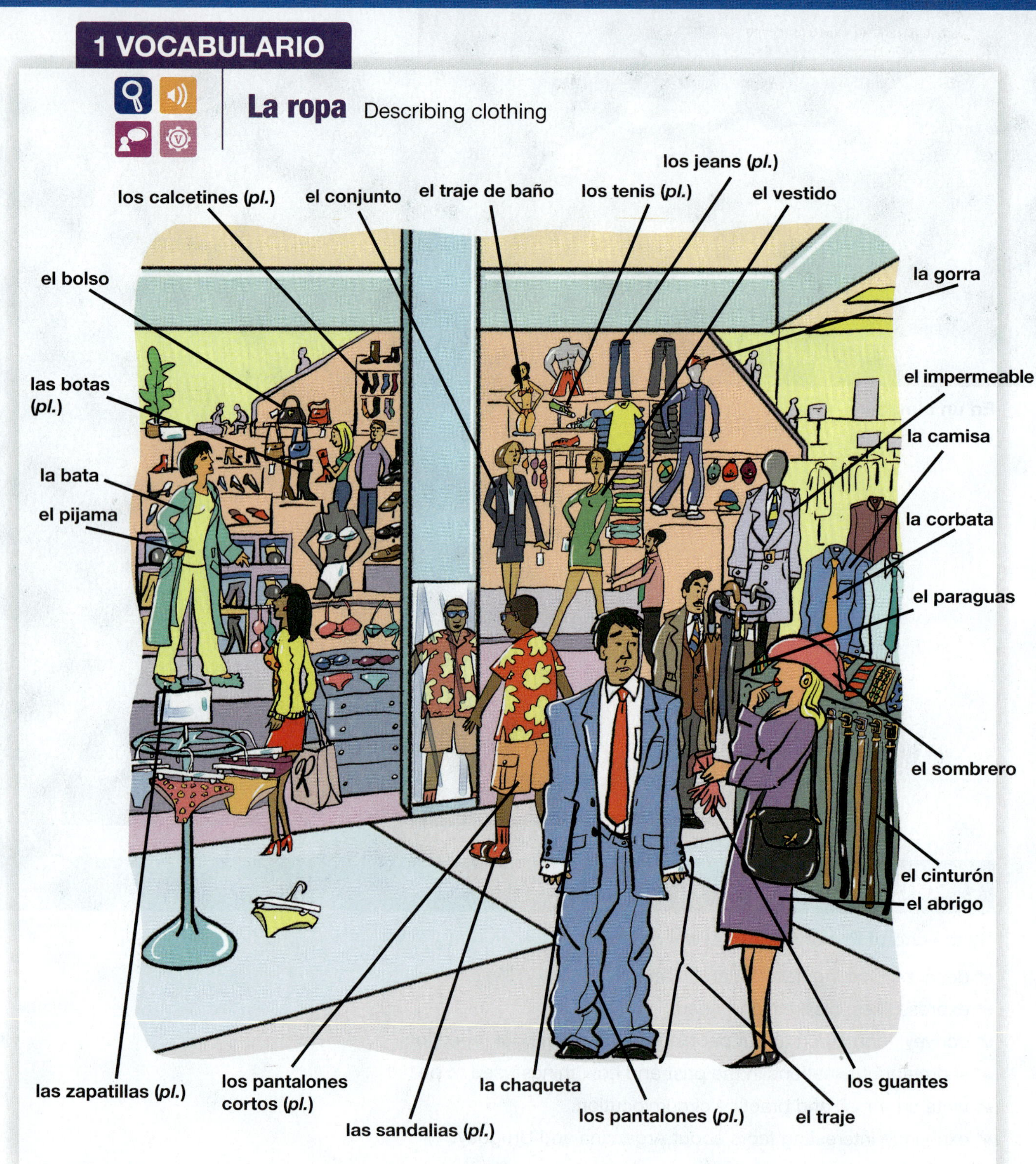

Fíjate

Note that *ropa* is a singular noun. All verb forms and adjectives used with it should be singular. Think *clothing* instead of *clothes.*

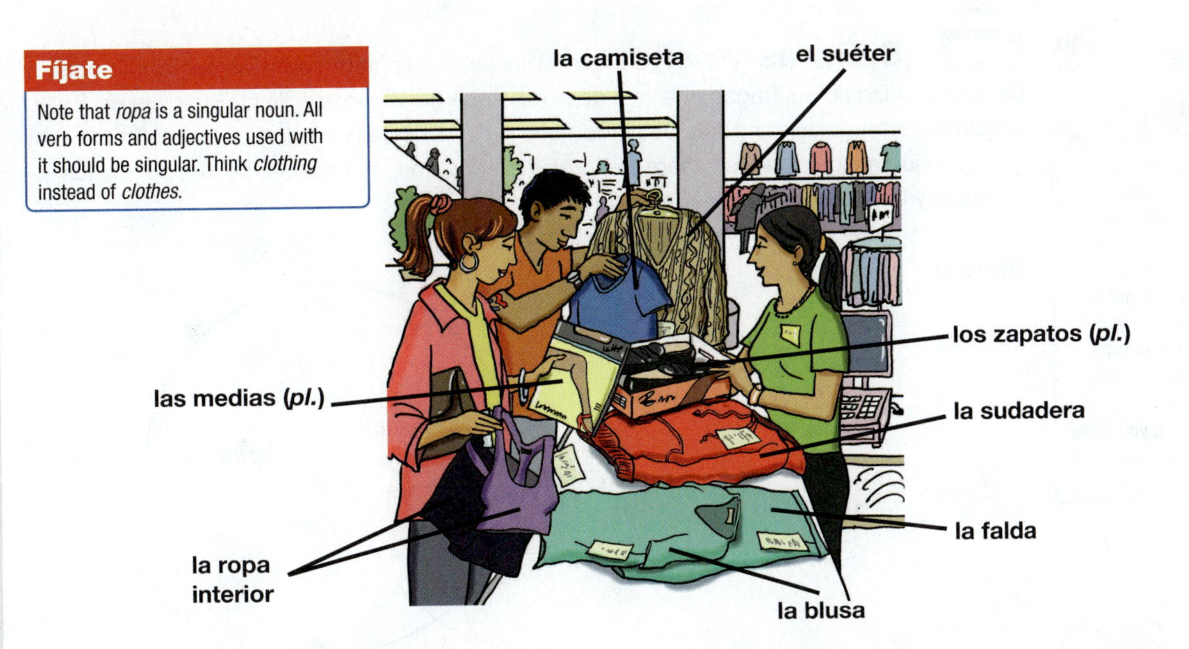

Algunos verbos	*Some verbs*
llevar	*to wear; to take; to carry*
prestar	*to lend, to loan*

Algunos sustantivos	*Some verbs*
la moda	*fashion; style*
las prendas	*articles of clothing*

Fíjate

In your vocabulary list you see the letters (*pl.*) beside words such as *las medias* or *los jeans* to indicate that they are plural in Spanish. You will also notice (*pl.*) beside *los calcetines.* Each sock is a *calcetín.*

Now you are ready to complete the ***Preparación y práctica*** activities for this chunk online.

PRONUNCIACIÓN

The letters *ll* and *ñ*

Go to *¡Anda!* online to learn about the letters *ll* and *ñ*.

8-1 Categorías Escribe todas las palabras nuevas del vocabulario que corresponden a las siguientes categorías. Luego, compara tu lista con la de un/a compañero/a.

¿Qué ropa usas para…?

1. hacer ejercicio y jugar a los deportes
2. ir a la cama
3. cubrir (*to cover*) los pies (*feet*)
4. ir a clase
5. trabajar en una oficina
6. ir a cenar a un restaurante elegante

8-2 ¡Señoras y señores!

Dibujen un diagrama de Venn según el modelo. En el círculo izquierdo, hagan una lista de la ropa que generalmente llevan las mujeres. En el círculo derecho, hagan una lista de la ropa que generalmente llevan los hombres. En el centro donde se juntan los círculos (*where the circles overlap*), hagan una lista de la ropa que los hombres y las mujeres llevan. ¿Qué lista es la más larga?

Fíjate

You have noticed that *¡Anda! Curso elemental* makes extensive use of pair and group work in the classroom to provide you with many opportunities during the class period to practice Spanish. When working in pairs or groups, it's imperative that you make every effort to speak only Spanish.

MODELO

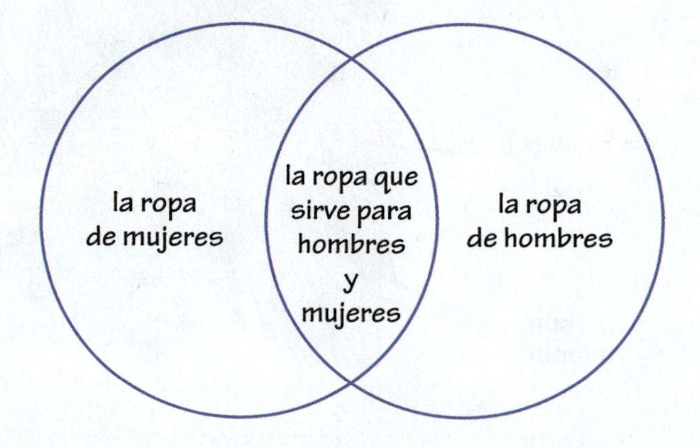

8-3 ¿Cómo se visten?

Túrnense para describir qué ropa llevan las personas en las fotos.

Capítulo 3. Los colores, pág. 119.

MODELO *El hombre y los chicos llevan sombreros…*

Estrategia

Remember that adjectives describe nouns and agree in number (singular/plural) and gender (masculine/feminine) with the nouns they are describing.

Una familia guatemalteca

Una señora peruana

8-4 El juego del viaje (*travel*)

Formen un círculo de cinco estudiantes o más. Primero, decidan adónde quieren ir de viaje. Después, túrnense para decir sus nombres y un artículo de ropa que quieren llevar. Cada estudiante tiene que repetir lo que dijeron los estudiantes anteriores. **¡OJO!** Si no recuerdan (*If you don't remember*), tienen que preguntar: **¿Qué dijiste, por favor?** o **¿Puedes repetir, por favor?**

Estrategia

It is important to be supportive of your fellow classmates during these activities, which includes making suggestions and helpful comments and corrections. Because you will be learning from each other, it is good to know the following expressions to help you interact with each other:

(No) Estoy de acuerdo.	*I agree. / I don't agree.*
Yo pienso que es…	*I think it's…*
¿No debería ser…?	*Shouldn't it be…?*

MODELO Vamos a Cancún.

E1: *Soy Beverly y voy a llevar un traje de baño.*

E2: *Soy Tim y voy a llevar una camiseta blanca. Beverly va a llevar un traje de baño.*

E3: *Soy Kelly y voy a llevar una chaqueta. Tim va a llevar una camiseta blanca. Beverly va a llevar un traje de baño.*

E4: …

8-5 Señora, ¿qué debo llevar?

Trabajas para una agencia de viajes y, para ayudar a tus clientes, tienes que preparar una lista de la ropa que deben llevar a cada destino (*destination*). Compara tu lista con la de un/a compañero/a.

Capítulo A Para empezar. Los días, los meses y las estaciones, pág. 21.

MODELO la República Dominicana en agosto

los trajes de baño, los pantalones cortos, las camisetas, los jeans, los tenis y el paraguas

1. Argentina en julio
2. Costa Rica en junio
3. México en septiembre
4. Cuba en diciembre
5. Uruguay en marzo
6. España en febrero

Fíjate

Remember that the seasons south of the equator are the opposite of those in the northern hemisphere, so that when it is summer in the northern hemisphere it is winter in the southern hemisphere.

Capítulo 3. Los colores, pág. 119; Capítulo 4. *Ir + a + infinitivo*, pág. 156; Capítulo 5. Los pronombres de complemento directo, pág. 202.

8-6 ¿Tienes un presupuesto (*budget*)? Completa el siguiente cuadro con las prendas que acabas de comprar (*have just bought*) y con las que necesitas comprar. Luego, comparte tus respuestas con un/a compañero/a.

Fíjate

The expression *acabar de + infinitive* means "to have just done something." Use this expression in the present tense when you want to refer to the very recent past. As in the *modelo*, this expression is useful for establishing a context for the use of the preterit.

MODELO *Acabo de comprar una blusa blanca muy elegante. La compré en la tienda Alta Moda la semana pasada. Pagué cuarenta y cinco dólares. Necesito comprar una falda negra.*

ACABO DE COMPRAR...	LO(S)/LA(S) COMPRÉ...	PAGUÉ...	VOY A / NECESITO COMPRAR...
1. una blusa blanca	en Alta Moda	$45	una falda negra
2.			
3.			

Zara: la moda internacional

En España, uno de los negocios más florecientes (*flourishing*) es la empresa de ropa Zara. El fundador, Amancio Ortega Gaona, empezó el negocio (*business*) en La Coruña, en el norte de España, con unas 5.000 pesetas (el equivalente de unos 30 euros). Ahora el Sr. Ortega es uno de los hombres más ricos del mundo. Una de las razones del gran éxito del negocio es que continuamente ofrece lo que la gente quiere. Su filosofía es vender ropa "barata y de buena calidad". Tiene unos doscientos diseñadores (*designers*) que son los responsables de crear la moda Zara. Las diferentes líneas creadas por los diseñadores proporcionan un *look* completo para hombres, mujeres y niños.

Fíjate

In 2002, Spain converted to the *euro*. Previously, its currency was the *peseta*.

Gran parte de la ropa se hace en una fábrica (*factory*) muy moderna en La Coruña, España o en otros lugares de Europa. Desde el momento que surge la idea hasta que la prenda llega a la tienda, solo pasan unas tres o cuatro semanas. Dos veces por semana llegan productos nuevos a las tiendas y así se renueva más del cuarenta por ciento del inventario.

Ahora se puede comprar la moda Zara en más de 2.000 tiendas en 88 países, por catálogo y por Internet. Para conocer la moda internacional del momento, hay que conocer Zara.

Preguntas

1. ¿Quién empezó la empresa Zara y dónde? ¿Cuánto costó?
2. ¿Por qué tiene tanto éxito el negocio?

2 GRAMÁTICA

Los pronombres de complemento indirecto

Stating to whom and for whom things are done

The indirect object indicates *to whom* or *for whom* an action is done. Note these examples:

A: My mom bought this dress *for whom*?
B: She bought this dress *for you*.
A: Yes, she bought *me* this dress.

Review the chart of the indirect object pronouns and their English equivalents:

Los pronombres de complemento indirecto

me	*to / for me*
te	*to / for you*
le	*to / for you* (Ud.)
le	*to / for him, her*
nos	*to / for us*
os	*to / for you all* (vosotros)
les	*to / for you all* (Uds.)
les	*to / for them*

¡Explícalo tú!

Now study the sentences and answer the questions that follow.

Mi madre **me** compra mucha ropa.
Mi madre **te** compra mucha ropa.
Mi madre **le** compra mucha ropa a usted.
Mi madre **le** compra mucha ropa a mi hermano.
Mi madre **nos** compra mucha ropa.
Mi madre **os** compra mucha ropa.
Mi madre **les** compra mucha ropa a ustedes.
Mi madre **les** compra mucha ropa a mis hermanos.

In each of the above sentences:

1. Who is *buying* the clothing?
2. Who is *receiving* the clothing?

 Check your answers to the preceding questions in Appendix 1.

Now, look at the following examples. Identify the **direct objects** and the **indirect object pronouns**.

¿Me traes la falda gris?	*Will you bring me the gray skirt?*
Su novio le regaló la chaqueta más formal.	*Her boyfriend gave her the more formal jacket.*
Mi hermana me compró la blusa elegante.	*My sister bought me the elegant blouse.*
Nuestra compañera de cuarto nos lavó la ropa.	*Our roommate washed our clothes for us.*

(*continued*)

Some things to remember:

> **Fíjate**
> Object pronouns can also be attached to present participles (forms ending in *-ando, -iendo*). You will learn about present participles in *Capítulo 11*.

1. Like direct object pronouns, indirect object pronouns *precede* verb forms and can also be *attached to infinitives*.

   ¿**Me** quieres dar la chaqueta?
   ¿Quieres dar**me** la chaqueta? } *Do you want to give me the jacket?*

   ¿**Me** vas a dar la chaqueta?
   ¿Vas a dar**me** la chaqueta? } *Are you going to give me the jacket?*

   Manolo **te** puede comprar la gorra en la tienda.
   Manolo puede compra**rte** la gorra en la tienda. } *Manolo can buy you the cap at the store.*

   Su hermano **le** va a regalar una camiseta.
   Su hermano va a regalar**le** una camiseta. } *Her brother is going to give her a T-shirt.*

2. To clarify or emphasize the indirect object, a prepositional phrase (**a** + *prepositional pronoun*) can be added, as in the following sentences. Clarification of **le** and **les** is especially important since they can refer to different people (*him, her, you, them, you all*).

   Le presto el abrigo **a él** pero no **le** presto nada **a ella**. — *I'm loaning him my coat, but I'm not loaning her anything*. (clarification)
   ¿**Me** preguntas **a mí**? — *Are you asking me?* (emphasis)

3. It is common for Spanish speakers to include both an indirect object noun and pronoun in the same sentence, especially when the third person form is used. This is most often done to clarify or emphasize something.

> **Fíjate**
> Remember that indirect object pronouns indicate to whom (*a quién*) and for whom (*para quién*) something is done.

¿? Now you are ready to complete the ***Preparación y práctica*** activities for this chunk online.

8-7 ¿Para quién? Juntos escriban las oraciones de nuevo, sustituyendo las palabras subrayadas con pronombres de complemento indirecto. Sigan el modelo.

MODELO El diseñador ___ preparó un conjunto de verano precioso para la modelo.
El diseñador le preparó un conjunto de verano precioso.

1. Mi pareja _____ compró un abrigo muy bonito para su madre.
2. Mis amigas _____ encontraron unas botas negras para mí.
3. Yo _____ busqué unos paraguas para mis padres.
4. Tara y Tim _____ dieron unas gorras de béisbol a mi hermano y a mí.
5. Nosotros _____ regalamos un traje nuevo a mi hermano.

8-8 **Amigos perfectos** Cuando tus mejores amigos y tú celebran sus cumpleaños, Uds. siempre organizan las fiestas. Juntos escriban oraciones sobre las cosas que hacen, usando **me, te, nos, le** y **les**. Sigan el modelo.

MODELO E1: yo / preparar / las fiestas de cumpleaños / para mis amigos

E2: *Yo preparo las fiestas de cumpleaños <u>para mis amigos</u>. / <u>Les</u> preparo las fiestas.*

1. yo / preparar / una fiesta sorpresa (*surprise*) / para él
2. yo / mandar / invitaciones / a todos nuestros amigos
3. mis amigos y yo / comprar / unos regalos (*gifts*) cómicos / para ella
4. tú / hacer / una torta / para nosotros
5. nosotros / cantar / una canción especial / a ti
6. nuestros amigos / dar / unas rosas bonitas / a mí

8-9 **De compras** Mira el dibujo. Elena y Manolo van de compras a la tienda Primera Moda en Buenos Aires. Sonia, una dependienta de la tienda, los ayuda. Primero, lee las oraciones y después escucha la conversación entre ellos. Finalmente indica si las oraciones son ciertas (**C**) o falsas (**F**). **¡Ojo!** Los precios son en pesos argentinos.

C	F	
☐	☐	1. Manolo y Elena son hermanos.
☐	☐	2. Manolo necesita comprar ropa de deportes.
☐	☐	3. A Sonia le gusta el conjunto azul.
☐	☐	4. El precio de la sudadera roja es 400 pesos.
☐	☐	5. A Manolo no le gusta el suéter amarillo y negro.
☐	☐	6. De todas las cosas que Manolo y Elena compran, el conjunto de Elena cuesta más.

8-10 ¿Qué me recomienda? Una persona hace el papel de consejero/a y la otra de estudiante de primer año (*freshman*). Deben hacer y contestar las siguientes preguntas según el modelo. Luego, cambien de papel.

MODELO E1: ¿Me recomienda usted la clase de Conversación 101?
E2: *No, no le recomiendo esa clase. Le recomiendo la clase de civilización española.*

1. ¿Me pide usted información sobre mi familia?
2. ¿Me recomienda usted algunas clases fáciles?
3. ¿Me ayuda usted con mis estudios?
4. ¿Me recomienda usted jugar algún deporte?
5. ¿Me recomienda usted hablar con mis profesores fuera de clase?
6. ¿Me recomienda usted la cafetería?

Capítulo 3. Los quehaceres de la casa, pág. 117; Capítulo 5. El pretérito, págs. 197, 200.

8-11 ¡Qué suerte! Haz una lista de por lo menos **cuatro** cosas que tú hiciste por tu compañero/a de cuarto o tu familia la semana pasada. Después, haz otra lista de tres o cuatro cosas que esa persona hizo por ti. Compara tus listas con las de un/a compañero/a.

MODELO E1: *A mi compañero de cuarto le arreglé la sala, le contesté el teléfono...*
E2: *Mi compañera de cuarto me buscó unos libros en la biblioteca. También me preparó la comida...*

Capítulo 5. El pretérito, págs. 197, 200; Capítulo 7. Algunos verbos irregulares en el pretérito, pág. 284.

8-12 Los regalos ¿Te regalaron muchas cosas este año? ¿Regalaste muchas cosas tú? Escribe una lista de **cuatro** regalos que te dieron y de **cuatro** cosas que tú les regalaste. Luego, comparte tu lista con un/a compañero/a según el modelo. ¡Hay que ser creativos/as!

MODELO E1: *Le di una corbata a mi padre.*
E2: *¿Ah sí? ¿De qué color? ¿Le gustó a tu padre?*
E1: *Sí, le gustó mucho la corbata azul. Y mis padres me regalaron una bicicleta.*
E2: *¡Qué suerte! ¿Te gusta montar en bicicleta?*

Fíjate

As in English, there are word "families." *El regalo* (noun) means "gift" and *regalar* (verb) means "to give a gift."

3 GRAMÁTICA

Gustar y verbos como *gustar*

Expressing likes, dislikes, needs, etc.

As you already know, the verb **gustar** is used to express likes and dislikes. **Gustar** functions differently from other verbs you have studied so far.

- The person, thing, or idea that is liked is the *subject* (S) of the sentence.
- The person who likes the other person, thing, or idea is the *indirect object* (IO).

Consider the chart below:

(A mí)	**me**	gusta el traje.	*I like the suit.*
(A ti)	**te**	gusta el traje.	*You like the suit.*
(A Ud.)	**le**	gusta el traje.	*You like the suit.*
(A él)	**le**	gusta el traje.	*He likes the suit.*
(A ella)	**le**	gusta el traje.	*She likes the suit.*
(A nosotros/as)	**nos**	gusta el traje.	*We like the suit.*
(A vosotros/as)	**os**	gusta el traje.	*You (all) like the suit.*
(A Uds.)	**les**	gusta el traje.	*You (all) like the suit.*
(A ellos/as)	**les**	gusta el traje.	*They like the suit.*

Note the following:

1. The construction **a** + *pronoun* (**a mí, a ti, a él,** etc.) or **a** + *noun* is optional most of the time. It is used for clarification or emphasis. Clarification of **le gusta** and **les gusta** is especially important since the indirect object pronouns **le** and **les** can refer to different people (*him, her, you, them, you all*).

   A él le gusta llevar ropa cómoda. (clarification) — *He likes to wear comfortable clothes.*
   A Ana le gusta llevar pantalones cortos. (clarification) — *Ana likes to wear shorts.*
   Me gustan esos pantalones largos. — *I like those long pants.*
   A mí me gustan más esos cortos. (emphasis) — *I like those short ones even more.*

2. Use the plural form **gustan** when what is liked (the subject of the sentence) is plural.

   Me gusta **el traje.** → Me gustan **los trajes.**
   I like the suit. — *I like the suits.*

3. To express the idea that one likes *to do* something, **gustar** is followed by an infinitive. In that case you always use the singular **gusta,** even when you use more than one infinitive in the sentence:

   Me gusta ir de compras por la mañana. — *I like to go shopping in the morning.*
   A Pepe **le gusta leer** revistas de moda y **llevar** ropa atrevida. — *Pepe likes to read fashion magazines and wear daring clothing.*
   Nos gusta llevar zapatos cómodos cuando hacemos ejercicio. — *We like to wear comfortable shoes when we exercise.*

The verbs listed below function like **gustar:**

encantar	*to love; to like very much*
fascinar	*to fascinate*
hacer falta	*to need; to be lacking*
importar	*to matter; to be important*
molestar	*to bother*

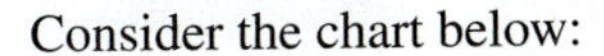

(continued)

Me encanta ir de compras. — *I love to go shopping. (I like shopping very much.)*

A Doug y a David **les fascina** la tienda de ropa Rugby. — *The Rugby clothing store fascinates (is fascinating to) Doug and David.*

¿**Te hace falta** dinero para comprar el vestido? — *Do you need (Are you lacking) money to buy the dress?*

A Juan **le importa** el precio de la ropa, no la moda. — *The price of the clothing, not the style, matters (is important) to Juan.*

Nos molestan las personas que llevan sandalias en invierno. — *People who wear sandals in the winter bother us.*

¿? Now you are ready to complete the ***Preparación y práctica*** activities for this chunk online.

8-13 Ideas incompletas

Completa las siguientes oraciones. Después, compártelas con un/a compañero/a.

1. En invierno me encanta(n)…
2. A mis profesores les molesta(n)…
3. A mi mejor amigo/a no le importa(n)…
4. A los estudiantes de español les fascina(n)…
5. A mis compañeros de clase y a mí nos hace(n) falta…

8-14 Lo que nos gusta…

Digan oraciones lógicas, escogiendo uno de los verbos como **gustar**. Sigan el modelo.

MODELO a mí, la ropa nueva
A mí me encanta la ropa nueva.

1. al niño, las corbatas
2. a los hombres, las camisetas
3. a las mujeres, la moda
4. a ti, los trajes de baño
5. a la niña, la bata
6. a nosotros, los jeans
7. al/a la profesor/a, las gorras
8. a mi mejor amiga, el vestido
9. a ti y a mí, el traje

8-15 Hablando de la música…

A Jaime y a Celia les gusta mucho la música. Completa las siguientes oraciones para descubrir sus preferencias. Después, comparte tu párrafo con un/a compañero/a.

Capítulo 5. El mundo de la música, pág. 182.

MODELO A nosotros *nos fascina* (fascinar) la música rap.

A nosotros (1) __________ __________ (encantar) la música rock. A mí (2) __________ __________ (gustar) los grupos como Slipknot y Anthrax. Mi cantante favorita es Haley Williams y (3) __________ __________ (gustar) su grupo también. A Celia (4) __________ __________ (fascinar) el grupo Mastodon. Celia tiene casi toda su música, pero (5) __________ __________ __________ (hacer falta) un álbum que se llama *Once More 'Round the Sun*. A nuestros compañeros (6) __________ __________ (molestar) tener que escuchar nuestra música favorita. Ellos prefieren la música jazz. A Celia y a mí no (7) __________ __________ (importar) su opinión. ¡Somos amigos, pero no nos tienen que gustar las mismas cosas siempre!

8-16 ¿Qué opinas? Escribe tu opinión sobre esta ropa en la columna apropiada de cada hilera (*row*). Luego, comparte tu opinión con un/a compañero/a.

MODELO E1: *¿Te fascinan los vestidos de Carolina Herrera?*
E2: *Sí, me fascinan. / No, no me importan mucho. / No sé, no los conozco.*

	(NO) ME FASCINA(N)	(NO) ME ENCANTA(N)	NO ME IMPORTA(N) MUCHO	NO LO(S)/LA(S) CONOZCO
1. los vestidos de Carolina Herrera				
2. los trajes de Armani				
3. una camisa y una corbata de Zara				
4. la ropa deportiva				
5. un conjunto elegante				

Capítulo 2. Las materias y las especialidades, pág. 66; En la universidad, pág. 80; Los deportes y los pasatiempos, pág. 89.

8-17 En mi opinión…

¿Qué te gusta y no te gusta de tu universidad? Completa los siguientes pasos.

Paso 1 Completa el siguiente cuadro según tu opinión.

ME MOLESTA(N)…	ME ENCANTA(N)…	NOS HACE(N) FALTA…
1.	1.	1.
2.	2.	2.
3.	3.	3.

Paso 2 Ahora, circula por la clase para pedirles a tres compañeros sus opiniones.

MODELO E1: *¿Qué te molesta?*

E2: *Me molesta la comida de la cafetería.*

A _____ LE MOLESTA(N)…	A _____ LE ENCANTA(N)…	NOS HACE(N) FALTA…
1.	1.	1.
2.	2.	2.
3.	3.	3.

4 GRAMÁTICA

Los pronombres de complemento directo e indirecto usados juntos

Conveying information about people and things

You have worked with two types of object pronouns, direct and indirect. Now, note how they are used together in the same sentence.

Paula **nos** está devolviendo **las botas**.	→	Paula **nos las** está devolviendo.
Paula is giving us back the boots.		*Paula is giving them back to us.*
Ella nunca **nos** presta **sus zapatos**.	→	Ella nunca **nos los** presta.
She never loans us her shoes.		*She never loans them to us.*
Paula **me** pide **el bolso** ahora.	→	Paula **me lo** pide ahora.
Paula is asking me for my purse now.		*Paula is asking me for it now.*
Mi novio **me** compró **una blusa blanca**.	→	Mi novio **me la** compró.
My boyfriend bought me a white blouse.		*My boyfriend bought it for me.*

¡Explícalo tú!

1. You know that direct and indirect objects come after verbs. Where do you find the direct and indirect object pronouns?
2. Reading from left to right, which pronoun comes first (direct or indirect)? Which pronoun comes second?

 Check your answers for the preceding questions in Appendix 1.

¡OJO! A change occurs when you use **le** or **les** along with a direct object pronoun that begins with **l:** (**lo, la, los, las**): **le** or **les** changes to **se.**

le → se

Paula **le** pide **el bolso** a mi hermana.	→	Paula **se lo** pide.
Su novio no **le** compró **una chaqueta**.	→	Su novio no **se la** compró.
Su novio **le** va a comprar **un traje**.	→	Su novio **se lo** va a comprar.

les → se

Paula **les** devuelve **las botas**.	→	Paula **se las** devuelve.
Yo **le** presto **mis zapatos**.	→	Yo **se los** presto.
Paula nunca **les** presta **sus cosas**.	→	Paula nunca **se las** presta.

Direct and indirect object pronouns may also be attached to infinitives. Note that when attached, an accent is placed over the final vowel of the infinitive.

¿Aquel abrigo? Mi madre **me lo** va a comprar.
¿Aquel abrigo? Mi madre va a comprár**melo**.
} *That coat over there? My mother is going to buy it for me.*

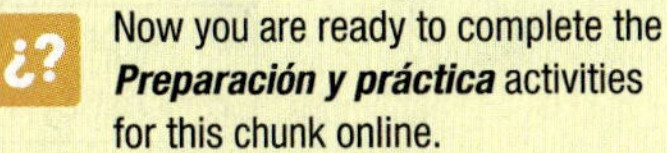

Now you are ready to complete the ***Preparación y práctica*** activities for this chunk online.

Capítulo 5. El pretérito, pág. 197; Capítulo 7. Algunos verbos irregulares en el pretérito, págs. 277, 284.

8-18 Favores Escribe oraciones completas sobre lo que dijo Pablo de su hermano Antonio. Sigue el modelo, primero usando el complemento indirecto y después los pronombres de complemento indirecto y directo juntos. Comparte tus oraciones con un/a compañero/a.

MODELO mi hermano Antonio / prestar / (a mí) / sus zapatos favoritos / ayer

Mi hermano Antonio ***me*** *prestó* ***sus zapatos favoritos*** *ayer.*

Mi hermano Antonio ***me los*** *prestó ayer.*

1. yo / dar / (a Antonio) / unos jeans / la semana pasada
2. mis padres / regalar / (a Antonio) / un traje formal / el año pasado
3. Antonio / lavar / (para nosotros) / la ropa / anteayer
4. Antonio / pedir / (a mí) / dinero para comprar una gorra / anoche
5. Antonio y yo / buscar / (para los niños) / unas sudaderas / ayer

8-19 Antonio, ¿me prestas...? Ahora Pablo va a una fiesta y quiere usar la ropa de su hermano Antonio. Túrnense para hacer los papeles de Pablo y Antonio usando los pronombres de complemento directo e indirecto.

MODELO prestar / un abrigo

E1 (PABLO): *¿Me prestas el abrigo?*

E2 (ANTONIO): *Sí, te lo presto. / No, no te lo presto.*

1. prestar / los zapatos negros
2. prestar / la corbata azul
3. prestar / una camiseta blanca y una camisa azul de manga larga (*long-sleeved*)
4. prestar / el cinturón negro
5. prestar / tu abrigo nuevo

8-20 Mis recomendaciones ¿Qué recomiendas? Lee la lista y pon una equis (**X**) en la columna apropiada. Después, comparte tus opiniones con un/a compañero/a según el modelo.

MODELO los libros de Tom Clancy (a tus primas)

E1: *¿Les recomiendas los libros de Tom Clancy a tus primas?*

E2: *Sí, se los recomiendo. / No, no se los recomiendo.*

	SÍ	NO
1. las novelas de J.K. Rowling (a tus tíos)		
2. la música de Pitbull (a tu compañero/a de cuarto)		
3. el restaurante Taco Bell (a nosotros)		
4. la tienda Macy's (a tu amigo/a que le gusta mucho la moda)		
5. la película *Drácula* (a tus primos de cinco años)		
6. Disney World (a tu hermano/a)		
7. el Museo de Arte Moderno (a tu profesor/a)		
8. la clase de español (a tu mejor amigo/a)		

8-21 ¿En qué puedo servirle? Acabas de empezar una pasantía (*internship*). En vez de (*Instead of*) tareas asociadas con tu carrera, te dan el trabajo de ayudante de una de las vicepresidentas. Túrnense para contestar sus preguntas.

Estrategia

Remember that when addressing an employer, you would use *usted*, not *tú*. Also, be sure to practice both ways of structuring the sentence with two object pronouns, as in the *modelo*.

MODELO E1: *¿Me puede comprar un periódico?*
E2: *Sí, se lo puedo comprar. / Sí, puedo comprárselo.*

1. ¿Me puede traer un café?
2. ¿Me puede comprar los boletos (*tickets*) para un viaje a Nueva York?
3. ¿Me puede arreglar los apuntes y los papeles para la reunión de esta tarde?
4. ¿Me puede buscar un artículo en el periódico?
5. ¿Me puede reservar una mesa en un restaurante elegante para esta noche?
6. ¿Me puede comprar unas rosas para la recepcionista? Es su cumpleaños hoy.

¿Cómo andas? I

Having completed **Comunicación I**, I now can…	Feel confident	Need to review
• describe clothing. (p. 308)	☐	☐
• pronounce the letters *ll* and *ñ*. (p. 309 and online)	☐	☐
• recount information about a Spanish clothing company. (p. 312)	☐	☐
• state to whom and for whom things are done. (p. 313)	☐	☐
• express likes, dislikes, needs, etc. (p. 317)	☐	☐
• convey information about people and things. (p. 321)	☐	☐

Comunicación II

5 VOCABULARIO

Las telas y los materiales

Providing details about clothing

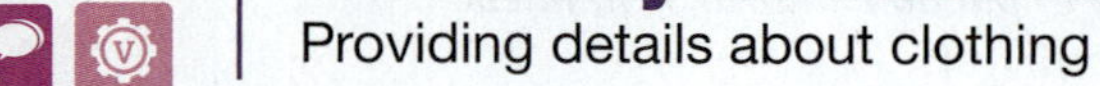

Más telas y materiales	*More fabrics and materials*
el algodón	*cotton*
la lana	*wool*
el poliéster	*polyester*
la seda	*silk*

Otras palabras	*Other words*
ancho/a	*wide*
atrevido/a	*daring*
claro/a	*light (colored)*
(in)cómodo/a	*(un)comfortable*
estrecho/a	*tight*
oscuro/a	*dark*
quedarle bien/mal	*to fit well/badly*

Fíjate

The expressions *quedarle bien* / *quedarle mal* follow the same forms as *gustar*.

¿? Now you are ready to complete the ***Preparación y práctica*** activities for this chunk online.

8-22 Los opuestos

Túrnense para decir el opuesto de cada una de las siguientes palabras.

1. ancho
2. formal
3. quedarle bien
4. claro
5. corto
6. liso

8-23 Definiciones

Túrnense para elegir una palabra o expresión para completar cada oración.

1. Cuando hace mucho frío, prefiero llevar un abrigo de __________.
   a. rayas   b. poliéster   c. lana
2. Ana tiene una entrevista de trabajo (*job interview*) en el banco. Ella no debe llevar un traje __________.
   a. elegante   b. atrevido   c. formal
3. La tela de __________ viene de una planta.
   a. algodón   b. cuero   c. poliéster
4. A mi madre no le importa mucho __________. Siempre prefiere llevar ropa cómoda y barata.
   a. el modelo   b. la moda   c. el algodón
5. Mi padre quiere proteger (*protect*) a los animales. Por eso nunca lleva ropa __________.
   a. lisa   b. estampada   c. de cuero
6. A mi amigo le encanta la ropa __________ porque dice que "su color" es el negro.
   a. lisa   b. clara   c. oscura

8-24 ¡A dibujar!

Completa los siguientes pasos.

Paso 1 Dibuja a un hombre o una mujer con cualquier (*whatever*) ropa que quieras. Incluye diferentes telas y materiales en el dibujo.

Paso 2 Descríbele tu dibujo a un/a compañero/a, quien tiene que dibujar lo que tú le dices. Luego cambien de papel.

MODELO *El hombre lleva un sombrero negro muy elegante. Lleva un traje azul oscuro muy elegante, una camisa blanca y una corbata azul con rayas rojas…*

8-25 ¿Cuál es tu conjunto favorito? Usa las siguientes preguntas para entrevistar a un/a compañero/a sobre su conjunto favorito.

1. ¿Cuál es tu conjunto favorito?
2. ¿De qué color es?
3. ¿De qué tela es?
4. ¿De qué estilo es?
5. ¿Lo compraste tú? Si no, ¿quién te lo compró?
6. ¿Cuándo lo compraste o cuándo te lo compraron?
7. ¿Dónde lo compraste o dónde te lo compraron?
8. ¿Cuándo lo llevas?
9. ¿Por qué te gusta tanto?

8-26 ¿Qué está de moda? Trae a la clase tres o cuatro fotos de modelos; pueden ser de una revista (*magazine*), un catálogo o de Internet. Túrnate con un/a compañero/a para describir en por lo menos **tres** oraciones la ropa que llevan los modelos. Digan qué ropa les gusta más y qué ropa no les gusta. ¿Están de acuerdo?

MODELO *La primera modelo lleva un conjunto de invierno blanco y gris. El suéter es blanco con...*

8-27 ¿Quién puede ser? Escoge a una persona de tu clase y piensa en la ropa que lleva incluyendo el estilo (*style*), el color y la tela. Describe **cuatro** de sus prendas a tu compañero/a, quien tiene que adivinar a quién describes. Túrnense para describir a **tres** compañeros de clase.

Capítulo 3. Los colores, pág. 119.

MODELO E1: *Esta persona lleva unos pantalones largos de rayas blancas, una camiseta oscura, una chaqueta informal y unos tenis blancos.*

E2: *Es Mayra.*

Los centros comerciales en Latinoamérica

Ir de compras en Latinoamérica se asocia muchas veces con los mercados al aire libre donde se vende la artesanía y la comida típica de la región. Es cierto que estos lugares existen y son muy populares, sobre todo con los turistas. Pero en las últimas décadas ha surgido (*has emerged*) la cultura del centro comercial y los grandes almacenes en las sociedades latinoamericanas.

Los grandes centros comerciales, como los Unicentros en El Salvador y los centros Sambil en Venezuela, las tiendas de Falabella en Chile, Argentina y Perú, y los almacenes Liverpool en México, son buenos ejemplos de mercados modernos que atraen a la población latina de varias clases económicas. Estas tiendas son modernas y ofrecen de todo a los clientes que buscan una gran variedad de productos como, por ejemplo, ropa, artículos y aparatos domésticos y muebles.

La gente va a los centros comerciales para pasear, mirar y entretenerse (*to entertain oneself*). En muchos hay hipermercados donde se puede comprar comida y artículos diversos para el hogar. Los centros comerciales son lugares para citas (*dates*), para pasar el tiempo, para ir al cine, para reunirse con amigos, para observar a la gente, para mirar las vitrinas (*window shop*) y para enterarse de las últimas tendencias de la moda. Verdaderamente, estos centros han cambiado (*have changed*) mucho el estilo de vida de la gente hoy en día.

Preguntas

1. Antes de leer "Los centros comerciales en Latinoamérica", ¿qué entendías tú (*did you understand*) por "mercado latinoamericano"? ¿Qué imagen tenías (*did you used to have*)?
2. ¿Qué hace la gente en los centros comerciales latinoamericanos? ¿Cómo se comparan estas actividades con las de los centros comerciales estadounidenses?

6 GRAMÁTICA

El imperfecto Sharing about situations in the past and how things used to be

Cuando Pepe vivía en la playa, nadaba en el mar todas las mañanas.

In **Capítulos 5** and **7** you learned how to express certain ideas and notions that happened in the past with the preterit. Spanish has another past tense, **el imperfecto**, that *expresses habitual or ongoing past actions, provides descriptions,* or *describes conditions.*

	-ar: hablar	-er: comer	-ir: vivir
yo	habl**aba**	com**ía**	viv**ía**
tú	habl**abas**	com**ías**	viv**ías**
Ud.	habl**aba**	com**ía**	viv**ía**
él, ella	habl**aba**	com**ía**	viv**ía**
nosotros/as	habl**ábamos**	com**íamos**	viv**íamos**
vosotros/as	habl**abais**	com**íais**	viv**íais**
Uds.	habl**aban**	com**ían**	viv**ían**
ellos/as	habl**aban**	com**ían**	viv**ían**

Estrategia

Focus on the forms and when to use the *imperfecto.* Note that the *-er* and *-ir* forms are exactly the same, and that they have accents in every form. Also note that in the *-ar* verbs the *nosotros/nosotras* form has an accent.

There are only *three irregular verbs* in the imperfect: **ir**, **ser**, and **ver**.

	ir	ser	ver
yo	iba	era	veía
tú	ibas	eras	veías
Ud.	iba	era	veía
él, ella	iba	era	veía
nosotros/as	íbamos	éramos	veíamos
vosotros/as	ibais	erais	veíais
Uds.	iban	eran	veían
ellos/as	iban	eran	veían

The imperfect is used to:

1. **provide background information, set the stage, or express a condition that existed**

Llovía mucho.	*It was raining a lot.*
Era una noche oscura y nublada.	*It was a dark and cloudy night.*
Estábamos en el segundo año de la universidad.	*We were in our second year of college.*
Adriana **estaba** enferma y no **quería** levantarse.	*Adriana was ill and didn't want to get up / get out of bed.*

2. **describe habitual or often repeated actions**

Íbamos al centro comercial todos los viernes. — *We went (used to go) to the mall / shopping district every Friday.*

Cuando **era** pequeño, Lebron **jugaba** al básquetbol por lo menos dos horas al día. — *When he was little, Lebron played (used to play) basketball for at least two hours a day.*

Mis padres siempre **llevaban** ropa muy elegante los domingos para ir a la iglesia. — *My parents always wore elegant clothing on Sundays to go to church.*

Fíjate

Repeated actions are usually expressed in English with *used to*… or *would*…

Some words or expressions for describing habitual and repeated actions are:

a menudo	*often*	**muchas veces**	*many times*
casi siempre	*almost always*	**mucho**	*a lot*
frecuentemente	*frequently*	**normalmente**	*normally*
generalmente	*generally*	**siempre**	*always*
mientras	*while*	**todos los días**	*every day*

3. **express *was* or *were* + *ing***

¿Dormías? — *Were you sleeping?*

Me duchaba cuando Juan llamó. — *I was showering when Juan called.*

Alberto **leía** mientras Alicia **escuchaba** música. — *Alberto was reading while Alicia was listening to music.*

4. **tell time in the past**

Era la una y yo todavía **estudiaba.** — *It was 1:00 and I was still studying.*

Eran las diez y los niños **dormían.** — *It was 10:00 and the children were sleeping.*

Now you are ready to complete the ***Preparación y práctica*** activities for this chunk online.

8-28 ***Tic-tac-toe*** Escucha mientras tu profesor/a te explica el juego para practicar el imperfecto.

8-29 Cuando era joven

Completa el párrafo sobre Eva Perón para saber cómo pudo ser su vida cuando era joven. Después, compara tus respuestas con las de un/a compañero/a.

ayudar	encantar	gustar	llegar	poder
preferir	querer	ser	tener	trabajar

María Eva Duarte, como primero se llamaba, nació en una provincia de Buenos Aires en el año 1919. Cuando (1) _______________ seis o siete años su padre murió. Para Eva y sus cuatro hermanos la vida (2) _______________ muy difícil porque les faltaban dinero y comida. La madre (3) _______________ como costurera (*seamstress*) y los niños la (4) _______________ mucho en la casa porque siempre (5) _______________ muy cansada. Nos imaginamos que a Eva le (6) _______________ el verano cuando (7) _______________ estar en casa con sus hermanos. No le (8) _______________ las muñecas (*dolls*) y (9) _______________ inventar juegos o imaginar situaciones diferentes. Parece que desde el principio (*from the start*) Eva (10) _______________ ser actriz.

8-30 Mi día de ayudante

Mira el dibujo en la página 324 y después lee las oraciones a continuación. Escucha mientras Estela nos habla sobre su día como ayudante en un taller de costura (*seamstress shop*). Finalmente selecciona la opción correcta para completar cada oración, según lo que dice Estela.

1. Estela trabajó en el taller…
   a. toda la mañana el lunes. b. el sábado. c. casi todo el día el viernes.
2. Estela y las otras personas trabajaron casi todo el día con…
   a. ropa informal y cara. b. vestidos de algodón. c. ropa formal y telas muy buenas.
3. Estela trabajó toda la mañana para terminar…
   a. un traje de hombre muy caro. b. un elegante vestido azul. c. un vestido ancho y corto.
4. Mientras Estela hacía su trabajo, las otras personas trabajaban con…
   a. trajes para un hombre y una mujer. b. unos pantalones largos. c. unos trajes de niños.
5. El traje para el hombre…
   a. no le quedaba bien. b. no necesitaba muchos cambios. c. era muy pequeño.
6. La esposa del señor no estaba allí porque…
   a. no necesita ropa. b. trabajaba como modelo en Nueva York. c. estaba en Paraguay.
7. Por la tarde, Estela trabajó en…
   a. un vestido largo y elegante. b. unos pantalones negros con rayas blancas.
   c. un vestido de lunares.
8. Estela piensa que va a poder trabajar en el taller durante el verano porque la señora le dijo que…
   a. estaba enojada con el hombre y su esposa. b. estaba muy contenta con su trabajo.
   c. no le gustaban los otros empleados.

8-31 En la escuela... ¿Qué hacías cuando estabas en la escuela primaria? ¿Con qué frecuencia? Escribe una equis (**X**) en la columna apropiada de cada hilera (*row*). Luego, compara tus respuestas con las de un/a compañero/a.

MODELO E1: *¿Escuchabas música?*

E2: *No, nunca escuchaba música. / Sí, a veces escuchaba música.*

	TODOS LOS DÍAS	MUCHAS VECES	A VECES	NUNCA
1. limpiar el cuarto				
2. leer los cuentos de los hermanos Grimm				
3. ver la tele por la noche				
4. ir al cine				
5. dormir ocho horas				
6. comer verduras				
7. jugar con los amigos				
8. tocar un instrumento				
9. hacer la tarea				
10. querer ir a la escuela				

8-32 Mi primera casa ¿Cómo era tu primera casa o la casa de tu amigo/a? Descríbesela a un/a compañero/a dándole por lo menos **cinco** detalles. Luego, cambien de papel.

Capítulo 3. La casa, pág. 106; Los colores, pág. 119.

MODELO *Mi primera casa estaba en una ciudad pequeña. Tenía dos dormitorios. La cocina era amarilla. El comedor blanco y la sala azul eran pequeños. Tenía solamente* (only) *un baño.*

8-33 ¡Cómo cambia la vida! Miren el dibujo y escriban **siete** oraciones que contesten la pregunta "¿cómo era la vida en los años setenta?". Usen verbos como **tener, estar, ser, haber, ayudar, limpiar** y **jugar**. ¡Sean creativos/as!

8-34 Preguntas personales Cuando tenían dieciséis años, ¿qué hacían tus compañeros/as de clase? Circula por la clase para preguntárselo.

MODELO E1: ¿Jugabas al fútbol con los amigos?
E2: *Sí, jugaba todos los días después de salir de la escuela.*
E3: *Sí, jugaba con el equipo del colegio.*
E4: *No, nunca jugaba al fútbol. No me gustaba.*

	ESTUDIANTE 1	ESTUDIANTE 2	ESTUDIANTE 3
1. ¿Preferías estar en casa los fines de semana?			
2. ¿Qué hacías los fines de semana?			
3. ¿Manejabas (*Did you drive*)?			
4. ¿Tenías carro?			
5. ¿Trabajabas?			
6. ¿Qué hacías cuando hacía mal tiempo?			
7. ¿Qué hacías cuando hacía buen tiempo?			
8. ¿Qué hacías cuando tenías dinero?			
9. ¿Qué hacías cuando no tenías dinero?			
10. ¿Adónde ibas con tus amigos?			

Escucha

En el centro comercial

Estrategia	
Guessing meaning from context	You do not need to know every word to understand a listening passage or to get the gist of a conversation. Think about the overall message, then use the surrounding words or sentences to guess at meaning.

8-35 Antes de escuchar Beatriz, la prima de Marisol, es estudiante de intercambio en Buenos Aires. Va de compras con su "hermana" argentina, Luz. Están en la tienda Zara, comprando ropa.

1. ¿Cómo es la tienda Zara?
2. ¿Piensas que ir de compras a Zara en Buenos Aires es igual que ir de compras a Zara en Nueva York (o en cualquier otra ciudad)?

Beatriz y Luz van de compras.

8-36 A escuchar Completa las siguientes actividades.

1. Escucha la conversación entre Beatriz y Luz y después selecciona la opción que mejor conteste la pregunta. ¿De qué se trata (*What is the gist of*) la conversación?
   a. A Beatriz no le gustan las blusas de la tienda y tampoco la tienda. Jamás va de compras allí.
   b. A Beatriz le encanta el dependiente. Vive cerca de Luz.
   c. A Luz le gustan los perros (*dogs*) negros. Alguien tiene un perro que se llama Toro o posiblemente Goro.
2. Escucha una vez más y termina las siguientes oraciones.
   a. Marisol y Beatriz visitaron una de las tiendas Zara… (dónde y cuándo)
   b. Marisol y Beatriz no compraron nada porque…
   c. Luz no quiere comprar la blusa de seda o la falda de lana porque…
   d. Beatriz reconoce (*recognizes*) al dependiente porque…
3. ¿Qué significa "dependiente"?

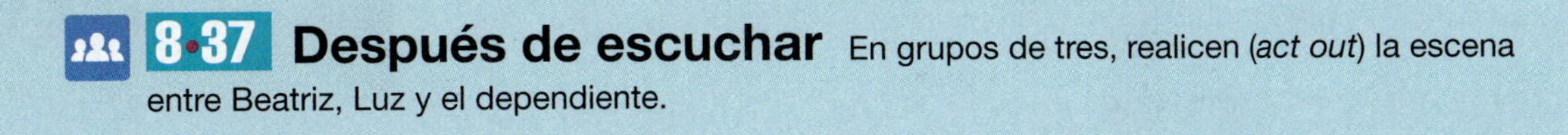

8-37 Después de escuchar En grupos de tres, realicen (*act out*) la escena entre Beatriz, Luz y el dependiente.

¡Conversemos!

8-38 Los modelos Crea un desfile de moda (*fashion show*) con un/a compañero/a. Describe la ropa que lleva tu compañero/a. Si quieres, trae fotos de ropa de unas revistas y descríbela como si fueras (*as if you were*) un/a comentarista de moda para un canal de televisión. Incluye **por lo menos diez** oraciones.

8-39 ¿Qué llevaban? Piensa en la ropa que tus amigos, tu familia y tú llevaban cuando eran más jóvenes. ¿Cómo se compara el estilo de antes con el estilo de ahora? Describe con detalles la ropa que se llevaba en **por lo menos diez** oraciones.

Escribe

Un e-mail

Estrategia

Circumlocution

It is common when learning a language not to know or remember the exact word(s) you need to communicate an idea. Thinking of another way to express something is called "circumlocution"—essentially using several words to describe something simple. For example, if you don't know or remember the word for *tía*, you could say *la hermana de mi padre*. If you can't remember the word for *cine*, you could get your point across by writing *todos los sábados íbamos al centro para ver una película*.

8-40 Antes de escribir ¿Qué te gustaba hacer de niño/a? ¿Jugabas con tus amigos todos los días? ¿Tus padres te dejaban comer caramelos y otros dulces a menudo? Haz una lista de las **ocho** cosas que más te gustaba hacer cuando eras niño/a, usando *circumlocution* cuando sea necesario.

8-41 A escribir Organiza tus ideas y escribe un e-mail a tu hermano/a (o a tu mejor amigo/a), recordando las cosas que hacías en tu niñez.

8-42 Después de escribir Tu profesor/a va a leer los e-mails a la clase para ver si ustedes pueden adivinar quiénes los escribieron.

¿Cómo andas? II

Having completed **Comunicación II**, I now can…	**Feel confident**	**Need to review**
• provide details about clothing. (p. 324)	☐	☐
• consider shopping practices in the Spanish-speaking countries. (p. 327)	☐	☐
• share about situations in the past and how things used to be. (p. 328)	☐	☐
• guess the meanings of unfamiliar words, when listening, from the context. (p. 333)	☐	☐
• communicate about clothing and fashion. (p. 334)	☐	☐
• write an e-mail, practicing circumlocution. (p. 335)	☐	☐

Vistazo cultural

Explore more about Argentina with *Club cultura* online.

Argentina

 Les presento mi país

María Graciela Martelli Paz

Mi nombre es María Graciela Martelli Paz y soy *porteña*, es decir, soy de Buenos Aires. Como yo, muchos argentinos tienen apellidos italianos a causa de la gran inmigración europea a fines del siglo diecinueve. **¿De qué herencia sos vos, che?** Mi país es grande y la geografía es muy variada: desde la montaña más alta del hemisferio occidental, el Cerro Aconcagua, hasta la ciudad más sureña *(del sur)* del mundo, Ushuaia. También tenemos lugares naturales como los glaciares, las pampas, la región de la Patagonia, las cataratas del Iguazú y unas playas hermosas, como la de Mar del Plata. **¿Qué regiones y riquezas naturales hay en tu país?** En mi tiempo libre, me gusta leer, tomar café y comprar libros en el Ateneo, una librería famosa de Buenos Aires. **¿Qué lugares son populares en tu ciudad?**

El Ateneo es un antiguo teatro convertido en librería y café.

Las cataratas del Iguazú en la frontera con Brasil y Argentina

El tango en San Telmo, un antiguo barrio en la capital

ALMANAQUE

Nombre oficial:	República de Argentina
Gobierno:	República
Población:	41.343.201 (2010)
Idioma:	español
Moneda:	Peso argentino ($)

¿Sabías que...?

- El **lunfardo** es un dialecto o jerga que tuvo su origen en los barrios de Buenos Aires a finales del siglo XIX. Es la lengua del tango y también la jerga de las prisiones a principios del siglo XX. Se forman palabras diciendo las sílabas al revés (*reversing the syllables*): "tango" en lunfardo es *gotán*.

Preguntas

1. ¿Cuáles son tres de las distintas regiones geográficas del país? Cuando es verano en Argentina, ¿en qué estación estamos aquí? ¿Por qué?
2. ¿Qué es el lunfardo? ¿Cómo funciona? ¿Puedes dar algunos ejemplos?
3. ¿Qué tiene Argentina en común con otros países de Sudamérica?

Vistazo cultural

Uruguay

Les presento mi país

Francisco Tomás Bacigalupe Bustamante

Mi nombre es Francisco Tomás Bacigalupe Bustamante y soy de Montevideo, la capital de Uruguay. Mi país es pequeño, pero también es tranquilo y bonito. El ochenta por ciento de la población vive en los centros urbanos. El clima templado (no hace mucho calor ni mucho frío) es perfecto para nuestras playas increíbles. Cuando era niño las playas eran nuestro destino favorito para ir de vacaciones. **¿Dónde ibas tú de vacaciones?** Como a los argentinos, a los uruguayos nos gusta mucho la yerba mate, la bebida nacional de Uruguay. Tenemos otras cosas en común con los argentinos, como el tango, los gauchos y una dieta que contiene mucha carne. También comemos mucha pizza y pasta, debido a nuestra herencia italiana. **¿Qué comida de otros países te gusta comer?**

ta del Este es un balneario *ort*) muy turístico.

Unos amigos comparten un mate en un parque en Uruguay.

El puerto de Montevideo

ALMANAQUE

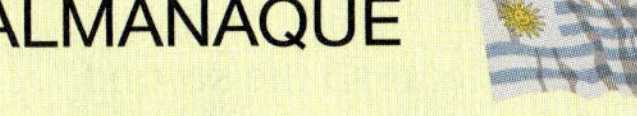

Nombre oficial:	República Oriental del Uruguay
Gobierno:	República democrática
Población:	3.510.386 (2010)
Idiomas:	español (oficial); portuñol/brasilero
Moneda:	Peso uruguayo ($U)

¿Sabías que...?

- Debido al índice de alfabetización (*literacy*), el clima agradable y templado, la belleza del paisaje y la hospitalidad de la gente, a Uruguay se le conoce como "la Suiza de América".

Preguntas

1. ¿Dónde vive la mayoría de los uruguayos?
2. Muchos uruguayos son de herencia italiana. ¿Qué evidencia hay de esta herencia en Uruguay?
3. ¿Qué tiene en común Uruguay con su país vecino (*neighboring*) Argentina?

Lectura

Consejos de moda

8-43 Antes de leer Elegir la ropa adecuada para ciertas situaciones puede ser difícil, especialmente cuando se trata del mundo del trabajo. Para prepararte bien para la lectura, contesta las siguientes preguntas.

1. ¿Qué te pones cuando vas a clase, al trabajo, a una fiesta?
2. ¿Por qué es importante vestirse (*to dress*) bien para una entrevista o reunión (*meeting*) de trabajo? Explica.

Estrategia

Guessing meaning from context
Before consulting a dictionary, always try to guess the meaning of an unfamiliar word from the context. Look closely at the surrounding words and sentences to help you determine the meaning. Even without an exact translation, you can get the general idea of what the word means.

Estrategia

The new strategy *guessing meaning from context* is especially useful for beginning language students. It is much easier to focus on what you can understand and make logical guesses about the new information than to try to focus on what you cannot understand and attempt to look up every word. Only look up a word if it interferes with your ability to comprehend the sentence, question, or the main idea.

8-44 Mientras lees Complete the following activities.

1. In the reading you will encounter some unknown words. For example, read the second sentence of the article. Look at the phrase **entre su banco y una nueva sucursal de Buenos Aires**. What is the meaning of **sucursal**? What other words in the sentence can help you determine the meaning? How is **sucursal** related to **banco**? In reality, **sucursal** means *branch*, that is, another location of the same bank.
2. Read the article and underline the words you do not know. Try to guess their meaning according to the context. (Follow the process in item 1.) Then compare your list with a classmate's.

¿Qué me pongo? *por Joelle Meire*

Estimados lectores, hoy hablaba con mi mejor amiga cuando me pidió consejos sobre qué llevar en un viaje de negocios a Argentina. Ella trabaja para un banco internacional y ahora tiene la oportunidad de ir a Argentina con una delegación bancaria para finalizar unos acuerdos entre su banco y una nueva sucursal en Buenos Aires. La eligieron porque entiende bien las finanzas, habla español perfectamente y conoce muy bien Buenos Aires. Estaba preocupada porque en Miami hace calor y en Buenos Aires es invierno y no sabía qué llevar para las reuniones de trabajo y luego para las cenas con los ejecutivos del banco.

Este era un dilema bastante grande porque en Miami en julio es caluroso y en Buenos Aires hace frío. Tuve que pensarlo bien porque las primeras impresiones son muy importantes. Decidí que los diseñadores estadounidenses no iban a tener nada para el invierno todavía en las tiendas. Le sugerí el diseñador argentino Pablo Ramírez porque tiene una tienda de ropa en Internet. Este diseñador se inspiró en el pasado de Hollywood y su nueva colección es la moda del pasado con una visión moderna. A mi amiga le recomendé un traje de falda y pantalón, gris azulado de lana y seda, con blusas blancas y azules de seda. Para salir a cenar, le recomendé un vestido negro de tafeta negro con finas rayas grises y un abrigo blanco de lana para dar contraste. Además necesita muchos pañuelos° de diferentes colores para combinar con el traje. Esta ropa va a poder usarla en enero y en febrero en Miami. Esta recomendación se la di a ella y ustedes, amigos lectores, también pueden usarla.

° *scarves*

8-45 Después de leer Contesta las siguientes preguntas.

1. ¿Qué consejos le pidió una amiga a Joelle Meire?
2. ¿Qué experiencia tiene su amiga para ser parte de la delegación bancaria?
3. ¿Por qué estaba preocupada por el viaje?
4. ¿Qué diseñador le recomendó a su amiga? ¿Por qué?
5. ¿Cómo es la nueva colección de Pablo Ramírez?
6. En tu opinión, ¿son buenos los consejos de la editora? ¿Sugerirías lo mismo (*Would you suggest the same*)? Explica.

8-46 ¡Qué horror! Ahora tú vas a ser el/la editor/a de *¡Vístete bien!* Mira esta foto de Néstor Hoyos, un actor famoso. Escribe un breve artículo en el que criticas su ropa y haz algunas recomendaciones para mejorar su estilo. Al final, debes ponerle un título interesante a tu artículo. ¡Sé creativo/a!

Néstor Hoyos

MODELO *Queridos lectores, hoy vi esta foto del actor Néstor Hoyos. No entiendo; es una persona famosa y tiene mucho dinero. ¿Por qué se viste de esta manera? ¡No tiene estilo! Su ropa… Recomiendo…*

8-47 Las entrevistas de trabajo Estas personas tienen entrevistas de trabajo esta semana y no saben qué ropa deben llevar. Selecciona un hombre y una mujer de la lista y haz recomendaciones sobre la ropa que debe usar cada uno para su entrevista.

- Carmen Valencia – consejera en un campamento de niños
- Enrique Lozada – diseñador de sitios web
- Antonio Delgado – reportero en la televisión
- Victoria Betancourt – abogada (*lawyer*)

For additional *Lectura* activities, go to *¡Anda!* online.

Y por fin, ¿cómo andas?

Having completed this chapter, I now can...	Feel confident	Need to review
Comunicación I		
• describe clothing. (p. 308)	☐	☐
• pronounce *ll* and *ñ* correctly. (p. 309 and online)	☐	☐
• state to whom and for whom things are done. (p. 313)	☐	☐
• express likes, dislikes, needs, etc. (p. 317)	☐	☐
• convey information about people and things. (p. 321)	☐	☐
Comunicación II		
• provide details about clothing. (p. 324)	☐	☐
• share about situations in the past, and how things used to be. (p. 328)	☐	☐
• guess the meanings of unfamiliar words, when listening, from the context. (p. 333)	☐	☐
• communicate about clothing and fashion. (p. 334)	☐	☐
• write an e-mail, practicing circumlocution. (p. 335)	☐	☐
Cultura		
• recount information about a Spanish clothing company. (p. 312)	☐	☐
• consider shopping practices in Spanish-speaking countries. (p. 327)	☐	☐
• share information about Argentina and Uruguay. (pp. 336–337)	☐	☐
Lectura		
• read an article from a fashion magazine. (p. 338)	☐	☐
Comunidades		
• use Spanish in real-life contexts. (online)	☐	☐

Vocabulario activo

La ropa	Clothing
el abrigo	*overcoat*
la bata	*robe*
la blusa	*blouse*
el bolso	*purse*
las botas (*pl.*)	*boots*
los calcetines (*pl.*)	*socks*
la camisa	*shirt*
la camiseta	*T-shirt*
la chaqueta	*jacket*
el cinturón	*belt*
el conjunto	*outfit*
la corbata	*tie*
la falda	*skirt*
la gorra	*cap*
los guantes	*gloves*
el impermeable	*raincoat*
los jeans (*pl.*)	*jeans*
las medias (*pl.*)	*stockings; hose*
la moda	*fashion; style*
los pantalones (*pl.*)	*pants*
los pantalones cortos (*pl.*)	*shorts*
el paraguas	*umbrella*
el pijama	*pajamas*
las prendas	*articles of clothing*
la ropa interior	*underwear*
las sandalias (*pl.*)	*sandals*
el sombrero	*hat*
la sudadera	*sweatshirt*
el suéter	*sweater*
los tenis (*pl.*)	*tennis shoes*
el traje	*suit*
el traje de baño	*swimsuit; bathing suit*
el vestido	*dress*
las zapatillas (*pl.*)	*slippers*
los zapatos (*pl.*)	*shoes*

Algunos verbos	Some verbs
llevar	*to wear; to take; to carry*
prestar	*to loan; to lend*

Algunos verbos como *gustar*	Verbs similar to gustar
encantar	*to love; to like very much*
fascinar	*to fascinate*
hacer falta	*to need; to be lacking*
importar	*to matter; to be important*
molestar	*to bother*

Las telas y los materiales	Fabrics and materials
el algodón	*cotton*
el cuero	*leather*
la lana	*wool*
el poliéster	*polyester*
la seda	*silk*
la tela	*fabric*

Algunos adjetivos	Some adjectives
ancho/a	*wide*
atrevido/a	*daring*
claro/a	*light (colored)*
cómodo/a	*comfortable*
corto/a	*short*
de cuadros	*checked*
de lunares	*polka-dotted*
de rayas	*striped*
elegante	*elegant*
estampado/a	*print; with a design or pattern*
estrecho/a	*narrow; tight*
formal	*formal*
incómodo/a	*uncomfortable*
informal	*casual*
largo/a	*long*
liso/a	*solid-colored*
oscuro/a	*dark*

Otras palabras	Other words
el/la modelo	*model*
quedarle bien/mal	*to fit well/poorly*

Algunas palabras y expresiones	Some words and expressions
a menudo	*often*
casi siempre	*almost always*
frecuentemente	*frequently*
generalmente	*generally*
mientras	*while*
muchas veces	*many times*
mucho	*a lot*
normalmente	*normally*
siempre	*always*
todos los días	*every day*

Yoga por la mañana

9 Estamos en forma

Todos queremos tener una buena calidad de vida y prolongarla lo más posible. No podemos cambiar nuestra herencia genética transmitida de padres a hijos, pero sí tenemos control sobre decisiones que pueden afectar nuestro estilo de vida: el ejercicio, la dieta, la prevención de accidentes y el uso de sustancias adictivas como el tabaco.

Preguntas

1. ¿Vives una vida sana (*healthy*)? ¿Qué haces (o no haces) para tener una vida más sana?
2. ¿Cuáles son algunas de las decisiones específicas que tomamos que pueden afectar nuestra salud (*health*)?
3. ¿Qué tipo de ejercicio te gusta hacer?

¿Sabías que...?

Vilcabamba, Ecuador, es conocido como "el valle de la longevidad" porque hay un alto número de personas que viven más de 100 años... y algunas ¡hasta 130!

¡Achís! **Está enferma.**

Hacen abdominales.

Learning Outcomes

By the end of this chapter, you will be able to:

- ✔ describe the human body.
- ✔ discuss ailments and treatments.
- ✔ relate daily routines.
- ✔ narrate in the past.
- ✔ communicate about ailments and healthy living.
- ✔ write a summary, sequencing past events.
- ✔ exchange interesting facts about Peru, Bolivia, and Ecuador.
- ✔ read a magazine article about health.

Comunicación I

1 VOCABULARIO

El cuerpo humano Describing the human body

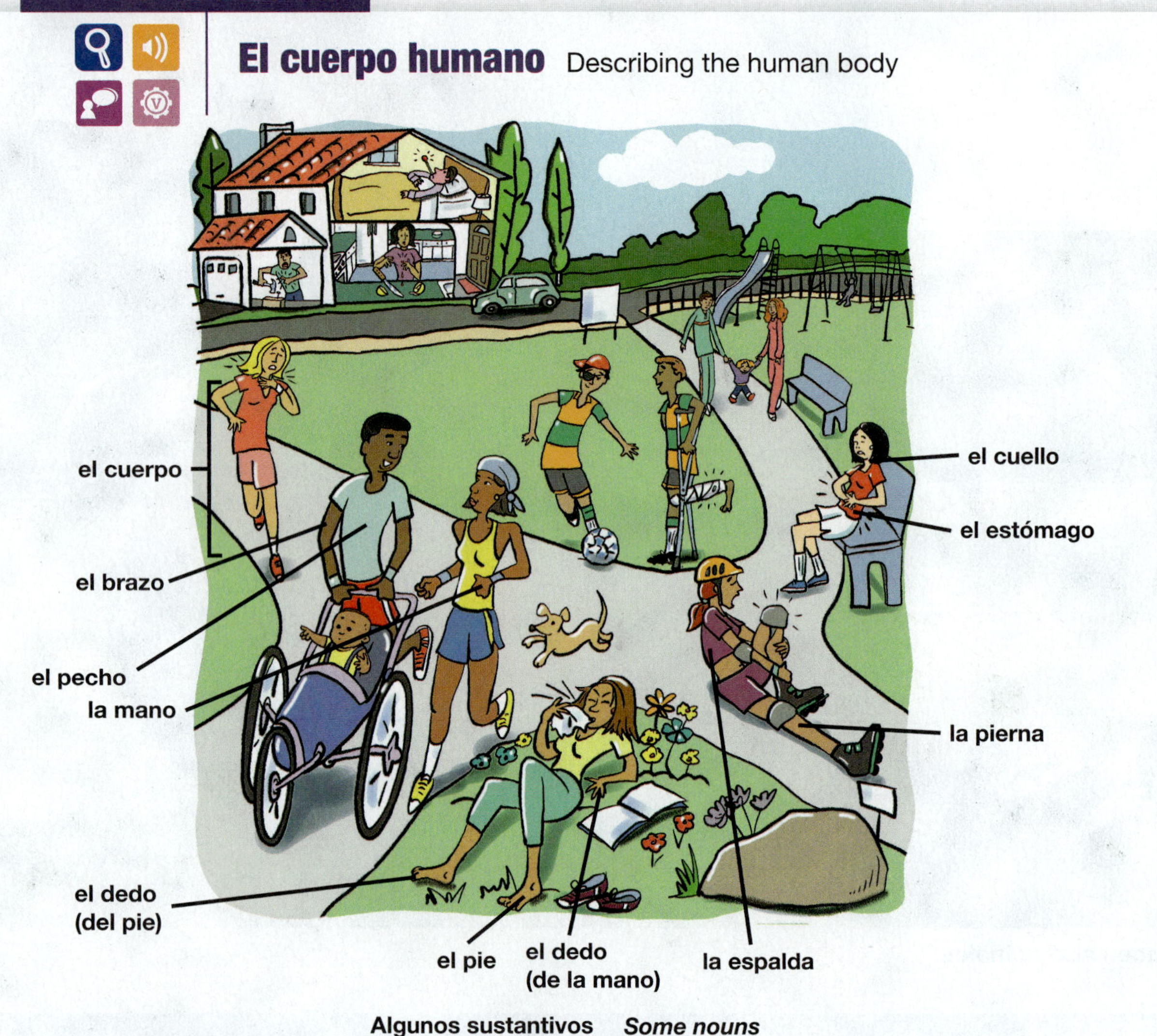

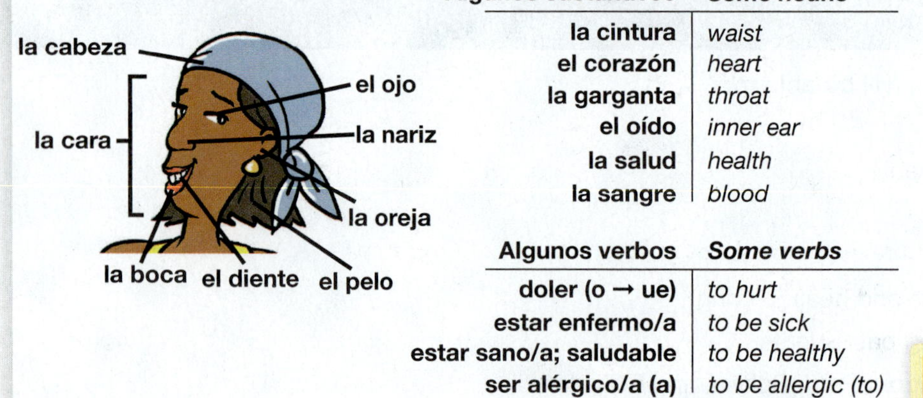

Algunos sustantivos	*Some nouns*
la cintura	*waist*
el corazón	*heart*
la garganta	*throat*
el oído	*inner ear*
la salud	*health*
la sangre	*blood*

Algunos verbos	*Some verbs*
doler (o → ue)	*to hurt*
estar enfermo/a	*to be sick*
estar sano/a; saludable	*to be healthy*
ser alérgico/a (a)	*to be allergic (to)*

¿? Now you are ready to complete the ***Preparación y práctica*** activities for this chunk online.

PRONUNCIACIÓN

The letters *d* and *t*

Go to *¡Anda!* online to learn about the letters *d* and *t*.

9-1 Simón dice Escuchen mientras su instructor/a les da las instrucciones de esta actividad.

9-2 ¿Cómo se escribe? Escribe la primera y la última letra de una de las palabras del vocabulario. Un/a compañero/a tiene que terminarla. Túrnense para practicar la ortografía de por lo menos **ocho** palabras en total.

MODELO E1: e _ _ _ _ _a

E2: e s p a l d a

9-3 ¿Cómo nos vestimos? Túrnense para decir qué partes del cuerpo asocian con la ropa indicada.

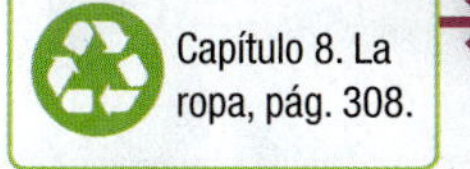

Capítulo 8. La ropa, pág. 308.

MODELO E1: los zapatos

E2: *los pies*

1. las botas
2. los guantes
3. los pantalones
4. la gorra
5. la corbata
6. la camiseta
7. los tenis
8. la chaqueta

9-4 Categorías Juntos escriban todas las palabras del vocabulario nuevo que corresponden a las siguientes partes del cuerpo.

MODELO E1: la cabeza

E2: *la cara, el pelo, etc.*

1. la cabeza
2. de la cintura para arriba (*from the waist up*)
3. de la cintura para abajo (*from the waist down*)
4. la cara

9-5 ¿Qué te duele?

Con un/a compañero/a, creen preguntas y respuestas para ver lo que les duele a las siguientes personas.

Fíjate

The verb *doler* functions like *gustar*.

Me duelen los brazos.
My arms hurt (me).

MODELO a Ricardo / los brazos

E1: *¿Qué le duele a Ricardo?*

E2: *Le duelen los brazos.*

1. a Julia / la cabeza
2. a Marco y a Miguel / las piernas
3. a ti / el estómago
4. a tu primo / la garganta
5. a ustedes / los ojos

9-6 Una obra de arte

Miren el cuadro y descríbanlo usando las siguientes preguntas como guía.

Capítulo 3. *Hay*, pág. 128.

Fíjate

Note that *la mano* is irregular; it ends in *o* but the word is feminine.

1. ¿Cuántas personas hay en el cuadro?
2. ¿Cuántas caras hay?
3. ¿Cuántas manos pueden ver?
4. ¿Cuántos ojos pueden ver?
5. ¿Cuántas narices hay?
6. ¿Qué otras cosas ven en el cuadro?
7. Estas personas son…
8. El cuadro representa…

9-7 ¿Es un monstruo o una obra de arte?

Su instructor/a va a dibujar un monstruo. Descríbele a un/a compañero/a cómo es el monstruo y él/ella tiene que dibujarlo. Al terminar, cambien de papel para describir un monstruo nuevo.

El monstruo tiene…

a la derecha	a la izquierda	encima de	debajo de

Estrategia

Being an "active listener" is an important skill in any language; it means that you have heard and understood what someone is saying. Being able to demonstrate that you have understood correctly, as in reproducing this drawing of the monster, helps you practice and perfect the skill of active listening.

2 GRAMÁTICA

Las construcciones reflexivas

Relating daily routines

Study the captions for the following drawings.
In each drawing:

- Who is performing / doing the action?
- Who or what is receiving the action?

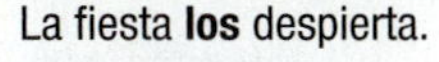

La fiesta **los** despierta.

Alberto **la** acuesta.

Beatriz **lo** lava.

When the subject both performs and receives the action of the verb, a reflexive verb and pronoun are used.

- Which of the drawings and captions demonstrate reflexive verbs?

Raúl y Gloria **se** despiertan.

Alberto **se** acuesta.

Beatriz **se** lava.

Look at the following chart: the reflexive pronouns are highlighted.

Reflexive pronouns

Yo	**me**	divierto	en las fiestas.
Tú	**te**	diviertes	en las fiestas.
Usted	**se**	divierte	en las fiestas.
Él / Ella	**se**	divierte	en las fiestas.
Nosotros	**nos**	divertimos	en las fiestas.
Vosotros	**os**	divertís	en las fiestas.
Ustedes	**se**	divierten	en las fiestas.
Ellos / Ellas	**se**	divierten	en las fiestas.

Reflexive pronouns follow the same rules for position as other object pronouns. Reflexive pronouns:

1. precede conjugated verbs.
2. can be attached to *infinitives* (and present participles (**-ando, -iendo**) [*Capítulo 11*]).

Te vas a dormir.
Vas a dormir**te**. } *You are going to fall asleep.*

¿**Se** van a dormir esta noche?
¿Van a dormir**se** esta noche? } *Are they going to fall asleep tonight?*

¿**Se** están durmiendo?
¿Están durmiéndo**se**? } *Are you all falling asleep?*

(*continued*)

Algunos verbos reflexivos

acordarse de (o → ue)	*to remember*
arreglarse	*to get ready*
caerse	*to fall down*
callarse	*to get / keep quiet*
cortarse	*to cut oneself*
curarse	*to be cured*
divertirse (e → ie → i)	*to enjoy oneself; to have fun*
enfermarse	*to get sick*
irse	*to go away; to leave*
lastimarse	*to get hurt*
lavarse	*to wash oneself*
levantarse	*to get up; to stand up*
llamarse	*to be called*
mejorarse	*to improve; to get better*
ponerse (la ropa)	*to put on (one's clothes)*
ponerse (nervioso/a)	*to get (nervous)*
probarse (o → ue) la ropa	*to try on clothing*
quedarse	*to stay; to remain*
quemarse	*to get burned*
quitarse (la ropa)	*to take off (one's clothes)*
reunirse	*to get together; to meet*
romperse	*to break (a bone)*
sentarse (e → ie)	*to sit down*
sentirse (e → ie → i)	*to feel*
vendarse	*to bandage oneself*

Note: To identify all of the previous verbs as *reflexive,* the infinitives end in **-se**.

Estrategia

When a new infinitive is presented, if it is a stem-changing verb, the irregularities will be given in parentheses. For example, if you see *divertirse* (*e → ie → i*) you know that this infinitive is an *-ir* stem-changing verb, that the first *e* in the infinitive changes to *ie* in the present indicative, and that the *e* changes to *i* in the third-person singular and plural of the preterit.

Fíjate

Some verbs change their meanings slightly between non-reflexive and reflexive verbs, for example: *dormir* (to sleep) and *dormirse* (to fall asleep); *ir* (to go) and *irse* (to leave).

¿? Now you are ready to complete the ***Preparación y práctica*** activities for this chunk online.

9-8 El juego de la asociación

Juntos decidan qué verbos reflexivos asocian con las siguientes palabras y expresiones.

1. no decir nada
2. una silla
3. recordar algo
4. tener sueño
5. no recordar algo
6. triste o alegre, por ejemplo
7. un sombrero
8. estar sucio
9. no ir a ningún lugar

9-9 Tres en línea

Vas a jugar con un/a compañero/a a *tic-tac-toe*. Escriban un verbo reflexivo diferente en cada espacio. Túrnense para decir un verbo reflexivo hasta que uno tenga tres en línea. Jueguen tres veces.

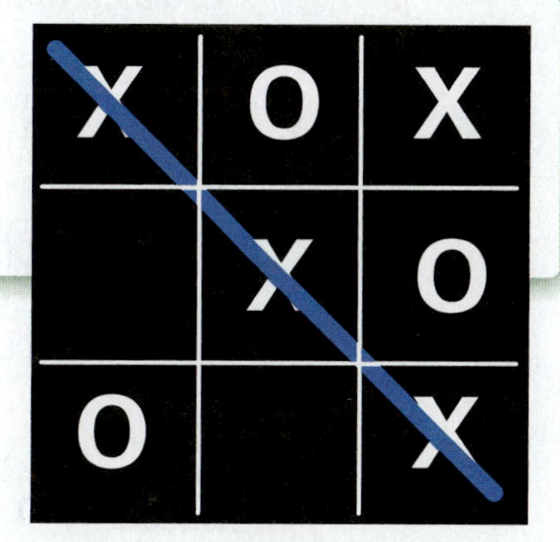

9-10 Mímica

Hagan mímica (*charades*) en grupos de cuatro. Túrnense para escoger un verbo reflexivo para representar al grupo. El grupo tiene que adivinar qué verbo es. Sigan jugando hasta que cada estudiante represente **tres** verbos diferentes.

9-11 Un día en la vida Ordena las actividades diarias de María y Tomás, estudiantes universitarios en Argentina, de forma cronológica. Luego, compara tu lista con la de un/a compañero/a.

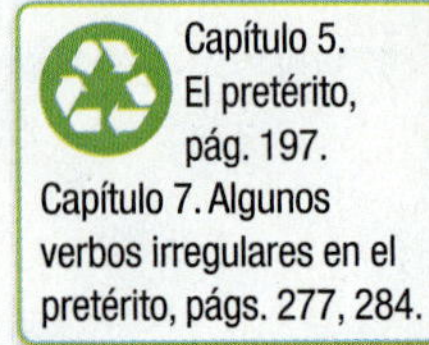

El día de María

1. Antes de irse a la universidad, se acordó de la tarea que no hizo para su clase de historia.
2. Se duchó.
3. Se maquilló.
4. Llegó a la clase de historia y se quitó el abrigo.
5. Se vistió.
6. Se secó.
7. Se levantó.

El día de Tomás

1. Se acostó tarde.
2. Se levantó rápidamente a las ocho.
3. Se despertó tarde.
4. No se durmió inmediatamente.
5. Se divirtió con sus amigos.
6. Después de las clases se fue con los amigos para pasar el fin de semana en la playa.
7. Se fue para la clase de química.

9-12 Un día normal Escribe por lo menos **cinco** actividades que haces normalmente y a qué hora las haces. Usa verbos reflexivos. Después, comparte tu lista con un/a compañero/a.

Capítulo A Para empezar. La hora, pág. 18.

9-13 Los nervios Ramón quiere ser médico. Te habla de lo que le pasó ayer. Lee las oraciones a continuación y después escucha a Ramón. Indica si cada oración es cierta (**C**) o falsa (**F**).

C	F	
☐	☐	1. Ramón tenía una entrevista para trabajar en el hospital.
☐	☐	2. Cuando se despertó, no se sentía bien.
☐	☐	3. Le dolían la garganta y el oído.
☐	☐	4. No comió nada pero tomó un café.
☐	☐	5. Se arregló en menos de una hora pero tuvo tiempo para afeitarse y ducharse.
☐	☐	6. Decidió vestirse bien y se puso un traje.
☐	☐	7. Caminó a la entrevista y por eso (*for that reason*) llegó tarde.
☐	☐	8. La secretaria vio que Ramón llevaba dos zapatos diferentes.

9-14 Para conocerte mejor

Túrnense para hacerse esta entrevista y conocer mejor sus hábitos.

MODELO E1: ¿Qué te pones cuando estás enfermo/a y te acuestas en la cama?
E2: *Me pongo el pijama o una camiseta grande. ¿Y tú? ¿Qué te pones?*
E1: *Generalmente me pongo el pijama o pantalones cortos con una sudadera.*
E2: ¿Qué…?

1. ¿Qué te pones cuando vas a la clínica?
2. ¿Te rompiste el brazo, la pierna, el pie, etc. alguna vez?
3. ¿Te cortaste alguna vez?
4. ¿Te quemaste alguna vez?
5. ¿Cuándo te lastimaste la última vez? ¿Qué pasó?
6. Cuando estás durmiéndote, ¿te acuerdas de las cosas que no hiciste durante el día?
7. ¿Cómo te diviertes?
8. ¿Cuándo te pones nervioso/a?
9. ¿Cuándo te sientes feliz?

9-15 ¿Conoces bien a tus compañeros?

Trabajen en grupos de cuatro para hacer esta actividad. Completen los siguientes pasos.

Paso 1 Un/a compañero/a debe salir de la sala de clase por un momento. Los otros estudiantes escriben **cinco** preguntas sobre la vida diaria del/de la compañero/a, usando los verbos reflexivos.

MODELO *¿A qué hora te despiertas?*
¿Te duchas todos los días?

Paso 2 Antes de entrar el/la compañero/a, el grupo de estudiantes debe adivinar cuáles van a ser las respuestas a esas preguntas.

MODELO *Se despierta a las siete.*
Sí, se ducha todos los días.

Paso 3 Entra el/la compañero/a y los otros le hacen las preguntas.

Paso 4 Comparen las respuestas del grupo con las del/de la compañero/a. ¿Tenían razón? Pueden repetir la actividad con los otros miembros del grupo.

3 GRAMÁTICA

Un resumen de los pronombres de complemento directo e indirecto y reflexivos

Sharing about people, actions, and things

You have already learned the forms, functions, and positioning of the *direct* and *indirect object pronouns,* as well as the *reflexive pronouns*. The following is a review:

LOS PRONOMBRES DE COMPLEMENTO **DIRECTO**

Direct object pronouns tell *what* or *who* receives the action of the verb. They replace direct object nouns and are used to avoid repetition.

me	*me*
te	*you*
lo, la	*you*
lo, la	*him/her/it*
nos	*us*
os	*you (all)*
los, las	*you (all)*
los, las	*them/you*

Compré la medicina ayer. **La** compré en la Farmacia Fénix. Tengo que dár**sela** a mi hijo.

I bought the medicine yesterday. I bought it it at Fénix Pharmacy. I have to give it to my son.

LOS PRONOMBRES DE COMPLEMENTO **INDIRECTO**

Indirect object pronouns tell *to whom* or *for whom* something is done or given.

me	*to/for me*
te	*to/for you*
le (se)	*to/for you*
le (se)	*to/for him/her*
nos	*to/for us*
os	*to/for you (all)*
les (se)	*to/for you (all)*
les (se)	*to/for them/you*

Le compré la medicina ayer. **Le** voy a dar la medicina esta noche.

I bought him the medicine yesterday. I am going to give him the medicine tonight.

LOS PRONOMBRES **REFLEXIVOS**

Reflexive pronouns indicate that the *subject* of a sentence or clause *receives the action of the verb.*

me	*myself*
te	*yourself*
se	*yourself*
se	*himself/herself*
nos	*ourselves*
os	*yourselves*
se	*yourselves*
se	*themselves/yourselves*

Me cepillo los dientes tres veces al día.

I brush my teeth three times a day.

Remember the following guidelines on position and sequence:

Position

- Object pronouns and reflexive pronouns come **before** the verb.

El doctor Sánchez **le** dio una inyección a David. — *Dr. Sánchez gave David a shot.*

Después **se** sintió aliviado. — *Then he felt relieved.*

- Object pronouns and reflexive pronouns can also be placed before or be attached to the end of infinitives.

La enfermera **me** va a llamar.
La enfermera va a llamar**me**. } *The nurse is going to call me.*

Después **se** va a ir a su casa.
Después va a ir**se** a su casa. } *Then she is going to go home.*

Fíjate

As with direct and indirect object pronouns, reflexive pronouns can also be attached to present participles (**-ando**, **-iendo**). You will learn about present participles in *Capítulo 11*.

Sequence

- When a direct (DO) and indirect object (IO) pronoun are used together, ***the indirect object precedes the direct object.***
- If both the direct and the indirect object pronouns begin with the letter **l**, the indirect object pronoun changes from **le** or **les** to **se,** as in the following example.

Quiero mandar la carta al director ahora. — *I want to send the letter to the director now.*

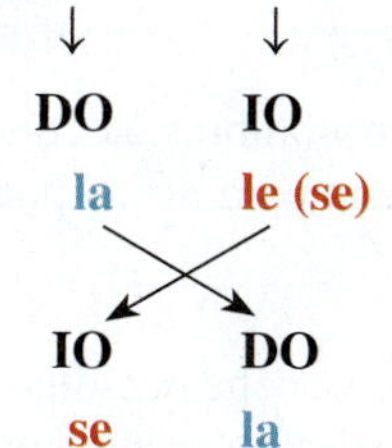

DO — **IO**

Se la quiero mandar ahora mismo.
Quiero mandár**sela** ahora mismo. } *I want to send it to him right now.*

¿? Now you are ready to complete the ***Preparación y práctica*** activities for this chunk online.

9-16 Un animal muy extraño

Capítulo 1. Los adjetivos descriptivos, pág. 44.

Juntos respondan a las siguientes oraciones exclamativas con el pronombre de complemento directo apropiado y un adjetivo.

MODELO E1: ¡Mira la nariz!
E2: *Sí, la tiene muy grande (pequeña/fea/bonita...).*

1. ¡Mira la boca!
2. ¡Mira las orejas!
3. ¡Mira los dientes!
4. ¡Mira las patas!
5. ¡Mira la cabeza!
6. ¡Mira el estómago!
7. ¡Mira la cara!
8. ¡Mira el cuello!

Fíjate

In Spanish, an animal's legs are referred to as *patas. Pierna(s)* is only used for people.

9.17 Las preferencias

Capítulo 8. *Gustar* y verbos como *gustar*, pág. 317.

Escribe oraciones completas usando los pronombres de complemento indirecto. Después compara tus oraciones con las de un/a compañero/a.

MODELO a Betty / gustar despertarse temprano
A Betty le gusta despertarse temprano.

1. a mis padres / importar la salud
2. a nuestro/a profesor/a / molestar ser alérgico/a
3. a Manolo / encantar los documentales sobre el cuerpo humano
4. a nosotros / hacer falta ir al médico más a menudo (*more often*)
5. a mí / fascinar el pelo largo

9.18 En el restaurante

¿Qué les pasó ayer a Paco y a Pati en el restaurante Boca Grande? Completa los siguientes pasos.

Paso 1 Completa las siguientes oraciones con los pronombres de complemento directo, indirecto o reflexivo apropiados. Después, compara tus respuestas con las de un/a compañero/a.

Paco y Pati se conocieron en el gimnasio el mes pasado. Anoche decidieron salir juntos. Llegaron al restaurante con mucha hambre. (1) __________ sentaron en una mesa grande al lado de las ventanas. Primero pidieron el menú. El camarero (2) __________ (3) __________ trajo en seguida (inmediatamente). Después, (4) __________ recomendó unos platos muy ricos. Paco pidió un bistec para él y a Pati (5) __________ pidió pollo asado con ajo. ¡Pati no (6) __________ podía creer! ¡Paco ni (7) __________ preguntó qué quería! Ella (8) __________ sentía muy incómoda —ningún hombre, excepto su padre, (9) __________ había tratado (*had treated*) así antes. Pati (10) __________ calló mientras Paco hablaba de su día, su trabajo y su familia. Cuando por fin el camarero (11) __________ sirvió la comida, Pati miró su plato y (12) __________ levantó muy enojada. ¡Su plato era del "Menú para niños"!

Paso 2 Digan qué tipo de pronombre usaron en cada oración.

9-19 ¿Quién...?

Jacobo está enfermo y no puede levantarse de la cama. Es un poco exigente (*demanding*) y quiere saber quiénes lo van a atender (*wait on him*). Contesta sus preguntas y después comparte tus respuestas con un/a compañero/a.

Capítulo 4. *Ir* + *a* + infinitivo, pág. 156.

MODELO ¿Quién va a traerme la tarea? (hermano)
Tu hermano te la va a traer. / Tu hermano va a traértela.

1. ¿Quién va a traerme los libros que pedí? (Patricia)
2. ¿Quién me compra la medicina que necesito? (Marcelo)
3. ¿Quién me va a limpiar el cuarto? (Guadalupe y Lina)
4. ¿Quién me lava la ropa? (tu madre)
5. ¿Quién me prepara la comida? (Tina y Luisa)
6. ¿Quién me va a hacer la tarea? (nadie)

9-20 Hay que ayudar a Pepito

Pepito tiene tres años y necesita ayuda para hacerlo todo. Túrnense para formar los pedidos (*requests*) del niño y las respuestas.

MODELO los dedos / limpiar
E1: *¿Me los limpias?*
E2: *Sí, te los limpio.*

1. el pelo / secar
2. las manos / lavar
3. las orejas / limpiar
4. los dientes / cepillar
5. los ojos / mirar

El agua y la buena salud

¿Sabías que tres cuartas partes de tu peso corporal (*body weight*) son de agua? Tu vida empezó en un mar de líquido amniótico y ahora, como adulto, alrededor del 85 por ciento de la sangre, el 70 por ciento de los músculos y el 22 por ciento de tu cerebro consisten en agua.

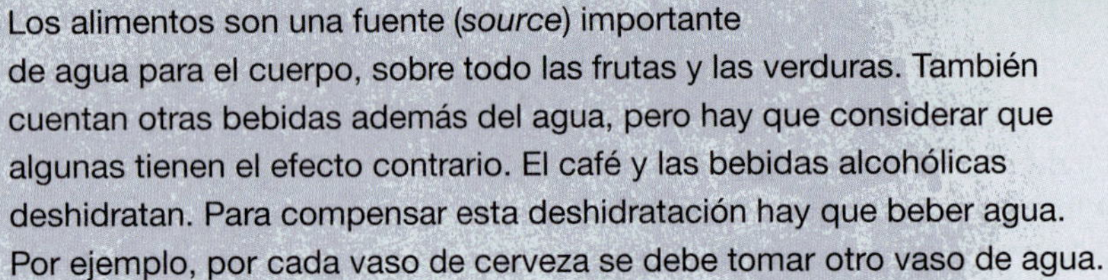

Para mantener la buena salud se debe beber por lo menos dos litros (seis a ocho vasos) de agua al día. El cuerpo elimina de unos 500 a 700 centímetros cúbicos diarios de agua al sudar (*sweat*) y es muy importante reponer esa cantidad y más.

Los alimentos son una fuente (*source*) importante de agua para el cuerpo, sobre todo las frutas y las verduras. También cuentan otras bebidas además del agua, pero hay que considerar que algunas tienen el efecto contrario. El café y las bebidas alcohólicas deshidratan. Para compensar esta deshidratación hay que beber agua. Por ejemplo, por cada vaso de cerveza se debe tomar otro vaso de agua.

Preguntas

1. ¿Por qué es importante beber tanta (*so much*) agua? ¿Cuántos vasos de agua bebes al día?
2. ¿Qué otros beneficios tiene beber suficiente agua al día?

¿Cómo andas? I

Having completed **Comunicación I**, I now can...	**Feel confident**	**Need to review**
• describe the human body. (p. 346)	☐	☐
• pronounce the letters *d* and *t*. (p. 347 and online)	☐	☐
• relate daily routines. (p. 349)		
• share about people, actions, and things. (p. 354)	☐	☐
• relate the importance of water in maintaining good health. (p. 358)	☐	☐

Comunicación II

4 VOCABULARIO

Algunas enfermedades y tratamientos médicos

Explaining ailments and treatments

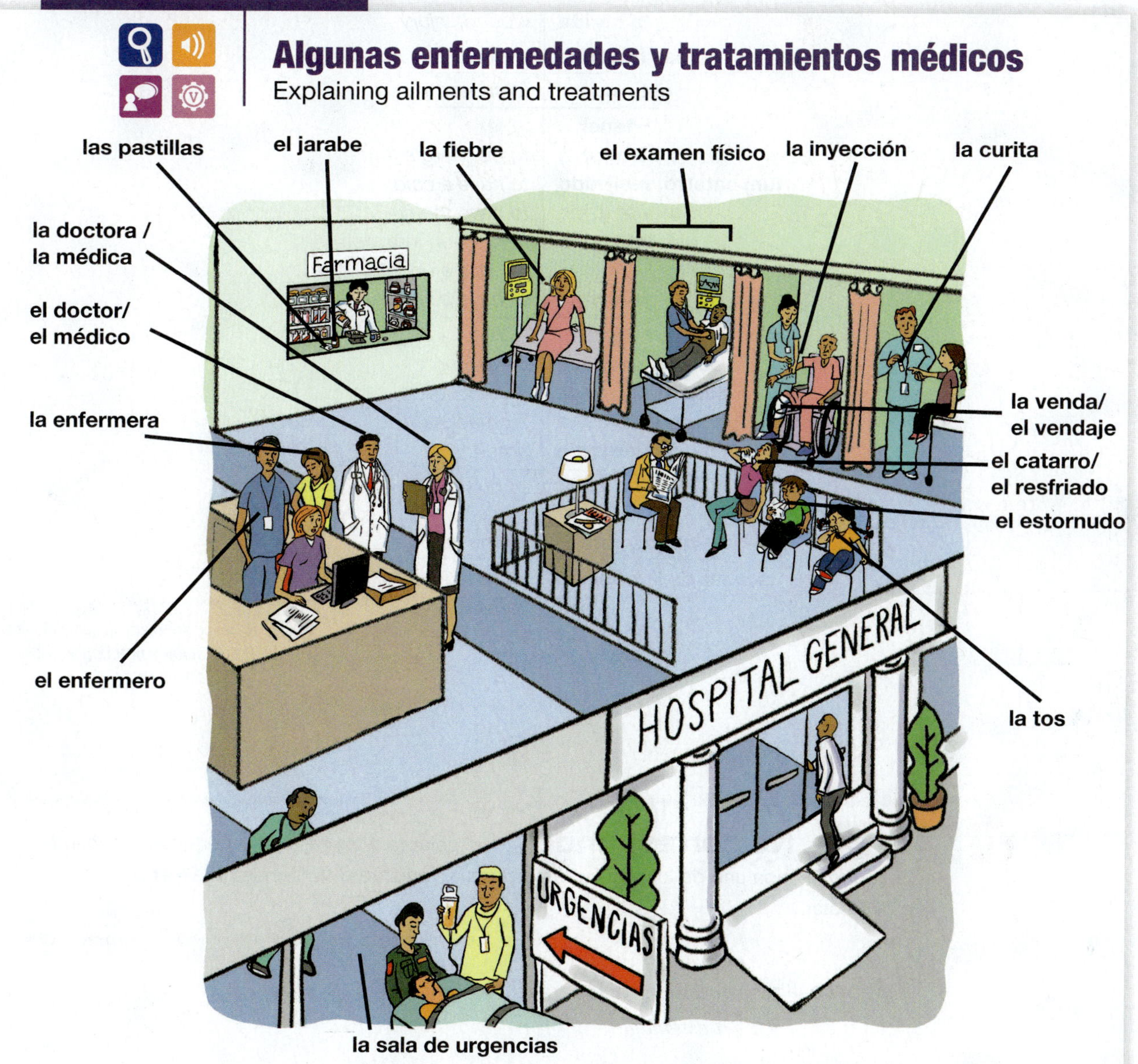

Los tratamientos	*Treatments*
el antiácido	*antacid*
el antibiótico	*antibiotic*
la aspirina	*aspirin*
la receta	*prescription*
evitar	*to avoid*
guardar cama	*to stay in bed*

(*continued*)

Los síntomas y las enfermedades	Symptoms and illnesses
el dolor	*pain*
la gripe	*flu*
la herida	*wound; injury*
las náuseas	*nausea*
estornudar	*to sneeze*
tener...	
alergia (a)	*to be allergic (to)*
(un) catarro, resfriado	*to have a cold*
(la/una) gripe	*to have the flu*
una infección	*to have an infection*
tos	*to have a cough*
un virus	*to have a virus*
tener...	*to have a...*
dolor de cabeza	*headache*
dolor de espalda	*backache*
dolor de estómago	*stomachache*
dolor de garganta	*sore throat*
toser	*to cough*

Algunos verbos	Some verbs
acabar de + *infinitivo*	*to have just finished (something)*
ocurrir	*to occur*
tratar de	*to try to*

¿? Now you are ready to complete the ***Preparación y práctica*** activities for this chunk online.

9-21 No corresponde ¿Qué palabra o expresión no pertenece (*doesn't belong*) a cada uno de los siguientes grupos de palabras? Túrnense para leer la lista y contestar.

MODELO E1: el estómago, la cara, el ojo, la nariz
E2: *el estómago*

1. el hospital, el doctor, el enfermero, el oído
2. toser, estornudar, la receta, tener catarro
3. el jarabe, la farmacia, las pastillas, quemarse
4. lastimarse, la sala de urgencias, la tos, romperse la pierna
5. la venda, la herida, cortarse, el resfriado

9-22 Algunos tratamientos

¿Adónde tienes que ir para poder curarte o buscar tratamiento? Pon una equis (**X**) en la columna apropiada. Después, túrnate con un/a compañero/a para decir adónde van.

MODELO un brazo roto (*broken*)

E1: *Si tengo un brazo roto, voy a la sala de urgencias.*

Fíjate

Parts of the body are usually referred to with an article, not a possessive adjective.

*Me duele **la** mano.*
My hand hurts.

SÍNTOMA/ENFERMEDAD	A LA CAMA	A LA FARMACIA	AL CONSULTORIO DEL MÉDICO	AL HOSPITAL	A LA SALA DE URGENCIAS
1. tos					
2. náuseas					
3. (la) gripe					
4. (un) dolor de garganta					
5. una infección de la sangre					
6. una herida en la pierna					
7. (un) catarro					
8. fiebre					

9-23 ¿Por qué?

Túrnense para describir lo que les pasa a estas personas, ofreciendo (*offering*) siempre una causa posible de su(s) problema(s). Después, sugieran un posible tratamiento.

MODELO *Selena tiene una herida porque se cortó con un cuchillo. Necesita vendarse.*

Selena

1. 
Antonio

2. 
Humberto y Ricardo

3. 
Juliana y Memo

4. 
María Jesús

5. 
Rafael

9.24 El soroche Nina está en Bolivia como voluntaria para ayudar a construir una escuela en el altiplano (*high plateau*). Completen los siguientes pasos.

El altiplano en los Andes de Bolivia

Paso 1 Juntos terminen la conversación entre Nina y su padre con las palabras de la lista.

corazón	enfermedad	estómago	evitar
me duele	mejorar	náuseas	pastillas

NINA: Hola, papá.
PAPÁ: ¡Ay, Nina! ¿Cómo estás, hija? ¿Llegaste bien?
NINA: Sí. Ayer llegamos bien pero hoy me siento enferma. (1) __________ la cabeza. No me duele mucho el (2) __________, pero tengo (3) __________ cuando pienso en la comida, me entran ganas (*I get the urge*) de vomitar.
PAPÁ: Pobrecita. ¿Qué te pasa? ¿Comiste ayer?
NINA: Sí, un poco. Pero desde que (*since*) llegamos no tengo mucha hambre.
PAPÁ: ¿Tienes otros síntomas?
NINA: Sí. El (4) __________ me late (*is beating*) rápidamente y no puedo respirar (*breathe*) muy bien. ¿Crees que tengo alguna (5) __________?
PAPÁ: Nina, me parece que tienes soroche.
NINA: ¿Soroche? ¿Qué es eso?
PAPÁ: Es el mal de altura (*altitude sickness*). Debes empezar a sentirte mejor en un par de días. Mientras tanto, necesitas intentar relajarte, tomar mucha agua y (6) __________ el alcohol y el tabaco. También puedes tomar unas (7) __________ de ibuprofeno y beber un té medicinal hecho de (*made from*) hojas de coca (*coca leaves*).
NINA: Gracias, papá. Ya que entiendo qué me ocurre, creo que voy a (8) __________ pronto.

Paso 2 Ahora, contesten las siguientes preguntas.

1. ¿Qué es el soroche?
2. ¿Cuáles son los síntomas?
3. ¿Qué tratamiento le recomienda su papá?

9-25 ¿Qué debemos hacer? En grupos de cuatro o cinco, cada estudiante escribe dos enfermedades u otros problemas médicos que tuvo, acaba de tener o que podría (*could*) tener. Después túrnense para compartir la información mientras los compañeros dicen lo que debe hacer.

MODELO E1: *Tengo una pierna rota* (broken).
E2: *Debes ir a la sala de urgencias.*
E3: *Debes guardar cama.*
E4: *Debes tomar medicina para el dolor.*

9-26 Para evitar lo inevitable ¿Cómo tratan de evitar tus compañeros las siguientes enfermedades y situaciones? Circula por la clase para hacerles las siguientes preguntas. Necesitas **tres** respuestas para cada pregunta.

MODELO TÚ: ¿Cómo tratas de evitar el dolor de garganta?
E1: *Bebo mucho jugo de naranja.*
E2: *Llevo una bufanda* (scarf) *en el cuello.*
E3: *Tomo mucha vitamina C.*

1. ¿Cómo tratas de evitar el dolor de cabeza? E1: ____________ E2: ____________ E3: ____________	4. ¿Cómo evitas enfermarte? E1: ____________ E2: ____________ E3: ____________
2. ¿Cómo tratas de evitar el dolor de estómago? E1: ____________ E2: ____________ E3: ____________	5. ¿Cómo evitas cortarte? E1: ____________ E2: ____________ E3: ____________
3. ¿Cómo tratas de evitar el dolor de espalda? E1: ____________ E2: ____________ E3: ____________	6. ¿Cómo evitas caerte? E1: ____________ E2: ____________ E3: ____________

5 GRAMÁTICA

El pretérito y el imperfecto Narrating in the past

Fuimos a Cuzco y subimos a Machu Picchu. Hacía buen tiempo.

In **Capítulos 5, 7,** and **8** you learned about two aspects of the past tense in Spanish, **el pretérito** and **el imperfecto,** which are not interchangeable. Their uses are contrasted below.

THE **PRETERIT** IS USED:	THE **IMPERFECT** IS USED:
1. To relate an event or occurrence that refers to *one specific time in the past* • **Fuimos** a Cuzco el año pasado. *We went to Cuzco last year.* • **Comimos** en el restaurante El Sol y **nos gustó** mucho. *We ate at El Sol Restaurant and liked it a lot.*	**1.** To express *habitual* or often *repeated actions* • **Íbamos** a Cuzco todos los veranos. *We used to go to Cuzco every summer.* • **Comíamos** en el restaurante El Sol todos los lunes. *We used to eat at El Sol Restaurant every Monday.*
2. To relate an act *begun* or *completed in the past* • **Empezó** a llover. *It started to rain.* • **Comenzaron** los juegos. *The games began.* • La gira **terminó.** *The tour ended.*	**2.** To express *was/were + -ing* • **Llovía** sin parar. *It was raining continuously.* • **Comenzaban** los juegos cuando llegamos. *The games were beginning when we arrived.* • La gira **transcurría** sin ningún problema. *The tour was going on without any problems.*
3. To relate a *sequence of events or actions,* each completed and moving the narrative along toward its conclusion • **Llegamos** en avión, **recogimos las maletas y fuimos al hotel**. *We arrived by plane, picked up our luggage, and went to the hotel.* • Al día siguiente **decidimos** ir a Machu Picchu. *The next day we decided to go to Machu Picchu.* • **Vimos** muchos ejemplos de la magnífica arquitectura incaica. Después **anduvimos** un poco por el camino de los incas. **Nos divertimos** mucho. *We saw many examples of the magnificent Incan architecture. Afterward we walked a bit on the Incan road. We had a great time.*	**3.** To provide *background information, set the stage,* or *express a pre-existing condition* • **Era** un día oscuro. **Llovía** de vez en cuando. *It was a dark day and it rained once in a while.* • Los turistas **llevaban** pantalones cortos y lentes de sol. *The tourists were wearing shorts and sunglasses.* • El camino **era** estrecho y **había** muchos turistas. *The path was narrow and there were many tourists.*

THE **PRETERIT** IS USED:	THE **IMPERFECT** IS USED:
4. To relate an action that took place within a specified or *specific amount* (segment) *of time* **Caminé** (por) dos horas. *I walked for two hours.* **Hablamos** (por) cinco minutos. *We talked for five minutes.* **Contemplaron** el templo un rato. *They contemplated the temple for a while.* **Viví** en Ecuador (por) seis años. *I lived in Ecuador for six years.*	**4.** To *tell time* in the past **Era** la una. *It was 1:00.* **Eran** las tres y media. *It was 3:30.* **Era** muy tarde. *It was very late.* **Era** la medianoche. *It was midnight.*
	5. To describe physical and emotional states or characteristics Después del viaje **queríamos** descansar. Yo **tenía** dolor de cabeza y no **me sentía** muy bien. *After the trip we wanted to rest. I had a headache and did not feel well.*

Fíjate

The use of *por* is optional in these cases.

WORDS AND EXPRESSIONS THAT COMMONLY SIGNAL:

PRETERIT	IMPERFECT
anoche	a menudo
anteayer	cada semana/mes/año
ayer	con frecuencia
de repente (*suddenly*)	de vez en cuando (*once in a while*)
el fin de semana pasado	frecuentemente
el mes pasado	mientras
el lunes pasado/el martes pasado, etc.	muchas veces
esta mañana	siempre
una vez, dos veces, etc.	todos los lunes/martes, etc.
	todas las semanas
	todos los días/meses/años

Fíjate

Some verbs change their meaning in the preterit:

conocer	conozco / *know (someone, some place)*	conocí / *met (someone)*
saber	sé / *know (information, how to do something)*	supe / *found out, discovered*
poder	puedo / *can, am able to*	pude / *succeeded, managed to*
no poder	no puedo / *can't, I'm not able*	no pude / *failed to*
querer	quiero / *want*	quise / *tried to*
no querer	no quiero / *don't want*	no quise / *refused to*

NOTE: The **pretérito** and the **imperfecto** can be used in the same sentence.

Veían la televisión cuando **sonó el teléfono.** — *They were watching television when the phone rang.*

In the preceding sentence, an action was going on (**veían**) when it was interrupted by another action (**sonó el teléfono**).

¿? Now you are ready to complete the ***Preparación y práctica*** activities for this chunk online.

9-27 Una (muy) breve historia de los incas

Completen los siguientes pasos.

Los países actuales (*present-day*) donde se encontraba el imperio de los incas

Paso 1 Lean el siguiente fragmento.

El imperio de los incas fue uno de los imperios más importantes de las civilizaciones precolombinas. Se encontraba (*It was located*) en lo que es hoy Perú, Bolivia, el norte de Chile y parte de Ecuador. El imperio se dividía en tres partes iguales: una tercera parte pertenecía (*belonged*) a los indígenas y pasaba de padre a hijo; otra tercera parte era del Inca, o sea, del Gobierno; la otra tercera parte pertenecía al clero (*clergy*).

Los incas adoraban al hijo del Sol. Según la leyenda (*legend*), el hijo cayó en algún lugar cerca del lago Titicaca. Con él llegó su hermana y según la leyenda, ellos eran los padres de todos los incas. Esta civilización practicaba sacrificios de animales y algunas veces sacrificios humanos. También le ofrecían objetos preciosos y joyas (*jewels*) al Sol. El último cacique (o jefe político) famoso de los incas fue Atahualpa.

Paso 2 Subrayen los verbos.

Paso 3 Digan cuáles son **pretéritos** y cuáles son **imperfectos** y expliquen por qué se usó cada uno de estos tiempos verbales.

Machu Picchu, la ciudad perdida de los incas

9-28 Un cuento de hadas

En grupos de tres o cuatro personas, pongan las siguientes oraciones en orden cronológico para terminar el cuento de Ricitos de Oro (*Goldilocks*). Después, analicen los usos **del pretérito** y **el imperfecto** dentro del cuento y expliquen por qué usaron cada uno de estos tiempos verbales.

Había una vez una niña muy curiosa. Un día, mientras caminaba por el bosque (*forest*), encontró una casa muy bonita. En la casa vivían tres osos. Mientras los osos no estaban…

_____ Los osos la asustaron (*scared her*).
_____ Entró en el dormitorio de los osos.
_____ Mientras ella dormía, entraron los osos.
_____ La niña se levantó y salió con mucha prisa de la casa.
_____ Tenía sueño.
_____ Buscó una cama.
_____ La niña entró en la casa.
_____ Vio que una cama era muy grande, otra era muy pequeña y la otra tenía el tamaño perfecto.
_____ Encontraron a la niña dormida en la cama.
_____ Se acostó.

9-29 El trabajo de Raúl

Mira el dibujo en la página 359. Raúl, uno de los enfermeros en el dibujo, trabaja en el Hospital General de Quito. Habla ahora con su novia, Sara, sobre lo que ocurrió en el trabajo ayer. Completa los siguientes pasos.

Paso 1 Lee las oraciones a continuación y después escucha a Raúl.

Paso 2 Completa las oraciones con la palabra o frase correcta, según la conversación.

1. Raúl está muy cansado porque ayer fue un día muy ___________________.
2. Raúl trabajó catorce horas en (qué parte del hospital) ___________________.
3. Raúl empezó a trabajar a las ___________________.
4. Su primer/a paciente fue ___________________.
5. Los síntomas del / de la paciente fueron dolores fuertes del estómago, náuseas y ___________________.
6. Después de examinar al / a la paciente y hacer unas pruebas (*tests*) de sangre, el médico decidió que tenía ___________________.
7. El tratamiento fue una inyección de antibiótico y unas pastillas para el dolor y ___________________.
8. Raúl quiere dormir ahora porque esta noche tiene que ___________________.

9-30 En el consultorio

Completa el siguiente pasaje con la forma correcta **del pretérito** o **el imperfecto** de cada verbo entre paréntesis. Después, comparte las respuestas con un/a compañero/a y explícale por qué usaste el pretérito o el imperfecto.

Esta mañana cuando llegué al consultorio del Dr. Fuentes (1. haber) ____________ mucha actividad. Muchos pacientes (2. esperar) ____________ al médico y yo no (3. encontrar) ____________ dónde sentarme. Dos horas (4. pasar) ____________ lentamente. (5. Ser) ____________ las once cuando por fin la recepcionista me (6. llamar) ____________ y la enfermera (7. salir) ____________ para buscarme. Juntas (8. entrar) ____________ al cuarto donde (9. estar) ____________ el médico. El Dr. Fuentes (10. levantarse) ____________ y me (11. mirar) ____________ con mucha curiosidad. (12. Empezar) ____________ a examinarme y a hacerme preguntas.

Yo (13. ponerse) ____________ nerviosa y (14. callarse) ____________ . Solo (15. esperar) ____________ un examen anual típico pero las preguntas (16. ser) ____________ demasiado específicas. Por ejemplo, me (17. preguntar) ____________ si (18. sentirse) ____________ mareada (*faint*) por la mañana y si (19. comer) ____________ bien cuando (20. tener)____________ hambre.

Por fin (21. darse cuenta [*to realize*]: yo) ____________ de lo que (22. ocurrir) ____________ . ¡El Dr. Fuentes (23. pensar) ____________ que yo (24. estar) ____________ embarazada (*pregnant*)! Por lo visto la enfermera (25. equivocarse [*to be mistaken*]) ____________ y ¡le (26. dar) ____________ al médico la información de otra paciente!

9-31 En el pasado

Termina las siguientes oraciones. Después, compártelas con un/a compañero/a.

MODELO Cuando era niño/a…

E1: *Cuando era niño, hacía ejercicio todos los días. Y tú, ¿qué hacías?*

E2: *Cuando era niña, siempre jugaba en el parque con mi hermana.*

1. Cuando era niño/a…
2. Cuando tenía dieciséis años, frecuentemente…
3. Una vez el verano pasado…
4. Ayer tenía ganas de ________ pero…
5. Anoche…
6. Cuando vivía con mis padres, todas las semanas…

9-32 Nuestro cuento

En grupos de tres, van a contar una historia (en el pasado) basada en los dibujos. Al terminar van a compartir sus historias con los otros miembros de la clase.

Estrategia

In this variation of "Cinderella," remember to use the *imperfect* for *description* and *background* information. Use the *preterit* for *sequences of actions.*

La Cenicienta

9-33 Y en el hospital

Imagina que trabajas como enfermero/a en la sala de urgencias de un hospital. Un día entra un joven de unos veinte años con unos síntomas raros. Completa los siguientes pasos.

Paso 1 Llena el siguiente formulario médico para el joven enfermo como si fueras un/a enfermero/a.

FORMULARIO MÉDICO

Por favor, complete este formulario con la mayor precisión posible. Toda la información en este formulario es confidencial y será utilizada en caso de emergencia. Por favor, escriba legiblemente.

HISTORIA CLÍNICA

Nombre ____________________
Dirección ____________________
Ciudad y estado ____________________
Código postal ____________________
Número de teléfono ____________________
Edad ____________________
Fecha de nacimiento ____________________
Sexo ________ Peso ________ Altura ________
Grupo sanguíneo ____________________

1. ¿Está bajo tratamiento por alguna enfermedad? Explique.____________________
2. ¿Toma algún tipo de medicamento? ____________________
3. ¿Tiene algún tipo de alergia?____________________
4. ¿Ha tenido cirugía alguna vez?____________________

ANTECEDENTES MÉDICOS

Por favor, marque cualquier enfermedad que haya tenido en el pasado y la fecha en que comenzó.

______artritis	______asma	_____dolor de espalda
______mareos	______tos crónica	_____dolor de pecho
______diabetes	______epilepsia	_____fracturas
______dolor de cabeza	______hernia	_____presión alta

¿Ha tenido otra enfermedad que no hemos mencionado?____________________

Paso 2 Crea **seis** preguntas para determinar cuál es su problema, según el modelo.

MODELO E1: ¿Dar / todos sus datos / en recepción?
E2: *¿Dio todos sus datos en recepción?*

1. ¿A qué hora / llegar / la sala de urgencias?
2. ¿Cuándo / empezar / a dolerle?
3. ¿Qué / hacer / cuando / empezar / a dolerle?
4. ¿Quién / estar / con Ud.?
5. ¿Cómo / sentirse / cuando / acostarse / anoche?
6. ¿Qué / causar / el dolor?

Paso 3 Crea un diálogo con un/a compañero/a entre el joven y el/la enfermero/a usando las preguntas que escribiste.

9-34 La última vez que nos enfermamos

Túrnense para describir la última vez que ustedes, un/a amigo/a o un pariente se enfermaron.

Fíjate

Use the term *médico* when referring to the profession of a doctor. Use *doctor* for the title of the person.

El doctor Ramírez es un médico excelente.

- ¿Cuándo fue?
- ¿Cómo se sentían?
- ¿Cuáles fueron los síntomas?
- Si fueron al médico, ¿qué les hizo? ¿Qué les dijo?
- ¿Les recetó (recetar = *to prescribe*) algo? ¿Cuánto pagaron por la visita? Si no fueron al médico, ¿qué hicieron para curarse?
- ¿Cuánto tiempo duró (durar = *to last*) la enfermedad?

9-35 ¿Y ayer?

Descríbele a un/a compañero/a tu día de ayer en por lo menos **cinco** oraciones.

MODELO *Ayer hacía mal tiempo cuando me desperté. No quería levantarme, pero por fin salí de la cama y fui a mi clase de español. El profesor nos dio mucha tarea. Luego fui a la biblioteca. Estudiaba cuando llegó mi mejor amigo, Jeff.*

Fíjate

When the preterit and imperfect are used together in narratives in which events are retold, you will notice that the *imperfect* provides the background information such as the time, weather, and location. The *preterit* relates the specific events that occurred.

9-36 Luces, cámara, acción

Capítulo 5. El mundo del cine, pág. 193.

¿Te gustan las películas? ¿Vas al cine a menudo? Cuéntale (*Narrate*) a un/a compañero/a la última película que viste. Usa por lo menos **siete** oraciones. ¡Recuerda! Generalmente **el imperfecto** se usa para la descripción y **el pretérito** para la acción.

Las farmacias en el mundo hispanohablante

En Latinoamérica, las farmacias son, por la mayor parte, dispensarios de medicina únicamente. El farmacéutico (*pharmacist*) muchas veces ofrece consejos sobre los medicamentos (medicinas). Es fácil conseguir muchos tipos de medicina sin receta en las farmacias. Por ejemplo, puedes ir a la farmacia, describir los síntomas que tienes (como tos y fiebre) y pedir que te den unos antibióticos. Todo ello sin consultar al médico. Muchos países tienen *farmacias de turno* o *de guardia* que atienden al público las veinticuatro horas del día.

En algunos países (como Argentina, Chile y Perú) hay un nuevo tipo de farmacia al estilo estadounidense, que vende de todo. Estas farmacias pertenecen a grandes cadenas (Farmacity en Argentina, Farmacias Ahumada [FASA] en Chile, Inka Farma en Perú) que atraen a los consumidores con una gran variedad de productos, aparte de los medicamentos.

Preguntas

1. ¿Qué es una "farmacia de turno" o "farmacia de guardia"? ¿Existe este sistema en los Estados Unidos?
2. ¿Qué diferencias hay entre las farmacias hispanas tradicionales y las de los Estados Unidos?

Escucha

Síntomas y tratamientos

Estrategia	
Asking yourself questions	A useful tool for boosting comprehension is asking yourself check questions to help you organize information and summarize what you have heard. You will practice this strategy in the **A escuchar** section.

9-37 Antes de escuchar

Marisol no se siente bien y llama a su madre para pedirle consejo. Cuando tú no te sientes bien, ¿qué haces generalmente: llamas al médico, hablas con un/a amigo/a, llamas a tu madre u otro pariente o te cuidas solo/a (*take care of yourself*)?

Marisol llama a su madre.

9-38 A escuchar

Completa las siguientes actividades.

1. La conversación entre Marisol y su madre se divide en tres partes. Escucha la primera parte y después escoge la pregunta que mejor resuma (*summarizes*) lo que escuchaste. Repite el proceso con cada parte.

   PRIMERA PARTE
   a. ¿Por qué llama Marisol a su madre?
   b. ¿Cuáles son los síntomas de Marisol?
   c. ¿Qué hizo Marisol cuando se levantó?

   SEGUNDA PARTE
   a. ¿Con quiénes salió Marisol anoche?
   b. ¿A Marisol le gustan las galletas?
   c. ¿Qué comió Marisol anoche?

   TERCERA PARTE
   a. ¿Debe ir a clase?
   b. ¿Debe comer mucho hoy?
   c. ¿Qué puede hacer Marisol para sentirse mejor?

2. Escucha una vez más para averiguar si escogiste las preguntas apropiadas. Compáralas con las de un/a compañero/a. Expliquen por qué son las mejores preguntas.
3. Ahora escucha la conversación por última vez para contestar las siguientes preguntas.
   a. ¿Por qué llama Marisol a su madre?
   b. ¿Cuáles son sus síntomas?
   c. ¿Qué comió Marisol anoche?
   d. ¿Cuál es el consejo de su mamá?

9-39 Después de escuchar

Realicen la escena entre Marisol y su madre.

¡Conversemos!

9-40 Los pacientes

Tienes un trabajo como voluntario/a en un hospital. Describe a tres pacientes (ficticios) con quienes estuviste ayer. Tu compañero/a te hace las siguientes preguntas para guiar tu descripción:

1. ¿Cómo son?
2. ¿Cuáles son las enfermedades o los síntomas de los pacientes?
3. ¿Qué tratamientos recibieron?

Incluye por lo menos **diez** oraciones en tu descripción.

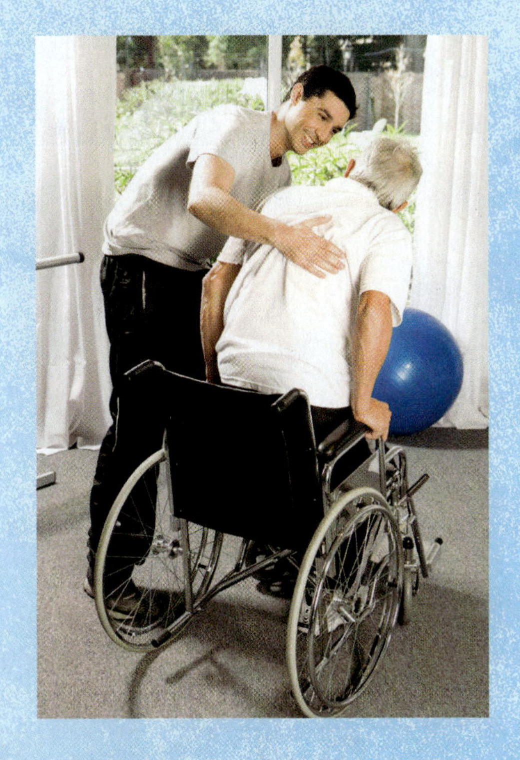

9-41 ¿Qué hicieron?

Piensa en alguien que conoces que antes no vivía una vida sana, pero que recientemente cambió su estilo de vida. Descríbele a tu compañero/a de clase qué hacía antes y qué hizo para cambiar. Piensa bien si debes usar **el pretérito** o **el imperfecto** para explicar su situación. Tu compañero/a te va a hacer preguntas para clarificar y recibir más información.

Escribe

Un resumen

Estrategia

Sequencing events

When writing a summary in Spanish about things that occurred in the past, you must choose appropriately between the preterit and the imperfect. For example, if you are relating a chain or sequence of events—actions that occurred one after the other—you will most likely need to use the preterit. If you are describing situations, what used to happen, or what was going on when something else happened, you will most likely use the imperfect. At this stage of your learning, it is a good idea to bookmark the list of words and expressions that commonly signal the preterit and the imperfect on page 365 to also help guide you.

9-42 Antes de escribir Piensa en tus libros o cuentos favoritos de la niñez. Escoge uno y haz una lista de los **ocho** acontecimientos (*events*) más importantes de ese libro o cuento.

9-43 A escribir Escribe un resumen del libro o cuento, utilizando tu lista e incorporando un poco de descripción sobre los personajes y la escena: dónde estaban, qué hacían, cómo se sentían, etc.

9-44 Después de escribir Comparte tu resumen con un/a compañero/a. Enfóquense en los verbos. ¿Usaron de manera correcta el pretérito y el imperfecto?

¿Cómo andas? II

Having completed **Comunicación II**, I now can…	**Feel confident**	**Need to review**
• explain ailments and treatments. (p. 359)	☐	☐
• narrate in the past. (p. 364)		
• consider pharmacies in Spanish-speaking countries and how they differ from those in the United States. (p. 371)	☐	☐
• ask myself questions when listening in order to organize and summarize what I hear. (p. 372)	☐	☐
• communicate about ailments and healthy living. (p. 373)	☐	☐
• write a summary, sequencing past events. (p. 374)	☐	☐

Vistazo cultural

Explore more about Peru with *Club cultura* online.

Perú

Les presento mi país

Diana Ávila Peralta

Mi nombre es Diana Ávila Peralta y soy de Ayacucho, Perú. Hay muchas ruinas de la civilización incaica en mi país, como las de Machu Picchu y Cuzco, la antigua capital del imperio inca. Cuando era más joven, visité Cuzco con mi familia y la arquitectura e historia de esta ciudad me inspiraron mucho. Ahora estudio historia en la Universidad Nacional Mayor de San Marcos en Lima y quiero ser profesora para compartir mi pasión con otras personas. **¿Qué profesión quieres tener en el futuro?** Perú es un país de extremos geográficos: tenemos la costa, las montañas impresionantes de los Andes, cañones profundos, la selva y el nacimiento (*source*) del río Amazonas con flora y fauna magníficas. ¡Puedes hacer mucho ejercicio caminando por estas zonas! **¿Qué haces tú para mantenerte en forma?**

'uzco se puede
ciar la arquitectura
y colonial.

Loros en la selva amazónica

Miraflores, en las afueras de Lima, Perú

ALMANAQUE

Nombre oficial: República del Perú
Gobierno: República constitucional
Población: 29.907.003 (2010)
Idiomas: español (oficial); quechua (oficial); idiomas indígenas
Moneda: Sol (S/)

¿Sabías que...?

- Las líneas de Nazca, que se encuentran en un desierto del sur del país, son un enigma. Consisten en una serie de dibujos de diferentes animales, plantas y flores, y figuras geométricas que se reconocen solamente desde el aire.
- Hay casi 3,5 millones de llamas en los Andes.

Preguntas

1. ¿Qué estudia Diana?
2. ¿Por qué se dice que Perú es un país de geografía muy variada?
3. ¿Qué otros países comparten algunas de las características geográficas de Perú?

Vistazo cultural

Bolivia

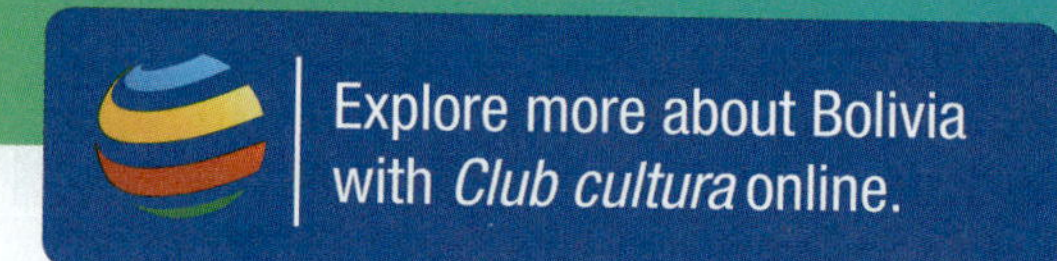

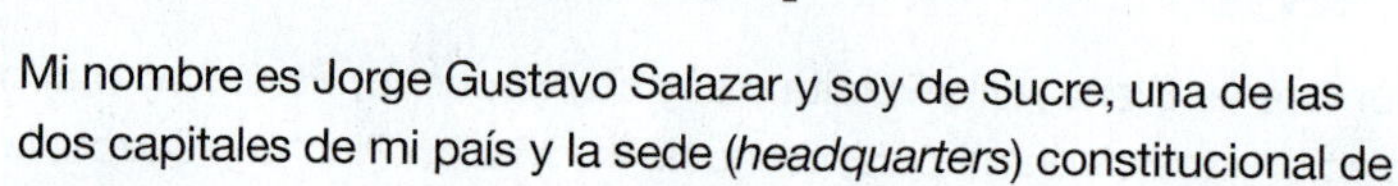

Les presento mi país

Fíjate

The abbreviation *m.s.n.m* means *metros sobre el nivel del mar*, or meters above sea level.

Jorge Gustavo Salazar

Mi nombre es Jorge Gustavo Salazar y soy de Sucre, una de las dos capitales de mi país y la sede (*headquarters*) constitucional de Bolivia. La Paz, la capital administrativa, es la capital más alta del mundo, a unos 3.650 m.s.n.m. en los Andes. **¿A qué altura está tu ciudad?** En Bolivia más del cincuenta por ciento de la población es indígena, como los aymara que viven en la zona del altiplano cerca del lago Titicaca. Desde tiempos remotos, los pueblos indígenas usaron las plantas y los rituales para tratar enfermedades, y el uso de la medicina tradicional es común en Bolivia hoy día. Por ejemplo, algunos bolivianos mastican (*chew*) las hojas de coca (*coca leaves*) para aliviar el hambre, el cansancio y el mal de altura (*altitude sickness*) **¿Es popular la medicina tradicional donde vives tú?**

El lago Titicaca está en la frontera entre Bolivia y Perú y es el lago navegable más alto del mundo.

Una mujer aymara con ropa tradicional

Unas hojas de coca a la venta en un mercado de La Paz

ALMANAQUE

Nombre oficial:	República de Bolivia
Gobierno:	República
Población:	9.947.418 (2010)
Idiomas:	37 lenguas oficiales, incluyendo español, quechua y aymara
Moneda:	Boliviano (Bs)

¿Sabías que...?

- La papa, nativa de Sudamérica, es un alimento básico en Bolivia. Se cultivan más de doscientos tipos de papa en el país.
- Aunque no tiene salida (*access*) al mar, Bolivia tiene una fuerza marina: la Armada Boliviana.

Preguntas

1. ¿Por qué crees que Bolivia tiene varios idiomas oficiales?
2. ¿Qué distinción tiene La Paz como capital?
3. Además de Bolivia, ¿en qué otros países sudamericanos puede una persona sufrir de mal de altura? ¿Por qué?

Vistazo cultural

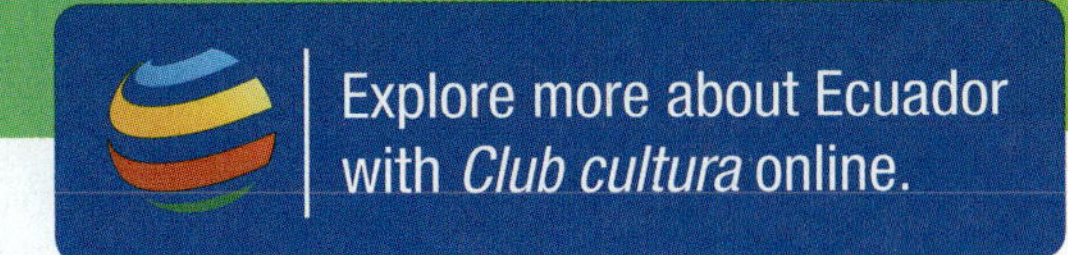

Ecuador

Les presento mi país

Yolanda Pico Briones

Mi nombre es Yolanda Pico Briones y soy de Quito, la capital de Ecuador. Quito fue la capital del norte del imperio inca y por eso hay ruinas de esta civilización en mi ciudad, como el Templo del Sol y una avenida principal que formó parte del antiguo sistema de carreteras que conectaban el imperio. **¿Qué evidencia de las civilizaciones antiguas se encuentra en tu país?** Ecuador tiene tres diferentes tipos de geografía: la costa, las montañas y el oriente o la selva. La población ecuatoriana, que es principalmente mestiza e indígena, se concentra en las montañas y la costa. **¿Dónde vive la mayoría de la población en tu país?**

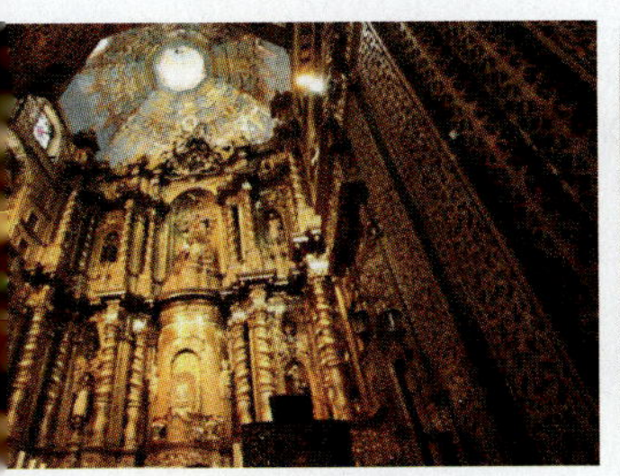
La Iglesia de la Compañía de Jesús en Quito está cubierta de oro (*gold*) en su interior.

Una iguana de las islas Galápagos

Un viaje en canoa en la región amazónica

ALMANAQUE

Nombre oficial:	República del Ecuador
Gobierno:	República
Población:	14.790.608 (2010)
Idiomas:	español (oficial), quechua y otros idiomas indígenas
Moneda:	El dólar estadounidense ($)

¿Sabías que…?

- Hay más de 80 especies endémicas de pájaros, peces, reptiles y mamíferos en las islas Galápagos. Esto significa que estas especies no se pueden encontrar en ningún otro lugar del mundo.
- El volcán Cotopaxi es uno de los volcanes más altos del mundo.

Preguntas

1. ¿Por qué son únicos algunos animales en las islas Galápagos?
2. ¿Qué tiene Ecuador en común geográficamente con Perú y Bolivia?
3. ¿En qué otros países se encuentra evidencia de la civilización inca?

Lectura

Test de salud

9-45 Antes de leer Piensa en tu salud en este momento. Contesta las siguientes preguntas.

- En general, ¿llevas una vida saludable?
- En tu opinión, ¿duermes lo suficiente?
- ¿Hay armonía entre tu vida académica y tu vida social? Explica.

Estrategia

Skipping words

If you have attempted to guess the meanings of unfamiliar words from context and are still having problems understanding, you may want to skip unfamiliar words and follow these steps where appropriate:

1. Identify the subject and main verb of each sentence.
2. Find descriptions of the subject in the sentence(s).
3. Identify words and phrases that indicate time and place, cause and effect.
4. Ignore words set off by commas.
5. Summarize the content of each paragraph and look for information to fill in gaps.

9-46 Mientras lees Completa las siguientes actividades.

1. Lee superficialmente la lectura y subraya (*underline*) las palabras que no conoces.
2. A continuación hay unas oraciones con posibles palabras problemáticas subrayadas. Léelas y responde.

   a. *Llevar una vida saludable, especialmente en un mundo ajetreado, puede ser muy difícil.*
   - La palabra *ajetreado* es…

     un sustantivo (*noun*). un verbo. un adjetivo.
   - Si ignoras la frase entre comas, ¿puedes entender la oración?

   b. *Ver mucha televisión o pasar tiempo pegado a las "pantallas" (tabletas, computadoras o teléfonos) justo antes de dormir.*
   - ¿Por qué *no* es crítico saber lo que significa *pegado* en esta oración?
3. Lee la lectura otra vez, empleando la estrategia con cualquier otra palabra que no comprendas (*you do not understand*).

Test: ¿Llevas una vida saludable?

Llevar una vida saludable, especialmente en un mundo ajetreado, puede ser muy difícil. A veces no tenemos tiempo de detenernos a pensar en nuestra salud porque siempre estamos corriendo, no nos cuidamos, no comemos bien y sufrimos de estrés. ¿Cómo está tu salud? Completa el siguiente cuestionario.

1. ¿Cuántas veces a la semana comes comida rápida?
a. 0–1 b. 2–4 c. 5–6 d. 7 o más

2. ¿Cuántas comidas balanceadas comes al día?
a. 3 o más b. 2 c. 1 d. 0

3. ¿Cuántas frutas o verduras comes al día?
a. 6 o más b. 3–5 c. 2–3 d. 0–1

4. ¿Cuántas horas duermes normalmente?
a. 9 b. 8 c. 6–7 d. 5 o menos

5. ¿Cuántos pasos caminas al día?
a. 10.000 o más b. 8.000 c. 5.000 d. 2.000 o menos

6. ¿Cuántas veces por semana haces ejercicio?
a. 5 b. 4 c. 2–3 d. 0–1

7. ¿Cuántas veces por semana sufres de dolor de cabeza, tensión o ansiedad?
a. 1 b. 2–3 c. 4–5 d. 6 o más

8. ¿Cuántas veces a la semana haces algo para relajarte?
a. todos los días b. 4–5 c. 2–3 d. 0–1

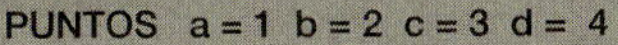

PUNTOS a = 1 b = 2 c = 3 d = 4
8–16: ¡Buena salud! Vives una vida saludable.
17–23: Tienes buena salud pero necesitas tener cuidado.
24–32: ¡Piensa en tu salud! ¡Inmediatamente!

RECOMENDACIONES

LO QUE DEBES HACER…	LO QUE *NO* DEBES HACER…
✔ Comer comidas equilibradas en porciones pequeñas. Comer muchas verduras, frutas, cereales integrales y proteínas sin grasa.	✘ Comer comidas procesadas ni alimentos con mucha grasa ni comida rápida. Ingerir productos con mucho azúcar.
✔ Beber ocho vasos de agua todos los días. Ingerir leche con 2% de grasa o descremada para fortificar los huesos. Consumir cafeína con moderación.	✘ Consumir refrescos con mucho azúcar o ingredientes artificiales.
✔ Hacer ejercicio 30 minutos como mínimo cada día. Usar las escaleras en vez del ascensor cada vez que puedas.	✘ Hacer ejercicio sin estirar los músculos o hacer calentamiento.
✔ Dormir de siete a nueve horas todas las noches. Dormirse y levantarse a la misma hora todos los días.	✘ Pasar noches sin dormir. Ver mucha televisión o pasar tiempo pegado a las "pantallas" (tabletas, computadoras o teléfonos) justo antes de dormir.
✔ Realizar actividades que ayuden a controlar el estrés: practicar yoga, meditación o pasar tiempo con amigos.	✘ Ignorar los síntomas del estrés, la ansiedad y la depresión.

9·47 Después de leer
Contesta las siguientes preguntas según la lectura.

1. ¿Qué comidas debes evitar?
2. ¿Cuáles son dos bebidas saludables?
3. ¿Cuánto ejercicio debes hacer al día?
4. ¿Qué no debes hacer justo antes de dormir?
5. ¿Para qué sirve practicar yoga o meditación?
6. ¿Cuántos puntos sacaste en el test? ¿Estás de acuerdo con los resultados?

9·48 Tu salud
Vuelve a leer las recomendaciones del artículo. ¿Cuáles sigues ya en tu vida diaria? ¿Hay cosas que debes evitar? ¿Por qué? ¿Qué otros hábitos debes incorporar para llevar una vida más sana? Prepara una presentación en la que contestes estas preguntas en detalle.

9·49 Al final del semestre
Al final de cada semestre los estudiantes tienen mucho estrés porque tienen que terminar ensayos, proyectos de laboratorio y tomar muchos exámenes. ¿Manejas (*Do you manage*) bien el estrés? Describe en detalle lo que haces o no para mantener una vida equilibrada durante los últimos días del semestre. Comparte tus ideas con un/a compañero/a.

For additional *Lectura* activities, go to *¡Anda!* online.

Y por fin, ¿cómo andas?

Having completed this chapter, I now can...	Feel confident	Need to review
Comunicación I		
• describe the human body. (p. 346)	☐	☐
• pronounce the letters *d* and *t*. (p. 347 and online)	☐	☐
• relate daily routines. (p. 349)	☐	☐
• share about people, actions, and things. (p. 354)	☐	☐
Comunicación II		
• explain ailments and treatments. (p. 359)	☐	☐
• narrate in the past. (p. 364)	☐	☐
• ask myself questions when listening in order to organize and summarize what I hear. (p. 372)	☐	☐
• communicate about ailments and healthy living. (p. 373)	☐	☐
• write a summary, sequencing past events. (p. 374)	☐	☐
Cultura		
• relate the importance of water in maintaining good health. (p. 358)	☐	☐
• consider pharmacies in Spanish-speaking countries and how they differ from those in the United States. (p. 371)	☐	☐
• share information about Peru, Bolivia, and Ecuador. (pp. 375–377)	☐	☐
Lectura		
• read a magazine article about health. (p. 378)		
Comunidades		
• use Spanish in real-life contexts. (online)	☐	☐

Vocabulario **activo**

El cuerpo humano	*The human body*
el brazo	*arm*
la cintura	*waist*
el corazón	*heart*
el cuello	*neck*
el cuerpo	*body*
el dedo (de la mano)	*finger*
el dedo (del pie)	*toe*
la espalda	*back*
el estómago	*stomach*
la garganta	*throat*
la mano	*hand*
el oído	*inner ear*
el pecho	*chest*
el pie	*foot*
la pierna	*leg*
la boca	*mouth*
la cabeza	*head*
la cara	*face*
el diente	*tooth*
la nariz	*nose*
el ojo	*eye*
la oreja	*ear*
el pelo	*hair*
la salud	*health*
la sangre	*blood*

Algunos verbos	*Some verbs*
doler (o → ue)	*to hurt*
estar enfermo/a	*to be sick*
estar sano/a; saludable	*to be healthy*
ser alérgico/a (a)	*to be allergic (to)*

Algunos verbos reflexivos	*Some reflexive verbs*
acordarse de (o → ue)	*to remember*
acostarse (o → ue)	*to go to bed*
afeitarse	*to shave*
arreglarse	*to get ready*
bañarse	*to bathe*
caerse	*to fall down*
callarse	*to get / keep quiet*
cepillarse (el pelo, los dientes)	*to brush (one's hair, teeth)*
cortarse	*to cut oneself*
curarse	*to be cured*
despertarse (e → ie)	*to wake up; to awaken*
divertirse (e → ie → i)	*to enjoy oneself; to have fun*
dormirse (o → ue → u)	*to fall asleep*
ducharse	*to shower*
enfermarse	*to get sick*
irse	*to go away; to leave*
lastimarse	*to get hurt*
lavarse	*to wash oneself*
levantarse	*to get up; to stand up*
llamarse	*to be called*
maquillarse	*to put on make up*
mejorarse	*to improve; to get better*
peinarse	*to comb one's hair*
ponerse (la ropa)	*to put on (one's clothes)*
ponerse (nervioso/a)	*to get (nervous)*
probarse (o → ue) la ropa	*to try on clothing*
quedarse	*to stay; to remain*
quemarse	*to get burned*
quitarse (la ropa)	*to take off (one's clothes)*
reunirse	*to get together; to meet*
romperse	*to break (a bone)*
secarse	*to dry off*
sentarse (e → ie)	*to sit down*
sentirse (e → ie → i)	*to feel*
vestirse (e → i → i)	*to get dressed*
vendarse	*to bandage oneself*

Algunas enfermedades y tratamientos médicos	Illnesses and medical treatments
En el hospital	*In the hospital*
el/la doctor/a	*doctor*
el/la enfermero/a	*nurse*
el examen físico	*physical exam*
la farmacia	*pharmacy*
el hospital	*hospital*
el/la médico/a	*doctor*
la sala de urgencias	*emergency room*
Los tratamientos	*Treatments*
el antiácido	*antacid*
el antibiótico	*antibiotic*
la aspirina	*aspirin*
la curita	*adhesive bandage*
la inyección	*shot*
el jarabe	*cough syrup*
las pastillas	*pills*
la receta	*prescription*
la venda / el vendaje	*bandage*
evitar	*to avoid*
guardar cama	*to stay in bed*
Los síntomas y las enfermedades	*Symptoms and illnesses*
el catarro / el resfriado	*cold*
el dolor	*pain*
el estornudo	*sneeze*
la fiebre	*fever*
la gripe	*flu*
la herida	*wound; injury*
las náuseas	*nausea*
la tos	*cough*
estornudar	*to sneeze*

Algunas enfermedades y tratamientos médicos	Illnesses and medical treatments
Los síntomas y las enfermedades	*Symptoms and illnesses*
tener...	
alergia (a)	*to be allergic (to)*
(un) catarro, resfriado	*to have a cold*
(la/una) gripe	*to have the flu*
una infección	*to have an infection*
tos	*to have a cough*
un virus	*to have a virus*
tener...	*to have a...*
dolor de cabeza	*headache*
dolor de espalda	*backache*
dolor de estómago	*stomachache*
dolor de garganta	*sore throat*
toser	*to cough*

Algunos verbos	Some verbs
acabar de + *infinitivo*	*to have just finished (something)*
ocurrir	*to occur*
tratar de	*to try to*

Cartagena, Colombia: moderna y colonial

10 ¡Viajemos!

Viajar a lugares nuevos te puede ampliar tu visión del mundo y de la vida. También los viajes te dan nuevas perspectivas sobre tu identidad y tu lugar de origen. La gente viaja por diversas razones: visitar a la familia, explorar lugares diferentes, conocer otras culturas, divertirse, descansar, hacer negocios... ¿Cuál es tu razón para viajar?

Preguntas

1. ¿Cuándo viajas? ¿Con quién?
2. Cuando viajas, ¿adónde vas generalmente?
3. En el futuro, ¿adónde quieres ir?

¿Sabías que...?

Avianca, una aerolínea colombiana, es la más antigua de las Américas. Fue fundada el 5 de diciembre de 1919.

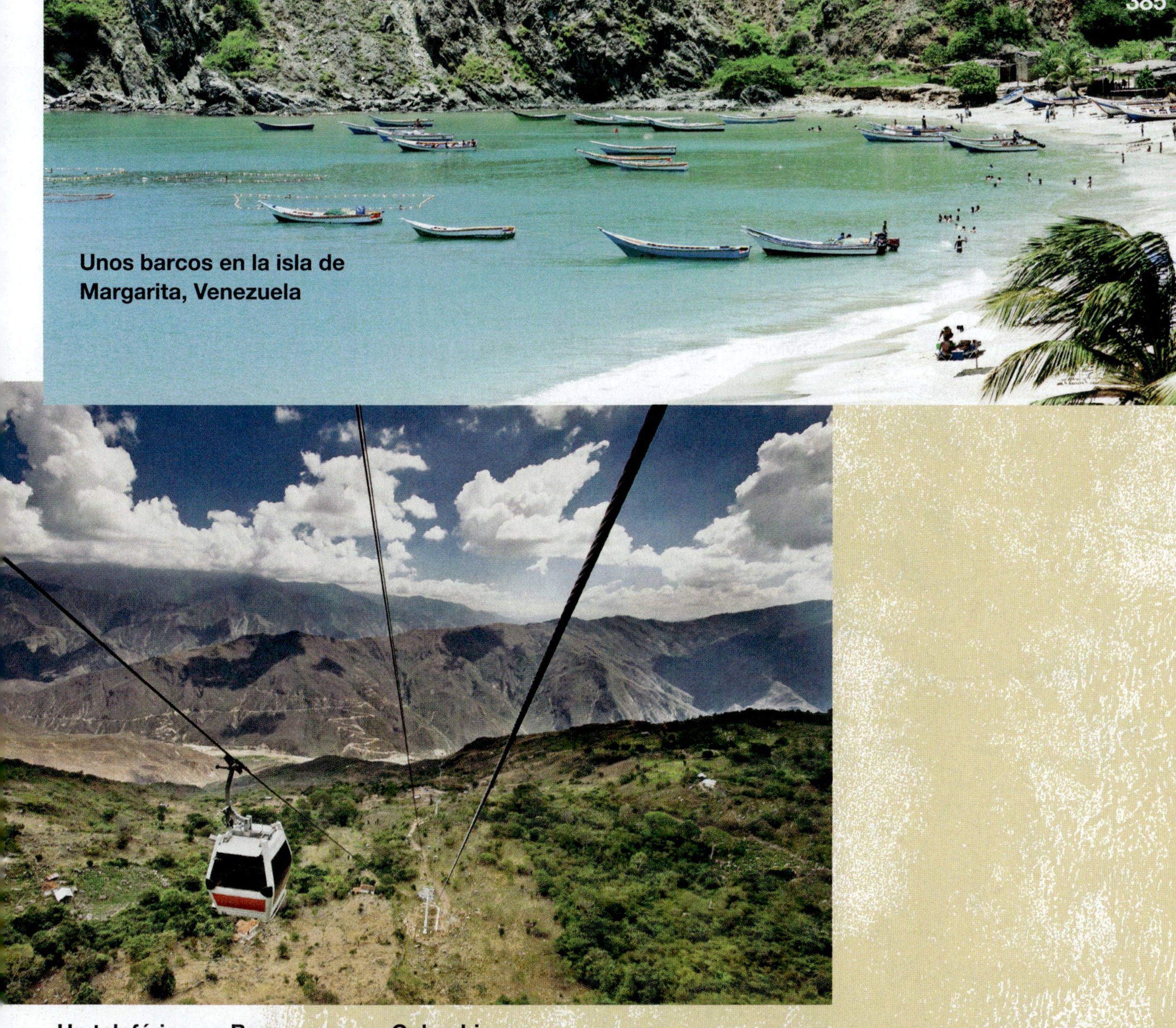

Unos barcos en la isla de Margarita, Venezuela

Un teleférico en Bucaramanga, Colombia

Learning Outcomes

By the end of this chapter, you will be able to:

- ✔ discuss modes of transportation.
- ✔ share about travel.
- ✔ give orders and instructions.
- ✔ compare people, places, and things.
- ✔ communicate about travel plans.
- ✔ write and present a report.
- ✔ exchange interesting facts about Colombia and Venezuela.
- ✔ read a fragment of a letter by Hernán Cortés.

Comunicación I

1 VOCABULARIO

Los medios de transporte Discussing modes of transportation

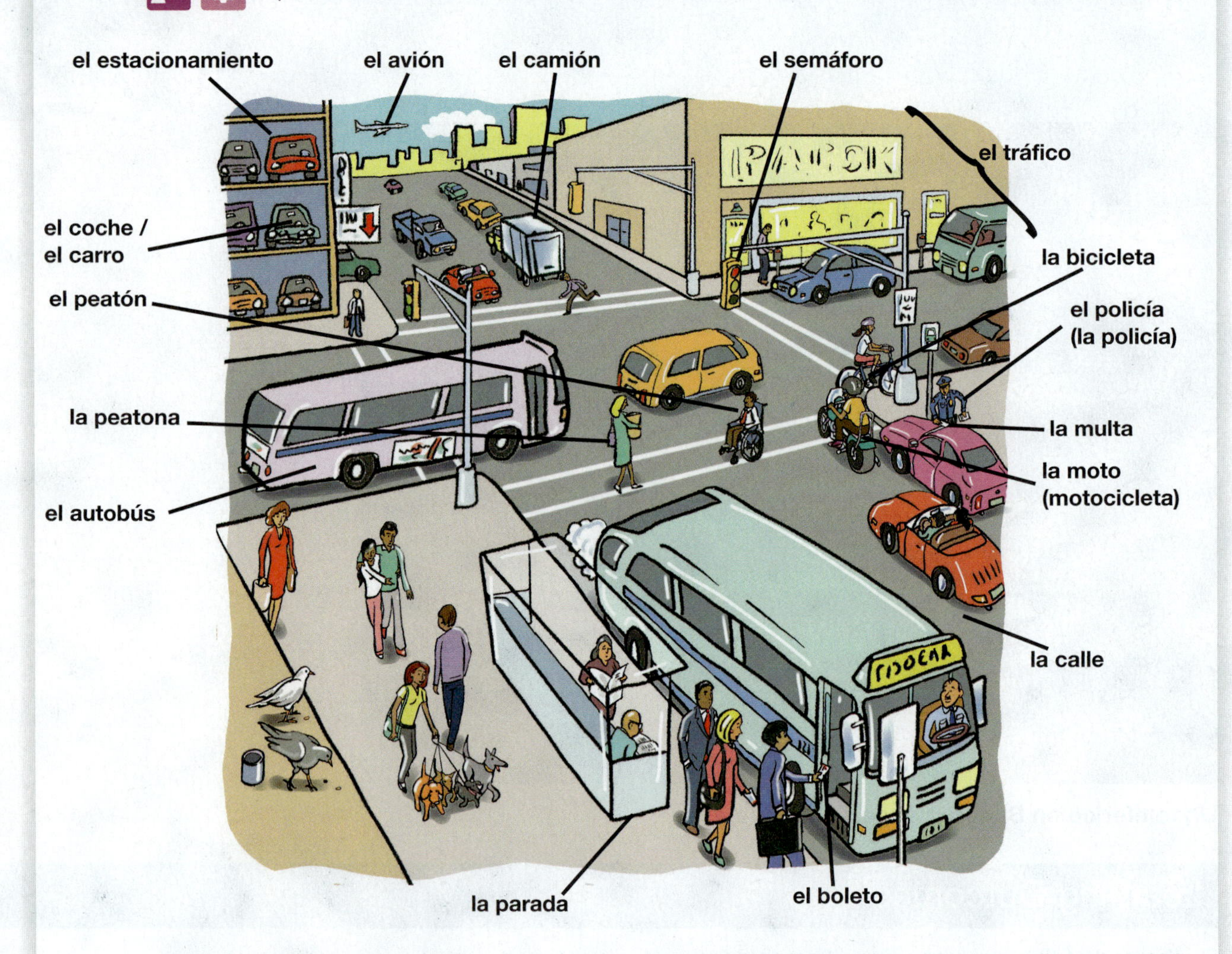

Algunos verbos	Some verbs
bajar (de)	*to get down (from); to get off (of)*
cambiar	*to change*
doblar	*to turn*
entrar	*to enter*
estacionar	*to park*
funcionar	*to work; to function*
hacer (la) cola	*to stand in line*
llenar el tanque	*to fill up; to fill the tank*
manejar/conducir	*to drive*
revisar	*to check; to overhaul*
sacar la licencia	*to get a driver's license*
subir (a)	*to go up; to get on*
viajar	*to travel*
visitar	*to visit*

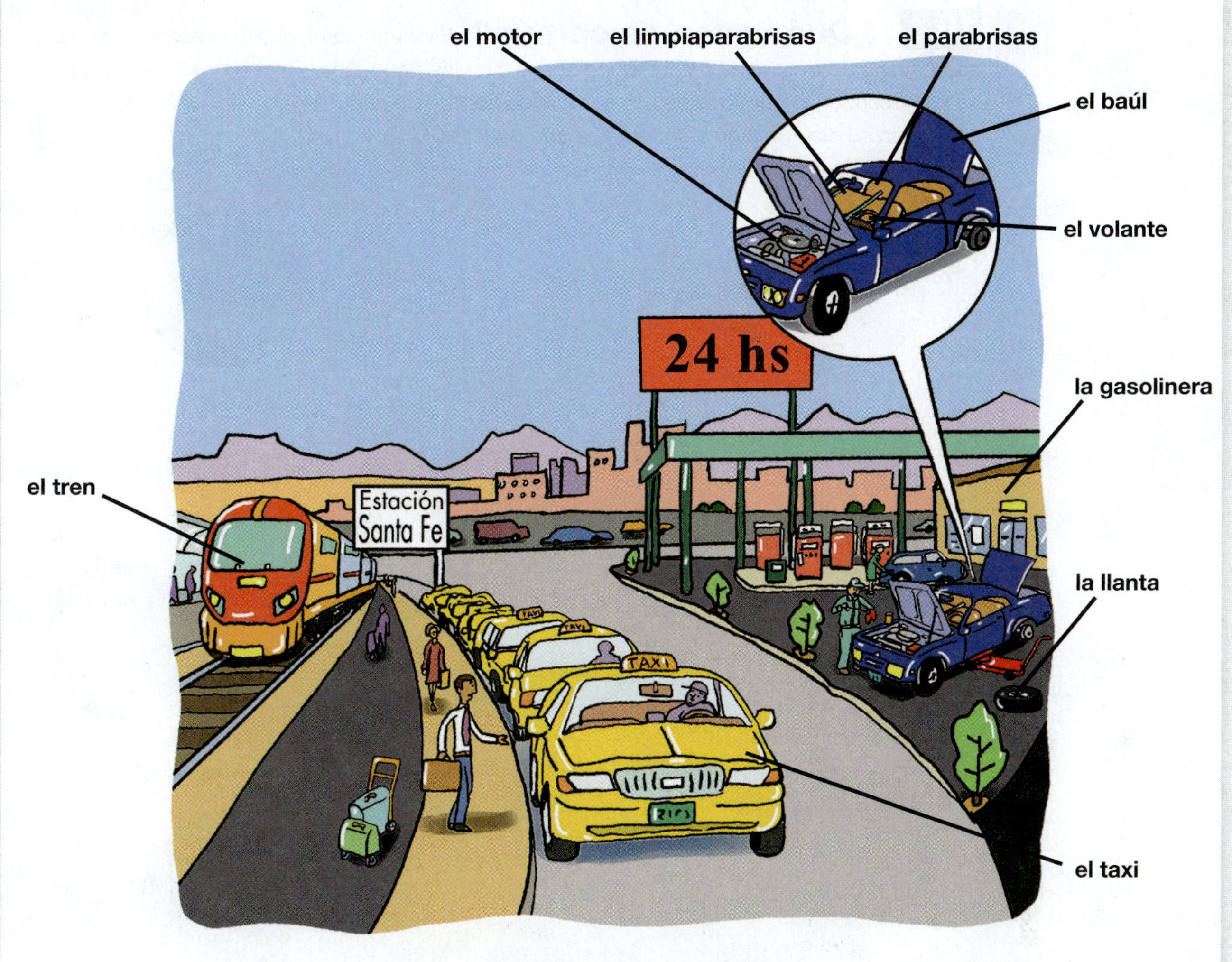

Algunos sustantivos	*Some nouns*
el aire acondicionado	*air conditioning*
la autopista	*highway; freeway*
el barco	*boat*
la calefacción	*heat*
la licencia (de conducir)	*driver's license*
la llave	*key*
el metro	*subway*
el ruido	*noise*
el taller mecánico	*auto repair shop*

Now you are ready to complete the ***Preparación y práctica*** activities for this chunk online.

PRONUNCIACIÓN

The letters *b* and *v*

Go to *¡Anda!* online to learn about the letters *b* and *v*.

10-1 ¿Qué tienen en común? Escriban características específicas de cada medio de transporte en cada uno de los círculos pequeños. En el círculo grande del centro, escriban lo que todos estos medios de transporte tienen en común. Después comparen su diagrama con los de otros compañeros.

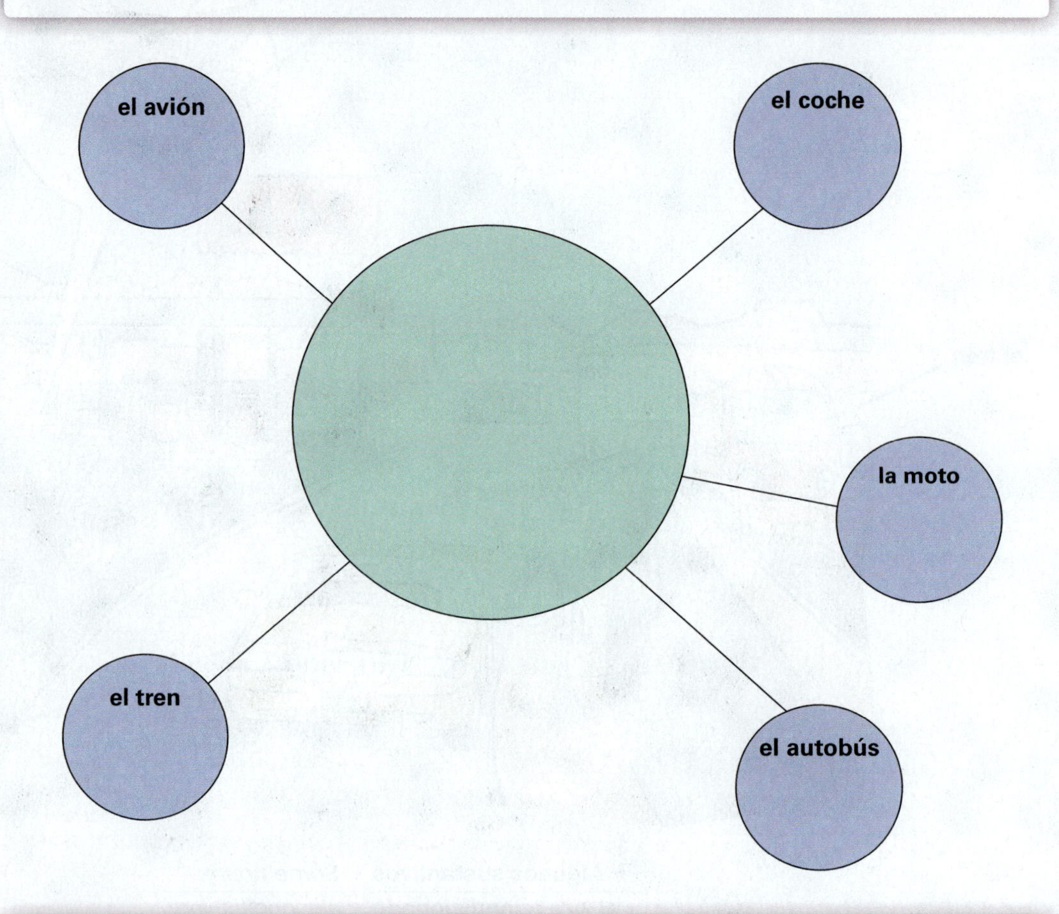

10-2 ¿Es verdad? Decide si las siguientes oraciones son ciertas (**C**) o falsas (**F**). Si son falsas, corrígelas (*correct them*). Compara tus respuestas con las de un/a compañero/a.

Estrategia

When correcting true/false statements, instead of simply adding a negative word, correct the word that is false to make the statement true.

MODELO Un carro tiene seis llantas.

E1: *Un carro tiene seis llantas.*

E2: *Falso. Un carro tiene cuatro llantas.*

1. Hay semáforos en las autopistas.
2. Para llegar a la universidad yo puedo tomar el autobús o ir a pie.
3. Ir en avión es más rápido que ir en tren.
4. Un coche no puede funcionar sin (*without*) limpiaparabrisas.
5. Hay que cambiar el aceite de un coche cada 100.000 millas.
6. Puedes llenar el tanque con gasolina en la gasolinera.
7. Usamos la calefacción en el verano.
8. Si manejamos muy rápido, el policía nos puede dar una llave.

10-3 ¿Cómo vas? Completa los siguientes pasos.

Paso 1 Pon una equis (**X**) en la columna apropiada. Después, pregúntale a un/a compañero/a qué medios de transporte usa él/ella.

¿QUÉ USAS…?	A MENUDO	A VECES	NUNCA
bicicleta			
autobús			
avión			
carro			
tren			

MODELO E1: *¿Qué medio de transporte usas a menudo?*
E2: *Uso el autobús a menudo. ¿Y tú?*
E1: *Uso el carro.*
E2: *¿Qué medio de transporte usas a veces?*
E1: *Uso la bicicleta a veces. ¿Y tú?*

Paso 2 Túrnense para hacerse y contestar las siguientes preguntas.
¿Qué medio de transporte usas…

1. más?
2. menos?
3. para ir a la universidad?
4. para ir al centro comercial?
5. para ir a visitar a tus amigos?
6. para ir a la casa de tus padres o de unos parientes?
7. para ir a Los Ángeles?
8. para ir a Caracas, Venezuela?
9. para ir a Europa?

10-4 Cinco preguntas En grupos de tres o cuatro estudiantes, escriban **cinco** preguntas interesantes relacionadas con **Los medios de transporte**. Después, para cada pregunta, deben escoger a una persona de otro grupo para contestarla.

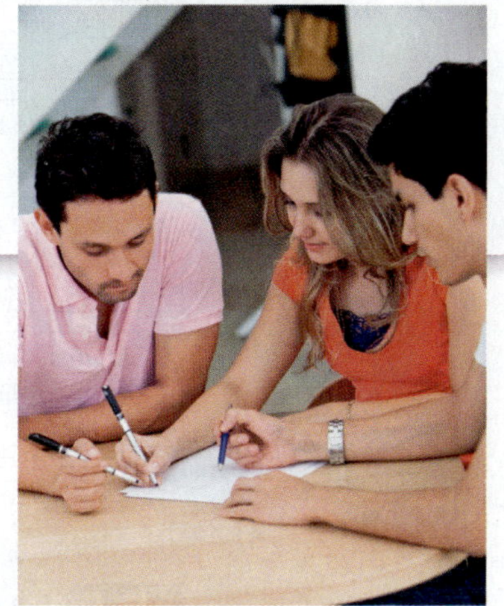

MODELO GRUPO 1: *¿Cambiaste el aceite del coche la semana pasada?*
GRUPO 2 (PHILLIP): *No, no cambié el aceite la semana pasada, pero tengo que cambiarlo pronto.*
GRUPO 1: *¿Viajaste a México el verano pasado?*
GRUPO 2 (GENA): *Sí, fui a Cancún con mi familia.*

10-5 Firma aquí Circula por la clase hasta encontrar a un/a estudiante que pueda contestar afirmativamente a tu pregunta. **¡OJO!** Debes usar **el pretérito** en la mayoría de las preguntas.

Estrategia

When performing a signature search (or *Firma aquí*) activity, remember to circulate around the classroom, speaking to many different classmates. You should try to have a different student's signature for each item.

MODELO manejar un camión el verano pasado

E1: *¿Manejaste un camión el verano pasado?*

E2: *Sí, manejé un camión el verano pasado.*

E1: *Pues, firma aquí.*

Rosario

manejar un camión el verano pasado __________	ir a una gasolinera esta mañana __________	saber manejar un barco __________
tener más de tres llaves contigo __________	ir a la universidad por la autopista __________	tener un coche sin calefacción __________
perder las llaves alguna vez __________	viajar a algún lugar exótico durante las últimas vacaciones __________	recibir una multa el año pasado __________
tener un accidente de coche en los últimos dos años __________	llevar el coche al taller mecánico el mes pasado __________	viajar en tren el año pasado __________

10-6 ¡No funciona! Necesitan llevar su coche a un mecánico. Hagan los papeles del conductor y el mecánico. Tienen que descubrir qué problema tiene el coche, hablar de posibles soluciones y decidir cuánto tiempo se necesita para repararlo.

2 GRAMÁTICA

Los mandatos informales

Influencing others and giving advice

When you need to give orders, advise, or ask people to do something, you use commands. If you are addressing a friend or someone you normally address as **tú,** you use informal commands. You have been responding to **tú** commands since the beginning of ***¡Anda! Curso elemental*:** **escucha, escribe, abre tu libro en la página,** etc.

1. **The affirmative *tú* command form is the same as the *él, ella, Ud.* form of the present tense of the verb:**

Infinitive		Present tense	Affirmative *tú* command
llen**ar**	él, ella, Ud.	llen**a**	llena
le**er**	él, ella, Ud.	le**e**	lee
ped**ir**	él, ella, Ud.	pid**e**	pide

Llen**a** el tanque.	*Fill the tank.*
Dobl**a** a la derecha.	*Turn to the right.*
Conduc**e** con cuidado.	*Drive carefully.*
Pid**e** permiso.	*Ask permission.*

There are eight common verbs that have irregular affirmative *tú* commands:

decir → **di**	ir → **ve**	salir → **sal**	tener → **ten**
hacer → **haz**	poner → **pon**	ser → **sé**	venir → **ven**

Sé respetuoso con los peatones.	*Be respectful of pedestrians.*
Ten cuidado al conducir.	*Be careful when driving.*
Ven al aeropuerto con tu pasaporte.	*Come to the airport with your passport.*
Pon las llaves en la mesa.	*Put the keys on the table.*

(*continued*)

2. To form the negative *tú* (informal) commands:

1. Take the **yo** form of the present tense of the verb.
2. Drop the **-o** ending.
3. Add ***-es*** for **-ar** verbs, and add ***-as*** for **-er** and **-ir** verbs.

Infinitive	Present tense		Negative *tú* command
llen**ar**	yo llenø	+ es	no llen**es**
le**er**	yo leø	+ as	no le**as**
ped**ir**	yo pidø	+ as	no pid**as**

No llen**es** el tanque. *Don't fill the tank.*
No dobl**es** a la derecha. *Don't turn to the right.*
No conduzc**as** muy rápido. *Don't drive very fast.*
No pid**as** permiso. *Don't ask permission.*

Fíjate

The verb *conducir* has an irregular *yo* form, similar to *conocer* (conocer → cono**zc**o; conducir → condu**zc**o).

Verbs ending in **-car, -gar,** and **-zar** have a spelling change in the negative **tú** command in order to preserve the sounds of the infinitive endings.

Infinitive	Present tense		Negative *tú* command
sa**car**	yo saco	**c → qu**	no sa**qu**es
lle**gar**	yo llego	**g → gu**	no lle**gu**es
empe**zar**	yo empiezo	**z → c**	no empie**c**es

Fíjate

These are the same spelling changes with which you were presented when you learned the irregular preterit tense of these verbs.

3. Object and reflexive pronouns are used with *tú* commands in the following ways:

a. They are *attached* to the ends of *affirmative* commands. When the command is made up of more than two syllables, a written accent mark is placed over the stressed vowel.

Se me pinchó una llanta. **¡Cámbiamela!** *I got a flat tire. Change it for me!*
Tu bicicleta no funciona. **Revísala.** *Your bike does not work. Check it.*
Me gusta tu coche. **Préstamelo.** *I like your car. Lend it to me.*
Es tarde. **Duérmete** mientras conduzco. *It's late. Fall asleep while I drive.*

b. They are placed *before negative* **tú** commands.

No se nos pinchó la llanta. *We don't have a flat tire.*
¡No **me la** cambies! *Don't change it for me!*

Tu bicicleta funciona. No **la** revises. *Your bicycle works. Don't check it.*

No me gusta tu coche. No **me lo** prestes. *I don't like your car. Don't lend it to me.*

No es tarde. No **te** duermas mientras conduzco. *It's not late. Don't fall asleep while I drive.*

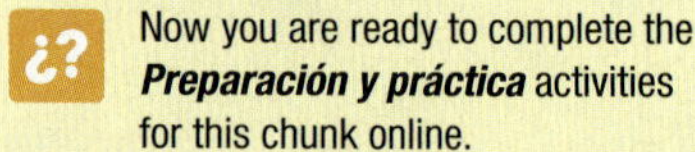
Now you are ready to complete the ***Preparación y práctica*** activities for this chunk online.

10-7 ¿Qué diría el profesor?

Túrnense para decir cuál de los dos mandatos diría (*would say*) un/a profesor/a de una escuela de conducir.

MODELO a. Toma apuntes mientras hablo.
b. No tomes apuntes mientras hablo.
E1: *Toma apuntes mientras hablo.*

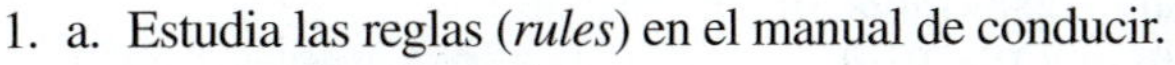

1. a. Estudia las reglas (*rules*) en el manual de conducir.
   b. No estudies las reglas.
2. a. Ven tarde a la clase.
   b. No vengas tarde a la clase.
3. a. Lee el manual con cuidado.
   b. No leas el manual con cuidado.
4. a. Practica fuera de la clase.
   b. No practiques fuera de la clase.
5. a. Ponte nervioso/a.
   b. No te pongas nervioso/a.
6. a. Conduce con cuidado.
   b. No conduzcas con cuidado.
7. a. Sal de la clase antes de tiempo.
   b. No salgas de la clase antes de tiempo.
8. a. Trae tu manual a clase.
   b. No traigas tu manual a clase.

10-8 Hazlo, por favor

Túrnense para expresar mandatos afirmativos y negativos usando los pronombres de complemento directo.

Capítulo 5. Los pronombres de complemento directo, pág. 202.

Estrategia

For activities like **10-8**, you can take turns; one student does the even-numbered items while the other does the odd ones.

MODELO esperar el autobús
E1: *¡Espéralo!*
E2: *¡No lo esperes!*

1. tomar el autobús
2. prestarme las llaves
3. conducir el carro
4. usar la calefacción
5. hacer ruido
6. limpiar el parabrisas
7. subir la ventana
8. estacionar el coche en el garaje
9. buscar un estacionamiento

10-9 Los consejos de un padre

Mira la foto y piensa en lo que los padres normalmente dicen a los conductores jóvenes. Joaquín acaba de sacar la licencia de conducir y su padre le da consejos. Escucha al padre y ordena los consejos.

_____ No estacionar muy cerca de los otros carros.
_____ Tener cuidado en los semáforos.
_____ Mirar bien antes de doblar.
_____ Llenar el tanque de gasolina.
_____ Llamar a su padre si tiene problemas.
_____ Mirar siempre los otros carros.
_____ No manejar rápido.
_____ No usar el teléfono.
_____ Revisar las llantas.

10-10 El sobrinito Tu hermana está enferma y necesita ir al médico. Tú tienes que quedarte en su casa con Abel, su hijo de cuatro años. Dile lo que puede y no puede hacer en las siguientes situaciones.

MODELO Abel quiere comer un plato de donas (*donuts*).
¡No comas todas las donas!

Abel quiere…

1. mirar un programa de *Sesame Street*
2. llamar por teléfono a Big Bird
3. dibujar en la pared
4. limpiar su cuarto
5. mirar una película de terror
6. poner el gato (*cat*) en la lavadora
7. beber un refresco
8. dormir la siesta

10-11 ¡Ayúdame! ¡Tu compañero/a de apartamento te vuelve loco/a!

Paso 1 Usa los siguientes verbos para decirle lo que debe y no debe hacer y compara tus respuestas con las de un/a compañero/a.

MODELO no poner tus libros en mi cama
No pongas tus libros en mi cama.

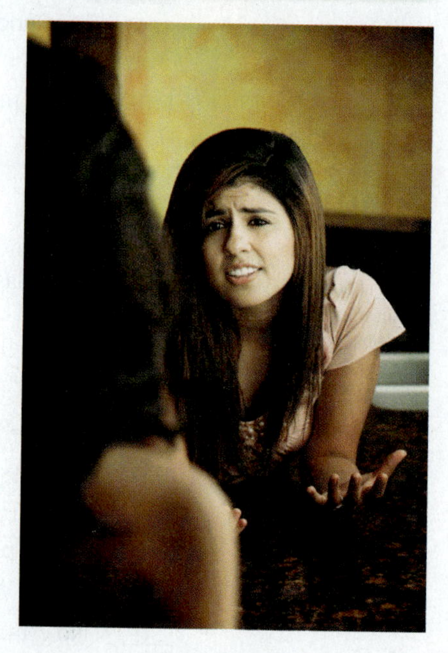

1. no dormirse en el sofá
2. sacar la basura
3. no comer en la sala
4. no beber de mi vaso
5. decirme la verdad siempre
6. no vestirse en la cocina
7. tener más paciencia con mi gato
8. no invitar siempre a los amigos después de las once de la noche

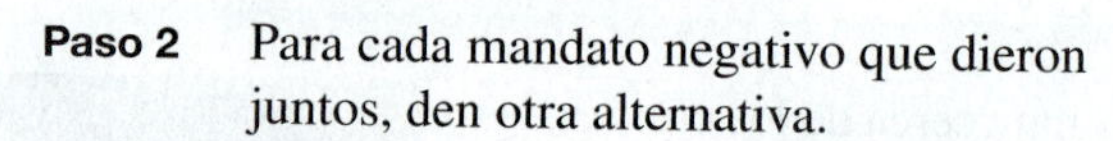

Paso 2 Para cada mandato negativo que dieron juntos, den otra alternativa.

MODELO E1: *No pongas tus libros en mi cama.*
E2: *Ponlos en la mesa.*

10-12 ¡Una fiesta! Tu compañero/a y tú organizan una fiesta para sus amigos. Tienen mucho que hacer: limpiar el apartamento, organizar la música, comprar y preparar la comida, vestirse, etc. Un amigo se ofrece a ayudarles. Hagan una lista de ocho cosas que él puede hacer.

MODELO

1. Organiza la música.

10-13 El transporte Revisa el vocabulario de **Los medios de transporte**. Escoge seis de los verbos y haz una lista de mandatos afirmativos y negativos, usando los verbos. ¡Sé creativo/a! Después, comparte tu lista con un/a compañero/a.

MODELO revisar → *Revisa el motor de tu coche.*

3 GRAMÁTICA

Los mandatos formales Giving orders and instructions

When you need to influence others by making a request, giving advice, giving instructions, or giving orders to people you normally treat as **Ud.** or **Uds.,** you are going to use a different set of commands: **formal** commands. The forms of these commands are similar to the negative **tú** command forms.

1. To form the *Ud.* and *Uds.* commands:

1. Take the **yo** form of the present tense of the verb.
2. Drop the **-o** ending.
3. Add ***-e(n)*** for **-ar** verbs, and add ***-a(n)*** for **-er** and **-ir** verbs.

Infinitive	Present tense		*Ud.* commands	*Uds.* commands
limpi**ar**	yo limpiø	+ e(n)	(no) limpi**e**	(no) limpi**en**
l**eer**	yo leø	+ a(n)	(no) le**a**	(no) le**an**
ped**ir**	yo pidø	+ a(n)	(no) pid**a**	(no) pid**an**

Llene el tanque. **Llénelo.** — *Fill up the tank. Fill it.*
No limpie el parabrisas. **No lo limpie.** — *Don't clean the windshield. Don't clean it.*
Conduzca el camión. **Condúzcalo.** — *Drive the truck. Drive it.*
No ponga esa gasolina cara en el coche. — *Don't put that expensive gasoline in the car.*
No la ponga en el coche. — *Don't put it in the car.*
Traiga su licencia. **Tráigala.** — *Bring your license. Bring it.*
No busquen sus llaves. **No las busquen.** — *Don't look for your keys. Don't look for them.*

¡Explícalo tú!

1. Where do the object pronouns appear in affirmative commands? Where do they appear in negative commands? In what order?
2. Why are there written accents added to some of the commands and not to others?

 Check your answers to the preceding questions in Appendix 1.

2. Verbs ending in *-car, -gar*, and *-zar* have a spelling change in the *Ud.* and *Uds.* commands. These spelling changes are needed to preserve the sounds of the infinitive endings.

Infinitive	Present tense		*Ud/Uds.* commands
sac**ar**	yo sac**o**	**c → qu**	sa**que**(n)
lleg**ar**	yo lleg**o**	**g → gu**	lle**gue**(n)
empez**ar**	yo empiez**o**	**z → c**	empie**ce**(n)

3. These verbs also have irregular forms for the *Ud./Uds.* commands:

dar	→	**dé (den)**	ir	→	**vaya(n)**	ser	→	**sea(n)**
estar	→	**esté(n)**	saber	→	**sepa(n)**			

4. Finally, compare the forms of the *tú* and *Ud./Uds.* commands:

	***Tú* commands**		***Ud./Uds.* commands**	
	affirmative	**negative**	**affirmative**	**negative**
hablar	habl**a**	no habl**es**	habl**e**(**n**)	no habl**e**(**n**)
comer	com**e**	no com**as**	com**a**(**n**)	no com**a**(**n**)
pedir	pid**e**	no pid**as**	pid**a**(**n**)	no pid**a**(**n**)

¿? Now you are ready to complete the ***Preparación y práctica*** activities for this chunk online.

10-14 Consejos Dos estudiantes de intercambio (*exchange students*) van a llegar a su universidad y necesitan la ayuda de ustedes con lo que deben y no deben hacer antes de venir a tu país. Túrnense para dar los consejos.

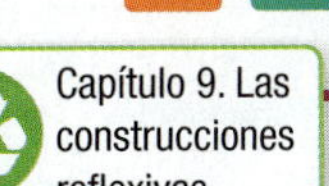

Capítulo 9. Las construcciones reflexivas, pág. 349.

MODELO E1: acostarse temprano la noche antes de viajar

E2: *Acuéstense temprano la noche antes de viajar.*

1. levantarse temprano el día del viaje
2. preparar el equipaje (*luggage*) el día anterior
3. llevar ropa cómoda
4. no ponerse nervioso/a
5. evitar el alcohol
6. tener su pasaporte a mano (*on hand*)
7. sentarse en el asiento correcto
8. dormirse en el avión

10-15 La multa

Termina el diálogo entre Mayra y el policía. Después presenta la escena con un/a compañero/a.

Capítulo 9. Un resumen de los pronombres de complemento directo, indirecto y reflexivos, pág. 354.

MAYRA: Buenas noches. ¿Iba muy rápido, señor policía?

POLICÍA: Sí, señorita. (1) _________ (mostrarme) su licencia, por favor.

MAYRA: Aquí la tiene (*here you go*), señor. Sé que la foto es muy mala.

POLICÍA: No (2) _________ (preocuparse). Ahora, (3) _________ (contarme), señorita: ¿A qué velocidad (*speed*) iba?

MAYRA: Pues… la verdad es que no estoy segura. (4) _________ (decírmelo) usted.

POLICÍA: Iba a ochenta kilómetros por hora y el límite aquí es sesenta y cinco.

MAYRA: ¡Ay! ¡Mi padre me va a matar! Por favor, no (5) _________ (darme) una multa. Perdóneme. Le aseguro que voy a manejar mucho más lento ahora.

POLICÍA: No es mi decisión. Es la ley (*law*).

MAYRA: Entonces, por lo menos no (6) _________ (escribir) ochenta kilómetros por hora en la multa. (7) _________ (poner) setenta, por favor.

POLICÍA: No puedo hacer eso. Bueno, (8) _________ (tomarla).

MAYRA: (*silencio*)

POLICÍA: Y no (9) _________ (manejar) tan rápido en el futuro. (10) _______ (tener) más cuidado.

10-16 El transporte rápido

El TransMilenio es un sistema de transporte masivo de pasajeros (*passengers*) en autobús que permite llegar rápidamente a cualquier (*any*) lugar de la ciudad de Bogotá. Lee las siguientes reglas del TransMilenio y completa la lista con mandatos formales. Luego, compártela con un/a compañero/a.

entrar	llevar	pagar	pararse (*to stand*)
permitir	respetar	evitar	transitar (*to enter/exit*)

MODELO Siempre <u>evite</u> correr.

Instrucciones para el uso adecuado (*suitable*) del sistema:

1. Cuando espere al autobús, ________ detrás de la línea amarilla de seguridad.
2. Antes de entrar, ________ que salgan los pasajeros.
3. _______ con su tarjeta al entrar.
4. Al usar las rampas, túneles o plataformas, ________ por la derecha.
5. No ______ paquetes (*packages*) grandes ni mascotas (*pets*).
6. No ______ en el autobús en estado de embriaguez (*intoxication*).
7. ______ las sillas azules que son para personas con discapacidad, mujeres embarazadas, niños pequeños y ancianos.

¿Cómo nos movemos?

El saber manejar un auto no suele ser tan importante en los países hispanohablantes como en los Estados Unidos. Por lo general, la gente camina más y usa el transporte público, ya sea el autobús, el metro o el taxi. Las personas que sí quieren conducir generalmente tienen que tomar un curso en una escuela privada de conducir.

En Colombia, por ejemplo, para obtener (*get*) una licencia de conducir es necesario:

- tener 16 años.
- saber leer y escribir.
- aprobar un examen teórico o presentar un certificado de aptitud en conducción (*driving*) emitido por una escuela aprobada (*approved*) por el Ministerio de Educación Nacional en coordinación con el Ministerio de Transporte.
- presentar un certificado de aptitud física y mental expedido por (*completed by*) un médico.

Una de las escuelas de conducir más conocidas en Colombia es Conducir Colombia. Los cursos y los precios varían según el tipo de licencia que necesita el conductor. Para una licencia básica, ofrecen 20 clases por unos 200 dólares, y para una licencia comercial, hay cursos de 30 clases por unos 325 dólares.

Preguntas

1. ¿Sabes conducir? ¿Cuándo aprendiste? ¿Quién te enseñó? ¿Cuándo sacaste la licencia de conducir?
2. Según la lectura, ¿crees que es generalmente más fácil o más difícil obtener una licencia en Colombia que en los Estados Unidos? Explica.

10-17 La gasolinera

Capítulo 8. Los pronombres de complemento indirecto, pág. 313; Los pronombres de complemento directo e indirecto usados juntos, pág. 321.

Ustedes acaban de llegar a una gasolinera con taller mecánico. Túrnense para decirle al mecánico lo que necesitan.

MODELO No pueden abrir el baúl.
Ábranos el baúl, por favor. / Ábranoslo, por favor.

1. Necesitan gasolina.
2. El parabrisas está sucio.
3. El limpiaparabrisas no funciona.
4. El motor tiene un ruido extraño.
5. Las llantas necesitan aire.
6. El aceite está sucio.

10-18 ¿Cómo contestaría tu profe de español?

Capítulo 2. La sala de clase, pág. 69.

Túrnense para hacer los papeles de estudiante (**E**) y profesor/a (**P**).

MODELO E: ¿Debemos hacer la tarea para mañana?

P: *Sí, hagan la tarea para mañana. / Sí, háganla para mañana.*

1. ¿Debemos traer el cuaderno a la clase?
2. ¿Podemos llegar cinco minutos tarde?
3. ¿Hay que hablar en español todo el tiempo?
4. ¿Tenemos que tomar un examen mañana?
5. ¿Podemos usar nuestros apuntes durante el examen?
6. ¿Está bien si no venimos a clase mañana?
7. ¿Podemos desayunar en la sala de clase?
8. ¿Buscamos la lectura en Internet?
9. ¿Empezamos la tarea en clase?
10. ¿Podemos salir temprano?

10-19 ¡A su servicio!

Capítulo 3. La casa, pág. 106; Los muebles y otros objetos de la casa, pág. 114; Los quehaceres de la casa, pág. 117.

Ustedes son compañeros/as de apartamento y acaban de ganar el concurso ¡A su servicio! Reciben como premio (*award*) la ayuda de Jaime, un mayordomo (*butler*), por una semana. Díganle **ocho** cosas que quieren que haga (*you want him to do*) para ayudarlos hoy con los quehaceres. Después, díganle **tres** cosas que no debe hacer.

MODELO *Jaime, saque la basura, por favor.*

¿Cómo andas? I

Having completed **Comunicación I,** I now can…

	Feel confident	Need to review
• discuss modes of transportation. (p. 386)	☐	☐
• pronounce the letters *b* and *v*. (p. 387 and online)	☐	☐
• influence others and give advice. (p. 391)	☐	☐
• give orders and instructions. (p. 396)	☐	☐
• list some public transportation options and discuss procedures for getting a driver's license. (p. 399)	☐	☐

Comunicación II

4 VOCABULARIO

El viaje Sharing about travel

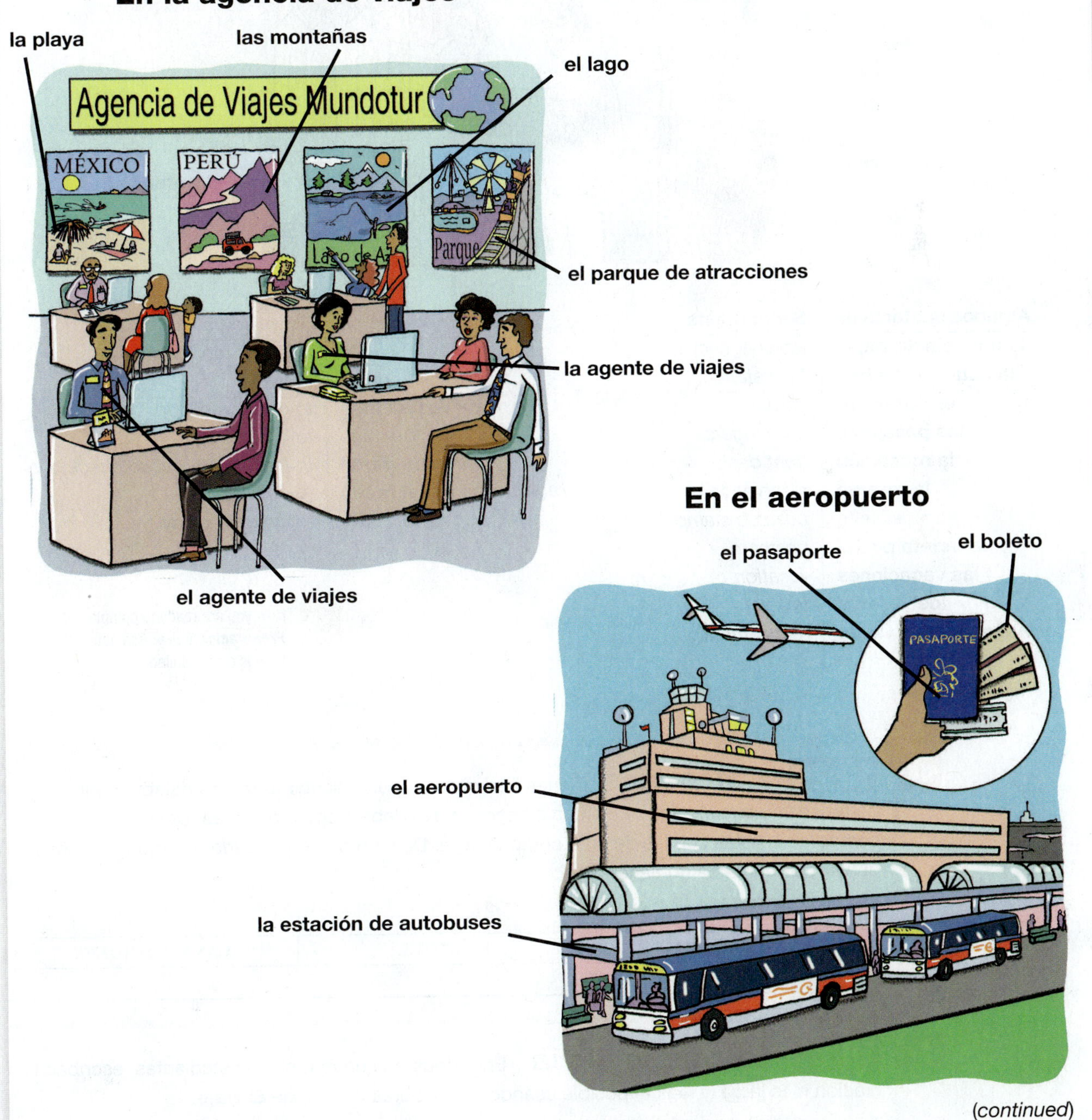

(*continued*)

En el hotel

Algunos sustantivos	*Some nouns*
la agencia de viajes	*travel agency*
la estación de tren	*train station*
el extranjero	*abroad*
los pasajeros	*passengers*
la recepción	*front desk*
la reserva	*reservation*
el sello	*postage stamp*
la tarjeta postal	*postcard*
las vacaciones	*vacation*
los viajeros	*travelers*
el vuelo de ida y vuelta	*round-trip flight*

Algunos verbos	*Some verbs*
ir a pie	*to go on foot*
dejar	*to leave*
ir de vacaciones	*to go on vacation*
ir de viaje	*to go on a trip*
irse del hotel	*to leave the hotel; to check out*
registrarse (en el hotel)	*to check in*
volar (o → ue)	*to fly; to fly away*

¿? Now you are ready to complete the ***Preparación y práctica*** activities for this chunk online.

10-20 Categorías

Tienes tres minutos para escribir todas las palabras que pertenecen (*pertain*) a las siguientes categorías. No debes repetir palabras. Después, compara tus listas con las de un/a compañero/a. Date un punto por cada palabra que tienes que tu compañero/a no tiene.

EL AEROPUERTO	EL HOTEL	LAS VACACIONES

10-21 La competencia

En grupos de cuatro o cinco estudiantes, escriban la oración más larga (y lógica) posible usando las palabras nuevas de **El viaje**.

10-22 El Hotel Gran Marqués David Aragón tiene que hacer un viaje de negocios a Santa Marta, Colombia. Su esposa lo va a acompañar. La agente de viajes acaba de dejarles un mensaje con información sobre un hotel muy bueno en Santa Marta. Completa cada oración con la palabra o expresión apropiada.

1. Según la agente de viajes, el hotel no está muy lejos del __________.
2. Se puede tomar un __________ para ir del aeropuerto al centro de la ciudad.
3. En total, el hotel tiene __________ cuartos.
4. La agente piensa que el hotel tiene los mejores __________ de la ciudad.
5. Los restaurantes del hotel sirven comida típica de __________ y también comida __________.
6. Los restaurantes están abiertos desde las __________ de la mañana hasta las __________ de la noche.
7. La gente puede hacer ejercicio en el gimnasio las __________ horas del día.
8. También el hotel tiene una ____________ donde se pueden organizar excursiones.

10-23 ¿Quiénes lo hacen? Circula por la clase hasta encontrar a un/a estudiante que pueda contestar afirmativamente a tu pregunta. **¡OJO!** Debes usar el pretérito (**P**) en algunas de las preguntas.

Capítulo 5. El pretérito, pág. 197; Capítulo 7. Algunos verbos irregulares en el pretérito, pág. 284.

MODELO ¿Quién…?

siempre dejar una buena propina para el/la camarero/a (*housekeeper*) cuando va a un hotel

TIFFANY: *¿Siempre dejas una buena propina para el camarero cuando vas a un hotel?*

ROB: *Sí, siempre dejo una buena propina.*

TIFFANY: *Pues, firma aquí.*

_____Rob_____

¿QUIÉN…?		
siempre dejar una buena propina para el/la camarero/a cuando va a un hotel __________	ir a un parque de atracciones el año pasado __________	viajar al extranjero __________
ir a la playa el verano pasado __________	volar en avión __________	recibir tarjetas postales __________
quedarse en un hotel elegante una vez __________	esquiar en las montañas __________	tener más de dos maletas __________

10-24 Antes de ir Tu amigo/a tiene que ir a Venezuela para una reunión (*meeting*) de negocios. Dale **cinco** consejos sobre lo que debe o no debe hacer para prepararse para el viaje y compara tu lista con la de tu compañero/a.

MODELO 1. *Busca tu pasaporte.*

10-25 Un joven increíble Su profesor/a les va a dar información sobre Jordan Romero, un alpinista mexicoamericano muy interesante. Luego, van a preparar una entrevista entre Jordan y un/a reportero/a. Completen los siguientes pasos.

Paso 1 Preparen una lista de preguntas para Jordan.

MODELO
1. ¿Cuándo y dónde naciste?
2. ¿Adónde viajaste cuando tenías diez años?
3. ¿Cómo viajaste... ?

Paso 2 Inventen respuestas lógicas para las preguntas.

MODELO E1: *¿Cuándo y dónde naciste?*
E2: *Nací en Bear Lake, California, el doce de julio del año 1996.*

Paso 3 Hagan los papeles de Jordan y el/la reportero/a.

10-26 Las mejores vacaciones Piensa en tus mejores vacaciones al contestar las siguientes preguntas. Después, circula por la clase para entrevistar a tus compañeros/as.

1. ¿Adónde fuiste?
2. ¿Cómo viajaste?
3. ¿Dónde te quedaste?
4. ¿Cuánto tiempo estuviste allí?
5. ¿Qué hiciste durante aquellas vacaciones especiales?
6. ¿A quién le mandaste mensajes de texto?, ¿fotos?
7. ¿Publicaste fotos o videos en una red social?

Venezuela, país de aventuras

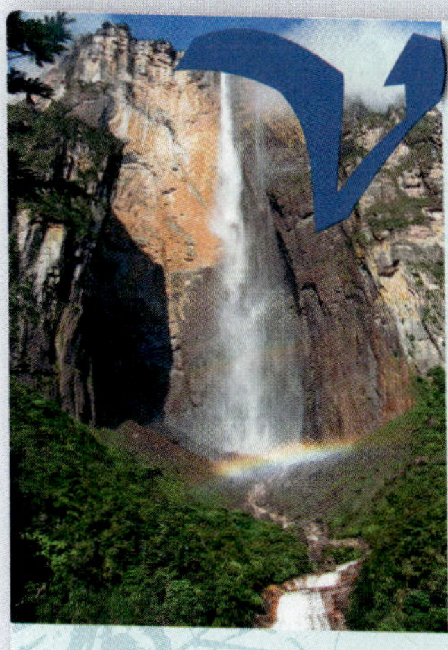

Venezuela, país de aventuras

¿Es Ud. aventurero/a? En Venezuela tenemos muchas oportunidades para conocer nuestro país a base de la aventura. Le proponemos *(propose)* una excursión de dos días en el Canaima. El primer día le ofrecemos un paseo en barco por la laguna Ucaima y una visita al Salto Ucaima. La excursión del segundo día le permite conocer el Salto Ángel, donde podemos nadar al pie de la cascada *(waterfall)*.

Si le gusta hacer trekking, puede disfrutar de una excursión a los tepuyes (una palabra indígena que significa "montaña"). Se puede subir el Pico Humboldt; a unos 4.942 m.s.n.m.; es el segundo pico más alto del país. Una excursión de este tipo está dentro de los considerados "deportes extremos" que se pueden practicar.

Si quiere combinar la aventura con una estancia en un hotel de lujo *(luxury)*, debe considerar la isla de Margarita. Está situada al norte de Caracas a sólo treinta y cinco minutos en avión o a un par de horas en ferry. Allí puede disfrutar de todos los deportes de agua, pescar, jugar al golf y explorar las numerosas y variadas playas. Por la noche hay restaurantes, clubes de baile, bares y casinos. Para informarse mejor, póngase en contacto hoy con su agencia de viajes preferida.

Preguntas

1. ¿Qué puedes hacer durante la excursión en el Canaima?, ¿en la excursión a los tepuyes?, ¿en la isla de Margarita?
2. De las aventuras que ofrece Venezuela, ¿cuál prefieres? ¿Por qué?
3. ¿Eres aventurero/a? ¿Cuál es la aventura más atrevida que has tenido (*you have had*)?

5 GRAMÁTICA

El comparativo y el superlativo

Comparing people, places, and things

El comparativo

Just as English does, Spanish uses comparisons to specify which of two people, places, or things has a lesser, equal, or greater degree of a particular quality.

1. The formula for comparing unequal things follows the same pattern as in English:

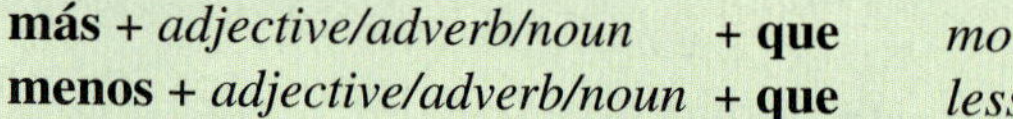

más + *adjective/adverb/noun*	+ **que**	*more… than*
menos + *adjective/adverb/noun*	+ **que**	*less… than*

Los hoteles son **más** caros **que** los moteles. — *Hotels are **more** expensive **than** motels.*

Este botones sube las maletas **más** rápidamente **que** aquel botones. — *This bellhop brings up the suitcases **faster than** that bellhop.*

En esta ciudad hay **menos** hoteles **que** moteles. — *In this city there are **fewer** hotels **than** motels.*

- When comparing numbers, **de** is used instead of **que**:

  El Hotel Estrella de Bogotá tiene **más de** doscientos cuartos. — *The Estrella Hotel has **more than** two hundred rooms.*

2. The formula for comparing two or more *equal* things also follows the same pattern as in English:

tan + *adjective/adverb* + **como**	*as… as*
tanto(a/os/as) + *noun* + **como**	*as much/many… as*

La agencia de viajes Mundotur es **tan** conocida **como** la agencia Sol. — *The Mundotur travel agency is **as** well known **as** the Sol travel agency.*

Estos vuelos son **tan** caros **como** esos. — *These flights are **as** expensive **as** those.*

Mi coche va **tan** rápido **como** un coche de carreras. — *My car goes **as** fast **as** a race car.*

No tengo **tantas** maletas **como** tú. — *I don't have **as many** suitcases **as** you (do).*

No hay **tanto** tráfico **como** ayer. — *There isn't **as** much traffic **as** yesterday.*

El superlativo

1. **To compare three or more people or things, use the superlative. The formula for expressing the superlative is:**

   el, la, los, las (*noun*) + **más/menos** + *adjective* (+ **de**)

La agencia de viajes Viking es **la** agencia **más** popular **de** nuestro pueblo. — *The Viking Travel Agency is **the most** popular (travel) agency **in** our town.*

—¿Es el aeropuerto Hartsfield de Atlanta **el** aeropuerto **más** concurrido **de** los Estados Unidos? — *Is Atlanta's Hartsfield Airport **the busiest** airport **in** the United States?*

—Sí, ¡y el aeropuerto de mi ciudad es **el menos** concurrido! — *Yes, and my city's airport is **the least** busy!*

2. **The following adjectives have irregular comparative and superlative forms.**

Adjective		Comparative		Superlative	
bueno/a	*good*	**mejor**	*better*	**el/la mejor**	*the best*
malo/a	*bad*	**peor**	*worse*	**el/la peor**	*the worst*
joven	*young*	**menor**	*younger*	**el/la menor**	*the youngest*
viejo/a	*old*	**mayor**	*older*	**el/la mayor**	*the eldest*

Comparative:

Mi clase de español es **mejor que** mis otras clases. — *My Spanish class is **better than** my other classes.*

Superlative:

Mi clase de español es **la mejor de** mis clases. — *My Spanish class is **the best (one) of** my classes.*

¿? Now you are ready to complete the ***Preparación y práctica*** activities for this chunk online.

10-27 ¿Cierto o falso?

¿Qué sabes de geografía? Indica si las siguientes oraciones son ciertas (**C**) o falsas (**F**); si son falsas, corrígelas. Después, compara tus oraciones con las de un/a compañero/a siguiendo el modelo.

MODELO México es más grande que Uruguay.

E1: *¿Es México más grande que Uruguay?*

E2: *Sí. México es mucho más grande que Uruguay.*

1. México es más pequeño que Colombia.
2. Venezuela es casi tan grande como Colombia.
3. Panamá es más grande que Venezuela.
4. De estos países, Panamá es el más pequeño.
5. Colombia es más grande que los Estados Unidos.
6. Caracas es tan grande como México, D.F.

10-28 ¡Así son!

Completa los siguientes pasos.

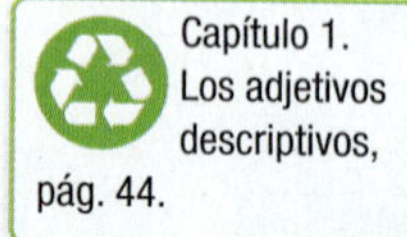
Capítulo 1. Los adjetivos descriptivos, pág. 44.

Paso 1 Piensa en una persona para cada categoría y escribe el nombre. Después, escribe un adjetivo para describir a la persona.

MODELO persona de la clase

Adela, alta

1. actriz de la televisión
2. actor del cine
3. jugador de fútbol/béisbol/tenis/etc.
4. cantante de rock/jazz/ópera
5. profesor/a de la universidad
6. persona de la política

Paso 2 En parejas, túrnense para hacer comparaciones de las personas para cada categoría.

E1: *Tengo Adela, y ella es alta.*

E2: *Tengo Daniel y es simpático.*

E1: *Adela es más alta que Daniel.*

E2: *Sí, y Daniel es tan simpático como Adela.*

Paso 3 Ahora júntense dos parejas para formar grupos de cuatro. Revisen los adjetivos que usaron para cada categoría, y entre todos, creen un superlativo.

MODELO

E1: *persona de la clase, alta*

GRUPO: *La persona más alta de la clase es Adela.*

E2: *simpático*

GRUPO: *La persona más simpática de la clase es Elena.*

10-29 ¿El mejor o el peor?

Circula por la clase para averiguar qué opinan tus compañeros sobre "los mejores" y "los peores". Necesitas al menos **dos** opiniones para cada categoría.

Estrategia

You can also use the following expressions to express your opinions: *Pienso que…*, *Creo que…*, *Estoy de acuerdo*, *No estoy de acuerdo*, and *En mi opinión…*

MODELO E1: *¿Cuál es el mejor supermercado?*

E2: *En mi opinión, Healthy Foods es el mejor supermercado. Y tú, ¿qué piensas?*

E1: *Creo que el mejor supermercado es Alpine Grocery.*

	ESTUDIANTE 1	ESTUDIANTE 2
1. el mejor supermercado		
el peor supermercado		
2. el mejor almacén		
el peor almacén		
3. el mejor restaurante		
el peor restaurante		
4. el mejor aeropuerto		
el peor aeropuerto		
5. el mejor hotel		
el peor hotel		
6. el mejor parque de atracciones		
el peor parque de atracciones		
7. la mejor playa		
la peor playa		
8. el mejor lugar para la luna de miel (*honeymoon*)		
el peor lugar para la luna de miel		
9. la mejor aerolínea (*airline*)		
la peor aerolínea		
10. el mejor coche		
el peor coche		
11. la mejor pizza		
la peor pizza		
12. la mejor clase		
la peor clase		
13. el mejor día de la semana		
el peor día da la semana		
14. el mejor café		
el peor café		

10-30 Adivina, adivinanza Trae un objeto personal a la clase y escribe **cinco** oraciones sobre él, usando las formas comparativas. No digas el nombre de tu objeto. Lee las oraciones en grupos de cuatro o cinco estudiantes para ver si tus compañeros pueden adivinar (*guess*) lo que es.

Estrategia

One way to approach **10-30** is to arrange your clues from most general to most specific.

MODELO un bolígrafo

E1: 1. Es más grande que un anillo.
2. Es tan importante como un libro.
3. Es menos largo que mi zapato.
4. Seguramente ustedes lo usan tanto como yo.
5. Es tan útil como un lápiz.

E2: *¡Es un bolígrafo!*

10-31 El transporte Habla con un/a compañero/a sobre todos los medios de transporte que usan o han usado (*have used*) y compárenlos, pensando en los aspectos positivos y negativos de cada uno.

MODELO E1: *Uso el coche más que el metro pero el metro es más rápido que el coche.*

E2: *Nunca voy en metro porque no hay metro en mi ciudad. Voy mucho en autobús porque es más barato que un taxi y es más rápido que mi bicicleta.*

10-32 Los mejores recuerdos (*memories*) Túrnense para escoger uno de los siguientes temas y describirle la situación a tu compañero/a. Debes mencionar cuándo y dónde ocurrió, quiénes estaban contigo y qué pasó.

Capítulo 5. El pretérito, págs. 197, 200; Capítulo 7. Algunos verbos irregulares en el pretérito, págs. 277, 284; Capítulo 8. El imperfecto, pág. 328; Capítulo 9. El pretérito y el imperfecto, pág. 364.

1. el mejor regalo que recibí
2. el mejor regalo que regalé (*gave*)
3. el mejor día de mi vida
4. el peor día de mi vida
5. las mejores vacaciones que tomé
6. las peores vacaciones que tomé

Escucha

Algunos viajes

Estrategia	
Listening for linguistic cues	You can enhance comprehension by listening for linguistic cues. For example, verb endings can tell you who is participating and whether the incident is taking place now, already took place in the past, or will take place in the future.

10-33 Antes de escuchar

Contesta las preguntas, pensando en viajes pasados y futuros.

1. ¿Cuáles fueron tus viajes más memorables?
2. ¿Hay un viaje en particular que le puedes recomendar a un/a amigo/a?
3. ¿Adónde quieres ir en tu próximo viaje?

Memo, Cristina y Rosa hablan de unos viajes interesantes.

10-34 A escuchar

Paso 1 Memo, Cristina y Rosa charlan sobre algunos viajes que ya tomaron y otros viajes que quieren tomar en el futuro. Escucha su conversación para tener una idea general de lo que dicen.

Paso 2 Cristina habla de Venezuela. Escucha otra vez y apunta todos los verbos que puedas que ella usa. ¿Cuál es el tiempo verbal que usa más? Entonces, es un viaje que…

a. hizo ya.

b. va a hacer.

c. quiere hacer.

Paso 3 Escucha una vez más para poder completar la siguiente actividad.

1. ¿Quién sale mañana para Colombia? Escribe los verbos que usa esta persona para hablar de su viaje.
2. ¿Habla Rosa de un viaje que hizo ya, va a hacer o quiere hacer? ¿Cómo lo sabes?

10-35 Después de escuchar

En grupos de tres o cuatro estudiantes, hablen de dos o tres lugares turísticos diferentes que conozcan (*you know*). ¿Qué tienen en común?

¡Conversemos!

10-36 Ayudante indispensable

Tu jefe/a viaja mucho para el negocio y necesita que tú le hagas los arreglos (*make the arrangements*) para su próximo viaje a Colombia. Crea un itinerario para tu jefe/a y dile lo que necesita hacer y cuándo, usando por lo menos **siete** mandatos. Tu compañero/a de clase va a ser el/la jefe/a y tiene que responder a tus arreglos, usando mandatos cuando sea necesario. ¿Van a usar mandatos formales o informales?

10-37 ¡Buen viaje!

Tienes fondos (*funds*) sin límite para tus próximas vacaciones. Planea un viaje para tu compañero/a de clase y tú. Después, descríbele el viaje a tu compañero/a y dile qué necesita hacer y cuándo, usando por lo menos **siete** mandatos. Tu compañero/a tiene que responder, también usando mandatos cuando sea necesario. ¿Van a usar mandatos formales o informales?

Escribe

Un reportaje

Estrategia

Using linking words

Linking words help you connect ideas and sentences so you can communicate more effectively. As you write your travel review, practice linking your ideas and sentences. Linking words you know include *y*, *o*, *pero*, *porque*, *que*, *cuando*, *antes de*, *después de*, *durante*, *para empezar*, *entonces*, *antes*, *después*, *de repente*, *finalmente*, *al final*, *por fin*, and *mientras*.

10-38 Antes de escribir Escoge un lugar turístico de Colombia o Venezuela e investígalo en Internet. Toma apuntes sobre los aspectos que encuentres más interesantes del lugar.

10-39 A escribir Organiza tus ideas y escribe un reportaje para una revista turística que incluya como mínimo la siguiente información:

1. dónde está
2. cómo llegar allí
3. qué actividades se pueden hacer
4. dónde uno puede quedarse (hotel de lujo, etc.)
5. el precio del viaje
6. este lugar es más interesante que…
7. este lugar es más/menos barato que…
8. este lugar es el más ______ porque…

10-40 Después de escribir Presenta tu reportaje a los compañeros de clase. Después de todas las presentaciones deben votar para elegir los **tres** lugares que desean visitar.

¿Cómo andas? II

Having completed **Comunicación II,** I now can…	Feel confident	Need to review
• share about travel. (p. 401)	☐	☐
• investigate travel and tourism opportunities in Venezuela. (p. 405)	☐	☐
• compare people, places, and things. (p. 406)	☐	☐
• focus on linguistic cues. (p. 411)	☐	☐
• communicate about travel plans. (p. 412)	☐	☐
• write and present a report using linking words. (p. 413)	☐	☐

Vistazo cultural

Colombia

Les presento mi país

Rosa María Gutiérrez Murcia

Mi nombre es Rosa María Gutiérrez Murcia y soy de Medellín, la segunda ciudad más grande de Colombia. El setenta y cinco por ciento de la población colombiana se concentra en los centros urbanos y las regiones montañosas del país. En Medellín disfrutamos del único sistema de metro del país que proporciona transporte a la gente que vive en las afueras de la ciudad. **¿Qué tipos de transporte público hay en tu pueblo o ciudad?** Bogotá, la capital, tiene el sistema más extenso de ciclorrutas (caminos para bicicletas) del país; gracias a este sistema, la gente puede circular y disfrutar de los espacios públicos y verdes de la capital. Mi país es muy bello y tiene muchas atracciones para los turistas. Además, es el único país de Sudamérica que tiene costa en el Océano Pacífico y en el Mar Caribe.

El café es un producto de exportación importante en Colombia.

Objeto del Museo del Oro en Bogotá

El teleférico de Medellín conecta el centro de la ciudad con las zonas más altas.

ALMANAQUE

Nombre oficial: República de Colombia
Gobierno: República
Población: 44.205.293 (2010)
Idioma: español
Moneda: Peso colombiano (COP/$)

¿Sabías que...?

- En Zipaquirá, Colombia, hay una catedral única. ¡La catedral está situada a 600 pies adentro de una montaña de sal!
- Medellín fue la primera ciudad en el mundo en implementar un sistema de teleférico como medio de transporte público de tiempo completo (*full-time*).

Preguntas

1. ¿Qué tiene Colombia que no tiene ningún otro país del continente?
2. ¿Cómo se comparan los medios de transporte de Medellín y Bogotá con los de tu área?
3. ¿Qué tienen en común Colombia, Perú y Chile?

Vistazo cultural

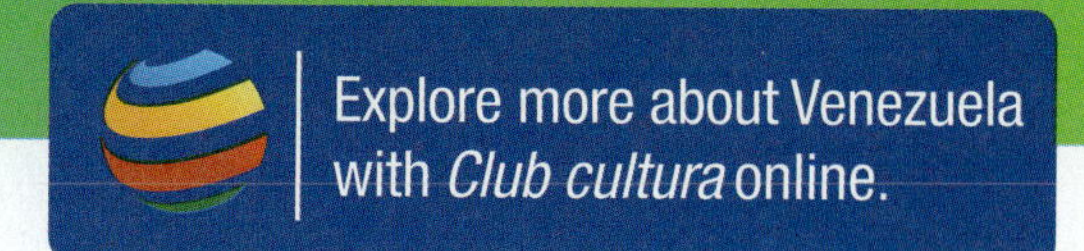

Venezuela

Les presento mi país

Joaquín Navas Posada

Mi nombre es Joaquín Navas Posada y soy de Maracaibo, Venezuela. Vivo con mi hermano mayor en la capital, Caracas, porque estudio arte en la Universidad Central de Venezuela. Mi hermano es ingeniero y trabaja en la industria petrolera. El petróleo es muy importante para la economía de Venezuela: es nuestro principal producto de exportación. **¿Qué industrias son importantes en tu región?** Vivir en la capital es agradable porque hay mucho que hacer, tanto para nosotros como para los turistas. Los turistas pueden visitar las playas de la costa caribeña o conocer uno de nuestros numerosos parques nacionales, como el Parque Nacional Canaima donde están los famosos tepuyes y el Salto Ángel, la catarata más alta del mundo. **¿Adónde te gusta viajar cuando tienes vacaciones?**

El área metropolitana de Caracas tiene más de cinco millones de habitantes.

A unos 978 metros de altura, el Salto Ángel es casi 20 veces más alto que las cataratas del Niágara.

Una estatua de Simón Bolívar, "El libertador"

ALMANAQUE

Nombre oficial:	República Bolivariana de Venezuela
Gobierno:	República federal
Población:	27.223.228 (2010)
Idiomas:	español (oficial); lenguas indígenas
Moneda:	Bolívar (Bs.)

¿Sabías que...?

- Simón Bolívar es considerado un héroe en Colombia, Venezuela, Ecuador, Perú, Panamá y Bolivia, por sus contribuciones a la independencia de estos países.
- En Mérida hay una heladería reconocida por los Récords Guinness por el mayor número de helados: tienen más de 600 sabores.

Preguntas

1. ¿Dónde vive Joaquín? ¿Le gusta? Explica.
2. ¿Cuál es la base principal de la economía venezolana?
3. Compara las banderas de Venezuela, Colombia y Ecuador. ¿Por qué son similares? ¿Qué diferencias hay?

Lectura

Carta al rey Carlos I

10-41 Antes de leer

Empareja cada término con su descripción apropiada.

1. Tenochtitlán _____
2. Hernán Cortés _____
3. 1519 _____
4. Moctezuma _____
5. Salamanca _____
6. la Ciudad de México _____
7. 1521 _____

a. una ciudad española
b. el líder azteca
c. un conquistador
d. año en que Cortés toma Tenochtitlán para España
e. ciudad construida sobre (*on*) las ruinas de Tenochtitlán
f. la capital del imperio azteca
g. año en que Cortés llega a la península de Yucatán

Estrategia

Asking yourself questions
Ask yourself check questions as you read, in order to help you summarize and organize information.

10-42 Mientras lees

Completa los siguientes pasos.

Paso 1 Lee el primer párrafo y elige la pregunta que mejor lo resuma (*summarizes it*).

a. ¿Tiene la ciudad múltiples entradas?
b. ¿Son grandes sus calles?
c. ¿Es una ciudad grande similar a otras en España?

Paso 2 Ahora lee el segundo párrafo y elige la pregunta que mejor lo resuma.

a. ¿Es un mercado muy popular con muchas mercancías?
b. ¿Es un mercado de comidas?
c. ¿Tiene la plaza portales grandes?

Paso 3 Continúa leyendo y escribe una pregunta para cada una de las secciones 3 a 5. Compara tus preguntas con las de tus compañeros.

Segunda carta al rey Carlos I de España (Descripción de Tenochtitlán, fragmento)

por Hernán Cortés

1 [...] Esta gran ciudad de Temixtitan (Tenochtitlán) está fundada en esta laguna salada, y desde la Tierra-Firme hasta el cuerpo (centro) de la dicha ciudad, por cualquier° parte que quisieren (quieren) entrar en ella, hay dos leguas*. Tiene cuatro entradas, todas de calzada (calle) hecha a mano, tan ancha como dos lanzas jinetas. Es tan grande la ciudad como Sevilla y Córdoba. Son las calles de ella, digo las principales, muy anchas y muy derechas,° [...] son la mitad (el 50%) de tierra,° y por la otra mitad es agua, por la cual andan en sus canoas [...] hay puentes° de muy anchas y muy grandes vigas recias;° por muchas de ellas pueden pasar diez a caballo [...]

any

straight / earth, dirt
bridges /
thick beams

2 Tiene esta ciudad muchas plazas, donde hay continuos mercados y trato de comprar y vender.° Tiene otra plaza tan grande como dos veces la de la ciudad de Salamanca, toda cercada (encerrada) de portales, donde hay cotidianamente arriba de setenta mil ánimas (personas) comprando y vendiendo; donde hay todos los géneros de mercaderías que en todas las tierras hay, [...] vituallas (provisiones), joyas de oro y de plata,° [...] de piedras, huesos,° conchas° y de plumas. También venden todo linaje (especie) de aves que hay en la tierra [...] y de algunas aves venden los cueros con su pluma y cabezas y pico. Venden conejos,° venados y perros pequeños, que crían° para comer.

sell

gold and silver
jewelry
bones / shells

rabbits / they raise

3 Hay calles de herbolarios,° donde hay todas las raíces° y yerbas medicinales que hay en la tierra. Hay casas como de boticarios (farmacéuticos) donde se venden las medicinas, así potables como ungüentos° [...]

herbalists / roots

salves

4 Hay casas como de barberos, donde lavan y rapan (afeitan) las cabezas. Hay casas donde dan de comer y beber por precio. [...]

5 Hay en esta gran plaza una [...] audiencia (tribunal), donde están siempre sentadas 10 o 12 personas, que son jueces° y libran (resuelven) todos los casos y cosas que en mercado acaecen (pasan), y mandan castigar (sentencian) los delincuentes.

judges

El emperador azteca Moctezuma y Hernán Cortés en Tenochtitlán

*Una legua es la distancia que una persona puede caminar en una hora (aproximadamente tres millas).

10-43 Después de leer Completa las siguientes actividades.

1. Lee las oraciones y decide si cada una es **cierta** o **falsa.**

C	F	
☐	☐	a. La ciudad está situada en las montañas.
☐	☐	b. La distancia entre una entrada y el centro de la ciudad son seis millas.
☐	☐	c. Tenochtitlán es similar a Sevilla.
☐	☐	d. Los residentes de Tenochtitlán solo pueden viajar por canales de agua.
☐	☐	e. En el mercado puedes comprar cualquier tipo de ave.
☐	☐	f. En el mercado puedes comprar ingredientes, pero no hay lugares para comer.
☐	☐	g. Los aztecas tienen un sistema de justicia.

2. Identifica los artículos que se pueden comprar en el mercado.
   a. joyas de plumas
   b. perros
   c. barcos
   d. zapatos
   e. medicinas
   f. caballos
   g. lanzas
   h. comidas y bebidas
3. ¿Cuál es la función de los jueces en el mercado?
   a. poner el precio
   b. castigar a los criminales
   c. colectar multas
4. En tu opinión, ¿qué parte de Tenochtitlán es la más interesante? Explica.

10-44 Visita de Cortés

Imagina que Hernán Cortés visita tu ciudad. Escribe una descripción desde el punto de vista de Cortés de sus primeras impresiones sobre tu ciudad. Puedes usar la lectura como modelo.

Media Share

10-45 Un cartel de Tenochtitlán

Con base en las descripciones que Cortés da en la *Lectura*, haz un cartel (*poster*) para ilustrar sus primeras impresiones de Tenochtitlán. Puedes usar dibujos, fotos de revistas o de Internet y otros materiales. Presenta tu cartel a la clase. ¡Sé creativo/a!

For additional *Lectura* activities, go to *¡Anda!* online.

Y por fin, ¿cómo andas?

Having completed this chapter, I now can...

	Feel confident	Need to review
Comunicación I		
• discuss modes of transportation. (p. 386)	☐	☐
• pronounce the letters *b* and *v*. (p. 387 and online)	☐	☐
• influence others and give advice. (p. 391)	☐	☐
• give orders and instructions. (p. 396)	☐	☐
Comunicación II		
• share about travel. (p. 401)	☐	☐
• compare people, places, and things. (p. 406)	☐	☐
• focus on linguistic cues. (p. 411)	☐	☐
• communicate about travel plans. (p. 412)	☐	☐
• write and present a report using linking words. (p. 413)	☐	☐
Cultura		
• list some public transportation options and discuss procedures for getting a driver's license. (p. 399)	☐	☐
• investigate travel and tourism opportunities in Venezuela. (p. 405)	☐	☐
• share information about Colombia and Venezuela. (pp. 414–415)	☐	☐
Lectura		
• read a fragment from *Segunda carta al rey Carlos I de España* by Hernán Cortés. (p. 416)	☐	☐
Comunidades		
• use Spanish in real-life contexts. (online)	☐	☐

Vocabulario **activo**

Los medios de transporte	*Modes of transportation*
el autobús	*bus*
el avión	*airplane*
el barco	*boat*
la bicicleta	*bicycle*
el camión	*truck*
el carro / el coche	*car*
el metro	*subway*
la moto (motocicleta)	*motorcycle*
el taxi	*taxi*
el tren	*train*

Algunos sustantivos	*Some nouns*
la autopista	*highway; freeway*
el boleto	*ticket*
la calle	*street*
el estacionamiento	*parking*
la gasolinera	*gas station*
la licencia (de conducir)	*driver's license*
la multa	*traffic ticket; fine*
la parada	*bus stop*
el peatón / la peatona	*pedestrian*
el/la policía	*policeman/policewoman*
el ruido	*noise*
el semáforo	*traffic light*
el taller mecánico	*auto repair shop*
el tráfico	*traffic*

Algunas partes de un vehículo	*Parts of a vehicle*
el aire acondicionado	*air conditioning*
el baúl	*trunk*
la calefacción	*heat*
el limpiaparabrisas	*windshield wiper*
la llanta	*tire*
la llave	*key*
el motor	*motor; engine*
el parabrisas	*windshield*
el volante	*steering wheel*

Algunos verbos	*Some verbs*
arreglar / hacer la maleta	*to pack a suitcase*
bajar (de)	*to get down (from); to get off (of)*
cambiar	*to change*
dejar	*to leave*
doblar	*to turn*
entrar	*to enter*
estacionar	*to park*
funcionar	*to work; to function*
hacer (la) cola	*to stand in line*
ir a pie	*to go on foot*
ir de vacaciones	*to go on vacation*
ir de viaje	*to go on a trip*
irse del hotel	*to leave the hotel; to check out*
llenar el tanque	*to fill up; to fill up the tank*
manejar / conducir	*to drive*
registrarse (en el hotel)	*to check in*
revisar	*to check; to overhaul*
sacar la licencia	*to get a driver's license*
subir (a)	*to go up; to get on*
viajar	*to travel*
visitar	*to visit*
volar (o → ue)	*to fly; to fly away*

El viaje	*The trip*
el aeropuerto	*airport*
la agencia de viajes	*travel agency*
el/la agente de viajes	*travel agent*
la estación (de tren, de autobús)	*(train, bus) station*
el extranjero	*abroad*
la maleta	*suitcase*
el pasaporte	*passport*
los pasajeros	*passengers*
la reserva	*reservation*
el sello	*postage stamp*
la tarjeta postal	*postcard*
las vacaciones	*vacation*
los viajeros	*travelers*
el vuelo de ida y vuelta	*round-trip flight*

El hotel	*The hotel*
el botones	*bellhop*
el cuarto doble	*double room*
el cuarto individual	*single room*
la propina	*tip*
la recepción	*front desk*

Algunos lugares	*Some places*
el lago	*lake*
las montañas	*mountains*
el parque de atracciones	*theme park*
la playa	*beach*

Un arrecife de coral

11 El mundo actual

¿Qué peligros (*dangers*) existen hoy en día para el medio ambiente (*environment*)? Hay más de 16.000 especies de animales y plantas en peligro de extinción. Las selvas (*jungles*), las cuales contienen más del 50% de todas las especies de plantas y animales existentes, se reducen drásticamente cada año. Hay una isla de plástico dos veces el tamaño de Texas en el océano Pacífico.

Preguntas

1. ¿Dónde hay selvas tropicales?
2. ¿En qué ciudades o países hay mucha contaminación del aire?
3. ¿Puedes nombrar algunos animales que están en peligro de extinción?

¿Sabías que...?

En el pueblo de Bañado Sur, Paraguay, hay una "Orquesta Reciclada" formada por niños y jóvenes. En esta sinfónica única, todos los instrumentos musicales son elaborados con materiales sacados del vertedero (*landfill*) de Cateura.

El zunzuncito (*hummingbird*) cubano, el más pequeño del mundo

Las tres Rs: reducir, reciclar, reutilizar

Learning Outcomes

By the end of this chapter, you will be able to:

- ✔ communicate details about the environment, animals, and their habitats.
- ✔ share information about politics and current affairs.
- ✔ describe what is happening at the moment, and specify location and other information.
- ✔ comment on what is necessary, possible, probable, and improbable.
- ✔ communicate about world issues.
- ✔ employ persuasive writing to create a public announcement.
- ✔ exchange interesting facts about Cuba, Puerto Rico, and the Dominican Republic.
- ✔ read a legend from Mexico.

Comunicación I

1 VOCABULARIO

Los animales Describing animals and their habitats

Los animales de la granja

Algunos sustantivos	*Some nouns*
los animales de la granja	*farm animals*
los animales domésticos / las mascotas	*domesticated animals; pets*
el insecto	*insect*
la mosca	*fly*
la rata	*rat*
el ratón	*mouse*
la granja / la finca	*farm*

Algunos verbos	*Some verbs*
cuidar	*to take care of*
preocuparse (por)	*to worry about; to concern oneself with*

Los animales salvajes

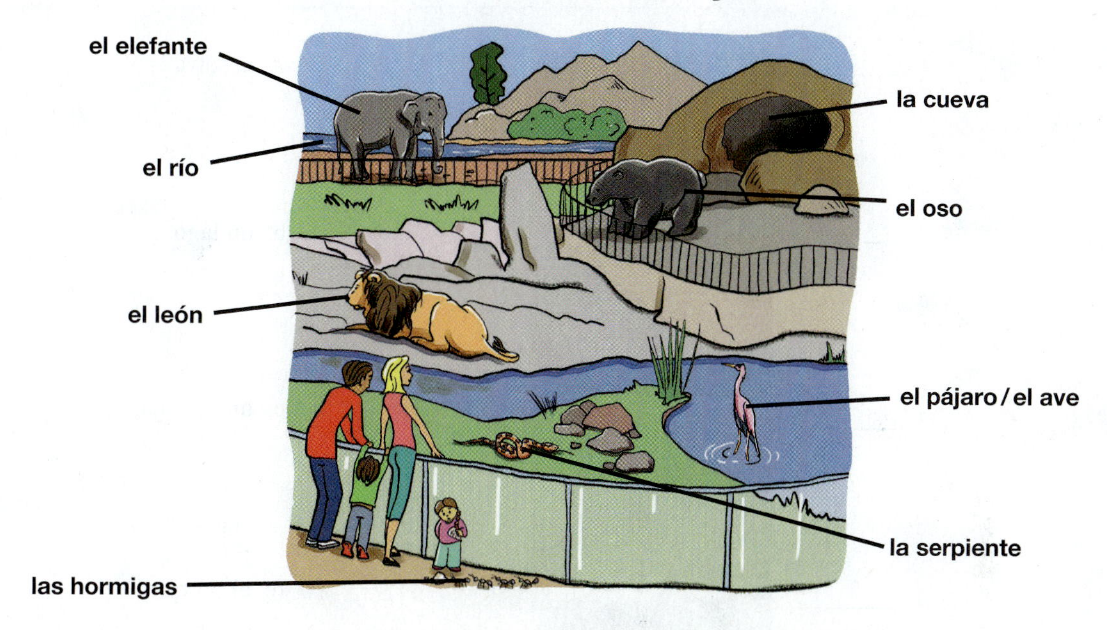

Otras palabras	Other words
los animales salvajes	*wild animals*
los animales en peligro de extinción	*endangered animals*
el océano	*ocean*
peligroso/a	*dangerous*
la selva	*jungle*

¿? Now you are ready to complete the ***Preparación y práctica*** activities for this chunk online.

PRONUNCIACIÓN

Review of Word Stress and Accent Marks

Go to *¡Anda!* online to review word stress and accent marks.

11·1 La fauna Organiza los animales del vocabulario con un/a compañero/a según las siguientes categorías: **insecto, reptil, mamífero, ave** y **anfibio**.

INSECTO	REPTIL	MAMÍFERO	AVE	ANFIBIO

11·2 ¿Dónde viven?

Digan en qué lugar viven los siguientes animales.

1. ________ 
2. ________ 
3. ________ 
4. ________  
5. ________ 
6. ________ 

a. la selva
b. un lago
c. una granja
d. el bosque
e. un hoyo
f. un árbol

11·3 ¿Qué sabemos?

Termina las siguientes oraciones con lo que sabes de los animales y dónde viven. Después compara tus oraciones con las de un/a compañero/a.

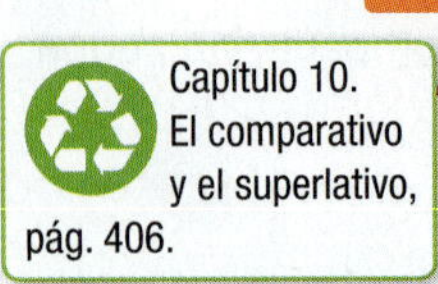

Capítulo 10. El comparativo y el superlativo, pág. 406.

MODELO Los insectos más molestos son…

Los insectos más molestos son las moscas y los mosquitos.

1. Los animales de la granja más grandes son…
2. Los animales de la granja más pequeños son…
3. Los animales domésticos más comunes en mi familia y entre mis amigos son…
4. El animal salvaje más peligroso es…
5. El animal salvaje más grande es…
6. Los animales del bosque más interesantes son…

11-4 Las preferencias Completa los siguientes pasos.

Estrategia

When you write in Spanish you are not expected to be as articulate as you are in your native language. Try to limit, as much as possible, your responses to the vocabulary you know, and as always, you can circumlocute (see *Capítulo 8, Escribe* section).

Paso 1 Escribe los nombres de los **tres** animales que más te gustan y de los **tres** que menos te gustan y explica por qué. Usa verbos como **gustar, fascinar, encantar** y **molestar**. Después, comparte tus respuestas con un/a compañero/a.

MODELO *El animal que más me gusta es el caballo porque es muy fuerte y me encanta montar a caballo* (go horseback riding). *También me gustan los gatos y los perros porque puedo tenerlos en casa. Los tres animales que menos me gustan son… porque…*

Paso 2 Presenten sus respuestas a los compañeros de la clase. ¿Cuál es el animal que más les gusta? ¿Y el que menos les gusta?

11-5 ¿Qué opinas? Circula por la clase para averiguar (*find out*) con quiénes asocian tus compañeros las siguientes actividades.

Estrategia

Remember that when completing signature search activities like **11-5**, it is important to move quickly around the room, trying to get as many different signatures as possible, while asking and answering all questions in Spanish.

MODELO tener miedo de las serpientes

E1: *Hola, Sarah. ¿Quién tiene miedo de las serpientes?*

E2: *Hola, Tomás. Mi madre tiene mucho miedo de las serpientes.*

¿(A) QUIÉN…?		
tener miedo de las serpientes E1: La madre de Sarah E2: _____ E3: _____	ver un oso el año pasado E1: _____ E2: _____ E3: _____	gustarle los perros E1: _____ E2: _____ E3: _____
tener un animal doméstico E1: _____ E2: _____ E3: _____	odiar (*to hate*) los insectos E1: _____ E2: _____ E3: _____	saber ordeñar (*to milk*) una vaca E1: _____ E2: _____ E3: _____
ver un elefante o un león de niño/a E1: _____ E2: _____ E3: _____	gustarle cuidar animales E1: _____ E2: _____ E3: _____	tener un caballo E1: _____ E2: _____ E3: _____

11-6 Una encuesta Completen los siguientes pasos.

Paso 1 Háganse preguntas sobre los siguientes animales.

MODELO los perros

E1: *Meghan, ¿tienes perros?*

E2: *Sí, tengo dos perros. Se llaman Duke y Spot. ¿Y ustedes?*

E3: *Sí, en mi casa tenemos dos perros grandes. Se llaman Sissie y Pepper. Son viejos porque ya tienen ocho años.*

E4: *Nosotros no tenemos perros. Tenemos dos gatos que se llaman Snuggles y Lucky.*

E1: *Tengo un perro pequeño. Es chihuahua y se llama Bullet…*

1. los perros
2. los gatos
3. los caballos
4. los pájaros
5. las serpientes
6. los osos
7. las vacas
8. ¿?

Paso 2 Organicen las respuestas y compártanlas con los otros grupos.

MODELO *En nuestro grupo todos tenemos perros menos Jack. Los perros se llaman Duke, Spot, Sissie, Pepper y Bullet. Jack tiene dos gatos…*

2 VOCABULARIO

El medio ambiente Sharing details about the environment

Los desastres

El reciclaje

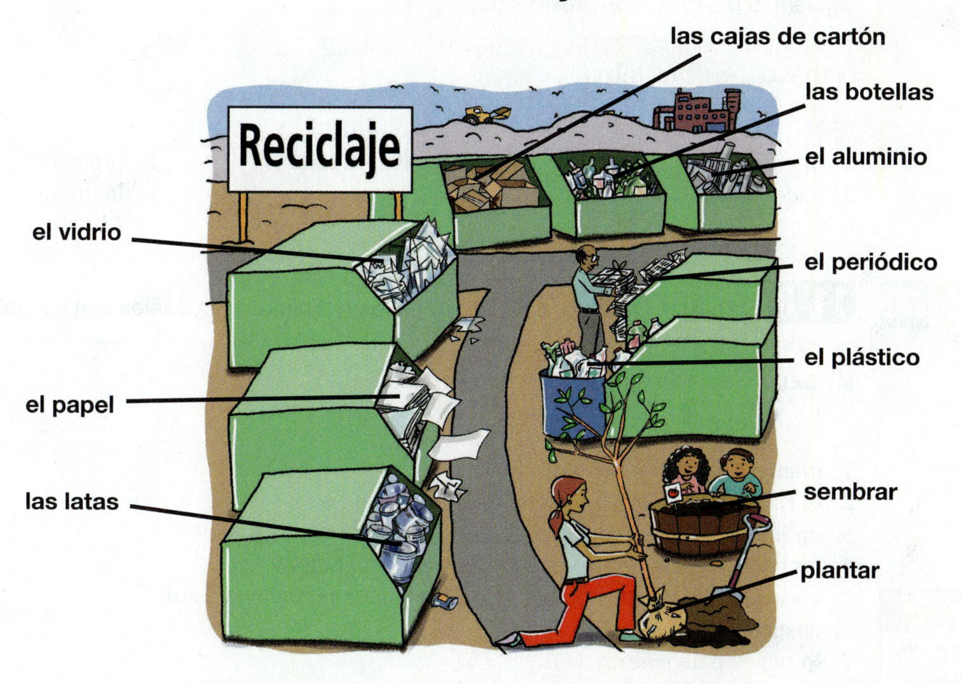

El planeta	*The planet*
el cielo	*sky; heaven*
la naturaleza	*nature*
el recurso natural	*natural resource*
la selva (tropical)	*(tropical) rain forest*
la tierra	*land; soil*
la Tierra	*Earth*

Los desastres	*Disasters*
el cambio climático	*climate change*
la destrucción	*destruction*
el efecto invernadero	*greenhouse effect*
la lluvia ácida	*acid rain*
la tragedia	*tragedy*

Otras palabras	*Other words*
el aire	*air*
la basura	*garbage*
la calidad	*quality*
la ecología	*ecology*
el vertedero	*dump*
puro/a	*pure*
vivo/a	*alive; living*

Algunos verbos	*Some verbs*
botar	*to throw away*
contaminar	*to pollute*
hacer daño	*to (do) damage; to harm*
matar	*to kill*
proteger	*to protect*
reciclar	*to recycle*
reforestar	*to reforest*
reutilizar	*to reuse*

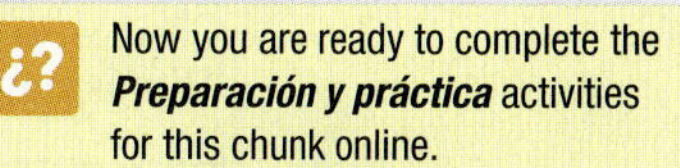
Now you are ready to complete the ***Preparación y práctica*** activities for this chunk online.

11-7 Asociaciones

Túrnense para decir qué asocian con cada una de las siguientes palabras o expresiones.

MODELO E1: reutilizar
E2: *reciclar*

1. la basura
2. hacer daño
3. el recurso natural
4. puro
5. proteger
6. la lluvia ácida

11-8 ¿Qué es...?

Aquí tienen las definiciones. ¿Cuáles son las palabras?

MODELO E1: lo opuesto de *contaminado*
E2: *puro*

1. plantar árboles donde antes los había
2. el estudio de la protección del medio ambiente
3. un lugar designado donde botamos la basura
4. no botar; buscar un uso nuevo para una lata, botella, etc.
5. estas plantas grandes protegen la Tierra de la potencia del sol
6. ensuciar el agua o el aire
7. lo opuesto de *muerto*
8. el posible resultado de la contaminación del aire

Fíjate

Note that *la Tierra* (Earth) is capitalized in Spanish, but *la tierra* (land, soil) is not.

11-9 Una presentación muy importante

Tomás tiene que dar una pequeña presentación sobre el medio ambiente en su clase de español mañana. Te llama para practicar lo que va a decir. Completa los siguientes pasos.

Paso 1 Mira los dibujos en las páginas 428–429 y repasa el vocabulario.

Paso 2 Escucha la presentación de Tomás y completa las oraciones con la palabra o expresión apropiada.

1. Muchos animales en Latinoamérica están en peligro de extinción a causa de la ____________________ y la destrucción de los hábitats.
2. Tres animales en peligro de extinción que Tomás menciona son los cocodrilos, las ____________________ y los ____________________ .
3. El ____________________ contribuye (*contributes*) a la destrucción del medio ambiente.
4. Tomás menciona que debemos ____________________ muchos materiales, como el ____________________ y las latas.
5. No podemos evitar algunos ____________________, como los huracanes.

11-10 Hay que reciclar

¿Qué hacen tu familia, tu comunidad y tu universidad para proteger el medio ambiente? Explícale a un/a compañero/a quién hace qué para proteger el medio ambiente. Después, cambien de papel.

MODELO *Yo voy a la universidad en bicicleta para evitar la contaminación del aire. Mi familia y yo reciclamos el plástico. Mi pueblo ofrece programas de prevención contra incendios. La universidad dio un seminario sobre el efecto invernadero y la destrucción de la capa de ozono.*

11-11 Entrevista

Circula por la clase haciéndoles a tus compañeros las siguientes preguntas.

1. ¿Cuáles son los recursos naturales más importantes donde vivimos?
2. ¿Dónde está el vertedero más cerca de aquí?
3. ¿Qué haces con tu basura?
4. ¿Dónde podemos reciclar en nuestra universidad?
5. ¿Qué reciclamos en nuestra universidad?
6. ¿Cómo es la calidad del aire donde vivimos?

11-12 El reportaje

¿Cómo podemos proteger el medio ambiente? Completa los siguientes pasos.

Paso 1 Escribe un párrafo de **seis** a **ocho** oraciones sobre qué podemos hacer en el futuro para proteger el medio ambiente. Puedes usar las ideas de la siguiente lista.

- sembrar muchas plantas
- reciclar o reutilizar el plástico, el vidrio, el papel y el cartón
- usar carros eléctricos
- proteger los animales en peligro de extinción
- apoyar las instituciones de conservación de los recursos naturales
- proteger la selva tropical
- reforestar los bosques
- usar el carro lo menos posible
- usar energía solar
- no prender (*turn on*) a menudo el aire acondicionado

MODELO *Para evitar la destrucción de los bosques y la selva tropical, no debemos cortar más árboles. En el futuro, debemos plantar más árboles para reforestar el bosque…*

Paso 2 Después, en grupos pequeños, comparen sus oraciones y juntos escriban un reportaje corto con sus recomendaciones para proteger el medio ambiente.

El Yunque: tesoro tropical

El Bosque Nacional del Caribe también se conoce como El Bosque Lluvioso de El Yunque, en honor al dios bondadoso (*kind*) indígena Yuquiyú. El Yunque es el único bosque lluvioso (selva) tropical que pertenece al Sistema de Bosques Nacionales de los Estados Unidos. Más de 100 billones de galones de agua de lluvia caen anualmente en el bosque sobre el monte El Toro (a 1.076 metros).

El Yunque es el bosque nacional más viejo y pequeño de las Américas. Sin embargo, cuenta con la mayor diversidad de flora. Hay más de 240 especies de árboles en un área de poco más de 11.760 hectáreas (28,000 acres). Además, sirve de refugio a muchas especies de pájaros incluyendo la cotorra o loro (*parrot*) puertorriqueño, el cual está en peligro de extinción. Desde 1975 el número de loros en El Yunque no sobrepasa (*doesn't exceed*) los 50, y después del huracán Hugo en el año 1989 quedaron solo 23 loros. Gracias a un programa para salvarlos, hoy en día existen unos 80. La ranita (rana pequeña) llamada *coquí* es original de Puerto Rico y hay muchas clases diferentes de coquíes en El Yunque.

El Bosque Nacional del Caribe es el lugar de Puerto Rico más frecuentado por los turistas. También lo frecuentan mucho las familias puertorriqueñas durante los fines de semana para pasar el día.

Preguntas

1. ¿Por qué es tan importante El Yunque?
2. ¿Cuáles son algunas de las características de El Yunque que lo hacen tan especial?

3 GRAMÁTICA

El presente progresivo

Describing what is happening at the moment

If you want to emphasize that an action is **occurring at the moment and is in progress**, you can use the ***present progressive*** tense rather than the present indicative.

The English present progressive is made up of a form of the verb ***to be* + *present participle* (*-ing*)**. Look at the following sentences and formulate a rule for creating the present progressive in Spanish. Use the questions on p. 434 to guide you.

—¿Qué *estás* **haciendo** este verano?	*What are you doing this summer?*
—*Estoy* **trabajando** en una granja, **cuidando** muchos animales.	*I'm working on a farm, taking care of a lot of animals.*
—¿Qué *están* **haciendo** Uds. para proteger el medio ambiente?	*What are you all doing to protect the environment?*
—*Estamos* **reciclando** el plástico y el vidrio y **reutilizando** el papel.	*We are recycling plastic and glass and reusing paper.*

Direct object pronouns, indirect object pronouns, and reflexive pronouns can either be placed before the conjugated form of **estar** or attached to the present participle:

—¿El plástico y el vidrio? **Los** estamos reciclando para proteger el medio ambiente.
—¿El plástico y el vidrio? Estamos reciclándo**los** para proteger el medio ambiente.

} *Plastic and glass? We are recycling them to protect the environment.*

Fíjate

The present progressive is *not* used to express the future.
Present progressive: *Estoy trabajando.* I am working (right now).
Future: *Voy a trabajar mañana.* I am going to work tomorrow.

(*continued*)

¡Explícalo tú!

1. In the first group of sample sentences in Spanish, what is the infinitive of the first verb in each sentence that is in *italics*?
2. What are the infinitives of **haciendo, trabajando, cuidando, reciclando,** and **reutilizando**?
3. How do you convert the infinitives to this new form of the verb?
4. In this new tense, the *present progressive*, do any words come between the two parts of the verb?
5. Therefore, your formula for forming the *present progressive* is:

   a form of the verb __________ + a verb ending in __________ or __________

Check your answers to the preceding questions in Appendix 1.

NOTE: The following are some verbs that have irregular present participles.

decir → diciendo
mentir → mintiendo
pedir → pidiendo
preferir → prefiriendo
perseguir → persiguiendo
repetir → repitiendo
seguir → siguiendo
servir → sirviendo

dormir → durmiendo
morir → muriendo

creer → creyendo
ir → yendo
leer → leyendo

Fíjate

For the *-ir* stem-changing verbs only, these vowel changes occur in the stem: *e* → *i* (*diciendo*) and *o* → *u* (*durmiendo*).

Fíjate

When the stem of an *-er* or *-ir* verb ends in a vowel, e.g. *creer* and *leer,* the present participle ends in *-yendo* (the *i* changes to *y*).

¿? Now you are ready to complete the ***Preparación y práctica*** activities for this chunk online.

11-13 Progresando Escuchen mientras su instructor/a les da las instrucciones de esta actividad. ¡Diviértanse!

MODELO E1: *sembrar, yo*
E2: *estoy sembrando*
E2: *proteger, nosotros*
E3: *estamos protegiendo*

11-14 ¿Tienes telepatía?

Es sábado. Túrnense para decir qué está haciendo su profesor/a en varios momentos del día.

Capítulo 8. *Gustar* y verbos como *gustar*, pág. 317.

MODELO E1: Le encantan los animales.
E2: *Está visitando el zoológico.*

1. Le gustan mucho las flores.
2. Le fascinan los carros eléctricos.
3. Dio una fiesta anoche. Le molesta tener tantas botellas y latas en la basura.
4. Le importa estar bien informado/a sobre lo que está ocurriendo en el mundo.
5. Le gusta servir a la comunidad.
6. Le encanta su gato. El gato se escapó durante la fiesta anoche.

11-15 ¿Qué está ocurriendo?

Túrnense para decir qué están haciendo estas personas.

MODELO E1: Felipe
E2: *Felipe está preparando su comida y está comiendo también.*

1. Manuel
2. Sofía
3. Raúl y Mari Carmen
4. José
5. Mercedes y Guillermo

11-16 Amantes de la naturaleza

Formen siete oraciones lógicas utilizando elementos de cada columna.

MODELO yo sembrar muchas plantas para el jardín
Estoy sembrando muchas plantas para el jardín.

yo	buscar	la gente que sufre desastres naturales
Lourdes	sacar fotos de	las mascotas de mi vecino
Ángeles y Rocío	participar en	el papel y el cartón
tú y yo	ayudar a	una campaña para proteger los animales en peligro de extinción
mi mejor amigo	reforestar	unos animales salvajes y peligrosos
los estudiantes	llevar basura a	soluciones para la contaminación
Antonia	reutilizar	el vertedero
el gobierno	cuidar	los bosques tropicales

11-17 ¡Qué creativo!

Juntos escriban la letra de una canción popular usando **el presente progresivo** un mínimo de **ocho** veces. Deben usar verbos de la siguiente lista.

apoyar	decir	proteger
ayudar	hacer daño	reciclar
botar	ir	reforestar
contaminar	matar	reutilizar
creer	plantar	servir
cuidar	preocuparse	

11-18 ¿Qué estamos haciendo...?

Completa el cuadro con las acciones que tu familia, tus amigos y tú están tomando para mejorar el medio ambiente. Después, comparte tu información con un/a compañero/a.

PARA PROTEGER LOS RÍOS, LOS OCÉANOS Y LOS BOSQUES	PARA EVITAR LA CONTAMINACIÓN DEL AIRE	PARA MANTENER LAS CALLES LIMPIAS
1. No estamos botando la basura en los ríos.	1.	1.
2.	2.	2.
3.	3.	3.

¿Cómo andas? I

Having completed **Comunicación I**, I now can...	**Feel confident**	**Need to review**
• describe animals and their habitats. (p. 424)	☐	☐
• pronounce words following the rules for accentuation and stress. (p. 425 and online)	☐	☐
• share details about the environment. (p. 428)	☐	☐
• describe El Yunque, the rain forest of Puerto Rico. (p. 432)	☐	☐
• describe what is happening at the moment. (p. 433)	☐	☐

Comunicación II

4 VOCABULARIO

La política Discussing government and current affairs

Los cargos	*Posts*
el alcalde / la alcaldesa	*mayor*
la dictadora	*dictator*
el/la diputado/a	*deputy; representative*
el/la gobernador/a	*governor*
el/la juez/a	*judge*
la presidenta	*president*
el/la senador/a	*senator*

Las administraciones y los regímenes	*Administrations and regimes*
el congreso	*congress*
la democracia	*democracy*
la dictadura	*dictatorship*
el estado	*state*
el gobierno	*government*
la ley	*law*
la monarquía	*monarchy*
la presidencia	*presidency*

Las cuestiones políticas	*Political matters*
el bienestar	*well-being; welfare*
la corte	*court*
la defensa	*defense*
la delincuencia	*crime*
el desempleo	*unemployment*
la deuda (externa)	*(foreign) debt*
el discurso	*speech*
las elecciones	*elections*
la encuesta	*survey*
el impuesto	*tax*
la inflación	*inflation*
el juicio	*trial*
el partido político	*political party*

Algunos verbos	*Some verbs*
apoyar	*to support*
combatir	*to fight; to combat*
elegir	*to elect*
estar en huelga	*to be on strike*
llevar a cabo	*to carry out*
luchar	*to fight; to combat*
meterse en política	*to get involved in politics*
resolver (o → ue)	*to resolve*
votar	*to vote*

¿? Now you are ready to complete the ***Preparación y práctica*** activities for this chunk online.

11-19 Al revés

Generalmente recibes las definiciones y tienes que advinar la palabra o expresión. Esta vez vas a escribir las definiciones. Completa los siguientes pasos.

Paso 1 Elige **seis** palabras o expresiones de **La política** y escribe las definiciones.

MODELO el impuesto

El dinero que tenemos que pagar al gobierno cuando compramos algo. Es un porcentaje del costo.

Paso 2 Lee tus definiciones a un/a compañero/a, quien tiene que adivinar la palabra.

11-20 La política de hoy

Completa los siguientes pasos.

Paso 1 Completa cada parte del cuadro con el nombre de un lugar o una persona según la descripción.

1. una reina ________	5. un país con alta inflación ________	9. el nombre del segundo presidente de los Estados Unidos ________
2. un estado del noreste de los Estados Unidos ________	6. un país con baja inflación ________	10. el nombre de un/a senador/a de tu estado ________
3. un país con monarquía ________	7. una ciudad de los Estados Unidos con mucha delincuencia ________	11. el nombre de una guerra muy larga ________
4. un rey ________	8. un alcalde / una alcaldesa ________	12. un/a juez/a de la Corte Suprema de los Estados Unidos ________

Paso 2 Ahora, compara tus respuestas con las de un/a compañero/a. Dense un punto por cada acierto (*match*).

Capítulo 5. El pretérito, págs. 197, 200.

11-21 Reportando Imagínense que son periodistas y tienen que hacer un reportaje sobre unas charlas (*talks*) y discursos de unos políticos. Formen oraciones lógicas, escogiendo palabras de cada columna y añadiendo otras palabras cuando sea necesario. Usen el pretérito.

MODELO encuesta mostrar el 65% de las personas no votar elecciones

La encuesta mostró que el 65% de las personas no votaron en las elecciones.

alcalde	preocuparse por	problemas de…
jefe, partido político	dedicarse a luchar contra	combatir alta inflación
senadora	(no) resolver	votar por nuevos impuestos
reyes	confirmar	el bienestar de las personas de las provincias
presidente	meterse en política	la delincuencia, el desempleo, la deuda externa

Nota cultural: La política en el mundo hispano

La historia política de Latinoamérica es la historia de la lucha dramática del ser humano contra fuerzas destructivas como la colonización, el imperialismo, la esclavitud y el genocidio en siglos anteriores y, en épocas más recientes, la pobreza, la corrupción, el nepotismo, la división rígida de clases y el militarismo. Muchos países hispanohablantes han sufrido severas dictaduras o democracias débiles e ineficaces. Esta lucha ahora se traduce en la búsqueda de una relación más justa con el mundo desarrollado y en particular con los Estados Unidos.

John Kerry, el Secretario de Estado de los Estados Unidos, con Bruno Rodríguez, el Ministro de Relaciones Exteriores de Cuba

En décadas recientes, España ha surgido (*has emerged*) como un país moderno y avanzado, con un rey progresista y amante de la democracia. Latinoamérica, a su vez, experimentó un periodo de paz y esperanza (*hope*) en la segunda mitad del siglo XX. Hasta Cuba, una dictadura aislada (*isolated*) durante cinco décadas, restableció relaciones diplomáticas con los Estados Unidos en 2015, abriendo paso al turismo y al comercio libre. En la ceremonia de reapertura (*reopening*) de la embajada estadounidense en La Habana, el Secretario de Estado John Kerry expresó la esperanza de ver una democracia auténtica en Cuba.

Preguntas

1. ¿Cuáles fueron algunos de los problemas en la historia política de los países hispanos?
2. ¿Qué cambios han experimentado (*have they experienced*) muchos de los países hispanos en los últimos 15 o 20 años?

11-22 ¿Qué sabes de…? Juntos contesten las siguientes preguntas para mostrar sus conocimientos políticos.

1. ¿En qué año fue la última campaña para la presidencia de los Estados Unidos?
2. ¿Cómo se llama el/la gobernador/a de tu estado?
3. ¿Quién fue un/a dictador/a infame? ¿De qué país? ¿Cuándo fue dictador/a?
4. ¿Qué países tienen un rey o una reina? ¿Cómo se llaman?
5. ¿Cuántos senadores hay en el senado de los Estados Unidos?
6. ¿Cuántos jueces hay en la Corte Suprema de los Estados Unidos?

11-23 El futuro político Escribe algunas ideas sobre lo que debe pasar en el futuro en tu ciudad, estado, país o en el mundo. Después, en grupos de tres, escriban un párrafo colectivo para la clase.

MODELO *Los partidos políticos no deben combatir tanto entre sí (*among themselves*). También es importante resolver problemas económicos como la inflación. Es difícil reducir la deuda nacional porque todos quieren dinero para sus programas.*

11-24 Los partidos políticos En grupos de cinco o seis estudiantes van a crear un partido político nuevo. Tienen que determinar el nombre del partido y el programa (*platform*). Después, presenten sus partidos a los otros grupos y juntos decidan cuál(es) de los partidos mejor representa(n) las opiniones de la clase.

5 GRAMÁTICA

El subjuntivo Commenting on what is necessary, possible, probable, and improbable

In Spanish, *tenses* such as the present, past, and future are grouped under two different moods, the **indicative** mood and the **subjunctive** mood.

Up to this point you have studied tenses grouped under the *indicative* mood (with the exception of commands) to report what happened, is happening, or will happen. The *subjunctive* mood, on the other hand, is used to express doubt, insecurity, influence, opinion, feelings, hope, wishes, or desires that can be happening now, have happened in the past, or will happen in the future. In this chapter you will learn the present tense of the *subjunctive mood.*

Es una lástima que no quieran reciclar el plástico, el vidrio, el aluminio y el papel.

Fíjate

You are already somewhat familiar with the subjunctive forms from your practice with *usted* (*¡Estudie!*) and negative *tú* (*¡No hables!*) commands.

Present subjunctive

To form the subjunctive, take the **yo** form of the present indicative, drop the final **-o**, and add the following endings.

Present indicative	*yo* form		Present subjunctive
estudiar	estudiø	+ e	**estudie**
comer	comø	+ a	**coma**
vivir	vivø	+ a	**viva**

	estudiar	comer	vivir
yo	estudi**e**	com**a**	viv**a**
tú	estudi**es**	com**as**	viv**as**
Ud.	estudi**e**	com**a**	viv**a**
él, ella	estudi**e**	com**a**	viv**a**
nosotros/as	estudi**emos**	com**amos**	viv**amos**
vosotros/as	estudi**éis**	com**áis**	viv**áis**
Uds.	estudi**en**	com**an**	viv**an**
ellos/as	estudi**en**	com**an**	viv**an**

Irregular forms

- Verbs with irregular **yo** forms maintain this irregularity in all forms of the present subjunctive.

	conocer	**hacer**	**poner**	**venir**
yo	conozca	haga	ponga	venga
tú	conozcas	hagas	pongas	vengas
Ud.	conozca	haga	ponga	venga
él, ella	conozca	haga	ponga	venga
nosotros/as	conozcamos	hagamos	pongamos	vengamos
vosotros/as	conozcáis	hagáis	pongáis	vengáis
Uds.	conozcan	hagan	pongan	vengan
ellos/as	conozcan	hagan	pongan	vengan

- Verbs ending in **-car, -gar,** and **-zar** have a spelling change in all present subjunctive forms, in order to maintain the sound of the infinitive.

		Present indicative	**Present subjunctive**
buscar	**c → qu**	**yo** busco	busque
pagar	**g → gu**	**yo** pago	pague
empezar	**z → c**	**yo** empiezo	empiece

	buscar	**pagar**	**empezar**
yo	busque	pague	empiece
tú	busques	pagues	empieces
Ud.	busque	pague	empiece
él, ella	busque	pague	empiece
nosotros/as	busquemos	paguemos	empecemos
vosotros/as	busquéis	paguéis	empecéis
Uds.	busquen	paguen	empiecen
ellos/as	busquen	paguen	empiecen

Stem-changing verbs

In the present subjunctive, stem-changing **-ar** and **-er** verbs make the same vowel changes that they do in the present indicative: **e → ie** and **o → ue**. Also, as in the present indicative, the **nosotros** and **vosotros** forms do not have a stem change.

	pensar (e → ie)	**poder (o → ue)**
yo	piense	pueda
tú	pienses	puedas
Ud.	piense	pueda
él, ella	piense	pueda
nosotros/as	pensemos	podamos
vosotros/as	penséis	podáis
Uds.	piensen	puedan
ellos/as	piensen	puedan

(continued)

The pattern is different with the **-ir** stem-changing verbs. In addition to their usual changes of **e → ie, e → i,** and **o → ue,** in the **nosotros** and **vosotros** forms the stem vowels change **ie → i** and **ue → u**.

	sentir (e → ie, i)	**dormir (o → ue, u)**
yo	sienta	duerma
tú	sientas	duermas
Ud.	sienta	duerma
él, ella	sienta	duerma
nosotros/as	sintamos	durmamos
vosotros/as	sintáis	durmáis
Uds.	sientan	duerman
ellos/as	sientan	duerman

The **e → i** stem-changing verbs keep the change in all forms.

	pedir (e → i, i)
yo	pida
tú	pidas
Ud.	pida
él, ella	pida
nosotros/as	pidamos
vosotros/as	pidáis
Uds.	pidan
ellos/as	pidan

Irregular verbs in the present subjunctive

- The following verbs are irregular in the subjunctive.

	dar	**estar**	**saber**	**ser**	**ir**
yo	dé	esté	sepa	sea	vaya
tú	des	estés	sepas	seas	vayas
Ud.	dé	esté	sepa	sea	vaya
él, ella	dé	esté	sepa	sea	vaya
nosotros/as	demos	estemos	sepamos	seamos	vayamos
vosotros/as	deis	estéis	sepáis	seáis	vayáis
Uds.	den	estén	sepan	sean	vayan
ellos/as	den	estén	sepan	sean	vayan

Dar has a written accent on the first- and third-person singular forms **(dé)** to distinguish them from the preposition **de**. All forms of **estar**, except the **nosotros** form, have a written accent in the present subjunctive.

Using the subjunctive

One of the uses of the subjunctive is with fixed expressions that communicate opinion, doubt, probability, and wishes. They are always followed by the subjunctive.

¡Es increíble que este capítulo sea el último!

Opinion

Es bueno/malo/mejor que…	*It's good / bad / better that…*
Es importante que…	*It's important that…*
Es increíble que…	*It's incredible that…*
Es una lástima que…	*It's a pity that…*
Es necesario que…	*It's necessary that…*
Es preferible que…	*It's preferable that…*
Es raro que…	*It's rare that…*

Doubt and probability

Es dudoso que…	*It's doubtful that…*
Es imposible que…	*It's impossible that…*
Es improbable que…	*It's unlikely that…*
Es posible que…	*It's possible that…*
Es probable que…	*It's likely that…*

Wishes and hopes

Ojalá (que)…	*Let's hope that… / Hopefully…*

Fíjate

The expression *Ojalá (que)* comes from the Arabic expression meaning *May it be Allah's will.* The conjunction *que* is optional in this expression.

Es necesario que votemos en todas las elecciones.	*It's necessary that we vote in all elections.*
Es una lástima que algunas personas no se metan en la política.	*It's a shame that some people don't get involved in politics.*
Ojalá (que) haya menos delincuencia en nuestra ciudad con el nuevo alcalde.	*Let's hope that there is less crime in our city with our new mayor.*

Fíjate

The subjunctive of *hay* is *haya.*

¡Explícalo tú!

1. What is the difference between the subjunctive and the indicative moods?
2. What other verb forms look like the subjunctive?
3. Where does the subjunctive verb come in relation to the word **que**?

 Check your answers to the preceding questions in Appendix 1.

 Now you are ready to complete the ***Preparación y práctica*** activities for this chunk online.

 **11-25 ¡Corre!** Escuchen mientras su profesor/a les explica cómo jugar con las formas de los verbos en el subjuntivo.

11-26 Opciones Túrnense para crear oraciones completas usando los sujetos indicados en cada frase.

MODELO es preferible que ella / nosotros / tú (apoyar al nuevo candidato)

E1: *Es preferible que ella apoye al nuevo candidato.*

E2: *Es preferible que nosotros apoyemos al nuevo candidato.*

E3: *Es preferible que tú apoyes al nuevo candidato.*

1. es dudoso que tú / Marta y yo / ella (combatir el desempleo)
2. es necesario que el gobierno / ellos / Uds. (luchar contra los impuestos altos)
3. ojalá que ellos / él / nosotros (elegir un buen presidente)
4. es posible que yo / tú / Uds. (estar en huelga esta semana)
5. es importante que los políticos del país / el congreso / nosotros (pensar en la defensa de nuestros derechos)
6. es una lástima que papá / tú / tus hermanos (no poder resolver todos los problemas)

11-27 El cocodrilo Completa el siguiente párrafo con la forma correcta del verbo apropiado en el subjuntivo. Algunos verbos se pueden usar más de una vez. Después, compara tus respuestas con las de un/a compañero/a.

El cocodrilo cubano

Fíjate

The *yo* form of the present tense (indicative mood) of *proteger* is *protejo*. Therefore, the subjunctive of *proteger* is *proteja, protejas*, etc.

estar	haber	poder	ser
existir	matar	proteger	vivir

Es raro que los cocodrilos (1) ______________ en el hemisferio occidental. ¡Siempre pienso en el continente de África como hábitat para este animal! Es una lástima que el cocodrilo americano y el cocodrilo cubano (2) ______________ en peligro de extinción. Es bueno que el cocodrilo americano (3) ______________ en varias partes del hemisferio (Florida, algunas islas del Caribe y varias zonas costeras del Golfo de México y el océano Pacífico), porque así tiene menos peligro de extinción que el cocodrilo cubano, el cual (*which*) existe solamente en el sureste de Cuba. Es posible que el cocodrilo americano (4) ______________ peligroso para los humanos. Son tan grandes que pueden atacar y comer animales de gran tamaño cuando se acercan a beber agua. Es improbable que el cocodrilo cubano (5) ______________ a una persona porque es mucho más pequeño y prefiere aves, pequeños mamíferos, peces y otros animales acuáticos. Es increíble que el cocodrilo americano (6) ______________ caminar distancias cortas, lo que significa que puede matar fuera del agua también. Es necesario que nosotros (7) ______________ a estos reptiles y ojalá que (8) ______________ muchos más en el futuro.

11-28 ¿Para quién es necesario que...?

Túrnense para hacer y contestar las preguntas sobre las siguientes situaciones usando las expresiones de la pág. 445.

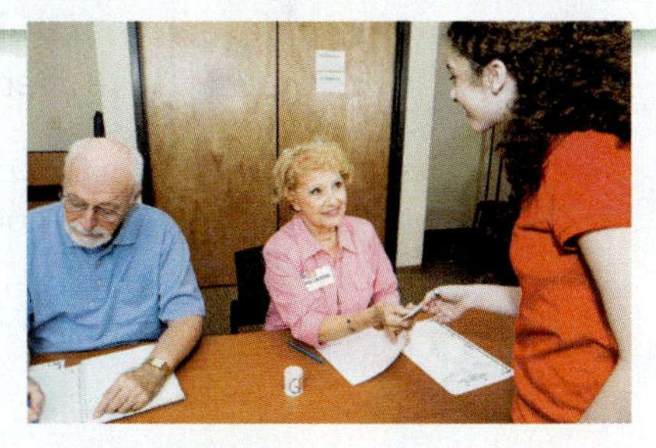

MODELO votar en las próximas elecciones

E1: *Es probable que vote en las próximas elecciones. ¿Y tú?*

E2: *No tengo dieciocho años, pero es necesario que vote en el futuro.*

1. apoyar al candidato
2. meterse en un partido político
3. luchar contra el desempleo
4. preocuparse por el bienestar de todos
5. combatir la delincuencia
6. bajar la deuda externa
7. buscar más maneras de proteger el medio ambiente
8. dar dinero a una campaña política

11-29 Posibles determinaciones

¿Cuáles pueden ser tus determinaciones (*resolutions*) para el próximo año? Descríbelas y después compártelas con un/a compañero/a.

Estrategia

Use activities like **11-29** to challenge yourself to provide as much pertinent information as you can.

MODELO *No debo comer tanto chocolate el próximo año, pero no sé si puedo evitarlo. ¡Me fascina el chocolate! Es importante que haga más ejercicio. Es una lástima que no me guste hacerlo.*

11-30 Es importante que...

Juntos escojan una de las siguientes situaciones para desarrollar en forma de diálogo. Usando las expresiones que acaban de aprender, den consejos según la situación. Después, presenten el diálogo a la clase.

Situación A

La doctora Pérez es especialista en nutrición. María Cecilia es una joven universitaria de dieciocho años que va a hacerle una consulta a la doctora sobre cómo mejorar el cutis (*complexion*).

Situación B

Bruno quiere comprar un carro usado y le pide a su amigo Manolo, quien trabaja en una agencia de carros, que lo ayude.

Situación C

El sargento López está enamorado de la muy simpática Carolina, pero es tan tímido que nunca la invita a salir con él. Su amiga Carmen trata de ayudarlo.

Situación D

Patricio se mata estudiando para el examen de matemáticas. Un día antes del examen se da cuenta (*he notices*) de que no tenía un examen de matemáticas, ¡sino de español! Va a su consejero para ver qué le aconseja.

6 GRAMÁTICA

Por y para Expressing time, deadlines, movement, destination, means, purpose, etc.

As you have seen, Spanish has two main words to express *for*: **por** and **para**. They have distinct uses and are not interchangeable.

¿Por cuánto tiempo ocupa el presidente la presidencia?

POR is used to express:

1. **Duration of time (*during, for*)**

   El presidente ocupa la presidencia **por** cuatro años consecutivos.

   The president holds the presidency for four consecutive years.

   El alcalde habló **por** más de media hora.

   The mayor spoke for more than a half hour.

2. **Movement or location (*through, along, past, around*)**

   Los candidatos andan **por** la calle y hablan con la gente.

   The candidates are going through the streets talking with the people.

   El rey saluda **por** la ventana.

   The king is waving through the window.

3. **Motive (*on account of, because of, for*)**

   Decidimos meternos en política **por** nuestros hijos. Queremos asegurarles un futuro mejor.

   We decided to get involved in politics because of our children. We want to assure them a better future.

   En resumen, nos dijeron que hay que reciclar **por** el futuro de nuestro planeta.

   In short, they told us that we must recycle for the future of our planet.

4. **Exchange (*in exchange for*)**

   Gracias **por** su ayuda, señora Presidenta.

   Thank you for your help, Madam President.

   Limpiaron el vertedero **por** diez mil dólares.

   They cleaned the dump for ten thousand dollars.

PARA is used to express:

1. **Point in time or a deadline (*for, by*)**

   Es dudoso que todos los problemas se solucionen **para** el final de su presidencia.

   It is doubtful that all problems will be solved by the end of her presidency.

   Es importante que bajemos los impuestos **para** el próximo año.

   It is important that we lower taxes by next year.

2. **Destination (*for*)**

   La reina sale hoy **para** Puerto Rico.

   The queen leaves for Puerto Rico today.

   Los diputados se fueron **para** el Capitolio.

   The representatives left for the Capitol.

3. **Recipients or intended person or persons (*for*)**

   Mi hermano escribe discursos **para** la gobernadora.

   My brother writes speeches for the governor.

   Necesitamos un avión **para** el dictador.

   We need a plane for the dictator.

4. **Comparison (*for*)**

   Para un hombre que sabe tanto de la política, no tiene ni idea sobre la delincuencia de nuestras calles.

   For a man who knows so much about politics, he has no idea about the crime on our streets.

   La tasa de desempleo es bastante baja **para** un país en desarrollo.

   The unemployment rate is quite low for a developing country.

5. Means (*by*)

Los diputados discutieron los resultados de las elecciones **por** teléfono.

The representatives argued about the election results over the phone.

¿Los reyes van a viajar **por** barco o **por** avión?

Are the king and queen going to travel by ship or by plane?

5. Purpose or goal (*to, in order to*)

Para recibir más votos, la candidata necesita proponer soluciones **para** los problemas con la deuda externa.

(In order) to receive more votes, the candidate needs to propose solutions for the problems with foreign debt.

Hay que luchar contra la contaminación **para** proteger el medio ambiente.

One needs to fight pollution to protect the environment.

¿? Now you are ready to complete the ***Preparación y práctica*** activities for this chunk online.

11-31 Los políticos Hoy en día, los políticos son muy activos y están en todas partes. Completen las oraciones de manera lógica.

MODELO La candidata Dávila tuvo una entrevista y habló por…
La candidata Dávila tuvo una entrevista y habló por tres horas.

1. El alcalde dijo que se metió en política para…
2. Las diputadas Meana y Caballero dijeron que hay que elegir a un gobernador nuevo para…
3. Nuestro presidente les dio las gracias a las organizadoras por…
4. El dictador se comunicó por…
5. Después del discurso el rey salió para…
6. La senadora, acompañada por _____, caminó por…

11-32 Razones Túrnense para decir para quiénes están haciendo ustedes las siguientes cosas.

MODELO comprar / libro sobre la inflación
E1: *¿Para quién estás comprando el libro sobre la inflación?*
E2: *Estoy comprando el libro para mis padres.*

1. hacer / campaña
2. escribir / discurso
3. pedir / donación (*contribution*)
4. buscar / empleo
5. circular / peticiones
6. proteger / el medio ambiente

11-33 Mi hermana Leonor

Mi hermana Leonor me dio una gran sorpresa para mi cumpleaños.

Paso 1 Para saber qué pasó, completa cada espacio en blanco del siguiente párrafo con **por** o **para**.

Leonor, mi hermana, estuvo en mi casa (1) __________ un mes el verano pasado. Vino (2) __________ mi cumpleaños. Leonor llegó con tres maletas y una enorme caja misteriosa. El día de mi cumpleaños me dijo que (yo) tenía que estar lista (3) __________ las cinco de la tarde. Efectivamente, a las cinco en punto estaba sentada en la sala cuando vi (4) __________ la ventana a un grupo de amigos. Venían con un trío de guitarras. ¡Era una serenata (5) __________ mí! ¡Qué emoción tan grande! La serenata comenzó y Leonor bajó (6) __________la escalera con una caja.

—Es (7) __________ ti —me dijo. La abrí y ¡qué sorpresa! Era una hamaca de yute (*jute hammock*) de la República Dominicana, donde Leonor había vivido (*had lived*) (8) __________ varios meses.

—¡Una hamaca (9) __________ el patio —exclamé— (10) __________ leer y dormir al sol! ¡Qué delicia! —Y en seguida pregunté:— Pero, Leonor, ¿cómo trajiste esta hamaca desde Santo Domingo? ¿La trajiste (11) __________ avión o la mandaste (12) __________ correo?

Leonor se rió y me contestó: —(13) __________ una hermana como tú, todo es posible. Me la traje en avión. (14) __________ ser una caja tan grande, la verdad es que no me causó tantos problemas. ¡Feliz cumpleaños!

Paso 2 Comparte tus respuestas con un/a compañero/a y explícale por qué usaste **por** o **para** en cada una.

11-34 Preguntas personales

Túrnense para contestar las siguientes preguntas.

Capítulo 5. El pretérito, pág. 197; Capítulo 7. Algunos verbos irregulares en el pretérito, pág. 284; Capítulo 8. El imperfecto, pág. 328.

1. ¿Por cuánto tiempo viste las noticias en la televisión anoche?
2. ¿Por cuánto tiempo estudiaste anoche?
3. ¿Qué veías por la ventana de tu cuarto cuando eras joven?
4. Cuando estabas en la escuela primaria, ¿ibas al colegio en autobús, carro o a pie?
5. ¿Por quién votaste la primera vez que pudiste votar?
6. ¿Qué puede hacer un estudiante universitario para ser más activo en la política?
7. ¿Sabes si hay un centro de reciclaje por aquí? ¿Por dónde voy para llegar allí?
8. ¿Qué necesitamos hacer para evitar la contaminación?

7 GRAMÁTICA

Las preposiciones y los pronombres preposicionales Specifying location and other information

Besides the prepositions **por** and **para**, there is a variety of useful prepositions and prepositional phrases, many of which you have already been using throughout ***¡Anda! Curso elemental***. Study the following list to review the ones you already know and to acquaint yourself with those that may be new to you.

a	*to; at*	**después de**	*after*
a la derecha de	*to the right of*	**detrás de**	*behind*
a la izquierda de	*to the left of*	**en**	*in*
acerca de	*about*	**encima de**	*on top of*
(a)fuera de	*outside of*	**enfrente de**	*across from; facing*
al lado de	*next to*	**entre**	*among; between*
antes de	*before (time/space)*	**hasta**	*until*
cerca de	*near*	**lejos de**	*far from*
con	*with*	**para**	*for; in order to*
de	*of; from; about*	**por**	*for; through; by; because of*
debajo de	*under; underneath*	**según**	*according to*
delante de	*in front of*	**sin**	*without*
dentro de	*inside of*	**sobre**	*over; about*
desde	*from*		

El centro de reciclaje está **a la derecha del** supermercado. — *The recycling center is to the right of the supermarket.*

La alcaldesa va a hablar **acerca de** los problemas que tenemos con la protección del cocodrilo cubano. — *The mayor is going to speak about the problems we are having with the protection of the Cuban crocodile.*

Vimos un montón de plástico **encima del** papel. — *We saw a mountain of plastic on top of the paper.*

Quieren sembrar flores **enfrente del** vertedero. — *They want to plant flowers in front of the dump.*

El proyecto no puede tener éxito **sin** el apoyo del gobierno local. — *The project cannot be successful without the support of the local government.*

(continued)

Los pronombres preposicionales

Study the list of pronouns that are used with prepositions.

Fíjate

This list of pronouns that follow prepositions is the same as the list of subject pronouns, except for the first two (*mí* is used instead of *yo*, and *ti* instead of *tú*).

mí	*me*	**nosotros/as**	*us*
ti	*you*	**vosotros/as**	*you*
usted	*you*	**ustedes**	*you*
él	*him*	**ellos**	*them*
ella	*he*	**ellas**	*them*

Para mí, es muy importante resolver el problema de la lluvia ácida. — *For me, it's really important to solve the problem of acid rain.*

¿Qué candidato está sentado **enfrente de ti**? — *Which candidate is seated in front of you?*

Se fueron de la huelga **sin nosotros**. — *They left the strike without us.*

Trabajamos **con ellos** para proteger el medio ambiente. — *We work with them to protect the environment.*

Note that **con** has two special forms:

1. con + mí = **conmigo** *with me*
   —¿Vienes **conmigo** al discurso?
   Are you coming with me to the speech?

2. con + ti = **contigo** *with you*
   —Sí, voy **contigo**.
   Yes, I'm going with you.

Now you are ready to complete the ***Preparación y práctica*** activities for this chunk online.

11-35 Hablando del candidato Completa la conversación entre Celia y Manolo sobre el candidato Carlos Arroyo con los pronombres preposicionales apropiados. Después comparte tus respuestas con un/a compañero/a.

CELIA: Manolo, ¿qué opinas tú de (1) _________?

MANOLO: Pues, te digo que para (2) ___________ está muy claro. El señor Arroyo no piensa en (3) ___________ ni en nuestros problemas.

CELIA: Sí, siempre está con las personas ricas e influyentes (*influential*), tratando de conseguir dinero de (4) __________ para su campaña.

MANOLO: También creo que vive parte del año aquí y parte en la costa. Para (5) ___________ eso significa que quiere ser nuestro líder pero no quiere vivir con (6) ___________ . ¿Y para (7) __________ , Celia?

CELIA: Creo que tienes razón. Me gusta hablar con (8) ________ porque me haces pensar en las cosas que no son tan obvias.

11-36 Descríbemelo

Juntos describan el dibujo usando las siguientes preposiciones.

MODELO *El gato está al lado del árbol.*

1. al lado de
2. a la derecha de
3. a la izquierda de
4. cerca de
5. debajo de
6. delante de
7. detrás de
8. lejos de

11-37 Una política joven

Completa el párrafo sobre Martina Peña, una candidata nueva en el mundo político, con las preposiciones de la lista. Después compara tu párrafo con el de un/a compañero/a.

a	antes de	con (2 veces)	de
después	entre	sobre	sin

(1) _________ meterse en la política, Martina compartió sus ideas (2) __________ mucha gente. (3) ___________ otras personas, se reunió (4) __________ políticos importantes y (5) __________ ellos aprendió mucho (6) ___________ el bienestar, los derechos humanos, la violencia, el desempleo y la inflación. (7) __________ de escuchar todo lo que tenían que decir, ella volvió (8) ________ su casa y empezó a convertir sus ideas en discursos. El próximo paso fue buscar apoyo y dinero. Sabía perfectamente que (9) __________ ese apoyo no iba a ser posible ganar las elecciones.

11-38 Una charla con Martina Peña

Decides asistir a una charla con Martina Peña (Actividad **11-37**) sobre el desempleo y la delincuencia. Vas con tu compañera de apartamento, Christina, quien te acaba de dejar un mensaje de voz. Completa los siguientes pasos.

Paso 1 Escucha el mensaje y después indica si las oraciones son ciertas (**C**) o falsas (**F**).

C	F	
☐	☐	1. La charla es lejos del campus.
☐	☐	2. Para llegar, necesitas doblar a la derecha en la Avenida Central.
☐	☐	3. La charla es en el segundo piso de la biblioteca.
☐	☐	4. Necesitas llevarle a Christina un cuaderno rojo y un libro.
☐	☐	5. Christina piensa que la computadora está debajo de los libros de biología.
☐	☐	6. Christina va a esperar en la puerta principal de la biblioteca pública.

Paso 2 Corrige las oraciones falsas.

11-39 ¿Dónde están?

Expliquen dónde están estos lugares en El Viejo San Juan en Puerto Rico, usando las preposiciones apropiadas.

MODELO E1: *¿Dónde está el Campo del Morro?*

E2: *Está entre el Castillo y La Casa Blanca, al lado del Cementerio de San Juan.*

1. La Fortaleza, casa del gobernador
2. El Capitolio, edificio de las oficinas de los senadores y representantes
3. La Plaza de Armas
4. El Castillo de San Felipe del Morro
5. La Casa Blanca, casa de la familia de Juan Ponce de León
6. La Alcaldía / El Ayuntamiento, edificio donde el alcalde tiene sus oficinas
7. Correos
8. El Banco Popular
9. La puerta de San Juan
10. La catedral de San Juan

11-40 La universidad Túrnense para explicar dónde están los siguientes lugares en su universidad.

MODELO *La biblioteca está detrás del centro estudiantil.*

1. la biblioteca
2. el gimnasio
3. el centro estudiantil
4. la librería
5. la cafetería
6. tu cuarto o residencia estudiantil
7. el centro de salud
8. el estadio de fútbol

11-41 ¿Con quién...? Decide quién hace las siguientes actividades contigo y después comparte las respuestas con un/a compañero/a.

MODELO E1: *¿Quién... habla contigo por teléfono todos los días?*
E2: *Mi madre habla conmigo por teléfono todos los días.*

¿Quién...?

1. viene a clase contigo
2. se sienta contigo en la sala de clase
3. hace las actividades de clase contigo
4. estudia contigo fuera de clase
5. almuerza o cena contigo
6. sale contigo por la tarde (para ir al cine / bar / club de baile, etc.)

8 GRAMÁTICA

El infinitivo después de preposiciones

Providing more information about location, time, and other subjects

In Spanish, if you use a verb immediately after a preposition, it must always be in the **infinitive** form.

Antes de reciclar las latas debes limpiarlas.	*Before recycling the cans, you should clean them.*
Después de pisar la hormiga, la niña lloró.	*After stepping on the ant, the little girl cried.*
Es fácil decidir **entre reciclar** y **botar**.	*It is easy to decide between recycling and throwing away.*
Necesitamos trabajar con personas de todos los países **para proteger** mejor la Tierra.	*We need to work with people from all countries in order to better protect the Earth.*
Ganaste el premio **por estar** tan interesado en el medio ambiente.	*You won the prize for being so interested in the environment.*
No podemos vivir **sin trabajar** juntos.	*We cannot live without working together.*

Now you are ready to complete the ***Preparación y práctica*** activities for this chunk online.

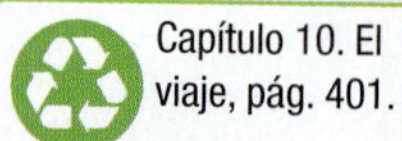

Capítulo 10. El viaje, pág. 401.

11-42 De viaje

Forma oraciones lógicas usando **antes de** o **después de**. Después compártelas con un/a compañero/a.

MODELO salir / hacer la maleta

Antes de salir, necesito hacer la maleta. / Antes de salir, tengo que hacer la maleta.

1. comprar el boleto / ir al banco
2. pasar por recepción / ir al cuarto
3. llegar al aeropuerto / mostrar el pasaporte
4. hacer la maleta / lavar la ropa
5. ir de vacaciones / dejar el gato con mis padres

Fíjate

The sentences for **11-42** can be written two ways. Start the sentence with *antes de + infinitive* or *después de + infinitive* and finish the sentence, as in *Antes de salir necesito hacer la maleta.* Or end the sentence with the prepositional phrase, e.g., *Necesito hacer la maleta antes de salir.*

11-43 Lo que pasó con el perro

Termina las siguientes oraciones de forma lógica según el modelo. Después, comparte tus respuestas con un/a compañero/a.

MODELO Es importante que sepas que el perro se escapó para…

Es importante que sepas que el perro se escapó para jugar con esa perra bonita del vecino.

1. Es mejor que busquemos el perro antes de…
2. Es probable que el perro nos evite para…
3. Es posible que el perro tenga hambre después de…
4. Sí, es raro que no venga para…
5. Es dudoso que se vaya con otra persona después de…
6. Ojalá que lo encontremos sin…

11·44 Mis decisiones

Termina las siguientes oraciones y después compártelas con un/a compañero/a.

MODELO No me voy de aquí sin…
No me voy de aquí sin terminar la tarea.

1. Necesito pensar en el futuro antes de…
2. Quiero hablar con mis padres / mi mejor amigo sobre…
3. Voy a buscar un trabajo después de…
4. Tengo que escoger entre…
5. Me quedo en este lugar hasta…
6. Después pienso ir a ______ para…

11·45 El medio ambiente

Oswaldo y Fania, dos amigos de la República Dominicana, conversan sobre los problemas del medio ambiente. Completen la conversación entre ellos con la forma correcta del **subjuntivo** o del **infinitivo**.

FANIA: Es muy bueno que los dominicanos (1) ______________ (querer) proteger el medio ambiente.

OSWALDO: Sí, pero es una lástima que muchas personas (2) ______________ (botar) basura por las calles todavía (*still*). ¡Qué sucios!

FANIA: Es necesario que mi familia y yo (3) ______________ (buscar) alguna manera de reciclar más.

OSWALDO: Mi familia y yo necesitamos (4) ______________ (caminar) más y no usar tanto ni el carro ni el autobús.

FANIA: Es cierto. Cada uno debe hacer su parte para (5) ______________ (proteger) el medio ambiente contra la contaminación. Es imposible que los gobiernos solos (6) ______________ (poder) controlar adecuadamente el uso de procesos y materiales que contaminan.

OSWALDO: Nos preocupamos por el reciclaje y la limpieza de las calles y del aire, pero también es necesario que nuestro gobierno (7) ______________ (pensar) en cómo proteger los ríos y los océanos. Pero como tú dices, no podemos solucionar todos estos problemas sin (8) ______________ (trabajar) juntos. Todos debemos (9) ______________ (hacer) algo para cambiar las cosas.

FANIA: ¡Sí! Ojalá que nosotros (10) ______________ (disfrutar) de este paraíso natural por muchos años.

Escucha

Un anuncio político

Estrategia		
Using visual organizers	Once you know the topic or gist of a passage, it may be helpful to mentally organize what you are about to hear.	Determine whether a list, chart, or diagram could be useful in helping you keep track of the information.

11-46 Antes de escuchar

Fania Marte Lozada tiene un anuncio político en la radio.

1. ¿Qué es un anuncio político?
2. ¿Escuchaste alguna vez un anuncio político de un candidato en la radio o viste uno de estos anuncios en la televisión?
3. ¿Qué información contiene generalmente un anuncio de este tipo?

Fania Marte Lozada, candidata

11-47 A escuchar

Completa los siguientes pasos.

1. Escucha el anuncio para sacar la idea general.
2. Decide de qué forma quieres organizar la información (*list, chart, diagram,* etc.).
3. Escucha otra vez para completar tu diagrama o lista con la información esencial.
4. Escucha una vez más para añadir algunos detalles.

11-48 Después de escuchar

En grupos de tres o cuatro, compartan su información y juntos decidan si la Dra. Marte Lozada sería (*would be*) una buena alcaldesa. Expliquen.

¡Conversemos!

11-49 Nuestro mundo Junto con un/a compañero/a, creen una conversación entre una persona y un candidato sobre los problemas más críticos del medio ambiente y las posibles soluciones y fondos (*funding*). Necesitan incluir por lo menos **diez** oraciones y usar el **subjuntivo por lo menos cinco veces**. Después, presenten la entrevista para los compañeros de la clase.

11-50 La política Tu compañero/a y tú son reporteros de noticias. Juntos creen un reportaje sobre algún aspecto de la política del mundo y de lo que pasó hoy. Incluyan por lo menos **diez** oraciones.

Escribe

Un anuncio de servicio público

Estrategia

Persuasive writing

In writing a public announcement, your goal is to influence the listeners to support your cause and become better environmentalists. To create the most effective announcement, consider the elements of persuasive writing: appeal to reason, emotions, and good character (ethical, morals, and concern for the well-being of the audience); define any key terms that may not be clear; reference an authority and/or supporting evidence to back your claims; and anticipate counterarguments and address them. You must develop a rational argument, making sure the conclusion logically follows the claims you make.

11-51 Antes de escribir Vas a crear un anuncio de publicidad para la radio sobre algún aspecto de la protección del medio ambiente. Debe durar (*last*) unos quince segundos. Decide de qué quieres hablar y haz una lista de los puntos más importantes que quieres incluir.

11-52 A escribir Organiza tus ideas y escribe un anuncio. Debe estar dirigido (*directed*) a los adultos jóvenes.

11-53 Después de escribir Presenta tu anuncio a los compañeros de clase.

¿Cómo andas? II

Having completed **Comunicación II**, I now can…	Feel confident	Need to review
• discuss government and current affairs. (p. 438)	☐	☐
• relate specific facts about politics in the Spanish-speaking world. (p. 440)		
• comment on what is necessary, possible, probable, and improbable. (p. 442)	☐	☐
• express time, deadlines, movement, destination, means, purpose, etc. (p. 448)	☐	☐
• specify location and other information. (p. 451)	☐	☐
• provide more information about location, time, and other subjects. (p. 455)	☐	☐
• listen to a radio announcement and practice using visual organizers to enhance comprehension. (p. 458)	☐	☐
• communicate about world issues. (p. 459)	☐	☐
• employ persuasive writing to create a public announcement. (p. 460)	☐	☐

Vistazo cultural

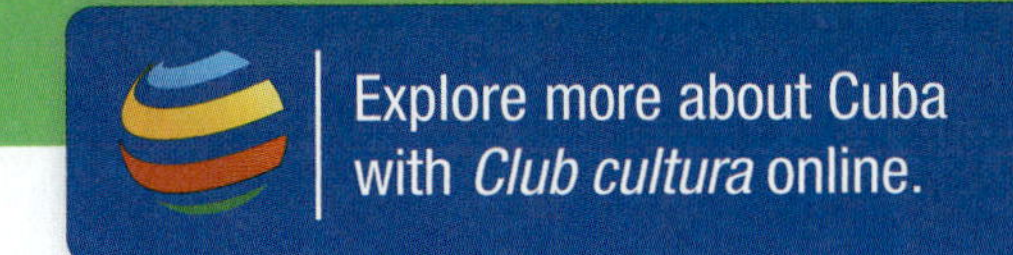

Cuba

Les presento mi país

Alicia Ortega Mujica

Mi nombre es Alicia Ortega Mujica y soy de La Habana, la capital de Cuba. La mayoría de los cubanos tenemos herencia española, africana o una mezcla (*mixture*) de las dos. La influencia africana se nota en muchos aspectos de la cultura cubana, sobre todo en la música. La salsa es un estilo musical muy popular que mezcla las melodías europeas con los ritmos de los tambores africanos. **¿Qué influencia africana se siente en la música de tu país?** Antes, la economía cubana dependía mayormente de productos agrícolas como el azúcar y el tabaco, pero ahora el turismo es muy importante y el gobierno invierte (*invest*) recursos para atraer a más visitantes al país.

La Plaza de la Revolución

Los puros cubanos son famosos en todo el mundo por su buena calidad.

La música cubana incorpora instrumentos africanos, como el tambor.

ALMANAQUE

Nombre oficial:	República de Cuba
Gobierno:	Estado/Régimen comunista
Población:	11.477.459 (2010)
Idioma:	español
Moneda:	Peso cubano ($) y Peso convertible (CUC$)

¿Sabías que…?

- El zunzuncito, el pájaro más pequeño del mundo, es endémico (*native*) de Cuba. Mide menos de seis centímetros y pesa menos de dos gramos. Es una especie de colibrí (*hummingbird*).
- Después de décadas de restricciones, los estadounidenses pueden viajar a Cuba para cuestiones de trabajo, estudios o visitas a familiares.

Preguntas

1. ¿Cuál es la composición étnica de la población cubana?
2. ¿Cuáles son las bases principales de la economía cubana?
3. ¿Qué tipo de música es popular en Cuba? ¿Es popular en otras partes del mundo?

Vistazo cultural

Puerto Rico

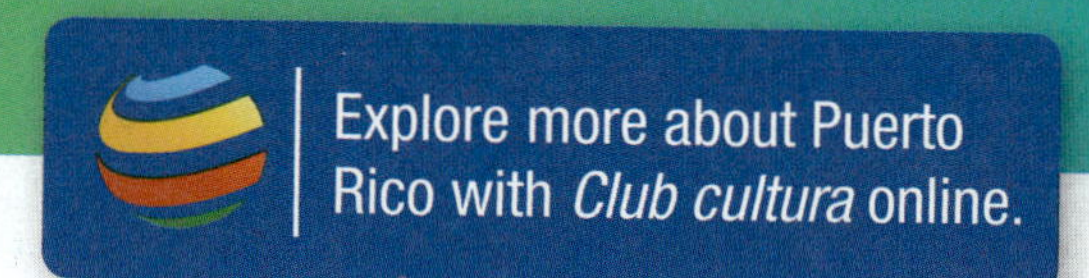

Les presento mi país

Pablo Colón Padín

Mi nombre es Pablo Colón Padín y soy de San Germán, Puerto Rico, conocido como la Ciudad de las Lomas (*hills*). Actualmente soy estudiante del Recinto Universitario de Mayagüez, donde estudiaron, entre muchos otros, algunos ingenieros de la NASA. **¿Te interesan los estudios del espacio y de los planetas?** El Observatorio de Arecibo, sitio del radiotelescopio de un solo plato más grande del mundo, está a unas setenta millas de mi universidad. También se puede estudiar una naturaleza muy diversa en mi isla en El Yunque, un bosque lluvioso del este donde vive el coquí, una rana que es un símbolo importante de la isla. Puerto Rico es territorio de los Estados Unidos pero la independencia y la estadidad (*statehood*) se siguen debatiendo. **¿Qué opinas tú de esta cuestión?**

El radiotelescopio del Observatorio de Arecibo

El coquí, el famoso símbolo de Puerto Rico

Vista de San Juan, la capital

ALMANAQUE

Nombre oficial:	Estado Libre Asociado de Puerto Rico
Gobierno:	Territorio de los Estados Unidos; Estado Libre Asociado
Población:	3.978.702 (2010)
Idiomas:	español e inglés
Moneda:	Dólar estadounidense ($)

¿Sabías que...?

- Puerto Rico tiene tres bahías (*bays*) fosforescentes habitadas por millones de microorganismos (dinoflagelados) que emanan luz cuando se agitan. Se puede observar este fenómeno por la noche. ¡Qué maravilla!

Preguntas

1. ¿Qué evidencia del desarrollo avanzado de las ciencias hay en Puerto Rico?
2. ¿Cómo es el clima de El Yunque?
3. ¿Hay otros países de Centroamérica y el Caribe que tienen bosques lluviosos?

Vistazo cultural

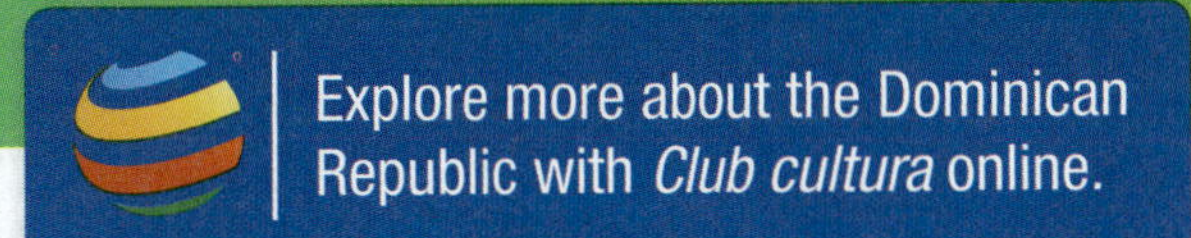

La República Dominicana

Les presento mi país

Amparo Burgos Báez

Mi nombre es Amparo Burgos Báez y soy de la República Dominicana, que comparte la isla de La Española con Haití. Mi país es muy montañoso con cuatro sistemas principales de cordilleras (*mountain ranges*), pero también tiene unas playas increíbles de arena fina y agua cristalina. **¿Prefieres las montañas o la playa?** Uno de nuestros platos más típicos es *la bandera dominicana,* que consiste en arroz, habichuelas (*beans*) rojas, carne, ensalada y tostones (*plantain chips*)… Si nos visitas, vas a escuchar el merengue y la bachata con sus ritmos contagiosos. Otras aficiones del país son los deportes acuáticos y el béisbol. **¿Sabes qué jugadores dominicanos juegan para equipos estadounidenses?**

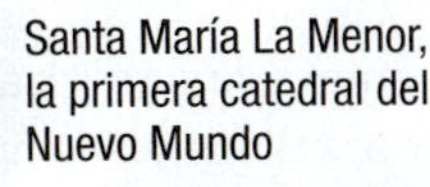

Santa María La Menor, la primera catedral del Nuevo Mundo

Las playas dominicanas atraen a muchos turistas.

El béisbol es el deporte nacional.

ALMANAQUE

Nombre oficial:	La República Dominicana
Gobierno:	Democracia representativa
Población:	9.823.821 (2010)
Idioma:	español (oficial)
Moneda:	Peso dominicano (RD$)

¿Sabías que…?

- Cristóbal Colón descubrió la isla en su primer viaje y la nombró La Española. Santo Domingo fue la primera ciudad europea fundada en el Nuevo Mundo.
- En 1586 el pirata Francis Drake asaltó la ciudad de Santo Domingo. Él y sus hombres robaron y vandalizaron la Catedral Santa María La Menor extensamente antes de salir.

Preguntas

1. ¿Cómo es la geografía dominicana y qué tiene de especial?
2. ¿Qué es "la bandera dominicana"?
3. ¿Qué sabes de la historia de Santo Domingo?
4. ¿Qué tienen en común la República Dominicana y los otros países del Caribe?

Lectura

Una leyenda mexicana

11-54 Antes de leer Contesta las siguientes preguntas.

1. ¿Qué leyendas conoces? ¿Cuál es tu favorita?
2. Generalmente, ¿qué función tienen las leyendas? ¿Qué características tienen?

Estrategia

Using visual organizers

After you have read a text, it may be useful to create a visual organizer for the information contained therein. In ***¡Anda! Curso elemental***, you have already worked with timelines, semantic maps (or web diagrams), charts, and Venn diagrams in completing activities. Look for ways to incorporate these organizers as you read.

11-55 Mientras lees Lee rápidamente la lectura. Usa las expresiones temporales y las frases como guía para completar esta línea de tiempo y resumir la historia con tus propias palabras.

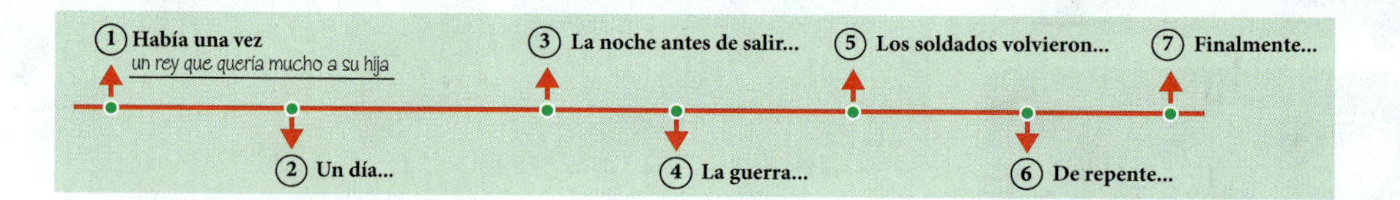

Fíjate

This legend uses several verbs in the future tense, which is used to tell what *will happen*. You can easily recognize these verbs because the endings are the same for all *-ar, -er,* and *-ir* verbs: *-é, -ás, á, -emos, -áis, án.* These endings are simply added to the infinitive of the verb: *yo daré, tú darás,* etc.

La leyenda de los volcanes (adaptación)

1

Había una vez un emperador azteca cuyo° mayor tesoro° era su hija Iztaccíhuatl. Un día, él recibió malas noticias. Sus enemigos planeaban un ataque. Por eso, reunió a todos los guerreros° del Imperio. Y les dijo:

—Tengo noticias terribles. Nuestros enemigos están planeando un ataque. Elijan al guerrero más valiente, más fuerte y más inteligente, y yo lo nombraré capitán de mis ejércitos°. Si ganamos° la guerra, le daré mi Imperio y también mi hija, la bella princesa Iztaccíhuatl.

whose / treasure

warriors

armies

we win

Todos los guerreros gritaron°: — shouted

—Popocatépetl es el más valiente, el más fuerte y el más inteligente. ¡Viva Popocatépetl!

Los jóvenes guerreros levantaron a Popocatépetl y lo llevaron al emperador. Este lo miró y le dijo:

—Popocatépetl, nuestro pueblo está en tus manos. Si ganas, te daré mi trono° y la mano de mi hija Iztaccíhuatl. Pero si somos derrotados°, no vuelvas. — throne / defeated

Popocatépetl tenía una tarea muy difícil. Estaba preocupado y feliz: preocupado por la guerra, pero… ¿por qué estaba feliz? Nadie lo sabía. El secreto era que él e Iztaccíhuatl se amaban. La guerra iba a ser dura, difícil y terrible; pero con la victoria, sus sueños de amor se verían cumplidos°. — would be fulfilled

2 La noche antes de salir para la lucha, Popocatépetl fue a despedirse de Iztaccíhuatl. La princesa estaba muy triste. Le dijo:

—Tengo miedo de que mueras. Ten mucho cuidado, mi amor. Regresa sano y salvo°. No puedo vivir sin ti. — safe

—Volveré por ti. Nos casaremos° y permaneceré° a tu lado—contestó Popocatépetl. — We will get married / I will stay

Los volcanes Popocatépetl e Iztaccíhuatl, México

Popocatépetl salió de la capital con jóvenes soldados°. La guerra resultó sangrienta°, larga y feroz. Con Popocatépetl, el ejército azteca triunfó sobre sus enemigos. Todos los guerreros se alegraron, pero uno de ellos tenía celos° de Popocatépetl. Deseaba todo lo que Popocatépetl poseía. Él quería ser el nuevo jefe del ejército y casarse con la princesa Iztaccíhuatl. — soldiers / bloody / was jealous

Los soldados aztecas se prepararon para regresar a la capital. El guerrero celoso salió más pronto y corrió tan rápidamente que llegó un día antes del ejército. Fue al emperador, se arrodilló° a sus pies y anunció que Popocatépetl había muerto°; que él, y no Popocatépetl, fue el guerrero más fuerte y valiente, y que fue el jefe del ejército en la batalla. — he kneeled / had died

3 El emperador, quien apreciaba a Popocatépetl, se entristeció. Pero él había hecho° una promesa y él tenía que cumplirla. Le ofreció al guerrero celoso todo el Imperio azteca y la mano de su hija. Al día siguiente fueron las bodas° de Iztaccíhuatl y el guerrero. De repente°, en mitad° de la ceremonia, Iztaccíhuatl gritó: "¡Ay, mi pobre Popocatépetl! No podré vivir sin ti". Y ella cayó muerta en el suelo. — he had made / wedding / Suddenly / middle

(continued)

Entonces, los otros guerreros con Popocatépetl entraron en el palacio. Popocatépetl vio a Iztaccíhuatl. Corrió a su lado. La tomó en brazos, le acarició el pelo y llorando° le dijo: *crying*

—No te dejaré nunca sola. Estaré a tu lado hasta el fin del mundo.

La llevó a las montañas más altas. La puso entre las flores y se sentó a su lado para siempre. Pasó el tiempo y, por fin, uno de los buenos dioses transformó a los dos amantes° en volcanes. *lovers*

Desde entonces, Iztaccíhuatl ha sido° un volcán tranquilo y silencioso que permanece dormido. Pero Popocatépetl tiembla° de vez en cuando. Entonces, todo México sabe que Popocatépetl llora por su amor, la bella Iztaccíhuatl. *has been* *shakes*

11·56 Después de leer

Contesta las siguientes preguntas.

1. ¿Qué problema tenía el emperador azteca? ¿Qué decidió hacer para solucionarlo?
2. ¿Quién era Popocatépetl? ¿Quién era Iztaccíhuatl?
3. ¿Qué prometió el emperador azteca?
4. ¿Quiénes ganaron la guerra?
5. Después de la victoria, ¿qué hizo el guerrero celoso?
6. ¿Qué le pasó a Iztaccíhuatl en la boda?
7. ¿Por qué permaneció Popocatépetl con Iztaccíhuatl?
8. ¿Te gustó el final de la leyenda? Explica.

Media Share

11·57 Una novela gráfica

Ahora tú vas a ser el/la autor/a de la leyenda de los volcanes, pero en forma de una novela gráfica. Debes incluir por lo menos ocho viñetas y una mezcla de diálogo y narración. Luego prepara una presentación para la clase en la que presentes tu novela.

11·58 Dos leyendas

En la leyenda que leíste, Popocatépetl e Iztaccíhuatl se transforman en volcanes. Piensa en otra leyenda que conoces que trata de la naturaleza o de unos amantes. Usa un diagrama de Venn para comparar y contrastar las dos leyendas.

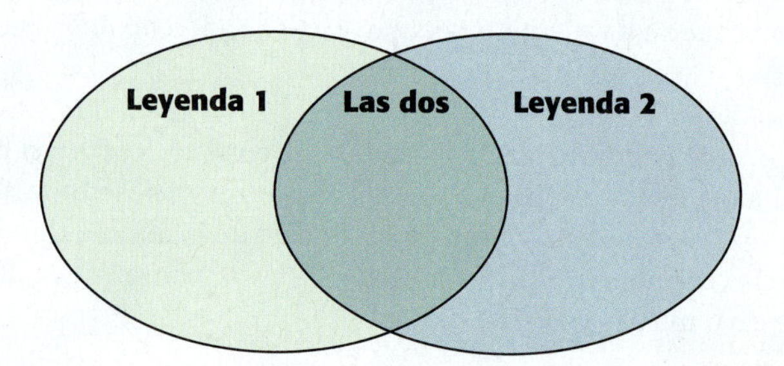

For additional *Lectura* activities, go to *¡Anda!* online.

Y por fin, ¿cómo andas?

Having completed this chapter, I now can...	Feel confident	Need to review
Comunicación I		
• describe animals and their habitats. (p. 424)	☐	☐
• pronounce words following the rules for accentuation and stress. (p. 425 and online)	☐	☐
• share details about the environment. (p. 428)	☐	☐
• describe what is happening at the moment. (p. 433)	☐	☐
Comunicación II		
• discuss government and current affairs. (p. 438)	☐	☐
• comment on what is necessary, possible, probable, and improbable. (p. 442)	☐	☐
• express time, deadlines, movement, destination, means, purpose, etc. (p. 448)	☐	☐
• specify location and other information. (p. 451)	☐	☐
• provide more information about location, time, and other subjects. (p. 455)	☐	☐
• listen to a radio announcement and practice using visual organizers to enhance comprehension. (p. 458)	☐	☐
• communicate about world issues. (p. 459)	☐	☐
• employ persuasive writing to create a public announcement. (p. 460)	☐	☐
Cultura		
• describe El Yunque, the rain forest of Puerto Rico. (p. 432)	☐	☐
• relate specific facts about politics in the Spanish-speaking world. (p. 440)	☐	☐
• share information about Cuba, Puerto Rico, and the Dominican Republic. (pp. 461–463)	☐	☐
Lectura		
• read a legend from Mexico. (p. 464)	☐	☐
Comunidades		
• use Spanish in real-life contexts (online)	☐	☐

Vocabulario **activo** 

Los animales — *Animals*

Los animales de la granja	*Farm animals*
los animales domésticos / las mascotas	*domesticated animals; pets*
el caballo	*horse*
el cerdo	*pig*
el conejo	*rabbit*
la gallina	*chicken; hen*
el gato	*cat*
el insecto	*insect*
la mosca	*fly*
el mosquito	*mosquito*
el perro	*dog*
el pez (*pl.*, los peces)	*fish*
la rana	*frog*
la rata	*rat*
el ratón	*mouse*
el toro	*bull*
la vaca	*cow*

Los animales salvajes	*Wild animals*
los animales en peligro de extinción	*endangered animals*
el elefante	*elephant*
la hormiga	*ant*
el león	*lion*
el oso	*bear*
el pájaro / el ave	*bird*
la serpiente	*snake*

Otras palabras — *Other words*

el árbol	*tree*
el bosque	*forest*
la cueva	*cave*
la finca	*farm*
la granja	*farm*
el hoyo	*hole*
el océano	*ocean*
el río	*river*
la selva	*jungle*
peligroso/a	*dangerous*

Algunos verbos — *Some verbs*

cuidar	*to take care of*
preocuparse (por)	*to worry about; to concern oneself with*

El medio ambiente — *The environment*

Los desastres	*Disasters*
el cambio climático	*climate change*
la contaminación	*pollution*
el derrame de petróleo	*oil spill*
la destrucción	*destruction*
el efecto invernadero	*greenhouse effect*
el huracán	*hurricane*
el incendio	*fire*
la inundación	*flood*
la lluvia ácida	*acid rain*
la tragedia	*tragedy*
el terremoto	*earthquake*
la tormenta	*storm*
el tornado	*tornado*
el tsunami	*tsunami*

El reciclaje	*Recycling*
el aluminio	*aluminum*
la botella	*bottle*
la caja (de cartón)	*(cardboard) box*
la lata	*can*
el papel	*paper*
el periódico	*newspaper*
el plástico	*plastic*
el vidrio	*glass*

El planeta	*The planet*
el cielo	*sky; heaven*
la naturaleza	*nature*
el recurso natural	*natural resource*
la selva (tropical)	*(tropical) rain forest*
la tierra	*land; soil*
la Tierra	*Earth*

Algunos verbos	*Some verbs*
botar	*to throw away*
contaminar	*to pollute*
hacer daño	*to (do) damage; to harm*
matar	*to kill*
plantar	*to plant*
proteger	*to protect*
reciclar	*to recycle*
reforestar	*to reforest*
reutilizar	*to reuse*
sembrar (e → ie)	*to sow*

Otras palabras	*Other words*
el aire	*air*
la basura	*trash*
la calidad	*quality*
la ecología	*ecology*
el vertedero	*dump*
puro/a	*pure*
vivo/a	*alive; living*

La política — *Politics*

Los cargos	*Posts*
el alcalde / la alcaldesa	*mayor*
el/la candidato/a	*candidate*
el/la dictador/a	*dictator*
el/la diputado/a	*deputy; representative*
el/la gobernador/a	*governor*
el/la juez/a	*judge*
el/la presidente/a	*president*
el rey / la reina	*king / queen*
el/la senador/a	*senator*

Las administraciones y los regímenes	*Administrations and regimes*
el congreso	*congress*
la democracia	*democracy*
la dictadura	*dictatorship*
el estado	*state*
el gobierno	*government*
la ley	*law*
la monarquía	*monarchy*
la presidencia	*presidency*

Las cuestiones políticas	*Political matters*
el bienestar	*well-being; welfare*
la corte	*court*
la defensa	*defense*
la delincuencia	*crime*
el desempleo	*unemployment*
la deuda (externa)	*(foreign) debt*
el discurso	*speech*
las elecciones	*elections*
la encuesta	*survey; poll*
la guerra	*war*
la huelga	*strike*
el impuesto	*tax*
la inflación	*inflation*
el juicio	*trial*
el partido político	*political party*
el voto	*vote*

Algunos verbos	*Some verbs*
apoyar	*to support*
combatir	*to fight; to combat*
elegir	*to elect*
estar en huelga	*to be on strike*
llevar a cabo	*to carry out*
luchar	*to fight; to combat*
meterse en política	*to get involved in politics*
resolver (o → ue)	*to resolve*
votar	*to vote*

Las preposiciones — *Prepositions*

See pages 451–452.

12 Y por fin, ¡lo sé!

This final chapter is designed for you to see just how much Spanish you have acquired thus far. The *major points* of **Capítulos 7–11** are recycled in this chapter. No new vocabulary is presented.

All learners are different in terms of what they have mastered and what they still need to practice. Take the time with this chapter to determine what you feel confident with, and what you personally need to work on. And remember, language learning is a process. Like any skill, learning Spanish requires practice, review of the basics, and then more practice!

Before we begin revisiting the important grammar concepts, go to the end of each chapter, to the **Vocabulario activo** summary sections, and review the vocabulary that you have learned. Doing so now will help you successfully and creatively complete the following recycling activities. Consult the **Vocabulario activo** pages at the end of each chapter as needed as you progress through this chapter.

Learning Outcomes

After reviewing Chapters 7–11, you will be able to:

- ✔ communicate preferences and express ideas on topics such as food, clothing, health, travel, animals, the environment, and politics.
- ✔ relate ideas about past experiences and your daily routine.
- ✔ convey information about people and things.
- ✔ describe what is happening at the moment.
- ✔ make requests, give advice, and articulate desires and opinions on a variety of topics.
- ✔ exchange interesting facts about Chile, Paraguay, Argentina, Uruguay, Peru, Bolivia, Ecuador, Venezuela, Colombia, Cuba, Puerto Rico, and the Dominican Republic.
- ✔ review and reflect on readings from these chapters.

Estrategia

Beyond reading these suggestions carefully, you will want to review the rubric for each section prior to beginning the activities. The first rubric can be found on page 475.

Organizing Your Review

There are processes used by successful language learners for reviewing a world language. The following tips can help you organize your review. There is no one correct way, but these are some suggestions that will best utilize your time and energy.

1 Reviewing Strategies

1. Make a list of the *major* topics you have studied and need to review, dividing them into categories: *vocabulary, grammar,* and *culture.* These are the topics where you need to focus the majority of your time and energy.
   Note: The two-page chapter openers can help you determine the *major* topics.
2. Allocate a minimum of an hour each day over a period of days to review. Budget the majority of your time with the major topics. After beginning with the major grammar and vocabulary topics, review the secondary/supporting grammar topics and the culture. Cramming the night before a test is *not* an effective way to review and retain information.
3. Many educational researchers suggest that you start your review with the most recent chapter, or for this review, **Capítulo 11**. The most recent chapter is the freshest in your mind, so you tend to remember the concepts better, and you will experience quick success in your review.
4. Spend the most amount of time on concepts in which you determine *you* need to improve. Revisit the self-assessment tools from **Y por fin, ¿cómo andas?** in each chapter to see how you rated yourself. Those tools are designed to help you become good at self-assessing what *you* need to work on the most.

2 Reviewing Grammar

1. When reviewing grammar, begin with the *major* points, that is, begin with the *preterit, imperfect, pronouns (direct, indirect, and reflexive), commands, present progressive,* and the *subjunctive*. After feeling confident using the major grammar points correctly, then proceed with the additional grammar points and review them.
2. Good ways to review include redoing activities in your textbook, redoing activities in ***¡Anda!*** online.

3 Reviewing Vocabulary

1. When studying vocabulary, it is usually most helpful to look at the English word, and then say or write the word in Spanish. Make a special list of words that are difficult for you to remember, writing them in a small notebook or in an electronic file. Pull out the notebook every time you have a few minutes (in between classes, waiting in line at the grocery store, etc.) to review the words. The **Vocabulario activo** pages at the end of each chapter will help you organize the most important words of each chapter.
2. Saying vocabulary (which includes verbs) out loud helps you retain the words better.

4 Overall Review Technique

1. Get together with someone with whom you can practice speaking Spanish. It is always good to structure the oral practice. If you need something to spark the conversation, take the drawings from each vocabulary presentation in ***¡Anda! Curso elemental*** and say as many things as you can about each picture. Have a friendly challenge to see who can make more complete sentences or create the longest story about the pictures. This will help you build your confidence and practice stringing sentences together to speak in paragraphs.
2. Yes, it is important for you to know "mechanical" pieces of information such as verb endings, or how to take a sentence and replace the direct object with a pronoun. *But*, it is *much more important* for you to be able to take those mechanical pieces of information and put them all together, creating meaningful and creative samples of your speaking and writing on the themes of **Capítulos 7–11**.
   Also remember that **Capítulos 7–11** are built upon previous knowledge that you acquired in the beginning chapters of ***¡Anda! Curso elemental.***
3. You are on the road to success if you can demonstrate that you can speak and write in paragraphs, using a wide variety of verbs and vocabulary words correctly. Keep up the good work!

Comunicación

Capítulo 7

12-1 ¡Fiesta! Ustedes decidieron tener una fiesta y tienen que trabajar mucho para prepararlo todo. Organicen la fiesta siguiendo el modelo y utilizando **el pretérito**.

Estrategia

Before beginning each activity, make sure that you have reviewed carefully the concepts in each given chapter so that you are able to move through the activities seamlessly as you put it all together.

MODELO ¿preparar / tu compañero / los perros calientes?

E1: *¿Preparó tu compañero los perros calientes?*

E2: *Sí, los preparó esta mañana.*

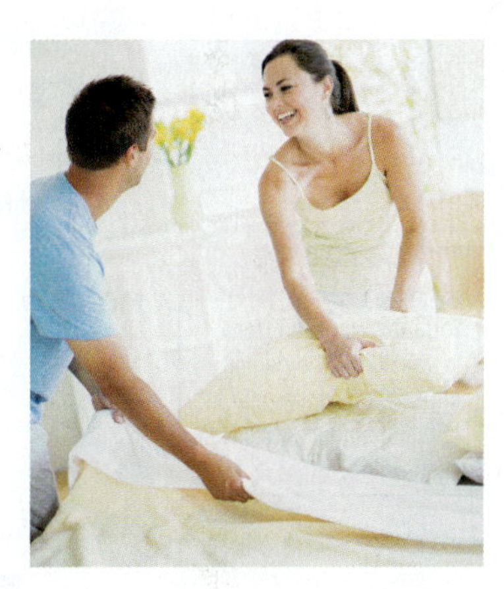

1. ¿sacar / tú / dinero del banco?
2. ¿pedir / ustedes / los mariscos?
3. ¿buscar / tú / el pastel?
4. ¿traer / Jorge / la música?
5. ¿poner / ustedes / los manteles?
6. ¿encontrar / Manuel y Manuela / las servilletas?
7. ¿empezar a limpiar / tú / el apartamento?
8. ¿hacer / Rafael y tú / las camas?

12-2 Después de la fiesta

¡La fiesta de la actividad **12-1** fue un éxito! Describan lo que pasó en la fiesta y qué hicieron cuando se fueron los invitados. Sean creativos/as y usen por lo menos **siete** oraciones.

MODELO *¡Nuestra fiesta fue un éxito! Vinieron muchos invitados. La gente bailó, comió y se divirtió mucho. Escuchamos música salsa y rock. Después, tuvimos que pasar la aspiradora…*

12-3 La semana pasada

Túrnense para describir qué hicieron y adónde fueron la semana pasada, usando por lo menos **siete** oraciones en **el pretérito** con verbos diferentes.

MODELO *La semana pasada hice muchas cosas. Por ejemplo, vi una película en la televisión. Estudié mucho también. Conduje a la universidad el martes en vez de tomar el autobús porque tuve que ir al médico por la tarde. El miércoles por la noche mi amigo y yo fuimos al concierto de Juanes. Dormí muy poco toda la semana…*

l	m	m	j	v	s	d
estudiar, ver una película	ir al médico	ir al concierto de Juanes			ir al café Chulo	

12-4 Una comida especial

Túrnense para describir una comida especial que prepararon recientemente, usando por lo menos siete oraciones en **el pretérito** con verbos diferentes.

Estrategia

You may want to refer to *También se dice…* in Appendix 3 for specific food vocabulary for your description.

MODELO *Anoche preparé una cena muy especial para mis padres. Primero compré muchas cosas deliciosas en el supermercado como melón, peras, patatas, lechuga…*

En casa lavé las verduras y las peras muy bien. Después preparé la carne con ajo, sal y pimienta para cocinarla a la parrilla. Decidí cocinar las patatas al horno y…

A mi padre le gusta la carne roja, con sangre, entonces la hice poco hecha…

Rúbrica

Estrategia

You and your instructor can use this rubric to assess your progress for activities **12-1** through **12-4**.

All aspects of our lives benefit from self-reflection and self-assessment. Learning Spanish is an aspect of our academic and future professional lives that benefits greatly from just such a self-assessment. Also coming into play is the fact that as college students, you personally are being held accountable for your learning and are expected to take ownership for your performance. Having said that, we instructors can assist you greatly by letting you know what we will expect of you. It will help you determine how well you are doing with the recycling of **Capítulo 7**. This rubric is meant first and foremost for you to use as a self-assessment, but you also can use it to peer-assess. Your instructor may use the rubric to assess your progress as well.

	3 EXCEEDS EXPECTATIONS	2 MEETS EXPECTATIONS	1 APPROACHES EXPECTATIONS	0 DOES NOT MEET EXPECTATIONS
Duración y precisión	• Has at least 8 sentences and includes all the required information. • May have errors, but they do not interfere with communication.	• Has 5–7 sentences and includes all the required information. • May have errors, but they rarely interfere with communication.	• Has 4 sentences and includes some of the required information. • Has errors that interfere with communication.	• Supplies fewer sentences and little of the required information in *Approaches Expectations*. • If communicating at all, has frequent errors that make communication limited or impossible.
Gramática nueva del *Capítulo 7*	• Makes excellent use of the chapter's new grammar (e.g., **irregular verbs in the preterit**). • Uses a wide variety of verbs when appropriate.	• Makes good use of the chapter's new grammar (e.g., **irregular verbs in the preterit**). • Uses a variety of verbs when appropriate.	• Makes use of some of the chapter's new grammar (e.g., **irregular verbs in the preterit**). • Uses a limited variety of verbs when appropriate.	• Uses little, if any, of the chapter's new grammar (e.g., **irregular verbs in the preterit**). • Uses few, if any, of the chapter's verbs.
Vocabulario nuevo del *Capítulo 7*	• Uses many of the new vocabulary words (e.g., foods, food preparation, and restaurants).	• Uses a variety of the new vocabulary words (e.g., foods, food preparation, and restaurants).	• Uses some of the new vocabulary words (e.g., foods, food preparation, and restaurants).	• Uses few, if any, new vocabulary words (e.g., foods, food preparation, and restaurants).
Gramática y vocabulario reciclado de los capítulos anteriores	• Does an excellent job using recycled grammar and vocabulary to support what is being said. • Uses a wide array of recycled verbs. • Uses some recycled vocabulary, but focuses predominantly on new vocabulary.	• Does a good job using recycled grammar and vocabulary to support what is being said. • Uses an array of recycled verbs. • Uses some recycled vocabulary, but focuses predominantly on new vocabulary.	• Does an average job using recycled grammar and vocabulary to support what is being said. • Uses a limited array of recycled verbs. • Uses mostly recycled vocabulary and some new vocabulary.	• If speaking at all, relies almost completely on a few isolated words. • Usage of previously learned grammar is inconsistent.
Esfuerzo	• Clearly the student made his/her best effort.	• The student made a good effort.	• The student made an effort.	• Little or no effort went into the activity.

Capítulo 8

12-5 La boda del siglo

David y Adriana se casan. Tu compañero/a y tú están invitados y están planeando cómo vestirse. Sigan el modelo.

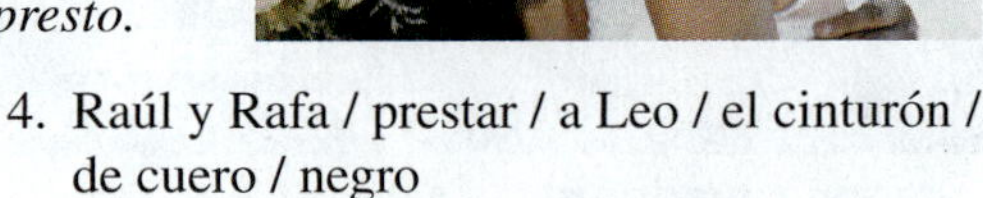

MODELO tú / prestar / a mí / pantalones / amarillo

E1: *¿Me prestas tus pantalones amarillos?*

E2: *Sí, te los presto. / No, no te los presto.*

1. tú / prestar / a mí / zapatos / negro
2. tú / prestar / a Julieta / blusa / azul / seda
3. ellas / prestar / a Mariela / falda / corto / atrevido
4. Raúl y Rafa / prestar / a Leo / el cinturón / de cuero / negro
5. Ud. / prestar / a Jaime / coche / nuevo

12-6 La recomendación fue...

Túrnense para formar preguntas y contestar según el modelo.

Estrategia

You can elaborate on your answers as to why you recommended or did not recommend something by adding **porque** and a short explanation. In the model, you could say *No, no se las recomendé porque son muy caras.*

MODELO tú / las blusas de seda (a tus primas)

E1: *¿Les recomendaste las blusas de seda a tus primas?*

E2: *No, no se las recomendé. / Sí, se las recomendé.*

1. ellos / los museos de arqueología (a tu profesor/a)
2. tú / el café donde te encuentras con tus amigos (a tus padres)
3. tu hermano / un hotel de cinco estrellas (a su amiga que no tiene dinero)
4. nosotros / la música de Shakira (a unos compañeros)
5. yo / la película *Shrek* (a mis primos de cinco años)
6. ustedes / las novelas de Gabriel García Márquez (a sus tíos)
7. tú / la clase de español (a tu mejor amigo/a)

12-7 Encuesta

Usa estas expresiones para crear una encuesta de **diez** preguntas. Hazles las preguntas a diez personas diferentes y comparte tus resultados con la clase.

PREGUNTA	ME ENCANTA(N)	ME MOLESTA(N)	ME IMPORTA(N)	ME HACE(N) FALTA	ME FASCINA(N)
¿Te gustan los animales salvajes? ¿Cuáles?					Erika: Sí, me fascinan los leones.
¿Te gusta la ropa elegante?		Alex: No, me molesta. Prefiero la ropa informal.			

12-8 Para conocerte mejor

Cuando tenías quince años, ¿qué hacías en las siguientes situaciones? Completa los siguientes pasos.

Paso 1 Contesta las siguientes preguntas.

1. ¿Qué te ponías cuando salías con esa "persona especial"?
2. Antes de dormirte, ¿pensabas en tu día?
3. ¿Tenías un perro?
4. ¿Cómo te divertías?
5. ¿Siempre te acordabas de hacer toda la tarea?
6. Si tenías tiempo, ¿con quién(es) te reunías?
7. ¿Dónde te gustaba sentarte en el cine, adelante o atrás? ¿Por qué?
8. ¿Qué querías ser de mayor?
9. ¿En qué situaciones te ponías nervioso/a?
10. ¿Cuándo te sentías feliz?

Estrategia

It is rare that people remember *everything* that they hear! It is important that you feel comfortable asking someone to repeat information or asking for clarification.

Paso 2 Escucha las respuestas de tu compañero/a. ¿Cuántas preguntas contestaron ustedes de manera similar? ¿De manera diferente?

MODELO E1: ¿Qué hacías por las tardes, después de salir del colegio?

E2: *Yo jugaba al tenis. ¿Qué hacías tú?*

E1: *Hacía la tarea y ayudaba a mi madre con los quehaceres de la casa.*

12-9 Mi primera casa

¿Cómo era tu primera casa o la de un/a amigo/a de tu infancia? Descríbesela a un/a compañero/a en por lo menos **diez** oraciones incluyendo todos los detalles posibles (los muebles, los colores, etc.).

MODELO *Mi primera casa estaba en una ciudad grande. Tenía dos dormitorios. La cocina era amarilla. El comedor y la sala eran pequeños. Tenía solamente* (only) *un baño…*

Estrategia

You and your instructor can use this rubric to assess your progress for activities **12-5** through **12-9**.

Rúbrica

	3 EXCEEDS EXPECTATIONS	2 MEETS EXPECTATIONS	1 APPROACHES EXPECTATIONS	0 DOES NOT MEET EXPECTATIONS
Duración y precisión	• Has at least 8 sentences and includes all the required information. • May have errors, but they do not interfere with communication.	• Has 5–7 sentences and includes all the required information. • May have errors, but they rarely interfere with communication.	• Has 4 sentences and includes some of the required information. • Has errors that interfere with communication.	• Supplies fewer sentences and little of the required information in *Approaches Expectations*. • If communicating at all, has frequent errors that make communication limited or impossible.
Gramática nueva del *Capítulo 8*	• Makes excellent use of the chapter's new grammar (e.g., **the imperfect, object pronouns,** and **verbs like *gustar***). • Uses a wide variety of verbs when appropriate.	• Makes good use of the chapter's new grammar (e.g., **the imperfect, object pronouns,** and **verbs like *gustar***). • Uses a variety of verbs when appropriate.	• Makes use of some of the chapter's new grammar (e.g., **the imperfect, object pronouns,** and **verbs like *gustar***). • Uses a limited variety of verbs when appropriate.	• Uses little, if any, of the chapter's new grammar (e.g., **the imperfect, object pronouns,** and **verbs like *gustar***). • Uses few, if any, of the chapter's verbs.
Vocabulario nuevo del *Capítulo 8*	• Uses many of the new clothing-related vocabulary words.	• Uses a variety of the new clothing-related vocabulary words.	• Uses some of the new clothing-related vocabulary words.	• Uses few, if any, new clothing-related vocabulary words.
Gramática y vocabulario reciclado de los capítulos anteriores	• Does an excellent job using recycled grammar and vocabulary to support what is being said. • Uses a wide array of recycled verbs. • Uses some recycled vocabulary, but focuses predominantly on new vocabulary.	• Does a good job using recycled grammar and vocabulary to support what is being said. • Uses an array of recycled verbs. • Uses some recycled vocabulary, but focuses predominantly on new vocabulary.	• Does an average job using recycled grammar and vocabulary to support what is being said. • Uses a limited array of recycled verbs. • Uses mostly recycled vocabulary and some new vocabulary.	• If speaking at all, relies almost completely on a few isolated words. • Usage of previously learned grammar is inconsistent.
Esfuerzo	• Clearly the student made his/her best effort.	• The student made a good effort.	• The student made an effort.	• Little or no effort went into the activity.

Capítulo 9

12-10 Un diálogo Creen un diálogo entre un/a médico/a y un/a paciente con respecto a sus síntomas y su tratamiento. Escriban por lo menos **catorce** oraciones.

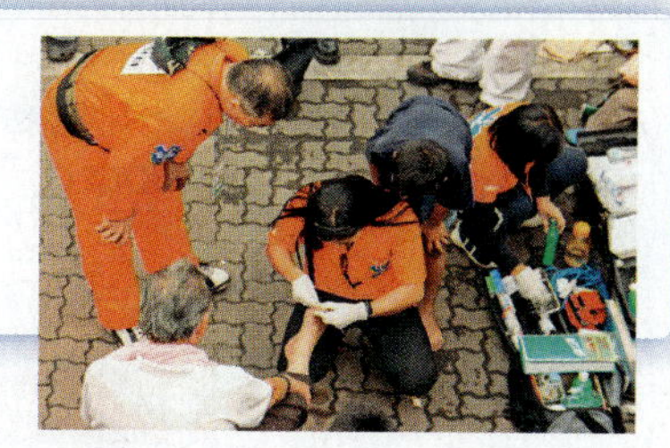

MODELO
E1 (MÉDICO/A): *¿Cómo está? ¿Qué le duele?*
E2 (PACIENTE): *Creo que tengo catarro o un virus. Me duele todo.*
E1: *¿Tiene fiebre? ¿Tose? ¿Estornuda?*
E2: *No, no tengo fiebre pero sí tengo tos. Y sí, estornudo mucho. ¡También me quemé!*
E1: *¿Se quemó? ¿Cómo?*
E2: ...

12-11 ¡Me enfermé! Completa los siguientes pasos.

Estrategia

Being a good listener is an important life skill. Repeating what your classmate said gives you practice in demonstrating how well you listened.

Paso 1 Descríbele a un/a compañero/a tu última enfermedad en por lo menos **diez** oraciones.

MODELO *Me enfermé la semana pasada. Tuve gripe y guardé cama por una semana. Mi madre me llevó al médico porque me dolía el cuerpo y tenía fiebre...*

Paso 2 Describe en tus propias (*own*) palabras la enfermedad de tu compañero/a de clase.

12-12 El e-mail de Carla Carla le escribe a su hermana sobre sus vacaciones en Sudamérica. Completa el párrafo con las formas correctas de los verbos en **el pretérito** o **el imperfecto**, según el caso. Después comparte tus respuestas con un/a compañero/a, explicando siempre por qué elegiste el pretérito o el imperfecto.

¡Hola, hermana!

¿Cómo estás? ¡Sudamérica es increíble! La gente, la comida, el paisaje, el tiempo —todo es maravilloso. Te cuento un poco:

En las montañas de Perú (1) ___________ (hacer) mucho frío por la noche, pero en las playas de Ecuador el sol (2) ___________ (ser) muy agradable. En los Andes nosotros (3) ___________ (hacer) muchas actividades. Primero, (4) ___________ (subir) a un volcán famoso de Ecuador, el Cotopaxi. Después, (5) ___________ (ir) a explorar los picos más altos de los Andes. No (6) ___________ (poder) llegar a la cumbre (*mountain top*), porque (7) ___________ (haber) mucha nieve. En Argentina yo (8) ___________ (esquiar) un poco y después (9) ___________ (visitar) un pueblo pequeño cerca de la estación de esquí. Yo (10) ___________ (sacar) muchas fotos. Después de pasar unas horas en el pueblo, el grupo (11) ___________ (decidir) volver al hotel porque todos nosotros (12) ___________ (estar) cansados.

Escribo más mañana,
Carla

12-13 **¿Qué hiciste ayer?** Escribe un párrafo sobre lo que hiciste ayer. Incluye por lo menos **diez** actividades usando un mínimo de **siete** verbos reflexivos. Después, léeselo a un/a compañero/a.

MODELO *Ayer me levanté a las seis de la mañana. Me duché en tres minutos. Me puse los pantalones rojos con rayas blancas…*

Estrategia

You and your instructor can use this rubric to assess your progress for activities **12-10** through **12-13**.

Rúbrica

	3 EXCEEDS EXPECTATIONS	2 MEETS EXPECTATIONS	1 APPROACHES EXPECTATIONS	0 DOES NOT MEET EXPECTATIONS
Duración y precisión	• Has at least 8 sentences and includes all the required information. • May have errors, but they do not interfere with communication.	• Has 5–7 sentences and includes all the required information. • May have errors, but they rarely interfere with communication.	• Has 4 sentences and includes some of the required information. • Has errors that interfere with communication.	• Supplies fewer sentences and little of the required information in *Approaches Expectations.* • If communicating at all, has frequent errors that make communication limited or impossible.
Gramática nueva del *Capítulo 9*	• Makes excellent use of the chapter's new grammar (e.g., **preterit and imperfect, reflexive verbs**). • Uses a wide variety of verbs when appropriate.	• Makes good use of the chapter's new grammar (e.g., **preterit and imperfect, reflexive verbs**). • Uses a variety of verbs when appropriate.	• Makes use of some of the chapter's new grammar (e.g., **preterit and imperfect, reflexive verbs**). • Uses a limited variety of verbs when appropriate.	• Uses little, if any, of the chapter's new grammar (e.g., **preterit and imperfect, reflexive verbs**). • Uses few, if any, of the chapter's verbs.
Vocabulario nuevo del *Capítulo 9*	• Uses many of the new vocabulary words (e.g., **the body** and **medical terms**).	• Uses a variety of the new vocabulary words (e.g., **the body** and **medical terms**).	• Uses some of the new vocabulary words (e.g., **the body** and **medical terms**).	• Uses few, if any, new vocabulary words (e.g., **the body** and **medical terms**).
Gramática y vocabulario reciclado de los capítulos anteriores	• Does an excellent job using recycled grammar and vocabulary to support what is being said. • Uses a wide array of recycled verbs. • Uses some recycled vocabulary, but focuses predominantly on new vocabulary.	• Does a good job using recycled grammar and vocabulary to support what is being said. • Uses an array of recycled verbs. • Uses some recycled vocabulary, but focuses predominantly on new vocabulary.	• Does an average job using recycled grammar and vocabulary to support what is being said. • Uses a limited array of recycled verbs. • Uses mostly recycled vocabulary and some new vocabulary.	• If speaking at all, relies almost completely on a few isolated words. • Usage of previously learned grammar is inconsistent.
Esfuerzo	• Clearly the student made his/her best effort.	• The student made a good effort.	• The student made an effort.	• Little or no effort went into the activity.

Capítulo 10

12-14 El blog de *Viajes por el mundo* Escribe una entrada en un blog sobre un lugar interesante que ya conoces o que quieres conocer. Incluye dónde está, cómo se llega allí, qué puedes hacer, dónde puedes quedarte y comer, cómo son los alojamientos (*accommodations*) y restaurantes, tus recomendaciones para una estancia (*stay*) fenomenal, etc. Necesitas escribir por lo menos **diez** oraciones y usar una variedad de verbos. Después léesela a un/a compañero/a.

MODELO *Durante las últimas vacaciones fui a Punta Cana. Fue la primera vez que visité la República Dominicana. Fui en avión desde Miami. Todos los días iba a la playa. Allí nadaba…*

12-15 Mis vacaciones favoritas ¿Adónde fuiste y cómo fueron tus vacaciones favoritas? Descríbeselas a un/a compañero/a en por lo menos **siete** oraciones usando el pretérito y una variedad de verbos.

MODELO *Mis vacaciones en Argentina fueron mis mejores vacaciones. Fuimos a la playa, donde mi familia y yo anduvimos muchas horas. Bebí mate por primera vez…*

12-16 Y también...

Imagina que tienes un hijo y que, por primera vez, él va a salir solo con sus amigos y se va a llevar el coche. ¿Qué le aconsejas? Túrnense para hacer **mandatos informales** con los siguientes verbos.

MODELO E1: leer / el manual
E2: *Lee el manual.*

1. conducir / con cuidado
2. llevar / la licencia
3. tener cuidado / los peatones
4. llenar el tanque / gasolina
5. no mandar / mensajes de texto
6. no perder / llaves
7. no abrir / ventanas / si llueve
8. estacionar / en lugares seguros
9. no doblar a la izquierda / sin mirar
10. no comer ni beber / en el coche
11. limpiar / parabrisas
12. no ir / muy rápido

12-17 ¡Me molestas!

¿En tu vida hay alguien que te está volviendo loco/a (*is driving you crazy*)? Túrnense para decirle a tu compañero/a lo que debe y no debe hacer. Pueden usar las palabras y expresiones de la lista y otras también. ¡Sean creativos/as!

Estrategia

Organize your thoughts in chronological order, and use transitions in your paragraphs. Consider words like *primero, segundo, tercero, próximo, después*, and *finalmente*.

guardar tu comida	tener más paciencia
no dejar la ropa sucia en el piso	no estornudar
lavar los platos	mejorarte
sacar la basura	cuidarte
no invitar siempre a tus amigos	no ponerte mi ropa

MODELO *Raúl, por favor, ¡me estás volviendo loca! Primero, guarda tu comida en el refrigerador, no la pongas en el sofá. Segundo, ¡no estornudes encima de la comida! Ponte el abrigo porque hace frío. Cuídate, por favor...*

12-18 En la gasolinera

Están en una gasolinera. Túrnense para decirle al empleado (*attendant*) lo que necesitan. Usen por lo menos **diez** mandatos formales.

MODELO *Ponga aire en las llantas, por favor. También, abra el baúl, por favor. Yo no puedo abrirlo...*

12-19 ¡Por fin!

¡Este es el momento que esperabas! ¡Por fin ustedes son los profesores de español! Túrnense para decirles a sus estudiantes por lo menos **ocho** cosas que deben o no deben hacer. ¡Sean creativos/as!

MODELO *Hagan la tarea para mañana. También, hablen en español durante toda la clase…*

12-20 En mi opinión

Hagan por lo menos **diez** comparaciones usando las siguientes acciones, una variedad de adjetivos y adverbios y las comparaciones (**más… que, menos… que, tan… como** y **tanto/a/os/as… como**). Después comparte tus oraciones con un/a compañero/a para saber si tienen las mismas opiniones.

MODELO ir en bicicleta ir a pie
Ir en bicicleta es más rápido que ir a pie.

viajar por avión	viajar por barco
ir por autobús	ir en motocicleta
ir a pie	ir en bicicleta
ir en carro	ir a la playa
ir a las montañas	quedarse en un hotel elegante
quedarse en un hotel barato	visitar un parque de atracciones
visitar un bosque nacional	visitar una selva tropical

12-21 Comparando

Estás planeando unas vacaciones. Dile a tu compañero/a cuáles son, en tu opinión, los mejores y los peores servicios y destinos. Usa comparaciones y superlativos. Crea por lo menos **diez** oraciones.

MODELO *El aeropuerto de Austin es más pequeño que el aeropuerto de Dallas, pero en mi opinión es mejor porque no es muy grande. Para mí, la agencia Travel Experts es la mejor porque los agentes de viajes saben preparar unos viajes estupendos. Por ejemplo, la playa de Ixtapa en México es tan bonita como la playa de Cancún, y los hoteles no cuestan tanto como los hoteles de Cancún…*

Estrategia

You and your instructor can use this rubric to assess your progress for activities **12-14** through **12-21.**

Rúbrica

	3 EXCEEDS EXPECTATIONS	2 MEETS EXPECTATIONS	1 APPROACHES EXPECTATIONS	0 DOES NOT MEET EXPECTATIONS
Duración y precisión	• Has at least 8 sentences and includes all the required information. • May have errors, but they do not interfere with communication.	• Has 5–7 sentences and includes all the required information. • May have errors, but they rarely interfere with communication.	• Has 4 sentences and includes some of the required information. • Has errors that interfere with communication.	• Supplies fewer sentences and little of the required information in *Approaches Expectations*. • If communicating at all, has frequent errors that make communication limited or impossible.
Gramática nueva del *Capítulo 10*	• Makes excellent use of the chapter's new grammar (e.g., **formal and informal commands, the comparative** and **superlative**). • Uses a wide variety of verbs when appropriate.	• Makes good use of the chapter's new grammar (e.g., **formal and informal commands, the comparative** and **superlative**). • Uses a variety of verbs when appropriate.	• Makes use of some of the chapter's new grammar (e.g., **formal and informal commands, the comparative** and **superlative**). • Uses a limited variety of verbs when appropriate.	• Uses little, if any, of the chapter's new grammar (e.g., **formal and informal commands, the comparative** and **superlative**). • Uses few, if any, of the chapter's verbs.
Vocabulario nuevo del *Capítulo 10*	• Uses many of the new travel-related vocabulary words.	• Uses a variety of the new travel-related vocabulary words.	• Uses some of the new travel-related vocabulary words.	• Uses few, if any, new travel-related vocabulary words.
Gramática y vocabulario reciclado de los capítulos anteriores	• Does an excellent job using recycled grammar and vocabulary to support what is being said. • Uses a wide array of recycled verbs. • Uses some recycled vocabulary, but focuses predominantly on new vocabulary.	• Does a good job using recycled grammar and vocabulary to support what is being said. • Uses an array of recycled verbs. • Uses some recycled vocabulary, but focuses predominantly on new vocabulary.	• Does an average job using recycled grammar and vocabulary to support what is being said. • Uses a limited array of recycled verbs. • Uses mostly recycled vocabulary and some new vocabulary.	• If speaking at all, relies almost completely on a few isolated words. • Usage of previously learned grammar is inconsistent.
Esfuerzo	• Clearly the student made his/her best effort.	• The student made a good effort.	• The student made an effort.	• Little or no effort went into the activity.

Capítulo 11

12-22 Acciones comunes

Completen los siguientes pasos.

Paso 1 En parejas, escriban en un papel limpio una lista de diez infinitivos de verbos de acción de los **Capítulos 7–11**.

Paso 2 Intercambien papeles con otra pareja. Escriban una oración para cada infinitivo, usando el presente progresivo.

MODELO plantar

Hoy mis padres están plantando muchas flores en su jardín.

12-23 Me imagino que...

Escribe una lista de diez personas que conoces bien. Después túrnense para describir lo que está haciendo cada persona en este momento.

MODELO mi padre

Son las ocho y media de la mañana. Mi padre está haciendo ejercicio.

12-24 Mis deberes

Siempre hay algo que podemos hacer para mejorar. Dile a tu compañero/a por lo menos **diez** cosas que debes hacer ahora o que te propones (*you intend*) hacer en el futuro. Usa **el subjuntivo** cuando sea necesario.

MODELO *Primero, es necesario que estudie más en el futuro. También es importante que no coma tanto chocolate, pero es dudoso que pueda evitarlo. Entonces, es importante que compre cosas saludables. Pero, ¡qué lástima! ¡Me fascina el chocolate! Pues, como me gusta tanto, es importante que haga más ejercicio. ¡Es una lástima que no me guste hacerlo!*

12.25 Mi casa ideal

¿Cómo esperas que sea tu casa en diez años? Completa los siguientes pasos.

You may want to draw the floor plan of your house and label the rooms. That way, it will be easier to talk about where each room is located in relation to other rooms. When working with a partner, you might want to draw your partner's house as you hear it described, taking note of the prepositions he/she has mentioned.

Paso 1 Descríbele a un/a compañero/a con todo detalle tu casa ideal (los cuartos, los muebles, los colores, etc.). Incluye por lo menos **cinco** preposiciones diferentes en la descripción.

MODELO *Espero que mi casa tenga cinco dormitorios. Al lado de la puerta quiero que haya una sala y una cocina detrás de la sala. ¡Ojalá que tenga una cocina muy grande!*

Paso 2 Repite lo que tu compañero/a te dijo. Es importante que uses y practiques las preposiciones.

12.26 El medio ambiente

Andrew y Sarah conversan sobre los problemas del medio ambiente después de un viaje a las islas Galápagos. Termina la conversación con la forma correcta de los verbos o en **el subjuntivo** o **el infinitivo**.

ANDREW: Es increíble que los ecuatorianos (1) __________ (intentar) proteger tanto el medio ambiente.

SARAH: Es una lástima que todavía muchos estadounidenses no (2) __________ (reciclar) ni el plástico ni el aluminio. Es necesario que yo personalmente (3) __________ (buscar) alguna manera de reciclar más. También es importante que tú (4) __________ (reducir) el uso de envases de vidrio. Además, me molesta (5) __________ (tener) que respirar tanto humo (*fumes*) en las calles.

ANDREW: Es cierto. Cada uno debe hacer un esfuerzo para (6) __________ (proteger) el medio ambiente contra la contaminación. Es imposible que los gobiernos (7) __________ (controlar) adecuadamente el uso de procesos y materiales que contaminan.

SARAH: Es dudoso que los gobiernos solos (8) __________ (resolver) los problemas. No podemos solucionar estos problemas sin (9) __________ (trabajar) juntos. Todos debemos hacer algo para cambiar las cosas.

ANDREW: ¡Qué aire tan puro respirábamos en las islas!

SARAH: ¡Sí! Ojalá que la gente (10) __________ (disfrutar) de este paraíso natural por muchos años.

12-27 Hechos, datos y opiniones Juntos terminen las oraciones con **por** o **para** y otra información necesaria. Después compartan sus oraciones con otra pareja. Expliquen por qué usaron **por** o **para** en cada caso.

1. Ayer trabajé en el centro de reciclaje por/para…
2. Luis y yo anduvimos por la granja por/para…
3. Decidí votar en las elecciones por/para…
4. Hay que luchar contra la delincuencia por/para…
5. El Presidente va viajar por Latinoamérica por/para…
6. El Presidente ofrece soluciones por/para…
7. Este dinero es por/para la campaña del Sr. García por/para…
8. Él decidió meterse en la política por/para…
9. Es honesto por/para un hombre…
10. Pero a veces propone soluciones difíciles por/para…

Estrategia

You and your instructor can use this rubric to assess your progress for activities **12-22** through **12-27**.

Rúbrica

	3 EXCEEDS EXPECTATIONS	2 MEETS EXPECTATIONS	1 APPROACHES EXPECTATIONS	0 DOES NOT MEET EXPECTATIONS
Duración y precisión	• Has at least 8 sentences and includes all the required information. • May have errors, but they do not interfere with communication.	• Has 5–7 sentences and includes all the required information. • May have errors, but they rarely interfere with communication.	• Has 4 sentences and includes some of the required information. • Has errors that interfere with communication.	• Supplies fewer than 4 sentences and little of the required information. • If communicating at all, has frequent errors that make communication limited or impossible.
Gramática nueva del *Capítulo 11*	• Makes excellent use of the chapter's new grammar (e.g., **the present progressive, the subjunctive**, and **prepositions**). • Uses a wide variety of verbs when appropriate.	• Makes good use of the chapter's new grammar (e.g., **the present progressive, the subjunctive**, and **prepositions**). • Uses a variety of verbs when appropriate.	• Makes use of some of the chapter's new grammar (e.g., **the present progressive, the subjunctive**, and **prepositions**). • Uses a limited variety of verbs when appropriate.	• Uses little, if any, of the chapter's new grammar (e.g., **the present progressive, the subjunctive**, and **prepositions**). • Uses few, if any, of the chapter's verbs.
Vocabulario nuevo del *Capítulo 11*	• Uses many of the new vocabulary words (e.g., **animals, the environment**, and **politics**).	• Uses a variety of the new vocabulary words (e.g., **animals, the environment**, and **politics**).	• Uses some of the new vocabulary words (e.g., **animals, the environment**, and **politics**).	• Uses few, if any, new vocabulary words (e.g., **animals, the environment**, and **politics**).
Gramática y vocabulario reciclado de los capítulos anteriores	• Does an excellent job using recycled grammar and vocabulary to support what is being said. • Uses a wide array of recycled verbs. • Uses some recycled vocabulary, but focuses predominantly on new vocabulary.	• Does a good job using recycled grammar and vocabulary to support what is being said. • Uses an array of recycled verbs. • Uses some recycled vocabulary, but focuses predominantly on new vocabulary.	• Does an average job using recycled grammar and vocabulary to support what is being said. • Uses a limited array of recycled verbs. • Uses mostly recycled vocabulary and some new vocabulary.	• If speaking at all, relies almost completely on a few isolated words. • Usage of previously learned grammar is inconsistent.
Esfuerzo	• Clearly the student made his/her best effort.	• The student made a good effort.	• The student made an effort.	• Little or no effort went into the activity.

Un poco de todo

12-28 Un reportaje para la televisión

Completen los siguientes pasos.

Paso 1 Con un/a compañero/a, escojan uno de los siguientes temas y preparen un reportaje para la televisión.

Temas

1. el medio ambiente
2. la política
3. el tiempo
4. el arte, la música, los deportes y otros eventos

Paso 2 Presenten su reportaje a la clase.

12-29 ¿Cómo eres? Conoces un poco a los estudiantes de los países que estudiamos en los capítulos anteriores. ¿Qué más quieres saber de ellos? Escribe por lo menos **diez** preguntas que quieras hacerles. Usa **el pretérito**, **el imperfecto** y **el subjuntivo** en tus preguntas.

MODELO

1. ¿Qué estudiaste el semestre pasado?
2. ¿Adónde fuiste el verano pasado?
3. ¿Es posible que viajes este verano?
4. …

Gino Breschi Arteaga

Sandra Manrique Esquivel

María Graciela Martelli Paz

Francisco Tomás Bacigalupe Bustamante

Diana Ávila Peralta

Jorge Gustavo Salazar

Yolanda Pico Briones

Rosa María Gutiérrez Murcia

Joaquín Navas Posada

Alicia Ortega Mujica

Pablo Colón Padín

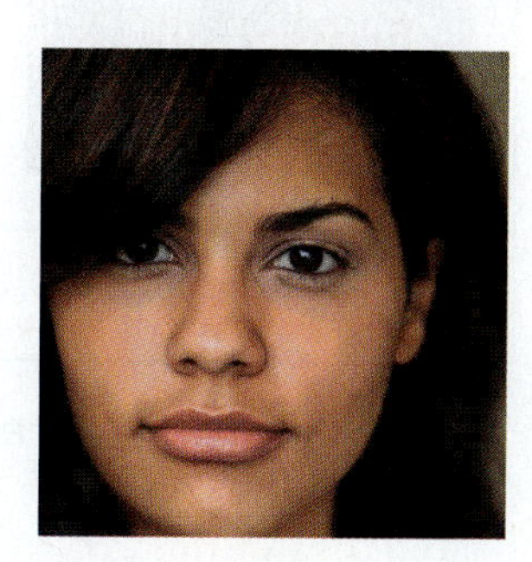
Amparo Burgos Báez

12-30 ¿Sabías que...? Completa los siguientes pasos.

Paso 1 Escribe dos cosas interesantes que no sabías antes pero que aprendiste de tu libro, de tus investigaciones propias y de la sección *Vistazo cultural* (junto con *Club cultura*) sobre cada uno de los siguientes países.

CHILE	PARAGUAY	ARGENTINA	URUGUAY
1.	1.	1.	1.
2.	2.	2.	2.

PERÚ	BOLIVIA	ECUADOR	COLOMBIA
1.	1.	1.	1.
2.	2.	2.	2.

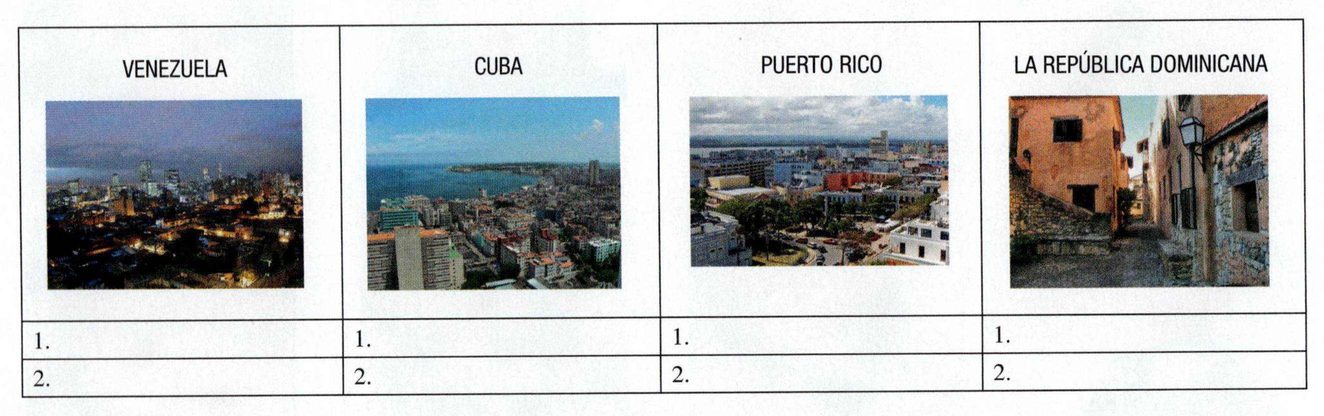

VENEZUELA	CUBA	PUERTO RICO	LA REPÚBLICA DOMINICANA
1.	1.	1.	1.
2.	2.	2.	2.

Paso 2 Compara la información con el lugar donde vives. ¿Qué cosas son similares? ¿Qué diferencias hay?

12·31 ¡A cocinar! Vas a preparar una cena latina para tus amigos con platos representativos de varios países. Selecciona por lo menos **tres** platos y **una** bebida. Indica el país de origen de cada plato y los ingredientes. Si varios países comparten el plato, menciónalos también.

La parrillada

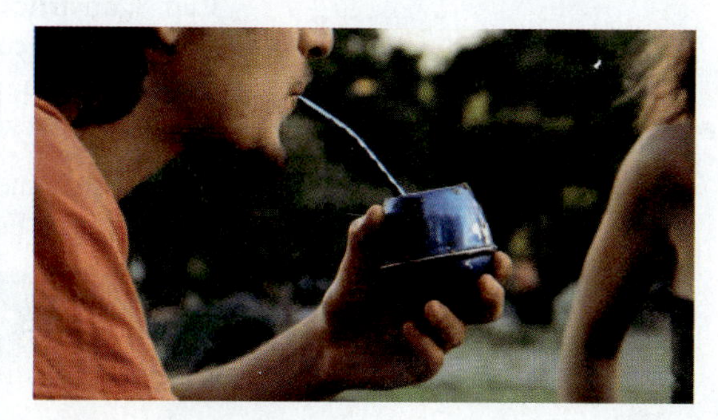
El mate

12·32 Los símbolos nacionales Escoge **tres** países distintos y un símbolo para cada uno de ellos. Describe estos símbolos nacionales y habla de cómo y por qué son representativos del país. Después, haz una comparación entre los países y sus símbolos.

12·33 ¿El ecoturismo o una expedición arqueológica?
¡Qué suerte! Recibiste la distinción de ser el/la mejor estudiante de español y puedes elegir entre un viaje de ecoturismo o una expedición arqueológica. Piensa en lo que aprendiste de cada país y decide adónde quieres ir para divertirte e investigar más. Después, describe el lugar específico que vas a visitar y di por qué, cómo, cuándo, etc. Si hay dos países con lugares similares, compáralos e indica por qué seleccionaste uno en particular.

12.34 Reflexiones Completa los siguientes pasos.

Paso 1 Elige tu lectura favorita de los **Capítulos 7–11**. Usa el formato de esa lectura como modelo para escribir tu propia versión, pero con un tema diferente.
Cap. 7, una solicitud para un concurso de cocina
Cap. 8, un artículo de una revista de moda
Cap. 9, un artículo sobre la vida sana
Cap. 10, un fragmento de la *Segunda carta al rey Carlos I* de Hernán Cortés
Cap. 11, una leyenda mexicana

Paso 2 En la clase reúnete con los compañeros que eligieron la misma lectura para comparar sus versiones. Escojan la mejor lectura del grupo para publicarla en MediaShare.

Y por fin, ¿cómo andas?

Having completed this chapter, I now can...	Feel confident	Need to review
Comunicación		
• communicate preferences regarding food and clothing.	☐	☐
• relate ideas about past experiences and my daily routine.	☐	☐
• convey information about people and things.	☐	☐
• express ideas on topics such as health, travel, animals, the environment, and politics.	☐	☐
• describe what is happening at the moment.	☐	☐
• make requests and give advice using commands.	☐	☐
• make equal and unequal comparisons and use comparatives and superlatives.	☐	☐
• articulate desires and opinions on a variety of topics.	☐	☐
Cultura		
• share information about Chile, Paraguay, Argentina, Uruguay, Peru, Bolivia, Ecuador, Venezuela, Colombia, Cuba, Puerto Rico, and the Dominican Republic.	☐	☐
• compare and contrast the countries I learned about in **Capítulos 7–11.**	☐	☐
• explore further cultural themes (online).		
Lectura		
• share information about the readings from **Capítulos 7–11**.	☐	☐
Comunidades		
• use Spanish in real-life contexts. (online)	☐	☐

APÉNDICES

APPENDIX 1

Answers to *¡Explícalo tú!* (Inductive Grammar Answers)

Capítulo A Para empezar

12. *Gustar*

1. To say you like or dislike one thing, what form of **gustar** do you use?
   gusta
2. To say you like or dislike more than one thing, what form of **gustar** do you use?
   gustan

Capítulo 2

9. El verbo *gustar*

1. To say you like or dislike one thing, what form of **gustar** do you use?
   gusta
2. To say you like or dislike more than one thing, what form of **gustar** do you use?
   gustan
3. Which words in the examples mean *I?* **(Me)** *You?* **(Te)** *He/she?* **(le)**
4. If a verb is needed after **gusta,** what form of the verb do you use?
   the infinitive form of the verb

Capítulo 4

4. Los verbos con cambio de raíz

1. Which verb forms look like the infinitive **cerrar**?
   nosotros, vosotros
2. Which verb forms have a spelling change that differs from the infinitive **cerrar**?
   yo, tú, usted, él, ella, ustedes, ellos, ellas

1. Which verb forms look like the infinitive **pedir**?
   nosotros, vosotros
2. Which verb forms have a spelling change that differs from the infinitive **pedir**?
   yo, tú, usted, él, ella, ustedes, ellos, ellas

1. Which verb forms look like the infinitive **encontrar**?
   nosotros, vosotros
2. Which verb forms have a spelling change that differs from the infinitive **encontrar**?
   yo, tú, usted, él, ella, ustedes, ellos, ellas

1. Which verb forms look like the infinitive **jugar**?
   nosotros, vosotros
2. Which verb forms have a spelling change that differs from the infinitive **jugar**?
   yo, tú, usted, él, ella, ustedes, ellos, ellas
3. Why does **jugar** not belong with the verbs like **encontrar**?
   because the change is *u* → *ue*, not *o* → *ue* like *encontrar*

To summarize…

1. What rule can you make regarding all four groups of stem-changing verbs and their forms?
   ***Nosotros/vosotros* look like the infinitive. All the other forms have the spelling change.**
2. With what group of stem-changing verbs would you put **querer**?
   e → ie
3. With what group of stem-changing verbs would you put the following verbs?

demostrar	*to demonstrate* **o → ue**
devolver	*to return (an object)* **o → ue**
encerrar	*to enclose* **e → ie**
perseguir	*to chase* **e → i**

6. *Ir* + *a* + infinitivo

1. When do the actions in the previous sentences take place: in the *past, present,* or *future?*
   future
2. What is the first bold type verb you see in each sentence?
   a form of *ir*
3. In what form is the second bolded verb?
   infinitive
4. What word comes between the two verbs?
   a

   Does this word have an equivalent in English?
   no
5. What is your rule, then, for expressing future actions or statements?
   use a form of *ir* + *a* + infinitive

8. Las expresiones afirmativas y negativas

1. When you use a negative word (**nadie, nunca,** etc.) in a sentence, does it come before or after the verb?
   The negative word can go either before or after the verb.
2. When you use the word **no** and then a negative word in the same sentence, does **no** come before or after the verb?
   ***No* comes before the verb.**

   Where does the negative word come in these sentences?
   The negative word can go either before or after the verb.
3. Does the meaning change depending on where you put the negative word (e.g., **Nadie llama** *vs.* **No llama nadie**)?
   No, the meaning stays the same.

9. Un repaso de *ser* y *estar*

1. Why do you use a form of **ser** in the first sentence?
   because it describes a physical or personality characteristic that remains relatively constant
2. Why do you use a form of **estar** in the second sentence?
   because it describes a physical or personality characteristic that can change, or a change in condition

Capítulo 5

2. Los adjetivos y los pronombres demostrativos

1. When do you use **este, ese,** and **aquel**?
   when you want to point out *one* masculine person or object
2. When do you use **esta, esa,** and **aquella**?
   when you want to point out *one* feminine person or object
3. When do you use **estos, esos,** and **aquellos**?
   when you want to point out *two or more* masculine persons or objects, or a mix of masculine and feminine persons or objects
4. When do you use **estas, esas,** and **aquellas**?
   when you want to point out *two or more* feminine persons or objects

5. El pretérito: los verbos regulares *-ar*

1. What do you notice about the endings?
   They all begin with -a except for the *yo* and the *él/ella* forms. In present tense, the *yo* ending was -o. Here, the -o ending is the *él/ella* forms and it has an accent mark.
2. Where are accent marks needed?
   Accent marks are needed on the *yo* and *él/ella/usted* forms.

Capítulo 6

Major grammar points to be reviewed

1. Present tense of:
   Regular **-ar, -er, -ir** verbs
   Irregular verbs
   Stem-changing verbs **e → ie, e → i, o → ue, u → ue**
2. Expressing the future with ***ir + a* + infinitive**
3. Use of direct object pronouns
4. Use of **ser** and **estar**
5. Use of **gustar**
6. Preterit tense of regular verbs

Major vocabulary to be reviewed

1. The *Vocabulario activo* at the end of each chapter

Major cultural information to be reviewed

1. At least two facts about each of the feature countries
2. At least one point about each of the two culture presentations in each chapter

Capítulo 7

2. Repaso del complemento directo

1. What are direct objects?
   Direct objects receive the action of verbs, answering the questions *what* and *whom*.
   What are direct object pronouns?
   Direct object pronouns replace direct objects.
2. What are the pronouns (forms)? With what must they agree?
   The pronoun forms are *me, te, lo, la, nos, los, las*. They must agree with direct objects.
3. Where are direct object pronouns placed in a sentence?
   They are placed either before verbs or attached to infinitives.

Capítulo 8

2. Los pronombres de complemento indirecto

1. Who is *buying* the clothing?
   mi madre
2. Who is *receiving* the clothing?
   Mi madre **me** compra mucha ropa.
   I am receiving the clothing.
   Mi madre **te** compra mucha ropa.
   You are receiving the clothing.
   Mi madre **le** compra mucha ropa a usted.
   You are receiving the clothing.
   Mi madre **le** compra mucha ropa a mi hermano.
   My brother is receiving the clothing.
   Mi madre **nos** compra mucha ropa.
   We are receiving the clothing.
   Mi madre **os** compra mucha ropa.
   You all are receiving the clothing.
   Mi madre **les** compra mucha ropa a ustedes.
   You all are receiving the clothing.
   Mi madre **les** compra mucha ropa a mis hermanos.
   My brothers are receiving the clothing.

4. Los pronombres de complemento directo e indirecto usados juntos

1. You know that direct and indirect objects come after verbs. Where do you find the direct and indirect object pronouns?
   The pronouns come before verbs or attached to infinitives.
2. Reading from left to right, which pronoun comes first (direct or indirect)? Which pronoun comes second?
   The indirect object pronoun comes first, and the direct object pronoun comes second.

Capítulo 9

2. Las construcciones reflexivas

In each drawing:

Who is performing / doing the action?

- **a. La fiesta**
- **b. Alberto**
- **c. Beatriz**
- **d. Raúl y Gloria**
- **e. Alberto**
- **f. Beatriz**

Who or what is receiving the action?

- **a. neighbors**
- **b. daughter**
- **c. car**
- **d. Raúl and Gloria**
- **e. Alberto**
- **f. Beatriz**

Which of the drawings and captions demonstrate reflexive verbs?

the bottom row (Raúl y Gloria se despiertan. / Alberto se acuesta. / Beatriz se lava.)

Capítulo 10

3. Los mandatos formales

1. Where do the object pronouns appear in affirmative commands?
   attached to the command
   Where do they appear in negative commands?
   before the command and not attached
   In what order?
   The indirect object pronoun comes first, and the direct object pronoun comes second.
2. Why are there written accents added to some of the commands and not to others?
   because some commands would change pronunciation without the accent marks

Capítulo 11

3. El presente progresivo

1. In the first group of sample sentences in Spanish, what is the infinitive of the first verb in each sentence that is in *italics*?
   estar
2. What are the infinitives of **haciendo, trabajando, cuidando, reciclando,** and **reutilizando**?
   hacer, trabajar, cuidar, reciclar, reutilizar
3. How do you convert the infinitives to this new form of the verb?
   Take the infinitive, drop the *-ar* or *-er,* add *-ando* or *-iendo*.
4. In this new tense, the *present progressive*, do any words come between the two parts of the verb?
   no
5. Therefore, your formula for forming the present progressive is:
   a form of the verb *estar* + a verb ending in *-ando* or *-iendo*

5. El subjuntivo

1. What is the difference between the subjunctive and the indicative moods?
   The subjunctive expresses concepts such as opinions, doubt and probability, and wishes and hopes. The indicative reports events and happenings.
2. What other verb forms look like the subjunctive?
   The *usted* and *ustedes* (formal) commands, and the negative *tú* (informal) commands.
3. Where does the subjunctive verb come in relation to the word **que**?
   after the word *que*

Capítulo 12

Major grammar points to be reviewed

1. Past tenses:
   Irregular preterit
   Regular and irregular imperfect
   Uses of the preterit and imperfect
2. Pronouns:
   Direct object
   Indirect object
   Reflexive
   Placement of pronouns
3. Commands:
   Informal affirmative and negative
   Formal affirmative and negative
4. Subjunctive:
   Formation
   Usage
5. Present progressive

Major vocabulary to be reviewed

1. The *Vocabulario activo* at the end of each chapter

Major cultural information to be reviewed

1. At least two facts about each of the feature countries
2. At least one point about each of the two culture presentations in each chapter

APPENDIX 2

Verb Charts

Regular Verbs: Simple Tenses

Infinitive Present Participle Past Participle	Indicative					Subjunctive		Imperative
	Present	Imperfect	Preterit	Future	Conditional	Present	Imperfect	Commands
hablar hablando hablado	hablo hablas habla hablamos habláis hablan	hablaba hablabas hablaba hablábamos hablabais hablaban	hablé hablaste habló hablamos hablasteis hablaron	hablaré hablarás hablará hablaremos hablaréis hablarán	hablaría hablarías hablaría hablaríamos hablaríais hablarían	hable hables hable hablemos habléis hablen	hablara hablaras hablara habláramos hablarais hablaran	habla (tú), no hables hable (usted) hablemos hablad (vosotros), no habléis hablen (Uds.)
comer comiendo comido	como comes come comemos coméis comen	comía comías comía comíamos comíais comían	comí comiste comió comimos comisteis comieron	comeré comerás comerá comeremos comeréis comerán	comería comerías comería comeríamos comeríais comerían	coma comas coma comamos comáis coman	comiera comieras comiera comiéramos comierais comieran	come (tú), no comas coma (usted) comamos comed (vosotros), no comáis coman (Uds.)
vivir viviendo vivido	vivo vives vive vivimos vivís viven	vivía vivías vivía vivíamos vivíais vivían	viví viviste vivió vivimos vivisteis vivieron	viviré vivirás vivirá viviremos viviréis vivirán	viviría vivirías viviría viviríamos viviríais vivirían	viva vivas viva vivamos viváis vivan	viviera vivieras viviera viviéramos vivierais vivieran	vive (tú), no vivas viva (usted) vivamos vivid (vosotros), no viváis vivan (Uds.)

Regular Verbs: Perfect Tenses

Indicative										Subjunctive			
Present Perfect		Past Perfect		Preterit Perfect		Future Perfect		Conditional Perfect		Present Perfect		Past Perfect	
he has ha hemos habéis han	hablado comido vivido	había habías había habíamos habíais habían	hablado comido vivido	hube hubiste hubo hubimos hubisteis hubieron	hablado comido vivido	habré habrás habrá habremos habréis habrán	hablado comido vivido	habría habrías habría habríamos habríais habrían	hablado comido vivido	haya hayas haya hayamos hayáis hayan	hablado comido vivido	hubiera hubieras hubiera hubiéramos hubierais hubieran	hablado comido vivido

Irregular Verbs

Infinitive Present Participle Past Participle	Indicative					Subjunctive		Imperative
	Present	Imperfect	Preterit	Future	Conditional	Present	Imperfect	Commands
andar andando andado	ando andas anda andamos andáis andan	andaba andabas andaba andábamos andabais andaban	anduve anduviste anduvo anduvimos anduvisteis anduvieron	andaré andarás andará andaremos andaréis andarán	andaría andarías andaría andaríamos andaríais andarían	ande andes ande andemos andéis anden	anduviera anduvieras anduviera anduviéramos anduvierais anduvieran	anda (tú), no andes ande (usted) andemos andad (vosotros), no andéis anden (Uds.)
caer cayendo caído	caigo caes cae caemos caéis caen	caía caías caía caíamos caíais caían	caí caíste cayó caímos caísteis cayeron	caeré caerás caerá caeremos caeréis caerán	caería caerías caería caeríamos caeríais caerían	caiga caigas caiga caigamos caigáis caigan	cayera cayeras cayera cayéramos cayerais cayeran	cae (tú), no caigas caiga (usted) caigamos caed (vosotros), no caigáis caigan (Uds.)
dar dando dado	doy das da damos dais dan	daba dabas daba dábamos dabais daban	di diste dio dimos disteis dieron	daré darás dará daremos daréis darán	daría darías daría daríamos daríais darían	dé des dé demos deis den	diera dieras diera diéramos dierais dieran	da (tú), no des dé (usted) demos dad (vosotros), no deis den (Uds.)
decir diciendo dicho	digo dices dice decimos decís dicen	decía decías decía decíamos decíais decían	dije dijiste dijo dijimos dijisteis dijeron	diré dirás dirá diremos diréis dirán	diría dirías diría diríamos diríais dirían	diga digas diga digamos digáis digan	dijera dijeras dijera dijéramos dijerais dijeran	di (tú), no digas diga (usted) digamos decid (vosotros), no digáis digan (Uds.)

Irregular Verbs (continued)

Infinitive Present Participle Past Participle	Indicative					Subjunctive		Imperative
	Present	Imperfect	Preterit	Future	Conditional	Present	Imperfect	Commands
estar estando estado	estoy estás está estamos estáis están	estaba estabas estaba estábamos estabais estaban	estuve estuviste estuvo estuvimos estuvisteis estuvieron	estaré estarás estará estaremos estaréis estarán	estaría estarías estaría estaríamos estaríais estarían	esté estés esté estemos estéis estén	estuviera estuvieras estuviera estuviéramos estuvierais estuvieran	está (tú), no estés esté (usted) estemos estad (vosotros), no estéis estén (Uds.)
haber habiendo habido	he has ha hemos habéis han	había habías había habíamos habíais habían	hube hubiste hubo hubimos hubisteis hubieron	habré habrás habrá habremos habréis habrán	habría habrías habría habríamos habríais habrían	haya hayas haya hayamos hayáis hayan	hubiera hubieras hubiera hubiéramos hubierais hubieran	
hacer haciendo hecho	hago haces hace hacemos hacéis hacen	hacía hacías hacía hacíamos hacíais hacían	hice hiciste hizo hicimos hicisteis hicieron	haré harás hará haremos haréis harán	haría harías haría haríamos haríais harían	haga hagas haga hagamos hagáis hagan	hiciera hicieras hiciera hiciéramos hicierais hicieran	haz (tú), no hagas haga (usted) hagamos haced (vosotros), no hagáis hagan (Uds.)
ir yendo ido	voy vas va vamos vais van	iba ibas iba íbamos ibais iban	fui fuiste fue fuimos fuisteis fueron	iré irás irá iremos iréis irán	iría irías iría iríamos iríais irían	vaya vayas vaya vayamos vayáis vayan	fuera fueras fuera fuéramos fuerais fueran	ve (tú), no vayas vaya (usted) vamos, no vayamos id (vosotros), no vayáis vayan (Uds.)
oír oyendo oído	oigo oyes oye oímos oís oyen	oía oías oía oíamos oíais oían	oí oíste oyó oímos oísteis oyeron	oiré oirás oirá oiremos oiréis oirán	oiría oirías oiría oiríamos oiríais oirían	oiga oigas oiga oigamos oigáis oigan	oyera oyeras oyera oyéramos oyerais oyeran	oye (tú), no oigas oiga (usted) oigamos oíd (vosotros), no oigáis oigan (Uds.)

Irregular Verbs (continued)

Infinitive Present Participle Past Participle	Indicative					Subjunctive		Imperative
	Present	Imperfect	Preterit	Future	Conditional	Present	Imperfect	Commands
poder pudiendo podido	puedo puedes puede podemos podéis pueden	podía podías podía podíamos podíais podían	pude pudiste pudo pudimos pudisteis pudieron	podré podrás podrá podremos podréis podrán	podría podrías podría podríamos podríais podrían	pueda puedas pueda podamos podáis puedan	pudiera pudieras pudiera pudiéramos pudierais pudieran	
poner poniendo puesto	pongo pones pone ponemos ponéis ponen	ponía ponías ponía poníamos poníais ponían	puse pusiste puso pusimos pusisteis pusieron	pondré pondrás pondrá pondremos pondréis pondrán	pondría pondrías pondría pondríamos pondríais pondrían	ponga pongas ponga pongamos pongáis pongan	pusiera pusieras pusiera pusiéramos pusierais pusieran	pon (tú), no pongas ponga (usted) pongamos poned (vosotros), no pongáis pongan (Uds.)
querer queriendo querido	quiero quieres quiere queremos queréis quieren	quería querías quería queríamos queríais querían	quise quisiste quiso quisimos quisisteis quisieron	querré querrás querrá querremos querréis querrán	querría querrías querría querríamos querríais querrían	quiera quieras quiera queramos queráis quieran	quisiera quisieras quisiera quisiéramos quisierais quisieran	quiere (tú), no quieras quiera (usted) queramos quered (vosotros), no queráis quieran (Uds.)
saber sabiendo sabido	sé sabes sabe sabemos sabéis saben	sabía sabías sabía sabíamos sabíais sabían	supe supiste supo supimos supisteis supieron	sabré sabrás sabrá sabremos sabréis sabrán	sabría sabrías sabría sabríamos sabríais sabrían	sepa sepas sepa sepamos sepáis sepan	supiera supieras supiera supiéramos supierais supieran	sabe (tú), no sepas sepa (usted) sepamos sabed (vosotros), no sepáis sepan (Uds.)
salir saliendo salido	salgo sales sale salimos salís salen	salía salías salía salíamos salíais salían	salí saliste salió salimos salisteis salieron	saldré saldrás saldrá saldremos saldréis saldrán	saldría saldrías saldría saldríamos saldríais saldrían	salga salgas salga salgamos salgáis salgan	saliera salieras saliera saliéramos salierais salieran	sal (tú), no salgas salga (usted) salgamos salid (vosotros), no salgáis salgan (Uds.)

Irregular Verbs (continued)

Infinitive Present Participle Past Participle	Indicative					Subjunctive		Imperative
	Present	Imperfect	Preterit	Future	Conditional	Present	Imperfect	Commands
ser siendo sido	soy eres es somos sois son	era eras era éramos erais eran	fui fuiste fue fuimos fuisteis fueron	seré serás será seremos seréis serán	sería serías sería seríamos seríais serían	sea seas sea seamos seáis sean	fuera fueras fuera fuéramos fuerais fueran	sé (tú), no seas sea (usted) seamos sed (vosotros), no seáis sean (Uds.)
tener teniendo tenido	tengo tienes tiene tenemos tenéis tienen	tenía tenías tenía teníamos teníais tenían	tuve tuviste tuvo tuvimos tuvisteis tuvieron	tendré tendrás tendrá tendremos tendréis tendrán	tendría tendrías tendría tendríamos tendríais tendrían	tenga tengas tenga tengamos tengáis tengan	tuviera tuvieras tuviera tuviéramos tuvierais tuvieran	ten (tú), no tengas tenga (usted) tengamos tened (vosotros), no tengáis tengan (Uds.)
traer trayendo traído	traigo traes trae traemos traéis traen	traía traías traía traíamos traíais traían	traje trajiste trajo trajimos trajisteis trajeron	traeré traerás traerá traeremos traeréis traerán	traería traerías traería traeríamos traeríais traerían	traiga traigas traiga traigamos traigáis traigan	trajera trajeras trajera trajéramos trajerais trajeran	trae (tú), no traigas traiga (usted) traigamos traed (vosotros), no traigáis traigan (Uds.)
venir viniendo venido	vengo vienes viene venimos venís vienen	venía venías venía veníamos veníais venían	vine viniste vino vinimos vinisteis vinieron	vendré vendrás vendrá vendremos vendréis vendrán	vendría vendrías vendría vendríamos vendríais vendrían	venga vengas venga vengamos vengáis vengan	viniera vinieras viniera viniéramos vinierais vinieran	ven (tú), no vengas venga (usted) vengamos venid (vosotros), no vengáis vengan (Uds.)
ver viendo visto	veo ves ve vemos veis ven	veía veías veía veíamos veíais veían	vi viste vio vimos visteis vieron	veré verás verá veremos veréis verán	vería verías vería veríamos veríais verían	vea veas vea veamos veáis vean	viera vieras viera viéramos vierais vieran	ve (tú), no veas vea (usted) veamos ved (vosotros), no veáis vean (Uds.)

Stem-Changing and Orthographic-Changing Verbs

Infinitive Present Participle Past Participle	Indicative					Subjunctive		Imperative
	Present	Imperfect	Preterit	Future	Conditional	Present	Imperfect	Commands
almorzar (ue) (c) almorzando almorzado	almuerzo almuerzas almuerza almorzamos almorzáis almuerzan	almorzaba almorzabas almorzaba almorzábamos almorzabais almorzaban	almorcé almorzaste almorzó almorzamos almorzasteis almorzaron	almorzaré almorzarás almorzará almorzaremos almorzaréis almorzarán	almorzaría almorzarías almorzaría almorzaríamos almorzaríais almorzarían	almuerce almuerces almuerce almorcemos almorcéis almuercen	almorzara almorzaras almorzara almorzáramos almorzarais almorzaran	almuerza (tú), no almuerces almuerce (usted) almorcemos almorzad (vosotros), no almorcéis almuercen (Uds.)
buscar (qu) buscando buscado	busco buscas busca buscamos buscáis buscan	buscaba buscabas buscaba buscábamos buscabais buscaban	busqué buscaste buscó buscamos buscasteis buscaron	buscaré buscarás buscará buscaremos buscaréis buscarán	buscaría buscarías buscaría buscaríamos buscaríais buscarían	busque busques busque busquemos busquéis busquen	buscara buscaras buscara buscáramos buscarais buscaran	busca (tú), no busques busque (usted) busquemos buscad (vosotros), no busquéis busquen (Uds.)
corregir (i, i) (j) corrigiendo corregido	corrijo corriges corrige corregimos corregís corrigen	corregía corregías corregía corregíamos corregíais corregían	corregí corregiste corrigió corregimos corregisteis corrigieron	corregiré corregirás corregirá corregiremos corregiréis corregirán	corregiría corregirías corregiría corregiríamos corregiríais corregirían	corrija corrijas corrija corrijamos corrijáis corrijan	corrigiera corrigieras corrigiera corrigiéramos corrigierais corrigieran	corrige (tú), no corrijas corrija (usted) corrijamos corregid (vosotros), no corrijáis corrijan (Uds.)
dormir (ue, u) durmiendo dormido	duermo duermes duerme dormimos dormís duermen	dormía dormías dormía dormíamos dormíais dormían	dormí dormiste durmió dormimos dormisteis durmieron	dormiré dormirás dormirá dormiremos dormiréis dormirán	dormiría dormirías dormiría dormiríamos dormiríais dormirían	duerma duermas duerma durmamos durmáis duerman	durmiera durmieras durmiera durmiéramos durmierais durmieran	duerme (tú), no duermas duerma (usted) durmamos dormid (vosotros), no durmáis duerman (Uds.)
incluir (y) incluyendo incluido	incluyo incluyes incluye incluimos incluís incluyen	incluía incluías incluía incluíamos incluíais incluían	incluí incluiste incluyó incluimos incluisteis incluyeron	incluiré incluirás incluirá incluiremos incluiréis incluirán	incluiría incluirías incluiría incluiríamos incluiríais incluirían	incluya incluyas incluya incluyamos incluyáis incluyan	incluyera incluyeras incluyera incluyéramos incluyerais incluyeran	incluye (tú), no incluyas incluya (usted) incluyamos incluid (vosotros), no incluyáis incluyan (Uds.)

Stem-Changing and Orthographic-Changing Verbs (continued)

Infinitive Present Participle Past Participle	Indicative					Subjunctive		Imperative
	Present	Imperfect	Preterit	Future	Conditional	Present	Imperfect	Commands
llegar (gu) llegando llegado	llego llegas llega llegamos llegáis llegan	llegaba llegabas llegaba llegábamos llegabais llegaban	llegué llegaste llegó llegamos llegasteis llegaron	llegaré llegarás llegará llegaremos llegaréis llegarán	llegaría llegarías llegaría llegaríamos llegaríais llegarían	llegue llegues llegue lleguemos lleguéis lleguen	llegara llegaras llegara llegáramos llegarais llegaran	llega (tú), no llegues llegue (usted) lleguemos llegad (vosotros), no lleguéis lleguen (Uds.)
pedir (i, i) pidiendo pedido	pido pides pide pedimos pedís piden	pedía pedías pedía pedíamos pedíais pedían	pedí pediste pidió pedimos pedisteis pidieron	pediré pedirás pedirá pediremos pediréis pedirán	pediría pedirías pediría pediríamos pediríais pedirían	pida pidas pida pidamos pidáis pidan	pidiera pidieras pidiera pidiéramos pidierais pidieran	pide (tú), no pidas pida (usted) pidamos pedid (vosotros), no pidáis pidan (Uds.)
pensar (ie) pensando pensado	pienso piensas piensa pensamos pensáis piensan	pensaba pensabas pensaba pensábamos pensabais pensaban	pensé pensaste pensó pensamos pensasteis pensaron	pensaré pensarás pensará pensaremos pensaréis pensarán	pensaría pensarías pensaría pensaríamos pensaríais pensarían	piense pienses piense pensemos penséis piensen	pensara pensaras pensara pensáramos pensarais pensaran	piensa (tú), no pienses piense (usted) pensemos pensad (vosotros), no penséis piensen (Uds.)
producir (zc) (j) produciendo producido	produzco produces produce producimos producís producen	producía producías producía producíamos producíais producían	produje produjiste produjo produjimos produjisteis produjeron	produciré producirás producirá produciremos produciréis producirán	produciría producirías produciría produciríamos produciríais producirían	produzca produzcas produzca produzcamos produzcáis produzcan	produjera produjeras produjera produjéramos produjerais produjeran	produce (tú), no produzcas produzca (usted) produzcamos producid (vosotros), no produzcáis produzcan (Uds.)
reír (i, i) riendo reído	río ríes ríe reímos reís ríen	reía reías reía reíamos reíais reían	reí reíste rio reímos reísteis rieron	reiré reirás reirá reiremos reiréis reirán	reiría reirías reiría reiríamos reiríais reirían	ría rías ría riamos riáis rían	riera rieras riera riéramos rierais rieran	ríe (tú), no rías ría (usted) riamos reíd (vosotros), no riáis rían (Uds.)

Stem-Changing and Orthographic-Changing Verbs (continued)

Infinitive Present Participle Past Participle	Indicative					Subjunctive		Imperative
	Present	Imperfect	Preterit	Future	Conditional	Present	Imperfect	Commands
seguir (i, i) (ga) siguiendo seguido	sigo sigues sigue seguimos seguís siguen	seguía seguías seguía seguíamos seguíais seguían	seguí seguiste siguió seguimos seguisteis siguieron	seguiré seguirás seguirá seguiremos seguiréis seguirán	seguiría seguirías seguiría seguiríamos seguiríais seguirían	siga sigas siga sigamos sigáis sigan	siguiera siguieras siguiera siguiéramos siguierais siguieran	sigue (tú), no sigas siga (usted) sigamos seguid (vosotros), no sigáis sigan (Uds.)
sentir (ie, i) sintiendo sentido	siento sientes siente sentimos sentís sienten	sentía sentías sentía sentíamos sentíais sentían	sentí sentiste sintió sentimos sentisteis sintieron	sentiré sentirás sentirá sentiremos sentiréis sentirán	sentiría sentirías sentiría sentiríamos sentiríais sentirían	sienta sientas sienta sintamos sintáis sientan	sintiera sintieras sintiera sintiéramos sintierais sintieran	siente (tú), no sientas sienta (usted) sintamos sentid (vosotros), no sintáis sientan (Uds.)
volver (ue) volviendo vuelto	vuelvo vuelves vuelve volvemos volvéis vuelven	volvía volvías volvía volvíamos volvíais volvían	volví volviste volvió volvimos volvisteis volvieron	volveré volverás volverá volveremos volveréis volverán	volvería volverías volvería volveríamos volveríais volverían	vuelva vuelvas vuelva volvamos volváis vuelvan	volviera volvieras volviera volviéramos volvierais volvieran	vuelve (tú), no vuelvas vuelva (usted) volvamos volved (vosotros), no volváis vuelvan (Uds.)

APPENDIX 3

También se dice…

Capítulo A Para empezar

Los saludos/*Greetings*

¿Cómo andas? *How are you doing?*
¿Cómo vas? *How are you doing?*
El gusto es mío. *Pleased to meet you; The pleasure is all mine.*
Hasta entonces. *Until then.*
¿Qué hay? *What's up?*
¿Qué hubo? *How's it going? What's happening? What's new?*
¿Qué pasa? *How's it going? What's happening? What's new?*
¿Qué pasó? *How's it going? What's happening? What's new?*

Las presentaciones/*Introductions*

¿Cuál es su nombre y apellido? *What is your name and last name? (formal)*
¿Cuál es tu nombre y apellido? *What is your name and last name? (familiar)*
Mi apellido es… *My last name is…*
Mi nombre es… *My name is…*
Me gustaría presentarle a… *I would like to introduce you to… (formal)*
Me gustaría presentarte a… *I would like to introduce you to… (familiar)*
Un placer. *Delighted.*

Las despedidas/*Farewells*

Nos vemos. *See you.*
Que te vaya bien. *Hope everything goes well.*
Que tenga(s) un buen día. *Have a nice day.*
Te veo. *I'll see you around.*
Vaya con Dios. *Go with God.*

Expresiones útiles para la clase/*Useful classroom expressions*

Preguntas y respuestas/*Questions and answers*

(No) entiendo. *I (don't) understand.*
¿Puede repetir, por favor? *Could you repeat, please?*

Expresiones de cortesía/*Polite expressions*

Muchas gracias. *Thank you very much.*
No hay de qué. *Not at all.*

Mandatos para la clase/*Classroom instructions*

Levántense. *Stand up.*
Pongan sus cosas en su mochila/bolso/bolsa. *Put your things in your backpack/purse/bag.*
Saque(n) un bolígrafo/papel/lápiz. *Take out a pen/a piece of paper/a pencil.*
Siéntense. *Sit down.*

Las nacionalidades/*Nationalities*

argentino/a *Argentine*
boliviano/a *Bolivian*
chileno/a *Chilean*
colombiano/a *Colombian*
costarricense *Costa Rican*
dominicano/a *Dominican*
escocés/a (Escocia) *Scottish*
ecuatoriano/a *Ecuadorian*
griego/a (Grecia) *Greek*
guatemalteco/a *Guatemalan*
hondureño/a *Honduran*
irlandés/a (Irlanda) *Irish*
italiano/a (Italia) *Italian*
nicaragüense *Nicaraguan*
panameño/a *Panamanian*
peruano/a *Peruvian*
portugués/a (Portugal) *Portuguese*
ruso/a (Rusia) *Russian*
uruguayo/a *Uruguayan*
venezolano/a *Venezuelan*

Expresiones del tiempo/*Weather expressions*

el arco iris *rainbow*
el chirimiri *drizzle (Spain)*
Está despejado. *It's clear.*
Hace fresco. *It's cool.*
Hay neblina/niebla. *It's foggy.*
Hay tormenta. *There is a storm.*
la humedad *humidity*
los copos de nieve *snowflakes*
las gotas de lluvia *raindrops*
el granizo *hail*
el hielo *ice*
el huracán *hurricane*
la llovizna *drizzle*
el pronóstico *weather forecast*
el/los rayo/s, el relámpago *lightning*
la tormenta *storm*
el tornado *tornado*
el/los trueno/s *thunder*

Capítulo 1

La familia/*Family*

el/la ahijado/a *godchild*
el bisabuelo *great-grandfather*
la bisabuela *great-grandmother*
el/la cuñado/a *brother-in-law/sister-in-law*
la familia política *in-laws*
el/la hermanastro/a *stepbrother/stepsister*
el /la hijastro/a *stepson/stepdaughter*
el/la hijo/a único/a *only child*
la madrina *godmother*
el/la medio/a hermano/a *half brother/half sister*
los medios hermanos *half brothers and sisters*
la mami *Mommy; Mom (Latin America)*
el marido *husband*
la mujer *wife*
los nietos *grandchildren*
la nuera *daughter-in-law*
el padrino *godfather*
el papi *Daddy; Dad (Latin America)*
el pariente *relative*
el/la prometido/a *fiancé(e)*
el/la sobrino/a *niece/nephew*
los sobrinos *nieces and nephews*
el/la suegro/a *father-in-law/mother-in-law*
los suegros *parents-in-law*
la tatarabuela *great-great-grandmother*
el tatarabuelo *great-great-grandfather*
la tía abuela *great-aunt*
el tío abuelo *great-uncle*
el/la viudo/a *widower/widow*
el yerno *son-in-law*

La gente/*People*

el bato *friend; guy (in SE USA slang)*
el/la chaval/a *young man/young woman (Spain)*
el chamaco *young man (Cuba, Honduras, Mexico, El Salvador)*
el/la fulano/a *what's-his/her-name*

Los adjetivos descriptivos/*Descriptive adjectives*

La personalidad y otros rasgos/*Personality and other characteristics*

amable *nice; kind*
bobo/a *stupid; silly*
el/la bromista *jokester; prankster*
cariñoso/a *loving; affectionate*
chistoso/a *funny*
cursi *pretentious; affected*
divertido/a *funny*
educado/a *well mannered; polite*
elegante *elegant*
empollón/a *bookworm; nerd (Spain)*
encantador/a *charming; lovely*
espabilado/a *smart; vivacious; alert (Latin America)*
frustrado/a *frustrated*
gracioso/a *funny*
grosero/a *unpleasant*
histérico/a *crazed*
impaciente *impatient*
indiferente *indifferent*
irresponsable *irresponsible*
maleducado/a *ill mannered, rude*
malvado/a *evil; wicked*
majo/a *pretty; nice (Spain)*
mono/a *pretty; nice (Spain, Caribbean)*
odioso/a *unpleasant*
pesado/a *annoying (person)*
pijo/a *posh; snooty (Spain)*
progre *liberal; progressive (Spain)*
sabelotodo *know-it-all*

Las características físicas/*Physical characteristics*

atlético/a *athletic*
bello/a *beautiful (Latin America)*
blando/a *soft; weak*
esbelto/a *slender*
flaco/a *thin*
frágil *fragile*
hermoso/a *beautiful; lovely*
menor *younger*
musculoso/a *muscular*
robusto/a *hardy*
viejo/a *old*

Otras palabras/*Other words*

demasiado/a *too much*
divorciado/a *divorced*
separado/a *separated*
suficiente *enough*

Capítulo 2

Las materias y las especialidades/*Subjects and majors*

la agronomía *agriculture*
la antropología *anthropology*
el cálculo *calculus*
las ciencias políticas *political science*
las comunicaciones *communications*
la contabilidad *accounting*
el diseño *design*
la economía *economics*
la educación física *physical education*
la enfermería *nursing*
la filosofía *philosophy*
la física *physics*
la geografía *geography*

la geología *geology*
la historia *history*
la ingeniería *engineering*
la lingüística *linguistics*
la literatura comparada *comparative literature*
la medicina del deporte *sports medicine*
el mercadeo *marketing (Latin America)*
la mercadotecnia (el márketing) *marketing (Spain)*
la microbiología *microbiology*
la química *chemistry*
la química orgánica *organic chemistry*
los servicios sociales *social work*
la sociología *sociology*
la terapia física (fisioterapia) *physical therapy*

En la sala de clase/*In the classroom*

el aula *classroom*
el/la alumno/a *student*
la bombilla *light bulb*
la cámara proyectora *overhead camera*
el cielorraso *ceiling*
el enchufe *wall socket*
el interruptor *light switch*
las luces *lights*
el ordenador *computer (Spain)*
la pantalla *screen*
el proyector *projector*
la prueba *test*
el pupitre *student desk*
el rotulador *marker*
el sacapuntas *pencil sharpener*
el salón de clase *classroom*
el suelo *floor*
la tarima *dais; platform*

Los verbos/*Verbs*

apuntar *to take notes*
asistir a clase *to attend class*
beber *to drink*
entender *to understand*
entrar *to enter*
entregar *to hand in*
matricularse *to register*
practicar *to practice*
prestar atención *to pay attention*
repasar *to review*
respónder *to answer*
sacar *to take out*
sacar buenas/malas notas *to get good/bad grades*
tomar apuntes *to take notes*

Las palabras interrogativas/*Interrogative words*

¿Con cuánto/a/os/as? *With how many…?*
¿Con qué? *With what…?*
¿Con quién/es? *With whom…?*
¿De qué? *About what…?*
¿De quién/es? *About/from whom…?*

En la universidad/*At college/university*

Los lugares/*Places*

el apartamento estudiantil *student apartment*
el campo de fútbol *soccer field*
el campus *campus*
la cancha de tenis/baloncesto *tennis/basketball court*
la/s casa/s de hermandad/es *fraternity and sorority housing*
el centro comercial *mall*
el comedor estudiantil *student dining hall*
el mercado *market*
el museo *museum*
la oficina de consejeros *guidance/advising office*
el supermercado *supermarket*
el teatro *theater*

La residencia/*The dorm*

los bafles *speakers (Spain)*
el calendario *calendar*
la cama *bed*
la habitación *room*
el iPod *iPod*
Internet *Internet*
las literas *bunk beds*
la llave *key*
el llavero *keychain*
la mesita de noche *nightstand*
el móvil *cell phone (Spain)*
la redacción/la composición *essay*
la tarjeta de crédito *credit card*
la tarjeta de identidad; el carné *ID card*
los videojuegos *video games*
el wifi *wifi, wireless connection*

Los deportes y los pasatiempos/*Sports and pastimes*

el/la aficionado/a *fan*
el bate *bat*
el campo *field*
el campo de golf *golf course*
cazar *to hunt*
conversar con amigos *to talk with friends*
escalar montañas *to go mountain climbing*
esquiar *to ski*
estar en forma *to be in shape*
hablar por teléfono *to talk on the phone*
hacer alpinismo *to go mountain climbing (Spain)*
hacer andinismo *to go mountain climbing (Latin America)*
hacer footing *to go jogging (Spain)*
hacer gimnasia *to exercise*
hacer senderismo *to hike*
hacer pilates *to do Pilates*
hacer yoga *to do yoga*
ir al centro *to go downtown*
ir al centro comercial *to go the mall*
ir a fiestas *to go to parties*
ir a navegar *to go sailing*
ir a un partido de… *to go to a… game*
el juego de mesa *board game*

jugar a las damas *to play checkers*
jugar a videojuegos *to play video games*
jugar al ajedrez *to play chess*
jugar al boliche *to bowl*
jugar al ráquetbol *to play racquetball*
leer libros de… *to read… books*
 acción *action*
 autoayuda *self-help*
 aventura *adventure*
 ciencia-ficción *science fiction*
 cuentos cortos *short stories*
 ficción *fiction*
 espías *spy*
 misterio *mystery*
 romance *romance*
 terror *horror*
levantar pesas *to lift weights*
montar a caballo *to go horseback riding*
el palo de golf *golf club*
pasear *to go out for a ride; to take a walk*
pasear en barco *to sail*
la pelota de tenis/béisbol *tenis ball; baseball*
pescar *to fish*
la pista *track*
la pista y el campo *track and field (Spain)*
practicar boxeo *to box*
practicar ciclismo *to cycle*
practicar lucha libre *to wrestle*
practicar las artes marciales *to do martial arts*
la raqueta *racket*
salir a cenar/comer *to go out to dinner/eat*
tirar un disco volador *to throw a Frisbee*
ver películas *to watch movies*

Emociones y estados/*Emotions and states of being*

agotado/a *exhausted*
agradable *nice*
alegre *happy*
asombrado/a *amazed; astonished*
asqueado/a *disgusted*
asustado/a *scared*
deprimido/a *depressed*
desanimado/a *discouraged; disheartened*
disgustado/a *upset*
dormido/a *sleepy*
emocionado/a *moved; touched; excited*
entusiasmado/a *delighted*
fastidiado/a *annoyed; bothered*
ilusionado/a *thrilled*
optimista *optimistic*
pesimista *pessimistic*
retrasado/a *late*
sonriente *smiling*
soñoliento/a *sleepy (Spain)*

Capítulo 3

La casa/*The house*

la alcoba *bedroom*
el armario empotrado *closet (Spain)*
el ático *attic*
la bodega *cellar*
la buhardilla *attic*
el clóset *closet (Latin America)*
el corredor *hall*
el despacho *office*
el desván *attic*
el pasillo *hallway*
el patio *patio; yard*
el placar *closet (Argentina)*
el portal *porch*
el porche *porch*
la recámara *bedroom (Mexico)*
el salón *salon; lounge; living room*
el tejado *roof*
la terraza *terrace; porch*
el vestíbulo *entrance hall*

Los muebles y otros objetos de la casa/*Furniture and other objects*

La sala y el comedor/*The living room and dining room*

la banqueta/el banquillo *small seating stool*
la estantería *bookcase*
la mecedora *rocking chair*
la moqueta *carpet (Spain)*

La cocina/*The kitchen*

el congelador *deep freezer*
el fregadero *kitchen sink*
el friegaplatos *dishwasher*
el frigorífico *refrigerator (Spain)*
el horno *oven*
el lavavajillas *dishwasher (Spain)*
la nevera *refrigerator*
el taburete *bar stool*

El baño/*The bathroom*

el espejo *mirror*
el grifo *faucet*
la jabonera *soap dish*
el toallero *towel rack*

El dormitorio/*The bedroom*

las cortinas *curtains*
el edredón *comforter*
la frazada *blanket (Latin America)*

Otras palabras/*Other words*

el aparato eléctrico *electric appliance*
la chimenea *chimney; fireplace*
el espejo *mirror*
los gabinetes *cabinets*
la lavadora *washer*
la secadora *dryer*

el librero *bookcase (Mexico)*
las persianas *shutters; window blinds*

Los quehaceres de la casa/*Household chores*

barrer *to sweep*
cortar el césped *to cut the grass*
fregar los platos *to wash the dishes*
fregar el suelo/piso *to wash the floor*
guardar la ropa *to put away clothes*
lavar la ropa *to do laundry*
ordenar *to organize*
planchar la ropa *to iron*
quitar el polvo *to dust*
recoger *to clean up (in general)*
recoger la mesa *to clear the table*
regar las plantas *to water the plants*
sacudir las alfombras *to shake out the rugs*
sacudir el polvo *to dust*

Los colores/*Colors*

azul/verde claro *light blue/green*
azul/verde oscuro *dark blue/green*
color café *brown*
color crema *ivory; cream-colored*
naranja *orange*
púrpura *purple (Spain)*
rosa *pink (Spain)*

Expresiones con *tener*/*Expressions with* tener

tener cansancio *to be tired*
tener celos *to be jealous*
tener novio/a *to have a boyfriend/girlfriend*

Capítulo 4

Los lugares/*Places*

la alberca *swimming pool (Mexico)*
el ambulatorio *medical clinic (Spain)*
el aseo *public restroom*
la catedral *cathedral*
el campo de golf *golf course*
la capilla *chapel*
la clínica *clinic*
el consultorio *doctor's office*
el convento *convent*
la ferretería *hardware store*
la frutería *fruit store*
la gasolinera *gas station*
la heladería *ice cream shop*
el mercado al aire libre *open-air market*
la mezquita *mosque*
la papelería *stationary store*
la panadería *bread store*
la pastelería *pastry shop*
la pescadería *fish shop; fishmonger*
la piscina *pool*
el polideportivo *sports center*
el quiosco *newsstand*
los servicios *public restrooms*
la sinagoga *synagogue*
la tienda de juguetes *toy store*
la tienda de ropa *clothing store*
el zócalo *plaza (Mexico)*

Otras palabras/*Other words*

la cuadra *city block (Latin America)*
la fogata *bonfire*
la fuente *fountain*
la manzana *city block (Spain)*

Capítulo 5

El mundo de la música/*The world of music*

la armónica *harmonica*
el arpa *harp*
el bajo eléctrico *bass guitar*
el címbalo/el platillo *cymbal*
el clarinete *clarinet*
la corneta *cornet*
el coro *choir*
el cuarteto *quartet*
la flauta *the flute*
la guitarra eléctrica *electric guitar*
el/la mánager *manager*
el/la organista *organist*
la pandereta *tambourine*
el saxofón *saxophone*
los/las seguidores/as *groupies*
el trombón *trombone*
el teclado *keyboard*
la tuba *tuba*
el violín *violin*
el violonchelo *cello*

Algunos géneros musicales/*Some musical genres*

el merengue *merengue*
la música alternativa *alternative music*
la música bluegrass *bluegrass music*

El mundo del cine/*The world of film*

Gente/*People*

el/la cineasta *cinematographer*
el/la director/a *director*
el equipo de cámara/sonido *camera/sound crew*
el/la guionista *scriptwriter*

Las películas/*Movies*

el cortometraje *short (film)*
los dibujos animados *cartoons*

el guión *script*
el montaje *montage*

Otras palabra/*Other word*

la pandilla *gang; posse*

Capítulo 7

La comida/*Food*

Las carnes y las aves/*Meat and poultry*

las aves de corral *poultry*
la carne de cerdo *pork*
la carne de cordero *lamb*
la carne de res *beef*
la carne molida *ground beef*
la carne picada *ground beef (Spain)*
el chorizo *spicy pork sausage*
la chuleta *chop*
el chuletón *T-bone steak (Spain)*
el jamón serrano *cured ham (Spain)*
el pavo *turkey*
la salchicha *sausage; hot dog*
el salchichón *seasoned sausage (Spain)*
la ternera *veal*
el tocino *bacon*

El pescado y los mariscos/*Fish and seafood*

las almejas *clams*
las anchoas *anchovies*
los calamares *squid*
el cangrejo *crab*
el chillo *red snapper (Puerto Rico)*
las gambas *shrimp (Spain)*
el huachinango *red snapper (Mexico)*
la langosta *lobster*
el lenguado *flounder*
el mero *grouper*
la ostra *oyster*
el róbalo *bass*
el pulpo *octopus*
el salmón *salmon*
la sardina *sardine*
la trucha *trout*
las vieiras *scallops*

Las frutas/*Fruit*

el aguacate *avocado*
el albaricoque *apricot*
el ananá *pineapple (Latin America)*
el arándano *blueberry; cranberry*
el banano *banana; banana tree*
la cereza *cherry*
la china *orange (Puerto Rico)*
la ciruela *plum*
el durazno *peach*
la fresa *strawberry*
el melocotón *peach*
la papaya *papaya*
la piña *pineapple*
el pomelo *grapefruit*
la sandía *watermelon*
la toronja *grapefruit*

Las verduras/*Vegetables*

las aceitunas *olives*
las alcaparras *capers*
el apio *celery*
la berza *cabbage (Spain)*
el brócoli *broccoli*
el calabacín *zucchini*
la calabaza *squash; pumpkin*
los champiñones *mushrooms*
la col *cabbage*
la coliflor *cauliflower*
los espárragos *asparagus*
las espinacas *spinach*
los guisantes *peas*
las habichuelas *kidney beans*
los hongos *mushrooms (Latin America)*
las judías verdes *green beans (Spain)*
el pepinillo *pickle*
el pepino *cucumber*
el pimiento *pepper*
el plátano *plantain*
el repollo *cabbage*
las setas *wild mushrooms (Spain)*
la zanahoria *carrot*

Los postres/*Desserts*

el arroz con leche *rice pudding*
la batida *milkshake*
el batido *milkshake (Spain)*
los bollos *sweet bread*
el bombón *sweets; candy*
el caramelo *sweets; candy*
los chocolates *chocolates*
los chuches *candies (Spain)*
la dona *donut*
el flan *caramel custard*
la natilla *custard*
los pastelitos *turnover; pastry; finger cakes*
la tarta *cake*

Las bebidas/*Beverages*

el champán *champagne*
la sidra *cider*
el zumo *juice (Spain)*

Más comidas/*More foods*

la avena *oatmeal*
los bocaditos *bite-size sandwiches*
el caldo *broth*
el consomé *clear soup*
los fideos *noodles (in soup)*
el gofre *waffle*
la harina *flour*
la jalea *jelly; marmalade (Spain, Puerto Rico)*
la margarina *margarine*

la miel *honey*
el pan dulce *sweet roll*
el panqueque *pancake*
la salsa *sauce*
las tortas americanas *pancakes (Spain)*

Verbos/*Verbs*

aclararse *to thin*
agregar *to add*
añadir *to add*
asar *to roast; to broil*
batir *to beat*
calentar *to heat*
cocer *to cook*
derretir *to melt*
echar (algo) *to add (something)*
espesarse *to thicken*
freír *to fry*
hervir *to boil*
mezclar *to mix*
recalentar *to reheat*
remover *to stir (Spain)*
revolver *to stir*
unir *to combine*
verter *to pour*

Las comidas/*Meals*

el aperitivo *appetizer*
las tapas *hors d'oeuvres*

La preparación de comidas/*Food preparation*

Algunos términos de la cocina/*Cooking terms*

el fuego (lento, mediano, alto) *(low, medium, high) heat*

En el restaurante/*In the restaurant*

el batidor *beater*
la batidora *hand-held mixer*
la cacerola *saucepan*
la copa *goblet; wine glass*
la cucharilla *teaspoon (Spain)*
el cuenco *bowl; mixing bowl*
el/la friegaplatos *dishwasher (person)*
la fuente *serving platter/dish*
el ingrediente *ingredient*
el kilogramo *kilogram (or 2.2 pounds)*
el/la mesero/a *waiter/waitress (Latin America)*
el nivel *level*
la olla *pot*
el pedazo *piece*
el/la pinche *kitchen assistant*
el platillo *saucer*
el plato hondo *bowl*
el plato sopero *soup bowl*
el procesador de alimentos *food processor*
la receta *recipe*
la reserva *the reservation*
la sartén *frying pan*
el/la sopero/a *soup serving bowl*

Capítulo 8

La ropa/*Clothing*

el albornoz *bathrobe (Spain)*
las alpargatas *espadrille sandals (Spain)*
el anorak *rain-proof coat*
los aretes *earrings*
la bolsa *bag*
las bragas *panties*
la bufanda *scarf*
los calzoncillos *men's underwear*
la capa de agua *raincoat (Puerto Rico)*
la cartera *pocketbook, purse*
el chándal *tracksuit (Spain)*
el chubasquero *raincoat (Spain)*
el collar *necklace*
la correa *belt*
el gorro *wool cap; hat*
los mahones *jeans (Puerto Rico)*
las pantallas *earrings (Puerto Rico)*
el peine *comb*
la peinilla *comb (Latin America)*
los pendientes *earrings*
la pulsera *bracelet*
la sombrilla *parasol; umbrella*
el sostén *bra*
el sujetador *bra (Spain)*
los vaqueros *jeans*
las zapatillas de tenis *sneakers; tennis shoes (Spain)*
los zapatos planos/de cuña *flat/wedge shoes*

Algunos verbos/*Some verbs*

desnudarse *to get undressed*
desvestirse *to get undressed*
ponerse la ropa *to get dressed*
quitarse la ropa *to get undressed*
vestirse *to get dressed*

Las telas y los materiales/*Fabrics and materials*

la goma *rubber*
el lino *linen*
el nilón *nylon*
el oro *gold*
la plata *silver*
el platino *platinum*

Algunos adjetivos/*Some adjectives*

amplio/a *wide*
apretado/a *tight*

de buena/mala calidad *good/poor quality*
de manga corta/larga/media *short-/long-/half-sleeved*
de puntitos *polka-dotted*

Otras palabras/*Other words*

el escaparate *store window*
el/la dependiente/a *clerk*
la ganga *bargain*
la liquidación *clearance sale*
el maniquí *mannequin*
el mostrador *counter*
la oferta *offer; sale*
la rebaja *sale; discount*
el tacón alto/bajo *high/low heel*
la venta *(clearance) sale*
la vitrina *store window*

Capítulo 9

El cuerpo humano/*The human body*

la arteria *artery*
el cabello *hair*
la cadera *hip*
la ceja *eyebrow*
el cerebelo *cerebellum*
el cerebro *brain*
la cintura *waist*
el codo *elbow*
la costilla *rib*
la frente *forehead*
el hombro *shoulder*
el hueso *bone*
el labio *lip*
la lengua *tongue*
las mejillas *cheeks*
la muñeca *wrist*
el músculo *muscle*
el muslo *thigh*
las nalgas *buttocks*
los nervios *nerves*
las pestañas *eyelashes*
la piel *skin*
el pulmón *lung*
la rodilla *knee*
el talón *heel*
el tobillo *ankle*
la uña *nail*
las venas *veins*
el vientre *belly*

Algunas enfermedades y tratamientos médicos/*Illnesses and medical treatments*

En el hospital/*In the hospital*

el análisis *analysis, test*
la camilla *stretcher*
operar *to operate*
el/la paciente *patient*
las pruebas médicas *medical tests*
el pulso *pulse*
los puntos *sutures, stitches*
la radiografía *X-ray*
respirar *to breathe*
el resultado *result*
sacar la sangre *to draw blood*
tomarle la presión *to take someone's blood pressure*
tomarle el pulso *to take someone's pulse*
tomarle la temperatura *to check someone's temperature*

Los tratamientos/*Treatments*

el antihistamínico *antihistamine*
la cura *cure*
la dosis *dose; dosage*
enyesar *to put on a cast*
las gotas para los ojos *eyedrops*
hacer gárgaras *to gargle*
el medicamento *medicine*
las muletas *crutches*
la penicilina *penicillin*
recetar *to prescribe*
el termómetro *thermometer*
la tirita *bandage (Spain)*
la vacuna *vaccination*

Los síntomas y las enfermedades/*Symptoms and illnesses*

la acidez *heartburn*
el alcoholismo *alcoholism*
las alergias *allergies*
la alta/baja tensión *high/low blood pressure*
el ataque al corazón *heart attack*
el cáncer *cancer*
contagiarse de *to catch (an illness)*
la depresión *depression*
desmayarse *to faint*
desvanecerse *to faint*
la diabetes *diabetes*
doblarse *to sprain*
el/la drogadicto/a *drug addict*
el esguince *sprain*
fracturar(se) *to break; to fracture*
hinchar *to swell*
la hipertensión *high blood pressure*
el infarto *heart attack*
la inflamación *inflammation*
el mareo *dizziness*
la narcomanía *drug addiction*
pegársele (Se me pegó…) *to catch something (I caught…)*
la presión alta/baja *high/low blood pressure*
la quemadura *burn*
sangrar *to bleed*
el sarampión *measles*
el sida *AIDS*
torcerse *to sprain*
vomitar *to vomit*
la varicela *chicken pox*

Capítulo 10

Los medios de transporte/*Modes of transportation*

el camión *bus (Mexico)*
la camioneta *pickup truck; van; station wagon*
la guagua *bus (Caribbean)*
el tranvía *streetcar, trolley*

Algunos sustantivos/*Some nouns*

el aparcamiento *parking lot*
el atasco *traffic jam*
la autoescuela *driving school*
el camino *dirt road*
el carné *driver's license (Spain)*
la carretera *highway*
el cruce *crossing, intersection*
el paso de peatones *crosswalk*
el seguro del coche *car insurance*
la señal de tráfico *traffic sign, street light*
la velocidad *speed*

Algunas partes de un vehículo/*Parts of a vehicle*

el acelerador *accelerator; gas pedal*
el cinturón de seguridad *seat belt*
el claxon *horn*
el espejo retrovisor *rearview mirror*
los frenos *brakes*
la goma *tire (Latin America)*
el guía *steering wheel*
las luces *lights*
el maletero *car trunk (Spain)*
el parachoques *bumper*
la transmisión *transmission*

Algunos verbos/*Some verbs*

cambiar de marchas *to change gears*
cambiar el aceite *to change the oil*
echar marcha atrás *to go in reverse*
frenar *to brake*
perderse *to get lost*

El viaje/*The trip*

la aduana *customs*
el billete *ticket*
los cheques de viajero *traveler's checks*
la dirección *address*
el equipaje *luggage*
la oficina de turismo *tourist office*
el pasaje *ticket*

El hotel/*The hotel*

la caja fuerte *safe*
el/la camarero/a *housekeeper, chambermaid*
el/la guardia de seguridad *security guard*
el/la portero/a *doorman/woman*
el/la recepcionista *receptionist*
el servicio *room service (cleaning)*
el servicio de habitaciones *room service (food)*

Capítulo 11

Los animales/*Animals*

Los animales de la granja/*Farm animals*

la abeja *bee*
la cabra *goat*
el cochino *pig*
el gallo *rooster*
el marrano *pig*
la oveja *sheep*
el pato *duck*
el puerco *pig*

Los animales salvajes/*Wild animals*

la ardilla *squirrel*
la ballena *whale*
el cangrejo *crab*
el ciervo *deer*
la culebra *snake*
la foca *seal*
el gorila *gorilla*
la iguana *iguana*
la jirafa *giraffe*
el lobo *wolf*
el loro *parrot*
la mariposa *butterfly*
el mono *monkey*
la paloma *pigeon; dove*
el pulpo *octopus*
el puma *puma*
el rinoceronte *rhinoceros*
el tiburón *shark*
el tigre *tiger*
la tortuga *turtle*
el venado *deer*
el zorro *fox*

Otras palabras/*Other words*

el dinosaurio *dinosaur*
el nido *nest*

El medio ambiente/*The environment*

el aerosol *aerosol*
el agua subterránea *ground water*
la Antártida *Antarctica*
el Ártico *the Arctic*
la atmósfera *atmosphere*
el aumento *increase*
el carbón *coal*
la central nuclear *nuclear plant*
el clorofluorocarbono *chlorofluorocarbon (CFCs)*

el combustible fósil *fossil fuel*
la cosecha *crop; harvest*
la descomposición *decomposition*
el desperdicio de jardinería *yard waste*
el dióxido de carbono *carbon dioxide*
el ecosistema *ecosystem*
la energía *energy*
la energía eólica (molinos de viento) *wind power (windmills)*
la industria *industry*
insostenible *unsustainable*
el oxígeno *oxygen*
el pesticida *pesticide*
el petróleo *petroleum; oil*
la piedra *rock; stone*
las placas solares *solar panels*
la planta eléctrica *power plant*
el plomo *lead*
el rayo de sol *ray of sunlight*
el rayo ultravioleta *ultraviolet ray*
el riesgo *risk*

Algunos verbos/*Some verbs*

atrapar *to trap*
conseguir *to achieve*
corroer *to corrode*
dañar *to damage*
desarrollar *to evolve; to develop*
descongelarse *to melt; melt down*
destruir *to destroy*
hacer huelga *to go on strike*
hundirse *to sink*
luchar en contra *to fight against*
prevenir *to prevent*
realizar *to achieve*
tirar *to throw away (Spain)*

La política/*Politics*

el concejal/la concejala *city/town councilor*
la constitución *constitution*
la ciudadanía *citizenship*
el/la ciudadano/a *citizen*
el/la congresista *congressman/woman*
el golpe de estado *coup d'état*
la monarquía constitucional *constitutional monarchy*
el paro general *general strike*
el/la primer/a ministro/a *prime minister*
el/la secretario/a de estado *secretary of state*

Las cuestiones políticas/*Political matters*

el aborto *abortion*
el abuso de menores *child abuse*
el asesinato *assasination*
los derechos de los trabajadores *workers' rights*
los derechos humanos *human rights*
la eutanasia *euthanasia*
el genocidio *genocide*
el/la indocumentado/a *undocumented immigrant/worker*
la inmigración ilegal *illegal immigration*
el/la inmigrante *immigrant*
la pena capital *death penalty*
la seguridad social *social security*
la violencia doméstica *domestic violence*

APPENDIX 4

Spanish-English Glossary

Fíjate

This glossary includes all words and expressions presented in the text, except for words spelled the same in English and Spanish. The number in bold following each entry corresponds to the **capítulo** in which the word is first introduced for active mastery. Numbers that are not bold indicate that the word is presented for receptive use.

A

a to; at (**11**); ~ **cambio** in exchange (4, B); ~ **eso de** around (7); ~ **la derecha** (de) to the right (of) (3, 7, **11**); ~ **la... /** ~ **las...** At... o'clock (**A**); ~ **la izquierda (de)** to the left (of) (3, 7, **11**); ~ **la parrilla** grilled (**7**); ~ **mano** on hand (10); ~ **menudo** often (2, 3, 8); **¿~ qué hora...?** At what time? (**A**); ~ **veces** sometimes; from time to time (2, 3, **4**)
abarcar to encompass (5)
abogado/a, el/la lawyer (8)
Abra(n) el libro en la página... Open your book to page... (**A**)
abrazo, el hug (A)
abrigo, el coat; overcoat (3, **8**)
abril April (**A**)
abrir to open (**2**)
abuelo/a, el/la grandfather/grandmother (**1**)
abuelos, los *(pl.)* grandparents (**1**)
aburrido/a boring; bored (*with* **estar**) (**1**, **2**, **5**)
acabar: ~ **con** to end (4); ~ **de + infinitivo** to have just finished + *(something)* (**9**)
aceite, el oil (**7**)
acerca de about (**11**)
acierto, el match (11)
acontecimiento, el event (9)
acordarse (ue) de to remember (**9**)
acostarse (ue) to go to bed (**9**)
actor, el actor (**5**)
actriz, la actress (**5**)
adecuado/a suitable (10)
además de furthermore (2, 7); in addition to (2, 7); besides (4)
aderezo, el salad dressing (**7**)
Adiós. Good-bye. (**A**)
adivinar to guess (5, 7)
adjetivos, los *(pl.)* adjectives (**1**)
administración de empresas, la business administration (**2**)
administraciones, las *(pl.)* administrations (**11**)
¿Adónde? To where? (**2**)
aerolínea, la airline (10)
aeropuerto, el airport (**10**)
afeitarse to shave (**9**)
aficionado/a, el/la fan (**5**)
afuera de outside of (**11**)
afueras, las *(pl.)* outskirts (3)
agencia de viajes, la travel agency (6, **10**)
agente de viajes, el/la travel agent (**10**)
agosto August (**A**)
agua, el water; ~ **(con hielo)** water (with ice) (5, **7**); ~ **dulce** fresh water (5)
ahora now (B); ~ **mismo** right now (2)
aire, el air (**11**); ~ **acondicionado** air conditioning (**10**)
aislado/a isolated (11)
ajo, el garlic (**7**)
al: ~ **aire libre** open air (4); ~ **horno** baked (**7**); ~ **lado (de)** beside; next to (3, 7, **11**)
alcalde, el mayor (**11**)
alcaldesa, la mayor (**11**)
alebrijes, los *(pl.)* painted wooden animals (2)
alfabetización, la literacy (8)
alfombra, la rug (**3**); carpet (**3**)
algo something (**4**)
algodón, el cotton (**8**)
alguien someone (**4**)
algún some (**4**); any (**4**)
alguno/a/os/as some (3, **4**); any (3, **4**)
aliño, el salad dressing (**7**)
allá over there *(and potentially not visible)* (6)
allí there / over there (6)
almacén, el department store (**4**)
almendra, la almond (7)
almohada, la pillow (**3**)
almorzar (ue) to have lunch (**4**)
almuerzo, el lunch (**7**)
alpargatas, las *(pl.)* espadrilles (8)
altillo, el attic (**3**)
altiplano, el high plateau (9)
alto/a tall (**1**)
aluminio, el aluminum (**11**)
amantes, los *(pl.)* lovers (11)
amarillo yellow (**3**)
ambiente, el environment (5)
ambulante roving (4)
amenazado/a endangered (7)
amigo/a, el/la friend (**1**)
amor, el love (4)
amueblado/a furnished (**3**)
anaranjado orange (**3**)
ancho/a wide (7, **8**)
andar to walk (**7**)
anillo, el ring (5)
animado/a animated (**5**)
animal, el animal (**11**); ~ **doméstico** domesticated animal (**11**); pet (**11**); ~ **en peligro de extinción** endangered animal (**11**); ~ **salvaje** wild animal (**11**)
año pasado, el last year (5, 7)
anoche last night (5, 7)
anteayer the day before yesterday (5, 7)
anterior previous (5)
antes (de) before *(time/space)* (6, **11**)
antiácido, el antacid (**9**)
antibiótico, el antibiotic (**9**)
antiguo/a old (3)
antipático/a unpleasant (**1**)
anuncio, el ad (3)
apartamento, el apartment (**2**)
apasionado/a passionate (**5**)
apéndice, el appendix (4)
apodo, el nickname (5)
apoyar to support (B, **11**)
aprender to learn (**2**)
aprobado/a approved (10)
apuntes, los *(pl.)* notes (**2**)
aquel/la that, that one *(way over there/ not visible)* (**5**)
aquellos/as those *(way over there/not visible)*; those ones (**5**)
aquí here (6)
árbol, el tree (**11**)
arbusto, el bush; shrub (7)
armario, el armoire; closet; cabinet (**3**)
arquitectura, la architecture (**2**)
arreglar to straighten up; to fix (**3**); ~**se** to get oneself ready (**9**); ~ **la maleta** to pack a suitcase (**10**)
arrodillarse to kneel (11)
arroz, el rice (**7**)
arte, el art (**2**)
artista, el/la artist (**5**)

asado/a roasted; grilled **(7)**
aspirina, la aspirin **(9)**
asunto, el matter (6)
asustar to scare (9)
atender (ie) to wait on (9)
atletismo, el track and field (2)
atrevido/a daring **(8)**
atentamente sincerely (4)
atún, el tuna **(7)**
aún más even more (1)
aunque even though (5)
autobús, el bus **(10)**
autopista, la highway; freeway **(10)**
ave, el bird **(11)**
averiguar to find out (4, B)
aves, las *(pl.)* poultry **(7)**
avión, el airplane **(10)**
ayer yesterday (5, 7)
ayudante, el/la assistant (5); **~ personal** personal assistant (6)
azúcar, el sugar **(7)**
ayudar to help **(3)**; **~ a las personas mayores/los mayores** to help elderly people (4)
azul blue **(3)**

B

la bahía bay (11)
bailar to dance **(2)**
bajar (de) to download (5); to get down (from); to get off (of) **(10)**
bajo/a short **(1)**
balcón, el balcony **(3)**
banana, la banana **(7)**
bañarse to bathe **(9)**
banco, el bank **(4)**
bañera, la bathtub **(3)**
baño, el bathroom **(3)**
bar, el bar **(4)**
barato/a inexpensive (3, 4), cheap **(7)**
barco, el boat (B, **10**)
barro negro, el black clay (2)
Bastante bien. Just fine. **(A)**
basura, la garbage **(11)**
bata, la robe **(8)**
batata, la yam (7)
batería, la drums **(5)**
baúl, el trunk **(10)**
beber to drink **(7)**
bebida, la drinks (5); beverage (B, **7**)
beige beige **(3)**
bello/a beautiful (4)
besito, el little kiss (A)
biblioteca, la library **(2)**
bicicleta, la bicycle **(10)**
bidé, el bidet **(3)**
bien: ~ cocido/a well done **(7)**; **~ hecho/a** well cooked **(7)**; **~, gracias.** Fine, thanks. **(A)**
bienestar, el well-being; welfare **(11)**
bienvenida, la welcome **(2)**
bija, la annatto (7)
biología, la biology **(2)**
bistec, el steak **(7)**
blanco white **(3)**
blusa, la blouse **(8)**
boca, la mouth **(9)**
boda, la wedding (4, 6, 11)
boleto, el ticket (8, **10**)
bolígrafo, el ballpoint pen **(2)**
bolso, el bag **(7, 8)**
bondadoso/a kind (11)
bonito/a pretty **(1)**
borrador, el eraser **(2)**
bosque, el forest (9, **11**)
botar to throw away **(11)**
botas, las *(pl.)* boots **(8)**
bote, el boat (4)
botella, la bottle **(11)**
botones, el bellhop **(10)**
brazo, el arm **(9)**
buceo, el scuba diving (4)
¡Buen provecho! Enjoy your meal! **(7)**
buenas: ~ noches. Good evening. **(A)** **~ tardes.** Good afternoon. **(A)**
bueno/a good **(1, 10)**
Buenos días. Good morning. **(A)**
bufanda, la scarf (9)
bullicio, el hubbub (4)
buscar to look for **(4)**

C

caballo, el horse **(11)**
cabeza, la head **(9)**
cada each (3, 4, B)
caer(se) to fall down **(9)**
café, el café; coffee **(4, 7)**
cafetería, la cafeteria **(2)**
caja, la (de cartón) (cardboard) box **(11)**
cajero automático, el ATM **(4)**
calcetines, los *(pl.)* socks **(8)**
calculadora, la calculator **(2)**
calefacción, la heat **(10)**
calidad, la quality **(11)**
caliente hot *(temperature)* (7)
callarse to get / keep quiet **(9)**
calle, la street (3, **10**)
cama, la bed **(3)**
camarero/a, el/la waiter/waitress **(7)**; housekeeper (10)
camarones, los *(pl.)* shrimp **(7)**
cambiar to change **(10)**; **~ de papel** to change roles (3)
cambio, el change *(monetary)* (4); **~ climático** climate change **(11)**
caminar to walk **(2)**
camión, el truck **(10)**
camisa, la shirt **(8)**
camiseta, la T-shirt **(8)**
campo, el country (3); countryside (4)
canción, la song **(5)**
candidato/a, el/la candidate **(11)**
cansado/a tired **(2)**
cantante, el/la singer **(5)**
cantar to sing **(5)**
cara, la face **(9)**
caracolas, las *(pl.)* conch (7)
cargos, los *(pl.)* posts **(11)**
caridad, la charity (3)
carne, la meat **(7)**
caro/a expensive **(7)**
carro, el car **(10)**
cartel, el poster (10)
casa, la house **(3)**
casado/a married **(1)**
casarse to get married (11)
cascada, la waterfall (10)
cáscara, la peel (7)
casi: ~ siempre almost always **(8)**; **~ todo** almost everything (2)
castillo, el castle (3)
catarro, el cold **(9)**
catorce fourteen **(A)**
cazuela, la pot; casserole (7)
cebolla, la onion **(7)**
cena, la dinner **(7)**
cenar to have dinner **(7)**
centro, el downtown **(4)**; **~ comercial** mall; business/shopping district **(4)**; **~ estudiantil** student center; student union **(2)**
cepillarse (el pelo, los dientes) to brush (one's hair, teeth) **(9)**
cerca (de) near (2, 7, **11**)
cerdo, el pig **(11)**
cereal, el cereal **(7)**
cerrar (ie) to close **(4)**
cerveza, la beer **(7)**
cestería, la basket weaving (2)
Chao. Bye. **(A)**
chaqueta, la jacket **(8)**
charla, la talk (11)
chicle, el gum **(2)**
chico/a, el/la boy/girl **(1)**

chicozapote, el sapodilla tree (2)
chile, el chili pepper (**7**)
chisme, el gossip (7)
cibercafé, el Internet café (**4**)
cielo, el sky; heaven (**11**)
cien one hundred (**1, 2**); ~ **mil** one hundred thousand (**3**); ~ **millones** one hundred million (**3**)
ciencias, las *(pl.)* science (**2**)
ciento: ~ **uno** one hundred and one (**2**); ~ **dos** one hundred and two (**2**); ~ **dieciséis** one hundred and sixteen (**2**); ~ **veinte** one hundred and twenty (**2**)
Cierre(n) el/los libros/s. Close your book/s. (**A**)
cierto true (**1**)
cinco five (**A**)
cincuenta fifty (**1**); ~ **y uno** fifty-one (**1**)
cine, el movie theater (**4**)
cintura, la waist (**9**); **de la ~ para arriba/abajo** from the waist up/down (9)
cinturón, el belt (**8**)
circular una petición to circulate a petition (**4**)
cita, la appointment (4, B); date (8)
ciudad, la city (3, **4**)
claro/a clear (5); light *(colored)* (**8**)
clero, el clergy (9)
cliente/a, el/la customer; client (**7**)
club, el club (**4**)
coche, el car (**10**)
cocido/a boiled; baked (**7**)
cocina, la kitchen (**3**)
cocinar to cook (**3, 7**); to prepare a meal (**3**)
cocinero/a, el/la chef (**4, 7**)
cognado, el cognate (**A**)
cola, la line *(of people)* (**10**)
colcha, la bedspread; comforter (**3**)
colgar to hang up (7)
colibrí, el hummingbird (11)
color, el color (**3**)
combatir to fight; to combat (**11**)
comedia, la comedy (**5**)
comedor, el dining room (**3**)
comenzar (ie) to begin (**4**)
comer to eat (**2**)
cómico/a funny; comical (**1**)
comida, la food; meal (**4, 5**, B, **7**); ~ **rápida** fast food (B)
como like (5)
¿cómo?: What? How? (**A, 2**); **¿~ andas?** How are you doing? (A); **¿~ está usted?** How are you? *(formal)* (**A**); **¿~ estás?** How are you? *(familiar)* (**A**); **¿~ se dice… en español?** How do you say… in Spanish? (**A**); **¿~ se escribe… en español?** How do you write… in Spanish? (**A**) **¿~ se llama usted?** What is your name? *(formal)* (**A**); **¿~ te llamas?** What is your name? *(familiar)*
cómoda, la dresser (**3**)
cómodo/a comfortable (**8**)
compañero/a, el/la ~ de clase classmate (**2**); ~ **de cuarto** roommate (**2**)
compartir to share (3, 5)
competencia, la competition (7)
composición, la composition (**2**)
comprar to buy (**2**)
comprender to understand (**2**)
Comprendo. I understand. (**A**)
computadora, la computer (**2**)
con with (**11**)
concha, la shell (10)
concierto, el concert (**5**)
concurso, el competition (7)
condimento, el condiment; seasoning (**7**)
conducción, la driving (10)
conducir to drive (8, **10**)
conejo, el rabbit (10, **11**)
congelador/a, el/la freezer (7)
congreso, el congress (**11**)
conjunto, el group; band (**5**); outfit (**8**)
conmovedor/a moving (**5**)
conocer to be acquainted with (**3**)
consejo, el advice (7)
contaminación, la pollution (**11**)
contaminar to pollute (**11**)
contar to narrate (9)
contemporáneo/a contemporary (3)
contento/a content; happy (**2**)
contestar to answer (**2**)
Conteste(n). Answer. (**A**)
corazón, el heart (**9**)
corbata, la tie (**8**)
cordillera, la mountain range (11)
corregir to correct (3, 10)
correos post office (**4**)
correr to run (**2**)
cortar(se) to cut (oneself) (**9**)
corte, la court (**11**)
cortejo, el courting (7)
corto/a short (**8**)
cosa, la thing (**3**)
cosecha, la crop (7)
costar (ue) to cost (3, **4**)
costurero/a, el/la tailor; seamstress (8)
crear to create (4, B)
creativo/a creative (**5**)
creer to believe (**2**)
crema batida, la whipped cream (7)
criar to raise *(children, animals, etc.)* (10)
crucero, el cruise ship (5)
crudo/a rare; raw (**7**)
cuaderno, el notebook (**2**)
cuadro, el picture; painting (**3**, 5)
cual which (11)
¿cuál?: What? Which (one)? (**2**); **¿~ es la fecha de hoy?** What is today's date? (**A**)
cualquier whatever (8); any (10)
¿Cuándo? When? (**2**)
¿Cuánto/a? How much? (**2**); **¿Cuántos/as?** How many? (**2**)
cuarenta forty (**1**); ~ **y uno** forty-one (**1**)
cuarto/a fourth (**3**)
cuarto, el room (**2, 3**); ~ **doble** double room (**10**); ~ **individual** single room (**10**)
cuatro four (**A**)
cuatrocientos four hundred (**2**)
cubrir to cover (8)
cuchara, la soup spoon; tablespoon (**7**)
cucharada, la spoonful (7)
cucharita, la teaspoon (**7**)
cuchillo, el knife (**7**)
cuello, el neck (**9**)
cuenta, la bill; account (**4**)
cuero, el leather (**8**)
cuerpo humano, el human body (**9**)
cuestiones políticas, las *(pl.)* political issues (**11**)
cueva, la cave (**11**)
cuidadosamente carefully (**2**)
cuidar to take care of (3, 9, **11**)
cumbre, la mountain top (12)
cumplido/a fulfilled (11)
curandero/a, el/la folk healer (4)
curar(se) to be cured (**9**)
curita, la adhesive bandage (**9**)
curso, el course (**2**)
cutis, el complexion (11)
cuyo whose (11)

D

dar to give (**3**); ~ **un concierto** to give/perform a concert (**5**); ~ **un paseo** to go for a walk (**4**); **~se cuenta** to realize (9); ~ **vida** to give life (5)
de of (1); from; about (**11**); ~ **cuadros** checked (**8**); **¿~ dónde?** From where? (2); ~ **espanto** scary (**5**); ~ **ida y vuelta** round-trip (**10**); ~ **la mañana** in the morning (**A**); ~ **la noche** in the

evening (**A**); ~ **nuevo** again (2); ~ **la tarde** in the afternoon (**A**); ~ **lunares** polka-dotted (**8**); ~ **manga larga** long-sleeved (8); ~ **nada.** You're welcome. (**A**); **¿~ qué se trata… ?** What is the gist of… ? (8); ~ **rayas** striped (**8**); ~ **repente** suddenly (B, 11); ~ **suspenso** suspenseful (**5**)

debajo (de) under; underneath (7, **11**)

deber ought to; should (**4**); **~, el** obligation; duty (**4**)

débil weak (**1**)

décimo/a tenth (**3**)

decir to say; to tell (**3**)

dedicar to devote (3)

dedo, el ~ (de la mano) finger (**9**); **~ (del pie)** toe (**9**)

defensa, la defense (**11**)

dejar to leave (**10**)

delante de in front of (**11**)

delgado/a thin (**1**)

delicioso/a delicious (**7**)

delincuencia, la crime (**11**)

demás, los *(pl.)* others (4)

democracia, la democracy (**11**)

demostrar (ue) to demonstrate (**4**)

dentro de inside of (**11**)

deporte, el sport (**2**)

deprimente depressing (**5**)

derecho, el law (**2**)

derecho/a straight (10)

derrame de petróleo, el oil spill (**11**)

derrotado/a defeated (11)

desastre, el disaster (**11**)

desayunar to have breakfast (**7**)

desayuno, el breakfast (**7**)

descansar to rest (7)

desde from (**11**); ~ **que** since (9)

desempleo, el unemployment (**11**)

desfile de moda, el fashion show (8)

desordenado/a messy (**3**)

despedida, la farewell (**A**)

despertador, el alarm clock (**2**)

despertarse (ie) to wake up; to awaken (**9**)

después afterward (6); after (**11**)

destacar to stand out (5); to distinguish (7)

destino, el destination (8)

destrucción, la destruction (**11**)

destruir to destroy (5)

determinaciones, las *(pl.)* resolutions (11)

detrás (de) behind (4, **11**)

deuda (externa), la (foreign) debt (**11**)

devolver (ue) to return *(an object)* (4)

día, el day (**A**)

dibujar to draw (**4**)

dibujo, el drawing (3)

diciembre December (**A**)

dictador/a, el/la dictator (**11**)

dictadura, la dictatorship (**11**)

diente, el tooth (**9**)

diez: ten; **dieciséis** sixteen; **diecisiete** seventeen; **dieciocho** eighteen; **diecinueve** nineteen (**A**)

difícil difficult (2)

dinero, el money (**2**)

diputado/a, el/la deputy; representative (**11**)

discurso, el speech (**11**)

discutir to discuss (B)

diseñador/a, el/la designer (8)

disfrutar de to enjoy (4, B)

divertirse (ie, i) to enjoy oneself (5, **9**); to have fun (6, **9**)

dividido por divided by (1)

doblar to turn (**10**)

doce twelve (**A**)

doctor/a, el/la doctor (**9**)

documental, el documentary (**5**)

dólar, el dollar (2)

doler (ue) to hurt (**9**)

dolor, el pain (**9**)

domingo, el Sunday (**A**)

donación, la contribution (11)

donas, las *(pl.)* donuts (10)

¿Dónde? Where? (**2**)

dormir (ue, u) to sleep (**4**)**; ~se** to fall asleep (**9**)

dormitorio, el bedroom (**3**)

dos two (**A**); ~ **millones** two million (**3**); **~cientos** two hundred (**2**)**; ~cientos uno** two hundred and one (**2**)

ducha, la shower (**3**)

ducharse to shower (**9**)

dulce, el candy; sweets (**7**)

durante during (B)

durar to last (9, 11)

duro/a hard-boiled (**7**)

DVD, el *(pl.* **los DVD***)* DVD/s (**2**)

E

ecología, la ecology (**11**)

edificio, el building (**2**)

efecto invernadero, el greenhouse effect (**11**)

ejército, el army (5)

ejércitos, los *(pl.)* armies (11)

él he, him (**A**, **11**)

el the (**1**)

elecciones, las *(pl.)* elections (**11**)

elefante, el elephant (**11**)

elegante elegant (**8**)

elegir to elect (**11**)

ella she (**A**); her (**11**)

ellos/as they (**A**); them (**11**)

embarazada pregnant (9)

embriaguez, la intoxication (10)

emocionante moving (**5**)

emociones, las *(pl.)* emotions (**2**)

empanada, la turnover (meat) (7)

empezar (ie) to begin (**4**)

empleado/a, el/la employee (5); attendant (12)

empresario/a, el/la agent; manager (**5**)

en in (**11**); ~ **frente de** in front of (2); ~ **vez de** instead of (8)

enamorarse de to fall in love (7)

Encantado/a. Pleased to meet you. (**A**)

encantar to love; to like very much (**8**)

encerrar (ie) to enclose (**4**)

encima (de) on top (of); above (3, 7, **11**)

encontrar (ue) to find (**4**)

encubierto/a undercover (5)

encuesta, la survey; poll (**11**)

endémico/a native (11)

enero January (**A**)

enfermar(se) to get sick (**9**)

enfermedad, la illness (**9**)

enfermero/a, el/la nurse (**9**)

enfermo/a ill; sick (**2**)

enfrente (de) in front (of) (4); across from; facing (**11**)

enojado/a angry (**2**)

ensalada, la salad (**7**)

ensayar to practice/rehearse (**5**)

enseñar to teach; to show (**2**)

entender (ie) to understand (**4**)

entonces then (**6**)

entrada, la ticket (**5**); entrance (5); entry (blog) (6)

entrar to enter (**10**); ~ **ganas** get the urge (9)

entre among; between (4, B, **11**); ~ **sí** among themselves (11)

entregar to turn in (7)

entretenerse to entertain oneself (8)

entretenido/a entertaining (**5**)

entrevista, la interview (3); ~ **de trabajo** job interview (8)

entrevistar to interview (5)

enviar to send (**4**)

envolver to wrap (7)

épico/a epic (**5**)

equipaje, el luggage (10)

equipo, el team (**2**)

equivocarse to be mistaken (9)

es: ~ **bueno/malo/mejor que…** It's good/bad/better that…; ~ **dudoso que…** It's doubtful that…; ~ **importante que…** It's important that…; ~ **imposible que…** It's impossible that…; ~ **improbable que…** It's unlikely that…; ~ **increíble que…** It's incredible that…; ~ **la… / Son las…** It's… o'clock. (**A**); ~ **una lástima que…** It's a pity that…; ~ **necesario que…** It's necessary that…; ~ **posible que…** It's possible that…; ~ **preferible que…** It's preferable that…; ~ **probable que…** It's likely that…; ~ **raro que…** It's rare that… (**11**); ~ **verdad.** It's true. (1)
escalera, la staircase (**3**, 11)
esclusa, la lock *(of a canal)* (5)
escoger to choose (4)
Escriba(n). Write. (**A**)
escribir to write (**2**)
escritorio, el desk (**2**)
escuchar música to listen to music (**2**)
Escuche(n). Listen. (**A**)
ese/a that, that one (**5**)
esos/as those *(over there)*; those ones (**5**)
espalda, la back (**9**)
especialidad de la casa, la specialty of the house (7)
especias, las *(pl.)* spices (**7**)
esperanza, la hope (11)
esperar to wait for; to hope (**2**)
esposo/a, el/la husband/wife (**1**)
Está nublado. It's cloudy. (**A**)
estación, la season (**A**); ~ **(de tren, de autobús)** (train, bus) station (**10**)
estacionamiento, el parking (**10**)
estacionar to park (**10**)
estadidad, la statehood (11)
estadio, el stadium (**2**)
estado, el state *(of being)* (**2**); state (**11**)
estampado/a print *(with a design or pattern)* (**8**)
estante, el bookcase (**3**)
estar to be (**2**); ~ **de acuerdo** to agree (4); ~ **en huelga** to be on strike (**11**); ~ **enfermo/a** to be sick (**9**); ~ **sano/a / saludable** to be healthy (**9**)
este/a this, this one (**5**)
estilo, el style (8)
estimado/a dear (4)
estómago, el stomach (**9**)
estornudar to sneeze (**9**)
estornudo, el sneeze (**9**)
estos/as these (**5**)
estrecho/a narrow; tight (**8**)
estrella, la star (**5**)
estrenar una película to release a film/movie (**5**)
estreno, el opening (**5**)
estudiante de intercambio, el/la exchange student (10)
estudiante, el/la student (**2**); ~ **de primer año** freshman (8)
estudiar to study (**2**, 6)
estufa, la stove (**3**)
estupendo/a stupendous (**5**)
euro(s), el euro (**2**)
evitar to avoid (**9**)
evolucionar to evolve (5)
examen, el (**2**); ~ **físico** physical exam (**9**)
exigente demanding (9)
expedir to complete (10)
experimentar to experience (11)
expresión de cortesía, la polite expression (**A**)
extranjero, el abroad (**10**)

F

fabada, la bean stew (7)
fábrica, la factory (8)
fácil easy (2)
falda, la skirt (**8**)
falso false (**1**)
faltar to miss (**4**, B)
fama, la fame (**5**)
familia, la family (**1**)
farmacéutico/a, el/la pharmacist (9)
farmacia, la pharmacy (**9**)
fascinar to fascinate (**8**)
febrero February (**A**)
feliz happy (**2**)
feo/a ugly (**1**)
fiebre, la fever (**9**)
fin de semana, el weekend (**3**, 7); ~ **pasado** last weekend (7)
finalmente finally (6)
finca, la farm (**11**)
fino/a fine; delicate (**5**)
firma, la signature (4)
flauta, la flute (5)
floreciente flourishing (8)
flores, las *(pl.)* flowers (7)
fondos, los *(pl.)* funds (10); funding (11)
formal formal (**8**)
foto, la photo (**1**)
frecuentemente frequently (**8**)
fresco/a fresh (**7**)
frijoles, los *(pl.)* beans (**7**)
frito/a fried (7)
fruta, la fruit (**7**)
fuente, la source (5, 9)
fuera outside (7); ~ **de** outside of (**11**)
fuerte strong (**1**); loud (3)
funcionar to work; to function (**10**)

G

galleta, la cookie; cracker (**7**)
gallina, la chicken; hen (7, **11**)
gallo, el rooster (7)
ganar to win (3, 6, 7)
garaje, el garage (**3**)
garganta, la throat (**9**)
gasolinera, la gas station (**10**)
gato, el cat (10, **11**)
generalmente generally (**8**)
género, el genre (**5**)
gente, la people (**1**)
gimnasio, el gymnasium (**2**)
gira, la tour (**5**)
gobernador/a, el/la governor (**11**)
gobierno, el government (**11**)
gordo/a fat (**1**)
gorra, la cap (**8**)
grabar to record (**5**)
Gracias. Thank you. (**A**)
gramo, el gram (7)
grande big; large (**1, 10**)
granja, la farm (**11**)
grasa, la fat (7)
gripe, la flu (**9**)
gris gray (**3**)
gritar to shout (11)
guantes, los *(pl.)* gloves (**8**)
guapo/a handsome/pretty (**1**)
guardar to put away; to keep (**3**); ~ **cama** to stay in bed (**9**)
guerra, la war (**11**)
guerreros, los warriors (11)
guía, la guide (5)
guitarra, la guitar (**5**)
guitarrista, el/la guitarist (**5**)
gustar to like (**A**)

H

habichuelas, las *(pl.)* beans (11)
habilidad, la ability; skill (**5**)
hablar to speak (**2**)
hace: ~ **buen tiempo.** The weather is nice.; ~ **calor.** It's hot.; ~ **frío.** It's cold.; ~ **mal tiempo.** The weather is bad.; ~ **sol.** It's sunny.; ~ **viento.** It's windy. (**A**)
hacer to do; to make (**3, 4, 9**); ~ **artesanía** to make arts and crafts

(4); ~ **daño** to (do) damage; to harm (**11**); ~ **ejercicio** to exercise (**2**); ~ **falta** to need; to be lacking (**8**); ~ **la cama** to make the bed (**3**); ~ **(la) cola** to stand in line (**10**); ~ **la maleta** to pack a suitcase (**10**); ~ **los arreglos** to make the arrangements (10); ~ **las compras** to do the shopping (7); ~ **mímica** to play charades (9); ~ **una gira** to tour (**5**); ~ **una hoguera** to light a campfire (**4**)
hamaca, la hammock (11)
hamburguesa, la hamburger (**7**)
hasta until (11); ~ **luego.** See you later.; ~ **mañana.** See you tomorrow.; ~ **pronto.** See you soon. (**A**)
hay there is (**3**); there are (**3**); ~ **que** + *infinitivo* it is necessary… / you must… / one must/should… (**3**)
hecho/a de made from (9)
helado, el ice cream (**7**)
herbolario, el herbalist (10)
herida, la wound; injury (**9**)
hermano/a, el/la *(pl.)* brother/sister (**1**)
hermanos, los brothers and sisters; siblings (**1**)
hervido/a boiled (**7**)
hijo/a, el/la son/daughter (**1**)
hijos, los *(pl.)* sons and daughters; children (**1**)
hilera, la row (8)
hispanohablante, el/la Spanish speaker (1)
hojalatería, la tin work (2)
hojas de coca, las *(pl.)* coca leaves (9)
¡Hola! Hi! (**A**)
hombre, el man (**1**)
homenaje, el tribute (5)
hora, la time (**A**)
horario (de clases), el schedule (of classes) (**2**)
hormiga, la ant (**11**)
hospital, el hospital (**9**)
hotel, el hotel (**10**)
hoy: ~ **es el 1° (primero) de septiembre.** Today is September first.; ~ **es lunes.** Today is Monday. (**A**)
hoyo, el hole (**11**)
huelga, la strike (**11**)
hueso, el bone (10)
huevo, el egg (**7**)
humilde humble (3)
humo, el fumes (12)
huracán, el hurricane (**11**)

I

idiomas, los *(pl.)* languages (**2**)
iglesia, la church (**4**)
Igualmente. Likewise. (**A**)
imaginativo/a imaginative (**5**)
impermeable, el raincoat (**8**)
importar to matter; to be important (**8**)
impresionante impressive (**5**)
impuesto, el tax (**11**)
incendio, el fire (**11**)
incluir to include (6)
incómodo/a uncomfortable (**8**)
inflación, la inflation (**11**)
influyente influential (11)
informal casual (**8**)
informática, la computer science (**2**)
inodoro, el toilet (**3**)
insecto, el insect (**11**)
inteligente intelligent (**1**)
intercambiar to exchange (6)
interesante interesting (**1**)
inundación, la flood (**11**)
invertir to invest (11)
invierno, el winter (**A**)
inyección, la shot (**9**)
ir to go (**4, 9**); ~ **a pie** to go on foot (**10**); ~ **de camping** to go camping (**4**); ~ **de compras** to go shopping (**2**); ~ **de excursión** to take a short trip (**4**); ~ **de vacaciones** to go on vacation (**10**); ~ **de viaje** to go on a trip (**10**); ~**se** to go away; to leave (**9**); ~**se del hotel** to leave the hotel; to check out (**10**)

J

jamás never; not ever *(emphatic)* (**4**)
jamón, el ham (**7**)
jarabe, el cough syrup (**9**)
jardín, el garden (**3**)
jazz, el jazz (**5**)
jeans, los *(pl.)* jeans (**8**)
joven young (**1, 10**); **el/la joven** young man/young woman (**1, 10**)
joya, la jewel (9)
jueves, el Thursday (**A**)
juez/a, el/la judge (7, **11**)
jugar (ue) to play (4); ~ **al básquetbol** to play basketball; ~ **al béisbol** to play baseball; ~ **al fútbol** to play soccer; ~ **al fútbol americano** to play football; ~ **al golf** to play golf; ~ **al tenis** to play tennis (**2**)
jugo, el juice (**7**)
juicio, el jury (**11**)
julio July (**A**)
junio June (**A**)
juntos/as together (2, 3)

L

la(s) the (**1**)
La cuenta, por favor. The check, please. (**7**)
laboratorio, el laboratory (**2**)
lago, el lake (**10**)
lámpara, la lamp (**3**)
lana, la wool (**8**)
lápiz, el pencil (**2**)
largo/a long (**8**)
lastimarse to get hurt (**9**)
lata, la can (**11**)
latir to beat *(heart)* (9)
lavabo, el sink (**3**)
lavaplatos, el dishwasher (**3**)
lavar: ~ **los platos** to wash dishes (**3**); ~**se** to wash oneself (**9**)
le: to/for him, her (**8**); ~ **saludo atentamente…** Best regards… (**2**)
Lea(n). Read. (**A**)
leche, la milk (**7**)
lechuga, la lettuce (**7**)
leer to read (**2**)
lejos (de) far (from) (7, **11**)
lento/a slow (3, **5**)
león, el lion (**11**)
les to/for them (**8**)
letra, la lyrics (**5**)
levantarse to get up; to stand up (**9**)
ley, la law (10, **11**)
leyenda, la legend (9)
leyes laws (2)
librería, la bookstore (**2**)
libro, el book (**2**)
licencia (de conducir), la driver's license (**10**)
ligero/a light *(meal)* (7)
limón, el lemon (**7**)
limpiaparabrisas, el windshield wiper (**10**)
limpiar to clean (**3**)
limpio/a clean (**3**)
liso/a solid-colored (**8**)
literatura, la literature (**2**)
llamarse to be called (**9**)
llanta, la tire (**10**)
llave, la key (**10**)
llegar to arrive (**2**)
llenar el tanque to fill up the tank (**10**)
llevar to wear; to take; to carry (**8**); ~ **a alguien al médico** to take someone to the doctor (**4**); ~ **a cabo** to carry out (**11**); ~ **ropa** to wear clothing (8)
llorar to cry (11)
Llueve. It's raining. (**A**)
lluvia, la rain (**A**); ~ **ácida** acid rain (**11**)

lo que what (3)
Lo sé. I know. **(A)**
lo, la him, her, it, you **(5)**
lomas, las *(pl.)* hills (11)
loro, el parrot (11)
los, las the **(1)**; them; you all **(5)**
lucha libre, la wrestling (2)
luchar to fight; to combat **(11)**
luego then (6)
lugar, el place **(2)**
lugareños, los *(pl.)* locals (4)
lujo, el luxury (10)
luna de miel, la honeymoon (10)
lunes, el Monday **(A)**

M

madrastra, la stepmother **(1)**
madre, la mother **(1)**
maíz, el corn **(7)**
mal de altura, el altitude sickness (9)
maleta, la suitcase **(10)**
malo/a bad **(1, 10)**
mamá, la mom **(1)**
mañana: ~ es el dos de septiembre. Tomorrow is September second. **(A)**
mandar una carta to send/mail a letter **(4)**
mandioca, la yucca (7)
manejar to drive (5, 8, **10**)
mano, la hand **(1, 9)**
manta, la blanket **(3)**
mantel, el tablecloth **(7)**
mantequilla, la butter **(7)**
manzana, la apple **(7)**
mapa, el map **(2)**
maquillarse to put on make up **(9)**
mareado/a faint (9)
mariscos, los *(pl.)* shellfish; seafood **(7)**
marrón brown **(3)**
martes, el Tuesday **(A)**
marzo March **(A)**
más plus (1); **~** + *adjective/adverb/noun* + **que** more… than **(10)**; **~ o menos.** So-so. **(A)**; **~ tarde que** later than (7); **~ temprano que** earlier than (7)
mascota, la domesticated animal; pet (10, **11**)
masticar to chew (9)
matar to kill **(11)**
matemáticas, las *(pl.)* mathematics **(2)**
materia, la subject **(2)**
material, el material **(8)**
mayo May **(A)**
mayonesa, la mayonnaise **(7)**
mayor old **(1)**; older **(10)**; **~, el/la** the eldest **(10)**
mayordomo, el butler (10)
me: me **(5)**; to/for me **(8)**; **~ llamo…** My name is… **(A)**
medianoche, la midnight **(A)**
medias, las *(pl.)* stockings; hose **(8)**
medicina, la medicine **(2)**
médico/a, el/la doctor **(9)**
medio ambiente, el environment **(11)**
mediodía, el noon **(A)**
mejor best (4, **10**); better **(9)**; **~, el/la** the best **(10)**
mejorar(se) to improve; to get better **(9)**
melón, el melon **(7)**
menor, el/la the youngest **(10)**
menos minus (1); **~** + *adjective/adverb/ noun* + **que** less… than **(10)**; **~ cinco** five minutes to the hour **(A)**; **¡~ mal!** Thank goodness! (4)
mentir (ie) to lie **(4)**
menú, el menu **(7)**
mercado, el market **(4)**
merendar (ie) to have a snack **(7)**
merienda, la snack **(7)**
mermelada, la jam; marmalade **(7)**
mes, el month **(A)**
mesa, la table **(2)**
meterse en política to get involved in politics **(11)**
metro, el subway **(10)**
mezcla, la mixture (7, 11)
mí me **(11)**
mi, mis my **(1)**
microondas, el microwave **(3)**
mientras while (3, **8**)
miércoles, el Wednesday **(A)**
mil one thousand **(2, 3)**
milla, la mile (2, B)
millón one million **(3)**
mirar to look (at); to watch **(2)**; **~ las vitrinas** to window shop (8)
mismo/a same (2)
mitad, la middle (11)
mochila, la book bag; backpack **(2)**
moda, la fashion; style **(8)**
modelo, el/la model **(8)**; **~ de ropa** fashion model (3)
moderno/a modern (3)
molestar to bother **(8)**
monarquía, la monarchy **(11)**
montaña, la mountain **(10)**
montañoso/a mountainous (4)
montar: ~ a caballo to go horseback riding (11); **~ en bicicleta** to ride a bike **(2)**; **~ una tienda de campaña** to put up a tent **(4)**
montón, el pile (7)
morado purple **(3)**
moreno/a dark-haired (5)
morir (ue) to die (**4,** 11)
mosca, la fly **(11)**
mosquito, el mosquito **(11)**
mostaza, la mustard **(7)**
mostrar (ue) to show **(4)**
moto(cicleta), la motorcycle **(1, 10)**
motor, el motor; engine **(10)**
muchacho/a, el/la boy/girl **(1)**
muchas veces many times **(8)**
mucho a lot **(8)**; **~ gusto.** Nice to meet you. **(A)**
mueble, el piece of furniture **(3)**; furniture *(pl.)* **(3)**
muerto/a dead **(11)**
mujer, la woman **(1)**
multa, la traffic ticket; fine **(10)**
mundo, el world (5, 11)
muñeca, la doll (8)
museo, el museum **(4)**
música, la music **(2)**; **~ clásica** classical music; **~ folklórica** folk music; **~ popular** pop music; **~ rap** rap music **(5)**
musical musical **(5)**
músico/a, el/la musician **(5)**
muy very **(1)**; **~ bien.** Really well. **(A)**

N

nacionalidad, la nationality (A)
nada nothing **(4)**
nadar to swim **(2)**
nadie no one; nobody **(4)**
naranja, la orange **(7)**
nariz, la nose **(9)**
naturaleza, la nature **(3, 11)**
náuseas, las *(pl.)* nausea **(9)**
necesitar to need **(2)**
negocio, el business (8)
negro black **(3)**
nervioso/a upset; nervous **(2)**
ni… ni neither… nor **(4)**
nieto/a, el/la grandson/granddaughter **(1)**
Nieva. It's snowing. **(A)**
nieve, la snow **(A)**
ningún none **(4)**
ninguno/a/os/as none (3, **4**)
niño/a, el/la little boy/little girl **(1)**
no: ~. No. **(A)**; **~ comprendo.** I don't understand. **(A)**; **~ lo sé.** I don't know. **(A)**; **~ es verdad.** It's not true. **(1)**; **¡~ me digan!** No way! (4)
normalmente normally **(8)**
nos us **(5)**; to/for us **(8)**
nosotros/as us **(A)**; we **(11)**
novecientos nine hundred **(2)**
noveno/a ninth **(3)**

noventa ninety (**1**)
noviembre November (**A**)
novio/a, el/la boyfriend/girlfriend (**1**)
nube, la cloud (**A**)
nuestro/a/os/as our/s (**1**)
nueve nine (**A**)
nuevo/a new (3)
número, el number (**A**)
nunca never (2, 3, **4**)

O

o… o either… or (**4**)
objeto, el object (**3**)
obra de teatro, la play (5)
obtener to get (10)
océano, el ocean (**11**)
ochenta eighty (**1**)
ocho eight (**A**); **~cientos** eight hundred (**2**)
octavo/a eighth (**3**)
octubre October (**A**)
ocupado/a busy (6)
ocurrir to occur (**9**)
odiar to hate (11)
oferta, la offer (3)
oficina, la office (**3**); **~ de correos** post office (**4**)
ofrecer offer (2)
oído, el inner ear (**9**)
oír to hear (**3**)
ojalá que let's hope that… / hopefully… (11)
ojo, el eye (**9**)
oler to smell (7)
once eleven (**A**)
ópera, la opera (**5**)
opuesto/a opposite (4)
oraciones, las *(pl.)* sentences (3)
ordeñar to milk (11)
oreja, la ear (**9**)
organizar to organize (**4**)
orgulloso/a proud (B)
oro, el gold (9)
orquesta, la orchestra (**5**)
os to/for you all (**5, 8**)
oscuro/a dark (**8**)
oso, el bear (**11**)
otoño, el fall (**A**)
otro/a another (**A**)

P

paciente, el/la patient (**1, 9**)
padrastro, el stepfather (1)
padre, el father (**1**)
padres, los *(pl.)* parents (**1**)
pagar to pay (**7**)
paisaje, el countryside (3)
pájaro, el bird (**11**)
palabra, la word (**A**)
palomitas, las *(pl.)* popcorn (5)
pan, el bread (**7**)
pantalla, la screen (**5**)
pantalones, los *(pl.)* pants (**8**); **~ cortos** *(pl.)* shorts (**8**)
pañuelo, el scarf (8)
papá, el dad (**1**)
papa, la potato (**7**)
papas fritas, las *(pl.)* french fries; potato chips (**7**)
papel, el paper (**2, 11**)
paquete, el package (10)
para for; in order to (**11**)
parabrisas, el windshield (**10**)
parada, la bus stop (**10**)
paraguas, el umbrella (**8**)
pararse to stand (10)
pared, la wall (**2**)
parientes, los *(pl.)* relatives (2, B)
parque, el park (**4**); **~ de atracciones** theme park (**10**)
participar: ~ en una campaña política to participate in a political campaign (4)
partido político, el political party (11)
pasajero/a, el/la passenger (**10**)
pasantía, la internship (8)
pasaporte, el passport (**10**)
pasar to spend *(time)* (6)
pasar la aspiradora to vacuum (**3**)
pasatiempos, los *(pl.)* pastimes (**2**)
pastel, el pastry; pie (**7**)
pastilla, la pill (**9**)
pata, la leg *(of an animal)* (9)
patata, la potato (**7**)
patinar to skate (**2**)
paz, la peace (5)
peatón/peatona, el/la pedestrian (**10**)
pecho, el chest (**9**)
pedagogía, la education (**2**)
pedido, el request (9)
pedir (i) to ask for (**4**); to order (**7**)
peinarse to comb one's hair (**9**)
pelar to peel (7)
película, la movie; film (3, **4**)
peligro, el danger (11)
peligroso/a dangerous (**11**)
pelo, el hair (**9**)
pelota, la ball (**2**)
pensar (ie) to think (**4**)
peor worse (4, **10**); **~, el/la** the worst (**10**)
pequeño/a small (**1, 10**)
pera, la pear (**7**)
perder (ie) to lose; to waste (**4**)
perezoso/a lazy (**1**)
periódico, el newspaper (**11**)
periodismo, el journalism (**2**)
permanecer to stay (11)
pero but (2)
perro dog (3, **11**); **~ caliente** hot dog (**7**)
perseguir (i) to chase (**4**)
personalidad, la personality (**1**)
pertenecer to belong (9); to pertain (10)
pescado, el fish (**7**)
peso corporal, el body weight (9)
pez, el *(pl.,* **los peces***)* fish (**11**)
pianista el/la pianist (**5**)
piano, el piano (**5**)
picante spicy (**7**)
pie, el foot (8, **9**)
piensa thinks (1)
pierna, la leg *(of a person)* (**9**)
pijama, el pajamas (**8**)
película, la film; movie (**4, 5**); **~ de acción** action movie; **~ de ciencia ficción** science fiction movie; **~ dramática** drama; **~ de guerra** war movie; **~ de misterio** mystery movie; **~ musical** musical; **~ romántica** romantic movie; **~ de terror** horror movie (**5**)
pimienta, la pepper (**7**)
piscina, la pool (**2**)
piso, el floor; story (**3**)
pizarra (interactiva), la chalkboard; (interactive) whiteboard (**2**)
placer, el pleasure (7)
planeta, el planet (**11**)
planta baja, la ground floor (**3**)
plantar to plant (**11**)
plástico, el plastic (**11**)
plato, el plate; dish (**7**)
playa, la beach (**10**)
plaza, la town square (**4**)
pobre poor (**1**)
poco: ~ hecho/a rare *(meat)* (**7**); **un ~** (a) little (**1**)
poder to be able to (**3**)
policía, el/la policeman/policewoman (**10**)
poliéster, el polyester (**8**)
política, la politics (**11**)
pollo, el chicken (**7**)
poner to put; to place (**3**); **~ la mesa** to set the table (**3**); **~se (la ropa)** to put on (one's clothes) (**9**); **~se (nervioso/a)** to get (nervous) (**9**)
por times; by (1); **~** for (**2**); through; by; because of (**11**); **~ eso** for that reason (9); **~ favor.** Please. (**A**); **~ lo menos**

at least (3); ~ **ciento** percent (1); **¿~ qué?** Why? (**2**)
postre, el dessert (**7**)
preferir (ie) to prefer (**4**)
preguntar to ask (a question) (**2**)
premio, el award (5, 10)
prendas, las *(pl.)* articles of clothing (**8**)
prender to turn on (11)
preocupado/a worried (**2**)
preocuparse to worry about; to concern oneself with (**11**)
preparar to prepare; to get ready (**2**); ~ **la comida** to prepare a meal (**3**); **~se** to prepare onself (B)
preparativo, el preparation (**5**)
presentación, la introduction (**A**)
presentar: ~ **una película** to show a film/movie (**5**)
presidencia, la presidency (**11**)
presidente/a, el/la president (**11**)
prestar to loan; to lend (**8**)
presupuesto, el budget (3, 8)
primavera, la spring (**A**)
primer, primero/a first (2, **3**) ~ **piso, el** first floor (**3**)
primo/a, el/la cousin (**1**)
principio, el start (8)
probarse (ue): ~ **la ropa** to try on clothing (**9**)
profesor/a, el/la professor (**2**)
programa, el platform (11)
promedio, el average (7)
propina, la tip (**7**)
propio/a own (12)
proponer to propose (5, 10)
propósito, el purpose (7)
proteger to protect (8, **11**)
prueba, la test (9)
psicología, la psychology (**2**)
pueblo, el town; village (**4**)
¿Puedes… ? Can you… ? (**1**)
puente, el bridge (10)
puerta, la door (**2**)
puro/a pure (**11**)

Q

¡Qué bueno! That's great! (**2**)
¿qué? What? (**2**); **¿~ día es hoy?** What day is today?; **¿~ es esto?** What is this?; **¿~ hora es?** What time is it?; **¿~ significa?** What does it mean?; **¿~ tal?** How's it going?; **¿~ tiempo hace?** What's the weather like? (**A**)
quedar to stay (11); ~ **le bien/mal** to fit well/poorly (**8**); **~se** to stay; to remain (**9**)
quehaceres, los *(pl.)* chores (**3**)
quemarse to get burned (**9**)
querer to want; to love (2, **3**)
queso, el cheese (**7**)
¿Quién/es? Who? (A, **2**)
quiero: ~ **presentarle a…** I would like to introduce you to… *(formal)* (**A**); ~ **presentarte a…** I would like to introduce you to… *(familiar)* (**A**)
quince fifteen (**A**)
quinientos five hundred (**2**)
quinto/a fifth (**3**)
quitarse (la ropa) to take off (one's clothes) (**9**)

R

radio: ~, **el/la** radio; broadcast (**2**)
raíces, las *(pl.)* roots (10)
rana, la frog (**11**)
rasgo, el characteristic (**1**)
rata, la rat (**11**)
ratón, el mouse (**11**)
realizar to act out (7)
reapertura, la reopening (11)
recepción, la front desk (**10**)
receta, la recipe (7); prescription (**9**)
recetar to prescribe (9)
recibir to receive (**2**)
reciclaje, el recycling (**11**)
reciclar to recycle (**11**)
recomendar (ie) to recommend (**4**)
reconocer to recognize (8)
recordar (ue) to remember (**4**)
recuerdo, el memento (3); memory (10)
recurso natural, el natural resource (**11**)
reforestar to reforest (**11**)
refresco, el soft drink (**7**)
refrigerador, el refrigerator (**3**)
regalar to give a gift (8)
regalo, el gift (8)
regatear to bargain; to negotiate the price (7)
regímenes, los *(pl.)* regimes (**11**)
registrarse: ~ **(en el hotel)** to check in (**10**)
regla, la rule (10)
regresar to return (**2**)
Regular. Okay. (**A**)
reina, la queen (**11**)
reloj, el clock; watch (**2**)
remedio casero, el homemade remedy (7)
remunerar to pay (**4**)
repartir: ~ **comidas** to hand out/deliver food (**4**)
repetir (i) to repeat (**4**)
Repita(n). Repeat. (**A**)
reportaje, el report (12)
reseña, la review (5)
reserva, la reservation (**10**)
reservar: ~ **una mesa** to reserve a table (**7**)
resfriado, el cold (**9**)
residencia, la dormitory (**2**); ~ **estudiantil** dormitory (**2**)
resolver (ue) to resolve (**11**)
respirar to breathe (9)
responsable responsible (**1**)
restaurante, el restaurant (**4**, **7**)
resumir to summarize (9)
reunión, la meeting (8, 10)
reunirse to get together; to meet (**9**)
reutilizar to reuse (**11**)
revisar to check; to overhaul (**10**)
revista, la magazine (8)
rey, el king (**11**)
Ricitos de Oro Goldilocks (9)
rico/a rich (**1**)
río, el river (**11**)
ritmo, el rhythm (**5**)
rock, el rock (**5**)
rojo red (**3**)
romperse to break *(a bone)* (**9**)
ropa, la clothes; clothing (**3**, **8**); ~ **interior** underwear (**8**)
rosado pink (**3**)
roto broken (9)
ruido, el noise (B, **10**)

S

sábado, el Saturday (**A**)
sábana, la sheet (**3**)
saber to know (**4**); ~ **bien/mal** to taste good/bad (**7**)
sabroso/a tasty (**7**)
sacar: ~ **buenas notas** to get good grades (**4**); ~ **la basura** to take out the garbage (**3**); ~ **la licencia** to get a driver's license (10); ~ **una canción** to release a song (**5**)
sacudir: ~ **los muebles** to dust (**3**)
sal, la salt (**7**)
sala, la living room (**3**); ~ **de clase** classroom (**2**); ~ **de urgencias** emergency room (**9**)
salir to leave; to go out (**3**)
salsa, la salsa (**5**); ~ **de tomate** ketchup (**7**)
salud, la health (**9**)
saludo, el greeting (**A**)
salvo/a safe (11)
sandalias, las *(pl.)* sandals (**8**)
sangre, la blood (**9**)

sangriento/a bloody (11)
sano/a healthy (9)
secarse to dry off (**9**)
seda, la silk (**8**)
sede, la seat (of government) (9)
seguir (i) to follow; to continue (doing something) (**4**)
según according to (1, **11**)
segundo/a second (3); ~ **piso, el** second floor (**3**)
seguro/a sure (5)
seis six (**A**); ~**cientos** six hundred (**2**)
sello, el postage stamp (**10**)
selva, la jungle (**11**); ~ **(tropical)** (tropical) rain forest (**11**)
semáforo, el traffic light (**10**)
semana, la week (**A**); ~ **pasada** last week (5, 7)
sembrar (ie) to sow (**11**)
semejanza, la similarity (**4**, 6)
semestre, el semester (**2**)
senador/a, el/la senator (**11**)
señor, el (Sr.) man; gentleman; Mr. (**1**)
señora, la (Sra.) woman; lady; Mrs. (**1**)
señorita, la (Srta.) young woman; Miss (**1**)
sentarse (ie) to sit down (**9**)
sentido, el meaning (3)
sentir (ie, i) to feel (3, B); ~**se** to feel (**9**); ~**se perdido/a** to feel lost (4)
septiembre September (A)
séptimo/a seventh (**3**)
ser to be (**A**); ~ **alérgico/a (a)** to be allergic (to) (**9**)
serpiente, la snake (**11**)
servilleta, la napkin (**7**)
servir (i) to serve (**4**)
sesenta sixty (**1**)
setecientos seven hundred (**2**)
setenta seventy (**1**)
sexto/a sixth (**3**)
si if (4)
Sí. Yes. (**A**)
siempre always (2, 3, **4**, **8**)
siete seven (**A**)
siglo, el century (3)
siguiente, el following (2, 3)
silla, la chair (**2**)
sillón, el armchair (**3**)
simpático/a nice (**1**)
sin without (4, B, 10, **11**); ~ **embargo** nevertheless (2, 3, 6)
sobrar to be left over (5)
sobre on; on top (of); over; about (3, **11**); ~ **todo** above all (5)
sobrepasar to exceed (11)
sofá, el sofa (**3**)
sol, el sun (**A**)
solamente only (8, 12)
soldados, los *(pl.)* soldiers (11)
solicitud, la application (2, 7)
solicitar to apply (4)
sombrero, el hat (**8**)
son equals (1)
sopa, la soup (**7**)
sorprendente surprising (**5**)
sorpresa, la surprise (8)
sótano, el basement (**3**)
Soy… I am… (**A**)
su/s his, her, its, your, their (**1**)
suave smooth (**5**)
subir (a) to go up; to get on (**10**)
subrayar to underline (7)
sucio/a dirty (**3**)
sucursal, la branch (8)
sudadera, la sweatshirt (**8**)
sudar to sweat (9)
suelo, el floor (**3**)
suéter, el sweater (**8**)
supermercado, el supermarket (**4**)
surgir to emerge (8)

T

tableta, la tablet (**2**)
tarjeta, la: ~ **de crédito** credit card (**7**); ~ **de débito** debit card (**7**); ~ **postal** postcard (4, **10**)
taller, el ~ **de costurera** seamstress shop (8); ~ **mecánico** auto repair shop (**10**)
tamaño size (3)
también too; also (2)
tambor, el drum (**5**)
tan: ~ + *adjective/adverb* + **como** as… as (**10**)
tanto: so much (9); **tanto (a/os/as)** + *noun* + **como** as much/many… as (**10**)
tarde late (2, 3)
tarea, la homework (**2**)
taxi, el taxi (**10**)
taza, la cup (**7**)
te to/for you (**5**, **8**)
té, el (helado/caliente) tea (iced/hot) (**7**)
teatro, el theater (**4**)
techo, el roof (**3**)
tela, la fabric (**8**)
teléfono celular, el cell phone (**2**)
televisión, la television (**2**)
tema, el topic; gist (5)
temblar to shake (11)
temperatura, la temperature (**A**)
templo, el temple (**4**)
temprano early (3)
tenedor, el fork (7)
tener to have (**1**); ~ **alergia (a)** to be allergic (to) (**9**); ~ **… años** to be… years old (**3**); ~ **calor** to be hot (**3**); ~ **celos** to be jealous (11); ~ **cuidado** to be careful (**3**); ~ **dolor de cabeza** to have a headache (**9**); ~ **dolor de estómago** to have a stomachache (**9**); ~ **dolor de espalda** to have a backache (**9**); ~ **éxito** to be successful (**3**); ~ **frío** to be cold (**3**); ~ **ganas de** + *(infinitive)* to feel like + (verb) (**3**); ~ **dolor de garganta** to have a sore throat (**9**); ~ **hambre** to be hungry (**3**); ~ **(la/una) gripe** to have the flu (**9**); ~ **miedo** to be afraid (**3**); ~ **prisa** to be in a hurry (3); ~ **que** + *(infinitive)* to have to + *(verb)* (**3**); ~ **razón** to be right (**3**); ~ **resfriado** to have a cold (**9**); ~ **sed** to be thirsty (**3**); ~ **sueño** to be sleepy (**3**); ~ **suerte** to be lucky (**3**); ~ **tos** to have a cough (**9**); ~ **(un) catarro** to have a cold (**9**); ~ **un virus** to have a virus (**9**); ~ **una infección** to have an infection (**9**); ~ **vergüenza** to be embarrassed (**3**)
tenis, los *(pl.)* tennis shoes (**8**)
tercer, tercero/a third (**3**); ~ **piso, el** third floor (**3**)
terminar to finish; to end (**2**, 3)
término medio medium *(meat)* (**7**)
terremoto, el earthquake (5, **11**)
tesoro, el treasure (11)
ti you (11)
tiburón, el shark (5)
tiempo completo, el full-time (10)
tienda, la store (**2**)
tierra, la earth, dirt (10); land; soil (**11**)
Tierra, la Earth (**11**)
tío/a, el/la uncle/aunt (**1**)
tíos, los *(pl.)* aunts and uncles (**1**)
tiza, la chalk (**2**)
tocar: ~ **un instrumento** to play an instrument (**2**)
todavía still (11)
todos los días every day (**8**)
tomar to take; to drink (**2**); ~ **el sol** to sunbathe (**2**)
tomate, el tomato (**7**)
tonto/a silly; dumb (**1**)
tormenta, la storm (**11**)
tornado, el tornado (**11**)
torneo, el tournament (**4**)
toro, el bull (**11**)

torre, la tower (3)
torta, la cake (**7**)
tos, la cough (**9**)
toser to cough (**9**)
tostada, la toast (**7**)
tostones, los *(pl.)* plantain chips (11)
trabajador/a hard-working (**1**)
trabajar to work (**2**); **~ como consejero/a** to work as a counselor (**4**); **~ como voluntario/a en la residencia de ancianos** to volunteer at a nursing home (**4**); **~ en el campamento de niños** to work in a summer camp (**4**); **~ en política** to work in politics (**4**)
trabajo, el job (4)
tradicional traditional (3)
traer to bring (**3**)
tráfico, el traffic (**10**)
tragedia, la tragedy (**11**)
trágico/a tragic (**5**)
traje, el outfit (5); suit (**8**); **~ de baño** swimsuit; bathing suit (**8**)
transitar to enter/exit (10)
transporte, el transportation (**10**)
tratamiento médico, el medical treatment (**9**)
tratar de to try to (3, **9**)
trece thirteen (**A**)
treinta thirty (**A, 1**); **~ y uno** thirty-one; **~ y dos** thirty-two; **~ y tres** thirty-three; **~ y cuatro** thirty-four; **~ y cinco** thirty-five; **~ y seis** thirty-six; **~ y siete** thirty-seven; **~ y ocho** thirty-eight; **~ y nueve** thirty-nine (**1**)
tren, el train (**10**)
tres three (A); **~cientos** three hundred (**2**)
triste sad (**2**)
trompeta, la trumpet (**5**)
trono, el throne (11)
tsunami, el tsunami (**11**)
tú you *(familiar)* (**A, 1**)
tu/s your (**1**)
turnarse to take turns (3)

U

un/a/os/as a, an, some (**1**)
ungüento, el salve (10)
uno one (**A**)
usar to use (**2**, 4)
usted/es you *(formal)* (**A, 11**)
útil useful (**A**)

V

vaca, la cow (**11**)
vacaciones, las *(pl.)* vacation (**10**)
vaso, el glass (**7**)
Vaya(n) a la pizarra. Go to the board. (**A**)
¡Vaya! Wow! (4)
vecino/a neighboring (8)
vehículo, el vehicle (**10**)
veinte twenty; **veintiuno** twenty-one; **veintidós** twenty-two; **veintitrés** twenty-three; **veinticuatro** twenty-four; **veinticinco** twenty-five; **veintiséis** twenty-six; **veintisiete** twenty-seven; **veintiocho** twenty-eight; **veintinueve** twenty-nine (**A**)
velas, las *(pl.)* candles (**7**)
velocidad, la speed (10)
venda, la bandage (**9**)
vendaje, el bandage (**9**)
vendarse to bandage oneself (**9**)
vendedor/a, el/la seller (7)
vender to sell (7)
venir to come (**3**)
ventana, la window (**2**)
ver to see (**2**); **~ la televisión** to watch television (**3**)
verano, el summer (**A**)
verdad, la truth (3)
verde green (**3**)
verdura, la vegetable (**7**)
vertedero, el dump (**11**)
vestido, el dress (**8**)
vestirse (i, i) to get dressed (**9**)
vez: una ~ once (**4**)
viajar to travel (**10**); **~ en canoa** to canoe (**4**)
viaje, el trip (**10**)
viajero/a, el/la traveler (**10**)
vidrio, el glass (**11**)
viejo/a old (3)
viento, el wind (**A**)
viernes, el Friday (**A**)
vigas recias, las *(pl.)* thick beams (10)
vinagre, el vinegar (**7**)
vino, el wine (**7**)
visitar to visit (**10**)
vivir to live (**2**)
vivo/a alive; living (**11**)
volante, el steering wheel (**10**)
volar (ue) to fly; to fly away (**10**)
voluntariado, el volunteerism (**4**)
volver (ue) to return (**4**); **~le loco/a** to drive him/her crazy (12)
vosotros/as you *(fam. pl. Spain)* (**A**)
votar to vote (**11**)
voto, el vote (**11**)
voz, la voice (**5**)
vuelo, el flight (**10**); **~ de ida y vuelta** round-trip flight (**10**)
vuestro/a/os/as your/s *(fam. pl. Spain)* (1)

Y

y and (2); **~ cinco** five minutes after the hour (**A**); **¿~ tú?** And you? *(familiar)* (**A**); **¿~ usted?** And you? *(formal)* (**A**)
yo I (**A**)
yogur, el yogurt (**7**)

Z

zapatillas, las *(pl.)* slippers (**8**)
zapatos, los *(pl.)* shoes (**8**)

APPENDIX 5

English-Spanish Glossary

Fíjate

This glossary includes all words and expressions presented in the text, except for words spelled the same in English and Spanish. The number in bold following each entry corresponds to the **capítulo** in which the word is first introduced for active mastery. Numbers that are not bold indicate that the word is presented for receptive use.

A

a un/a/os/as (**1**)
a lot mucho (**8**)
ability la habilidad (**5**)
able to, to be poder (**3**)
about acerca de (**11**)
above encima (de) (3, 7, **11**)
abroad el extranjero (**10**)
according to según (1, **11**)
account la cuenta (**4**)
acquainted with, to be conocer (**3**)
act out, to realizar (7)
actor el actor (**5**)
actress la actriz (**5**)
ad el anuncio (3)
adjectives los adjetivos (**1**)
administrations las administraciones (**11**)
advice el consejo (7)
afraid, to be tener miedo (**3**)
after después (**11**)
afterward después (**6**)
agent el/la empresario/a (**5**)
agree, to estar de acuerdo (4)
airline la aerolínea (10)
airplane el avión (**10**)
airport el aeropuerto (**10**)
alarm clock el despertador (**2**)
alive vivo/a (**11**)
allergic (to), to be ser alérgico/a (a); tener alergia (a) (**9**)
almond la almendra (7)
almost always casi siempre (**8**)
also también (**2**)
altitude sickness el mal de altura (9)
aluminum el aluminio (**11**)
always siempre (2, 3, **4**, **8**)
an un/a/os/as (**1**)
and y (2)
angry enojado/a (**2**)
animated animado/a (**5**)
annatto la bija (7)
another otro/a (**A**)
answer, to contestar (**2**); **Answer.** Conteste(n). (**A**)
ant la hormiga (**11**)
antacid el antiácido (**9**)
antibiotic el antibiótico (**9**)
any algún (**4**); alguno/a/os/as (3, **4**); cualquier (10)
apartment el apartamento (**2**)
appendix el apéndice (4)
apple la manzana (**7**)
application la solicitud (2, 7)
apply, to solicitar (**4**)
appointment la cita (4, B)
approved aprobado/a (10)
April abril (**A**)
architecture la arquitectura (**2**)
arm el brazo (**9**)
armchair el sillón (**3**)
armies los ejércitos (11)
armoire el armario (**3**)
army el ejército (5)
arrive, to llegar (**2**)
art el arte (**2**)
articles of clothing las prendas (**8**)
artist el/la artista (**5**)
ask (a question), to preguntar (**2**)
ask for, to pedir (i) (**4**)
aspirin la aspirina (**9**)
assistant el/la ayudante (5)
ATM el cajero automático (**4**)
attendant el/la empleado/a (12)
attic el altillo (**3**)
August agosto (**A**)
aunt la tía; **aunts and uncles** los tíos (*pl.*) (**1**)
average el promedio (7)
avoid, to evitar (**9**)
awaken, to despertarse (e, ie) (**9**)
award el premio (5, 10)

B

back la espalda (**9**)
backpack la mochila (**2**)
bad malo/a (**1**, **10**)
bag el bolso (7, **8**)
baked cocido/a (**7**)
balcony el balcón (**3**)
ball la pelota (**2**)
ballpoint pen el bolígrafo (**2**)
banana la banana (**7**)
band el conjunto (**5**)
bandage la venda; el vendaje; (**9**); **bandage (adhesive)** la curita (**9**); **to bandage (oneself)** vendar(se) (**9**)
bank el banco (**4**)
bar el bar (**4**)
bargain, to regatear (7)
basement el sótano (**3**)
basket weaving la cestería (2)
bathe, to bañarse (**9**)
bathroom el baño (**3**)
bathtub la bañera (**3**)
bays las bahías (11)
be, to estar (**2**); ser (**A**)
beach la playa (**10**)
bean stew la fabada (7)
beans los frijoles (*pl.*) (**7**); las habichuelas (11)
bear el oso (**11**)
beat *(heart)*, to latir (9)
beautiful bello/a (4)
bed la cama (**3**)
bedroom el dormitorio (**3**)
bedspread la colcha (**3**)
beer la cerveza (**7**)
before *(time/space)* antes (de) (6, **11**)
begin, to comenzar (ie); empezar (ie) (**4**)
behind detrás (de) (4, **11**)
beige beige (**3**)
believe, to creer (**2**)
bellhop el botones (**10**)
belong, to pertenecer (9)
belt el cinturón (**8**)
beside al lado (de) (3)
best mejor, **the best** el/la mejor (4)
beverage la bebida (5, **B**, **7**)
bicycle la bicicleta (**10**)
bidet el bidé (**3**)
big grande (**1**, **10**)
bill la cuenta (**4**)
biology la biología (**2**)
bird el ave; el pájaro (**11**)
black negro (**3**); **black clay** el barro negro (2)
blanket la manta (**3**)
blood la sangre (**9**)
bloody sangriento/a (11)
blouse la blusa (**8**)
blue azul (**3**)

boat el barco (**B**); el bote (**4**)
body weight el peso corporal (9)
boiled cocido/a; hervido/a (**7**)
bone el hueso (10)
book el libro (**2**)
book bag la mochila (**2**)
bookcase el estante (**3**)
bookstore la librería (**2**)
boots las botas *(pl.)* (**8**)
bored (*with* estar) aburrido/a (**2**)
boring aburrido/a (**1**, **2**, **5**)
bother, to molestar (**8**)
bottle la botella (**11**)
boy el chico; el muchacho (**1**)
boyfriend el novio (**1**)
branch la sucursal (8)
bread el pan (**7**)
break *(a bone)*, to romper(se) (**9**)
breakfast el desayuno (**7**)
breathe, to respirar (9)
bridge el puente (10)
bring, to traer (**3**)
broken roto (9)
brother el hermano (**1**); **brothers; brothers and sisters** los hermanos (**1**)
brown marrón (**3**)
brush (one's hair, teeth), to cepillarse (el pelo, los dientes) (**9**)
budget el presupuesto (3, 8)
building el edificio (**2**)
bull el toro (**11**)
bus el autobús (**10**)
bus stop la parada (**10**)
bush el arbusto (7)
business administration la administración de empresas (**2**); el negocio (8)
busy ocupado/a (6)
but pero (2)
butler el mayordomo (10)
butter la mantequilla (**7**)
buy, to comprar (**2**)
Bye. Chao. (**A**)

C

cabinet el armario (**3**)
café el café (**4**, **7**)
cafeteria la cafetería (**2**)
cake la torta (**7**)
calculator la calculadora (**2**)
called, to be llamarse (**9**)
can la lata (**11**); **Can you … ?** ¿Puedes… ? (**1**)
candidate el/la candidato/a (**11**)
candles las velas (**7**)
candy el dulce (**7**)
canoe, to viajar en canoa (**4**)
cap la gorra (**8**)
car el carro; el coche (**10**)
careful, to be tener cuidado (**3**)
carefully cuidadosamente (**2**)
carpet la alfombra (**3**)
carry, to llevar (**8**); **to carry out** llevar a cabo (**11**)
casserole la cazuela (7)
castle el castillo (3)
casual informal (**8**)
cat el gato (10, **11**)
cave la cueva (**11**)
cell phone el teléfono celular (**2**)
century el siglo (3)
cereal el cereal (**7**)
chair la silla (**2**)
chalk la tiza (**2**)
chalkboard la pizarra (**2**)
change, to cambiar (**10**); **to change roles** cambiar de papel (3)
characteristic el rasgo (**1**)
charity la caridad (3)
chase, to perseguir (i) (**4**)
check in, to registrarse (en el hotel) (**10**)
check out, to irse del hotel (**10**)
check, to revisar (**10**)
cheese el queso (**7**)
chef el/la cocinero/a (**4**, **7**)
chest el pecho (**9**)
chew, to masticar (9)
chicken el pollo (**7**); la gallina (7, **11**)
children los hijos (**1**)
chili pepper el chile (**7**)
choose, to escoger (**4**)
chores los quehaceres *(pl.)* (**3**)
church la iglesia (**4**)
circulate a petition, to circular una petición (**4**)
city la ciudad (1, 3, **4**)
clean limpio/a (**3**)
clean, to limpiar (**3**)
clear claro/a (5)
clergy el clero (9)
client el/la cliente/a (**7**)
climate change el cambio climático (**11**)
clock el reloj (**2**)
Close your book/s. Cierre(n) el/los libros/s. (**A**)
close, to cerrar (ie) (**4**)
closet el armario (**3**)
clothes la ropa (**3**, **8**)
clothing la ropa (**3**, **8**)
cloud la nube (**A**)
club el club (**4**)
coat el abrigo (3, **8**)
coca leaves las hojas de coca (9)
coffee el café (**4**, **7**)
cognate el cognado (**A**)
cold el catarro; el resfriado (**9**)
cold, to be tener frío (**3**)
color el color (**3**)
comb one's hair, to peinarse (**9**)
combat, to combatir (**11**); luchar (**11**)
come, to venir (**3**)
comedy la comedia (5)
comfortable cómodo/a (8)
comforter la colcha ([illegible]
comical cómico/a (**1**)
competition la competencia; el concurso (7)
complete, to expedir (10)
complexion el cutis (11)
composition la composición (**2**)
computer la computadora (**2**)
computer science la informática (**2**)
concern oneself with, to preocuparse (por) (**11**)
concert el concierto (**5**)
conch las caracolas (7)
condiment el condimento (**7**)
congress el congreso (**11**)
contemporary contemporáneo/a (3)
content contento/a (**2**)
continue (doing something), to seguir (i) (**4**)
contribution la donación (11)
cook, to cocinar (**3**, **7**)
cookie la galleta (**7**)
corn el maíz (**7**)
correct, to corregir (3, 10)
cost, to costar (ue) (3, **4**)
cotton el algodón (**8**)
cough la tos (**9**); **cough syrup** el jarabe (**9**)
cough, to toser (**9**)
country el campo (3)
countryside el campo (4); el paisaje (3)
course el curso (**2**)
court la corte (**11**)
courting el cortejo (7)
cousin el/la primo/a (**1**)
cover, to cubrir (8)
cow la vaca (**11**)
cracker la galleta (**7**)
create, to crear (4, B)
creative creativo/a (**5**)

crime la delincuencia (**11**)
crop la cosecha (7)
cruise ship el crucero (5)
cry, to llorar (11)
cup la taza (**7**)
cured, to be curar(se) (**9**)
customer el/la cliente/a (**7**)
cut (oneself), to cortar(se) (**9**)

D

dad el papá (**1**)
dance, to bailar (**2**)
danger el peligro (11)
dangerous peligroso/a (**11**)
daring atrevido/a (**8**)
dark oscuro/a (**8**)
dark-haired moreno/a (5)
date la cita (8)
daughter la hija (**1**); **daughters** las hijas (**1**)
day el día (**A**)
dead muerto/a (**11**)
dear estimado/a (**4**)
December diciembre (**A**)
defeated derrotado/a (11)
defense la defensa (**11**)
delicate fino/a (**5**)
delicious delicioso/a (7)
deliver food, to repartir comidas (**4**)
demanding exigente (9)
democracy la democracia (**11**)
demonstrate, to demostrar (ue) (**4**)
department store el almacén (**4**)
depressing deprimente (**5**)
deputy el/la diputado/a (**11**)
designer el/la diseñador/a (8)
desk el escritorio (**2**)
dessert el postre (**7**)
destination el destino (8)
destroy, to destruir (5)
destruction la destrucción (**11**)
devote, to dedicar (3)
dictator el/la dictador/a (**11**)
dictatorship la dictadura (**11**)
die, to morir (ue) (**4,** 11)
difficult difícil (2)
dining room el comedor (**3**)
dinner la cena (**7**)
dirt la tierra (10)
dirty sucio/a (**3**)
disaster el desastre (**11**)
discuss, to discutir (**B**)
dish el plato (**7**)
dishwasher el lavaplatos (**3**)
distinguish, to destacar (7)
divided by dividido por (1)
do the shopping, to hacer las compras (7)
damage, to (do) hacer daño (**11**)
do, to hacer (**3**, 4, **9**)
doctor el/la doctor/a; el/la médico/a (**9**)
documentary el documental (**5**)
dog perro (3, **11**)
doll la muñeca (8)
dollar(s) dólar(es) (**2**)
domesticated animal el animal doméstico; la mascota (10, **11**)
donuts las donas (10)
door la puerta (**2**)
dormitory la residencia (**2**)
download, to bajar (de) (5)
draw, to dibujar (**4**)
drawing el dibujo (3)
dress el vestido (**8**)
dresser la cómoda (**3**)
drink, to beber (**7**); tomar (**2**)
drive him/her crazy, to volver (ue) loco/a (12)
drive, to conducir (7, 8, **10**); manejar (5, 8, **10**)
driver's license la licencia (de conducir) (**10**)
driving la conducción (10)
drum el tambor (**5**); **drums** la batería (**5**)
dry off, to secarse (**9**)
dumb tonto/a (**1**)
dump el vertedero (**11**)
during durante (**B**)
dust, to sacudir los muebles (**3**)
duty el deber (**4**)
DVD/s el DVD (*pl.* los DVD) (**2**)

E

each cada (3, **4**, B)
ear la oreja; ***(inner)*** **ear** el oído (**9**)
earlier than más temprano que (7)
early temprano (3)
Earth la Tierra (**11**)
earth la tierra (10)
earthquake el terremoto (5, **11**)
easy fácil (2)
eat, to comer (**2**)
ecology la ecología (**11**)
education la pedagogía (**2**)
egg el huevo (**7**)
eight ocho (**A**); **eight hundred** ochocientos (**2**)
eighth octavo/a (**3**)
eighty ochenta (**1**)
either … or o… o (**4**)
elect, to elegir (**11**)
elections las elecciones (**11**)
elegant elegante (**8**)
elephant el elefante (**11**)
eleven once (**A**)
embarrassed, to be tener vergüenza (**3**)
emerge, to surgir (8)
emotions las emociones (**2**)
employee el/la empleado/a (5)
enclose, to encerrar (ie) (**4**)
encompass, to abarcar (5)
end, to terminar (**2,** 3)
endangered amenazado/a (7); **endangered animals** los animales en peligro de extinción (**11**)
engine el motor (**10**)
enjoy (oneself), to disfrutar de (**4, B**); divertirse (e, ie, i) (5, **9**)
Enjoy your meal! ¡Buen provecho! (**7**)
enter, to entrar (**10**); **enter/exit, to** transitar (10)
entertain oneself, to entretenerse (8)
entertaining entretenido/a (**5**)
environment el ambiente (5); el medio ambiente (**11**)
epic épico/a (**5**)
equals son (1)
eraser el borrador (**2**)
espadrilles las alpargatas (8)
euro el euro(s) (**2**)
even more aún más (1)
even though aunque (5)
event el acontecimiento (9)
every day todos los días (**8**)
evolve, to evolucionar (5)
exceed, to sobrepasar (11)
exchange student el/la estudiante de intercambio (10)
exchange, to intercambiar (6)
exercise, to hacer ejercicio (**2**)
exit, to transitar (10)
expensive caro/a (**7**)
experience, to experimentar (11)
eye el ojo (**9**)

F

fabric la tela (**8**)
face la cara (**9**)
factory la fábrica (8)
faint mareado/a (9)
fall el otoño (**A**)
fall down, to caer(se) (**9**)
fall in love, to enamorarse de (7)
false falso (**1**)

fame la fama (**5**)
family la familia (**1**)
fan el/la aficionado/a (**5**)
far (from) lejos (de) (7, **11**)
farewell la despedida (**A**)
farm la finca; la granja (**11**)
fascinate, to fascinar (**8**)
fashion la moda (**8**); **fashion show** el desfile de moda (8)
fat gordo/a (**1**); la grasa (7)
father el padre (**1**)
February febrero (**A**)
feel like + *(verb)*, to tener ganas de + *(infinitive)* (**3**)
feel lost, to sentirse perdido/a (**4**)
feel, to sentir (e, ie, i) (3, **B**); **to feel (oneself)** sentirse (**9**)
fever la fiebre (**9**)
fifteen quince (**A**)
fifth quinto (**3**)
fifty cincuenta (**1**); **fifty-one** cincuenta y uno (**1**)
fight, to combatir; luchar (**11**)
fill up the tank, to llenar el tanque (**10**)
film la película (3, **4**)
finally finalmente (**6**)
find out, to averiguar (4, **B**)
find, to encontrar (ue) (**4**)
fine la multa (**10**)
fine fino/a (**5**)
finish, to terminar (**2**, 3)
fire el incendio (**11**)
first primer, primero/a (**3**); **first floor** el primer piso (**3**)
fish el pescado (**7**); el pez (*pl.* los peces) (**11**)
fit well/poorly, to quedarle bien / mal (**8**)
five cinco (**A**); **five hundred** quinientos (**2**)
fix, to arreglar (**3**)
flight el vuelo (**10**); **round-trip flight** vuelo de ida y vuelta
flood la inundación (**11**)
floor el piso; el suelo (**3**)
flourishing floreciente (8)
flowers las flores (**7**)
flu la gripe (**9**)
flute la flauta (5)
fly la mosca (**11**)
fly, to volar (ue) (**10**)
folk healer el/la curandero/a (4)
follow, to seguir (i) (**4**)
following el siguiente (**2**, 3)
food la comida (**4, 5**, B, 7); **fast food** la comida rápida (B)
foot el pie (8, **9**)
for por (**11**); para (**11**)
for them les (**8**)
for us nos (**8**)
for you te (**5, 8**); **for you all** os (**5, 8**)
forest el bosque (9, **11**)
fork el tenedor (7)
formal formal (**8**)
forty cuarenta (**1**); **forty-one** cuarenta y uno (**1**)
four cuatro (**A**); **four hundred** cuatrocientos (**2**)
fourteen catorce (**A**)
fourth cuarto/a (**3**)
freeway la autopista (**10**)
freezer el/la congelador/a (7)
french fries las papas fritas (*pl.*) (**7**)
frequently frecuentemente (**8**)
fresh fresco/a (**7**)
freshman el/la estudiante de primer año (8)
Friday el viernes (**A**)
fried frito/a (**7**)
friend el/la amigo/a (**1**)
frog la rana (**11**)
from desde (**11**)
front desk la recepción (**10**)
fruit la fruta (**7**)
fulfilled cumplido/a (11)
full-time el tiempo completo (10)
fumes el humo (12)
function, to funcionar (**10**)
funding los fondos (11)
funds los fondos (10)
funny cómico/a (**1**)
furnished amueblado/a (3)
furniture los muebles (*pl.*) (**3**); **piece of furniture** el mueble (**3**)

G

garage el garaje (**3**)
garbage la basura (**11**)
garden el jardín (**3**)
garlic el ajo (**7**)
gas station la gasolinera (**10**)
generally generalmente (**8**)
genre el género (**5**)
gentleman el señor (Sr.) (**1**)
get, to obtener (10); **to get a driver's license** sacar la licencia (10); **to get better** mejorarse (**9**); **to get burned** quemar(se) (**9**); **to get down (from)** bajar (de) (**10**); **to get dressed** vestirse (e, i, i) (**9**); **to get good grades** sacar buenas notas (**4**); **to get hurt** lastimar(se) (**9**); **to get involved in politics** meterse en política (**11**); **to get married** casarse (11); **to get (nervous)** ponerse (nervioso/a) (**9**); **to get off (of)** bajar (de) (**10**); **to get on** subir (a) (**10**); **to get oneself ready** arreglarse (**9**); **to get quiet** callarse (**9**); **to get ready** preparar (**2**); **to get sick** enfermar(se) (**9**); **to get together** reunirse (**9**); **to get up** levantarse (**9**)
gift el regalo (8)
girl la chica; la muchacha (**1**)
girlfriend la novia (**1**)
gist el tema (5)
give, to dar (**3**); **to give a concert** dar un concierto (**5**); **to give a gift** regalar (5); **to give life** dar vida (8)
glass el vaso (**7**); el vidrio (**11**)
gloves los guantes (**8**)
Go to the board. Vaya(n) a la pizarra. (**A**)
go, to ir (**4, 9**); **to go away** irse (**9**); **to go camping** ir de camping (**4**); **to go for a walk** dar un paseo (**4**); **to go horse-back riding** montar a caballo (11); **to go on a trip** ir de viaje (**10**); **to go on foot** ir a pie (**10**); **to go on vacation** ir de vacaciones (**10**); **to go out** salir (**3**); **to go shopping** ir de compras (**2**); **to go to bed** acostarse (ue) (**9**); **to go up** subir (a) (**10**)
gold el oro (9)
Goldilocks Ricitos de Oro (9)
good bueno/a (**1, 10**)
Good morning. Buenos días. (**A**)
Good-bye. Adiós. (**A**)
gossip el chisme (7)
government el gobierno (**11**)
governor el/la gobernador/a (**11**)
gram el gramo (7)
granddaughter la nieta (**1**)
grandfather el abuelo (**1**)
grandmother la abuela (**1**)
grandparents los abuelos (**1**)
grandson el nieto (**1**)
gray gris (**3**)
green verde (**3**)
greenhouse effect el efecto invernadero (**11**)
greeting el saludo (**A**)
grilled asado/a (**7**)
ground floor la planta baja (**3**)
group el conjunto (**5**)
guess, to adivinar (5, 7)
guide la guía (5)
guitar la guitarra (**5**)

guitarist el/la guitarrista (**5**)
gum el chicle (**2**)
gymnasium el gimnasio (**2**)

H

hair el pelo (**9**)
ham el jamón (**7**)
hamburger la hamburguesa (**7**)
hammock la hamaca (11)
hand la mano (**1, 9**)
hand out food, to repartir comidas (**4**)
handsome guapo/a (**1**)
hang up, to colgar (7)
happy contento/a; feliz (**2**)
hard-boiled duro/a (**7**)
hard-working trabajador/a (**1**)
harm, to hacer daño (**11**)
hat el sombrero (**8**)
hate, to odiar (11)
have, to tener (**1**); **to have a backache** tener dolor de espalda (**9**); **to have a cold** tener resfriado; tener (un) catarro (**9**); **to have a cough** tener tos (**9**); **to have a headache** tener dolor de cabeza (**9**); **to have a snack** merendar (**7**); **to have a sore throat** tener dolor de garganta (**9**); **to have a stomachache** tener dolor de estómago (**9**); **to have a virus** tener un virus (**9**); **to have an infection** tener una infección (**9**); **to have breakfast** desayunar (**7**); **to have dinner** cenar (**7**); **to have fun** divertirse (e, ie, i) (6, **9**); **to have just finished** + *(something)* acabar de + *infinitivo* (**9**); **to have lunch** almorzar (ue) (**4**, 7); **to have the flu** tener (la/una) gripe (**9**); **to have to** + *(verb)* tener que + *(infinitive)* (**3**)
he él (**A, 11**)
head la cabeza (**9**)
health la salud (**9**)
healthy sano/a (9)
healthy, to be estar sano/a / saludable (**9**)
hear, to oír (**3**)
heart el corazón (**9**)
heat la calefacción (**10**)
heaven el cielo (**11**)
help, to ayudar (**3**); **to help elderly people** ayudar a las personas mayores/los mayores (4)
hen la gallina (7, **11**)
her su/s (**1**); la (**5, 11**)
herbalist el herbolario (10)
here aquí (**6**)
hers su/s (**1**)
Hi! ¡Hola! (**A**)
high plateau el altiplano (9)
highway la autopista (**10**)
hills las lomas (11)
him él (**A, 11**); lo (**5**)
him/her, to le (**8**)
his su/s (**1**)
hole el hoyo (**11**)
homemade remedy el remedio casero (7)
homework la tarea (**2**)
honeymoon la luna de miel (10)
hope la esperanza (11)
hope, to esperar (**2**)
hopefully… ojalá que (**11**)
horse el caballo (**11**)
hose las medias *(pl.)* (**8**)
hospital el hospital (**9**)
hot *(temperature)* caliente (**7**)
hot dog el perro caliente (**7**)
hot, to be tener calor (**3**)
hotel el hotel (**10**)
house la casa (**3**)
housekeeper el/la camarero/a (10)
hubbub el bullicio (4)
hug el abrazo (**A**)
human body el cuerpo humano (**9**)
humble humilde (3)
hummingbird el colibrí (11)
hungry, to be tener hambre (**3**)
hurricane el huracán (**11**)
hurt, to doler (ue) (**9**)
husband el esposo (**1**)

I

I yo (**A**); **I am …** Soy… (**A**); **I know.** Lo sé. (**A**); **I understand.** Comprendo. (**A**)
ice cream el helado (**7**)
if si (**4**)
ill enfermo/a (**2**)
illness la enfermedad (**9**)
imaginative imaginativo/a (**5**)
important, to be importar (**8**)
impressive impresionante (**5**)
improve, to mejorarse (**9**)
in a hurry, to be tener prisa (3)
in front of, enfrente (de) (4); delante de (**11**)
in order to para (**11**)
include, to incluir (6)
inexpensive barato/a (3, **4**, **7**)
inflation la inflación (**11**)
influential influyente (11)
injury la herida (**9**)
insect el insecto (**11**)
inside of dentro de (**11**)
intelligent inteligente (**1**)
interesting interesante (**1**)
Internet café el cibercafé (**4**)
internship la pasantía (8)
interview la entrevista (3); **job interview** la entrevista de trabajo (8)
interview, to entrevistar (5)
intoxication la embriaguez (10)
introduction la presentación (**A**)
invest, to invertir (11)
isolated aislado/a (11)
it lo, la (**5**)
it's: It's cloudy. Está nublado. (**A**); **It's raining.** Llueve. (**A**); **It's snowing.** Nieva. (**A**)
its su/s (**1**)

J

jacket la chaqueta (**8**)
jam la mermelada (**7**)
January enero (**A**)
jazz el jazz (**5**)
jealous, to be tener celos (11)
jeans los jeans *(pl.)* (**8**)
jewel la joya (9)
job el trabajo (**4**)
journalism el periodismo (**2**)
judge el/la juez/a (7, **11**)
juice el jugo (**7**)
July julio (**A**)
June junio (**A**)
jungle la selva (**11**)
jury el juicio (**11**)
Just fine. Bastante bien. (**A**)

K

keep quiet, to callarse (**9**)
keep, to guardar (**3**)
ketchup la salsa de tomate (**7**)
key la llave (**10**)
kill, to matar (**11**)
kind bondadoso/a (11)
king el rey (**11**)
kitchen la cocina (**3**)
kneel, to arrodillarse (11)
knife el cuchillo (**7**)
know, to saber (**4**)

L

laboratory el laboratorio (**2**)
lacking, to be necesitar (**2**); hacer falta (**8**)

lady la señora (Sra.) (**1**)
lake el lago (5, **10**)
lamp la lámpara (**3**)
land la tierra (**11**)
languages los idiomas *(pl.)* (**2**)
large grande (**1, 10**)
last night anoche (5, 7)
last year el año pasado (5, 7)
last, to durar (9, 11)
late tarde (2, 3); **later than** más tarde que (7)
law el derecho (**2**); la ley (10, **11**); **laws** las leyes (2)
lawyer abogado/a (8)
lazy perezoso/a (**1**)
learn, to aprender (**2**)
leather el cuero (**8**)
leave, to dejar (**10**); irse (**9**); salir (**3**); **to leave the hotel** irse del hotel (**10**)
left over, to be sobrar (5)
leg la pierna *(of a person)* (**9**); la pata *(of an animal)* (9)
legend la leyenda (9)
lemon el limón (**7**)
lend, to prestar (**8**)
let's hope that … ojalá que (**11**)
lettuce la lechuga (**7**)
library la biblioteca (**2**)
lie, to mentir (ie) (**4**)
light *(colored)* claro/a (**8**); **light** *(meal)* ligero/a (7)
light a campfire, to hacer una hoguera (**4**)
like como (5)
like, to gustar (**A**); **to like very much** encantar (**8**)
Likewise. Igualmente. (**A**)
line *(of people)* la cola (**10**)
lion el león (**11**)
listen music, to escuchar música (**2**)
Listen. Escuche(n). (**A**)
literacy la alfabetización (8)
literature la literatura (**2**)
little: little boy el niño (**1**); **little girl** la niña (**1**); **little kiss** el besito (**A**)
live, to vivir (**2**)
living vivo/a (**11**)
loan, to prestar (**8**)
locals *(pl.)* los lugareños (**4**)
lock *(of a canal)* la esclusa (5)
long largo/a (**8**)
look (at), to mirar (**2**); **to look for** buscar (**4**)
lose, to perder (ie) (**4**)
loud fuerte (3)
love el amor (4)
love, to encantar (**8**); querer (2, **3**)
lovers los amantes (11)
lucky, to be tener suerte (**3**)
luggage el equipaje (10)
lunch el almuerzo (**7**)
luxury el lujo (10)
lyrics la letra (**5**)

M

made from hecho de (9)
magazine la revista (8)
mail a letter, to mandar una carta (**4**)
make arts and crafts, to hacer artesanía (**4**)
make the arrangements, to hacer los arreglos (10)
make the bed, to hacer la cama (**3**)
make, to hacer (**3**, 4, **9**)
man el hombre; el señor (Sr.) (**1**)
manager el/la empresario/a (**5**)
many times muchas veces (**8**)
map el mapa (**2**)
March marzo (**A**)
market el mercado (**4**)
marmalade la mermelada (**7**)
married casado/a (**1**)
match el acierto (11)
material el material (**8**)
mathematics las matemáticas *(pl.)* (**2**)
matter el asunto (6)
matter, to importar (**8**)
May mayo (**A**)
mayonnaise la mayonesa (**7**)
mayor el alcalde; la alcaldesa (**11**)
me me (**5, 8**); **to/for me** mí (**11**)
meal la comida (**4, 5**, B, **7**)
meaning el sentido (3)
meat la carne (**7**)
medical treatment el tratamiento médico (**9**)
medicine la medicina (**2**)
medium *(meat)* término medio (**7**)
meet, to reunirse (**9**)
meeting la reunión (8, 10)
melon el melón (**7**)
memento el recuerdo (3)
memories *(pl.)* el recuerdo (10)
menu el menú (**7**)
messy desordenado/a (**3**)
microwave el microondas (**3**)
middle la mitad (11)
midnight la medianoche (**A**)
mile la milla (**2**, B)
milk la leche (**7**)
milk, to ordeñar (11)
minus menos (1)
Miss la señorita (Srta.) (**1**)
miss, to faltar (**4, B**)
mistaken, to be equivocarse (9)
mixture la mezcla (7, 11)
model el/la modelo (**8**); **fashion model** el/la modelo de ropa (3)
modern moderno/a (3)
mom la mamá (**1**)
monarchy la monarquía (**11**)
Monday el lunes (**A**)
money el dinero (**2**)
month el mes (**A**)
mosquito el mosquito (**11**)
mother la madre (**1**)
motor el motor (**10**)
motorcycle la moto(cicleta) (**1, 10**)
mountain la montaña (**10**); **mountain range** la cordillera (11); **mountain top** la cumbre (12)
mountainous montañoso/a (**4**)
mouse el ratón (**11**)
mouth la boca (**9**)
movie la película (3, **4**); **movie theater** el cine (**4**)
moving conmovedor/a (**5**); emocionante (**5**)
Mr. el señor (Sr.) (**1**)
Mrs. la señora (Sra.) (**1**)
museum el museo (**4**)
musical musical (**5**)
musician el/la músico/a (**5**)
mustard la mostaza (**7**)
my mi, mis (**1**)
My name is … Me llamo… (**A**)

N

napkin la servilleta (**7**)
narrate, to contar (9)
narrow estrecho/a (**8**)
nationality la nacionalidad (A)
native endémico/a (11)
natural resource el recurso natural (**11**)
nature la naturaleza (3, **11**)
nausea las náuseas (**9**)
near cerca (de) (2, 7, **11**)
neck el cuello (**9**)
need, to necesitar (**2**); hacer falta (**8**)
negotiate the price, to regatear (7)
neighboring vecino/a (8)
neither … nor ni… ni (**4**)
nervous nervioso/a (**2**)
never jamás (**4**); nunca (2, 3, **4**)
new nuevo/a (3)
newspaper el periódico (**11**)
nice simpático/a (**1**)
nickname el apodo (5)

nine nueve (**A**); **nine hundred** novecientos (**2**)
ninety noventa (**1**)
ninth noveno/a (**3**)
no one nadie (**4**)
nobody nadie (**4**)
noise el ruido (**B, 10**)
none ningún (**4**); ninguno/a/os/as (3, **4**)
noon el mediodía (**A**)
normally normalmente (**8**)
nose la nariz (**9**)
not ever (*emphatic*) jamás (**4**)
notebook el cuaderno (**2**)
notes los apuntes *(pl.)* (**2**)
nothing nada (**4**)
November noviembre (**A**)
now ahora (B); **right now** ahora mismo (2)
number el número (**A**)
nurse el/la enfermero/a (**9**)

O

object el objeto (3)
obligation el deber (**4**)
occur, to ocurrir (**9**)
ocean el océano (**11**)
October octubre (**A**)
offer ofrecer (2); la oferta (3)
office la oficina (**3**); **post office** la oficina de correos (**4**)
often a menudo (2, **8**)
oil el aceite (**7**); **oil spill** el derrame de petróleo (**11**)
Okay. Regular. (**A**)
old antiguo/a (3); mayor (**1**); viejo/a (**3, 10**)
older mayor (**10**)
on strike, to be estar en huelga (**11**)
on top (of) encima (de), sobre (3, 7, **11**)
once una vez (**4**)
one uno (**A**) ; **one million** millón (3); **one thousand** mil (**2 3**)
onion la cebolla (**7**)
only solamente (8, 12)
Open your book to page … Abra(n) el libro en la página… (**A**)
open, to abrir (**2**)
opening el estreno (**5**)
opera la ópera (**5**)
opposite opuesto/a (**4**)
orange anaranjado (**3**); la naranja (**7**)
orchestra la orquesta (**5**)
order, to pedir (i) (**7**)
organize, to organizar (**4**)
others los demás (**4**)
ought to deber (**4**)
our/s nuestro/a/os/as (**1**)
outfit el conjunto (**8**)
outside fuera (7); **outside of** afuera de (**11**)
outskirts las afueras (3)
over there *(and potentially not visible)* allá (**6**)
overcoat el abrigo (**8**)
overhaul, to revisar (**10**)
own propio/a (12)

P

pack a suitcase, to arreglar la maleta (**10**); hacer la maleta (**10**)
package el paquete (10)
pain el dolor (**9**)
painted wooden animals los alebrijes (2)
painting el cuadro (**3**)
pajamas el pijama (**8**)
pants los pantalones *(pl.)* (**8**)
paper el papel (**2, 11**)
parents los padres (**1**)
park el parque (**4**); **theme park** el parque de atracciones (**10**)
park, to estacionar (**10**)
parking el estacionamiento (**10**)
parrot el loro (11)
participate in a political campaign, to participar en una campaña política (**4**)
passenger el pasajero (**10**)
passionate apasionado/a (**5**)
passport el pasaporte (**10**)
pastimes los pasatiempos (**2**)
pastry el pastel (**7**)
patient paciente (**1**); el/la paciente (**9**)
pay, to pagar (**7**); remunerar (**4**)
peace la paz (5)
pear la pera (**7**)
pedestrian el/la peatón/peatona (**10**)
peel la cáscara (7)
peel, to pelar (7)
pencil el lápiz (**2**)
people la gente (**1**)
pepper la pimienta (**7**)
percent por ciento (1)
perform a concert, to dar un concierto (**5**)
personal assistant el/la ayudante personal (6)
personality la personalidad (**1**)
pertain, to pertenecer (10)
pet la mascota (10, **11**)
pharmacist el/la farmacéutico/a (9)
pharmacy la farmacia (**9**)
photo la foto (**1**)
pianist el/la pianista (**5**)
piano el piano (**5**)
picture el cuadro (**3,** 5)
pie el pastel (**7**)
pig el cerdo (**11**)
pile el montón (7)
pill la pastilla (**9**)
pillow la almohada (**3**)
pink rosado (**3**)
place el lugar (**2**)
place, to poner (**3**)
plantain chips los tostones (11)
planet el planeta (**11**)
plant, to plantar (**11**)
plastic el plástico (**11**)
plate el plato (**7**)
platform el programa (11)
play la obra de teatro (5)
play, to: jugar (ue) (**4**); **to play (a musical instrument)** tocar un instrumento (**2**); **to play baseball** jugar al béisbol (**2**); **to play basketball** jugar al básquetbol (**2**); **to play charades** hacer mímica (9); **to play football** jugar al fútbol americano (**2**); **to play golf** jugar al golf (**2**); **to play soccer** jugar al fútbol (**2**); **to play tennis** jugar al tenis (**2**)
Pleased to meet you. Encantado/a. (**A**)
pleasure el placer (7)
plus más (1)
police la policía (**10**); **policeman** el policía (**10**); **policewoman** la policía (**10**)
polite expression la expresión de cortesía (**A**)
political issues las cuestiones políticas (**11**)
political party el partido político (**11**)
politics la política (**11**)
poll la encuesta (**11**)
pollute, to contaminar (**11**)
pollution la contaminación (**11**)
polyester el poliéster (**8**)
pool la piscina (**2**)
poor pobre (**1**)
popcorn las palomitas *(pl.)* (5)
post office correos; la oficina de correos (**4**)
postage stamp el sello (**10**)
poster el cartel (10)
posts los cargos (**11**)
pot la cazuela (7)
potato la papa; la patata (**7**)
potato chips las papas fritas *(pl.)* (**7**)

poultry las aves **(7)**
practice, to ensayar **(5)**
prefer, to preferir (ie) **(4)**
pregnant embarazada (9)
preparation el preparativo (5)
prepare, to preparar **(2)**; **to prepare a meal** cocinar; preparar la comida **(3)**; **to prepare oneself** prepararse (B)
prescribe, to recetar (9)
prescription la receta **(9)**
presidency la presidencia **(11)**
president el/la presidente/a **(11)**
pretty guapo/a **(1)**
pretty bonito/a **(1)**
previous anterior (5)
print *(with a design or pattern)* estampado/a **(8)**
professor el/la profesor/a **(2)**
propose, to proponer (5,10)
protect, to proteger (8, **11**)
proud orgulloso/a (B)
psychology la psicología **(2)**
pure puro/a **(11)**
purple morado **(3)**
purpose el propósito (7)
put, to: poner **(3)**; **to put away** guardar **(3)**; **to put on (one's clothes)** ponerse (la ropa) **(9)**; **to put on make up** maquillarse **(9)**; **to put up a tent** montar una tienda de campaña **(4)**

Q

quality la calidad **(11)**
queen la reina **(11)**

R

rabbit el conejo (10, **11**)
rain la lluvia **(A)**; **acid rain** la lluvia ácida **(11)**; **rain forest (tropical)** la selva (tropical) **(11)**
raincoat el impermeable **(8)**
raise, to criar *(children, animals, etc.)* (10)
rare crudo/a (7)
rat la rata **(11)**
raw crudo/a (7)
read, to leer **(2)**
Read. Lea(n). **(A)**
realize, to darse cuenta (9)
Really well. Muy bien. **(A)**
receive, to recibir **(2)**
recipe la receta (7)
recognize, to reconocer (8)
recommend, to recomendar (ie) **(4)**
record, to grabar **(5)**
recycle, to reciclar **(11)**
recycling el reciclaje **(11)**
red rojo **(3)**
reforest, to reforestar **(11)**
refrigerator el refrigerador **(3)**
regimes los regímenes **(11)**
rehearse, to ensayar **(5)**
relatives los parientes (2, B)
release a film/movie, to estrenar una película **(5)**
release a song, to sacar una canción (5)
remain, to quedarse **(9)**
remember, to acordarse (ue) de **(9)**; recordar (ue) **(4)**
reopening la reapertura (11)
repeat, to repetir (i) **(4)**
Repeat. Repita(n). **(A)**
report el reportaje (12)
representative el/la diputado/a **(11)**
request el pedido (9)
reservation la reserva **(10)**
reserve a table, to reservar una mesa **(7)**
resolutions las determinaciones (11)
resolve, to resolver (ue) **(11)**
responsible responsable **(1)**
rest, to descansar (7)
restaurant el restaurante **(4, 7)**
return, to regresar **(2)**; **to return (an object)** devolver (ue) **(4)**; volver (ue) **(4)**
reuse, to reutilizar **(11)**
review la reseña (5)
rhythm el ritmo **(5)**
rice el arroz **(7)**
rich rico/a **(1)**
ride a bike, to montar en bicicleta **(2)**
right, to be tener razón **(3)**
ring el anillo (5)
river el río **(11)**
roasted asado/a **(7)**
robe la bata **(8)**
rock el rock **(5)**
roof el techo **(3)**
rooster el gallo (7)
roots las raíces (10)
roving ambulante **(4)**
row la hilera (8)
rug la alfombra **(3)**
rule la regla (10)
run, to correr **(2)**

S

sad triste **(2)**
safe salvo/a (11)
salad la ensalada **(7)**; **salad dressing** el aderezo; el aliño (7)
salsa la salsa **(5)**
salt la sal **(7)**
salve el ungüento (10)
same mismo/a **(2)**
sandals la sandalias *(pl.)* **(8)**
sapodilla tree el chicozapote (2)
Saturday el sábado **(A)**
say, to decir **(3)**
scare, to asustar (9)
scarf la bufanda (9); el pañuelo (8)
schedule (of classes) el horario (de clases) **(2)**
science las ciencias *(pl.)* **(2)**
screen la pantalla **(5)**
scuba diving el buceo (4)
seafood los mariscos **(7)**
seamstress el/la costurero/a (8)
seasoning el condimento **(7)**
seat *(of government)* la sede (9)
second segundo/a **(3)**; **second floor** el segundo piso **(3)**
see, to ver **(2)**
sell, to vender (7)
seller el/la vendedor/a (7)
semester el semestre **(2)**
senator el/la senador/a **(11)**
send, to enviar **(4)**; **to send/mail a letter** mandar una carta **(4)**
sentences las oraciones **(3)**
September septiembre **(A)**
serve, to servir (i) **(4)**
set the table, to poner la mesa **(3)**
seven siete **(A)**; **seven hundred** setecientos **(2)**
seventh séptimo/a **(3)**
seventy setenta **(1)**
shake, to temblar (11)
share compartir (3, 5)
shark el tiburón (5)
shave, to afeitarse **(9)**
she ella **(A)**
sheet la sábana **(3)**
shell la concha (10)
shellfish los mariscos **(4)**
shirt la camisa **(8)**
shoes los zapatos *(pl.)* **(8)**
short bajo/a **(1)**; corto/a **(8)**
shorts los pantalones cortos *(pl.)* **(8)**
shot la inyección **(9)**
should deber **(4)**
shout, to gritar (11)
show, to enseñar **(2)**; mostrar (ue) **(4)**; **to show a film/movie** presentar una película **(5)**
shower la ducha **(3)**
shower, to ducharse **(9)**

shrimp los camarones *(pl.)* **(7)**
shrub el arbusto (7)
siblings los hermanos (**1**)
sick enfermo/a (**2**)
sick, to be estar enfermo/a (**9**)
signature la firma (4)
silk la seda (**8**)
silly tonto/a (**1**)
similarity la semejanza (**4**, 6)
since desde que (9)
sincerely atentamente (**4**)
sing, to cantar (**5**)
singer el/la cantante (**5**)
sink el lavabo (**3**)
sister la hermana (**1**); **sisters** las hermanas (**1**)
sit down, to sentarse (e, ie) (**9**)
six seis (**A**); **six hundred** seiscientos (**2**)
sixth sexto/a (**3**)
sixty sesenta (**1**)
size tamaño (3)
skate, to patinar (**2**)
skill la habilidad (**5**)
skirt la falda (**8**)
sky el cielo (**11**)
sleep, to dormir (o, ue, u) (**4**); **to fall asleep** dormirse (**9**)
sleepy, to be tener sueño (**3**)
slippers las zapatillas *(pl.)* (**8**)
slow lento/a (3, **5**)
small pequeño/a (**1, 10**)
smell, to oler (7)
smooth suave (**5**)
snack la merienda (**7**)
snake la serpiente (**11**)
sneeze el estornudo (**9**)
sneeze, to estornudar (**9**)
snow la nieve (**A**)
socks los calcetines (*pl.*) (**8**)
sofa el sofá (**3**)
soft drink el refresco (**7**)
soil la tierra (**11**)
soldiers los soldados (11)
solid-colored liso/a (**8**)
some algún (**4**); alguno/a/os/as (3, **4**); un/a/os/as (**1**)
someone alguien (**4**)
sometimes a veces (2, **4**)
something algo (**4**)
son el hijo (**1**); **sons** los hijos (**1**)
soup la sopa (**7**); **soup spoon** la cuchara (**7**)
source la fuente (5, 9)
sow, to sembrar (e, ie) (**11**)
Spanish speaker el/la hispanohablante (1)
speak, to hablar (**2**)
specialty of the house la especialidad de la casa (7)
speech el discurso (**11**)
speed la velocidad (10)
spend ***(time)*****, to** pasar (6)
spices las especias (**7**)
spicy picante (**7**)
spoonful la cucharada (7)
sport el deporte (**2**)
spring la primavera (**A**)
stadium el estadio (**2**)
staircase la escalera (**3,** 11)
stand, to pararse (10); **to stand in line** hacer (la) cola (**10**); **to stand out** destacar (5); **to stand up** levantarse (**9**)
star la estrella (**5**)
start el principio (8)
state el estado (**11**); **state** ***(of being)*** (2)
statehood la estadidad (11)
stay, to permanecer (11); quedar (11); quedarse (**9**); **to stay in bed** guardar cama (**9**)
steak el bistec (**7**)
steering wheel el volante (**10**)
stepfather el padrastro (**1**)
stepmother la madrastra (**1**)
still todavía (11)
stockings las medias *(pl.)* (**8**)
stomach el estómago (**9**)
store la tienda (**2**)
storm la tormenta (**11**)
story el piso (**3**)
stove la estufa (**3**)
straight derecho/a (10)
straighten up, to arreglar (**3**)
street la calle (3, **10**)
strike la huelga (**11**)
strong fuerte (**1**)
student el/la estudiante (**2**)
study, to estudiar (**2**, 6)
stupendous estupendo/a (**5**)
style el estilo (8); la moda (**8**)
subject la materia (**2**)
subway el metro (**10**)
successful, to be tener éxito (**3**)
sugar el azúcar (**7**)
suitable adecuado/a (10)
suitcase la maleta (**10**)
summarize, to resumir (9)
summer el verano (**A**)
sun el sol (**A**)
sunbathe, to tomar el sol (**2**)
Sunday el domingo (**A**)
supermarket el supermercado (**4**)
support, to apoyar (B, **11**)
sure seguro/a (5)
surprise la sorpresa (8)
surprising sorprendente (**5**)
survey la encuesta (**11**)
sweat, to sudar (9)
sweater el suéter (**8**)
sweatshirt la sudadera (**8**)
sweets el dulce (**7**)
swim, to nadar (**2**)

T

table la mesa (**2**)
tablecloth el mantel (**7**)
tablespoon la cuchara (**7**)
tablet la tableta (**2**)
tailor el costurero (8)
take, to llevar (**8**); tomar (**2**); **to take a short trip** ir de excursión (**4**); **to take care of** cuidar (3, 9, **11**); **to take off (one's clothes)** quitarse (la ropa) (**9**); **to take out the garbage** sacar la basura (**3**); **to take someone to the doctor** llevar a alguien al médico (**4**); **to take turns** turnarse (3)
talk la charla (11)
tall alto/a (**1**)
taste good/bad, to saber bien/mal (**7**)
tasty sabroso/a (**7**)
tax el impuesto (**11**)
taxi el taxi (**10**)
tea (iced / hot) el té (helado / caliente) (**7**)
teach, to enseñar (**2**)
team el equipo (**2**)
teaspoon la cucharita (**7**)
television la televisión (**2**)
tell, to decir (**3**)
temperature la temperatura (**A**)
temple el templo (**4**)
tennis shoes los tenis *(pl.)* (**8**)
tenth décimo (**3**)
test la prueba (9)
Thank you. Gracias. (**A**)
that, that one ese/a (**5**); **that one** *(way over there/not visible)* aquel/la (**5**); **those** (*way over there/not visible*) aquellos/as (**5**)
That's great! ¡Qué bueno! (**2**)
the el/la/los/las (**1**); **The check please.** La cuenta por favor. (**7**) **the day before yesterday** anteayer (5, 7); **the best** el/la mejor (4); **the eldest** el/la mayor (**10**); **the worst** el/la peor (**10**); **the youngest** el/la menor (**10**)

the left (of), to a la izquierda (de) (3, 7, **11**)
the right (of), to a la derecha (de) (**3, 7, 11**)
theater el teatro (**4**)
their su/s (**1**)
them los, las (**5**); **to them** les (**8**)
then entonces (**6**); luego (**6**)
there is hay (**2**); **there are** hay (**1, 2**); **over there** allí (**6**)
these estos/as (**5**)
they ellos/as (**A**)
thin delgado/a (**1**)
thing la cosa (**3**)
think, to pensar (ie) (**4**)
thinks piensa (1)
third tercer, tercero/a (**3**)
thirsty, to be tener sed (**3**)
thirteen trece (**A**)
this, this one este/a (**5**)
those over there; those ones esos/as (**5**)
throat la garganta (**9**)
throne el trono (11)
throw away, to botar (**11**)
Thursday el jueves (**A**)
tie la corbata (**8**)
tight estrecho/a (**8**)
time la hora (**A**); **sometimes, from time to time** a veces (2, 3, **4**)
tin work la hojalatería (2)
tip la propina (**7**)
tire la llanta (**10**)
tired cansado/a (**2**)
toast la tostada (**7**)
together juntos (2, **3**)
toilet el inodoro (**3**)
tomato el tomate (**7**)
too también (2)
tooth el diente (**9**)
topic el tema (5)
tornado el tornado (**11**)
tour la gira (**5**)
tour, to hacer una gira (**5**)
tournament el torneo (**4**)
tower la torre (3)
town el pueblo (**4**)
town square la plaza (**4**)
track and field el atletismo (2)
traditional tradicional (3)
traffic el tráfico (**10**); **traffic light** el semáforo (**10**); **traffic ticket** la multa (**10**)
tragedy la tragedia (**11**)
tragic trágico/a (**5**)
train el tren (**10**)
transportation el transporte (**10**)
travel agency la agencia de viajes (6, **10**); **travel agent** el/la agente de viajes (**10**)
travel, to viajar (**10**)
traveler el/la viajero/a (**10**)
treasure el tesoro (11)
tree el árbol (**11**)
tribute el homenaje (5)
trip el viaje (**10**)
truck el camión (**10**)
true cierto (**1**)
trumpet la trompeta (**5**)
trunk el baúl (**10**)
truth la verdad (**3**)
try (to), to tratar de (3, **9**)
try on clothing, to probarse (ue) la ropa (**9**)
T-shirt la camiseta (**8**)
tsunami el tsunami (**11**)
Tuesday el martes (**A**)
tuna el atún (**7**)
turn, to doblar (**10**); **to turn in** entregar (7); **to turn on** prender (11)
turnover (meat) la empanada (7)
twelve doce (**A**)
twenty veinte (**A**)

U

ugly feo/a (**1**)
umbrella el paraguas (**8**)
uncle el tío (**1**)
uncomfortable incómodo/a (**8**)
under debajo (de) (7, **11**)
undercover encubierto/a (5)
underline, to subrayar (7)
underneath debajo (de) (7, **11**)
understand, to comprender (**2**); entender (ie) (**4**)
underwear la ropa interior (**8**)
unemployment el desempleo (**11**)
unpleasant antipático/a (**1**)
upset nervioso/a (**2**)
us nosotros/as (**A**); nos (**5**); **to us** nos(**8**)
use, to usar (**2**, 4)
useful útil (**A**)

V

vacation las vacaciones *(pl.)* (**10**)
vacuum, to pasar la aspiradora (**3**)
vegetable la verdura (**7**)
vehicle el vehículo (**10**)
very muy (**1**)
village el pueblo (**4**)
vinegar el vinagre (**7**)
visit, to visitar (**10**)
voice la voz (**5**)
volunteer at a nursing home, to trabajar como voluntario/a en la residencia de ancianos (**4**)
volunteerism el voluntariado (**4**)
vote el voto (**11**)
vote, to votar (**11**)

W

waist la cintura (**9**); **from the waist up/down** de la cintura para arriba/abajo (9)
wait for, to esperar (**2**)
wait on, to atender (9)
waiter el camarero (**7**)
waitress la camarera (**7**)
wake up, to despertarse (e, ie) (**9**)
walk, to andar (**10**); caminar (**2**)
wall la pared (**2**)
want, to querer (2, **3**)
war la guerra (**11**)
warriors los guerreros (11)
wash dishes, to lavar los platos (**3**)
wash oneself, to lavarse (**9**)
waste, to perder (ie) (**4**)
watch el reloj (**2**)
watch, to mirar (**2**); **to watch television** ver la televisión (**3**)
waterfall la cascada (10)
we nosotros/as (**11**)
weak débil (**1**)
wear, to llevar (**8**)
wedding la boda (4, 6, 11)
Wednesday el miércoles (**A**)
week la semana (**A**); **last week** la semana pasada (5, 7)
weekend el fin de semana (**3**, 7); **last weekend** el fin de semana pasado (5)
welcome la bienvenida (**2**)
welfare el bienestar (**11**)
well-being el bienestar (**11**)
what lo que (3); **What?** ¿Qué? (**2**)
whatever cualquier (8)
When? ¿Cuándo? (**2**)
Where to? ¿Adónde? (**2**)
Where? ¿Dónde? (**2**)
which cual (11)
while mientras (3, **8**)
whipped cream la crema batida (7)
white blanco (**3**)
whiteboard (interactive) la pizarra (interactiva) (**2**)
Who? ¿Quién/es? (**A, 2**)
whose cuyo (11)
wide ancho (7, **8**)

wife la esposa (**1**)
win, to ganar (3, 6, 7)
wind el viento (**A**)
window la ventana (**2**); **to window shop** mirar las vitrinas (8)
windshield el parabrisas (**10**); **windshield wiper** el limpiaparabrisas (**10**)
wine el vino (**7**)
winter el invierno (**A**)
with con (**11**)
woman la mujer; la señora (Sra.) (**1**)
wool la lana (**8**)
word la palabra (**A**)
work, to: funcionar (**10**); trabajar (**2**); **to work as a counselor** trabajar como consejero/a (**4**); **to work in a summer camp** trabajar en el campamento de niños (**4**); **to work in politics** trabajar en política (**4**)
world el mundo (11)
worried preocupado/a (**2**)
worry about, to preocuparse (por) (**11**)
worse peor (**4, 10**)
wound la herida (**9**)
Wow! ¡Vaya! (**4**)
wrap, to envolver (7)
wrestling la lucha libre (2)
write, to escribir (**2**)
Write. Escriba(n). (**A**)

Y

yam la batata (7)
yellow amarillo (**3**)
… years old, to be tener … años (**3**)
Yes. Sí. (**A**)
yesterday ayer (5, 7)
yogurt el yogur (**7**)
you lo, la (**5**); ti (11); tú *(familiar)* (**A, 1**); usted/es *(formal)* (**A, 11**); vosotros/as (*fam. pl. Spain*) (**A, 11**)
you, to te (**5, 8**); **to you all** os (**5, 8**)
young joven (**1, 10**); **young man** el joven (**1, 10**); **young woman** la joven (**1, 10**); la señorita (Srta.) (**1**)
your su/s; tu/s; **your/s** vuestro/a/os/as (*fam. pl. Spain*) (**1**)
yucca la mandioca (7)

CREDITS

Text Credits

Chapter 7

p **273**: ChooseMyPlate.gov, U. S. Department of Agriculture

Chapter 10

p. 417 “Cartas de relación”, Hernán Cortés. Dastin (2000).

Chapter 11

p. 446 “La Leyenda de los volcanos (adaptacion)”. Dr. Aitor Bikandi-Mejias

Photo Credits

Chapter A

p. 3: David Schaffer/Getty Images; **p. 4**: (l) Nyul/Fotolia; (c) Jupiterimages/Stockbyte/Getty Images; (r) Digital Vision/Photodisc/Getty Images; **p. 7**: (t) Stockbyte/Getty Images; (b) Comstock Images/Stockbyte/Getty Images; **p. 12**: Andres Rodriguez/Fotolia; **p. 15**: Jupiterimages/Stockbyte/Getty Images; **p. 16**: George Doyle/Stockbyte/Getty Images; **p. 20**: (t) Stockbyte/Getty Images; (lc) Jupiterimages/PHOTOS.com/Getty Images/Thinkstock; (cl) Jupiterimages/Stockbyte/Getty Images; (cr) Pete Saloutos; (rc) BananaStock/Getty Images/Thinkstock; (bl) James Woodson/Photodisc/Getty Images; (bl) BananaStock/Getty Images/Thinkstock; (br) Jupiterimages/Stockbyte/Getty Images; (br) BananaStock/Getty Images/Thinkstock; **p. 22**: (tl) Medioimages/Photodisc/Getty Images; (tr) Eva Madrazo/Shutterstock; (b) Eddie Gerald/Dorling Kindersley, Ltd.; **p. 26**: (t) Andi Berger/Shutterstock; (tl) iofoto/Shutterstock; (tc) resnak/Shutterstock; (tr) Brad Remy/Shutterstock; (cl) Jupiterimages/Stockbyte/Getty Images; (c) Brandon Seidel/Shutterstock; (cr) Stuart Miles/Fotolia/Fotolia; (bl) Paul Yates/Shutterstock; (bc) Ollyy/Shutterstock.

Chapter 1

p. 30: Kevin Kozicki/Getty Images; **p. 31**: (t) Mint Images - Tim Robbins/Getty Images; (b) Huntstock.com/Shutterstock; **p. 35**: monbibi/Shutterstock; **p. 36**: Monkey Business/Fotolia; **p. 46**: (t) anekoho/Fotolia; (tc) Barabas Attila/Fotolia; (c) Eugenio Marongiu/Fotolia; (bc) Patricia Marks/Shutterstock; (b) Caroline Schiff/Getty Images; **p. 47**: Rido/Shutterstock; **p. 48**: Sergey Ash/Shutterstock; **p. 49**: Grigory Kubatyan/Shutterstock; **p. 53**: (t) Pearson Education; (bl) nyul/Fotolia; (br) Karramba Production/Fotolia; **p. 56**: (t) ImageryMajestic/Shutterstock; (cl) David Heining-Boynton; (cr) David Heining-Boynton; (bl) Pearson Education; (br) Samot/Shutterstock; (t) nandyphotos/Fotolia; **p. 58**: oneinchpunch/Fotolia; **p. 59**: (b) Iakov Filimonov/Shutterstock; **p. 60**: Monkey Business/Fotolia.

Chapter 2

p. 64: Jeremy Woodhouse/Getty Images; **p. 65**: (t) Andrew Bowen; (b) PhotoAlto/Sigrid Olsson/Getty Images; **p. 68**: csp/Shutterstock; **p. 77**: (c) Kaesler Media/Shutterstock; (b) CREATISTA/Shutterstock; **p. 78**: (l) Poprugin Aleksey/Shutterstock; (lc) Romolo Tavani/Fotolia; (rc) zsuriel/Fotolia; (r) Comugnero Silvana/Fotolia; **p. 89**: (tl) Skylinephoto/Shutterstock; (t) David Heining-Boynton; (tr) expressiovisual/Fotolia; (tcr) WavebreakmediaMicro/Fotolia; (tc) pololia/Fotolia; (tcl) 103tnn/Fotolia; (bcl) David Heining-Boynton; (bc) Brocreative/Fotolia; (bcr) Stephen Mcsweeny/Shutterstock; (br) David Heining-Boynton; (bl) Andres Rodriguez/Fotolia; (b) frinz/Fotolia; **p. 90**: (r) Brian Jackson/Fotolia; (l) Maridav/Shutterstock; (c) David Heining-Boynton; (br) Zsolnai Gergely/Fotolia; (b) Syda Productions/Fotolia; **p. 91**: Zou Zheng Xinhua News Agency/Newscom; **p. 93**: RStollner/Shutterstock; **p. 94**: Monkey Business/Fotolia; **p. 96**: (t) Rob/Fotolia; (c) Pearson Education; (b) csp/Shutterstock; **p. 97**: (t) José Méndez/EPA/Newscom; (c) ElHielo/Shutterstock; (b) Francesca Yorke/Dorling Kindersley, Ltd.; **p. 99**: Pearson Education; **p. 100**: racorn/Shutterstock.

Chapter 3

p. 104: VanderWolf Images/Fotolia; **p. 105**: (t) Tatyana Vyc/Shutterstock; (b) David Heining-Boynton; **p. 108**: (tl) David Heining-Boynton; (tc) Evok20/Shutterstock; (tr) gary yim/Shutterstock; (bl) javarman/Shutterstock; (bc) Jarno Gonzalez Zarraonandia/Shutterstock; (br) David Heining-Boynton; **p. 112**: Mark Hayes/Shutterstock; **p. 113**: (t) David Heining-Boynton; (b) David Heining-Boynton; **p. 115**: David Heining-Boynton; **p. 119**: (tl) David Heining-Boynton; (tc) David Heining-Boynton; (tr) David Heining-Boynton; (cl) David Heining-Boynton; (c) David Heining-Boynton; (cr) David Heining-Boynton; (bl) David Heining-Boynton; (bc) Alberto Loyo/Shutterstock; (b) David Heining-Boynton; (br) David Heining-Boynton; **p. 120**: David Heining-Boynton; **p. 121**: David Heining-Boynton; **p. 125**: (tr) David Heining-Boynton; (bl) Natalia Belotelova/

Shutterstock; (bc) Pres Panayotov/Shutterstock; (br) David Heining-Boynton; **p. 126**: (tl) David Heining-Boynton; (br) David Heining-Boynton; (tr) David Heining-Boynton; (br) David Heining-Boynton; **p. 127**: (t) David Heining-Boynton; (b) David Heining-Boynton; **p. 129**: David Heining-Boynton; **p. 130**: imging/Shutterstock; **p. 132**: (t) Brand X Pictures/Stockbyte/Getty Images; (tc) Chris Nash/Getty Images; (bc) imageZebra/Shutterstock; (b) Vinicius Tupinamba/Shutterstock; **p. 133**: (tl) Sillycoke/Shutterstock; (tr) Joan Ramon Mendo Escoda/Shutterstock; (c) Pearson Education; (b) David Heining-Boynton; **p. 134**: Syda Productions/Fotolia; **p. 135**: Johner Images/Getty Images; **p. 136**: Naphat_Jorjee/Shutterstock.

Chapter 4

p. 140: Gallo Images/Getty Images; **p. 141**: (t) Professional Geographer/Getty Images; (b) Enzo Figueres/Getty Images; **p. 144**: (br) Ollyy/Shutterstock; (bl) David Heining-Boynton; (tl) Dorling Kindersley, Ltd.; **p. 145**: (t) Suzanne Long/Shutterstock; (b) Jennifer Stone/Shutterstock; **p. 147**: Jupiterimages/PHOTOS.com/Thinkstock/Getty Images; **p. 149**: Medioimages/Photodisc/Stockbyte/Getty Images; **p. 153**: ImageState Royalty Free/Alamy; **p. 155**: Medioimages/Photodisc/Getty Images; **p. 157**: Jack Hollingsworth/Stockbyte/Getty Images; **p. 160**: vadim kozlovsky/Shutterstock; **p. 162**: Getty Images; **p. 165**: Andresr/Shutterstock; **p. 167**: Pearson Education; **p. 168**: BananaStock/Thinkstock/Getty Images; **p. 171**: (t) Andresr/Shutterstock; (c) Christopher Poe/Shutterstock; (bl) Pearson Education; (bc) Shawn Talbot; (br) Pearson Education; **p. 172**: (t) Jupiterimages/liquidlibrary/Thinkstock/Getty Images; (cl) Pearson Education; (c) sunsinger/Shutterstock; (lc) Mike Cohen/Shutterstock; (bl) Bumbim/Shutterstock; **p. 173**: (t) iofoto/Shutterstock; (tl) rj lerich/Shutterstock; (bl) Yai/Shutterstock; (br) Pearson Education; (b) Bumbim/Shutterstock; **p. 175**: Alan Jeffery/Shutterstock; **p. 174**: soft_light/Shutterstock; **p. 176**: Olesia Bilkei/Fotolia.

Chapter 5

p. 180: Mathew Imaging/Getty Images; **p. 181**: (t) Amble Design/Shutterstock; (b) Jakez/Shutterstock; **p. 184**: Ollyy/Shutterstock; **p. 185**: (t) Andros68/Fotolia; (b) dwphotos/Shutterstock; **p. 189**: (t) David Heining-Boynton; (l) Kevin Mazur/Getty Images; (r) ISOPRESS/REX/Newscom; (b) Nick Pickles/Getty Images; **p. 195**: fcarniani/Fotolia; **p. 196**: (t) Denis Makarenko/Shutterstock; (bl) Denis Makarenko/Shutterstock; (bc) Denis Makarenko/Shutterstock; (br) Everett Collection/Newscom; **p. 198**: mrcats/Fotolia; **p. 201**: zinkevych/Fotolia; **p. 204**: Karwai Tang/WireImage/Getty Images; **p. 205**: Dana Nalbandian/Shutterstock; **p. 206**: Rock and Wasp/Fotolia; **p. 207**: DeshaCAM/Shutterstock; **p. 209**: (t) blvdone/Fotolia; (cl) rj lerich/Shutterstock; (c) rj lerich/Shutterstock; (bl) Pearson Education; **p. 210**: (t) nandyphotos/Fotolia; (cl) Sandra A. Dunlap/Shutterstock; (b) Franck Monnot/Fotolia; (c) Pearson Education; **p. 211**: (t) Jack Hollingsworth/Photodisc/Getty Images; (cl) searagen/Fotolia; (bl) rj lerich/Shutterstock; (c) Chris Howey/Shutterstock; **p. 212**: Top Photo Corporation/Shutterstock; **p. 213**: (tl) Jane Hobson/REX Shutterstock/Newscom; (bl) LEHTIKUVA OY/REX/Newscom; (tr) Melinda Nagy/Fotolia; (br) romakoma/Shutterstock; **p. 214**: Lsantilli/Fotolia.

Chapter 6

p. 218: Vinicius Tupinamba/Shutterstock; **p. 219**: (t) Pearson Education; (b) Pearson Education; **p. 221**: (tl) Creatas/Thinkstock/Getty Images; (tr) Ryan McVay/Photodisc/Getty Images; (b) Jack Hollingsworth/Photodisc/Getty Images; **p. 222**: (tl) ImageryMajestic/Shutterstock; (tcl) Rob/Fotolia; (tcr) Brand X Pictures/Stockbyte/Getty Images; (tr) Andresr/Shutterstock; (bl) Jupiterimages/liquidlibrary/Thinkstock/Getty Images; (bcl) iofoto/Shutterstock; (bc) blvdone/Fotolia; (bcr) nandyphotos/Fotolia; (bc) Jack Hollingsworth/Photodisc/Getty Images; **p. 225**: Ian Tragen/Shutterstock; **p. 228**: Steve Mason/Stockbyte/Getty Images; **p. 230**: dwphotos/Shutterstock; **p. 233**: Frontpage/Shutterstock; **p. 235**: (l) Pearson Education; (r) Pearson Education; **p. 236**: Santiago Cornejo; **p. 237**: (l) Joe Mercier/Shutterstock; (r) John Cordes/Icon Sportswire 506/John Cordes/Icon Sportswire/Newscom; **p. 238**: (Top Row 1) csp/Shutterstock; (Top Row 2) David Heining-Boynton; (Top Row 3) Pearson Education; (Top Row 4) Pearson Education; (Top Row 5) Pearson Education; (Top Row 6) David Heining-Boynton; (Top Row 7) Shawn Talbot; (Top Row 8) Mike Cohen/Shutterstock; (Top Row 1) rj lerich/Shutterstock; (Top Row 2) Pearson Education; (Top Row 3) Pearson Education; (Top Row 4) David Heining-Boynton; (Top Row 5) Pearson Education; (Top Row 6) rj lerich/Shutterstock; (Top Row 7) Brand X Pictures/Getty Images; (Top Row 8) rj lerich/Shutterstock.

Chapter B

p. 240-241: Rawpixel.com/Fotolia; **p. 242**: (tl) JackF/Fotolia; (tr) Monkey Business Images/Shutterstock; (bl) Julie Keen/Shutterstock; (br) Monkey Business/Fotolia; **p. 243**: Robert Kneschke/Fotolia; **p. 250**: (tl) IM_photo/Shutterstock; (tr) Pearson Education; (bl) imging/Shutterstock; (br) David Heining-Boynton; **p. 253**: (tl) David Heining-Boynton; (tr) russ witherington/Shutterstock; (bl) David Heining-Boynton; (bc) Pearson Education; (br) David Heining-Boynton; **p. 254**: (l) Cheryl Casey/Shutterstock; (c) Giordano Aita/Shutterstock; (r) Michael Shake/Shutterstock; **p. 257**: Dean Mitchell/Getty Images; **p. 258**: Scott Griessel/Fotolia; **p. 261**: Dario Sabljak/Shutterstock; **p. 263**: Syda Productions/Fotolia; **p. 264**: Scott Leman/Shutterstock.

Chapter 7

p. 266: Image Source/Getty Images; **p. 267**: (t) Andrew Bowen; (b) Image Source/Getty Images; **p. 272**: BillionPhotos.com/Fotolia; **p. 273**: BasheeraDesigns/Fotolia; **p. 274**: Digital Vision/Photodisc/Getty Images; **p. 276**: (tr) George Doyle/Stockbyte/Getty Images; (cr) catmanc/shutterstock; (tl) C.J. White/Shutterstock; (tc) David Heining-Boynton; (tr) Yellowj/Shutterstock; (cl) joingate/Shutterstock; (c) Valentyn Volkov/Shutterstock; (cr) Michal Zajac/Shutterstock; (bl) David Heining-Boynton; (bc) David Heining-Boynton; (br) David Heining-Boynton; **p. 282**: (t) Kiselev Andrey Valerevich; (bl) Valentyn Volkov/Shutterstock; (tcl) Andrey Jitkov/Shutterstock; (tcr) hfng/Shutterstock; (tr) Robyn Mackenzie/Shutterstock; (tl) Shebeko/Shutterstock; (bcl) Denis Vrublevski/Shutterstock; (bcr) epsylon_lyrae/Shutterstock; (br) David Heining-Boynton; **p. 283**: sunsinger/Shutterstock; **p. 289**: KPG_Payless/Shutterstock ; **p. 292**: David Heining-Boynton; **p. 293**: David Heining-Boynton; **p. 294**: David Heining-Boynton; **p. 295**: Jupiterimages/Getty Images; **p. 296**: (t) LuckyImages/Shutterstock; (b) kondratyuk/Shutterstock; (t) Jupiterimages/Thinkstock/Getty Images; **p. 298**: Pearson Education; (tr) David Heining-Boynton; (tc) Pearson Education; (c) Rhonda Klevansky/

The Image Bank/Getty Images; **p. 299**: (t) Daniel M Ernst/Shutterstock; (c) Mykola Gomeniuk/Shutterstock; (b) Pearson Education; (br) Claudia Otte/Shutterstock; Pearson Education.

Chapter 8

p. 306: Jeremy Woodhouse/Getty Images; **p. 307**: (b) Jim Arbogast/Getty Images; (t) Raphye Alexius/Getty Images; **p. 310**: (c) Suzanne Long/Shutterstock; (b) Joel Shawn/Shutterstock; **p. 311**: David Heining-Boynton; **p. 312**: Colin Sinclair/Dorling Kindersley, Ltd.; **p. 315**: Africa Studio/Fotolia; **p. 316**: Johner Images; **p. 319**: (t) Nata Sha/Shutterstock; (tc) Creatas/Thnikstock/Getty Images; (c) littleny/Shutterstock; (bc) Paul Sutherland/Photodisc/Getty Images; (b) Pavel L Photo and Video/Shutterstock; **p. 320**: WavebreakMediaMicro/Fotolia; **p. 326**: Rudy Lawidjaja/Sipa USA/Newscom; **p. 327**: jorisvo/Shutterstock; **p. 330**: Pictorial Press/Alamy; **p. 331**: Andresr/Shutterstock; **p. 333**: Digital Vision/Photodisc/Getty Images; **p. 334**: (t) lev radin/Shutterstock; (b) iofoto/Shutterstock; **p. 336**: (t) Daniel M Ernst/Shutterstock; (l) Larry Lee Photography/Corbis; (bc) veroxdale/Shutterstock; (tc) Pearson Education; Pearson Education; **p. 337**: (t) Daniel M Ernst/Shutterstock; (l) Brand X Pictures/Stockbyte/Thinkstock/Getty Images; (c) Pearson Education; (b) SF photo/Shutterstock; Pearson Education; **p. 339**: Schum/Fotolia; **p. 340**: Mimi Haddon/Getty Images.

Chapter 9

p. 344: uzhursky/Fotolia; (t) Dirima/Fotolia; (b) mr.markin/Fotolia; **p. 348**: Stephen Schildbach/Photodisc/Getty Images; **p. 352**: Dario Lo Presti/Fotolia; **p. 357**: AVAVA/Shutterstock; **p. 358**: Inna Vlasova/Fotolia; **p. 362**: Guido Amrein, Switzerland/Shutterstock; **p. 366**: (t) Galyna Andrushko/Shutterstock; (b) Regissercom/Shutterstock; **p. 370**: (t) WavebreakmediaMicro/Fotolia; (b) nyul/Fotolia; **p. 371**: TheThirdMan/Shutterstock; **p. 372**: Pearson Education; **p. 373**: (t) iceteastock/Fotolia; (b) Andresr/Shutterstock; **p. 375**: (t) Monkey Business Images/Shutterstock; (cl) Pearson Education; (c) terekhov igor/Shutterstock; (b) Maria Veras/Shutterstock; Pearson Education; **p. 376**: (t) Andresr/Shutterstock; (cl) Shanti Hesse/Shutterstock; (c) Paul Clarke/Shutterstock; (b) Pearson Education; Pearson Education; **p. 377**: (t) Andresr/Shutterstock; (c) nouseforname/Shutterstock; (b) Pearson Education; (cl) Pearson Education; **p. 379**: Aleksandr Markin/Shutterstock; **p. 380**: wavebreakmedia/Shutterstock.

Chapter 10

p. 384: alexmillos/Shutterstock; **p. 385**: (b) Carlos Bohorquez Nassar - www.stillformat.com/Getty Images; (t) ruidoblanco/Shutterstock; **p. 389**: Andresr/Shutterstock; **p. 390**: Ramona Heim/Shutterstock; **p. 393**: Monkey Business/Fotolia; **p. 394**: Creatista/Shutterstock; **p. 395**: clownbusiness/Fotolia; **p. 398**: (t) michaeljung/Fotolia; (b) gary yim/Shutterstock; **p. 399**: (t) Robert Kneschke/Shutterstock; (b) David Heining-Boynton; **p. 400**: Ysbrand Cosijn/Shutterstock; **p. 403**: Fabian_Agudelo/Fotolia; **p. 404**: Rawpixel.com/Fotolia; **p. 405**: (t) LysFoto/Shutterstock; (b) Attila JANDI/Shutterstock; (c) Robert Wroblewski/Shutterstock; **p. 410**: Andrey Yurlov/Shutterstock; **p. 411**: Monkey Business Images/Shutterstock; **p. 412**: (t) Pressmaster/Shutterstock; (b) nito/Shutterstock; **p. 414**: (t) A and N photography/Shutterstock; (l) Pearson Education; (b) Pearson Education; (c) javarman/Shutterstock; **p. 415**: (t) Rido/Shutterstock; (l) irabassi/Fotolia; (c) Pearson Education; (b) Pearson Education; Pearson Education; **p. 417**: Juulijs/Fotolia; **p. 416**: Everett Historical/Shutterstock; **p. 418**: Sean Pavone/Shutterstock.

Chapter 11

p. 422: vilainecrevette/Fotolia; **p. 423**: (t) Uryadnikov Sergey/Fotolia; (b) Lisa Johnson - Olive Productions/Getty Images; **p. 426**: (t) Ng Yin Jian/Shutterstock; (tc) john michael evan potter/Shutterstock; (ct) marilyn barbone/Shutterstock; (bt) Denis Pepin/Shutterstock; (bt) Narcis Parfenti/Shutterstock; (b) Hintau Aliaksei/Shutterstock; **p. 427**: Kaesler Media/Shutterstock; **p. 432**: Colin D. Young/Shutterstock; **p. 440**: U.S. State Department; **p. 441**: FotolEdhar/Fotolia; **p. 446**: Uryadnikov Sergey/Fotolia; **p. 447**: Lisa F. Young/Fotolia; **p. 452**: bernardbodo/Fotolia; **p. 453**: eurobanks/Fotolia; **p. 456**: absolut/Shutterstock; **p. 458**: Jupiterimages/Stockbyte/Getty Images; **p. 459**: (t) Stephen Coburn/Shutterstock; (b) michaeljung/Shutterstock; **p. 461**: (t) Kamira/Shutterstock; (l) Jeff Whyte/Shutterstock; (b) Pearson Education; (c) Pearson Education; Pearson Education; **p. 462**: (t) fStop Images GmbH/Shutterstock; (l) Israel Pabon/Shutterstock; (c) Pearson Education; (b) Pearson Education; **p. 463**: (t) Blend Images/Shutterstock; (l) Pearson Education; (bl) Pearson Education; (c) mayakova/Fotolia; **p. 465**: Jeremy Woodhouse/Getty Images.

Chapter 12

p. 470: Galyna Andrushko/Shutterstock; **p. 471**: (t) veroxdale/Shutterstock; (b) mayakova/Fotolia; **p. 473**: (l) Westend61 Premium/Shutterstock; (c) Blaj Gabriel/Shutterstock; (r) Tetra Images/Shutterstock; (b) Catalin Petolea/Shutterstock; **p. 474**: David Heining-Boynton; **p. 476**: (t) Tetra Images/Shutterstock; (b) Monkey Business Images/Shutterstock; **p. 477**: (l) David Heining-Boynton; (c) photobank.ch/Shutterstock; (r) Horst Petzold/Shutterstock; **p. 479**: Tony Magdaraog/Shutterstock; **p. 481**: (l) Cedric Weber/Shutterstock; (c) Galyna Andrushko/Shutterstock; (r) David Heining-Boynton; **p. 482**: (t) Monkey Business/Fotolia; (b) Tatagatta/Shutterstock; **p. 486**: (l) Pattie Steib/Shutterstock; (c) Vadym Andrushchenko/Shutterstock; (r) Galina Barskaya/Shutterstock; **p. 488**: withGod/Shutterstock; **p. 489**: (tl) Barbara Penoyar/Photodisc/Getty Images; (tcl) Daniel M Ernst/Shutterstock; (tcr) Daniel M Ernst/Shutterstock; (tr) Daniel M Ernst/Shutterstock; (cl) Monkey Business Images/Shutterstock; (cl) Andresr/Shutterstock; (cl) Andresr/Shutterstock; (cr) A and N photography/Shutterstock; (bl) Rido/Shutterstock; (bcl) Kamira/Shutterstock; (bcr) fStop Images GmbH/Shutterstock; (br) Blend Images/Shutterstock; **p. 490**: (tl) kwest/Shutterstock; (tcl) Alexander Chaikin/Shutterstock; (tcr) javarman/Shutterstock; (tr) jorisvo/Shutterstock; (cl) Yory Frenklakh/Shutterstock; (lc) gary yim/Shutterstock; (rc) JOSE ALBERTO TEJO/Shutterstock; (cr) Alexander Chaikin/Shutterstock; (bl) Marinko Tarlac/Shutterstock; (bcl) David Berry/Shutterstock; (bcr) Eugene Moerman/Shutterstock; (br) jovannig/123RF; **p. 491**: (tl) sunsinger/Shutterstock; David Heining-Boynton; (bl) fotum/Shutterstock; (br) worker/Shutterstock.

INDEX

Y

Z

TEXTBOOK RENTAL POLICY

1. Check your e-mail for specific deadlines, penalties, hours, etc.
2. Last day to return textbooks with no penalties is the 1st business day following the final exams.
3. A fine will be assessed on books returned from the 2nd business day through the 5th business day following final exams.
4. Books not returned by the fifth business day following the last day of finals will be assessed a purchase fee which is due and payable by the early fee payment deadline of the following semester.

   Failure to pay this debt will result in this account being turned over to an outside collection agency. Student is responsible for all related cost (collection/attorney fees in the amount of 33 1/3% of the principal, interest, late fees, and related court cost).
5. Books are issued by barcode number. Books with incorrect barcode will be confiscated and returned to the rightful renter.
6. Books are available for purchase at anytime. See store for details.

This book is the property of
Textbook Rental @ SLU

SPAN 101/ 102/ 201/SPAN_NTC1010/1(
Price 235.25
MBI:6427 Adpt:2178

64270015

México, América Central y el Caribe